THE PORTRAITS OF ALEXANDER POPE

To the Memory of

B. S. M. W. *and* M. E. L. H.

PREFACE: ACKNOWLEDGMENTS

FIRST TO TWO who have passed away. To C. B. Tinker, who near the outset, in 1949, told me some secrets and who insisted that the job *ought* to be done. To George Sherburn, who showed me his files, who midway said, "You *must* finish it," and whose five volumes of *The Correspondence of Alexander Pope,* appearing shortly thereafter, put the whole endeavor in a new light.

It would be gratifying to me to dwell on a Maytime expedition out of Oxford for the purpose of photographing a bust in the garden at Stowe; on a day in the Twickenham Church when a scaffolding was erected in the gallery before Bishop Warburton's monument; on the waning light of a summer evening spent in the library at Hartlebury Castle; on an auction at Christie's in which a painting of Pope as a boy came to light, and a friend was the last bidder.

But the writing of a book is a story that ought not to appear in the book itself.

There is some risk that the author will seem "inordinately proud," as George Sherburn thought, even in the acknowledgment of many favors. With the hope that whatever kind of pride may be present is forgivable, and for the reason mainly that it gives me pleasure to do this, I attempt the following gestures.

Among my benefactors, let me name first of all the owners and custodians of the Pope portraits, both private persons and the officers of institutions, who from the start have by their courteous and kindly responses to inquiry and request made possible the search and the book. The names of the institutions and private owners appear (some of them repeatedly) both in the legends that accompany the pictures and at the head of the corresponding entries in the catalogue. I hope these acknowledgments will be read as expressing my earnest thanks, not only for the privilege of reproducing the pictures and for information concerning them, but for many gracious personal receptions the memory of which I cherish.

One of my colleagues, James M. Osborn, uniquely placed as collector and editor of the manuscripts of Joseph Spence, and endowed with an extraordinarily generous disposition for the furtherance of such studies, has first and last been a chief encourager and promoter. His assistance could be acknowledged on almost any page of this book.

Another American friend, Dallas Pratt, took an early and keen interest in the subject and both from New York and London repeatedly sent valuable assistance. Other kindly travelers were Mrs. E. Talbot Donaldson, Robert E. Moore, Walter J. Ong, S.J., and Mrs. I. E. Pinder.

James T. Babb, James L. Clifford, Gordon Haight, Robert Halsband, Allen T. Hazen, F. W. Hilles, George L. Lam, W. S. Lewis, Herman Liebert, Maynard Mack, F. A. Pottle, Warren H. Smith, Aubrey Williams, and Marjorie Wynne are American colleagues and friends who, more often and in more ways than I can well summarize, have put me in their debt.

Mrs. Henry W. Howell, Jr., opened to me an early and important store of information at the Frick Art Reference Library. Elizabeth E. Roth and Karl Kup did the same at the Prints Division of the New York Public Library. Annie Reese Wedgwood, at the New York office of Wedgwood, was kind enough to obtain for me photographs of all the images of Pope preserved at the Barlaston Museum—concerning which William Billington, Curator of the Museum, has more recently sent me much information. The late R. H. Griffith, on learning of my inquiry, sent me a handwritten list of the portraits of Pope in a grangerized Carruthers' *Life of Pope* which he had brought to the University of Texas many years before. Fannie Ratchford and William Todd have subsequently been my expert informants about these and other materials at Texas.

In Britain I have found not only learned but generous correspondents at the British Museum, at the Victoria and Albert Museum, and in many other places. Let me name Geoffrey Beard, John Butt, Edward Croft-Murray, G. Nevin Drinkwater, David Foxon, J. W. Goodison, T. W. I. Hodgkinson, Frank Kermode, Peter Murray, C. J. Rawson, T. V. Roberts, Miss A. H. Scott-Elliot, B. C. Skinner, Geoffrey Tillotson, Ralph Walker, Francis J. B. Watson, the late Mrs. Geoffrey Webb, and John Woodward. Gladys Singers-Bigger has sent me many letters not only full of helpful information but written in a uniquely enthusiastic and friendly spirit. Alastair Smart and E. K. Waterhouse, happening to visit New Haven, gave me excellent advice.

I arrived in England for the first time in my life during the summer of 1960. How much would have been lost in inexpert fumbling without the year-long patient welcome and instruction I received from the staff of the National Portrait Gallery—C. K. Adams, the Director of the Gallery (Dean of Studies), J. F. Kerslake, Roy Strong, Mrs. Barbara Isherwood-Kay (I can do no less than name each professor), and David Piper, who after a correspondence with the remote inquirer stretching back many years, then undertook the main responsibility for opening the Gallery's endless resources. His advice has pervaded every part of the book (I hope in the senses which he intended). Without the archives of the National Portrait Gallery, or without the willingness of its experts in making these available, this book on the portraits of Pope could scarcely have been carried beyond the stages of a preliminary inquiry. About the exhibition of portraits of Alexander Pope which opened at the Gallery on 20 March, 1961, and ran to the end of April, I attempt to speak on a later page.

Others in Britain who, during the course of my year of inquiry and importunity, made especially kind responses were Miss E. D. Abbott and H. Bond, Mr. and Mrs. F. W. Bateson, Mr. and Mrs. Stephen Crawfurd, Robert J. Charleston, Donald Gordon, Rupert Gunnis, Jacob Isaacs, R. W. Ketton-Cremer, Jill Knight, Sir John Murray, Mr. and Mrs. J. H. P. Pafford, Mr. and Mrs. A. M. D. Perrins, G. H. Tait, Joseph B. Trapp, P. O. Troutman, Peter Ure, Professor and Mrs. Geoffrey Webb, Thomas S. Wragg, and Robert Mackworth-Young.

I owe a special kind of thanks to Philip Ritterbush, Alexander Mackinnon, and Charles Chadwick-Healy, all of Trinity College, Oxford, who were the planners and technicians of a trip to Stowe, and to Kim Meldrum of the Stowe faculty, who received us. And to Donald Miller, of the Twickenham Public Library, who erected a scaffolding in Twickenham Church and photographed the medallion of Pope on Warburton's monument.

Ronald Paulson has made himself an expert in the engravings of Hogarth in time to help me to the answers to several perplexing questions.

It is unlikely that the following list, which has grown in my memory and in my files for so long, will be complete. I present it with apology both for its probable omissions and for the meagerness of the acknowledgment after so many kindnesses exceeding the routine or the impersonal. I wish further to express my thanks to: Frederick B. Adams, Jr., Robert Barry, Sr., Robert Barry, Jr., Harry Berger, Professor and Mrs. Brand Blanshard, Benjamin Boyce, Imbrie Buffum, Professor and Mrs. Geoffrey Bullough, Herbert Cahoon, Malcolm Cormack, W. G. Constable, Rosemary E. Cowler, Marlies K. Danziger, the Rev. Mr. and Mrs. W. H. S. Davies, the Reverend Mr. and Mrs. W. John Davies, Vinton Dearing, E. S. Dewing, James Dickie, Emily Driscoll, Edmund Esdaile, Lady Agnes Eyston, Canon G. H. Fendick, Mrs. Nathan H. Fink, Elizabeth Gee, Phyllis M. Giles, Thomas Greene, A. P. Grimbly, Joseph Hamburger, D. Beatrice Harris, John P. Harthan, Dr. and Mrs. W. Houben, R. E. Hutchison, William Jackson, John Jacob, Elizabeth Johnson, Winifred Kennedy, Bernard Knox, Kenneth A. Lohf, Canon D. P. Low, J. V. G. Mallet, Jay Martin, Mabel Martin, Jonathan Mayne, David McKibbin, J. C. Masterman, A. E. Haswell Miller, Eva M. Millington, R. J. Minney, the Reverend P. C. Moore, Benjamin C. Nangle, Peter Pagan, Michael Papantonio, R. Patterson, Graham Pollard (of the Fitzwilliam Museum), John C. Pope, Martin Price, David A. Randall, Lawrence Richardson, Philip Robinson, Dale R. Roylance, Elsie A. Russ, R. M. Schmitz, Richard Shroyer, Clifford Simmons, J. S. G. Simmons, Allan Stevenson, Johanna Stuckey, G. L. Taylor, Eugene Waith, J. Robert Wall, A. Dayle Wallace, Robert Wark, David R. Watkins, Lydia H. Wentworth, John Weston, Josephine Wheeler, Margaret Whinney, R. Wittkower, H. Bunker Wright, Reginald W. M. Wright, and Jacob Zeitlin.

Fredrick Ludwig, Head of the Yale University Photographic Services, made all the photographs of engravings in the Yale Library and in other local collections, both those which appear in the book and many others which I needed for study. I wish to record my appreciation of his devoted artistry.

Several of my undergraduate helpers on the Bursary Foundation at Yale during the period 1949–1963 have worked on this book. I would acknowledge especially Charles Swartz, Michael Uhlman, Donald Graham, and Walter Guterbock. During the summer of 1963 Donald Graham not only continued to assist the research but typed a large part of the copy. A visitor from Britain, Kevin O'Sullivan, completed the typing.

I am grateful to the Modern Language Association of America for a grant which near the beginning eased the expense of photography, and to Yale University for a Senior Faculty Fellowship, which made possible my stay in England during 1960 and 1961, and for a later grant to aid the completion of the work.

Among the many ways in which I am indebted to my wife, I mention especially her skill and resolution as principal engineer of the expedition to Britain.

W. K. W.

Silliman College, Yale University
31 January 1964

I am grateful for the prompt and generous measures taken by George H. Healey and Donald D. Eddy to make possible the inclusion in this catalogue of the fifteen original drawings of Pope by Jonathan Richardson which came to the Cornell University Library for examination in September 1964.

Crimilda Pontes, Sarah Sullivan, and Edward McClellan converted typescript and photographs into the design for a physical object; I wish to record my appreciation of their skillful labors.

David Piper has added to the book's already immeasurable debt to him by reading the galley proof.

Mary Price made the index.

1 May 1965

CONTENTS

CONTENTS

INTRODUCTION

1. CHRONOLOGY

When Pope was born, 21 May 1688, the school of international Baroque portrait painting in England was at the beginning of a third generation. The native miniaturist Samuel Cooper, Pope's own uncle (portrayer of both Cromwell and Charles II), had died in 1672. Sir Peter Lely, the Dutch court painter and successor of the great Fleming Sir Anthony Van Dyck, had died in 1680. A few months after Pope's birth, in November 1688, when William of Orange landed near Torbay, the news is said to have interrupted King James II in a sitting to the recently "famous" German painter Godfrey Kneller.[1] Within a few weeks, on the success of the revolution, Godfrey Kneller and the veteran middle-class painter John Riley were jointly "sworn and admitted chief painter" to the crown. Riley died on 30 March 1791, bequeathing both a style and, through marriage with his niece, much of his property to his pupil Jonathan Richardson, who seems to have been a friend of the Pope family and who in later years would be the intimate friend and frequent portrayer of the poet. At the age of seven, and before the attack of the spinal disease which deformed him, Pope was the subject of a sparkling oil portrait by an anonymous artist, very likely a foreigner. At about the same time another little boy (within a few weeks the same age as Pope, and in his tall coiffure and fluffy bow tie presenting much the same pert appearance) Prince James Francis Edward, the Pretender, was painted in exile by Nicolas de Largillière.

In 1711, when Pope published in London his second notable poem, *An Essay on*

---

1. *The Diary of Samuel Pepys . . . Supplementary Volume, Pepysiana,* ed. Henry B. Wheatley (London, 1920), p. 88; George Vertue, *Note Books, 4* (Oxford: Walpole Society 24, 1936), 108.

Criticism, and was reviewed by Addison in *Spectator* 253, the first London Academy of Painting was founded in Great Queen Street, with Sir Godfrey Kneller its President and Jonathan Richardson one of the Directors. The Academy is greeted by Steele in *Spectator* 555, 6 December 1712. Kneller, who had been knighted by William in 1692, was created a baronet by George I in 1715.

Pope's first good friend among the painters was the fashionable ladies' painter Charles Jervas, who had worked briefly under Kneller. He gave Pope lessons in painting and was his face-painter, making at least two portraits of him, at about the time (1714–15) when Pope was getting out the first volume of his *Iliad*. Shortly thereafter Pope, becoming more and more famous, was painted three times by Kneller (1716, 1721, 1722). Doubtless he would have been painted more times, but Kneller died in 1723.

English portrait painting pursued a quiet way during the next three decades. The aging Swedish master Michael Dahl was perhaps for a few years the most eminent practitioner. He painted Pope once, in 1727. Richardson's pupil and son-in-law Thomas Hudson (who did not paint Pope) carried to the third generation the rounded, drab, metallic style of masculine bust-lengths, and he was momentarily (1740–43) the mentor of the young Devonshire aspirant Joshua Reynolds. An innovation in English portraiture of the time was the work of the Flemish sculptor Michael Rysbrack—who duly makes his appearance in Pope's catalogue, under the date 1730. At about the same time, a very different sort of artist, William Kent, Pope's friend and collaborator in landscape gardening, contrived to make a few marginal contributions even to the portraiture.

Jonathan Richardson, as George Vertue, the Boswell of English painting in this period, observes, was the last of the master painters of the great old generation. He died in 1745, a year after Pope—nearly twenty-five years older. For the last dozen years of Pope's life, his image is lavishly multiplied in the friendly drawings, etchings, and oils of Richardson. During the last six years appear the noble busts in terra cotta and marble by the rococo French sculptor L. F. Roubiliac (1738), the austere profile in copper by the Swiss medalist J. A. Dassier (1741), the oil portrait (1740—later multiplied in oil and pastel) by the Bath society artist William Hoare, and (in 1742) impressive twin oils by the visiting French royal painter J. B. Van Loo.

2. COMMONPLACES

The two main purposes of the book, as guide to the portraiture of Pope and as biography of Pope, do not require an introductory treatise on the practice of portrait art in the England of Pope's day. The book itself supplies illustrations of that practice in some of its aspects. I believe, however, that some of these aspects may be unfamiliar to the reader of today who comes with any degree of purity from a preoccupation with literary studies. I would suggest that the facts arranged in this catalogue will fit together most conveniently for a reader who brings with him a recollection of the following platitudes: the rising theoretical estate of graphic art in the Augustan era and the flourishing conception of the ancient and honorable sisterhood of the arts of painting and poetry; the vast importance of the vanity work of portrait painting in the aristocratic and upper bourgeois life of that time; the extensive multiplication of portrait replicas, even by the original artists or in their studios, and of engravings, especially mezzotints, after oil portraits; the frequency, nevertheless, with which during a few generations both artists' and subjects' names came to be detached from portraits and wrong names substituted; the immense fame of Alexander Pope and the importance to him of having an adequate image of himself made public, and his apparently persistent efforts toward that end. Pope was probably the most frequently portrayed English person of his generation, perhaps of the whole eighteenth century. He was surely the English poet most often portrayed before the romantic era.[2] And after that the advent of the daguerreotype puts the reckoning on a very different basis.

Some of the ideas just baldly enumerated may be improved by a trace of their contemporary color in the following small anthology of excerpts.[3] They are placed in a roughly chronological order:

I have observed that a reader seldom peruses a book with pleasure 'till he knows whether the writer of it be a black or a fair man, of a mild or choleric disposition, married or a bachelor, with other particulars of a like nature, that conduce very much to the right understanding of an author.

—Joseph Addison, *Spectator* 1, 1 March 1711

Painting gives us not only the persons, but the characters of great men. The air of the head and the mien in general give strong indications of the mind and illustrate what the historian says more expressly and particularly. Let a man read a character in my Lord Clarendon (and certainly never was there a better painter in that kind), he will find it improved by seeing a picture of the same person by Van Dyck.

—Jonathan Richardson, *An Essay on the Theory of Painting*, 1715, Introduction

pray get Sir Godfrey to write . . . on the backside of mine, John Locke 1704. This he did on Mr. Molyneux's and mine, the last he drew, and this is necessary to be done, as else the pictures of private persons are lost in two or three

2. In the next generation Samuel Johnson, despite his productive friendship with Reynolds, met the arts in general and met fame with a gruffness which was no doubt a main cause for a much lower total of life portrayals. I am not sure that any of the romantic poets outdid Pope in portraiture. With the eighty-one types which I present compare the catalogue in Frances

Blanshard, *Portraits of Wordsworth*, Ithaca, 1959; Donald Parsons, *Portraits of Keats*, New York, 1954; and the catalogue of portraits of Sir Walter Scott at the end of the *DNB* article on him by Leslie Stephen

3. I have pillaged several of these from a few of the best modern histories and catalogues of portraiture. The texts are normalized.

4. George White's mezzotint of 1723 after the Kneller type of 1722 (no. 7.8).

5. John Simon's mezzotint of 1728 after the Dahl type of painting, 1727 (no. 10.4).

6. Jonathan Richardson's original etching, "Amicitiae Causa," dated 1736 (no. 41).

7. Jonathan Richardson's original etching, "Amicitiae Causa," on the title page of Pope's *Letters,* 1737 (no. 43.1).

8. Jonathan Richardson's original etching, "ΟΥΤΟΣ ΕΚΕΙΝΟΣ," dated 1738 (no. 48.1).

9. John Faber the Younger's mezzotint of c. 1744 after Van Loo's painting of 1742 (no. 66.15).

Apparently the earliest collector of Pope portraits was his friend and patron Edward Harley, the Second Earl of Oxford, who not only purchased the poet Prior's oil portrait of Pope by Jervas and presented it to Oxford University in 1723 (no. 2.1) but had at Wimpole a Kneller of the 1716 type (Kit-cat size—see no. 5.1) and had also two portraits of Pope by Richardson (see Appendix 2). All three of these latter appeared in the London sale of Oxford's pictures in March 1742, after his death. This was surely the first important sale of Pope portraits, and probably the largest sale of oil portraits of Pope ever yet held. It has long been known that Joshua Reynolds as a young art student saw Pope at a picture sale about that time. More recently it has appeared that the sale was no other than Lord Oxford's, conducted by Cock in Covent Garden.[5] Thus Pope himself that day saw three portraits of himself under the hammer. "Reynolds was at the upper end of the room, near to the auctioneer, when he perceived a considerable bustle at the farther part of the room, near the door. . . . he soon heard the name of Mr. Pope, Mr. Pope, whispered from every mouth. . . . Immediately every person drew back to make a free passage for the distinguished poet, and all those on each side held out their hands for him to touch as he passed."[6] "Pope was seldom seen in public, so it was a great sight to see him. He got within the rails at the head of the room."[7]

Another early collector of Pope portraits was his friend, the physician and virtuoso Dr. Richard Mead, with his home and museum near Jonathan Richardson's house in Great Ormond Street, Queen Square. He seems to have owned two nearly identical oil profiles of Pope by Richardson, one of which passed into the possession of his daughter Sarah and her husband, the physician Sir Edward Wilmot, and is still in the collection of that family (no. 52.3); the other was in Dr. Mead's sale of March 1754 and came later to Petworth, where it remains (no. 52.1).

Like Lord Oxford's portrait in the Bodleian and the Wilmot portrait, a few other portraits of Pope acquired by his contemporaries have remained in their early homes

5. Boswell's record of the incident, taken from Reynolds as he lay dying, 20 December 1791 (*Portraits by Sir Joshua Reynolds,* ed. F. W. Hilles, New York, 1952, p. 24). Cf. James Prior, *Life of Edmond Malone* (London, 1860), pp. 428–29.

6. James Northcote, *Memoirs of Sir Joshua Reynolds, Knt.* (London, 1813), p. 14. "The above anecdote I heard from Sir Joshua himself."

7. Boswell, *Portraits,* p. 24.

to this day, or nearly so: the large oil of Pope and a lady, by Charles Jervas, which at a very early date passed from the widow of William Cleland into the collection at Elton Hall (no. 3.1); Lord Bathurst's version of the 1716 Kneller, at Cirencester Park (no. 5.2—and here, too, should be mentioned the painting of this type at Raby Castle, Lord Barnard's [no. 5.1], which I conjecture passed directly to its present home from the Oxford sale of 1742); Lord Harcourt's Kneller, the undisputed archetype of 1722 and one of the best documented of all Pope portraits, still at Stanton Harcourt (no. 7.1); Richardson's large oil of Pope and his dog Bounce, presumably a gift to Lord Lyttleton, still at Hagley (no. 9.1); William Kent's "round" of 1735, for a place over a door at Chiswick House (no. 18); the anonymous stone bust in the Temple of Worthies at Stowe, of c. 1735–40 (no. 19.a); the three-quarters to right face in a wig by Richardson which passed from the Harcourt collection to its present owner only in 1948 (no. 50); Lord Fitzwilliam's signed version of the Roubiliac bust dated 1740, which has presumably been all along at Milton (no. 59.1); Lord Mansfield's oil by Van Loo, which about 1922 moved from Kenwood to Scone Palace (no. 66.1). Lord Mansfield had also a bust of Pope—which, it seems there are good grounds for believing, left Kenwood only in the sale of 1922, and is the bust now at Temple Newsam (no. 58).

For about seventy years after the death of Pope, the most significant new evidence concerning his portraiture appears in the editions of his *Works*. In some copies of the reprint of Warburton's edition by the booksellers in 1769 or else in Ruffhead's *Life* which accompanies it, appears the mysterious engraving by Ravenet which gives us a bust-length wigged Pope, aged 24, purporting to be by Kneller, but on very good grounds assignable to Richardson (no. 8.2). In Warton's first volume of the 1797 *Works* appears for the first time an identified engraving of the profile by Richardson once owned by Dr. Mead, at the time of the edition owned by Mr. and Mrs. Benjamin Way, and later, as we have noted, at Petworth (no. 52.1). The same volume reveals for the first time, following the death at Bath of the aged William Hoare, his surreptitious drawing of Pope full-length made at Prior Park perhaps about 1742. These two pictures are repeated in the first volume of W. L. Bowles' edition of the *Works*, 1806; and in Bowles' second volume appears the first engraving ever made of the bust-length oil (by Hoare) in the Marquis of Buckingham's collection at Stowe (no. 63.1).

In the early nineteenth century a number of important second- and third-generation collectors emerge. About 1820 the wealthy M. P. George Watson Taylor owned not only an excellent version of Jervas' oil of Pope and the lady (most likely that now known at the National Portrait Gallery, no. 112), but also a marble Roubiliac bust signed and dated 1741. This bust apparently made the first public appearance of any Pope bust, in the British Institution Exhibition of 1820, and it was well engraved as a frontispiece to William Roscoe's first volume of Pope's *Works* in 1824. At Watson Taylor's great Erlestoke Sale of 1832, it was Sir Robert Peel who acquired this bust, which is today Lord Rosebery's (no. 61.1). Later, at the Stowe Sale of 1848, Peel acquired the then celebrated Buckingham oil, by Hoare, which disappeared quietly in 1917 in a sale of Peel's heirlooms (no. 63). Some years earlier the poetical banker Samuel Rogers had acquired another Roubiliac bust, the terra cotta, which for many years was a noted conversation piece in his breakfast room in St. James's Place. At his sale in 1857 it passed into the hands of John Murray III, by whose descendants it is held today, at Elton Hall (no. 57.1). In 1823 yet another Roubiliac signed marble came on the market, from the Garrick collection, passing into the hands of John George Lambton, later Earl of Durham, by whose descendants it was held, until in recent years it came to the Shipley Art Gallery. In 1842 the fine large version of the Van Loo portrait which had been in the Upper Ossory collection passed into that of the Marquis of Lansdowne, where it remained until 1930 (no. 66.2). In 1876 the oil portrait by Richardson (Pope as a Tory gentleman with wig, hands folded on a book) which had come down to the Marquis of Hastings at Donington Park, was acquired by the Boston litterateur James Fields, and may be seen in Boston to this day (no. 51).

The huge dispersal of Richardson drawings which had taken place at the sale of February 1772, following the death of his son, left few immediately discernible clues for the historian of Pope portraiture. But at the Walpolian Strawberry Hill sales of 1842, a large collection of Richardson drawings included a fine laureated pencil-on-vellum of Pope (no. 23.a). The collection is today in the British Museum. Perhaps this sale was likewise the source of three Richardson pencil drawings of Pope which before 1888 were acquired for the Royal Collection at Windsor Castle (nos. 25, 33, 35). Another drawing of Pope which came down at Strawberry Hill disappeared in the dispersal of 1842. But this drawing, luckily, had earlier inspired the Walpolian collector Richard Bull to insert an *original* substitute in his grangerized *Description of Strawberry Hill*, now at Farmington (no. 30).

A collection of fifteen Richardson drawings of Pope were lent to a memorial exhibition at Twickenham in 1888 by Titus Herbert Hibbert-Ware, but, after being returned to the owner, did not come to light again until September 1964, when they appeared at Cornell University, just in time to be included in this book—nos. 19(1)–19(14), 37(1).

The nineteenth century is also the era of the great portrait exhibitions which accompanied the maturing of the nation's consciousness of its personalities.[8] At Manchester in 1857, the artist and critic George Scharf played a prominent part, from which he went on to be the first Director of the National Portrait Gallery. Lord Harcourt's Kneller of 1722 was in that exhibition, and Lord Lyttelton's Hagley portrait of Pope and Bounce, and Sir Henry Wilmot's Richardson profile, descended from Dr. Mead. Then came the great series of National Portrait Exhibitions at the South Kensington Museum in 1866, 1867, and 1868. The same three portraits, the Harcourt Kneller, the Hagley Pope and Bounce, and the Wilmot Richardson, were seen again in 1867, along with one other, a small portrait by Richardson, signed and dated 1742, which had somewhat mysteriously arrived at the Fitzwilliam Museum in 1834 (no. 55.2). In 1868 came the Leeds Exhibition, where Lord Lyttelton's Pope and Bounce appeared a third time. In 1890 the Guelph Exhibition in London had the Harcourt

8. See the quotation from Carlyle (1854) which makes, with the passages from Addison and Richardson, quoted above in this Introduction, one of the epigraphs to the National Portrait Gallery Catalogue.

Kneller. The Twickenham bicentennial Pope Exhibition of 1888 appears in retrospect, with regard to Pope portraits, as either a comedy or a catastrophe. Of the several possibly original large Pope portraits which were listed, only two, Alfred Morrison's Kneller of 1721 (no. 6.5) and John Murray's terra cotta (no. 57.1), can today be identified. (The first public photograph of this terra cotta appeared in 1889 as frontispiece to Murray's volume 5 of the Elwin-Courthope edition of Pope.) Two paintings from Mapledurham which were seen at Twickenham in 1888 (if they were actually Pope)[9] are among those that have vanished.

Meanwhile, however, a number of important portraits of Pope had been finding their way into institutional collections. In 1868 the long-unknown Rysbrack marble bust was bequeathed by Edward Badeley to the Athenaeum Club. In 1860 the National Portrait Gallery had acquired its first Pope portrait, the Jervas of Pope and the lady (no. 112). In 1870 the Gallery received by bequest from the Reverend Edward Townsend, who had received it from Prince Hoare the younger, the blue pastel of the Stowe type (no. 299), which is so important a part of the evidence in that puzzle (nos. 63.1–2). In 1891 was acquired the red crayon drawing (no. 873) which had been engraved for Warton's edition in 1797, and in 1898 the mysterious and admirable laureated profile in oil (no. 1179) attributed to Richardson.

Nearly all of the best-known original portraits of Pope have been mentioned in the foregoing brief recital. The appearance of some of these—at exhibitions during the past sixty years, in photographic reproduction in books by and about Pope, and in journals—can to a great extent be traced in the entries of the catalogue. I mention here only a few of the most important moments. In 1932 the Roubiliac marble signed and dated 1738, now at Temple Newsam (which I conjecture, p. 235, may have been Lord Mansfield's) first came to public notice photographed at the home of G. D. Hobson in Bedford Square (no. 58). In 1934 the Rysbrack marble bust (no. 112) traveled the distance from the Athenaeum Club to Burlington House for the Exhibition of British Art, and was first publicly reproduced in the *Commemorative Catalogue*. In 1937 the Shipley Art Gallery at Gateshead acquired the Garrick bust (no. 60.1). This was seen at Burlington House in the Winter Exhibition of British Portraits, 1956–57. In the Burlington House Winter Exhibition, *English Taste*, of the year before, Earl Fitzwilliam's signed Roubiliac marble (no. 59.1) emerged for the first time to public view.

An apex of Pope portrait exhibition, surely not soon if ever to be equaled, was reached when from 20 March to 30 April 1961, the National Portrait Gallery held its public Exhibition, "Portraits of Alexander Pope." Fourteen oil paintings were assembled at this exhibition, or, to speak broadly, one for each of the main types. Jervas was represented by Lord Oxford's Bodleian bust-length (the only example of this type, no. 2.1) and by the National Portrait Gallery no. 112, Pope with the lady (no. 3.2). The Knellers were Lord Barnard's Kit-cat half-length of the 1716 type (with the curious

9. Information about the paintings at Mapledurham which has come to light in recent years suggests that the two male portraits seen at Twickenham may have been the poet Prior and Michael Blount, brother of Pope's two favorite nymphs, Martha and Teresa.

feature of a signature and date 1719—no. 5.1), Lord Home's signed and dated example of the 1721 laureated profile (no. 6.2), and Lord Harcourt's signed and dated Pope in a cap leaning on Homer, of 1722 (the most celebrated of all Kneller portraits of Pope —no. 7.1). From the earlier part of Pope's career there was also Lord Cobham's Pope and Bounce by Richardson (no. 9.1) and the Reading University example of the Dahl portrait of Pope in a cobalt blue robe (no. 10.2). From the later period of Richardson's relation with Pope, there were five oils: Dr. Mead's fur-collar profile from Petworth (no. 52.1) and along with it a lesser-known full face (no. 49); Mrs. Poore's three-quarter face in wig, formerly in the Harcourt collection (no. 50); the fine National Portrait Gallery 1179, a laureated profile (no. 54.1); and the small three-quarter face, signed and dated 1742, belonging to the Fitzwilliam Museum (no. 55.2). The Van Loo type of 1742 was represented by Mr. and Mrs. A. M. D. Perrins' excellent replica formerly in the Darnley Collection at Cobham (no. 66.3). The elusive Stowe type of portrait done by William Hoare in both oils and pastel was represented by National Portrait Gallery no. 299, a pastel in blues (no. 63.3). Finally, among the oil paintings the most surprising was the earliest in the series, Mr. James M. Osborn's spirited image of Pope at the age of seven, which had come to light in the preceding October at Christie's (no. 1).[10]

Eighteen drawings of Pope were shown. Thirteen of these were pencil-on-vellum drawings by Jonathan Richardson: three small ones from the Royal Collection at Windsor Castle (nos. 25, 33, 35), the laureated head which came via Strawberry Hill to the British Museum (no. 23), and nine hitherto unexhibited and almost unknown drawings, all dating between 1733 and about 1737, in a collection belonging to Mr. and Mrs. Roger Warner of Burford, Oxfordshire (nos. 8.1, 20, 22, 24, 27–29, 31, 32). The other five drawings were: Kneller's crayon pattern for the 1721 profile painting, from the British Museum (no. 6.1); William Kent's pen-and-wash drawing of Pope's Twickenham garden, with Pope standing full length with his dog, also from the British Museum (no. 14); a hitherto unexhibited and unknown pen-and-ink drawing of Pope at cards by Lady Burlington, from the Chatsworth Collection (no. 65); another from the same collection (no. 16), perhaps by Lady Burlington, perhaps by Kent, showing Pope seated in his grotto;[11] and William Hoare's celebrated surreptitious full-length drawing in red crayon, done about 1742 at Prior Park (National Portrait Gallery no. 873—*post* no. 64.1).

A magnificent feature of this exhibition was the assemblage of busts: Rysbrack's heroic marble of 1730 from the Athenaeum (no. 11.2) and also his terra-cotta pastiche of c. 1760, from the Fitzwilliam (no. 67.5); the noble Roubiliac terra cotta, from Elton Hall (no. 57.2); and all four of the known signed and dated marbles; that of 1738, from Temple Newsam (no. 58); Lord Fitzwilliam's dated 1740 (no. 59.1); the Garrick marble dated 1741, from the Shipley Museum (no. 60.1); and Lord Rosebery's, dated 1741 (no. 61.1). This was the first time Lord Rosebery's bust had been seen on exhibition since Watson Taylor lent it to the British Institution Exhibition in 1820; it has never

---

10. With the boy Pope and two other oils of Pope, by Richardson and Hoare (nos. 52.8 and 63.4), in his New Haven study, Mr. Osborn is surely the Lord Ox-ford among Pope collectors of the present age.

11. A second drawing of this kind (no. 15) was represented by a photograph.

been reproduced except in the engraving in Roscoe's *Pope* of 1824. The confrontation of these five closely related Roubiliac busts, all on a single table, was an event which a student of Pope portraiture might well have been content to dream about.

Other exhibits were the Dassier medal (no. 62.1), the hollow bronze relief of the Roubiliac type belonging to Mr. and Mrs. Francis J. B. Watson (no. 57–61.1), and from the Manchester Gallery William Blake's oil-and-tempera panel so curiously derived from the Van Loo type (no. 66.20). The most significant early engravings of Pope, including a few satires, were nearly all represented. An elaborate series of photographs and legends expounded topics relating to Augustan iconography, the sisterhood of the arts of painting and poetry, and the Homeric English poet. At the entrance to the inner of the two sections of the "Sculpture Gallery," where the Exhibition was held, potted plants illustrated the "critic's ivy" and the "poet's bays" which were the insistent theme of so much of the portraiture.

The more important Pope portraits which the present volume will illustrate for, I believe, the first time are the following:

Lord Barnard's Kneller of the 1716 type, at Raby Castle (no. 5.1).

Lord Crawford's Kneller of the same type, at Balcarres Palace (no. 5.3).

The oil of the Hagley Richardson type (no. 9.2) in the Beinecke Rare Book and Manuscript Library, Yale University.

The Reading example of the oil by Dahl (no. 10.2).

The garden bust at Stowe (no. 19).

Fourteen drawings on paper and one on vellum by Richardson at the Cornell University Library—nos. 19(1)—19(14), 37(1).

Eight of the nine pencil-on-vellum drawings by Richardson belonging to Mr. and Mrs. Roger Warner (nos. 8.1, 22, 24, 27–29, 31, 32).[12]

Three pencil-on-vellum drawings by Richardson belonging to Dr. Dallas Pratt, of New York City (nos. 26, 34, 37).

A pencil-on-vellum drawing by Richardson belonging to Mr. W. S. Lewis, Farmington, Connecticut (no. 30), and with this a pencil-on-vellum drawing by Richardson of Pope's mother (no. Ex. 9).

A pencil-on-vellum drawing by Richardson at the University of Texas Library (no. 36).

Ten etchings of Pope by Richardson, a few of them unique examples (nos. 38.a–42, 44 48).

12. The other drawing, no. 20, has been illustrated in Robert Halsband, *The Life of Lady Mary Wortley Montague* (Oxford, 1956), p. 144. A similar drawing, in crayon, at the Yale University Library (no. 21), has been illustrated as frontispiece to volume 1 of George Sherburn's *Correspondence of Alexander Pope* (Oxford, 1956).

The oil of Pope by Richardson, three-quarters to the right, with wig, belonging to Mrs. H. M. Poore (no. 50).

The Petworth profile by Richardson (no. 52.1—never before illustrated by photograph).

The Dyce profile by Richardson, at the Victoria and Albert Museum (no. 53.1).

Lord Rosebery's marble version of the Roubiliac bust (no. 61.1—never before illustrated by photograph).

James M. Osborn's oil by William Hoare, of the Stowe type (no. 52.8).

Lord Mansfield's oil by Van Loo, long at Kenwood, now at Scone Palace (no. 66.1).

The pen-and-ink profile of Pope playing cards, by the Countess of Burlington, at Chatsworth (no. 65); and from the same collection her fanciful self-portrait drawing (no. Ex. 6).

The medallion, by Prince Hoare, on the monument erected by Bishop Warburton in Twickenham Church (no. 67.3).[13]

4. POPE'S PHYSICAL APPEARANCE

Entry no. 1 of the catalogue quotes a passage from Spence's *Anecdotes* which describes Pope as a healthy child of ten, with a face round, plump, pretty, and of fresh complexion. It was about two years afterwards, the report goes on, that he fell into a "perpetual affliction" that "changed his form and ruined his constitution."[14] Pope himself told Spence that in four years' time this affliction reduced him to such a state of poor health that he expected to die. He was restored, on the advice of Dr. Radcliffe, by studying less and riding every day.[15] The period and the nature of the disease which deformed Pope seem not well documented. But during adult life he showed a stunted growth and a curvature of the spine, apparently the result of tubercular infection.[16] He described himself as "a lively little Creature, with long Arms and Legs: A spider is no ill Emblem of him."[17] Voltaire referred to him as "un petit homme contrefait, bossu par devant et par derrière."[18] From the attacks of his enemies, Dennis, Gildon, Lady Mary, Lord Hervey, and various Dunciad warriors, savage comments upon his physical misfortune may be multiplied. Nos. 12, 14, 64, and 65 show Pope in profile at full length, or nearly

13. Other portraits which I omit from this list have been reproduced before only ephemerally, as in newspaper illustrations to accounts of the 1961 exhibition. See nos. 1 (Mr. Osborn's Pope at the age of seven), 6.2 (Sir Alexander Douglas-Home's Kneller of the 1721 type), and 16 (grotto drawing at Chatsworth). An article which I prepared for *Antiques*, February 1964, borrows in advance from the list above several portraits in American collections.

14. Spence, *Anecdotes*, 1820, p. 26.

15. Spence, *Anecdotes*, 1820, p. 76. Cf. Sherburn, *Early Career*, pp. 42–43.

16. Sherburn, *Early Career*, p. 43.

17. ["The Club of Little Men"], *The Guardian*, No. 92, 26 June 1713 (*The Prose Works of Alexander Pope*, ed. Norman Ault, *1* [Oxford, 1936], 125). Pope almost certainly refers to himself.

18. *Oeuvres*, *42* (66 tomes, Paris, 1819–25), 157, quoted by G. B. Hill, ed., Johnson's *Lives of the Poets*, *3* (Oxford, 1905), 178, n. 2.

so, and suggest that Voltaire's plain phrase "par devant et par derrière" may be a slight exaggeration. Nos. 13.1 and 2 are examples of a kind of satiric image which need have no close correspondence to Pope's actual appearance; Appendix 3 lists some others. Samuel Johnson, in an account of Pope's appearance based in part on a reported interrogation of an aged female domestic of the Earl of Oxford, published in the *Gentleman's Magazine* for September 1775, stresses Pope's weakness, slenderness, and sensitivity to cold in later life, the heavy layers of clothes and laced supports he had to wear, and his need for help in dressing and undressing.[19]

"His hair," says Johnson, "had fallen almost all away, and he used to dine sometimes with Lord Oxford, privately, in a velvet cap."[20] Nos. 5 and 7 in the catalogue (by Kneller) illustrate the negligee cap in Pope's earlier years; and nos. 63.3–4 (by Hoare) show it toward the end.[21] His hair toward the end may have fallen away, but no. 30, a drawing by Richardson dated 1736, seems to show the hair cropped close as for a wig. And George Scharf reports noticing the same thing under the wig in Richardson's oil no. 51.[22] The entry for no. 52.1 gives us a glimpse of Pope in 1739 putting on a scarlet cloak such as appears (with brown fur trim) in several of Richardson's paintings of him.

But it was Joshua Reynolds, the young painter seeing Pope at Lord Oxford's sale in 1742, who seems to have retained the most vivid pictorial impression of him:

> [Pope] was, according to Sir Joshua's account, about four feet six high; very humpbacked and deformed; he wore a black coat; and according to the fashion of that time, had on a little sword; . . . he had a large and very fine eye, and a long handsome nose; his mouth had those peculiar marks which always are found in the mouths of crooked persons; and the muscles which ran across the cheek were so strongly marked as to appear like small cords. Roubiliac the statuary, who made a bust of him from life, observed that his countenance was that of a person who had been much afflicted with headache, and that he should have known the fact from the contracted appearance of the skin above the eyebrows, though he had not been otherwise apprised of it.[23]

> Sir Joshua said he had an extraordinary face, not an everyday countenance,— a pallidly studious look; not merely a sharp, keen countenance, but something grand, like Cicero's.[24]

19. *Lives of the Poets, 3* (ed. Hill, 1905), 197.

20. *Lives* 3.198.

21. The close-fitting jacket of no. 5 does not reappear. But the loose green gown which accompanies the cap in no. 7 (1722) has a near counterpart in the gown (blue or green), again with a cap, in the late portrait by Hoare (nos. 63.3–4). A bright blue gown with black fur trim appears in the painting by Dahl (no. 10).

See C. Willett [Cunnington] and Phillis Cunnington, *Handbook of English Costume in the Eighteenth Century* (London, Faber and Faber, 1957), pp. 43–105, for an informed account, with drawings, of the several sorts of male attire in vogue during the lifetime of Pope. See the same authors' *Dictionary of English Costume* (Philadelphia: Dufour Editions, 1960).

22. Charles Gildon, *Memoirs of the Life of William Wycherly, Esq.* (London: Printed for E. Curll, 1718), pp. 15–17, reports calling once on Wycherley (about 1704) and finding Pope present, a "little Aesopic sort of animal with his own cropt hair."

23. James Prior, *Life of Edmond Malone* (London, 1860), 428–429, "Maloniana." "His dress of ceremony," says Johnson, "was black, with a tye-wig and a little sword" (*Lives* 3 [ed Hill, 1905], 198). As early as 1713 Pope describes himself as going "generally in Black" (*Guardian* 92; see note 17 above).

24. James Boswell, *Portraits by Sir Joshua Reynolds*, ed. F. W. Hilles (New York, 1952), p. 24.

"His face," says Johnson, "was not displeasing, and his eyes were animated and vivid."[25] "Sir! you have an Eye," Pope quotes his flatterers, in the *Epistle to Arbuthnot*. And his executor Warburton annotates this passage: "his eye . . . was fine, sharp and piercing."[26] His eye and nose were indeed unusual. No. 5 (Kneller) and nos. 52.1 and 54 (Richardson) especially exploit the profile, an unusual procedure in male portraiture of the day. This extraordinary face could grow aged and have moments of homely, even comic, unpreparedness, as we see in the surreptitious drawings by Hoare and Lady Burlington (nos. 64 and 65), and in the recollection of Allen's sister quoted in the entry for no. 64. It could apparently give the impression of weakness. Spence records the remark of a Mr. T., made about 1740, that "The bust of Julius Caesar, in the long open gallery [of the Grand Duke's Palace at Florence] has a very weakly look, and resembles Mr. Pope as much as any bust that has been made on purpose for him."[27] Nos. 54 (profile in oil attributed to Richardson), 57.1, and 61.1 (the terra cotta and the polished marble bust by Roubiliac) are the artist's lie to the term "weakly." They are convincing presentations of Pope as the noble Roman, the laureated, the senatorial.

5. *SHORT TITLES AND BIBLIOGRAPHICAL NOTE*

The following is mainly a list of the most frequently cited sources of the book, with their short titles placed in the margin. As the short titles are readily scanned, the works are arranged not in alphabetical order but according to the several kinds of materials. A few notes on further sources are added.

1. Alexander Pope, editions, biographies, etc.

Elwin and Courthope
: Whitwell Elwin and W. J. Courthope, ed. *The Works of Alexander Pope*, 10 vols., London, John Murray, 1871–89; Letters in vols. 6–10; *Life* by Courthope in vol. 5.

Twickenham
: *The Twickenham Edition of the Poems of Alexander Pope*, 6 vols., London, Methuen and Co. Ltd., 1939–61; general editor John

25. *Lives 3.* 197.

26. Pope, *Works*, ed. Warburton, *4* (London, 1757), 17. Cf. "the lively Eye" of Pope's Swiftian *Imitation of Horace, Epistle I. vii* (*Twickenham 4.* 271).

27. Spence's editor in 1820, S. W. Singer, conjectures that "Mr. T." is Charles Townley, of Townley in Lancashire, author of an earlier anecdote about Garth (Spence's *Anecdotes* [1820], p. 115). This Townley was the father of Charles Townley (1737–1805), collector of the Townley marbles. Mr. James M. Osborn, in his forthcoming edition of the manuscripts of Spence, has written an extended commentary on the anecdote of the bust of Caesar (no. 1464). He believes that "Mr. T.," author of more than 70 anecdotes in Spence, cannot safely be identified.

Pope's friend Jonathan Richardson, Jr., visiting "the Great Duke's Gallery . . . on the upper floor of the Palace" at Florence in 1720, records (apparently the first object seen on his entering) among "Antique Busts" a "Julius Caesar; Brass" (*An Account of Some of the Statues . . . in Italy* [London, 1722], pp. 44–45). A white marble *busto* with a bronze head of Caesar which today is to be seen in the First Corridor near the entrance to the Uffizi Gallery is apparently recorded in Gallery inventories as far back as 1704. See Guido A. Mansuelli, *Galleria degli Uffizi Le Sculture, Parte II* (Roma, Instituto Poligrafico dello Stato, 1961), pp. 44 (no. 32), 175 (1704), 194 (1753), 248 (1784), and figures 32 *a,b*—front and profile views (the nose and the general profile aquiline).

Butt; vol. 1, *Pastoral Poetry and An Essay on Criticism,* ed. E. Audra and Aubrey Williams, 1961; vol. 2, *The Rape of the Lock and Other Poems,* ed. Geoffrey Tillotson, 1940 (revised edition, 1954); vol. 3, i, *An Essay on Man,* ed. Maynard Mack, 1950; vol. 3, ii, *Epistles to Several Persons,* ed. F. W. Bateson, 1951 (revised edition, 1961); vol. 4, *Imitations of Horace,* ed. John Butt, 1939; vol. 5, *The Dunciad,* ed. James Sutherland, 1943; vol. 6, *Minor Poems,* ed. Norman Ault and John Butt, 1954. Quotations from Pope's poems follow the text of this edition.

Earlier editions of Pope's *Works,* by William Warburton (9 vols., 1751, reprinted in 4 vols., with Owen Ruffhead's *Life,* 1769; vol. 6, 1807), Joseph Warton (10 vols., 1797), W. L. Bowles (10 vols., 1806), William Roscoe (10 vols., 1824), and Robert Carruthers (4 vols., including *Life,* 1853–54; revised *Life,* 1857), will be easily recognized in abbreviated local references.

Spence   Joseph Spence, *Anecdotes . . . Collected from the Conversation of Mr. Pope . . . ,* ed. S. W. Singer, London, W. H. Carpenter, 1820. James M. Osborn's forthcoming variorum edition of the manuscripts of Spence will supersede Singer.

Cunningham   Samuel Johnson, *Life of Pope,* in *Lives of the Most Eminent English Poets,* ed. Peter Cunningham, *3* (London, 1854), 95: a list of Pope portraits and locations, remarkably comprehensive for the date, though here and there mistaken in detail.

George Paston, *Mr. Pope, His Life and Times,* 2 vols., London, Hutchinson & Co., 1909, contains many reproductions of the Pope portraits best known at that date.

George Sherburn, *The Early Career of Alexander Pope,* Oxford, Clarendon Press, 1934, is still the most advanced account of the years up to 1727.

Griffith   R. H. Griffith, *Alexander Pope, a Bibliography,* 2 vols., Austin, University of Texas Press, 1922–27.

Correspondence George Sherburn, ed. *The Correspondence of Alexander Pope,* 5 vols., Oxford, Clarendon Press, 1956.

2. *Lists of Portraits (Chiefly Oil Paintings) of Pope and his Contemporaries*

A. TRAVEL GUIDES

Various guides to English estates, houses, and collections are cited throughout by readily identifiable titles. A few of the more frequent are Daniel Lysons, *The Environs of London,* London, 1795,

1810; John Britton, Edward W. Brayley, *et al.*, *The Beauties of England and Wales*, 18 vols., London, 1801–16; Gustave Friedrich Waagen, *Treasures of Art in Great Britain*, 3 vols., London, 1854, and *Galleries and Cabinets of Art in Great Britain . . . 1854 and 1856*, London, 1857.

B. EXHIBITIONS

British Institution, 1820	*The British Institution for Promotion of the Fine Arts in the United Kingdom*, London, 1820: pp. 15 ff., "A Catalogue of Portraits Representing Distinguished Persons."
Manchester, 1857	*Catalogue of the Art Treasures of the United Kingdom, Collected at Manchester in 1857*, London, 1857.
South Kensington, 1867	*South Kensington Museum, Catalogue of the Second Special Exhibition of National Portraits on Loan . . .* London, 1867.
Leeds, 1868	*National Exhibition of Works of Art at Leeds, Official Catalogue*, Leeds, 1868.
Twickenham, 1888	Pope Commemoration, 1888, Loan Museum. *Catalogue of the Books, Autographs, Paintings, Drawings, Engravings, and Personal Relics Exhibited in the Town Hall, Twickenham, July 31st to August 4th, 1888*, Richmond, Surrey, Edward King, 1888.
Guelph, 1891	*Exhibition of the Royal House of Guelph, The New Gallery, Regent Street*, London, 1891.
Oxford, 1906	[Oxford University], *Illustrated Catalogue of a Loan Collection of Portraits of English Historical Personages who Died between 1714 and 1837. Exhibited in the Examination Schools, Oxford, April and May, MDCCCCVI*, Oxford, 1906.

Later exhibitions, at the Bodleian (1920), at Chesterfield House (1934), at the Royal Academy, Burlington House (1934, 1955–56, 1956–57, 1960–61), at the Walker Art Gallery, Liverpool (1958), and at the Iveagh Bequest, Kenwood (1959), are cited by full titles.

C. COLLECTIONS

National Portrait Gallery Catalogues (see under NPG, p. xxxii).

F. R. Earp, *A Descriptive Catalogue of the Pictures in the Fitzwilliam Museum*, Cambridge: At the University Press, 1902.

Mrs. R. H. Poole, *Catalogue of Portraits in the Possession of the University, Colleges, City and County of Oxford*, 3 vols., Oxford, Clarendon Press, 1912 (vol. 1), 1925 (vols. 2 and 3).

Richard W. Goulding and C. K. Adams, *Catalogue of the Pictures Belonging to His Grace the Duke of Portland, K.G., at Welbeck Abbey . . .* Cambridge University Press, 1936.

Various house catalogues of paintings and the like are cited throughout by full titles.

3. Art Histories and Biographies

Vertue

George Vertue, *Note Books*, Oxford University Press, Walpole Society: vol. 1 (Walpole *18*, 1930); vol. 2 (Walpole *20*, 1932); vol. 3 (Walpole *22*, 1934); vol. 4 (Walpole *24*, 1936); vol. 5 (Walpole *26*, 1938); vol. 6, Index to 1–5 (Walpole *29*, 1947); vol. 6 [i.e. 7] (Walpole Society *30*, 1955). I have for the most part normalized quotations.

George Vertue (1684–1756), engraver and antiquary, in his series of Note Books kept from c. 1713 to 1750, tells us most of what we know about artists in England during this period.

Walpole, *Anecdotes*

Horace Walpole, *Anecdotes of Painting in England . . . Collected by the late Mr. George Vertue*, 4 vols., Strawberry Hill, 1762–71 [i.e. 1780]; ed. James Dallaway, 5 vols., 1826–28; ed. Ralph N. Wornum, 3 vols., London, 1849, and later editions to 1888; vol. 5 (Walpole's contemporary extracts, 1760–95), ed. F. W. Hilles and P. B. Daghlian, Yale University Press, 1937.

Wornum's edition has been quoted throughout from a three-volume printing, without date, published at London by Bickers and Son. But references are easily found in other printings.

Walpole acquired Vertue's manuscripts in 1758 for £100 (see Allen T. Hazen, *A Bibliography of the Strawberry Hill Press* [New Haven, Yale University Press, 1942], pp. 55–66; Vertue *1*. xii).

Waterhouse

Ellis [K.] Waterhouse, *Painting in Britain 1530–1790*, London, Penguin Books, 1953; pp. 247–52 contain a good bibliography.

Whinney and Millar

Margaret Whinney and Oliver Millar, *English Art 1625–1714*, Oxford, Clarendon Press, 1957.

An important earlier authority is C. H. Collins Baker, *Lely and the Stuart Portrait Painters*, 2 vols., London, The Medici Society, 1912.

William T. Whitley, *Artists and their Friends in England, 1700–1799*, 2 vols., London, The Medici Society, 1928, has been a frequent, if tantalizing, guide to incidents of eighteenth-century art history. Many of the sources can be discovered in the Whitley Papers, preserved at the Department of Prints and Drawings in the British Museum.

David Piper, *The English Face*, London, Thames and Hudson, 1957, less often cited in this book than it deserves, has been a presiding inspiration and perspective, however imperfect the realization.

Biographies of the several artists, Lord Killanin, *Kneller* (1948), W. Nisser, *Dahl* (1927), M. I. Webb, *Rysbrack* (1954), M. Jourdain, *Kent* (1948), and K. A. Esdaile, *Roubiliac* (1928), are cited locally by adequate titles.

4. Dictionaries

DNB
: *Dictionary of National Biography from the Earliest Times to 1900*, ed. Leslie Stephen and Sidney Lee, 62 vols., London, Smith, Elder, 1885–1900; reissue, in 21 vols., 1908–09.

Thieme-Becker
: U. Thieme and F. Becker, *Allgemeines Lexikon der Bildenden Künstler,* 37 vols., Leipzig, 1907–50.

A number of minor artists, mostly engravers, are identified, without citation of authority, from the above dictionaries or from Michael Bryan, *Dictionary of Painters and Engravers,* ed. G. C. Williamson, London, 1903–04, 5 vols., or Samuel Redgrave, *A Dictionary of Artists of the English School,* 2nd ed., London, 1878. Special dictionaries of great value are Rupert Gunnis, *Dictionary of British Sculptors 1660–1851,* Harvard University Press, 1954; and Basil S. Long, *British Miniaturists,* London, 1929. Data concerning the lives of peers are likely to be taken from G[eorge] E[dward] C[okayne], *The Complete Peerage,* 2nd ed., 13 vols., 1910–59. Various editions of J. B. Burke's *Peerage and Baronetage* and *Landed Gentry* have yielded similar information.

5. Art Sales

Lugt
: Frits Lugt, *Répertoire des Catalogues de Ventes Publiques Intéressant l'Art ou la Curiosité, 1* (1600–1825), *2* (1826–60), La Haye, Martinus Nijhoff, 1938–53. For the sake of firm reference I have often cited Lugt numbers.

Art Prices Current
: *Art Prices Current,* 9 vols. (1907–22), London, Office of the Fine Art Trade Journal; New Series, vol. 1–(1921–), London, London Art Trade Press.

Other works describing sales at which Pope portraits changed ownership are: George Redford, *Art Sales, A History of Sales of Pictures and Other Works of Art,* 2 vols., London, 1888; Algernon Graves, *Art Sales,* 3 vols., London, 1918–21; William T. Whitley, *Art in England 1821–1837,* Cambridge, 1930.

6. *Drawings*

Binyon — Laurence Binyon, *Catalogue of Drawings by British Artists and Artists of Foreign Origin Working in Great Britain Preserved in the Department of Prints and Drawings in the British Museum,* 4 vols. London, British Museum, 1898–1907. Vol. 2 (1902), pp. 224–28 contains an important list of Richardson drawings. For Kneller, this catalogue has been superseded by E. Croft-Murray and P. Hulton, *Catalogue of British Drawings,* vols. 1 [*1*], Text, and 1 [2], Plates, London, British Museum, 1960.

The Courtauld Institute of Art, *Hand-List of the Drawings in the Witt Collection,* London University, 1956.

Frits Lugt, *Les Marques de Collections de Dessins,* Amsterdam, 1921. (*Supplément,* La Haye, 1956) has important sections on the collecting activities of the Jonathan Richardsons, father and son, their marks and handwriting.

W. A. Churchill, *Watermarks in Paper,* Amsterdam, 1935.

7. *Engravings*

An early list of engravings of Pope appears in Mark Noble's *Continuation* (3 vols., 1806) of James Granger's *Biographical History of England,* 1st ed. 1769–74.

J. Ch. Smith — John Chaloner Smith, *British Mezzotint Portraits,* 5 vols., London, 1878–83.

Charles E. Russell, *English Mezzotint Portraits and Their States, Catalogue of Corrections and Additions to Chaloner Smith,* 2 vols., London, 1926.

BMEP — Freeman O'Donoghue and (Sir) Henry Hake, *Catalogue of Engraved British Portraits . . . in the British Museum,* 6 vols., London: British Museum, 1908–25. Vol. 3 lists more than sixty engravings of Pope.

BMP & PS — F. G. Stephens and E. Hawkins, *Catalogue of Prints and Drawings in the British Museum, Division I, Political and Personal Satires,* 2 (June 1689 to 1733), London, British Museum, 1873.

Grolier — *An Exhibition of the First Editions of Alexander Pope . . . with a Collection of the Engraved Portraits . . .* New York, The Grolier Club, 1911. It includes a catalogue of 125 Pope engravings plus some engravings of his contemporaries in the Beverly Chew Collection, bequeathed to the New York Public Library.

Several extra-illustrated sets of editions of Pope's *Works*, Spence's *Anecdotes,* and Johnson's *Life of Pope* (to be found at the Widener Library, Harvard; at W. S. Lewis's *Museum Arbuteanum,* Farmington, Conn.; at the Pierpont Morgan Library, New York; in the collection of Dr. Gordon N. Ray, New York; and in the Rare Books Collection at the University of Texas) contain valuable assemblages of Pope engravings. So also do the archives of the National Portrait Gallery.

NPG   National Portrait Gallery, London.

Scharf   Various published and unpublished materials are cited by abbreviated titles under this head. (Sir) George Scharf (1820–95) became the first Secretary of the National Portrait Gallery in 1857, and its Director in 1882. Beginning with the Manchester exhibition of 1857, he filled a series of pocket notebooks with sketches and notes on collections and exhibitions for many years. These are preserved at the National Portrait Gallery in two series, with the titles *Scharf Sketch Books* and *Trustees' Sketch Books.* Scharf also annotated many exhibition, sale, and house catalogues, now preserved in the archives of the Gallery. He was also the author of the Gallery's *Historical and Descriptive Catalogue,* eds. 1881, 1887, and of a

Catalogue, 1888.   "new and enlarged" *Historical and Descriptive Catalogue of the Pictures, Busts, &c. in the National Portrait Gallery, . . .* London, 1888.

Catalogue, 1949.   Subsequent catalogues of the Gallery are resumed in the latest edition: *Catalogue of the National Portrait Gallery 1856–1947,* London, National Portrait Gallery, 1949; *Supplement 1948–1959,* 1960.

Books illustrating pictures in the Gallery are: Lionel Cust, *The National Portrait Gallery,* 2 vols., London, Cassell and Company, 1901–02; and National Portrait Gallery, *British National Portraits, A Selection from the National Portrait Gallery with Biographical Notes,* Cambridge University Press, 1957.

Piper, *Seventeenth Century Portraits.*   A catalogue written in several new dimensions and amounting to an encyclopedia of English baroque portraiture: David Piper, *Catalogue of the Seventeenth-Century Portraits in the National Portrait Gallery 1625–1714,* Cambridge University Press, 1963.

6. ORDER OF THE CATALOGUE, LEGENDS, ENTRIES

The pictures of Pope, about 205 in number, are arranged in a nearly biographical or chronological order, under 81 primary numbers, for as many distinct types. The difficulty of defining the types according to an even rationale will be seen on examining such groups as the Kneller pattern drawing and the oils of 1721 (no. 6), the Richardson etchings (nos. 39–41, 42–45, 46–48), and the Roubiliac terra cotta and signed marbles (nos. 57–61). The numerous Richardson portraits dating from 1733 to 1742 are an exception to chronological order. They are put in four parallel sequences: drawings on paper, drawings on vellum, etchings, and oil paintings.

The portraits brought together under each primary number are also as far as possible arranged under that number in a chronological order, to suggest the development of the image during Pope's lifetime and for some time thereafter. But in a given group paintings precede engravings, even though the first engraving may well be earlier and more informative than many of the paintings. A further exception to the general chronological order within groups is that under the joint numbers "57–61" (the Roubiliac type) the images are put in four parallel sequences: marbles, plasters, ceramics, and engravings.

In the *order* of paintings themselves within a given group, provenance in general takes precedence over aesthetic quality.

The *legend* of each portrait is a *prima facie* report on the physical object, its materials, size, colors, inscriptions, and location. In a very few instances, this report is based on reliable information rather than first-hand inspection. Portraits which I have not seen are marked by a dagger in the legend.

The *entry* which complements and precedes each legend deals mainly with matters of documentary evidence. The heading of the entry, so far as it announces authorship and date, is a conclusion or hypothesis based on the evidence of the entry and the legend.

Dimensions given for paintings are generally those of the visible painted surface; for drawings, those of the sheet of paper, unless the image is specified. Dimensions of engravings are variously specified according to need or opportunity for precision. Height always precedes width. "Right" and "left" refer to the viewer, not the subject.

In transcribing from paintings, drawings, engravings, and sculpture throughout the book, I have tried to be faithful to spelling, punctuation, capitalization, abbreviation (within typographic limits), and lineation, but have ignored differences in style of letters, as roman, italic, gothic, cursive, outline, swash.

Some color notes in the legends have the identification "BCC." These are taken from the *British Colour Council Dictionary of Colour Standards* [2 vols.], 28, Sackville Street, London W.1, 1934.

I have used the terms "crayon drawing" and "crayon painting" (with appropriate explanations here and there in parentheses) instead of the usual three terms "chalk," "crayon," and "pastel." See Vertue's accounts of "crayon painting" (pastel) quoted in entry no. 7.6 and in the sketch of William Hoare; and see Waterhouse, *British Painting*, pp. 243–46.

THE PORTRAITS AND THE ARTISTS

· 1 ·

ANONYMOUS, c. 1695

1. OIL PAINTING, ARTIST UNKNOWN, C. 1695. MR. AND MRS. JAMES M. OSBORN, NEW HAVEN, CONNECTICUT.

Pope's uncle Samuel Cooper, the celebrated miniaturist, portrayer of Cromwell and Charles II, died in 1672. Some of his pictures are said to have hung in the boy's home at Binfield and to have become his property by delayed bequest in 1710. Mrs. Cooper (Christiana Turner, sister of Pope's mother) died when Pope was six years old; she was his godmother.[1] Here are slender enough grounds for talking about an influence on Pope's childhood, and such an influence in turn might have little enough to do with the fond parents' commissioning a portrait of the precocious boy at the age of seven. Still these suggestions of early artistic interest deserve notice and also perhaps the following anecdote of Pope as a schoolboy, aged less than twelve years: "At the Hours of Recreation [at Thomas Deane's School near Hyde Park Corner], whilst the Rest of his School-fellows were diverting themselves at such Games and Sports, as was usual with Boys of their Age, Mr. *Pope* used to amuse himself with Drawing, and such like improving and rational Accomplishments."[2] And also the following from a letter to a lady written by Pope while perhaps still in his teens: "You are but too good a painter already; and no Picture of *Raphael's* was ever so beautiful, as that which you have form'd in a certain heart of my acquaintance. . . . But I must complain to you of my hand, which is an arrant traitor to my heart; for having been copying your picture from thence and from *Kneller* these three days, it has done all possible injury to the finest Face that ever was made, and to the liveliest Image that ever was drawn."[3]

That a portrait of Pope as a young boy once existed has long been known from the

3

1. Oil on canvas. 29 x 24 in. Background and painted oval reddish-brown; area to left of head light gray; coat blue (like BCC 149 Stewart blue); tie and cloak scarlet (like BCC 208 Signal Red); branch of bay green; hair brown and gray; flesh tints pinkish; lips bright red; eyes blue. Inscribed in upper left corner in orange paint: "A. Pope. / Anno Ætatis. / 7." Mr. and Mrs. James M. Osborn, New Haven, Connecticut.

4

ANONYMOUS

Anecdotes of Joseph Spence. In May 1730 Pope's modest Boswell, Fellow of New College, Oxford, and also Professor of Poetry, spent a week in Pope's company, recording conversations with Pope, old Mrs. Pope, and other members of the family, among whom was William Mannick, resident priest in the family of Pope's half sister. Mannick is given as the authority for the following:

> He was a child of a particularly sweet temper, and had a great deal of sweetness in his look, when he was a boy. This is very evident in the picture; drawn for him when about ten years old: in which his face is round, plump, pretty and of a fresh complexion.—I have often heard Mrs. Pope say, that he was then exactly like that picture: as I have often been myself told that it was the perpetual application he fell into, about two years afterwards, that chang'd his form; and ruin'd his constitution.—The Laurel-branch, in that picture was not inserted originally; but was added, long after, by Jervas.[4]

At Christie's on 21 October 1960, in a sale of *Pictures of the 16th, 17th & 18th Centuries From Various Sources,* lot 19 (p. 5) was: "Van Loo Portrait of a Boy, said to be Alexander Pope, aged 7, bust length, in blue dress, white shirt, red bow and red cloak—in a painted oval—29 in. by 24 in." It was acquired by Mr. James M. Osborn of New Haven, Connecticut.

An inscription in orange paint in the upper left corner, "A. Pope. / Anno Ætatis. / 7," is presumably not original, but is nevertheless early. Mannick's reference to a "picture drawn for him when about ten years old" may indicate that the inscription is later than 1730. The face, plump and fair, while yet so manifestly Popean, is one good indication that this is indeed the picture described by Mannick. The laurel branch is another. It would hardly have been put in the hand of a seven-year-old boy. No doubt it *was* added by Jervas—following a tradition which may be sampled in William Marshall's engraving of Shakespeare in Shakespeare's *Poems* of 1640, or in Kneller's Dryden of 1698 (at Trinity College, Cambridge), though in the latter the poet holds not a branch but a wreath of bay.

The style of painting, the chevalier bearing of the child, the costume, and the coiffure, have an air that seems French. Pope was within a few weeks the same age as the Pretender, whose portrait, painted in France when he was seven years old, by Nicolas de Largillière, and now to be seen at the National Portrait Gallery (no. 976), has much the same shape of head and hair and the same bearing. Portraits of children in England at this period were not common, even in noble families. The emigré portrait-painter Simon Dubois (1632–1708), who came to England in 1785, and of whom Vertue has much to say, might plausibly be hazarded as the artist of this picture. We shall see later that some sort of acquaintance between the Pope family and that of the painter Richardson may be supported at a fairly early date. Pope's uncle, we have seen, was Samuel Cooper. There is no reason for surprise if we find the family in touch with good artists.

The picture is in a contemporary frame of gilt wood and gesso, a fact which tells against its being the portrait of "Mr. Pope when a boy in a black and gilt frame" which according to an inventory was in the Great Parlor at Twickenham when he died. See Appendix 2, no. 9.

This portrait was exhibited at the National Portrait Gallery Exhibition in 1961 and was illustrated in *The Sunday Telegraph*, 26 March 1961, p. 28, and in *The Times*, 15 April 1961, p. 3.

1. George Sherburn, *The Early Career of Alexander Pope* (Oxford, 1934), p. 102; Norman Ault, *New Light on Pope* (London 1949), p. 76; *Vertue* 2.41. Peter Cunningham, in *The Builder*, London, 5 September 1868, p. 655, quotes Mrs. Cooper's will: "To my nephew and godson, Alexander Pope, my painted china dish, with a silver foot, and a dish to set it in, and, after my sister Elizabeth Turner's decease, all my books, pictures, and medals set in gold."

2. *Life of Alexander Pope, Esq., Printed for Weaver Bickerton,* 1744, pp. 13–14, quoted in Ault, *New Light,* pp. 68–69; and in Sherburn, *Early Career,* p. 39.

3. 1 March 1704/5 (*Correspondence 1.*4). Cf. Ault, *New Light,* p. 69.

4. Joseph Spence, *Anecdotes,* ed. S. W. Singer (London 1820), pp. 25–26; J. M. Osborn, *New Year Greetings from the Osborns* [1962], quoting the manuscript in his possession.

· 2 ·

C. 1714-1715

CHARLES JERVAS (c. 1675-1739)

THE PRECOCIOUS YOUNG MAN who came in from the country to Will's Coffeehouse and within a few years published his *Pastorals,* his *Essay on Criticism,* his *Rape of the Lock,* and his *Windsor Forest* had, in common with many other poets (even blind singers like Homer and Milton), a distinctly pictorial imagination. Perhaps it is even worth arguing that Pope—far from being what the romantic and Victorian taste perceived in him, one of our less "imaginative" poets—was even in the pictorial sense one of the most vividly imaginative. There is a kind of truth in the plea that his *Pastorals* (1709) and his *Windsor Forest* (1713), rather than the traditionally named *Grongar Hill* of Dyer and the *Winter* of Thomson (both 1726), are the real beginnings of the "picturesque" tradition of English poetry. A modern critic who resorted to statistics has been able to establish at least one surprising fact, namely, that in those early descriptive poems, the *Pastorals* and *Windsor Forest,* Pope averaged two or three times as many names of *colors* as even the later and professed painter poets Dyer, Blake, and Rossetti.[1]

> The bright-ey'd Perch with Fins of *Tyrian* Dye,
> The silver Eel, in shining Volumes roll'd,
> The yellow Carp, in Scales bedrop'd with Gold,
> Swift Trouts, diversify'd with Crimson Stains. . . .
> —*Windsor Forest,* 11. 142-45

1. Norman Ault, *New Light on Pope* (London, 1949), pp. 80, 81, 85, 86. The following account is considerably indebted to Ault.

7

Pope was also a literary critic who liked well enough to bring in the painterly comparisons which were the clichés of the day:

> (to express my self like a Painter) their *Colouring* entertains the sight, but the *Lines* and *Life* of the Picture are not to be inspected too narrowly.[2]

> . . . the slightest Sketch, if justly trac'd,
> Is by ill *Colouring* but the more disgrac'd.[3]

He was the kind of young poet who would amuse a leisure hour by sketching on the back of a letter some classical figure in pen and ink;[4] he would, as we have seen, confess in a letter to a fine lady that he had been struggling unsuccessfully for three days to copy her portrait by Kneller;[5] he would make a drawing of the Madonna and present it to the wife of his best friend ("St Luke himself," she said, "never drew such a Madonna").[6] He would manufacture a gallant present for his lady—a fan painted with the story of Cephalus and Procris—and present it to her with a paper of verses. He would publish the verses in *The Spectator* (No. 527, 4 November 1712).[7]

All this perhaps does not add up to very much—hardly the stuff of which to make a Blake or a Rossetti. But here at least is a young Augustan poet who seems ripe for some kind of alliance with a painter. Hardly perhaps with the greatest of the day; hardly with the second greatest. Pope's choice of a painter, like the rest of that painter's somewhat specious eminence, seems to have been determined in large part by social and literary circumstance. George Vertue, the principal art chronicler of the time, had a rather limited admiration for Charles Jervas. Today he still shimmers somewhat unsubstantially upon the surface of Augustan art history. He was a Whiggish and freethinking Irishman who had appeared in England about 1694, had studied for a year with Kneller, had attracted some notice for his copies of the cartoons of Raphael at Hampton Court, and had been sent off to travel on the continent.[8] At Paris in 1699 he did a head of Prior in crayons (which has come down at Welbeck),[9] and at Rome about 1703[10] he made excellent copies of Carlo Maratti. Here also he studied to remedy his chief weakness, which was drawing.[11] Then, in April of 1709, at London, Jervas bursts upon us already mature in such special kind of glory as he was to attain—through the pen of Richard Steele in the fourth number of *The Tatler*.

2. Pope to Cromwell, 17 December 1710 (*Correspondence 1*.110).

3. *Essay on Criticism*, 11.23–24 (1711).

4. Ault, *New Light*, p. 75, alluding to Bodleian MS. Rawlinson letters, 90, f. 50V (Pope-Cromwell papers). Ault reports that the sketch measures about 3¼ x 2⅔ in., and that Edmund Curll, who had these papers in his possession, has written beneath it: "This Figure is the Delineation of Mr. Pope's Penmanship. E. Curll."

5. 1 March 1704/5 (*Correspondence 1*.4).

6. Pope to Caryll, 25 January 1710/11 (*Correspondence 1*.115).

7. *Twickenham 6, Minor Poems*, pp. 45–46.

8. Waterhouse, *Painting in Britain*, pp. 107–08; Lionel Cust, "Charles Jervas" in *Dictionary of National Biography*, 29.354; Walpole, *Anecdotes* 2.219–73; *Vertue* 3.15, 42.

9. Waterhouse, *Painting in Britain*, p. 107; H. Bunker Wright and Henry C. Montgomery, "The Art Collection of a Virtuoso in Eighteenth-Century England," *The Art Bulletin*, 27 (March 1945), 200.

10. Waterhouse, *Painting in Britain*, p. 107, n. 17, citing Oxford Historical Society, *Collectanea*, 2 (1890), 403 ff.

11. *Vertue* 3.16–17.

CHARLES JERVAS

White's Chocolate-house, April 18

All hearts at present pant for two ladies only, who have for some time en-
grossed the dominion of the town. . . . The beauty of Clarissa is soft, that of
Chloe piercing. When you look at Clarissa, you see the most exact harmony of
feature, complexion, and shape; you find in Chloe nothing extraordinary in
any one of those particulars, but the whole woman irresistible. Clarissa looks
languishing; Chloe, killing. . . . These different perfections are suitably represented by the last great painter Italy has sent us, Mr. Jervas. Clarissa is, by
that skilful hand, placed in a manner that looks artless, and innocent of the
torments she gives; Chloe drawn with a liveliness that shows she is conscious,
but not affected, of her perfections. Clarissa is a shepherdess; Chloe, a country
girl. I must own, the design of Chloe's picture shows, to me, great mastery in
the painter; for nothing could be better imagined than the dress he has given
her, of a straw hat and riband. . . .

It must have been about this time that Jervas began to fill a house in Cleveland Court,
near St. James's,[12] with an art collection and to make it the rendezvous of literary
friends. As Horace Walpole would put it, Jervas "sat at the top of his profession." He
enjoyed early and late high and fashionable patronage, from the time in 1711 when
he painted the Duke of Marlborough's daughters and Lord and Lady Strafford,[13]
through his incumbency as King's Painter (after Kneller) under both George I and
George II, to his commissions near the end of his life from Sir Robert Walpole.[14] His
vanity and his liberties in conversation with his noble sitters became notorious.

The two ladies celebrated in *Tatler* No. 4 are assigned in the annotation of an
early reader actual names, which unhappily lack verification.[15] The shepherdess Clarissa
survives for us, however, softly and brilliantly in Jervas's masterpiece, the Duchess of
Queensberry, holding a crook, with cows being milked in the distance (NPG 258), or
holding her hat (the version at Petworth).[16] A portrait by Jervas of Lady Louisa Smyth,
still to be seen at Ickworth in 1955, illustrates very well the innocent, frail charm of
the country girl Chloe—her wispy face and tapering laced bodice, over one arm her
basket of flowers, the other slender arm reaching up to secure her wide-brimmed hat,

12. It was known as Bridgewater House (Sherburn, *Early Career*, p. 69; Elwin and Courthope 8.91).

13. Waterhouse, *Painting in Britain*, p. 107, n. 18; citing *The Wentworth Papers*, ed. J. J. Cartwright (1883), 213, 279.

14. See Walpole, *Anecdotes* 2.273, n. 3, a list of four Walpole ladies by Jervas sold at the Strawberry Hill Sale.

15. "In a copy of the original edition of the *Tatler*, with MS notes written in the last century, which was sold at Messrs Sotheby's in April, 1887, the ladies here described were said to be Mrs. Chetwine [Chetwynd] and Mrs. Hales respectively." (*The Tatler*, ed. George A. Aitken, *1* [London, 1898], 39). "Mrs. Raines, a

Young Lady in the City & one of my Shepherdesses" (Jervas to Pope, 12 June 1715 [*Correspondence 1.295*]). And see Pope's *Moral Essay 2, On the Characters of Women*, Twickenham *3*, ii, *Moral Essays*, p. 47.

16. See C. H. Collins Baker, *Catalogue of the Petworth Collection* (1920), p. 63, no. 374; and Walker Art Gallery, *Painting and Sculpture in England 1700–1750* (Liverpool, 1958), p. 15, no. 24. For another of Jervas's shepherdesses, see this Lady Mary Pierrepont (later Lady Mary Wortley Montagu), owned by the Marquis of Bute, reproduced as frontispiece of Robert Halsband's *Life of Lady Mary Wortley Montagu*, Oxford, 1956.

9

as a suggestion of a Zephyr moves her flounced skirt and agitates a sapling silhouetted upon the skyline.[17] Often, however, Jervas's women were more buxom, with a solid, hour-glass contour of waist, bosom, and neck—statuesque, not unattractive large mannikins—like the half-reclining royal mistress Henrietta Howard, Lady Suffolk, once in the collections of Pope and of Horace Walpole;[18] or like Pope's own ladies,[19] once at Mapledurham, three-quarter length standing, one dark, one fair, caught in a pose of lively reaching arms, in the hands of one a wreath and a ribbon, bearing the appropriate Jervas-like words: "Martha Teresa Blount. Sic positae quoniam suaves 1716."[20] Or like the three Valkyrie portraits of Queen Caroline, superbly tall, blonde, silken, and bejewelled, a white hand resting on a crown on a table beside her.[21] At his best, says the modern historian, Jervas had a "pleasant soft and flowing quality to his silks and satins," learned no doubt from the Van Dycks and the Titians that he "assiduously copied."[22] He came off on the whole better with his women than with his men. But he cultivated the literary world and painted a number of the most noted authors and learned men, and not disgracefully. His Isaac Newton, seated, stiffly upright, pointing his finger at a large watch and fob lying on a table, still hangs at the Royal Society chambers, and his Dr. Arbuthnot is at the College of Physicians. Swift in his *Journal to Stella* records his sitting to Jervas and dining with him at Addison's country place during the year 1710,[23] and the picture of the clergyman seated in gown and fichu, three-quarter length, his hands engaged with quill and paper, his face wearing a somewhat severe, birch-rod expression, may be seen at the National Portrait Gallery (No. 278),[24] or at the Bodleian Library (reduced to a bust, No. 48), or in the Chesterfield Library Set.[25] In 1714 Jervas painted the picture of Joseph Addison now among the poets at Knole House—three-quarter length standing, before a folio book and papers, with a slender knuckly hand to his open coat, yet looking generally fair, sleek, and plump.[26] The portrait of Newton has a dark wig in addition to a dark gown, but Jervas' portraits of men generally seem to borrow something of the smoothness and fairness of his females—rounded faces, blond wigs, a wide shimmer of light on the black clerical gown of Swift.

17. NPG Photograph: Lady Louisa Smyth, daughter of John, First Earl of Bristol (48 x 39 in.), Ickworth, Lady Bristol, 1955.

18. NPG Photograph 1953: in the collection of the Earl of Buckinghamshire, on loan to the NPG. See Walpole, *Anecdotes* 2. 273, n. 3.

19. "I have just set the last hand to a couplet, for so I may call two Nymphs in One Piece. They are Pope's Favourites." (Jervas to Parnell, February 1715/16 [*Correspondence 1*.332]). The version at Mapledurham was exhibited at the Loan Exhibition at the South Kensington Museum in 1867 (No. 152); another version is at the Fitzwilliam Museum, Cambridge; and another, belonging to Mrs. Browne-Swinburne, Capheaton Hall, is on loan at King's College, Newcastle-on-Tyne. Carruthers, *Works 4* (1854) has as frontispiece a wood engraving "From the Picture in Stanton Harcourt."

20. In his copy of the South Kensington Catalogue of 1867 (p. 45, No. 152) George Scharf sketched the ribbon and inscription, which quotes Virgil's *Eclogue* 3.55. See a photograph facing vol. 1, p. 222 of George Paston, *Mr. Pope* (London, 1909).

21. At the Guildhall, London; NPG No. 369 (Studio of Charles Jervas), illustrated in the National Portrait Gallery's *British Historical Portraits* (Cambridge, 1957), Plate 118; and NPG Photograph 1951: Christie's, 19 January 1951, Lot 135, Duke of Bedford (by or after Jervas).

22. Waterhouse, *Painting in Britain*, p. 107.

23. Swift's *Journal to Stella*, ed. Harold Williams (Oxford, 1948), pp. 9, 13 (Letters II, III, 9 September 1710), 32 (Letter IV, 21 September), 71 (Letter VII, 19 October).

24. Illustrated in *British Historical Portraits*, plate 101; Waterhouse, *British Painting*, Plate 91b.

25. Now in the Sterling Library, London University. See no. 5.7.

26. NPG Photographs 1926 and 1960.

On the death of Sir Godfrey Kneller in the early autumn of 1723, Jervas succeeded to the post of Portrait Painter to His Majesty, with the salary of £200 per annum.[27] This brought him temporarily "a great increase of business."[28] Yet he failed notably to satisfy his royal patrons and suffered much humiliation. "Mr. Jervas, His Majesty's Painter," reports Vertue, "has had no success in painting their Majesties' pictures, and from thence he lost the favor and interest at Court." It seems the Queen with an entourage of nobles descended one morning from Kensington Palace to Jervas' house in Cleveland Court and from there swept on to "Mr. Wootton's in Cavendish Square." There she saw "a great picture of His Majesty painted on horseback, a gray horse . . . the face of the King by Mr. Jervas and all other parts by Mr. Wootton." The horse was "much approved of, but the King, not thought to be like, was much spoke against from thence."[29] Vertue adds that in his later years Jervas fell back much on copying.[30]

The fan which Alexander Pope (as a young man, before his study with Jervas) had painted and presented to Martha Blount, was pounced upon, after an auction sale, by Sir Joshua Reynolds, who then took it and displayed it with scorn to his classes: "work . . . taken up from idleness . . . laid aside when it ceases to amuse; . . . the work of one who paints only for amusement."[31] Fan-painting was, per se, scarcely the medium for Reynolds. At about the date when Pope's fan fell into the hands of Reynolds, Horace Walpole, in his *Anecdotes of Painting*, taking a cue from Vertue's *Note Books*, pronounced the following harsh but perhaps not grossly unfair judgment on Jervas: "In general his pictures are a light flimsy kind of fan-painting, as large as life."[32]

Pope's correspondence during March, May, and June of 1713—beginning just after he had sent to press his *Windsor Forest*—shows him in full pursuit of a new hobby, or "employ." He is a "lover of painting." He is "most particularly oblig'd to Mr. Gervase," who gives him "dayly instructions & examples." "You'll find me . . . painting at Mr. Gervase's in Cleveland Court, by St. James's. I generall[y] imploy the mornings this way."[33] In August the accounts ascend to a kind of sportive climax, with a certain gesture as of the hands cheerfully thrown up in defeat:

> I beg leave here to give you some notices of my self, who am so entirely immersed in the designing art, (the only sort of designing I shall ever be capable

27. *Daily Journal*, 4 November 1723 (Whitley Papers, Department of Prints and Drawings, British Museum); *Vertue* 3.16–17.

28. *Vertue* 3.16–17, 33, 35.

29. *Vertue* 3.59.

30. *Vertue* 3.99.

31. Allan Cunningham, *The Lives of the Most Eminent British Painters and Sculptors* (New York, 1831), *1*.233–34.

32. "his works rather appear to me like fan-painting: fine silks, fair flesh white and red, of beautiful colors, but no blood in them or natural heat or warmness; much a mannerist" (*Vertue* 3.16–17). In the summer of 1715 Pope presented fans to both Martha and Teresa Blount, but they were from the stock of Jervas (*Correspondence 1*.310, 315). "I . . . desire yourself &

your fair Sister to accept of these Fans. . . . I desir'd Mr Jervas to chuse two of the best he had, but if these do not chance to hitt your fancy, you'l oblige me by taking your own choice out of twenty when you go to London." The first part of Jervas' Sale *Catalogue* in March 1740 lists six "curious Italian leather Fan Mounts," decorated, Nos. 569, 599, 600, 601, 606, 607.

33. Pope to Caryll, March 1713(?), 30 April 1713, 12 June 1713 (*Correspondence 1*.170, 174, 177, 200). In a letter sold at the Parke-Bernet Galleries 31 March 1964, lot no. 166, and now in the Beinecke Rare Book and Manuscript Library, Yale University, Pope and Jervas address rival compliments to Sir William Trumbull at Easthamstead, in Berkshire. The letter is dated 6 June 1713, and Jervas's part is subscribed "Bridgwater House."

of) that I have not heard a rhyme of my own gingle this long time. My eyes have so far got the better of my ears, that I have at present no notion of any harmony besides that of colors. . . . They tell us, when St Luke painted, an angel came and finished the work; and it will be thought hereafter, that when I painted, the devil put the last hand to my pieces, they are so begrimed and smutted. 'Tis, however, some mercy that I see my faults; for I have been so out of conceit with my former performances, that I have thrown away three Dr Swifts, two Dutchesses of Montague, one Virgin Mary, the Queen of England, besides half a score earls and a Knight of the Garter. . . . I find my hand most successful in drawing of friends and those I most esteem; insomuch that my masterpieces have been one of Dr Swift, and one Mr Betterton.[34]

Pope's flirtation with painting in the studio of Jervas was carried on with delighted abandon; it was a golden, delirious interlude of escape from the other art, in which he was already beginning to experience the burden of actually being a master. His verse *Epistle to Jervas* (sent with a copy of Dryden's rules of painting translated from *Du Fresnoy*), is a blend of lush adulation and wistful retrospect:

> Smit with the love of Sister-arts we came,
> And met congenial, mingling flame with flame;
> Like friendly colours found them both unite,
> And each from each contract new strength and light.
> How oft' in pleasing tasks we wear the day,
> While summer suns roll unperceiv'd away?
> How oft' our slowly-growing works impart,
> While images reflect from art to art?[35]

But even during the autumn of 1713 Pope's allusions to the idyll begin to fade.[36] Pope is reported to have said, much later, that he had "learned to draw of Jervas for a year and a half."[37] But perhaps some allowance must be made for the expansion of reminiscence. The practical and professional concept of the *Iliad* translation was making an urgent claim by the spring of 1714:

> I shall now be very much taken up in this work which will keep me a poet (in spite of something I lately thought a resolution to the contrary) for some years longer.[38]

34. Pope to Caryll, 31 August 1713 (*Correspondence 1.*189). An earlier letter to Gay (23 August 1713) adds "two Lady Bridgewaters, a Duchess of Montague," and a Christ (*Correspondence 1.*187). The best known of the pictures attributed to Pope, apparently a copy of a portrait of Betterton by Kneller (cf. NPG 752), has come down in the possession of the Earls of Mansfield, at Kenwood until about 1922, and more recently at Scone Palace, Perth. This picture is reproduced and discussed with due caution by Benjamin Boyce, *The Character-Sketches in Pope's Poems* (Dur-

ham, N.C., 1962), frontispiece and pp. 131–32.

35. *Twickenham 6, Minor Poems*, pp. 156–58: 11. 13–20. Published in 1716. Ault, *New Light*, pp. 72–73, prints what appears to be a first draft from the Homer MSS in the British Museum (Add. MS. 4807, f.1286).

36. Pope to Caryll, 20 September [1713], 17 October 1713 (*Correspondence 1.*191, 194).

37. About 1728 (Spence, *Anecdotes*, ed. Singer, 1820, p. 23).

38. Pope to Caryll, 25 February 1713/14 (*Correspondence 1.*210).

The focus of mutual interest shifts, and Jervas the painter is now for a year or more all activity and concern in promoting subscriptions to Pope's Homer,[39] designing a head of Homer for the volume,[40] attempting to reconcile Pope and Addison,[41] gathering and forwarding reports of the warfare that ensued upon the simultaneous publications of Pope and Tickell in June 1715.[42] The year of discipleship had established a degree of intimacy which at moments, if one did not understand Pope's habitual facetiousness in correspondence, would seem sticky. ("I have scarce had an interval to think myself uneasy in the want of your company. I now and then just miss you as I step into bed.")[43] For a great many years, beginning presumably about the time of the painting lessons, but not ending when Pope moved in nearer to town at Chiswick in 1716, nor again when he moved out to Twickenham in 1718, Jervas' house in Cleveland Court was Pope's regular home when he was in town.[44] He would move in and share the "mansion" along with Jervas' servants Frank and Betty, even while Jervas was absent in Ireland—as he was much of the time from the summer of 1716 to apparently some time in 1720:[45]

> the spacious Mansion, like a *Turkish* Caravanserah, entertains the Vagabond with only bare Lodging. I rule the Family very ill, keep bad Hours, and lend out your Pictures about the Town. See what it is to have a Poet in your House! *Frank* indeed does all he can in such a Circumstance, for considering he has a wild Beast in it, he constantly keeps the Door chain'd.[46]

But the ten letters of Pope to Jervas and the eight letters of Jervas to Pope which are known today contain few serious words about the art of painting. The truth would seem to be that when Pope turned back to his professional concerns in the spring of 1714, he did not forget his love for Jervas and his sense of indebtedness to him, but, perhaps unconsciously at first, he did cease to look to this painter for serious inspiration or ideas about the art. A playfully extravagant sort of mutual complimentary relation seems to be set up, and on Pope's part perhaps to serve as a protection against more earnest exchanges which could no longer have any profit for him:

39. Jervas to Pope, after 27 May 1714 (*Correspondence 1*.226).

40. Jervas to Pope, 20 August 1714 (*Correspondence 1*.244); October 1714(?) (*Correspondence 1*.262).

41. Jervas to Pope, 20 August 1714 (*Correspondence 1*.244); Pope to Jervas, 27 August 1714 (*Correspondence 1*.244–45).

42. Jervas to Pope, 12 June 1715 (*Correspondence 1*.295–96); 28 June 1715 (*Correspondence 1*.300).

43. 16 August 1714 (*Correspondence 1*.243). "our morning Conferences in bed in the same Room, our evening Walks in the Park" (*Correspondence 2*.24: 1720?).

44. As late as 1725 and 1726 subscribers to the *Odyssey* were asked to send to Pope for their copies "at

Mr. Jervas's, Principal Painter to his Majesty, next Door to the Right Hon. the Lord Viscount Townshend's in Cleveland Court, St. James's" (Sherburn, *Early Career*, p. 270, citing *Evening Post*, 15 April 1725, 14 June 1726).

45. Jervas to Pope, 1716(?) (*Correspondence 1*.340–41); Pope to Jervas, 9 July 1716 (*Correspondence 1*.346–47); 14 November 1716 (*1*.370–71); 29 November 1716 (*1*.376–77); June–July 1717 (*1*.410); 1720(?) (*2*.23). In Ireland during 1716 Jervas seems to have boarded with Swift (*1*.370). When Swift visited Gay in London during 1726, extra sheets for him were borrowed from Jervas (Gay to Swift, 16 September 1726 [*Correspondence 2*.400]).

46. 29 November 1716 (*Correspondence 1*.377).

I am copying the great Master in one art, with the same love and diligence with which the Painters hereafter will copy you in another.[47]

I am pretty sure there never was a friendship of so easie a nature. We neither of us demand any mighty things from each other; what Vanity we have expects its gratifications from other people. It is not I, that am to tell you what an Artist you are, nor is it you that are to tell me what a Poet I am.[48]

In January of 1727 Jervas married Penelope Hume,[49] a lady whom Walpole describes as a widow worth £20,000,[50] and about this time we fail to trace Pope any more as a resident of Cleveland Court. We hear little more of Jervas, in fact, until the year 1738, when he is nearly ready to die. Perhaps a note of condescension creeps in with Pope's pity:

I have been very happy these 3 weeks & more, in the Company of . . . my Lord Bolingbroke . . . what adds to the obligation is, his being of a Rank in Understanding & Learning more above Others, than any Rank else can make a Man.
——It is with a *longo Intervallo,* that I name Another Old friend at this time, who gives me some Emotion, poor Jervas, whose Last Breathings are to be

Ex. 1. Etching. 8⅛ x 6¼ in. "The Collection of / Charles Jarvis Esq / Co[nsi]sting of Pictures / [Pri]nts Drawings Basso / Relievos &c. &c. / Heath / Auctioneer." ["G. V^dr Gucht In. et Fect"] *BMEP* Jervas 1. By permission of the Trustees of the British Museum.

47. 28 July 1714 (*Correspondence 1*.239).
48. 16 August 1714 (*Correspondence 1*.243). Cf. *Correspondence 1*.347, 376–77; 2.23, 99.
49. *Correspondence 3*.51, note 1. I have not found Professor Sherburn's source for the name of the lady.

50. *Anecdotes* 2.272 ("A Gentlewoman with 15 or 20 thousand pounds"—Vertue *3*.59). Pope said Jervas owed "almost everything" to her (to Bethel, 18 February 1740 [*Correspondence 4*.225]).

transferred to Italy, for he sets sail today, in hopes of some reprieve from his Asthma.[51]

Jervas returned from Italy in May 1739.[52] He died 3 November 1739, and surprised Pope by leaving him a legacy of £1000 if he outlived the widow. "an Old Friend from whom I had not the least imagination of such a thing, Mr. Jervas. . . . It is the first legacy I ever had, & I hope I shall never have another at the expense of any man's life, who would think so kindly of me."[53]

If the art of Jervas had ever extended, as it did with most painters of the era, to self-portraiture, today we have no trace of this. A few months after his death, on 11 March 1740, began the first part of a vast sale of his pictures and other art properties. On the etched cover (or title page)[54] of the catalogue, in a medallion on a pyramidal monument, appears a sketchy aquiline profile (Ex. 1) which is our only clue to the appearance of Pope's old friend and instructor, the painter of fans and shepherdesses.

51. Pope to Fortescue, 8 September, 1738 (*Correspondence 4*.135–36). Cf. Vertue *3*.85. Pope to Fortescue, 25 December 1738, and Pope to Swift, 17–19 May 1739 (*Correspondence 4*.155–56, 177), trace Jervas' travel over the Alps and return and a dinner with Pope.

52. Vertue *3*.93.

53. Pope to Bethel, 18 February 1740 (*Correspondence 4*.225).

54. This appears to be the source of the only other engraving (*BMEP* Jervas 2). The British Museum Library copy (C119.h3.14.15) of *A Catalogue of the Most Valuable Collection of Pictures, Prints, and Drawings Late of Charles Jarvis, Esq; deceased* [Part I] and *A Catalogue of the Valuable Collection of Prints and Drawings, in Architecture, History*, etc. [Part II], sold 11 March 1740, and days following, and 24 March and days following, lacks this frontispiece (or cover picture). In the Department of Prints and Drawings, a copy in the Anderdon Collectanea has the engraver's line partly trimmed off, and B. M. Crown 50–8–10–120, reproduced below, has lost it completely.

2.1 OIL PAINTING, BY CHARLES JERVAS. BODLEIAN LIBRARY, OXFORD.

The painting was apparently completed as early as the autumn of 1714. Vertue's engraving from it was published in the summer of 1715 and in 1717 was used as the frontispiece of Pope's first collected *Works*. See no. 2.2.

When the poet and virtuoso Matthew Prior died in 1721, one of the clauses of his will specified that his effects should be sold but that his patron Edward Lord Harley should have the preference if he wished to purchase any of them. Harley accordingly did acquire a number of pictures from Prior's collection, among them one described as "Gervais. Mr. Pope," appraised at £2, and listed as no. 104 in a manuscript catalogue drawn up by Prior's friend Adrian Drift.[1] This picture has been identified with a portrait of Pope which was in the collection of Harley (Second Earl of Oxford) at his death in 1741 and was sold by his widow in March 1742.[2] But this identification seems scarcely possible.[3] The portrait by Jervas acquired from Prior's estate in 1721 seems in all likelihood the same as a "picture of . . . Mr. Pope" for which Robert Shippen, Vice-Chancellor of Oxford University, sends his own and the University's thanks to Lord Harley in a letter of 1 April 1723.[4] In a notebook which he was keeping late in 1741 and in 1742, George Vertue drew up a "catalog of the Pictures in the picture Gallery

2.1. Oil on canvas. 29½ x 24 in. Background brown, wig yellowish gray, eyes blue-gray, coat dark blue (close to BCC 49 Oxford Blue). Bodleian Library, Oxford.

adjoyning to the Bodleian Library." This includes the entry "Mr. Alex. Pope—poet by Jarvis" (Vertue 5, 17).[5]

By the mid-nineteenth century the connection with Jervas seems to have been lost. In 1854 Cunningham assigns the portrait to Kneller.[6] And so too in 1906 does the *Burlington Magazine* reviewer of the Loan Collection of Historical Personages in the Examination Schools at Oxford.[7] But in the *Illustrated Catalogue* of this exhibition (Oxford, 1906), the portrait (no. 47, on p. 33, reproduced facing p. 25) is "Attributed to Charles Jervas."[8]

A large carved and gilt wooden label hangs below the frame, bearing a legend which both in style of lettering and in phrasing seems sufficiently contemporary:

Alexander Pope Armiger. / Et, quod Eximio apud Eruditos Nomini / Invidendam attulit Dignitatis Accensionem; / Effigiem dedit et Virum Cohonestavit / (A.D. 1722) / Hon[ssimus] Eduardus Comes Oxon et Mortimer.

A color reproduction of the picture may be seen in Lord David Cecil's *English Poets* (London, Collins, 1941), p. 32, and in the reprint of this work in the same publisher's *Impressions of English Literature,* edited by W. J. Turner (1944), p. 96.

The picture was exhibited, for the first time outside of Oxford,[9] at the National Portrait Gallery Exhibition of Pope in 1961.

1. Richard W. Goulding and C. K. Adams, *Catalogue of the Pictures Belonging to His Grace the Duke of Portland, K.G. at Welbeck Abbey* (Cambridge, 1936), pp. xxxii–xxxiv.

2. Goulding and Adams, *Catalogue of Pictures at Welbeck Abbey,* p. xxxiv; followed by H. Bunker Wright and Henry C. Montgomery, "The Art Collection of a Virtuoso in Eighteenth-Century England," *The Art Bulletin,* 27 (March 1945), 195, 200.

3. See no. 5.1.

4. Historical Manuscripts Commission, *Report of the Manuscripts of His Grace The Duke of Portland Preserved at Welbeck Abbey,* 5 (Norwich, 1899), 634. Shippen thanks Lord Harley also for two other pictures: one of Lord Dorset and one of Mr. Prior. The letter is fol. 255, vol. 34, *Harley Papers,* on loan at the British Museum.

5. *A Catalogue of the Several Pictures, Statues, and Busto's in the Picture Gallery Adjoining to the Bodleian Library,* Oxford, Printed for N. Bull, and sold by him at the Picture-Gallery, 1759, has (p. 12) "Alexander Pope, a Poet, by Jarvis."

6. In Walpole, *Anecdotes* 2.213, a note by "The Editor," listing portraits by Kneller, says "His own head and Pope's given to the Bodleian Library."

7. Sir Walter Armstrong, "Art in Georgian England: I—Historical Portraits at Oxford," *Burlington Magazine,* 9 (May 1906), 114. "If we allow for the effect on technique of a coarse, unprimed canvas, Kneller's authorship becomes unmistakable."

8. See also Mrs. R. L. Poole, *Catalogue of Portraits in the Possession of the University, Colleges, City, and County of Oxford,* Oxford, 1 (1912), 98, No. 243; and the same author's *Catalogue of Portraits Exhibited in the Reading Room & Gallery of the Bodleian Library* (Oxford, 1920), p. 98, no. 243.

9. It went to London for cleaning in 1905–06.

2.2 LINE ENGRAVING, BY GEORGE VERTUE AFTER CHARLES JERVAS.

By the autumn of 1714, apparently, a portrait of Pope by Jervas had been finished and was being engraved by George Vertue. For Jervas wrote to Pope, in a letter which Professor Sherburn places approximately in October 1714: "I intend this day to Call at Vertue's [to] see Swift's brought a little more like—And see what is doing to One Pope."[1] And again, in a letter of the following summer: "I am just going to Vertue to

give the last hand to that Enterprize which is our Concern."[2] The engraving was advertised in the *Daily Courant* for Saturday, 20 August 1715:

> On Tuesday next will be Published, A Print of Mr. Alexander Pope, done
> from the Original Painting of Mr. Jervasi, by Mr. Vertue. Printed for Bernard
> Lintott between the Temple Gates: where his Translation of Homer, and all
> his other Pieces may be had.[3]

The *Daily Courant* for 27 August advertised the same engraving as "this day . . . published." Jervas had recently also drawn (*Correspondence 1.* 244, 262), and Vertue had
engraved, the head of Homer which appears as frontispiece to the first volume of Pope's
Homer, published in June 1715. Vertue himself, in a manuscript list of his own works,
under the year 1715, recorded his engraving of both Pope and Homer—"Jervais p."
and "Jarvis del."[4]

In 1717, this engraving was used, folded, as the frontispiece to the first collected
volume of Pope's *Works,* in quarto and folio (*Griffith* nos. 79–86). In this volume Pope

2.2 Line engraving. 14 x 10 in. "Mr Pope / Geo: Vertue Sculpsit."
BMEP 61. *Grolier* 28. Frontispiece to Pope's *Works* 1717. Yale
University Library.

published for the first time his two most noteworthy poems in the pathetic mode, *Eloisa to Abelard* and *Verses* [later the *Elegy*] *to the Memory of an Unfortunate Lady*. The volume and the engraving were known to Mather Byles in Boston as early as 1728.[5]

Early derivatives from this engraving include a line engraving 5¼ x 3¼ inches with the lettering "Mr. Pope / D. Coster sculpsit,"[6] and another, 4¹¹⁄₁₆ x 2⅞, "Mr. Pope / Parr Sculp," which appears as frontispiece of a copy at Yale of *Mr. Pope's Literary Correspondence, Volume the Fourth . . . To which are added Muscovian Letters,* London; Printed for E. Curll, at Pope's-Head, in Rose Street, Covent Garden, 1736.[7] Curll's letter *To the Most Noble and Right Honourable Peers of Great Britain,* from Rose Street, Covent Garden, 22 May 1735, ends with the statement: "I have engraven a new plate of Mr. Pope's head from Mr. Jervas's painting; and likewise intend to hang him up in effigy for a sign to all spectators of his falsehood and my own veracity."[8]

The Vertue engraving is reproduced as frontispiece to R. K. Root's *Poetical Career of Alexander Pope,* Princeton, 1938. Professor Root speculates fondly (pp. 104–105) on the "completely romantic" image which would have lingered in our memory and "colored our reading" of the man and the poet had Pope died ten years before he published his *Dunciad*. The engraving is reproduced again as the frontispiece of the first volume of the Twickenham *Poems of Alexander Pope, Pastoral Poetry and An Essay on Criticism,* edited by E. Audra and Aubrey Williams, London and New Haven, 1961.

1. *Correspondence 1.162.* The second part of Jervas' sale in March 1740 catalogues 176 prints of "Dean Swift" in various lots.

2. *Correspondence 1.310* [31 July 1715?].

3. And in *The Post Man,* 23–25 August 1715: "This Day is publish'd, A Print of Mr. Alexander Pope, done from the Original Painting of Mr. Jervas, By Mr. Vertue. Printed for Bernard Lintott."

4. "A Collection of Engraved Prints The Works of G. Vertue from An.° Dom. M[D]CCVIII," drawn up apparently about the year 1740 (in the collection of

W. S. Lewis, Farmington, Connecticut.

5. *Correspondence 2.494.* See no. 5.11.

6. *Grolier* 30.

7. *Grolier* 29. The book is Griffith no. 415, but for the Wrenn Library copy, Griffith reports: "Frontispiece: portrait of Atterbury." And for the Ashley Library copy, Addison.

8. Carruthers, *Life of Pope,* 1857, Ch. 7, p. 324; and Elwin and Courthope 6.435–36. For "Pope's head" see further no. 5.16.

3.1. OIL PAINTING, BY CHARLES JERVAS. MAJOR SIR RICHARD PROBY, BART., ELTON HALL, HUNTINGDONSHIRE.

William Cleland (1674?–1741), Scottish soldier of fortune, Commissioner of Customs in Scotland and then of Taxes in England, was a close enough friend of Pope's to have his name subscribed to "A Letter to the Publisher Occasioned by the First Correct Edition of the Dunciad," dated at St. James's 22 December 1728, and prefixed to the *Dunciad Variorum* of 1729. Pope's footnote to the signature is an important source of Cleland's biography. Pope himself apparently presented the picture which is the subject of this entry to Cleland along with a set of his quarto *Odyssey* (1725–26) inscribed: "Mr Cleland, having read all other books, is / desired to read this by his most affectionate / humble servant A. Pope / Apr. 18. 1727." Cleland's wife Lucy had literary connections, notably with Swift. She was a sister of Margaret, Viscountess Allen, who was the mother-in-law of John Proby, First Baron Carysfort (1720–72). The picture and inscribed book seem to have passed into possession of the Proby family through Cleland's widow.[1] They come by descent to the present head of the family and resident of Elton Hall, Major Sir Richard Proby, Bart.

The picture is reported at Elton Hall by Cunningham in 1854 and by Carruthers in 1857.[2] At Mathews' in Birmingham on 24 November 1858, George Scharf, while sketching the picture which was to be NPG 112 (no. 3.2), noted: "A dup. of this belongs to Lord Carysfort of Elton Hall, Huntingdonshire. I saw it at Barker's."[3] Presumably Scharf refers to the dealer George Barker's establishment at 12 North Crescent, Bedford Square, where the picture may have been for cleaning.

In 1951 the picture was on loan to the Peterborough Museum, Priestgate, Peterborough.

1. Tancred Borenius and J. V. Hodgson, *A Catalogue of the Pictures at Elton Hall* (London, The Medici Society, 1924), p. 60, no. 72. The Preface, by Granville Proby, p. xxvii, gives details of Mrs. Cleland's relation to the Proby family and the text of Pope's inscription. A slightly different version of the inscription appears in Carruthers, *Life of Pope* (1857),

ch. 7, p. 260 (Cf. *Country Life*, 7 May 1957, p. 429.) I am indebted to Sir Richard Proby and Professor Maynard Mack for verification of the inscription and for the date.

2. P. 260, "by Jervas."

3. NPG Scharf *Sketch Books 54*. 103. See no. 3.2.

3.2. OIL PAINTING, BY CHARLES JERVAS. NATIONAL PORTRAIT GALLERY NO. 112.

George Watson Taylor, M.P., a wealthy West Indian speculator and a Governor and Director of the British Institution for Promoting the Fine Arts in the United King-

3.1. Oil on canvas. 77 x 49 in. Colors similar to those of no. 3.2.
Major Sir Richard Proby, Bart., Elton Hall, Huntingdonshire.

dom,[1] was the owner of perhaps the two portraits of Pope best known in that day, a large canvas of Pope with a lady, by Jervas, and a marble bust, by Roubiliac (see no. 61.1). The painting is first recorded in Taylor's possession by the engraving of 1819 (see no. 3.3). Samuel Weller Singer, in the dedication of his edition of Spence's *Anecdotes* in 1820 to Watson Taylor, alludes to both the bust and the painting. In June 1823 Taylor put up for sale at Christie's the "distinguished" collection of pictures at his town mansion in Cavendish Square; Pope, however, was not in this sale, and Taylor "bought in" a number of his literary pictures that were in the sale, including several by Reynolds of Johnson and his friends which he had acquired at the Streatham sale of Mrs. Piozzi's collection.[2] By the year 1832, however, Watson Taylor, bankrupt through the depreciation of West Indian properties, held sales in good earnest of the furniture and pictures of his town house (in Grafton Street) and of the immense collections at his country seat Erlestoke Park, near Devizes in Wiltshire. The latter sale attracted wide notice in the press,[3] was apparently one of the great events of the fashionable art world for that year (outdoing, by Beckford's admission, the sale at nearby Fonthill of nine years earlier), and, although it somehow escaped notice in the works on art sales compiled by both Redford and Graves, it has been celebrated at great length by W. T. Whitley in his *Art in England 1821–1837,* 1930.[4] George Robins, the auctioneer, engaged the virtuoso and Academy exhibitor W. H. Pyne (Ephraim Hardcastle, author of *Wine and Walnuts,* 1823) to draw up the elaborate catalogue.[5] On the fourteenth day (24 July), after Hogarth's self-portrait for the Foundling Hospital and the Shrimp Girl (both in the "Hogarth Room"), appears the canvas of Pope by Jervas (p. 160, lot 92).[6] A copy of this catalogue preserved at the Rijksbureau voor Kunsthistorische Documentatie, The Hague, has the annotation: "£17.17.0. Swaby." At the Winter Exhibition held the same year in Suffolk Street, Pall Mall, by The Society of British Artists, no. 35 was "Alexander Pope, & Martha Blount," by "Jervas," the "Proprietor" being "Mr. Swabey."[7]

I have been unable to close the gap between Mr. Swabey in 1832 and the person next to be mentioned who in 1849 owned the picture which is the subject of this entry. It appears to me all but certain, however, that we are dealing here with only one picture.

Edward Copleston, Bishop of Llandaff, died in 1849 leaving a portrait of Alexander Pope, which early in 1850 was sold by Toplis and Harding of 16 St. Paul's Church Yard to W. White, Printseller, in Brownlow Street, Holborn. (The picture was catalogued by Toplis and Harding as "Jervas—Portraits of Pope and Mrs. Blount full length.")[8] White of Brownlow Street apparently sold this painting along with another, of Sir Christopher Wren, to J. Mathews, apparently a dealer, at Edgbaston House, Birmingham. White "represented" both pictures "as coming from the collection of the Earl of Bessborough."[9] On 24 November 1858, George Scharf visited Mathews (on Hagley Road) in Birmingham and made sketches in his notebook of both Wren and Pope with his lady.[10] Both Wren (by Kneller, NPG 113) and Pope with the lady (NPG 112) were acquired by the Portrait Gallery from Mathews in 1860.[11] The portrait of Wren had indeed been part of the Bessborough Collection dispersed in 1850,

3.2. Oil on canvas. 76 x 49½ in. Flesh tints pink, eyes dark blue to hazel, eyebrows light brownish, wig gray with white highlights. Clothes metallic blue-gray, shoes black, buckles yellow, link at wrist black and yellow. Upholstery light red (near to BCC 96 Nasturtium; or 125 Brick Red), chair legs brownish, floor grayish. The lady has a golden to brownish dress (like BCC 115 and 116, Old Gold and Bronze), dark blonde hair, brownish eyes, swarthy flesh tints. The drapery is dark chartreuse green; the bust of Homer and pedestal are a greenish-white monochrome. National Portrait Gallery No. 112.

but a profile of Pope by "Kneller" which disappeared from that collection in 1801 has apparently nothing to do with Pope and his lady.[12]

In the National Portrait Gallery *Catalogue* of 1888 Scharf wrote (p. 360): "The Lady in the background, reaching a book from a shelf, most probably represents his friend Martha Blount, although conjectured by some to represent his sister-in-law Mrs. Rackett." A shade of anonymity and allegorization, perhaps most strongly hinted in the stockinged feet of the lady, is recognized in the description by George Pyne in the catalogue of the Erlestoke Sale of 1832 (p. 160): "Mrs. Martha Blount, introduced, on tiptoe, reaching a book from a shelf. The poet is represented as in a pleasing reverie, and the intended personification of the composition, may imply, that this fair and accomplished lady was the subject of his waking dream."

In 1740 Van Loo did a painting of Cibber (known today only in the mezzotint by Edward Fisher) in which the poet is seated at a table holding in his hand a quill which is either being offered or plucked away by an impish girl at his elbow, no doubt his daughter Charlotte. Hogarth painted Garrick quill in hand, his wife reaching over his shoulder as if to break a poetic reverie and summon him to supper (Windsor Castle). A painting by William Hoare of the Bath poet Christopher Anstey shows him seated with quill and paper but apparently suffering or enjoying a similar distraction from a little girl at his elbow reaching up a fancy doll (NPG 3084).

The lady in the picture of Pope seems to act as librarian, reaching up to return a book to the shelf. Her posture is Titianesque.[13]

The bust of Homer in the upper left corner bears a fairly close resemblance to the head which Jervas drew and Vertue engraved for the frontispiece of the first volume of Pope's *Iliad*, 1715: "G Vertue Sculp. / ΟΜΗΡΟΣ / Ex marmore antiquo in Ædibus Farnesianis, Romae." See this picture reproduced as no. 3.2X, and see no. 2.2.

NPG 112 has been reproduced in Lionel Cust, *The National Portrait Gallery, 1* (London, 1901), 215; as the frontispiece to George Paston, *Mr. Pope His Life and Times* (London, 1909), volume 1, and to George Sherburn, *The Early Career of Alexander Pope* (Oxford, 1934). It appears facing p. 146 of W. L. Macdonald, *Pope and His Critics*, London, 1951.

The picture, recently cleaned, was in the National Portrait Gallery Exhibition of 1961.

1. British Institution, *A Catalogue of Portraits Representing Distinguished Persons in the History and Literature of the United Kingdom* (London, 1820), pp. 5, 9, 19.

2. *Gentleman's Magazine, 93* (June, 1823), 546–48; and *Catalogue of the . . . Collection of . . . Pictures . . . of George Watson Taylor, Esq. . . . sold By Mr. Christie . . . Pall Mall . . . June 13th, 1823 and following Day* (British Museum Library and Victoria and Albert Museum).

3. E.g., *Devizes & Wiltshire Gazette*, 14 June 1823; *Times*, 16 June 1832, p. 8; *Gentleman's Magazine, 102* (August 1832), 162–63.

4. Pp. 239–244.

5. A newspaper extract dated 26 July 1832, and marked "M.C." in the Whitley Papers (Department of Prints and Drawings, British Museum), but not to be found in the *Morning Chronicle* or the *Morning Post* of that date. The index of Whitley's *Art in England 1821–1837* would suggest that these were main sources for his account of the Erlestoke sale, pp. 239–44.

6. *Catalogue of the Magnificent Assemblage of Property at Erlestoke Mansion Near Devizes . . . which will be sold at Auction by Mr. George Robins on Monday, the 9th Day of July, 1832. And Twenty Succeeding Days* (British Museum Library).

7. *Catalogue of the Winter Exhibition of the Works*

of Deceased and Living British Artists, Suffolk Street, Pall-Mall East, 1832, p. 8. On p. 15, no. 229 is R. B. Sheridan, by Reynolds, also lent by Mr. Swabey. In the Catalogue for 1833, p. 14, no. 191 is "Portrait of a Lady," by Reynolds, lent by Mr. Swabey, and p. 15, no. 206 is the Marchioness of Lansdowne, by Reynolds, lent by "Mr. Swaby" [sic]. Professor E. K. Waterhouse tells me that these pictures have not reappeared.

8. Letters to George Scharf from B. R.[?] Copleston, Barnes Rectory, 9 and 22 October 1860 (Reginald Edward Copleston was vicar of Barnes, Surrey, 1840–63.), and from Toplis and Harding, 11 October 1860 (NPG file 112). A slip of paper in Scharf's hand records that the picture had stencilled on the back of the frame: "W. White Printseller, Brownlow St. Holborn."

9. J. Mathews to George Scharf, 11 August 1859 (NPG file 112).

10. NPG Scharf *Sketch Book 54.* 103–05. Under the sketch of Pope and the lady, Scharf wrote: "Portraits of Alexander Pope & Mrs. Martha Blount by Jervas from Lord Bessborough" (for the rest of his inscription, see no. 3.1, note 3).

11. J. Mathews to Scharf, 25 August and 30 November 1860 (NPG files 112, 113).

12. Pope by "Kneller" was No. 5 in the sale of 1801. See Appendix 2, no. 15. I am indebted to a set of notes on these sales drawn up by Mr. C. K. Adams. The Portrait Gallery (Pope Iconographic Notes) has a letter from William Smith, Trustee of the Gallery, to George Scharf, 15 September 1860: "I fear the proprietor [of the *Athenaeum*] has made the mistake of supposing the picture belonged to Lord Bessborough because that of Wren really did."

13. Oskar Fischel, *Tizian* (Stuttgart, 1907), pp. 134–35, illustrates Titian's daughter Lavinia (Berlin, Kaiser Friedrich Museum) and the daughter of Herodias with the head of St. John the Baptist (Madrid, Prado Museum).

3.3. LINE ENGRAVING, BY J. H. ROBINSON AFTER CHARLES JERVAS, 1819.

Two states of this engraving, with and without Portuguese letters, correspond to two editions of Pope's *Essay on Man* which were published in 1819. *An Essay on Man, In Four Epistles, To Henry St. John, Lord Bolingbroke, By Alexander Pope,* London: Printed for Robert Jennings, in the Poultry, By James Moyes, Greville Street, 1819, a large folio of 77 pages, has the engraving, on India paper, without Portuguese letters, as frontispiece. An advertisement following the title, dated "2, Poultry, Dec. 1, 1819," explains that "there is now published a new translation [into Portuguese], from the pen of a nobleman of high rank in the court of Brazil . . . printed in this country in three volumes quarto. . . . For this elaborate work, of which only a very limited number of copies are intended for circulation in England . . . permission has been obtained to engrave . . . a most admirable and unique full-length portrait of Pope, from a painting, executed at an early period in his life, by his friend Jervas, in the valuable collection of George Watson Taylor, Esq. M.P.

"Previous to the insertion of the writing in these plates, a few proofs were taken on India paper, which the publisher has the satisfaction to offer to the public. . . . the interest that naturally attaches to an indisputably authentic, and hitherto unedited portrait of Pope, has induced him to accompany them with an edition of the poem."

The Portuguese translation of the *Essay on Man* appeared in three large quarto volumes entitled: *Ensaio Sobre O Homem de Alexandre Pope, Traduzido Verso Por Verso por Francisco Bento Maria Targini, Barão [Visconde] de Sao Lourenço . . . Dado a Luz por Huma Sociedade da Graõ-Bretanha . . . Londres: Na Officina Typographica de C. Whittingham, College House, Chiswick, 1819.* Pope faces page [33] of volume 1.

On 13 April 1823, Charles Lamb, writing to his young friend Bryan Waller Procter (Barry Cornwall), thanked him for a gift of a portrait of Pope (apparently this

above

3.2x. Line and stipple engraving. 8⅝ x 6¼ in. "G Vertue Sculp. / OMHPOΣ / Ex marmore antiquo in Ædibus Farnesianis, Romæ." Frontispiece to Pope's *Iliad*, vol. 1, 1715. See no. 2.2.

above, right

3.3. Line engraving. 6¹¹⁄₁₆ x 4⅞ in. frame around picture. "Jervas pinxit. / / J. H. Robinson sculp. / ALEXANDRE POPE / DE HUM RETRATO ORIGINAL, POR SEU AMIGO JERVAS, / QUE SE ACHA PRESENTE-MENTE EM PODER DO SENHOR / G. WATSON TAYLOR, MEMBRO DO PARLAMENTO BRITANICO. / FAC-SIMILE DA ESCRITURA DE POPE. / 'Approach, great Nature studiously behold,' / A. Pope." *BMEP* 6. *Grolier* 75–76. Facing p. [33] of vol. 1 of *Ensaio Sobre O Homem de Alexandre Pope,* by Francisco Bento Maria Targini, 1819; and (without "ALEXANDRE POPE . . . ESCRITURA DE POPE") frontispiece to Pope's *Essay on Man,* 1819. For the verse, see Pope's "Verses on a Grotto by the River Thames at Twickenham" (*Twickenham* 6.382–85). A holograph of this poem is apparently not known today.

right

4. Line engraving. 4¹¹⁄₁₆ x 2¾ in. "Pope. / Jarvis Pinxᵗ / / Caldwall sculp." *BMEP* 8. *Grolier* 77. Frontispiece to *The Works of the English Poets,* ed. Samuel Johnson, vol. 32, 1779. Yale University Library.

engraving), which he hung up in his town room, and which seems to have remained there until his death in 1835.[1]

The engraver has omitted the lady, has hidden Homer behind a large drape, and has added a book and a quill pen on the floor. George Pyne's Catalogue entry of 1732 (quoted in no. 3.2) informs us that Watson Taylor's painting included the lady.

1. *The Letters of Charles Lamb* . . . ed. E. V. Lucas, 2 (New Haven, 1935), 379–80, Letter 467 and annotation; cf. 2, 286; and J. M. Turnbull, "Charles Lamb: Some Side-Lights from Barry Cornwall," *The Book-* *man, 78* (August 1930), 270–73; Major S. Butterworth, "Charles Lamb: A Few More Details," *The Bookman, 61* (March 1922), 254–57.

4. LINE ENGRAVING, BY JAMES CALDWALL AFTER CHARLES JERVAS, 1781.

This engraving appears as the frontispiece to *The Poems of Pope,* volume 1, which is volume the Thirty-Second of *The Works of the English Poets With Prefaces, Biographical and Critical by Samuel Johnson,* London, Printed by W. and A. Strahan for C. Bathurst . . . 1779. (Vols. 32–37 of this set are a reprint of Warburton's edition of Pope, 1751. Johnson's Preface, the Life of Pope, was not of course published until 1781.) The engraver was presumably James Caldwall (1739–c. 1819). The countenance, wig, and clothing are similar enough to these features in NPG 112 to make the attribution to "Jarvis" convincing. It seems possible that the engraving is in fact a free derivation from a painting of that type.

1716, 1721, 1722
SIR GODFREY KNELLER
(1649[?]-1723)[1]

A MONTH OR TWO before Pope began to take lessons in painting from Charles Jervas (and hence presumably at a time before he copied Kneller's portrait[2] of Betterton), he was preparing for the press his politico-topographical poem *Windsor Forest* and got permission to dedicate it to the architect of the Tory Peace of Utrecht, his friend George Granville, Lord Lansdowne. In a letter of 10 January 1712/13, he conveyed the double compliment that the poem was in fact a portrait of Lansdowne and that it could be much improved if Lansdowne himself would correct the verses. And thus:

> I am in the circumstance of an ordinary painter drawing Sir Godfrey Kneller,
> who by a few touches of his own could make the piece very valuable.[3]

This early allusion by Pope to Kneller is not necessarily—perhaps not even likely—the expression of a young poet who had already been painted by Kneller or had any personal acquaintance with him.

Kneller was a more obvious figure in the London and court world, something more like a colossus, than anything we can readily imagine of a painter today. Many

---

1. Vertue (*1*.53) says on good authority that Kneller was 69 in 1718. But on his monument in Westminster Abbey he is said to have been 79 at his death in 1723. See Whinney and Millar, p. 192; Waterhouse, *Painting in Britain*, p. 109.

2. *Correspondence 1*.88n., 187n; see p. 12 and n. 34.

3. *Correspondence 1*.172.

smaller painters of the baroque era have had books written about them because no doubt they are easier to encompass, and bigger painters have had their several books when they made a warmer appeal to the modern imagination. The slightly comic, rather vulgar, and too successful German-born painter, about whom no adequately massive book has ever been written,[4] bulks as large in English painting of Pope's era as today in the First Presence Chamber at Hampton Court his equestrian and triumphant canvas of William III, painted to celebrate the sovereign's return from the Peace of Ryswyck:

> . . . great Nassau to Kneller's hand decreed
> To fix him graceful on the bounding Steed.

Kneller painted in five successive English courts. Ten reigning sovereigns sat to him. He went on missions abroad to paint Louis XIV of France (1684),[5] the Elector of Bavaria (c. 1697),[6] and the Archduke Charles, titular King of Spain (1703), afterwards the Emperor Charles VI.[7] For forty years he painted nearly everybody in England of rank, wealth, or accomplishment,[8] as well as a good many foreign visitors, including the Moroccan Ambassador (1684)[9] and Peter the Great of Russia (1698).[10] His effort was most largely spread, and he lives today most obviously if least sympathetically, in the huge official expanses of canvas—the equestrians, the 89-inch full-length royal elongations, the periwigged and armored admirals, the stately but pallid full-length "beauties" of Queen Mary's court—at Hampton, at Windsor, at Kensington, at Greenwich Hospital.

On the death of the veteran but uncourtly painter John Riley in 1691, Kneller had succeeded without partner as Principal Painter to the King. He enjoyed this title and that of Gentleman of the Privy Chamber through three reigns until his death in 1723. He became a Knight in 1692, later a Knight of the Holy Roman Empire (as a reward for his portrait of the Archduke Charles), and a Baronet in 1715. He had set up (c. 1703) a town house in Great Queen Street, Lincoln's Inn Fields, and a little later a magnificently decorated[11] country house at Whitton, near Hounslow and Twickenham, the resort of nobility and even of royalty. He was a Deputy Lieutenant and Justice

---

4. See, nevertheless, Lord Killanin's enthusiastic and highly colored *Sir Godfrey Kneller And His Times, 1646–1723* (London, Batsford Ltd., 1948).

5. Whinney and Millar, p. 194 and n. 2.

6. Life-size on horseback. See Lionel Cust, "Kneller," in *Dictionary of National Biography, 31.240*; Whinney and Millar, pp. 195–96. Vertue 2.119–23 provides a helter-skelter but vivid and reliable account of the splendid career of this "Morning Star for all other Portrait Painters" (p. 121). Edward Croft-Murray & Paul Hulton, *Catalogue of British Drawings, 1* (London, British Museum, 1960), 385–86, cite Baynbrigg Buckeridge, *An Essay Towards an English School of Painting*, in Roger de Piles, *The Art of Painting* (3rd ed., 1750), an early biographical account of Kneller which I have not seen, but which I infer is paralleled by Vertue.

7. Two full-lengths are still at Kensington Palace (Whinney and Millar, p. 194 n. 3).

8. From about 1683 until his death there is hardly a year in which half a dozen signed and dated works cannot be named (Waterhouse, *Painting in Britain*, p. 98).

9. A life-size equestrian portrait, signed and dated 1684, was long at Chatsworth (Whinney and Millar, p. 194 n. 3), but has lately been restored to the Domed Saloon at Chiswick House (John Charlton, *A History and Description of Chiswick House and Gardens* [London, 1958], p. 21).

10. At Kensington Palace.

11. A small staircase at Whitton was painted by Louis Laguerre; it was considered by Vertue to be one of his masterpieces (Vertue 2.125).

of the Peace in the County of Middlesex and a D.C.L. of Oxford University. From 1711 to 1716 he was the first Governor of the first Academy of Painting in London.[12]

The modern student will perhaps be astonished to discover the lively multiplication of replica portraits in which Kneller's studio engaged. His standard royal images, the State portraits of William and Mary, of Anne and George I, were in special demand. In 1705 he was paid for nine whole-lengths of Queen Anne, and about that same time also he petitioned for overdue payment of six whole-lengths of the late King. His court rate was £50 for a picture.[13] (Besides this, he had an annuity of £200 from the Crown.) He was noted for the rapidity of his personal execution and a talent for making his sitters enjoy the experience. He developed in his studio routine an elaborate division of labor, a factory or assembly-line method. He had specialists for perukes, for draperies, for lace, for architectural backgrounds, and for the landscape. It is notorious that in his later years he himself seldom painted more than the face[14]—or at most also the hands.

The star and garter, the sword-hilt, the full-bottomed wig, the brocaded or armored shoulder, the lace cravat and cuffs, the bravura posture and gesture, the classical bust in the background, the column or arch, the cloudy horizon, the overhanging cliff and umbrageous trees—these were the staples of invention in Kneller's aristocratic male portraits. The elongated bust rising from swirls of satin, the stately white neck, the narrow head and descending dark tresses were the traits of his peeresses. A certain conventional dullness, hardness, and gloss is a frequent result which is not difficult to understand. Yet at his best—at moments of special interest and effort, which occur all through his career—Kneller is a great painter: a sensitive technician, a cunning and various inventor, a much more acute psychologist than one might be led to suppose from the many anecdotes of his comic vanity. The Chinese Convert (1687, at Kensington Palace), which Kneller himself considered his masterpiece,[15] the elderly Mrs. Dunch (1689, at Parham Park), the actor Anthony Leigh as The Spanish Friar (1689, at the National Portrait Gallery), the two great ladies, the Duchess of Marlborough and Lady Fitzhardinge, playing cards (1691, at Blenheim), are examples of the kind of picture which the modern art historian will name to illustrate Kneller's versatile mastery.[16] During his youth in Holland he is said by Vertue to have worked briefly under the aged Rembrandt, and one critic has seen in the series of Greenwich Admirals painted by Kneller between 1690 and 1720 a mysteriously delayed Rembrandtesque development of open, fluent brushwork and interplaying broken color[17]—an extraordinarily direct translation of subject into the language of paint, an unprecedented English impressionism.

12. Waterhouse, *Painting in England*, p. 100; Whinney and Millar, pp. 196 97.

13. Whinney and Millar, p. 195 and n. 2.

14 On Kneller's factory, see Waterhouse, *Painting in Britain*, pp. 100, 109; Whinney and Millar, p. 195; W. T. Whitley, *Artists and Their Friends in England* (1928), *1*.4–6; Piper, *The English Face*, pp. 20–21, 145. About twelve of London's leading painters all relied on one expert (Joseph van Aken) to paint draperies in all their portraits.

15. Walpole, *Anecdotes* 3.2031 but see p. 211 n. 9. Kneller's opinion of his Dr. Wallis. The Chinese Convert is reproduced in color as frontispiece of Lord Killanin's *Kneller* (London, 1948).

16. Waterhouse, *Painting in Britain*, p. 99; Plate 87B is the ladies playing cards.

17. C. H. Collins-Baker, "The Craftsmanship of Kneller," *The Connoisseur*, *127* (March 1951), 29–32.

A refreshing contrast to Kneller's standard conception of the aristocratic male appears in a smaller gallery of intellectuals and men of letters which he painted from time to time over a long period. One encounters here an imposing sort of simplicity. Kneller inclined to paint such a man in his own hair, locks falling to his shoulders, without fancy background or other accessories, in a loose gown and open shirt collar—dégagé—a long half-length, facing full or three-quarters to the viewer and as if leaning slightly but intently forward, with hip against a table or counter edge or the frame of the picture. Such, for instance, are several of his self-portraits, and notably the earliest, signed and dated 1685, at the National Portrait Gallery[18]—a softly moulded but arrogant bright face, between luxuriant natural locks, looking back at the viewer nearly full over the left shoulder; or his two Isaac Newtons, the elder image of 1702, at the National Portrait Gallery ("Seen from a distance, a . . . wigged man . . . in the conventional . . . drapery. . . . Move closer. . . . almost . . . expressionistic . . . the loaded iris of the right eye too great for the lids to contain it, and the wig not stuffy . . . but lambent as an aura")[19] and the younger man in a simple robe, his own hair (or a long flaxy wig?) to the shoulders, a soft but lean and almost stern face, nearly full to the viewer, with his elbows on a table[20] and hands crossed; or the elderly John Locke, with drawn face, streaming white hair, aquiline nose, glowing dark eyes;[21] or the weirdly vertical, slender-headed and Greco-like, forward-sitting figure of Matthew Prior (at Trinity College, Cambridge)[22]—curious reminder of the mannerist tradition which back of Lely and Van Dyck was still a heritage of English baroque portraiture. Kneller painted at least two portraits of Dryden: one heroic, a bravo of an aristocrat, such a bear of a man as might have come off well enough in a Rose Alley Ambuscade, head tilted back, high arched eyebrows, wide jaws and mouth, the bay wreath loosely in the grasp of the left hand near the hip (at the National Portrait Gallery[23]); the other (probably Tonson's portrait, 1698, at Barn Elms, which has come to Trinity College, Cambridge), perhaps the masterpiece of all Kneller's painting: Dryden softly aged, but youthful, with still rounded cheek and liquid eye, silvery gray, at ease in his loose robe, proudly yet gracefully holding his laurel wreath in his lap.[24] This is the Dryden, unmistakably (if we may indulge ourselves for a moment), who, in the last year of his life, at the age of seventy, published the Preface to the *Fables* and the *Secular Ode*.

18. No. 3794; *British Historical Portraits*, Plate 83. The following seems apposite: "Sir Godfrey Kneller, in an oval, when young, by himself. Those who were acquainted with Sir Godfrey will easily recollect how characteristic the following lines were of him:

Qualis eram vultu Knellerius, quantus et arte,
Se pingens dixit, saecula longa sciant"

(*A Catalogue of Pictures—of the Late Richard Mead, M.D. Sold . . . March. . . . MDCCLIV* [London, 1755], p. vi).

19. Piper, *The English Face*, p. 146, illustrated Pl. 66; *NPG Catalogue*, 1949, No. 2881, Pl. XI; *British Historical Portraits*, Pl. 82.

20. Signed and dated 1689, Collection of the Earl of Portsmouth: The Royal Academy of Arts at Burlington House, *Winter Exhibition 1960–1961, The Age of Charles II*, p. 68, no. 217.

21. Formerly at Lincoln's Inn, sold at Sotheby's 19 February 1947 (NPG Photograph).

22. J. W. Goodison, "Cambridge Portraits II," *The Connoisseur, 140* (January 1958), 231–36, no. 6; illustrated facing p. 38 of Lord Killanin, *Kneller*, London, 1948.

23. No. 2083. Illustrated in *British Historical Portraits*, Plate 78. This portrait type (engraved anonymously for the 1709 edition of Dryden's *Virgil*) dates from 1693 (Piper, *Catalogue of the Seventeenth-Century Portraits*, p. 113 and Pl. 20a).

24. Whinney and Millar, p. 198, Pl. 56; Piper, *Catalogue of the Seventeenth-Century Portraits*, p. 114; J. W. Goodison, "Cambridge Portraits II," *The Connoisseur, 140* (January 1958), 231–36, no. 5.

The portrait of Dryden and another by Kneller, of Dryden's friend the Sixth Earl of Dorset, which also came into the collection of Jacob Tonson, were painted in a novel but convenient library size, 36 x 28 inches ("Kit-Cat size," as it came to be known), large enough to admit one of the sitter's hands, sometimes even two—larger than the conventional head and shoulders (30 x 25), yet not so large and imposing as the standard three-quarter-length (50 x 40). Tonson liked these portraits very well. At the time when Alexander Pope seems to have become a client and friend, Kneller was near the end of his celebrated series of forty-two Kit-Cat portraits (painted during a period of about twenty years—the earliest signed is 1702 and the latest is 1717).[25] Tonson's Club of Whig Lords, courtiers, landowners, soldiers, and M.P.'s included also a handful of literary men: Addison, Steele, Garth, Maynwaring, Vanbrugh. The aristocratic but equalizing frame of the periwigs, the lace, the heavy tight velvet coats, the big buttons and cuffs, the heroic outdoor decor, shade off in this series of pictures toward something slightly plainer, though still sleek and sufficiently self-assured: Sir John Vanbrugh and William Congreve in less formal velvet jackets and open shirt collars, but heavily wigged, Congreve smoothly curved and superbly gesturing, Vanbrugh wearing on a gold chain round his neck his Clarencieux herald's badge and fingering the architect's compasses; Sir Richard Steele, wigged, with a neckcloth, leaning with his elbow easily on a table against an outdoor background; Sir Samuel Garth, wigged too, but pudgy-faced, shrewdly smiling and squinting; Tonson (signed, 1717) the publisher and Secretary of the Club, homeliest of all, nearest to Hogarthian, in loose coat, plain neckcloth, and house cap, upright in a capacious dark chair, solid business head atilt, holding in his hands a gilt-backed folio of "Milton's Paradise Lost."[26] It is a fact which Pope may have found significant that in the Kit-Cat portrait of Addison and in at least two others (that signed and dated 1710 or 1716 at Northwick Park, or the Edinburgh portrait, seen there at the Exhibition in 1883),[27] Kneller painted him in the clothes, the posture and gesture, and with the accessories (drapes, panels, badges, table, letter, large tree) of one of his full Whig aristocrats.

Some time within a year or two of his publishing the first volume of his *Iliad* (in June 1715) and thus emerging as the champion Homeric poet of the English Augustan age, Pope might very plausibly have become both a client and a friend of the greatest painter of the age:

> . . . (thanks to *Homer*) since I live and thrive,
> Indebted to no Prince or Peer alive.

The date on the mezzotint of the earliest Kneller portrait of Pope is 1716 ("Kneller Pinxit"), and the mezzotint itself was engraved by J. Smith, Kneller's favorite engraver,

---

25. Piper, *Catalogue of the Seventeenth-Century Portraits*, p. 250 and Appendix, pp. 398–403.

26. Tonson, Congreve, and Vanbrugh are illustrated in the National Portrait Gallery's booklet *The Portraits of Members of the Kit-Cat Club. . . . Presented to the Nation in 1945 by the National Art-Collections Fund;* Tonson (NPG 3230), Vanbrugh (NPG 3231), Addison (NPG 3193), and Steele (NPG 3227) are il-

lustrated in *British Historical Portraits,* Plates 97, 98, 99, 100; and Addison in Piper, *The English Face,* p. 145, Pl. 63. Tonson and Garth are Plates 85 *a* and *b* in Waterhouse, *Painting in Britain.*

See the Appendix on the Kit-Cat Portraits in Piper, *Catalogue of the Seventeenth-Century Portraits.*

27. NPG Photograph.

in 1717. The acquaintance between the two eminent persons apparently soon kindled into a conflagration of mutual esteem—even if we make some allowances for Pope's habitual resources of ironic reserve. In August of 1717, when Pope was living at Chiswick, he regarded Sir Godfrey as one of half a dozen or more neighbors (Lord Burlington, Duchess Hamilton, and others) who had "indispensable claims" upon him "under penalty of the imputation of direct rudeness, living within 2 hours sail of Chiswick." Sir Godfrey had made him "a fine present of a picture."[28] And then we have a letter written by Pope to Sir Godfrey at Whitton on 18 February 1717/18:

> I can scarce repent my loss of your Company, when it was the occasion of the pleasure of your letter. . . . your praise of so unworthy a Subject as I. . . . The Elevation of Such a Genius is not to be measured by the Object it flies at. . . . You raise me to such a degree, that . . . I think myself *paulo minus ab Angelis.* . . . But this is no more than you daily do upon Canvas. . . . You will perceive Sir, that I am as much at [a loss] how to Express myself, as you pretend to be. But a Genius like yours . . . in the warmth with which [it is] agitated, let it but throw the Pen or [Pen]cil with never so careless a dash, all peop[le would] see 'tis a noble Frenzy, a Vaghezza, like the *Foam* of a Great Master.[29]

The peculiar savor of this flattery would be lost could we not read a few notes from the painter himself, written during the next few years—surviving on the backs of Pope's Homer manuscript sheets. By the summer of 1719, Pope had settled into the social life at Twickenham. Sir Godfrey was now his much closer neighbor, and the two between them were arranging for Sir Godfrey to rent a house to Mr. Edward Wortley Montagu and Lady Mary:

> Sir,—I am in Towne, and have louck'd for beds, and bed steads, which must cost ten pounds a year. . . .
>
> and am giving My most humble respects to My Lady Mary Whortley, (Sir) Your Most humble and most faithful Servant[30]

"I write this from Sir Godfrey's own mouth," wrote Pope to Mr. Montagu,[31] and a little later to Lady Mary: "Madam—you received, I suppose, the Epistle Sir Godfrey dictated to me, which (abating a few flowers) was word for word."[32]

> Pope and Kneller were apparently close cronies during this year:

> I believe ther will be Card playrs enoug, and we may do how we please. If you Come about 4: a Clock, you may see me paint.[33]

28. *Correspondence 1.417*: [6 August, 1717].
29. *Correspondence 1.466*: 18 February 1717/18.
30. *Correspondence 2.6*: 16 June 1719.
31. *Correspondence 2.12.*
32. *Correspondence 2.38.*
33. *Correspondence 2.9.*

Despite an accident which confined him to his own house for a while during the early autumn ("My body . . . has had no rest these two nights, but what it snadches . . . in thee day time. . . . I believe my left leg will be out of order a good wyle."[34]), Sir Godfrey about this time painted the three large grisaille panels for the Twickenham villa which Pope celebrated in his lines "To Sir Godfrey Kneller, on his painting for me the Statues of Apollo, Venus, and Hercules."[35] During the next year, 1720, he painted Lady Mary. Pope's letters, as he solicitously arranged the sittings at Twickenham, give glimpses not only of the poet's cultivated infatuation for the lady but of the society painter's extra-studio routine:

> allow me as much of your Person as Sir Godfrey can help me to.
>
> Upon conferring with him yesterday, I find he thinks it absolutely necessary to draw the Face first, which he says can never be set right on the figure if the Drapery & Posture be finishd before. To give you as little trouble as possible, he proposes to draw your face with crayons, & finish it up, at your own house in a morning; from whence he will transfer it to the Canvas, so that you need not go to sit at his house. This I must observe, is a manner in which they seldom draw any but Crown'd Heads & I observe it with a secret pride & pleasure.[36]
>
> Madam,—Sir Godfrey happening to come from London yesterday, (as I did myself) will wait upon you this morning at twelve to take a sketch of you in your dress, if you'l give leave. He is really very good to me: I heartily wish you will be so to.[37]

Sir Godfrey painted (or at least started to paint?) Pope himself again apparently during 1721. And in the spring of 1722, Pope, under pressure of Shakespeare editing, let a long time elapse between sittings for a portrait.[38] In late August of 1723, the "original" of a portrait dated 1722 was ready in Kneller's studio for Lord Harcourt to send and have his seal put on it. This was about two months before Kneller's death.[39] At the time of the accident to Kneller's leg in the autumn of 1719, Pope's friend James Craggs had comforted himself with the reflection that the painter's "hand & head" re-

---

34. *Correspondence* 2.15–16. The next letter in the series (James Craggs to Pope, 1 October 1719 [2.16]) establishes the approximate date of Sir Godfrey's confinement and the cause, an "Accident."

35. *Correspondence* 2.17–18 and n. Pope left the pictures to Lord Bathurst in his will, and they are still to be seen at Cirencester.

36. *Correspondence* 2.21–22. The portrait is apparently that of Lady Mary half-reclining, in Turkish head-dress, ermine cloak, and low-cut blue bodice, today in the collection of the Marquis of Bute. Pope had some portrait of her, perhaps this one, in his best room fronting the Thames at the time of his death. See Robert Halsband, *The Life of Lady Mary Wortley*

Montagu (Oxford, 1956), pp. 99–100; *Notes and Queries*, 6th Series, 5 (13 May 1882), 364.

37. *Correspondence* 2.22.

38. *Correspondence* 2.118: [16 or 23 May, 1722?]. The letter, preserved on the back of a Homer manuscript sheet, is addressed to Jacob Tonson II, like a later letter from Pope concerning his portrait by Michael Dahl (p. 93). A portrait of Pope, preferably by Kneller, would perhaps have been a welcome extension of the Kit-Cat gallery.

39. Cust, *Dictionary of National Biography*, says he died on 19 October and cites *Historical Register*, Chronological Diary, p. 56.

mained in their "former vigour & condition." In 1717, the year of the last dated Kit-Cat portraits, a rumor had apparently got about that his eyes were failing him.[40] Yet they seem to have held out well enough. The portrait of Pope, which may well have been one of the last he finished, shows "little diminution of his powers."[41]

In later life Pope would cherish a fund of droll stories about Sir Godfrey, his ignorance, his vanity, his rough equity as Justice of the Peace.[42] From the pen of Pope we get a last, strange, glimpse of the man "a few days before his death,"[43] in a culminating vanity.

> Sir Godfry sent to me. . . . He began by telling me, he was now convincd he could not live, & fell into a passion of tears. . . . The next word he said was this—*By God, I will not be buried in Westminster.* I askd him Why? he answer'd—*They do bury Fools there.* . . . Then proceeded to desire I would write his Epitaph, which I promis'd him. . . . Then he desird me that I would take down my Father's Monument. *For it was the best Place in the Church to be seen at a distance.* . . . He fell a crying again, & seem'd so violently moved, that In pure humanity to a dying man (as well as to one I thought *non Compos*) I would not directly persist in Denying it. . . .[44]

Ex. 2. Oil on canvas. 49 x 39½ in. Sir Godfrey Kneller, self-portrait, inscribed on the back with his name and titles, given to Oxford University by Kneller in September 1721. In the background appears Kneller's country house at Whitton, and he wears the gold medal of King William ("GVLIELMVS III: DEI G . . .") and gold chain presented to him when he was knighted in 1691. See Mrs. R. L. Poole, *Catalogue of Portraits in the Possession of . . . Oxford, 1* (Oxford, 1912), 89; Vertue *1*, 93; *2*, 121. The Bodleian Library, Oxford.

40. Waterhouse, *Painting in Britain*, p. 100.
41. Waterhouse, *Painting in Britain*, p. 100. Kneller is said to have left more than 500 portraits to be finished by his assistant Edward Byng (Walpole, *Anecdotes* 2.204 n. 3).
42. Spence, *Anecdotes* (ed. Singer, 1820), pp. 165, 180, 181 n., 227, 247, 335, 338, 368; *Epistle* 2.ii.24, *Twickenham* 4.167.
43. Pope to Lord Harcourt, 3 July 1725 (*Correspondence* 2.307).
44. Pope to the Earl of Strafford, 6 July [1725] (*Correspondence* 2.308–09).

Sir Godfrey's monument by Rysbrack (1729), which does boast an epitaph by Pope (the worst verses, he said later, he had ever written[45]), is actually to be found in Westminster Abbey, but that location was achieved only after a protracted squabble and litigation between Pope and the artist's widow.[46]

45. *Twickenham 6, Minor Poems*, p. 312; Spence, *Anecdotes*, p. 165.

46. It happened that Pope's monument (or tablet) to his father (planned for his mother, too, and himself) was affixed, where it remains today, to the wall in a gallery of Twickenham Church just above the pew of a noble friend, Lord Strafford, to whom in June 1725 Pope began an eloquent, and apparently effective, complaint: Lady Kneller wished to substitute a large monument "to Sir G and herself with both their Figures"—"overwhelming my Lady Strafford with . . . Immense Draperies & Stone Petticoats . . . & perhaps crushing to pieces your Lordships Posterity" (*Correspondence* 2.300). And see Pope to Lord Strafford, 6 July 1725 (*Correspondence* 2.308), and to Lord Harcourt, 3 July 1725 (*Correspondence* 2.307). Cf. *Correspondence* 2.27 (Pope to the sculptor Francis Bird about his own monument) and 2.288, 306, 327.

KNELLER 1716

5.1. OIL PAINTING, BY SIR GODFREY KNELLER. THE BARON BARNARD, RABY CASTLE, DURHAM.

Late in 1724 or early in 1725 George Vertue, on a visit to Wimpole, recorded among the paintings there: a "head," "Mr. Pope [G]K," and "Cleveland Poet Full[r]"[1] Pope himself, writing to Oxford in June 1730[2] about the completion of the new library at Wimpole, alludes playfully to the "Heads" of two poets, "Cleveland & Another," which he imagines seeing "in another room" (apparently neither the Library nor its "Antiroom") and which he says ought to be "kept at a convenient distance from the Library." On 1 October of the same year he rejoices that the "New Room, the Palace of Learning," is finished, and he wishes that his own "Head had as good right to be with the Authors there" as his "Heart has to be with the Master."[3] Then in 1733 or 1734 Vertue, again at Wimpole, lists "Mr. Pope" among pictures "in the anti room" to "the new great Library Room."[4] The second Lord Oxford sold Wimpole to Lord Hardwicke in 1740. But about the same time, household accounts show, a number of pictures were removed from Wimpole to Welbeck.[5] Among the portraits sold at the Oxford sale of March 1742 were a great many which had been recorded by Vertue at Wimpole in 1724–25 and 1733–34. On the third day, no. 36 was "Mr. Cleveland h.l. by Mr. Fuller,"[6] and, on the fourth day, no. 41 was "A Kit-Cat, of Mr. Pope." The presence of the monogram "[G]K" in Vertue's note of 1724–25 and the notation "Kit-Cat" in 1742 point strongly to a signed Kneller Portrait of size 36 x 28 inches. The only portrait known today which fits the requirement is the Kneller Pope of the 1716 type at Raby Castle, signed and dated "[G]Kneller / 1719." A considerable number of portraits by Kneller which are today among the heirlooms at Raby Castle may well have been collected in part by Gilbert Vane, the second Baron Barnard, who owned Raby Castle from 1723 to 1753 and was a first cousin of Lady Oxford. The "Kit-Cat" of Pope at the Oxford sale sold for £12.0.0, to "Money."[7] The picture at Raby Castle is recorded by Cunningham in 1854. It comes by descent to the present owner, the Tenth Baron Barnard. A printed label on the back reads: "Palace of Art / North East Coast Exhibi-

5.1. Oil on canvas. 35 x 26 in. Background dark brown, sky light blue and pink, trees and grass green, cap emerald green (BCC 213 Emerald), coat brownish purple (like BCC 40 Burgundy and BCC 136 Purple Brown), face pallid, eyes hazel. "ᴳKneller / 1719" in thin black paint, to right, above book; "ΙΛΙΑΔ. I." at top of page and initial Greek letters below. "[P]OPE" inscribed in orange paint is partly covered by the frame in the lower left corner. The Baron Barnard, Raby Castle, Staindrop, Darlington, Durham.

36

tion / Newcastle-upon-Tyne / 1929." The picture was exhibited at the National Portrait Gallery Exhibition of Pope in 1961. It is unique, among pictures of this type known today, in the signature and date and in having the second button above the hand unbuttoned and the Greek letters at the edge of the page. These are the first letters of the opening lines of *Iliad* IX (Iota). The third volume of Pope's *Iliad*, June 1717, begins with Book IX. For the date 1716, see no. 5.11, the mezzotint.

1. Vertue *1*.137–138.
2. *Correspondence* 3.115.
3. *Correspondence* 3.136.
4. Vertue *4*.56.
5. Goulding and Adams, *Catalogue of Welbeck*, p. xv.
6. The portrait of "Cleveland" by Isaac Fuller was bought by Bishop Percy (a collateral descendant of the poet) at the sale of James West the antiquary, begin-

ning 31 March 1773 (*Boswell for the Defence*, ed. W. K. Wimsatt, Jr. and F. A. Pottle [New York, 1959], p. 166 n. 2). The picture is today in the Tate Gallery. After removal of overpainting on a sheet of paper held in the subject's hand, he is seen to be not the poet Cleveland but an architect.

7. Annotated copy of the sale catalogue at the National Portrait Gallery.

5.2. OIL PAINTING, BY SIR GODFREY KNELLER. THE EARL BATHURST, CIRENCESTER PARK, GLOUCESTERSHIRE.

Pope's friendship with Allen, Lord Bathurst (First Baron, 1712), was probably well established at least as early as 1716 (when Kneller painted Pope's portrait for the first time).[1] But the earliest allusion to the portrait at Cirencester occurs in a volume of *The Beauties of England and Wales* published in 1803.[2] The portrait is attributed to Jervas in the *Catalogue of the Bathurst Collection of Pictures Compiled by Earl Bathurst* (Privately Printed, 1908), p. 72, and in *A Loan Exhibition Depicting Marlborough and the Reign of Queen Anne, Chesterfield House, 29 January–March 1934*, p. 40, no. 239.

1. See *Correspondence* 1.318–20 (1715?), 418 (1717), 476, 488, 515; and *Epistles to Several Persons* (Twickenham 3.ii. 81).
2. E. W. Brayley and J. Britton, *The Beauties of England and Wales*, 5 (1803), 619–20, account of

Oakley Grove, the seat of Henry, [Third] Earl Bathurst. "Bolingbroke, Prior, Atterbury, and Pope, may be seen here." The three chiaroscuros, of Apollo, Venus, and Hercules, painted by Kneller for Pope and bequeathed by Pope to Bathurst, are also mentioned.

5.3. OIL PAINTING, BY SIR GODFREY KNELLER. THE EARL OF CRAWFORD AND BALCARRES, BALCARRES PALACE, FIFE.

The First Baron Overstone (1796–1883) purchased this picture in 1857 from William Anthony of 1 Duke Street, St. James's.[1] It was later in the collection of his daughter Lady Wantage,[2] and then in that of her great-nephew, the 27th Earl of Crawford,[3] father of the present Earl of Crawford and Balcarres. On 19 May 1858 George Scharf saw this picture and entered a description of it in his notebook.[4] Thereafter, on seeing other portraits of this type (Rousham, 5.6; Mr. Davis, 5.9; Chesterfield, 5.7), Scharf noted "like Ld. Overstone's," "compare L. Overstone's," "same as Ld. Overstone type."[5] In his copy of Noble's *Continuation* of Granger, he annotated an engraving of the Kneller-Smith type: "Lord Overstone has the original of this picture."[6]

5.2. Oil on canvas. 35 x 27 in. Colors similar to those of no 5.1. The fifth buttonhole up has been crossed out with vertical strokes of reddish paint and is painted in just below, though its position with respect to the button is not improved. The left shoulder and the right waist, below the elbow, show similar *pentimenti,* or trial strokes. The Earl Bathurst, Cirencester Park, Gloucestershire.

5.3. Oil on canvas. 36 x 28 in. Colors similar to those of no. 5.1; cap bluish green. The Earl of Crawford and Balcarres, Balcarres, Colinsburgh, Fife.

The picture is reproduced as frontispiece of vol. 3 of *The Correspondence of Pope,* edited by George Sherburn, Oxford, 1957.

1. A list of pictures sold by Anthony to Lord Overstone, 1857–64, dated 24 August 1864, in possession of the Earl of Crawford and Balcarres, Balcarres, Colinsburgh, Fife. Along with the Pope, from the same dealer in the same year, came the portrait of Johnson by Opie, which is no. 167, p. 115, of the *Wantage Catalogue* (see above), and is there described as having been in the collection of Sir John St. Aubyn, sold at Lime Grove, Putney Hill, Surrey, after the death of Lady St. Aubyn in 1856.

2. *A Catalogue of Pictures Forming the Collection of Lord and Lady Wantage at 2 Carlton Gardens, London, Lockinge House, Berks, and Overstone Park and Ardington House* (London, George Bell & Sons, 1905), p. 88, no. 116.

3. MS. Catalogue of Haigh Hall, Wiggin, Lancashire, no. 171 (at Balcarres).

4. NPG *Scharf Sketch Book 51.59.*

5. NPG *Scharf Sketch Book 64.38; Trustees' Sketch Book 15.45; Scharf Sketch Book 80.51, 56.* The latter two entries are in June and September 1869. On 20 October 1869, Scharf saw and sketched the portrait at Raby Castle (no. 5.1), and noted simply "Pope, by Kneller, good." He seems not to have noticed the signature and date, which are indeed invisible from the floor with the present hanging of the picture at the second level in the dining room.

6. NPG copy of *A Biographical History of England . . . a Continuation of the Rev. J. Granger's Work,* ed. Rev. Mark Noble, *3* (1806), 290–94.

5.4. PHOTOGRAPH OF A PAINTING, BY OR AFTER SIR GODFREY KNELLER. *Orrery Papers,* 1903.

Pope's acquaintance with Swift's friend John Boyle, Fifth Earl of Orrery (1707–62), apparently had commenced not long before Pope's first letter to Orrery (12 July 1735), carefully preserved and numbered by Orrery in the bound volume now in the Morgan Library.[1] The portrait of Pope at Orrery's house, Marston, Somersetshire, does not, however, come to notice until the publication by the Countess of Cork and Orrery of *The Orrery Papers* in 1903.[2] At a sale for the Earl of Cork and Orrery at Christie's, 25 November 1905, lot 57 was described as "Portrait of Alexander Pope, in gray dress and blue cap, holding a book. 30 in. by 25 in. Presented by Pope to John, Earl of Orrery." It was bought by Gordon Fox.[3] Apparently the same picture was sold again at Christie's on 15 June 1923: attributed to "Sir G. Kneller" and described as "Portrait of Alexander Pope, in grey dress, blue cap, holding a book. 29½ in. by 24½ in. From the Collection of John, Earl of Orrery, to whom it was presented by Pope."[4] A copy of the photogravure from the *Orrery Papers,* no. 3 in a volume assembled by Sir Charles Firth, *Pope—Portraits and Caricatures* (Bodleian Library, Firth b10), bears the MS. inscription "Painted for John Earl of Orrery."

1. *Correspondence 3.469–470,* and notes.

2. *The Orrery Papers, Edited by the Countess of Cork and Orrery, in Two Volumes, 1* (London, Duckworth and Company, 1903), facing p. 234, photogravure (5 x 4⅜ in.) by Walker and Cockerell. The List of Illustrations identifies this as from a "Portrait at Marston."

3. Annotated copy in the Yale Library.

4. *Catalogue of Early English Portraits . . . Forming Part of the Private Collection of the Late W. Lockett Agnew, Esq. . . . Christie, Manson & Woods . . . Friday, June 15, 1923.* Pope is no. 141 (on p. 27), part of the "Property of a Lady."

5.5. PHOTOGRAPH OF A PAINTING, AFTER (?) SIR GODFREY KNELLER. FROM STONOR PARK, HENLEY.

Pope's letter to Caryll of 6 August 1717 names, among friends whom he feels "indispensably obliged" to visit, not only Kneller ("who has made me a fine present of a picture") and Bathurst but also "Mr. Stonor." Thomas Stonor, Esq., was one of Pope's Catholic neighbors; he had a house at Twickenham and another, Stonor Park, at Henley. Pope apparently passed some days with him at Twickenham during June or July 1717, and later, in September, on his journey to Oxford, felt a melancholy pleasure in riding past the "gloomy Verdure of Stonor," though the absence of the master prevented his stopping for the night.[1] Pope's portrait from Stonor Park came briefly to light in 1939 and 1940, when it was acquired and offered for sale by Dulau & Company, Ltd., with the description: "Portrait in Oils of Alexander Pope, by Sir Godfrey Kneller. . . . the sitter's turban olive green and his coat purple . . . Size 36 x 28 (feigned oval), outside measurements of frame, 45 x 37½. . . . from the collection of the Hon. Sherman Stonor, Stonor Park, Henley."[2]

1. *Correspondence 1*.411, 417, 429. Stonor had subscribed to Pope's *Iliad*, apparently through the soliciting of Pope's friend Caryll (*1*.221).

2. Dulau & Company, Ltd., 29 Dover Street, London, W.1, *Catalogue Number 281* (1940), p. 4, no. 12. Cf. *Art Prices Current*, New Series, *18*, no. 4153: "Kneller, Sir Godfrey, Alexander Pope, 35½ x 28," 26 July 1939, Sotheby's, bought by Dulau for £15.

5.6 a and b. OIL PAINTING, BY JAMES WORSDALE, AFTER SIR GODFREY KNELLER. THOMAS COTTRELL-DORMER, ESQ., ROUSHAM, OXFORD.

Pope's friendship with Colonel Robert Dormer, the master of Rousham, and with his brother Brigadier James Dormer (1679–1741), close friend of both the poet Gay and the artist Kent, is not traceable in the *Correspondence* until after about 1718,[1] but was no doubt solidly established a good many years earlier. The brothers were nephews-in-law of Pope's early encourager Sir William Trumbull of East Hampstead. William Kent's work for General Dormer on the house at Rousham was done between 1738 and 1741, and his plan for the gardens on the slope to the Cherwel, gardens admired so much by Walpole and still intact in their main outlines, seems to date from the same period.[2] The picture of Pope at Rousham is mentioned by Cunningham in 1854: "at Rousham, a copy by Worsdale, after Jervas." In June 1947, before relining of the canvas,[3] a photograph was made of the following inscription on the back (5.6b): "Alexander Pope Copy'd after / Sʳ Godfrey by his man / James Worsdale."

Vertue describes Worsdale as a "little cringing creature" (the son of a poor color grinder), whom Sir Godfrey took into his house to wait on him and at length was prevailed with to have him bound apprentice. This "chanting, canting" fellow married a niece of Sir Godfrey's wife and was turned out of "house and favor." Nevertheless, by "artful ways" and a "modest modish assurance" he "gained ground and friends." He "made a pretended picture by memory from her Majesty"—really a copy from an original sketch by Kneller. The Queen sat to him for the completion of the picture. The King "commended it highly, perhaps some ways to mortify Jervas." "We that have known this painter and have detected his barefaced mountebank lies are not surprised at his meeting encouragement in this age."[4] Worsdale became an actor, was associated with the stage in London and Dublin, was perhaps the author of a few farcical pieces, and was noted as a singer and mimic. Samuel Johnson in his *Life of Pope* says that

5.4. **Photogravure of a painting ascribed to Sir Godfrey Kneller. Said to be 30 x 25 in., dress gray, cap blue. "Mr Pope. 1716." in upper right corner.** *Orrery Papers,* 1903.

5.5. **Photograph of a painting ascribed to Sir Godfrey Kneller. Said to be 36 x 28 in.; cap olive green, coat purple. Dulau & Company, Ltd.,** *Catalogue 281,* 1940; **From Stonor Park, Henley.**

5.6a. **Oil on canvas. 33⅜ x 27⅜ in. Colors as in 5.1. "Alexander Pope" in upper left; "ΙΛΙΑΔ Ι" on book. Photograph made before restoration c. 1947. Thomas Cottrell-Dormer, Esq., Rousham, Oxfordshire.**

5.6b. **Inscription on back of 5.6a. "Alexander Pope Copyd after / Sr Godfrey by his man / James Worsdale."**

5.7. **Oil on canvas. 30 x 25 in. Colors of hat and coat similar to those of no. 5.1; background olive brown; spandrels; "Pope" in gold letters in lower left. Stirling Library, University of London.**

5.8. **Oil, presumably on canvas. 30 in. high. From a photograph in a catalogue,** *No. 63, New Series, Elizabethan Books and MSS.* . . . **issued by Bernard Halliday, of Leicester, in July 1923.**

Worsdale claimed to have been the emissary from Pope (disguised as a clergyman R. Smythe) who in May 1735 delivered printed sheets of Pope's letters to Curll.[5] Malone had it from Walpole that "Pope had an original picture of Bishop Atterbury painted by Kneller. Of this picture he used to make Worsdale the painter make copies for three or four guineas; and whenever he wished to pay a particular compliment to one of his friends, he gave him an *original* picture of Atterbury. Of these *originals*, Worsdale had painted five or six."[6] Ackermann's *Repository of Arts, Literature, Commerce* for 1812 quotes Worsdale's epitaph in Covent Garden Churchyard: "All that was mortal of James Worsdale, Esq. painter to his majesty's Board of Ordnance, lies under this stone:—who, during his whole life, was 'Eager to get but not to keep the pelf, / Friendly to all mankind, except himself.' Deceased June 10, 1767, aged 75."[7] At a Christie sale of 1829, a self-portrait of Worsdale sold for one pound and three shillings.[8]

1. *Correspondence* 1.468; 2.510 n., 513; 3.126.
2. Margaret Jourdain, *William Kent* (London, 1948), pp. 54, 80, 155.
3. Note on a photograph of the inscription at the National Portrait Gallery.
4. Vertue 3.59 (1732).
5. *Lives of the Poets*, ed. G. B. Hill, 3.158; *Correspondence* 3.476. Cf. Walpole, *Anecdotes* 4.117; Pope's *Works*, ed. Warton (1797), 2.339; ed. Elwin and Courthope 1, Introduction, p. lviii; 5.285; *The Athenaeum*, 8 September 1860, p. 319.
6. James Prior, *Life of Edmond Malone* (London, 1860), p. 385.
7. Rudolph Ackermann. *The Repository of Arts, Literature, Commerce*, 7 (April 1812), 198.
8. Lord Gwydir sale, Christie's, 8 May 1829, no. 8 (Victoria and Albert Museum).

5.7. OIL PAINTING, AFTER SIR GODFREY KNELLER. UNIVERSITY OF LONDON.

Vertue is the earliest to describe the portraits of the English poets assembled by the Fourth Earl of Chesterfield for the library of his house in Mayfair, completed about 1750: "Lord Chesterfield, having a fine room in his new builded house, . . . intends to call [it] the poets' room. Therein he designs to have the portraits of many most memorable poets' heads of this nation: Chaucer, Shakespeare, Jonson, Milton, Cowley, Dryden, Spenser, Waller, Rochester, Rowe. . . . He has some originals from the life he bought at several times from Lord Oxford, Lord Halifax's collection, etc. One particularly of Otway, painted by Riley—from the life. Many others are copied to the size he wants."[1] In another passage Vertue describes the portraits acquired by Chesterfield at the Halifax sale of March 1740.[2] This testimony and the catalogue of the Halifax sale[3] and that of the Oxford sale in March 1742[4] show that Chesterfield's portrait of Pope must have been among the "many others copied to the size he wants." In the nineteenth century [c. 1869] the Seventh Earl of Chesterfield sold Chesterfield House and removed the portraits to Bretby in Derbyshire. About 1918 the 6th Earl of Harewood recovered the portraits and replaced them in their original setting. They were again removed from Chesterfield house about 1932 and were for a time at Goldsborough Hall and then at Harewood House.[5] They were sold for the Earl of Harewood at Christie's on 29 June 1951, lot 43, and were acquired by the late Sir Louis Stirling, who bequeathed them to the University of London. A label on the back of the portrait of Pope records that it was lent by Sir Louis in September–October 1951 to the Exhibition *Le Livre*

Anglais at Paris. In January 1961 the seventeen pictures remaining from an original twenty-one of the Chesterfield set were placed in the Stirling Library at the University of London.

1. Vertue 5.70 (1748).

2. Vertue 4.165.

3. Lugt 497. I am indebted for this information and for general guidance in this entry to a dossier on the Chesterfield Collection drawn up by Mr. D. T. Piper (NPG file, Chesterfield House).

4. Lugt 553 (Scharf copy at the National Portrait Gallery). See no. 5.1.

5. *Bretby Hall near Burton-Upon-Trent Catalogue of the Valuable Contents . . . which will be sold by Auction (by instructions of the Right Hon. the Earl of Carnarvon), by Messrs. Leedam & Harrison . . . July 15–25, 1918*, p. 15, Lot 270b; and Tancred Borenius, *Catalogue of the Pictures and Drawings at Hare-*

wood House and Elsewhere in the Collection of the Earl of Harewood (Privately Printed at the University Press, Oxford, 1936), p. 197, No. 497.

A second collection of pictures, which was in the library at Chesterfield House during the latter part of the nineteenth century, included one of Alexander Pope (no. 17) ascribed to J. Richardson (a list dated 20 June 1893, with a letter of 5 June 1896, from Philip Norman, 45 Evelyn Gardens, S. Kensington, to Lionel Cust, in the National Portrait Gallery file on the Chesterfield Collection).

In H. W. Singer, *Neues Bildniskatalog* (1938), vol. 4, no. 28499 is a painting of Pope, "J. Richardson . . . Goldsborough Hall . . . Earl of Harewood."

5.8. OIL PAINTING, OVAL, BY OR AFTER SIR GODFREY KNELLER. OFFERED BY BERNARD HALLIDAY OF LEICESTER IN 1923.

The Times for Friday, 28 April 1916 (p. 9e), reports a sale by Messrs. Philips, Son, and Neale on the day before at New Lodge, a house in Windsor Forest which had been the residence of the American financier Joshua Bates, who died in 1864, and later of his daughter and heir, who married the Belgian diplomat Sylvain van de Weyer. Among continental pictures which had come into the collection apparently from the van de Weyer family, one which made this sale notable was a hitherto unnoticed portrait by Frans Hals, sold for 4,150 guineas. [Lot 348, on 27 April, the second day of the sale, was described as a portrait of John Gay by Hogarth.] In a catalogue entitled *No. 63, New Series. Elizabethan Books and MSS. And other Old-Time Literature. . . . Mostly privately purchased from a Nobleman's Library*, issued in July 1923[1] by Bernard Halliday, 14 High Cross Street, Leicester, item no. 197, on p. 20, is described as a portrait in oils of John Gay, by Hogarth, oval, 30 inches high, in a carved gilt frame. It is said to have come from the sale at New Lodge, Windsor Forest, 26 April 1916.[2] A photograph appears as Illustration No. 14 in this catalogue and is reproduced above, no. 5.8.

1. A copy received by the Yale University Library was mailed 20 July 1923.

2. The sale is identified unmistakably by allusion to the portrait by Frans Hals.

5.9. OIL PAINTING, KNELLER 1716 TYPE. SEEN BY GEORGE SCHARF, 1858.

On 11 May 1858, George Scharf "went to Highbury with old Mr. Dilke." There, "at the Revd. Mr. Gunnery's," he saw and sketched a portrait of the Kneller 1716 type, noting: "dk br gray" for the background, "greenblue" for the cap, "red brown" for the coat, "w" for the shirt cuff; and on the book "IΛIAΔ I." The attitude of the hand in the sketch suggests a table under it, but there is no indication of a scenic background.[1]

1. NPG *Scharf Sketch Book 51.59*. Cf. *Trustees' Sketch Book 15.45* and NPG Noble's *Granger 3.290*.

5.10. OIL PAINTING, KNELLER 1716 TYPE. SEEN BY GEORGE SCHARF, 1869.

Again, on 30 June 1869, George Scharf records: "Canvas life size shown [presumably at the Gallery] by Mr. Davis surgeon of Brentford—A Pope—compare L. Overstone's." Scharf's sketch of this portrait, in oval, has the notations: "green" on the hat, "w" on the shirt collar, "blue" near the cuff, and perhaps "y.br." on the coat sleeve.[1] At about the same date apparently Scharf went back to the notebook where he had eleven years before recorded Mr. Gunnery's picture and entered: "another repetition without landscape was shown by Mr. Davis, a surgeon residing at Brentford. The hands & book were absent a blue drapery came down from should[er] & concealed them."[2]

1. NPG *Trustees' Sketch Book 15.45*.
2. NPG *Scharf Sketch Book 51.58* verso.
On 16 March 1858, George Scharf "At Farrer's" made a sketch (presumably from a painting) of a young man, head and shoulders only, with very regular features, head and eyes turned left as in the Kneller 1716 type, cap "dull red," background "dark brown," garment "brown," shirt collar "w" and considerably more open than in Kneller 1716. Under this Scharf wrote "Pope." It seems uncertain, however, that it actually is Pope. If Pope, it is nearest to Kneller 1716 and may conceivably be a sketch having something to do with this type (NPG *Scharf Sketch Book 50.71*).

5.11. OIL PAINTING, AFTER KNELLER. COPENHAGEN, 1953.

In June 1953 the National Portrait Gallery received from Branner's Bibliofile Antikvariat A/s, of Copenhagen, Denmark, a photograph of an oil painting 38½ x 28 inches, "Alexander Pope. After Kneller," purchased in England about thirty years earlier. It appears to be a rather poorly painted replica of the Kneller 1716 type.[1]

1. A painting perhaps identical with 5.9, 5.10, or even 5.11, was sold by Knight, Frank, and Rutley, 18–20 September 1916, from the collection of Sir Henry Raphael, Bart., at Allestree Hall near Derby, lot 196: "Sir G. Kneller—A three-quarter life-size Portrait of Alexander Pope, 35 in. by 27 in an old carved frame" (National Portrait Gallery archives). H. F. Wolff, Jr., of Rumson, N.J., owns a 30 x 26″ oil of this type, without scenery, acquired in the 1930s from Sir Alec Lyle-Samuel, M.P.—5.11(1).

5.12. ENAMEL MINIATURE, AFTER KNELLER. GEORGE HOWARD, ESQ.,
        CASTLE HOWARD, YORKSHIRE.

In a letter of 15 August 1727 to Lord Oxford, Pope asks the interest of Lord Morpeth (Henry Howard, Fourth Earl of Carlisle, 1738) in getting a job for a friend. Lady Morpeth was the only daughter of a niece of Lady Oxford and had perhaps been brought up by Lady Oxford.[1] Two years later, 14 August 1729, Pope writes to Oxford: "I ought to have payd my thanks to my Lord & Lady Morpeth for the honour which thro your means I receivd from them."[2] Could the honor have been that of accepting, or commissioning, a miniature portrait of Pope? In an earlier letter to Lord Harcourt

Pope had used the expression: "the Honour you intend me, of filling a place in your Library with my Picture."[3] A large collection of pictures, accumulated apparently through three centuries by the Earls of Carlisle, and divided between Castle Howard in Yorkshire and Naworth Castle in Cumberland, was catalogued about 1895–1903. Among the miniatures at Castle Howard appears "Alexander Pope, the Poet, in brown coat, wearing a grey turban. . . . An enamel oval 3¾ x 2¾. By Christian Frederic Zincke."[4] The miniature was no. 717 in the Guelph Exhibition at the New Gallery, London, in 1891.[5] Mr. George Howard, of Castle Howard, tells me that it is now attributed to Jean André Rouquet.[6]

1. *Correspondence* 2.443.
2. *Correspondence* 2.46.
3. *Correspondence* 2.193. See no. 7.1.
4. Lord Hawkesworth, *Catalogue of the Portraits, Miniatures, &c., at Castle Howard, Yorkshire, and Naworth Castle, Cumberland,* in *The Transactions of the East Riding Antiquarian Society for the Year Ending October, 1903, 11* (Hull, Printed for the Society, 1904), 57, No. 12 in Case II. Basil S. Long, *British*

Portrait Miniaturists (London, 1929), pp. 471–74, lists a miniature by Christian Friedrich Zincke (1684?–1767) of Miss Arabella Fermor, signed on the back "CF Zincke fecit / 1716" (at the Victoria and Albert Museum).
5. P. 717 of the Catalogue.
6. Jean André Rouquet (1701–59) worked in England during the reign of George II, and was a pupil of Zincke. See Introduction, p. xvi.

5.13. STIPPLE ENGRAVING (1807), FROM A MINIATURE AFTER KNELLER.

A stipple engraving of Pope, bust length (3¾ x 3⅛), appearing in W. L. Bowles' edition of the *Works* of Pope (1806), vol. 3, frontispiece, or in vol. 1, facing p. [1], and also in the supplementary or 6th volume of "Ruffhead's" *Pope* (1807), follows the Kneller 1716 type very closely. It has the following legend: "Engraved by W. Evans, from a Drawing by Gardner. / Alexander Pope. / From an enamelled Painting in Miniature, / given by Pope, to Mrs. Nugent—Now / in the Marquis of Buckingham's Collection at Stowe. / Published by Cadell & Davies, Strand, and the other Proprietors May 1. 1807." Stowe guidebooks of this period show that the miniature was part of a large collection of family miniatures which apparently came to Stowe through the wife of the Marquis of Buckingham, Mary Nugent, daughter of Robert (Earl) Nugent (d. 1788), who had been third husband of Pope's friend Anne Craggs (Mrs. Newsham, Mrs. Knight). Earl Nugent had lived during his later years at the former seat of the Knight family, Gosfield Hall.[1]

The collection of family miniatures was witheld from the great Stowe sale of 1848. They appeared, however, 148 in all, in a sale by the Duke of Buckingham at Christie's, 14–16 March 1849, where Pope, lot 105, "painted in enamel. Presented by himself to Mrs. Knight, of Gosfield, afterwards the wife of Robert Earl Nugent," was sold for £8.15.[2]

1. See no. 63.1.
2. Lugt 19271, copy at the Rijksbureau voor Kunsthistorische Documentatie, The Hague.

5.14. MEZZOTINT ENGRAVING, BY JOHN SMITH (1717), AFTER SIR GODFREY KNELLER.

John Smith (1654–1742) was Kneller's favorite engraver. J. Chaloner Smith lists 287 mezzotint engravings by Smith, 124 of them after paintings by Kneller.[1] The lettering of this mezzotint constitutes the best contemporary external evidence for the author-ship of the painting and the only evidence for the date. Smith (*3.* 1209, John Smith no. 203) lists three states: 1. Before any inscription (British Museum); 2. As reproduced below, no. 5.13; 3. A "modern" or refurbished state.[2] State 2 is probably the mezzotint to which Mather Byles of Boston refers in a letter to Pope, 18 May 1728: "In our College Library at *Cambridge* . . . we have . . . your Poems in a large Folio: In which is the only picture I have seen of you in modern Dress [the line engraving of 1715 by Vertue], tho your smaller pictures in a poetical one are frequent, and most of our Genteel Rooms are embellished with your large mezzotint."[3] Among early simplified derivatives from this engraving are Pope in the mezzotint of four poets after Kneller (Addison, Prior, Pope, and Congreve) by J. Simon,[4] and in the four poets among the Worthies of Britain by F. Kyte (Dryden, Wycherley, Prior, Pope).[5] See also the next two entries, 5.14 and 5.15.

In the John G. Johnson Collection, Philadelphia, Pennsylvania, an oil painting on canvas, 29½ x 24 inches, illusionistic in style, represents a copy of this engraving ("Mr Alexander Pope. Æt^s 28. / G Kneller Pinx. 1716. // J. Smith fec. et ex. 1717.") tacked to a pine panel, with knife, letter, and quill stuck behind a pink ribbon tacked beneath. The painting is attributed to an unknown English artist of the mid-eighteenth century.[6]

1. J. Chaloner Smith, *British Mezzotint Portraits*, *3*, 1133–1241; Lord Killanin, *Sir Godfrey Kneller and His Times, 1646–1723* (London, 1948), chap. 7, "Kneller and the Early Mezzotint Artists."

2. Known to him through a Boydell *Catalogue* (1779–87; see J. Ch. Smith *1*.XV); perhaps this is

the altered state represented in an impression in the Widener Library at Harvard; a ray of sunlight being let in above the head from the right (Samuel Johnson, *Life of Pope*, 1825, extra-illustrated, 1874, vol. *1*, plate 1 after title, from the library of Clarence S. Bement).

3. *Correspondence* 2.494. Pope's portrait by Kneller

5.12. Enamel painting. 3¾ x 2¾ in. Coat brown; cap gray. George Howard, Esq., Castle Howard, Yorkshire.†

5.13. Stipple engraving. 3¾ x 3⅛ in. "Engraved by W. Evans, from a Drawing by Gardner. / ALEXANDER POPE. / From an enamelled Painting in Miniature, / given by Pope, to Mrs Nugent—Now / in the Marquis of Buckingham's Collection at Stowe. / Published by Cadell & Davies, Strand, and the other Proprietors May 1. 1807." *Works of Pope*, ed. W. L. Bowles (1806), vol. 3, frontispiece.

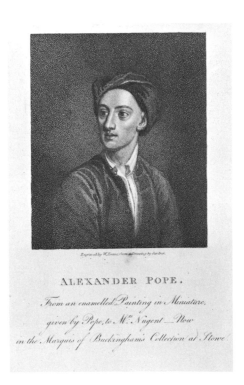

ALEXANDER POPE.

From an enamelled Painting in Miniature,
given by Pope, to Mrs Nugent—Now
in the Marquis of Buckingham's Collection at Stowe.

5.14. Mezzotint engraving. 13½ x 9⅝ in. plate mark (with lettering). "M.ͬ Alexander Pope Æt.ˢ 28. / G. Kneller S. R. Imp. et Mag. Brit. Baronet.ˢ Pinx. 1716. // J. Smith fec. et ex. 1717." *BMEP* Pope 9; *Grolier 1*; J. Ch. Smith 3.1209–10, John Smith no. 203, state 2.

right

5.15. Line engraving. 6¾ x 8⅜ in. "M.ͬ Alexander Pope. / [R.?A.?] Delin. Sculp. 1731. / Sold by H. Overton / without Newgate". *BMP&PS* 1880. By permission of the Trustees of the British Museum.

below

5.16. Line engraving. 1¹³⁄₁₆ x 1⁷⁄₁₆ in. "M.ͬ POPE". Top of first page of *Books Printed for E. Curll, At Pope's-Head, In Rose-Street, Covent-Garden*, 1 December 1735.

BOOKS
Printed for *E. CURLL,*
At *POPE's - HEAD,*

In *Rose - Street, Covent - Garden.*

dated 1722 was engraved in mezzotint by G. White in 1723, but there would seem to be some reason to think this mezzotint was better known upon republication in 1732. (See no. 7.8.) His portrait painted by Dahl in 1727 was engraved in mezzotint by J. Simon in 1728 (see no. 8.4), but this portrait was probably not well known in America as early as May 1728.

4. *BMEP* 5.80–81, "Poets and Philosophers of England"; J. Ch. Smith 3.1085.

5. *BMEP* 5.80, "Worthies of Britain"; J. Ch. Smith 2.793.

6. W. R. Valentiner, *Catalogue of a Collection of Paintings and Some Art Objects* (Philadelphia: John G. Johnson, 1914), 3.54–55, no. 825.

5.15. LINE ENGRAVING, AFTER KNELLER. SOLD BY H. OVERTON WITHOUT NEWGATE, 1731. DEPARTMENT OF PRINTS AND DRAWINGS, BRITISH MUSEUM.

This portrait of Pope is the central feature of an engraving which represents a "medley" or heap of engraved images and texts—described in the British Museum *Catalogue of Political and Personal Satires*, 2.753–755 (no. 1880). Pope lies on top of nine other partially showing sheets, which may be described, from top to bottom, in brief as follows: 1. a piece of sheet music; 2. a passage from Pope's *Windsor Forest* [2.33–42], ending with a compliment to Queen Anne—"And peace & plenty tell a STUART reigns"—beneath it a scene of lofty architecture and trees; 3. a passage from Pope's *Rape of the Lock* [4. 123–130], beneath it a portrait of "The Fop," Sir Plume; 4. a design of artificial leaf and flower scroll work, beneath it the signature (partly covered) and date: "[R.?A.?]Delin. Sculp. 1731"; 5. on a black ground a medallic profile of Queen Anne with the inscription "Anna.Dei.Gratia";[1] 6. a page printed in black letter; 7. a scene, apparently of villagers dancing about a Maypole; 8. a sheet of handwriting; 9. "An Encomium on Mr Pope and his Poems. By his Grace ye late Duke of Buckingham."[2] In the lower left corner appears: "Sold by H. Overton / without Newgate." An impression of this print belonging to the Oxford University Press and another in the Theatre Collection, Houghton Library, Harvard University, have instead: "London Printed / for Robt Sayer. at N^o / 53 in Fleet Street." In volume 1 of an extra-illustrated large-paper set of Singer's edition of Spence's *Anecdotes*, having the bookplate of Henry William Poor, acquired in 1963 by the University of Illinois Library from W. H. Lowdermilk & Co., booksellers in Washington, D.C., I have seen a similar medley centering on "Mr. Gay" ("W. Aikman pinx. G. Bickham sculp."), dated 1729, with the inscription "Our medley has a meaning—and no doubt / you all have sense enough to find it out." The medal or counter on a black ground is "Georgius II Dei Gratia."

1. The picture represents a copper "counter" of a sort issued at different times during and after the reign of Queen Anne. They bear the dates 1701, 1702, 1712, and so on; they vary in size from about one inch to three quarters of an inch in diameter. See British Museum, *Medallic Illustrations of the History of Great Britain and Ireland*, Plates CXXXI–CXL (London, 1911), Plate CXXXVII, nos. 14 and 17, and text; *Plates CXI–CXX* (1910), Plate CXV, nos. 10 (especially) and 11.

2. First published by Pope, at the front of his collected *Works*, 1717; also in vol. *1* of Pope's edition of Buckingham's *Works* in 1723. See *Twickenham* 6.188.

5.16. LINE ENGRAVING, "POPE'S HEAD." *Books Printed for E. Curll*, 1735.

Pope's piratical publisher Edmund Curll displayed a strong interest in the "head" of his favorite author, and especially in the head deriving from the Kneller portrait of

1716. As early as 13 July 1720, in the second volume of Giles Jacob's *Poetical Register*,[1] Curll had provided for Jacob's biographical sketch of Pope a small line cut of this type ("Clark & Pine Sc."—*Grolier* 6), Pope half length, standing in cap and unbuttoned coat, with open shirt collar. In this, Curll was a step ahead of Pope's legitimate publisher Bernard Lintot, who a month later, 15 August, used a similar derivative engraving ("G. Vertue S."—*Grolier* 15) in Volume 1 of his *Miscellaneous Poems*.[2] In copies of the first two volumes of his *Mr. Pope's Literary Correspondence* (published 23 May and 14 July 1735)[3] Curll used interchangeably as frontispiece two small line cuts of Pope, one of the Kneller 1722 type (no. 7.8) and the other yet a third version of the Kneller 1716 type ("Mr. Pope"—*Grolier* 10). In his public letter about Pope's *Correspondence*, addressed from his shop in Rose Street, Covent Garden, on 22 May 1735 "To the most Noble and Right Honourable the Peers of Great Britain," Curll ended with a flourish: "I have engraven a new plate of Mr. Pope's head from Mr. Jervas's painting [see no. 2.2]; and likewise intend to hang him up in effigy for a sign to all spectators of his falsehood and my own veracity."[4] By 26 July of the same year, in his letter "E. Curll to the Public" on the same themes, Curll was writing "From Pope's Head, in Rose Street" and boasting "I have hung up his head for my sign."[5] An engraved portrait of Pope which appears at the head of the first page of Curll's catalogue *Books Printed for E. Curll, At Pope's Head*, 1 December 1735,[6] suggests that a crude derivative from Kneller's portrait of 1716 was the effigy, no doubt painted on wood, which Curll had hung up for his sign.

This double triumph of sign and printed page was recognized by the *Grub-Street Journal* (no. 292) in the following epigram:

> Curst Cur—besieged by duns to raise the cash
> With P—s immortal busto stamps the trash
> So squandering coiners, to retrieve a loss
> Imprint their monarch's image on their dross.[7]

1. Griffith 123. The portrait faces p. 145. It reappears at the same place in the second edition of *The Poetical Register*, remainder sheets brought out by A. Butterworth and other booksellers in 1723.

2. Griffith 124. Griffith says the plate was used also in later editions, 1722, 1726–27, 1732, and in Lintot's *The Works of Alexander Pope, Esq.; Vol. I*, 1736, Griffith 413 (2.331).

3. Griffith 376 and 386. I base my statement on Griffith's descriptions, supplemented by my examination of copies of these two volumes in the Yale Library.

4. Carruthers, *Life of Pope* (1857), p. 324; Elwin and Courthope 4.435–36.

5. *Correspondence* 3.477.

6. A small octavo volume of sixteen pages, the date 1 December 1735 appearing at the foot of the last page (copy in the Yale Library). The cut of Pope is reproduced facing p. 188 of Ralph Straus, *The Unspeakable Curll* (London, 1927).

In his advertisement of Pope's works, p. 16, Curll lists: "IX. Four Prints of Mr. Pope, in different Attitudes. Price 6*d*. each." These four, which Curll advertises repeatedly hereafter, were no doubt the three which we have just noticed (Kneller 1716, *Grolier* 10; Kneller 1722, *Grolier* 20; Jervas 1714, *Grolier* 29) and a fourth (Kneller 1721, *Grolier* 31). Kneller 1716 and Kneller 1722 were used, as we have seen, in copies of Curll's *Volume the First* and *Volume the Second* of *Mr. Pope's Literary Correspondence*. Jervas 1714 and Kneller 1721 were used in copies of his *Volume the Third* and *Volume the Fourth* of *Mr. Pope's Literary Correspondence*, 1735 and 1736 (Griffith 402 and 415). See nos. 2.2, 6.13, 7.8. See my paper " 'Amicitiae Causa,' A Birthday Present from Curll to Pope," in *Restoration and Eighteenth-Century Literature*, ed. Carroll Camden (University of Chicago Press for William Marsh Rice University, 1963), pp. 341–49.

7. James T. Hillhouse, *The Grub-Street Journal* (Duke University Press, 1928), pp. 32–33.

PORTRAITS OF ALEXANDER POPE

KNELLER 1721

In the first of his three *Dialogues Upon Medals*, Addison had written: "I think there is a great affinity between Coins and Poetry, and that your Medallist and Critic are much nearer related than the world generally imagines. A reverse often clears up the passage of an old poet, as the poet often serves to unriddle a reverse."[1] "A cabinet of Medals is a collection of pictures in miniature. . . . You here see the *Alexanders*, *Caesars*, *Pompeys*, *Trajans*, and the whole catalogue of Heroes."[2] "You see on Medals not only the names and persons of Emperors, Kings, Consuls, Pro-Consuls, Praetors, and the like characters of importance, but of some of the Poets."[3] In his complimentary epistle *To Mr. Addison, Occasioned by his Dialogues on Medals* (drafted perhaps as early as 1713 but first published in an edition of Pope's *Works* in 1720 and then in Tickell's edition of Addison's *Works* in 1721),[4] Pope himself found the theme of numismatic poetics even more congenial:

> The verse and sculpture bore an equal part,
> And Art reflected images to Art.
> Oh when shall Britain, conscious of her claim,
> Stand emulous of Greek and Roman fame?
> In living medals see her wars enroll'd,
> And vanquish'd realms supply recording gold?
> Here, rising bold, the Patriot's honest face;
> There Warriors frowning in historic brass:
> Then future ages with delight shall see
> How Plato's, Bacon's, Newton's looks agree;
> Or in fair series laurell'd Bards be shown,
> A Virgil there, and here an Addison.[5]

This was the original conclusion of the poem. The sequence is brought to a point where, did not modesty forbid, and were not the poem addressed to Addison, Pope's own name, linked with a suitable one from antiquity, might well appear in another couplet. Instead, he added, about 1720, the coda on his friend James Craggs, who succeeded Addison as Secretary of State in 1718:

> Then shall thy CRAGS (and let me call him mine)
> On the cast ore, another Pollio, shine.

It may well have been, however, that the reworking and publication of this poem, c. 1719–21, had something to do with the fact that Kneller's second portrait of Pope (1721) is a highly stylized exploitation of numismatic motifs. Three iconographic features especially are to be noted: 1. The medallic imitation makes feasible the display of Pope's striking profile—an unusual pose in British male portraits of this period.

---

1. *Works* (1721), *1*.446.
2. *Works* (1721), *1*.438.
3. *Works* (1721), *1*.439.
4. *Twickenham* 6.205–06.
5. *Twickenham* 6.204.

2. The ancient symbol of eternity (see no. 6.6), the uroboros, a serpent biting its own tail,[6] is geometrized into a medallic frame. 3. Having appeared in the Kneller portrait of 1716 as the modern Homer, Pope apparently now elects another, if more modest, part of his classical heritage. This can be seen in the Roman toga and even more pronouncedly (if to the modern eye perhaps more cryptically) in the wreath of ivy leaves. The meaning had been in part determined by Pope himself in a couplet of the *Essay on Criticism:*

> Immortal *Vida!* on whose honour'd Brow
> The Poet's *Bays* and Critick's *Ivy* grow.[7]

Virgil's *Eclogue* 7 and Horace's First Ode stood behind a Renaissance idea that ivy was the apt symbol of the poet's learning and labor, the bay, or laurel, the symbol of his poetic genius and triumph. But Pope himself was apparently the first to reserve the ivy for the critic.[8] He was taken to task by one of his *Dunciad* enemies: "the Ancients always gave Ivy to the Poets . . . nor was it ever apply'd to Patrons or Criticks . . . by any but this ingenious Author."[9] In the *Dunciad* Pope made ivy "creeping, dirty," "dangling," and "courtly," the emblem of the Poet Laureate,[10] and he spoke with contempt of "all who since [monkish times], in mild benighted days, [had] mix'd the Owl's ivy

6. The highly geometrized serpent of Kneller may be seen again framing William Hoare's crayon of Newton and his similar etching ("Hoare f^t aquâ forti. 1734"), both in the Department of Prints and Drawings at the British Museum (1894–12–19–1 and P. 8–217). An engraving by J. Faber after a painting of Newton done by Vanderbank, for Martin Folkes, shows the same device attached to a wall in the background of the picture (Pierpont Morgan Library, Bessborough extra-illustrated Foulis *Pope,* 1785, 2.270). In St. Mary's Church at Twickenham, near Warburton's monument to Pope, is that of Admiral Sir Chaloner Ogle done by Rysbrack in 1751. Here an angel figure holds out a small marble hoop, which on close inspection is discovered to be the serpent biting its tail. In his second *Dialogue upon . . . Ancient Medals,* Addison remarks, "I have seen at *Rome* an antique Statue of Time, with a wheel or hoop of marble in his hand, as *Seneca* describes him, and not with a serpent as he is generally represented" (*Works* [1721], *1*.467). I am unable to point to any immediate or major model for Kneller. The symbol was associated with Saturn, the Medieval and Renaissance ancestor of our Father Time. See Erwin Panofsky, *Studies in Iconology* (1939: Harper Torchbook, 1962), pp. 78, 81, and figs. 3, 37, 45, 53. The neatest pictures which I have found in a Renaissance manual are those in Vincenzo Cartari, *Le Imagini De I Dei De Gli Antichi* (In Lione, 1581), pp. 24, 30, 34 (the last associated with Janus); cf. text pp. 26, 29, 36. For the archetypal theme of the eternal uroboros, see C. G. Jung, *Psychology and Alchemy* (London, 1953), pp. 45, 53, 99 (figs. 6, 13, 46, 47). See also George Boas, tr. *The Hieroglyphics of Horapollo* (New York, 1950), pp. 57–58; and George Hill, *Corpus of Italian Medals* (London, 1930),

1.273; 2, Plate 175, no. 1054, a medal of Lorenzo de' Medici, having a circled snake on the reverse.

7. *3*.705–06, *Twickenham 1*.320. In his Virgilian pastoral *Summer* (1709) Pope has conflated passages from *Eclogues* 7 and 8 in a compliment to a senior poet:

> Accept, O *Garth,* the Muse's early Lays,
> That adds this Wreath of Ivy to thy Bays.
> —ll. 9–10, *Twickenham 1*.72.

8. *Twickenham 1*.320–22. The Twickenham note is attributed to Mr. J. B. Trapp, whose learned essay "The Owl's Ivy and the Poet's Bays, An Inquiry into Poetic Garlands" in the *Journal of the Warburg and Courtauld Institutes, 21* (1958), 227–55, is my chief guide in this passage.

9. Matthew Concanen, *A Supplement to the Profound,* 1728, p. 13, quoted by Trapp in *Twickenham 1*.322 and in *Warburg,* p. 229. Thomas Cooke's *Battle of the Poets,* in his anonymous *Tales, Epistles, Odes, Fables, &c.* (London, 1729), pp. 136–37, has Dennis feeding the flames with various works of Pope, among them "that dull Strain / Where for the Critic's Wreath he strives in vain;" and *A New Miscellany* (London, printed for A. Moore, 1730) contains "On the Controversy Between Mr Pope and Mr Theobalds, 1729" (ascribed to William Duncombe by R. F. Jones, *Lewis Theobald,* 1919, p. 119). Here:

> In *Pope's* melodious Verse the Graces smile;
> In *Theobald's* is display'd sagacious Toil;
> The Critick's Ivy crowns his subtle Brow,
> While in Pope's Numbers Wit and Musick flow.

10. *Twickenham 5*.412 (*Of the Poet Laureate*) and 291 (Version B, *1*.304).

with the Poet's bays."[11] During the 1730s, with the help of his friend Jonathan Richardson, Pope's portraiture would gradually assume the Petrarchan bays.[12]

11. *Twickenham* 5.154 (Version A, 3.46).
12. For the coronation of Petrarch on the Capitol 8 April 1341, see Trapp, *Warburg*, pp. 239–41.

6.1. CRAYON (CHALK) DRAWING, BY SIR GODFREY KNELLER, C. 1721. DEPARTMENT OF PRINTS AND DRAWINGS, BRITISH MUSEUM.

The image is the same size as that in Sir Alexander Douglas-Home's oil (no. 6.2). The drawing has the appearance of being not a study for the oil portrait but a model, from which portraits of this type were no doubt multiplied. It was in a collection of materials which passed from Kneller to his chief assistant Edward Byng and by family descent to Mrs. E. A. Roberts, from whom it was purchased by the British Museum in 1888.[1] It is Kneller No. 14 in Lawrence Binyon, *Catalogue of Drawings by British Artists and Artists of Foreign Origin Working in Great Britain . . . in the British Museum, 3* (1902), 29; and Kneller no. 11 in Edward Croft-Murray & Paul Hulton, *Catalogue of British Drawings, 1* (1960), 390; plate 185 in vol. 1 (1960) of *Plates*. It was exhibited at the National Portrait Gallery Exhibition in 1961.

1. Croft-Murray and Hulton, *Catalogue of British Drawings, 1*.204, 390, 584.

6.2. OIL PAINTING, BY SIR GODFREY KNELLER, 1721. SIR ALEXANDER DOUGLAS-HOME, THE HIRSEL, COLDSTREAM.

This painting has come down among the heirlooms of the Earls of Home. It is no. 43 on p. 62 of a *List of Pictures at the Hirsel* compiled by Sir Hew Dalrymple (d. 1945). It was exhibited, apparently for the first time, at the National Portrait Gallery Exhibition in 1961, and was reproduced in the *Daily Telegraph and Morning Post,* 21 March 1961, p. 17, and in *The Illustrated London News,* 18 April 1961, p. 592.

6.3. PHOTOGRAPH OF A PAINTING, BY SIR GODFREY KNELLER.

At Christie's 22 November 1912, p. 13, no. 68 was a painting of this type, "in grey dress, in a sculptured oval," 29 x 23 inches (described as s. & d. "Kneller 1721" and sketched in a copy of the catalogue at the National Portrait Gallery), from the collection of the late H. N. Pym, Foxwold Chase, Brasted, Kent. A copy of the catalogue at Yale records: "Sold to Spencer for 5.5."

This was very likely, though not necessarily, the painting which was offered 1 October 1918, by Messrs. W. J. Thomson & Co., 6 Broad Street Place, London E.C.— photograph at the National Portrait Gallery reproduced below. The same painting appears in another photograph, as offered by Art Collectors Assoc[iation] Ltd., 1920 (at the Courtauld Institute Library).

The photograph of 1918 appeared in an Exhibition of photographs at the Warburg Institute in 1943 (Warburg micro-film negative VI.41).

6.1. Crayons (chalks) and lead pencil on yellowish (or buff) oiled paper. 18¼ x 14¾ in. A drawing in black, heightened with white and touched with rose and blue. The paper is "made up" in the lower left corner. By permission of the Trustees of the British Museum. Department of Prints and Drawings, 1888—7—19—65. Cf. *Catalogue of British Drawings*, 1960, p. 390.

6.2. Oil on canvas. 24½ x 22½ in. Painted frame and serpent greenish brown, background similar but darker at edges, toga coffee brown and shades of beige (similar to BCC 19 Coffee, 137 Chocolate, 18 Rose Beige, 168 Nutmeg), hair glossy dark brown, flesh tints sallow, eyes brownish, ivy leaves gray-green, veined with white; signed and dated to the left in front of the chest, "Kneller / 1721," with a fancy "K," in thin black paint. Sir Alexander Frederick Douglas-Home, The Hirsel, Coldstream, Berwickshire.

The photographs of 1918 and 1920 clearly represent the same picture, and in each the signature and date "Kneller/1721" are clearly discernible in the same position as in no. 6.2.[1]

1. At Christie's, 2 July 1887, p. 7, no. 29 was a portrait of Pope by Kneller, "profile to left, wearing wreath of ivy, encircled by painted serpent," from the collection of James Whatman, F.R.S., deceased, at Vinters, Maidstone. Scharf's third copy at the National Portrait Gallery has a slight pencil sketch and notes that the picture was bought by "Thibandeau" for 80 guineas.

6.4. OIL PAINTING, BY OR AFTER SIR GODFREY KNELLER. THE EARL OF SEFTON, CROXTETH HALL, LIVERPOOL.

A photograph of this painting at the National Portrait Gallery is inscribed "Ld. Sefton's Novr. 27, 1863." It is no. 100 in a typescript *Inventory of Paintings and Drawings at Croxteth Hall* drawn up by Lawrence Haward, dated January 1946.

6.5. OIL PAINTING, BY OR AFTER SIR GODFREY KNELLER. THE BARON MARGADALE, FONTHILL HOUSE, TISBURY, WILTSHIRE.

No. 150, on p. 31 of the Twickenham *Pope Commemoration Catalogue* of 1888, is " 'Alexander Pope,' Painted by C. Jervas. Lent by Mr. A. Morrison." The owner is identified on p. 56 as Mr. Alfred Morrison, 16 Carlton House Terrace, S.W. The noted virtuoso and art patron Alfred Morrison (1821–97), of Fonthill and Carlton House Terrace, was the son of James Morrison (1790–1857), whose collection of pictures is described by G. F. Waagen in his *Galleries and Cabinets of Art in Great Britain* (1857), pp. 105–13, 300–12. Alfred Morrison was the grandfather of John Granville Morrison, Baron Margadale, of Fonthill House, Tisbury, Wiltshire.

6.6. PAINTING, BY OR AFTER KNELLER. THE GROLIER CLUB, NEW YORK.

This portrait was presented to the Grolier Club by the late Beverly Chew, Esq. (d. 1924). It was exhibited at the Century Club in 1937 and reproduced in *Portraits Owned by Clubs of New York January 9 to February 3, 1937*, The Century Club, 7 West Forty-Third Street, New York, plate 2. On the back of the picture in black stencil are the numbers "769P" and "1001CK."

6.7. OIL PAINTING, BY OR AFTER SIR GODFREY KNELLER. CHRISTOPHER CALLAGHAN, ESQ., EAST TWICKENHAM.

This oil painting is said to have appeared c. 1957 at a sale of property from Elvetham Farm House, the family home of Brigadier Sir Richard Hamilton Anstruther-Gough-Calthorpe, at Hartley Wintney. The size is 29 x 24½ inches. The design, including the serpent, and the colors are similar to those of 6.2, but darker shades prevail, laid over the canvas somewhat thinly.

6.3. Photograph of a painting, by Kneller. W. J. Thomson & Co., 1918. "Kneller / 1721" (with a fancy "K," in front of the chest). National Portrait Gallery Archives.

6.4. Oil on canvas. 29 x 24 in. Colors similar to those of no. 6.2. The Earl of Sefton, Croxteth Hall, Liverpool.

6.5. Oil on canvas. 29½ x 24 in. Colors similar to those of nos. 6.2 and 6.4, but darker shades of olive and gray prevail. The Baron Margadale, Fonthill House, Tisbury, Wiltshire.

6.6. Oil on canvas. 30 x 25 in. Colors similar to those of no. 6.2, but brownish shades prevail. "ÆTERNITATI" is painted in a panel beneath. The Grolier Club, New York.

6.8. OIL PAINTING, AFTER KNELLER. NATIONAL MUSEUM OF WALES, CARDIFF.†

At the National Museum of Wales, Cardiff, is an oil-on-canvas oval of the Kneller 1721 type, 27¾ x 22½ inches, transferred from the Cardiff Museum, to which it was bequeathed by William Menelaus, of Dowlais, near Merthyr Tydfil, in 1882 (no. 19, p. 78, of the National Museum of Wales *Catalogue of Oil Paintings,* Cardiff, 1955).

6.9. OIL PAINTING, AFTER KNELLER. JAMES M. OSBORN, NEW HAVEN, CONNECTICUT.

Mr. James M. Osborn, of New Haven, Connecticut, has a small oil painting of Pope derived from the Kneller of 1721, on a wooden panel, on the back of which is an ink inscription dated 1744.

6.10. WATERCOLOR DRAWING, AFTER KNELLER. PIERPONT MORGAN LIBRARY, NEW YORK.

This drawing is found at the Pierpont Morgan Library in an album of Pope autographs and engravings (MA 561) rearranged in 1922 from materials once in the collection of Lord Bathurst, acquired by Mr. Morgan in 1909. The paper seems perhaps contemporary, though it is difficult to examine. The picture is underpainted with a cross-hatching of fine lines, as if to simulate the grain of canvas. It seems the work of an amateur, following the Kneller type of 1721. But the motto in the oval at top, "ΟΥΤΟΣ ΕΚΕΙΝΟΣ," doubtless postdates Richardson's etching of 1738 (below no. 48.1). In keeping with such a later date, the "critic's ivy" of Kneller's 1721 painting (see above, p. 51) has been replaced by the "poet's bays" (as in Richardson's profile, no. 54), which Pope was doubtless by 1738 felt to have securely earned. The signature "Bfc" seems possibly to point to Pope's friend the First Earl Bathurst (no. 5.2).

Miniatures by A. B. Lens

6.11. WATERCOLOR MINIATURE, OVAL, AFTER KNELLER, SIGNED, BY ANDREW BENJAMIN LENS. THE DUKE OF BUCCLEUCH AND QUEENSBERRY.†

Horace Walpole's *Description of . . . Strawberry Hill,* 1784, p. 25, has "Mr. Pope, by young Lens, in water-colours; round"; and this was no doubt no. 49 on the 11th day of the Strawberry Hill sale 6 May 1842: "Pope, by Lens." On 6 October 1857, at the Manchester Exhibition, George Scharf (NPG *Sketch Book* 48.76) noted among the miniatures lent by the Duke of Buccleuch, in case 14: "Alexander Pope. profile to l. crowned with laurel. signed ABL [monogram] in gold." The same miniature is noted in the Buccleuch Collection at Montague House, Whitehall, by George C. Williamson, *The History of Portrait Miniatures* (London, 1904), *1*.100, Plate LV; *2*.123 ("From Strawberry Hill"); it is said to be illustrated also in the Victoria and Albert Museum's

6.10. Watercolor on paper. 6⅝ x 5⅛ in. "ΟΥΤΟΣ // ΕΚΕΙΝΟΣ / Bfc". Shades of green and russet brown prevail in the background and garment. The hair is accented by pen-and-ink lines. The Pierpont Morgan Library, New York.

6.13. Mezzotint engraving. 12⅞ x 8⅞ in. plate mark. "G. Kneller Barᵗ Pinxᵗ 1721. // I. Faber fecit 1738. / Mʳ Pope / Sold by I. Faber at the Golden Head, Bloomsbury Square." *Grolier* 31. *BMEP* 23. J. Ch. Smith *1.*412, J. Faber Junior no. 293, state 1. Beverly Chew Bequest, Prints Division, The New York Public Library.

G. Kneller Barᵗ Pinxᵗ 1721.   I. Faber fecit 1738.

Mʳ Pope

Sold by I. Faber at the Golden Head, Bloomsbury Square

Eighty-Two Miniatures from the Collection Lent by the Duke of Buccleuch 1916–1917,
Plate 27; it is noticed and illustrated by A. Kennedy, *Early English Portrait Miniatures
in the Collection of the Duke of Buccleuch* (*The Studio,* Ltd., London, Paris, New
York, 1917), p. 41 and Plate LI (p. 44, "water-colour"). According to Kennedy, this
miniature was no. Q 27, wrongly attributed to Bernard Lens, in the *Catalogue* of the
Buccleuch Collection compiled by Andrew MacKay and privately printed in 1896. For
an account of Andrew Benjamin Lens, c. 1713–c. 1779, see Basil S. Long, *British Miniaturists* (London, 1929), pp. 265–66.

6.12. MINIATURE (OR MINIATURES) BY A. B. LENS.†

On 30 June 1859, George Scharf sketched a miniature of the same type as no. 6.11. He
recorded that this was later offered to the National Portrait Gallery by a Mr. Ainslie
and his son, from Brighton (NPG Scharf *Trustees' Sketch Books* 3.11). George C. Williamson, *The History of Portrait Miniatures, 2* (London, 1904), 134, says: "Lord Cathcart has . . . a [miniature] portrait of Alexander Pope by Lens." Colonel the Earl
Cathcart has kindly informed me that such a miniature is at present in his possession—
"a circular portrait of Pope wearing a brown coat and a crown of . . . leaves . . . signed
'A.B.L.' "

6.13. MEZZOTINT ENGRAVING, BY J. FABER, JUNIOR (1738), AFTER
      SIR GODFREY KNELLER 1721.

The Kneller 1721 type of painting has the distinction of having been apparently[1] *first*
reproduced in a small line engraving for the frontispiece of one of Curll's volumes of
Pope's letters (1735). A copy at Yale of *Mr. Pope's Literary Correspondence Volume
the Third* . . . London: Printed for E. Curll, at Pope's-Head, in Rose-Street, Covent-
Garden. M.DCC.XXXV (Griffith no. 402), has for frontispiece a line engraving, 5¼₀
x 3¼ inches (plate mark), Pope in profile to right, wearing toga and ivy wreath, within
an engraved oval serpent frame: "Kneller pinx. / / Parr Sculp. / Mr Pope / Horatius
Anglicanus." This is *Grolier 31.* The same engraving appears, though not as frontispiece, in Curll's *Mr. Pope's Literary Correspondence Volume the Fourth,* 1736 (Griffith
415). John Faber's mezzotint from the same type of painting is dated 1738. For the first
state, see the illustration above, no. 6.13. J. Ch. Smith *1.412* records a second state, with
"I. Faber fecit 1738" replaced by "John Faber fecit," and the address changed to
"Printed for Thos Bowles in St. Paul's Church Yard and Ino Bowles & Son at the Black
Horse in Cornhill." An example of this state is to be found in the Houghton Library at
Harvard University (Evert Jansen Wendell Bequest).

1. An unrecorded first state of Faber's mezzotint, much closer to 1721, is, I believe, strongly to be suspected.
See no. 7.8, the unique example of White's mezzotint dated 1723, after the Kneller of 1722.

KNELLER 1722

7.1. OIL PAINTING, BY SIR GODFREY KNELLER, 1722. THE VISCOUNT HARCOURT, STANTON HARCOURT, OXFORDSHIRE.

In a letter to Jacob Tonson, written most likely in May 1722, Pope complains that much business, including apparently the getting together of parties of his friends to collate plays of Shakespeare, has delayed his sitting for a portrait by Kneller. "I wish you'd inform Sir Godfry how busy I have been. I think it three Ages since I saw him and if my Features are altred, in proportion to the length of Time which it has seemd to me since I saw him, my Picture at next sitting, will be as old as Nestor."[1] Further delays must have occurred, for it was on 22 August 1723 that Pope wrote from Twickenham to Lord Harcourt that the "original" was ready for him:

> My Lord,—It is a Satisfaction to me to tell your Lordship, that I shall not be any way disappointed of the Honour you intend me, of filling a place in your Library with my Picture. I came to Town yesterday, & got admission to Sir Godfrey Kneller, who assur'd me the Original was done for Your Lordship, & that You, & no man but You, should have it. I saw the picture there afterwards, & was told then by his Man, that you had sent & put a Seal upon it. So I am certain this affair is settled. Give me leave, my Lord, with great sincerity, to thank you for so obliging a Thought, as thus to make me a Sharer in the Memory, as well as I was in the Love of a Person, who was justly the dearest object to you in the world: and thus to be Authorized by You to be calld his Friend, after both of us shall be Dust—I am ever with all good wishes to your Lordship & your Family (in which too I must do my Mother the justice to join her) / My Lord / Your most obligd & most faithfull Servant: / A. Pope.[2]

The portrait is mentioned in a second letter from Pope to Harcourt, 3 July 1725, part of Pope's battle to defeat Lady Kneller's plan of invading Twickenham Church with Sir Godfrey's monument. Lady Kneller alleged that Pope had received pictures from Sir Godfrey on a promise to put up the monument in the Church. But "She has annex'd this circumstance very falsely." "One of these pictures is that of myself which hangs in your Library, which your Lordship well knows was an Exchange of Sir Godfry's with you for another picture which you had long before, from Him & not from me, & of which he took the honour."[3]

In 1797 the Second Earl Harcourt published privately a now very rare little volume entitled *A Description of Nuneham Courtenay, in the County of Oxford;* it was reissued in 1806. This guidebook contained a list of pictures at Nuneham, based on a catalogue drawn up by Horace Walpole and Sir Joshua Reynolds. The entry for Kneller's portrait of Pope printed for the first time, from a transcription then on the back of the picture, Pope's letter to Harcourt of 22 August 1723. This entry is the basis for the later account of the picture in the third volume of *The Harcourt Papers,*

7.1. Oil on canvas. 28½ x 24 in. Background golden brown (a brownish light suffuses the picture); table yellowish brown, cap deep pink, lining of coat light salmon, as of silk, with green showing through; coat bright green (near to BCC 173 Sage Green, BCC 174 Moss Green, BCC 175 Cypress Green), deep black in shadows; eyes brownish to hazel, eyebrows brownish, flesh sallow and smooth, with brownish shadows; throat whitish with diffused light, as through buttonholes in shirt collar; book deep brown with gold pattern and "HOMER." "Alexander Pope" in brownish golden letters on table below book; signature and date, in thin black paint, "ᴳKneller / 1722" ("ᴳK" monogram). This has been read (e.g. *British Painting in the Eighteenth Century*, 1957–58, p. 47) as "GKneller f. / 1722." But after study of the painting at the Exhibition of 1961, I am convinced that the line read as "f." is a shadow stroke in the background. A correction stroke in the neck covers an originally higher shirt collar. The Viscount Harcourt, Stanton Harcourt, Oxfordshire.

edited by Edward William Harcourt (1825–91), grand-uncle of the present Viscount.[4]

The account in *The Harcourt Papers* tells of one occasion toward the end of the eighteenth century when a portrait of Pope in the Harcourt Collection was copied. In December of 1792 the Second Earl Harcourt wrote to Lady Harcourt: "Pray order Jacob to see that Mr. Pope's portrait be *carefully* placed in a packing-case, and brought to London with the waggon; for Lord Onslow wants a copy of it, and has a right to have one." (Lord Onslow, explains a footnote, had a right to this copy because he had allowed Lord Harcourt to have a copy of his picture of Milton, "which copy, now that the original is lost, has become a picture of much value").[5] There may be some reason to think, however, that the portrait of Pope which was copied was not that by Kneller, but another, by Richardson, then in Lord Harcourt's collection.[6]

The picture was one of two or three portraits of Pope best known during the nineteenth century.[7] In recent years it has been seen in the Exhibition of *British Painting in the Eighteenth Century*, which came to Canada and the United States during 1957 and 1958,[8] and in the Exhibition at the National Portrait Gallery in 1961.

1. *Correspondence* 2.118.

2. *Correspondence* 2.193, from the Harcourt Manuscripts. Pope's friend the Hon. Simon Harcourt, Jr., had died 1 July 1720.

3. *Correspondence* 2.307. So far as I am aware, this is the only surviving reference to a payment to an artist for a portrait of Pope. I venture a guess that Pope himself never paid for any portrait of himself. "Congreve and Delaval have at last prevailed on Sir Godfrey Kneller to intreat me to let him draw my picture for nothing; but I know not yet when I shall sit" (Jonathan Swift, *Journal to Stella*, ed. Harold Williams [Oxford, 1948], p. 114, Letter X, December 1710).

4. *The Harcourt Papers*, ed. Edward William Harcourt (privately printed, n.d.), *3*.220, 238, no. 27, follow the 1806 edition of *A Description of Nuneham Courtenay*. Cunningham, 1854, quotes Pope's letter from the edition of 1797, p. 27.

5. *The Harcourt Papers*, *3*.238. Whether Lord Harcourt's letter of 1792 is quoted originally in *A Description*, 1797 or 1806, is not clear.

6. See no. 50.

7. See *Pocket Companion to Oxford*, 1813, p. 147; J. N. Brewer, *The Beauties of England and Wales, 12*, Part ii (1813), 272–73; Cunningham, 1854; Waagen, *Galleries and Cabinets . . . Visited in 1854 and 1856*, 1857, p. 348; NPG Scharf *Sketch Book* 47.67, 27 September 1857; *Catalogue of the Art Treasures . . . at Manchester*, 1857, p. 127, no. 273; *Catalogue of the Second Special Exhibition . . . South Kensington Museum*, 1867, p. 43, no. 146; *Exhibition of the Royal House of Guelph*, 1891, p. 69, no. 204.

8. *British Painting in the Eighteenth Century, An Exhibition under the Gracious Patronage of Her Majesty the Queen*, The Montreal Museum of Fine Arts, The National Gallery of Canada, The Art Gallery of Toronto, the Toledo Museum of Art, 1957–58, in collaboration with The British Council, p. 47, no. 38, illustrated p. 74; illustrated also in the account of the Exhibition in *The Connoisseur, 141* (February 1958), 62.

7.2. OIL PAINTING, BY GEORGE KNAPTON, AFTER SIR GODFREY KNELLER. THE UNIVERSITY OF TEXAS, AUSTIN, TEXAS.

A sale at Christie's, 27 June 1924, was made up in part of heirlooms of the Sneyd family, of Keele Hall, Newcastle, Staffordshire. Lot 55 on p. 10 was a portrait of Pope, 29½ x 24 inches, "in green gown lined with red, leaning his right arm on a volume of 'Homer,'" attributed to G. Knapton. The entry says further that "This picture was purchased at Ashby Lodge, Ashby St. Legers, Northamptonshire."[1] Two notable collectors in the Sneyd family were Ralph Sneyd (d. 1870) and his brother the Rev. Walter Sneyd (d. 1888).[2]

At the sale of 1924, the picture was bought by C. J. Sawyer for nine guineas. The same painting appears in a mixed sale at the American Art Association, 28–29 April 1925, lot 521. It has for some years now been hanging in the Library at the University of Texas, Austin, Texas, and is said to have been a gift from Gabriel Wells. It is difficult to say on what grounds the attribution to Knapton rests, but it seems plausible enough. George Knapton (1698–1778), member of and first portrait-painter to the Society of Dilettanti, 1750–63, surveyor and keeper of the king's pictures, 1765, was a brother of Jonathan Richardson's friend John Knapton the publisher and with Thomas Hudson was a pupil of Richardson before 1725; in 1732 he returned to England after seven years in Italy.[3] For further relations of the Knapton family of publishers and artists with Pope and his friend Jonathan Richardson, see nos. 43.1 and 66.16.

1. From the Frick Art Reference Library archives, verified in part by a clipping from the catalogue at the Courtauld Institute. The photograph which I present (illustration 7.2 below) was made at the sale of 1924 and is available through courtesy of the Frick Art Reference Library.

2. The manuscript collection, sold at Sotheby's, 28 November 1927, is now at the John Rylands Library, Manchester (James H. Sledd and Gwin J. Kolb, *Dr. Johnson's Dictionary* (Chicago, 1955), pp. 117, 232–33).

See also Alfred J. Horwood, "The Manuscripts of the Rev. Walter Sneyd, of Keele Hall, Co. Stafford," *The Third Report of the Royal Commission on Historical Manuscripts* (London, 1872). Among photographs of paintings by George Knapton at the Courtauld Institute is a portrait (from the Lathom sale at Christie's 11 June, 1926) of John Sneyd, Esq. of Belmont, Staffordshire. For John Sneyd see Mary Alden Hopkins, *Dr. Johnson's Lichfield* (New York, 1952), 174, 184.

3. Vertue 3.62.

7.3. OIL PAINTING, AFTER SIR GODFREY KNELLER. DR. CALVIN H. PLIMPTON, AMHERST, MASSACHUSETTS.

This picture was in the collection of George Arthur Plimpton, of New York City and Berkeley, California, and was bequeathed by him in 1936 to his wife, who bequeathed it in 1950 to her estate. At one period during Mrs. Plimpton's lifetime, the picture was on loan to the Plimpton, Smith, and Dale Libraries at Columbia University, but after 1942 it was at Harvard University.[1] It was included in an exhibition of the Plimpton literary portraits at the Century Club, New York, in January 1956. It is now at the home of Dr. Calvin H. Plimpton, Amherst, Mass. On the back, a printed paper label, apparently torn from a catalogue, shows the picture to have been no. 217 in a sale "From General Bulwer's Collection." An ink inscription on the wood says the picture was purchased for $120.00 at a sale (the name of which seems illegible) in 1916. The illustration is from a photograph at the Frick Art Reference Library.

1. Information on file at the Frick Art Reference Library, from a letter of Mrs. George A. Plimpton, 31 December 1936, and letters of Miss Bertha Frick of the Columbia University Library, 17 and 21 June 1940; and information from Mr. Roland Baughman, Head of Special Collections, Columbia University Library, 8 September 1950.

7.4. OIL PAINTING, AFTER SIR GODFREY KNELLER. UNIVERSITY OF LONDON, KING'S COLLEGE.

The painting hangs in the Skeat and Furnivall Library at King's College, University of London. King's College was founded in 1829.

7.2. Oil on canvas. 29½ x 24 in. Colors similar to those of no. 7.1. The Library, The University of Texas, Austin, Texas.

7.3. Oil on canvas. 29½ x 24⅝ in. Colors similar to those of no. 7.1. Dr. Calvin H. Plimpton, Amherst College, Amherst, Massachusetts.

7.4. Oil on canvas. 29½ x 24½ in. Colors similar to those of no. 7.1. University of London, King's College.

7.5. Oil on canvas. 30 x 25 in. Robert B. Honeyman, Jr., Los Angeles, California, 1957.†

7.5. OIL PAINTING, AFTER SIR GODFREY KNELLER. ROBERT E. HONEYMAN, JR., LOS ANGELES, CALIFORNIA, 1957.

An old photograph of this painting discovered recently at the Library of the University of Texas bears on the back a stamp of Willett Studios, 115 West 57th Street, N.Y.C. In June 1957 the painting was in the possession of Mr. Robert B. Honeyman, Jr., Los Angeles, California. He remembered having acquired it some years earlier at a Parke-Bernet sale. This information and the photograph reproduced above came to me from Mr. Jacob Zeitlin of Los Angeles.[1]

1. Either no. 7.5 or no. 7.3 might be the picture sold at Christie's, 8 June 1923, the property of John Lewis Rutley, Esq., late of 5 Great Newport Street, W.C., lot 129 (p. 18): "Kneller, Portrait of Alexander Pope, in green cloak and red cap, 29 in. by 24 in., *From the Collection of Colonel Hayhurst*." The picture sold to Spiller for £4.14.6 (*Art Prices Current*, Second Series, 2, no. 5803).

Professor Geoffrey Bullough, of King's College, the

University of London, is the owner of an oil painting of Pope, found at Sheffield about 15 years ago, 29½ x 24½ in., in a flat wood frame stained brown. This portrait is a composite of features from several of the main types of Pope oil portraits (e.g., a small round black inkpot and a white quill seem to be derived from Michael Dahl—see no. 10.1–4), but the most obvious model, especially in face, cap, and shirt collar, is the Kneller type of 1722.

7.6. CRAYON PAINTING (PASTEL), AFTER KNELLER. W. S. LEWIS, FARMINGTON, CONNECTICUT.

After the initial dispersal of the Strawberry Hill collections in 1742, Lady Waldegrave, the wife of Walpole's collateral descendant, reassembled much of the original collection. At the sale of Strawberry Hill objects held in 1883, after her death, lot 978 was "An oval drawing of Alexander Pope by Richardson."[1] This was no doubt the small crayon drawing (11 x 8¼ inches) in an oval gilt wood frame, now in the collection of W. S. Lewis at Farmington, Connecticut. On the frame below the picture appears a partly obliterated inscription in black paint: "Strawberry Hill." On the back, someone has written in large letters in black ink: "Alexander Pope / Drawn by Richardson / from Strawberry Hill." This short bust-length image follows the Kneller type of 1722 in pose and colors. The technique of pastel (or "crayon painting," as Vertue calls it), practised by Rosalba in Italy and by Hoare, Pond, Lady Burlington, the Duchess of Queensberry, and others in England, c. 1740,[2] is quite unlike that of the many drawings, lead pencil on vellum or crayons on blue paper, which survive from the hand of Jonathan Richardson the Elder.

1. *Strawberry Hill, A Catalogue of the Contents of the Mansion . . . Sold by Auction, by Messrs. Vinton, Bull & Cooper, July 25th & Nine following Days* [1883] (transcript by courtesy of W. S. Lewis).

2. See Vertue 3.115 on crayon paintings by Lady

Burlington and the Duchess of Queensberry; and 5.73: "in her great room adornd with many crayon painted heads—the works of her Ladyship. mostly all of them Coppyd from excellent pictures." cf. Waterhouse, *Painting in Britain*, pp. 243–46.

7.7. GROUP PICTURE, THE WORTHIES OF GREAT BRITAIN, BY JAMES NORTHCOTE (POPE AFTER KNELLER). THOMAS CORAM FOUNDATION FOR CHILDREN (FORMERLY THE FOUNDLING HOSPITAL), LONDON.†

The picture appears under 1828, "Picture of a Gallery of the Worthies of Great Britain," in a list derived from a notebook kept by Northcote, in Stephen Gwynn's *Memo-*

rials of an Eighteenth Century Painter (London, 1898), p. 288 (cf. p. 4). R. H. Nichols and F. A. Wray, *The History of the Foundling Hospital* (London, 1935), reproduce the picture, facing p. 108 (it is mentioned p. 263). Mr. J. F. Kerslake, of the National Portrait Gallery, has prepared an unpublished Catalogue of the Foundling Hospital Collection, in which Northcote's picture, no. 62, is described as follows: "It shows two children seated, whole length in white, the nearer with a pencil in his right hand resting on a drawing after Lawrence of William IV; on the wall behind, a double row of portraits of celebrities, inscribed with their names below: top, from left to right, *Alfred the Great, Edward the Black Prince, Shakespeare,* (Francis Bacon, Milton, Locke); below *Newton, Dryden, Alexander Pope,* (two heads [Samuel Johnson 1769, by Reynolds, and another] partially obscured by the children), *Sir Joshua Reynolds.* In the bottom left-hand corner a vase of roses and behind it a rolled paper lettered *Sic Transit Gloria Mundi.* Signed and dated on the top book of a pile bottom right: *James Northcote Pinx* 1828." Mr. Kerslake adds that the picture was presented to the Hospital in 1836, by Newbold Kinton, a Governor, who was a friend and executor of Prince Hoare.

7.8. MEZZOTINT ENGRAVING, BY GEORGE WHITE, 1723, AFTER SIR GODFREY KNELLER. BEVERLY CHEW BEQUEST, THE NEW YORK PUBLIC LIBRARY.

J. Ch. Smith 4.1583, G. White no. 35, as corrected by Charles E. Russell, *English Mezzotint Portraits* (1926), 2.405, provides for four states of this engraving: 1. before any inscription; 2. before the publication line [but presumably with date 1732]; 3. with the inscription: "Mr Pope / G. Kneller S.R.I. et Mag. Brit. Eq. Aur. et Baronettus pinx. 1722. / / Sold by S. Sympson in the Strand near Catherine Street. / / G. White fec. 1732."; 4. Address after "in" erased; instead, "Maiden Lane Cov^t Garden." State 4 is apparently the most common, suggesting that the print had its greatest sale, after the death of White (c. 1732), from the later address of his publisher Samuel Sympson, in Maiden Lane.[1] I can verify the occurrence of state 3, with the earlier address, however, from an example in my own collection; and state 2, without publication line, but with the date 1732, is found, in a brilliant example, in the Yale University Library (formerly in the Hallam Murray collection). State 1, before lettering, is cited by J. Ch. Smith at the British Museum. It is important, however, to notice a further state, which I can illustrate only in an example to be found in the Beverly Chew collection at the New York Public Library. This was apparently added to the Chew collection later than the cataloguing of no. 122 in the *Grolier* 1911 Catalogue, which is state 4. This example, no. 122a in the present Chew collection (see below, illustration), represents a state of the plate between 1 and 2. With the Pope and Kneller parts of the inscription, but without the publication line, it has an earlier and more plausible date: "G. White fec. 1723." An example having apparently the same parts of the inscription and the same date, 1723, is described as no. 190, belonging to Austin Dobson, in the Twickenham *Commemoration Catalogue* of 1888, p. 36.

The earliest derivatives from this engraving seem to be the satiric prints of 1729 and c. 1734 which follow immediately below (nos. 7.9, 7.10, 7.11). But a line engraving, 4³⁄₁₆

7.6. Crayon painting (pastel). 11 x 8¼ in. The main colors, blue and pink, follow the pattern of no. 7.1. "STRAWBERRY HILL." (on frame). "Alexander Pope / Drawn by Richardson / from Strawberry Hill" (on back, in black ink). W. S. Lewis, Farmington, Connecticut.

7.8. Mezzotint engraving. 13⅝ x 9½ plate mark. "Mʳ Pope / G. Kneller S.R.I. et Mag. Brit. Eq. Aur. et Baronettus pinx. 1722. // G. White fec. 1723." State unrecorded in J. Ch. Smith 4.1583, G. White no. 35, and Russell 2.405. *Grolier* 122. *BMEP* 13. Beverly Chew Bequest, Prints Division, The New York Public Library.

x 3⅛₆, "Kneller pinx 1722. / / Parr sculp. / Mr. Pope," appears as frontispiece in one of two copies at Yale of *Mr Pope's Literary Correspondence For Thirty Years . . . Volume the First*. London: Printed for E. Curll, in Rose-Street, Covent-Garden, M. DCC. XXXV (Griffith no. 376), and in one of two copies at Yale of *Mr Pope's Literary Correspondence. Volume the Second . . .* London: Printed for E. Curll, in Rose-Street, Covent-Garden, M. DCC. XXXV (Griffith no. 386). The other Yale copy of each of these volumes has for frontispiece a line engraving of the Kneller 1716 (Smith 1717) type (see nos. 5.13 and 5.15).

A coarse imitation of White's work, a mezzotint, 8 x 6 inches, "G. Kneller Pinx. / Mʳ Pope / Sold by S. Sympson in Maiden Lane Covᵗ Garden," may be seen in the Boston Museum of Fine Arts Print Room and in the extra-illustrated Lord Derby's *Spence, 1.24*, in the collection of W. S. Lewis at Farmington. According to J. Ch. Smith, *4.1702* (no. 84 of early eighteenth-century anonymous engravings), the same print is found also with the address "Catherine Street, Strand."

Pope died on 30 May 1744. The following advertisement appeared in the *Daily Advertiser* for Tuesday, 12 June:

> *This day is publish'd, (Price 1s. 6d.)* A Curious Print of Mr. POPE, the famous Poet, done in Mezzotinto by Mr. *George White*, from a Picture of Sir *Godfrey Kneller*.
>
> Sold only by Samuel Sympson, at his Printshop in Maiden Lane, Covent Garden.

1. J. Ch. Smith *4.1572*, in the introductory note on White, points out that the latest date on engravings by White is 1732, and the address on the last in the list, no. 59, is the Strand near Catherine Street. Many of White's plates seem to have remained in Sympson's hands after White's death and to have been reissued, as may be seen from the address of Maiden Lane.

7.9. LINE ENGRAVING, *The Rival Printers*, C. 1734. DEPARTMENT OF PRINTS AND DRAWINGS, BRITISH MUSEUM.

In this satire of rival cheap editions of Shakespeare, the ghost of Shakespeare, after the Chandos portrait (E), rises through the pavement in a London street scene, where two printers, Walker (B—apprehended by a bailiff, C) and Tonson (A), and their printer's devils, and two editors, Pope (D) and his rival and corrector Theobald (D) with *Shakespeare Restored,* are set against each other, amid several incidental motifs ridiculing debasements of the contemporary stage (Harlequin, tumblers, fiddler and dancing dogs). See *BMP & PS 2.672–73*, no. 1811, for a more detailed exposition. Theobald's *Shakespeare Restored* appeared in March 1726. The date 1728, penned in before the price at the bottom, is assigned to the engraving by the British Museum editor. But Robert Walker's duodecimo edition of Shakespeare's *Dramatic Works* in seven volumes did not appear until 1734–1735. The pensive library posture of Kneller's 1722 portrait, mounted on a full-length figure and placed in the midst of the street scene, is an incongruity which is perhaps the best part of the joke.

7.10. LINE ENGRAVING, "THE PHIZ AND CHARACTER OF ———— THE HYPER-CRITICK
& COMENTATOR," 1729. BEVERLY CHEW BEQUEST, THE NEW YORK PUBLIC
LIBRARY.

The British Museum Catalogue of *Political and Personal Satires*[1] believes that the present engraving (or the altered state of it in the British Museum Collection, no. 1814) was "originally prepared" as a frontispiece for the satirical pamphlet *Pope Alexander's Supremacy*, 1729. But the length of the plate mark, 13½ inches, and also the publication line in the state of the print reproduced below, "Sold by the Print-sellers of London and Westminster. price 6ᵈ," refute that hypothesis. An indication that this print, in this state, is earlier than B.M. 1812, "Fronti Fides," the actual frontispiece to *Pope Alexander's Supremacy*, appears in the execution of the inkwell suspended from the donkey's ear. This and the quill pen would seem to be derived, not from the Kneller 1722 oil (from which the head and hand to the brow are clearly derived), but from Michael Dahl's portrait of 1727, engraved by Simon in 1728 (See no. 10.4). In the present engraving the inkwell is closer to that in Dahl's portrait; in "Fronti Fides," the frontispiece to *Pope Alexander's Supremacy*, the inkwell is flattened. Pope's *Dunciad Variorum* of April 1729 gives the earliest plausible date.

In the state of the engraving described here and illustrated below, five of the books piled on the pedestal have titles: "Rape of the Lock," "Art of Criticism," "Shake-

7.9. Line engraving. 12¼ x 7⅜ in. "THE RIVAL PRINTERS. / . . . . / Price 6ᵈ" For the inscriptions, see *BMP&PS* 2.672–73, no. 1811; and above, the entry for this picture. By permission of the Trustees of the British Museum.

speare," "Homer's Odysses," Homer's Iliads." In British Museum no. 1814, two of these titles have been expanded, and two added, one at each end of the pile, thus: "Temple of Fame," "Rape of the Lock," "Art of Criticism," "Shakespeare Mangled," "Undertaker of Homer's Odysses," "Homer's Iliads," "Pastorals." The two states of the print have in common the main inscriptions: "The Dunciad with Notes Variorum"[2] (on the top scroll), "A Letter to the Publisher"[3] (on the lower scroll), "His Holiness and his Prime Minister" (on the pedestal), and in the space below the picture the ten lines of blank verse, with ellipses, quoted with alterations from Dryden and Lee's *Oedipus* *1*.i.135–58.[4] The state represented by British Museum no. 1814 has, however, the following additions and changes: 1. the words "Nosce Te Ipsum.", just above the picture in the center; 2. "Art of Politicks 1731"[5] added on the lower part of the lower scroll; 3. "The Phiz and Character of —— the Hyper-critick & Conтentator" (below the picture) altered to "The Phiz and Character of an Alexandrine Hyper-critick & Conтentator."; 4. the quotation from "Psalms 36" (in the lower part of the lettering) removed and in its place two couplets from Pope's *Iliad* 2.257–58, 267–68: "Aw'd by no Shame, by no Respect controul'd, / In Scandal busy in Reproaches bold. / Spleen to Mankind his envious Heart possesst, / And much he hated All, but most the Best. / Pope's charact: of Thersites.";[6] 5. the words "Sold by the Print-sellers of London and Westminster" removed, "price 6ᵈ" remaining. The later state is reproduced in Paston 2.658.

The simian theme becomes well established in Augustan satire apparently after Edward Tyson's book on *Apes,* 1699.[7]

This engraving appears on the wall above the poet's head in Hogarth's painting, dated 1735, *The Distressed Poet.*[8]

1. 2.673–75, no. 1812, "Fronti Fides." See no. 7.11.

2. The first edition of Pope's *Dunciad Variorum* appeared on 10 April 1729 (Griffith no. 211).

3. The "Man William" of the title page to *Pope Alexander's Supremacy* is apparently William Cleland (see no. 3.1), whose name is attached to the "Letter to the Publisher" prefixed to the *Dunciad Variorum.*

4. The first act is by Dryden. See Hugh Macdonald, *Dryden Bibliography* (Oxford 1939), p. 118; Charles E. Ward, *The Life of John Dryden* (Chapel Hill, 1961), p. 133.

5. *The Art of Politicks, In Imitation of Horace's Art of Poetry,* [by James Bramston], was published by L. Gilliver in 1729. For the authorship, see Alexander Chalmers, *General Biographical Dictionary* (London, 1812–17), *6*.443.

6. *Homerides: or A Letter to Mr. Pope, Occasion'd by his intended Translation of Homer, By Sir Iliad Doggrel* [i.e. Thomas Burnet and George Duckett—see Sherburn, *Early Career,* p. 135], London, 1715, has on the title page four lines of Greek from *Iliad* 2.216–19, the portrait of Thersites.

7. H. W. Janson, *Apes and Apelore in the Middle Ages and the Renaissance* (London: The Warburg Institute, 1952) gives a broad background of simian symbolism.

8. At the City Museum and Art Gallery, Birmingham. See R. B. Beckett, *Hogarth* (London, 1949), p. 65, pl. 82; Frederick D. Leach, "Hogarth's Distressed Poet: The Riddle of the Garret," *The Ohio University Review,* 2 (1960), 8–11. Cf. Appendix 3.1.

7.11. LINE ENGRAVING, "MARTINI SCRIBLERI VERA EFFIGIES. / AD ORIGIN͞: DELINᵗ G. D. // HERMAN VAN KRUYS SCULP." FRONTISPIECE TO *Pope Alexander's Supremacy and Infallibility Examined,* 1729.

The book was advertised on 13 May 1729 in the *Monthly Chronicle.*[1] The title page reads: "Pope Alexander's Supremacy and Infallibility examin'd; And the Errors of Scriblerus and his Man William Detected. With the Effigies of His Holiness and his

Prime Minister, Curiously engrav'd on Copper. Obscene with Filth the Miscreant lies bewray 'd, / Fall'n in the Plash, his Wickedness had laid. / Dunciad, Lib. II, ver. 71, and 72. London: Sold by J. Roberts in Warwick-Lane. M. DCC. XXIX. Price 1*s.* 6*d.*"

The first of nine miscellaneous pieces of which this quarto volume is composed makes an elaborate play with the pretense that the frontispiece is taken from a "busto" on the pedestal of which there are four inscriptions—in Greek, Latin, Spanish, and English. The last is a composition in couplets (beginning "Artist, no longer let thy skill be shown"), slightly adapted from an attack on Rysbrack's bust of Pope in *The Weekly Journal* for 29 March 1729 (see no. 11).

The third piece in the volume, entitled "A Letter To A Noble Lord: Occasion'd by the late Publication of the Dunciad Variorum," is dated (p. 9) 5 April 1729 and signed (p. 18) "Will Flogg" (cf. p. v, first piece, "Gulielmus Flagellator"). This "Letter to A Noble Lord" tells, apparently for the first time[2] (p. 16), the story of Ambrose Philips hanging up the rod for Pope at Button's, and (p. 18) it alleges that Pope is not human, that he has never "been observ'd, since the Hour of his Birth, to have risen above a broad Grin, common to him with the Quadrupede, most resembling Human Nature."

Pope wrote to Lord Oxford, 16 May 1729: "I see a Book with a Curious Cutt calld Pope Alexrs Supremacy &c. 4°. In it are 3 or 4 things so false & scandalous that I think I know the Authors, and they are of a Rank to merit Detection. I therefore beg your Lordship to send a Careful hand to buy the Book of Lintot, (who must not be known to come from you) & to enter down the day of the month. I would fain have it bought of him, himself. The book is writ by Burnet, & a Person who has great obligations to me, & the Cut is done by Ducket. I would fain come at the proof of this, for Reasons of a Very High Nature.

"Let the same Man, after he has the book, go to Roberts the Publisher in Warwick Lane and threaten him, unless he declares the author; Or any other method your Lordship can judge best."[3] In the *Dunciad* of 1735 Pope ascribed the book to Duckett and Dennis.[4] The ascriptions are doubted by the modern editors of these authors.[5]

The phrase on the scroll at the top of the picture, "Fronti Fides," is apparently an adaptation, with reversed sense, of line 8 of Juvenal's *Satire 2*, "frontis nulla fides."

1. Robert W. Rogers, *The Major Satires of Alexander Pope* (University of Illinois Press, 1955), p. 138, citing *Monthly Chronicle.*

2. Sherburn, *Early Career,* pp. 120–21.

3. *Correspondence* 3.33–34.

4. *Twickenham* 5.212.

5. *Critical Works of John Dennis,* ed. E. N. Hooker (Baltimore, 1939–43), 2.ix–x; *Letters of Thomas Burnet to George Duckett, 1712–1722,* ed. D. N. Smith (Oxford, 1914), p. xix. Cf. Rogers, *Major Satires,* p. 138.

Alexander Pope. By Jonathan Richardson, c. 1718. Beinecke Rare Book and Manuscript Library, Yale University. See no. 9.2.

· 4 ·

c. 1718
JONATHAN RICHARDSON
(1665-1745)[1]

I

ACCORDING TO the slender story preserved for us in the *Note Books* of George Vertue, Richardson was apprenticed by an unsympathetic stepfather to a scrivener, but he ran away from his master and pretended to join the army of the Duke of Monmouth. Later, on the master's leaving off business, he took up the study of art in the studio of the uncourtly court painter John Riley. Shortly after Riley's death in 1691, Richardson married Riley's niece, and on the death of other members of the family, the young couple inherited some hundreds of pounds, together with Riley's collection of drawings by old masters.[2] Richardson no doubt inherited also some of Riley's patronage, and he continued to paint in Riley's sound prosaic style. It is not easy today to examine well-authenticated examples of Richardson's early work,[3] but he seems soon to have enjoyed,

1. My account of Richardson owes much for guidance to Gordon William Snelgrove's *The Work and Theories of Jonathan Richardson (1665–1745)*, unpublished thesis for the Ph.D. Degree at the University of London, June, 1936.

2. Vertue 3.23, 57, 67; 4.43; Walpole, *Anecdotes* 2.274. A couple of Richardson's careful pencil-on-vellum drawings of his wife in comely middle age were in the Witt collection, and are reproduced by C. H. Collins Baker in *The Connoisseur, 73* (December 1925), 195–202. See Riley's will in Collins Baker, *Lely and the Stuart Portrait Painters* (London, 1912), 2.33.

3. Waterhouse, *Painting in Britain*, p. 105, can point for the period up to 1700 only to "Lady Catherine Herbert and her brother Robert" at Wilton of c. 1698–1700, "in all probability his." At the Barber Institute, Mr. Waterhouse kindly showed me a photograph of a painting of the philanthropist Edward Colston (1636–1721), the property of the City Estates Committee, Bristol, and documented 1702. It was

side by side with Kneller and Dahl, a very flourishing and fashionable practice during the reigns of William and Mary and of Queen Anne. He was an original member and a director of the Academy of Painting founded in 1711 in Great Queen Street, of which Kneller was governor until his retirement in 1716.[4] From contemporary engravings and a few modern collections one may readily draw up an impressive sample list of persons who sat to Richardson during the earlier and middle part of his career: eminent churchmen, lawyers, judges and Barons of Exchequer, physicians and men of science, and members of the peerage.[5]

II

Richardson was always a quiet painter, "solid," "sober," "routine," "prosaic," as the art historians tell us—"essentially British, sturdy, and yeoman-like."[6] "The good sense of the nation was characterized in his portraits."[7] He had "the directness of Riley; but . . . little sense of colour."[8] His routine kind of mastery may be illustrated at the National Portrait Gallery equally well by his Sir Richard Steele (dated 1712 in the mezzotint by J. Smith)[9] or by his George Vertue (1738) or by his firmly modeled, apple-cheeked self-portrait in blue coat and cap (1729).[10] Now and then, however, he seems to have been "disturbed by artistic emotion"; he "surprises us by playing truant from his routine dullness."[11] Or at least he displays at moments a certain force, or fancy, or gaiety of color. The fancy effort is perhaps more conspicuous now and then in his earlier than in his later work. A picture which appeals to both the art historian and the biographer is his standing full-length of Lady Mary Wortley Montagu, in the collection of the Earl of Harrowby at Sandon. She wears a dress of draped golden satin, a low bodice and a jeweled girdle, a turban with feather and jewels; a blue cloak with ermine edges hangs over her arm; a negro page in red livery, carrying a large fan or umbrella,

engraved in mezzotint and in line during Richardson's lifetime (J. Ch. Smith 3.980, William Pether no. 5; *BMEP*, published by B. and S. Tooke, 1722). Another early painting by Richardson was that of Mordecai Abbott, 1657–1700, receiver-general of the customs, engraved by R. White for the frontispiece to Abbott's *Life* in 1700 (*BMEP*).

4. Vertue 3.7. See Steele, *Spectator* 555, 6 December 1712.

5. See J. Ch. Smith, *British Mezzotint Portraits*, vol. 4, Index of Painters; *BMEP* vol. 5, Index of Painters; Waterhouse, *Painting in Britain*, p. 106. The list includes, perhaps most notably, Bishop Fleetwood and Edmund Calamy, D.D.; Sir Thomas Bury, Chief Baron of the Court of Exchequer; Dr. William Cheselden (at the Royal College of Surgeons), Dr. Richard Hale (at the Bodleian and at the Royal College of Physicians), Martin Folkes, Sir Hans Sloane (at the Bodleian); Lord Chancellor Cowper (until recently, at Panshanger), the 1st Earl of Oxford (at Christ Church, Oxford), Charles Earl of Sunderland (at Althorp). Dryden's friend the 6th Earl of Dorset (d. 1706) pre-

sented by Lord Oxford to the University in 1723 and now in the Bodleian, and also Pope's friend the Duke of Buckingham, painted c. 1703–05, presented to Oxford by his widow, and now in the Examination Schools, have long been attributed to Richardson (Poole, *Catalogue of Oxford Portraits*, *1*, 1912, p. 76, no. 189 and p. 140, no. 341).

6. M. H. Spielmann, *British Portrait Painting* (Berlin, 1910), *1*.28, quoted by G. W. Snelgrove.

7. Walpole, *Anecdotes* 2.273.

8. Whinney and Millar, p. 191.

9. Piper, *Catalogue of the Seventeenth-Century Portraits*, p. 329, no. 160, and Pl. 15e; J. Ch. Smith, 3.1125, no. 244.

10. Vertue is no. 576, "as good a piece of solid and incisive prose as one could wish" (Waterhouse, *Painting in Britain*, p. 106; see Pl. 90B). The Richardson self-portrait is no. 706. I reproduce both, nos. Ex4, Ex6.

11. C. H. Collins Baker and M. R. James, *British Painting* (London, 1933), pp. 71–72.

completes the exotic effect.[12] Lady Mary had returned from Turkey in 1718. Another, and perhaps more typical because less exciting, example of Richardson's earlier fancy style may be seen in the full-length, elongate, and lavender Thomas Watson-Wentworth, First Marquis of Rockingham, at St. John's College, Cambridge, signed and dated 1714.[13] A flamboyant picture, to be dated apparently somewhat later, is the bust-length of his son at the Fitzwilliam Museum,[14] in olive and turquoise turban with gold tassel, head thrown back in full display of his cleft chin and glaring eyes. And Richardson's Sir Hans Sloane, 1730, at the Bodleian Library, is described by Professor Waterhouse as his "noblest experiment in the grand manner."[15] Among the literary persons whom Richardson painted, we have noted Steele. Apparently he also painted Addison and Gay.[16] His Vanbrugh, wearing the badge of Clarencieux King of Arms and holding a groundplan of Blenheim Palace, was done in 1725 according to the engraving by Faber in 1727, and is still to be seen in the College of Arms, London.[17]

Richardson seems to have been on a firm footing with Pope's friends and patrons Robert and Edward Harley, the First and Second Earls of Oxford.[18] They were patrons of Matthew Prior. And it seems likely that before the time when he became intimate with Pope, Richardson's most important literary connection was with Prior. Lord Harley paid him £21.10 s. in 1718 for the stately, large (48½ x 38¾ inches) portrait of Prior which came down at Welbeck Abbey in the Duke of Portland's collection—apparently an impressive study in the glossy blacks of coat and turban, offset by the sharp white of the neckcloth and full lace cuffs and quill in the right hand, and the red of the high-backed leather chair, tablecloth, and neat round center of the turban.[19]

---

12. The picture appears as frontispiece to George Paston, *Lady Mary Wortley Montagu and Her Times* (London, 1907), and again to Iris Barry, *Portrait of Lady Mary Wortley Montagu* (Indianapolis, 1928). See the Walker Art Gallery Catalogue *Painting and Sculpture in England 1700–1750* (Liverpool, 1958), no. 41, pp. 22–23. My color notes are taken from Snelgrove. The picture seems to be traditionally given to Richardson. I do not know the evidence for the attribution.

13. J. W. Goodison, "Cambridge Portraits II," *The Connoisseur*, 140 (1958), 231–36.

14. No. 926 on the frame, called a self-portrait of Richardson Senior. Richardson's very strong portrait of himself in a tricorne hat, admired by Collins Baker and James, is still to be seen at Polesden Lacy.

15. Waterhouse, *Painting in Britain*, p. 106; cf. Poole, *Catalogue of Oxford Portraits*, 1 (1912), 101, no. 252.

16. Snelgrove refers to an Addison in the collection of Lord Spencer at Althorp (*Catalogue of Pictures at Althorp House*, 1851). And see the plate in Pope's *Works*, vol. 6 (supplement to "Ruffhead's" edition), 1807, facing p. 57: "From a Picture by Richardson, in the Marquis of Buckingham's Collection at Stowe." An oil of Gay, dated 12 August 1732, was no. 177 in the South Kensington Exhibition of 1867 (p. 50 of

the *Catalogue*), lent by Viscountess Clifden; *BMEP*, vol. 2, Gay no. 13 is an engraving of 1812, after Richardson. Mr. Gerald Coke, Jenkyn Place, Bentley, Hampshire, is said to have a Gay by Richardson. In the Wellesley sale at Sotheby's, 1 July 1920, lot 652 was a Richardson drawing, "John Dryden . . . dated 1697."

17. J. Ch. Smith *1*.435, no. 358; Whinney and Millar, p. 192.

18. Richard W. Goulding and C. K. Adams, *Catalogue of Pictures Belonging to His Grace the Duke of Portland, K.G. at Welbeck Abbey* (Cambridge, 1936), p. 475, print Richardson's receipt for £99.16 from Lord Harley for pictures and frames, 10 January 1718/19. The *Catalogue* includes five pictures by Richardson: no. 450, Prior, signed, and four others unsigned: 324, the First Earl of Oxford; 451, his brother Edward Harley the Auditor; 571, the Second Earl of Oxford; 572, Abigail Harley. At Christ Church, Oxford, may be seen Robert Harley, First Earl of Oxford, painted by Richardson in 1712 (Poole, *Oxford Portraits, 3*, 1926, p. 48, no. 123).

19. My conception of the picture is based on color notes in Goulding and Adams, *Portland Catalogue*, p. 178, and a photograph at the National Portrait Gallery (no. 450 of the 1894 Welbeck Catalogue).

"Richardson," wrote Prior to Swift, "whom I take to be a better painter than any named in your letter, has made an excellent picture of me; from whence Lord Harley, whose it is, has a stamp taken by Vertue. He has given me some for you to give to our friends at or about Dublin."[20] The degree of reverence in which Richardson held the plenipotentiary and poet Matthew Prior will be seen below (p. 80) in a quotation from one of the painter's published works.

III

As early as 1715 Richardson had published the first fruits of a certain speculative artistic interest and gentlemanly leisure under the title *An Essay on the Theory of Painting.*[21] In 1719 he followed that with two other treatises, *The Whole Art of Criticism as it Relates to Painting* and *A Discourse on the Science of a Connoisseur.*[22] The first *Essay*, with some "retouching," was reprinted in 1725.[23] The principal change was a considerable enlargement of the last section, "Of the Sublime."

An enthusiastic blend of painterly and craftsmanly ideas with piety, morality, magnanimity, patriotism, and the loftiest classical idealism, the theories of Richardson had more effect than his practice[24] on the aesthetic consciousness of the eighteenth century. They have been reckoned among the "puffing" forces which, at one moment in the development of English history painting, affected the aim of Hogarth,[25] and they are said, on better authority, also to have had a share in arousing the ambitions of so

20. Westminster, 4 May 1720, in F. Elrington Ball, ed. *The Correspondence of Jonathan Swift, D.D., 3* (1910), 50.

A number of replicas or close derivations from this portrait may be identified. One at Cirencester is signed by Richardson. One is at the Bodleian Library. One is on loan to the Foreign Office from the National Portrait Gallery (no. 91). A fourth, at the Portrait Gallery (no. 562) and said to be by Hudson, has the same soberly poised, diplomatic head, nearly the same dress and chair, though the color scheme differs. A different portrait of Prior, in black skull-cap and dark greenish velvet coat, signed by Richardson on the back, is at Christ Church, Oxford. See *Portland Catalogue*, pp. 178, 382–83; Piper, *Catalogue of the Seventeenth-Century Portraits*, pp. 287–88; Poole, *Oxford Portraits, 1* (1912), 87, no. 217.

21. *By Mr. Richardson . . . London: Printed by W. Bowyer, for John Churchill at the Black-Swan in Pater-Noster-Row, 1715.* 8vo, pp. 1–240.

22. *Two Discourses. I. An Essay On the whole Art of Criticism as it relates to Painting. . . . II. An Argument in behalf of the Science of a Connoisseur. . . . Both by Mr. Richardson. London: Printed for W. Churchill at the Black Swan in Pater-Noster-Row, 1719,* 8vo. A second title page: *The Connoisseur: An Essay On the whole Art of Criticism as it relates to Painting. . . . By Mr. Richardson. . . . London* [as before] *1719,* is followed by the first essay, pp. 1–220.

A third title page: *A Discourse on the Dignity, Certainty, Pleasure and Advantage, of the Science of a Connoisseur. By Mr. Richardson. . . . London* [as before] *1719,* is followed by the second essay, pp. 3–234.

23. *An Essay on the Theory of Painting. By Mr. Richardson. The Second Edition, Enlarg'd, and Corrected. . . . London: Printed for A.C. and Sold by H. Meadows in Cornhill. M.DCC.XXV.* 8vo, pp. iii–viii, 1–279. The British Museum Catalogue gives this edition to A. Bettesworth. W. T. Lowndes, *Bibliographer's Manual, 4* (1864), 2088–89, reports editions of the *Theory of Painting* in 1720 and 1733 and a two-volume edition of *Works on Painting* in 1725. I have not been able to verify these.

24. "Though he wrote with fire and judgment, his paintings owed little to either" (Walpole *Anecdotes* 2.273).

25. MS. notes by Hogarth quoted in Allan Cunningham, *British Painters, 1* (New York, 1831), 90–91. "I entertained some thoughts of succeeding in what the puffers in books call the great style of history painting . . . I . . . commenced history painter, and on a great staircase at St. Bartholomew's Hospital painted . . . 'The Pool of Bethesda,' and 'The Good Samaritan.' " Charles R. Leslie and Tom Taylor, *Life and Times of Sir Joshua Reynolds* (London, 1865), *1.11,* identify "puffers" with Richardson. It is not clear to me that this is correct. Hogarth's pictures were put up in the Foundling Hospital during 1746 (Vertue *3.134*).

great a painter as Sir Joshua Reynolds. "The great Painter of the present age, had the first fondness for his art excited by the perusal of Richardson's treatise."[26]

> A *Rafaëlle* therefore is not only equal, but Superior to a *Virgil*, or a *Livy*, a *Thucydides*, or a *Homer*.
>
> —*The Theory of Painting*, 1715, p. 35

> A Time may come when Future Writers may be able to add the Name of an *English* Painter. . . . I cannot forbear wishing that some Younger Painter than my self, and one who has had Greater, and more Early Advantages would exert himself, and practice the Magnanimity I have been recommending. . . .
>
> —*The Theory of Painting*, "Of Grace and Greatness,"
> 1715, pp. 211–12

A peculiar shade of sober idealism (both Platonic and realistic, metaphysical and psychological, poetic and drab) enters into the more special part of his theory, that which concerns face-painting:

> To be a good Face-Painter, a degree of the Historical and Poetical Genius is requisite, and a great Measure of the other Talents and Advantages which a good History-Painter must possess. . . . 'Tis not enough to make a tame, insipid Resemblance of the Features, so that every body shall know who the Picture was intended for, nor even to make the Picture what is often said to be prodigious like: (This is often done by the lowest of Face-Painters, but then 'tis ever with the Air of a Fool, and an Unbred Person.) A Portrait-Painter must understand Mankind, and enter into their Characters, and express their Minds as well as their Faces: And as his Business is chiefly with People of Condition, he must Think as a Gentleman, and a Man of Sense, or 'twill be impossible for him to give such their true, and proper Resemblances.
>
> —*The Theory of Painting*, 1715, pp. 23–25

> Every one of His People must appear Pleas'd, and in Good-Humour.
>
> —*The Theory of Painting*, 1715, "Of Grace and Greatness," p. 173

At the same time:

> In making Portraits we must keep Nature in View; if we launch out into the Deep we are lost.
>
> —*The Theory of Painting*, 1715, "Of Grace and Greatness," p. 179

26. Samuel Johnson, *Life of Cowley*, in *Lives of the Poets*, ed. G. B. Hill (Oxford, 1905), I.2. Reynolds himself told Malone that Richardson's treatise on painting had "so delighted and inflamed his mind, that Raphael appeared to him superior to the most illustrious names of ancient or modern times, a notion which he loved to indulge all the rest of his life" (James Prior, *Life of Malone*, London, 1860, p. 403, "Maloniana," 10 July 1789). Cf. F. W. Hilles, *Portraits by Sir Joshua Reynolds* (New York, 1952), p. 23, 20 December 1791.

Lace, Embroydery, Gold, and Jewels must be sparingly employ'd. Nor are Flower'd Silks so much us'd by the best Masters as Plain.
—*The Theory of Painting,* 1715, "Of Grace and Greatness," p. 183

The character of the painter himself—both learned and virtuous—will necessarily be much involved. This was good humanistic and academic doctrine, in support of which Richardson seems to have felt that he could bring a special personal testimony:

A Painter should therefore read the Best Books. . . . *Homer, Milton.* . . . He should also frequent the Brightest Company, and avoid the rest.
—*The Theory of Painting,* 1715, "Of Grace and Greatness," pp. 190–91

A Painter ought to have a Sweet, and Happy Turn of Mind, that Great, and Lovely Ideas may have a Reception there.
—*The Theory of Painting,* 1715, "Of Grace and Greatness," p. 201

For (as it has been observed by Others before me, and must be true in the main from the Nature of things) *Painters paint themselves.*
—*The Theory of Painting,* 1715, "Of Grace and Greatness," p. 205

In the first of his two essays of 1719, on *The Art of Criticism,* Richardson flourished some novel ideas (though not quite so novel as he supposed).[27] He urged the importance of the true connoisseur's knowing how to discriminate the genuine "hand" and "idea" from the copy, the personality of one great painter from that of another. He wished him to observe the periods of life and the ups and downs shown in the work of even the greatest painter—even a Raphael—and the influence of painters on one another.[28] In the second of these essays, on *The Science of a Connoisseur,* he aimed with some boldness at the outlines of a new department of artistic activity, which in fact he did much to promote into one of the most flourishing cults of the age. This essay is the implementation of his artistic theory for the world of society and fashion. He writes of the pleasures of "Connoissance"—he offers "a plan for the happy life."[29] Connoisseurship would reform and improve the condition of England; it would persuade the nation to be more "Rational." It would save money otherwise lavished on luxuries. It would promote the importation of good pictures, increase the wealth of the nation, and even encourage an English school of painting. England would "make a more considerable Figure amongst the Polite Nations of the World."[30] The founding of *The Dilettante*

27. In his Introduction (pp. 8–10) he thinks his is "the only Book extant on the Subject, in any Language," but he has been anticipated in part by William Aglionby, *Painting Illustrated in Three Dialogues,* 1685, the Third Dialogue, "How to Know Good *Pictures.*" See Tancred Borenius, "An Early English Writer on Art," *Burlington Magazine, 39* (October 1921), 188–95.
28. See *The Art of Criticism,* 1719, second section,

"Knowledge of Hands," pp. 98–149, *passim;* third section, "Of Originals and Coppies," esp. pp. 178–80, 183, 186–88, 190–91. Cf. *The Science of a Connoisseur,* 1719, Section III, pp. 207–10, on the joy of knowing Raphael.
29. *The Science of a Connoisseur,* 1719, section 3, pp. 157–58.
30. *The Science of a Connoisseur,* 1719, section 1, pp. 41, 47–51.

Society in 1734[31] must have been to Richardson a gratifying evidence how far his ideas had been *en rapport* with the progressive spirit of the age.

The elder Richardson had yearned much toward Italy, but somehow could never manage the visit:

> O *Rome!* thou happy Repository of so many Stupendious Works of Art which my Longing Eyes have never seen, nor shall see. . . .
> — *The Theory of Painting,* 1715, "Of Grace and Greatness," p. 208

> would to God . . . I had seen, or could yet see *Italy!*
> — *The Art of Criticism,* 1719, Introduction, p. 6

In 1716, however, Richardson's son, Jonathan Richardson, Jr. (born 1694), travelled to Holland and Flanders,[32] and in 1720 he made a Grand Tour, going to Italy via France and returning via Germany. The young connoisseur wrote "Long and Frequent Letters" to his father and on his tour through Italy took notes in Italian, preserved today in the Department of Prints and Drawings at the British Museum. Thus the two Richardsons could collaborate to publish in 1722 *An Account of Some of the Statues, Bas-reliefs, Drawings and Pictures in Italy, &c. with Remarks.*[33] It was the first English guide to continental art treasures and became a standard for a century—"to every nobleman on the Grand Tour, the guide-book and gospel of art."[34] The work triumphantly completed the movement of Richardson's thought from the practical to the theoretic and back again. His earlier three essays and the *Account* were translated into French and published in three octavo volumes at Amsterdam in 1728 under the title *Traité de la Peinture et de la Sculpture.*[35]

31. Richardson's pupil George Knapton (1698–1778), brother of Pope's publishers, would become first portrait-painter to the Society, 1750–63. See no. 7.2.

32. Vertue 6.161 refers to "British Museum Add. MS. 23081.V.112–17. Extracts from Jonathan Richardson, the Younger. Memorandum book Holland and Flanders, 1716." The date 1718, as well as 1716, is given by Snelgrove in a "Chronology of Richardson." It seems plausible, but I do not know the evidence for it.

33. *By Mr. Richardson, Sen. and Jun. London: Printed for J. Knapton at the Crown in St. Paul's Church-Yard, 1722,* 8vo, pp. 1–357 of text. See the Preface for Richardson's account of his son's strenuous travels and letters and notes. He was at Florence and Rome during the summer [1720] when the plague at Marseilles occurred and thereby was prevented from coming home by way of Paris (A8r and v).

34. A. S. Turberville, *Johnson's England* (Oxford, 1952), 2.42.

35. For the translation of the *Account of the Statues,* the younger Richardson wrote a special introduction, which is consulted today as a valuable source of information about early English collecting. He owned a bound-up set of proof sheets of the whole French edition, which over the years he liberally enriched with annotations. The volumes are preserved today in the London Library and are described by F. J. B. Watson, "On the Early History of Collecting in England," *Burlington Magazine,* 85 (September 1944), 223–28.

An Account of the Statues was published alone in a second English edition, 8vo., in 1754. The three theoretical essays, "on Painting, Criticism, and Connoisseurship," were republished by T. Davies in 1773 (shortly after the death of Richardson Junior) in a single octavo volume under the title *Works,* "corrected and prepared for the press" by Richardson Junior and dedicated (by "the Editor," 4 May 1772) to Sir Joshua Reynolds. In 1792 the *Works* were reprinted in a quarto volume for several London booksellers, "Dedicated, by Permission, to Sir Joshua Reynolds. The Whole intended as a Supplement to the Anecdotes of Painters and Engravers [by Horace Walpole]. Printed at Strawberry-Hill" [!].

Another work by the two Richardsons, *Explanatory Notes and Remarks on "Paradise Lost,"* 1735, is noted p. 140.

In 1776 appeared an octavo volume of gossip and

Three times in the course of his essays Richardson quotes the newly established poet Alexander Pope. In the revised chapter "Of the Sublime," which concludes the *Theory of Painting* in 1725, appears a slightly misquoted line from "Pope's Abelard" (1717):

And more than Eccho talk'd along the Walls.[36]

If he noticed this, Pope was no doubt gratified to find this quotation linked with three from Shakespeare. In the second essay, on the *Art of Criticism*, 1719, appear the opening two lines of the Prologue to *Cato* (1713), with the identification "Mr. Pope."[37] And in the third essay, on the *Science of a Connoisseur*, 1719, three couplets of highest neo-classic doctrine, beginning with "Unerring nature still divinely bright," are quoted from "Pope's Essay on Criticism" (1711).[38]

The quotations suggest that Richardson was keeping up with new poetry or at least with Pope. But these quotations by themselves, like Pope's own allusion to Sir Godfrey Kneller in a letter of 1713, hardly argue any degree of intimacy. On the contrary they stand here in sharp contrast to the two-page outbreak in bold type with which Richardson in another passage of the essay on the *Science of a Connoisseur* proclaims his friendship with the poet Matthew Prior:

Here being a full Period, and the first Opportunity I have had, I will inform the Publick that I have at length found a Name for the Science of a *Connoisseur* of which I am treating, and which I observed at the entrance of this Subject wanted One. After some of these Sheets were printed I was complaining of this Defect to a Friend, who I knew, and Every Body will readily acknowledge was very proper to be advised with on This, or a Much Greater Occasion; and the next Day had the honour of Letter from him on another Affair, wherein however the Term CONNOISSANCE was us'd; This I immediately found was That he recommended, and which I shall use hereafter. . . . Perhaps 'tis not without some Mixture of Vanity in my self, but in Justice to my Friend I must not conceal his Name; 'tis Mr. *PRIOR*.[39]

Prior died in 1721.

In the collection of W. S. Lewis at Farmington, Connecticut, is a little-known drawing by Richardson of Pope's mother (see no. Ex. 9) inscribed on the back in Richardson's hand: "from a Dr: done by Candle light abᵗ the Year 1703." This drawing would

anecdotes by the younger Richardson, *Richardsoniana, or Occasional Reflections on the Moral Nature of Man.* See pp. 142–43.

W. T. Lowndes, *Bibliographer's Manual, 4* (1864), 2088–89, reports an octavo volume of poems by the elder Richardson published 1776: *Morning Thoughts; or Poetical Meditations, Moral, Divine and Miscellaneous; together with Several Other Poems on Various Subjects. By the Late Jonathan Richardson, Esq. with Notes by His Son, Lately Deceased.*

36. *Theory of Painting*, 1725, p. 237. Cf. *Twicken-*

ham 2.323, *1.*306.

37. *The Art of Criticism*, 1719, "I. Of the Goodness of a Picture," p. 43.

38. *The Science of a Connoisseur*, 1719, first section, p. 13. See *Twickenham 1.*236, 247. Richardson quotes Pope's couplets as they stand in the editions of the *Essay on Criticism* from 1711 through 1716.

39. The typography literally jumps from 14 to 20 points, the passage ending with the name *PRIOR* in large capital italics. *The Science of a Connoisseur,* 1719, first section, pp. 62–64.

seem to testify to some kind of acquaintance between the Richardson and Pope families at that early date. (Mrs. Pope was, indeed, sister-in-law of a renowned portrait artist, Samuel Cooper.) Another evidence that Richardson was a family friend of the Popes is that in 1717 he drew Pope's father on his deathbed.[40] In the absence of other clues, however, we need not suppose a very steady or close relation between Pope and Richardson during Pope's early years of success, when he was most assiduously cultivating the friendship of Jervas and then of Kneller. The two portraits of Alexander Pope by Richardson here catalogued, one dated approximately in 1718, represent perhaps a renewal of an earlier acquaintance which was thenceforth to ripen to warm friendship.

40. See no. 30.

8.1. PENCIL-ON-VELLUM DRAWING, BY JONATHAN RICHARDSON THE ELDER, 1736, FROM AN EARLIER PAINTING BY RICHARDSON. MR. AND MRS. ROGER WARNER, BURFORD, OXFORDSHIRE.

For a more general account of Richardson's drawings of Pope and of the Warner Collection, see pp. 148–154, 165–167, and no. 20. Among thirty-four drawings of Pope by Richardson known to me,[1] this drawing is unique in that it appears to have been derived from an earlier Richardson painting. Inscribed (or drawn) in lead pencil on the back, in Richardson's characteristically square and slightly faltering hand,[2] is "Alex Pope Esq. Painted / abt the year 171∞ / 14 Feb, 1735/6." (The old-fashioned ∞ is Richardson's usual symbol for 8.)

It is true that even during the 1730s, the period of his greatest creative activity with lead pencil and crayons, Richardson often enough copied works by other artists. And often he identified the work by suitable inscriptions. To name but a few among many: in the Warner Collection of drawings is found a lead-pencil drawing, inscribed in his own hand, "King Charles I—From the bust of Bernini. 19 June 1733." At the British Museum are two pencil drawings of Cromwell, "From Lely June 1739," and "after Sir P. Lely 20 June 1739."[3] Again at the British Museum, a drawing of Matthew Prior in chalks on blue paper is inscribed "After Sir Godfrey Kneller."[4]

But in contrast to Richardson's drawings with such inscriptions, stands another group of copied drawings. I can adduce six in all—besides the subject of the present entry—and it seems to me worth while to describe all six. In the collection of Dr. G. C. Williamson at Mount Manor House, Guildford, in the 1930s, was a lead-pencil drawing, one of Richardson's numerous self-portraits, said to have been inscribed: "Painted abt the year '95; 13 June 1730."[5] At the Victoria and Albert Museum, a lead-pencil drawing of a boy aged six or seven is inscribed on the back near the bottom in Richardson's hand, "Painted abt the year 1698 / 5 May 1735." Richardson's stamp "JR" appears nearby. (Near the top, apparently in the hand of Richardson the younger, appears in pencil "My Own," and near the lower inscription, with a light line connecting it to "1698," the expression "Miss date."[6] Jonathan Richardson, Jr. was born in 1694.) Once in the collection of Sir Robert Witt and now at the Courtauld Institute is a pencil drawing of a young man in a fur cap, inscribed in pencil on the back near the top, apparently in Richardson the younger's hand, "My Father," and below that (very faintly), "the Orig. done abt May 12 1697," and below that (more strongly), "3 Mar: 1734/5."[7] Another drawing, once in the Witt Collection but not now at the Courtauld, may be seen clearly reproduced in C. H. Collins Baker's article of 1925, "Some Drawings by Jonathan Richardson in the Witt Collection."[8] This is a pencil drawing, full face, of a youngish-looking, oval-faced lady. At the lower right appears very distinctly: "Painted ab[t] the year 1724 / My mother." In the British Museum a pencil drawing of the poet John Hughes (who seems to have been a friend of Richardson's)[9] is laid down on the mount so that the back cannot be examined. But in the Binyon Catalogue it is said to be inscribed on the back: "Mr John Hughes, Auth. of Siege of Damascus, IV April 1736. Painted ab[t] A[o] 1714."[10] Another pencil drawing at the British Museum (of a man "supposed J.R. Sen." in the Binyon Catalogue) is said to be inscribed "Painted abt. May 1692. 31 Jan 1734/5."[11]

It would seem clear that Richardson sometimes made drawings from earlier paintings by himself (especially paintings of persons in his immediate family or of his friends); and that these paintings might date from even twenty or thirty years earlier.

The present drawing of Pope was exhibited, with eight other pencil drawings of Pope in the Warner Collection, at the National Portrait Gallery Exhibition in 1961.

---

1. See nos. 19(1)–19(14), 20–37(1).

2. See p. 152.

3. British Museum 1902-8-22-26 and 1902-8-29-30. The drawings in the Richardson accession of 1902 were too late for the Binyon Catalogue.

4. British Museum 1885-5-9-1898; Binyon, 1902, 3.227, Richardson 26.

5. Gordon W. Snelgrove, *The Work and Theories of Jonathan Richardson (1665–1745), Thesis Presented . . . for the Ph.D. Degree at the University of London,* June, 1936 (Typescript, University of London Library), Catalogue of Drawings, No. 127.

6. Victoria and Albert, P. 114–1929 (in the R. H. Stephenson Bequest of 1928).

7. *Hand-List of the Drawings in the Witt Collection* (London University, 1956), pp. 39–40, no. 1660.

8. *The Connoisseur, 73* (December 1925), 195.

9. A verse quotation from "Mr. John Hughes M.S." appears in Richardson's *Science of a Connoisseur,* 1719, Section 3, p. 187.

10. British Museum 1880-6-12-337; Binyon Richardson 22.

11. British Museum 1872-10-12-3382; Binyon Richardson 9. Surely this round-faced gentleman in wig and lacy neck cloth is incorrectly "supposed J.R. Sen." Oddly enough, this drawing, of all that might have been found, seems to have been used for the engraving which stands at the head of the article on Jonathan Richardson in Dallaway and Wornum's edition of Walpole's *Anecdotes* 2.273.

8.2. LINE ENGRAVING, BY SIMON FRANÇOIS RAVENET. FRONTISPIECE TO OWEN RUFFHEAD'S *Life of Pope,* QUARTO, 1769.

In 1769 C. Bathurst, H. Woodfall, W. Strahan and other leading London booksellers brought out a four-volume quarto reprint of Warburton's edition of Pope's *Works,* "In Five Volumes." The fifth volume, not actually numbered or connected with the set on its own title page, was Owen Ruffhead's *Life of Alexander Pope, Esq. Compiled From Original Manuscripts; with a Critical Essay On His Writings and Genius,* published by the same booksellers in two formats, quarto and octavo, 1769. See also Appendix 1, no. 67.4. The line engraving of Pope which is the subject of this entry appears as frontis-

8.1. Lead pencil on vellum. 6 x 5½ in. In a contemporary mount and paper frame ruled with ink lines; watermark similar to Churchill 133, "Pro Patria," "Britannia" and lion in a stockade. See p. 299. Inscribed on the lower back with pencil in Richardson the elder's hand: "Alex. Pope Esq / Painted abᵗ the year 171∞/ 14 Feb: 1735/6." Stamp "℞." Mr. and Mrs. Roger Warner, Burford, Oxfordshire.

8.2. Line engraving. 9½ x 6¾ in. plate mark. "ALEXANDER POPE ESQᴿ / Ætatis 24. / Kneller pinx. // Ravenet sculp." *Grolier* 25. Cf. *BMEP* 21. Frontispiece to Owen Ruffhead's *Life of Pope,* quarto, 1769. Yale University Library.

piece to the *Life* in one set of the quarto *Life* and *Works* with which I am familiar (Yale University Library), and in another set (British Museum 77.l.3) it appears as frontispiece to volume 1 of the *Works,* Juvenile Poems, etc. Octavo copies of the *Life* are too small for the portrait; an engraving of Pope's monument, by Ravenet after Wale, appears instead as frontispiece (see Appendix 1, no. 67.4).

The attribution to Kneller is not supported by any other evidence and would seem to be ruled out by the inscription on Richardson's drawing (8.1). Reversal of direction from an original picture is suggested by the incorrect placing of the buttons on the subject's left side. *BMEP* 21 lacks "Alexander Pope Esqʳ / Aetatis 24." and has what is doubtless an earlier state of the credit line: "G. Kneller pinx. / / Ravenet sculp." "Ravenet" is doubtless Simon François Ravenet the elder (1706–74), who came to London about 1750 and had a well-established reputation as the leader of a school of line-engraving.

A second well-executed line engraving of this type (*BMEP* 22, *Grolier* 26b) seems more likely taken from no. 8.2 than from the original picture. The bust-length portrait, facing three-quarters to right, is framed in an oval surrounded by symbolic adjuncts. The lettering reads: "Sir Godfrey Kneller pinxᵗ / / Collyer sculpᵗ / ALEXANDER POPE Esqʳ / Etatis 24," some examples bearing in addition the address "London. Printed for J. Bell. British Library Strand July 10ᵗʰ 1787." The plate mark is 7⅞ x 5⅜ inches, but the paper is usually cut down to about 5⅝ x 3½ inches, to appear facing p. 6 of "*Bell's Edition of Shakespeare. Prolegomena to the Dramatick Writings of Will. Shakespeare. Volume the First* . . . London, Printed for and under the Direction of John Bell, British Library Strand . . . MDCC.LXXXVIII." The second volume of this edition has as frontispiece "E. Malone, Esqʳ," by Bartolozzi after Reynolds, 1787, and pp. 297–415, "Mr. Malone's Chronology" of Shakespeare's plays. Thus perhaps it happens that the Rev. Mark Noble's *Biographical History of England . . . a Continuation of the Rev. J. Granger's Work* (London, 1806), 3.290, includes in its list of Pope engravings: "5. Alexander Pope, AEt. 24, in Malone's Shakespear, 1787. G. Kneller p. J. Collyer sc." (Joseph Collyer the elder died in 1776; Joseph Collyer the younger lived from 1748 to 1827.)

The facts mentioned just above possibly have something to do with the description "From Malone's Sale" attached to a portrait sold at Christie's, 22 July 1871, lot 51 (p. 5), the property of Mr. John Green, removed from Evans's Rooms, Covent Garden.[1] Apparently the same painting, or at least a painting with a label on the frame bearing the inscription "Alex Pope / from E. Malone Sale," was in May 1952 in the possession of a Mrs. Donnelly at 9 Hope Park, Bromley, Kent.[2] The same painting apparently was acquired in 1954 from Cavendish Hood & Co. Ltd., 2 Baker Street, London W.1, by Dr. W. Houben, of W. & A. Houben, 18 Brewers Lane, Richmond, Surrey, and in 1961 was still in his possession. The painting is 24 x 18 inches. A young man in a bright blue coat with narrow gold buttonholes, a white fringed neckcloth, and grayish brown wig, faces the viewer with head and shoulders three-quarters to the left. A gilt wood label attached to a carved wood-and-gesso gilt frame has in black letters; "ALEX; POPE

/ from E. Malone Sale." In posture,[3] style of wig and clothing, and age of subject, the picture bears some resemblance to no. 8.1 and in reverse to no. 8.2.

1. Green was the proprietor for many years of Evans's Music and Supper Rooms, Covent Garden. See *Odds and Ends About Covent Garden*, by Mr. John Green (c. 1866?) (B.M. 11794.e.4); *Evans's Covent Garden. Minutes of Evidence Taken Before the Select Committee on Theatrical Licenses and Regulations* (B.M. 11795.f.7); and *Illustrated London News*, 28 February 1857, "Town & Table Talk on Literature and Art," on Green's *Odds and Ends* (Whitley papers, Department of Prints and Drawings, British Museum). Edmond Malone is known to have had a collection of fine pictures, chiefly portraits, at his house in Queen Street East (James Prior, *Edmond Malone*, 1860, p. 321), but no sale of the pictures is recorded, and *A Catalogue of the Greater Portion of the Library of the Late Edmond Malone . . .* Sotheby . . . 26 November 1818 (83 pages, 2544 lots, in eight days) includes no paintings.

2. National Portrait Gallery archives.

3. The right shoulder is not visible, nor are the buttons, which are behind the neckcloth. Only three buttonholes appear. The wig billows in front of the shoulders on both sides more than in the engravings.

8.3. OIL PAINTING, ATTRIBUTED TO FRANCIS HAYMAN.

A "portrait" said to be of Pope and attributed to F. Hayman (b. 1708) was sold at Christie's 14 March 1903, lot 116. A sketch of it by J. D. Milner in a copy of the Catalogue (p. 19) at the National Portrait Gallery shows it to be similar to no. 8.1 and (in reverse) to no. 8.2. Milner annotated the entry: "Seated holding a laurel wreath in his left hand, his left elbow resting on a table (unseen) large dark eyes. pale face. Youthful appearance."

9.1. OIL PAINTING, BY JONATHAN RICHARDSON, C. 1718. THE VISCOUNT COBHAM, HAGLEY PARK, STOURBRIDGE, WORCESTERSHIRE.

Evidence has long been available that Pope owned at least two Great Danes, both named Bounce, during the period 1728–44.[1] But until recently, there was no indication of his having had such a large dog earlier, though his general fondness for dogs could be shown in a letter of 19 October 1709, to Cromwell. A few years ago, however, C. J. Rawson published a letter of Gay to Parnell, dated convincingly in March 1716, when Pope was leaving Binfield forever; it contains a passing allusion to a dog named Bounce.[2] So there need be no difficulty in reconciling the large dog with the rather youthful countenance of Pope in this painting and a more exuberant or fancy style of painting than occurs in Richardson's later oils. I have already alluded to some similar features in Richardson's First Marquis of Rockingham, 1711, at St. John's College, Cambridge.[3] The portrait of Pope was recorded at Hagley and attributed to Richardson in *The English Connoisseur*, vol. 1 (London, 1766)[4]—within the lifetime of Pope's friend the First Baron Lyttelton. It was noted and attributed to Richardson, at about the same time, in a manuscript *Catalogue of Pictures & Portraits at Hagley Hall*, by Sir R. C. Hoare, Bart., of Stourhead.[5] It is mentioned in volume 15 of *The Beauties of England and Wales*, 1814.[6] It was one of the best-known portraits of Pope during the nineteenth century, being seen at the Manchester Exhibition of 1857, along with the

9.1 Oil on canvas. 39⅜ x 39¼ in. Coat and drapery light purple or lilac (the lighter parts like BCC 176 Lilac), light soft blue sky in distance, with streaks of white and pink; distant hill a soft darker blue; green foliage in nearer right background; he sits under a brownish cliff going back into near blackness behind his elbow. Woolly gray masses of wig; eyes dark blue-gray. Back of book yellowish brown, with red label showing; dog collar black, with yellow bands and letters "A. POPE." Dog yellow saddle-brown with white streak up nose and forehead. A branch of large green leaves edged with white (perhaps laurel) in lower left corner. The Viscount Cobham, Hagley Park, Stourbridge, Worcestershire.

86

9.2. Oil on canvas. 50 x 40 in. Colors similar to those of no. 9.1. Inscribed in lower left corner, in yellowish paint. "POPE". Beinecke Rare Book and Manuscript Library, Yale University.

four marble busts by Scheemakers, of Spenser, Shakespeare, Milton, and Dryden, presented to Pope by Frederick, Prince of Wales, and bequeathed by him to Lord Lyttelton;[7] at the South Kensington Museum in 1867;[8] and at Leeds in 1868.[9] It is no. 16, p. 10, in *A Catalogue of the Pictures at Hagley Hall* (London, Chiswick Press, 1900). It was damaged in a fire at Hagley in 1925, but has been restored. It was seen at the Midland Art Treasures Exhibition, Birmingham, 1934, no. 36.[10]

The Manchester *Catalogue* of 1857 (p. 127) says that the picture has been "engraved for the first time (by Mr. Doo) for Mr. Croker's forthcoming edition of Pope." The line engraving, by George T. Doo, R.A., bust-length, without the dog, appears as frontispiece to vol. 1 (1871) of Elwin and Courthope's edition of Pope.

In more recent times, the painting has been reproduced in the *Illustrated London News*, 3 November 1934, and as frontispiece of Norman Ault's *New Light on Pope* (London, 1949), and in the *TLS* review of that book, 14 November 1949.

In a note taken at the 1867 South Kensington Museum Exhibition, George Scharf recorded of this picture: "mellow in colour, slaty purple coat & drapery blue, Eyeballs dark slate, Eyebrows broad dark heavy grey, Hair light yellow grey, flowery curly wig, Complexion fair, Cheeks pale, Lips maddery pink touched with crimson."[11]

It was shown at the National Portrait Gallery Exhibition in 1961.

1. See Norman Ault, *New Light on Pope* (London, 1949), ch. 22, "Pope and His Dogs." The date 1728 for Pope's owning a Great Dane named Bounce depends on Spence's *Anecdotes* (1820), ed. Singer, p. 267.

2. C. J. Rawson, "Some Unpublished Letters of Pope and Gay; and Some Manuscript Sources of Goldsmith's *Life of Thomas Parnell*," *Review of English Studies*, New Series, *10* (November 1959), 380.

3. See p. 75.

4. *The English Connoisseur: Containing an Account of Whatever is Curious in Painting, Sculpture, &c. In the Palaces and Seats of the Nobility And Principal Gentry of England, Both in Town and Country, 1* (London, 1766), 70, Hagley Park, Library, "Pope, with his dog Bounce, Richardson."

5. Photostat at National Portrait Gallery.

6. J. Britton, J. Norris Brewer, J. Hodgson, and F. C. Laird, *The Beauties of England and Wales, 15* (London, 1814), 206 ff.

7. Manchester *Catalogue* (1757), p. 127, no. 271, and p. 136, **no. 117**. For the four busts, named in Pope's will and still at Hagley, see G. W. Beard, "Alexander Pope," *Apollo* 57 (January 1953), 4–6. The picture is listed by Cunningham in 1854 and by Waagen in the same year (*Treasures of Art*, 3.227).

8. South Kensington *Catalogue* (1867), p. 45, no. 154.

9. Leeds *Exhibition Catalogue* (1868), p. 74, no. 1260.

10. *Illustrated London News*, *185* (3 November 1934), 698–99.

11. National Portrait Gallery archives.

9.2. OIL PAINTING, BY JONATHAN RICHARDSON. BEINECKE RARE BOOK AND MANUSCRIPT LIBRARY, YALE UNIVERSITY.

This painting appeared briefly in the hands of Messrs. Frost & Reed, of Bristol, in 1938. It was said to come, "after a long period," from a private collection in Ireland and was attributed to Charles Jervas.[1] It was acquired in New York City, about 1942, by Mrs. Stefan Schnabel (later Mrs. John J. Rea III), and from her by Yale University in 1964. The painting of the face is perhaps stronger than in no. 9.1, and despite the absence of the dog (or partly because of it), this version may have some claim to priority in this group.

1. Photograph and correspondence in National Portrait Gallery archives.

9.3. PAINTING, AFTER RICHARDSON. CHRISTIE'S, 28 JUNE 1845.

At Christie's on 28 June 1845, lot 9 was "Jervis, Portrait of Pope, with his dog." *The Athenaeum,* 5 July 1845, p. 666, describes the picture as "very ill painted." Pope "sits in a pale drab riding coat, long black-topped boots, and a close powdered wig." "This small picture hung very high."

9.4, 9.4x, and 9.5. ENAMEL MINIATURES, AFTER RICHARDSON, BY HENRY PIERCE BONE, 1845, 1850.

9.4. No. 687, on p. 31 of *The Exhibition of the Royal Academy MDCCCXLV, The Seventy-Seventh,* London, was "Pope—enamel. From original by Richardson, in the collection of Lord Lyttelton, Hagley. H.P. Bone."

9.4x. An oval miniature (which may be no. 9.4 above) is illustrated by John Hales-Tooke, *The Connoisseur Year Book,* 1957, p. 67, no. 2, "Henry Pierce Bone, Enamel of Pope, coll. of Mrs. Layton-Bennett."

9.5. Miniature no. 107, at the Ashmolean Museum, Oxford, came by bequest to the Museum in 1897, from the Rev. W. Bentinck L. Hawkins (G. C. Williamson, "The Bentinck-Hawkins Collection of Enamels at the Ashmolean Museum, Oxford," *The Connoisseur, 56* [January 1920], 31–37). It is an oval miniature, about 2$^{7}\!/_{10}$ x 1$^{9}\!/_{10}$ in. Pope is dressed in a wine-colored coat and has a somewhat too thinnish face. On the back enameled in red are the words: "Pope / after Richardson / col. of Lord Lyttelton / Hagley: By Henry Pierce / Bone. Enamel Painter / to Her Majesty, Prince / Albert, &c. / Nov. 1850."

For Henry Pierce Bone (1799–1855), son of Henry Bone, R.A. (1755–1834), see Basil S. Long, *British Miniaturists* (London, 1929), pp. 40–41, an account which includes mention of no. 9.5 above.

9.6. WATERCOLOR, AFTER RICHARDSON. JOHN MURRAY, 1888.

At the Twickenham Exhibition of 1888, no. 181 (p. 35) was a "Water Colour Copy of Lord Lyttelton's portrait of Pope with his dog, at Hagley. Lent by Mr. John Murray." This copy was perhaps related to the engraving by Doo which appeared as frontispiece of vol. 1 (1871) of Elwin and Courthope's edition of Pope, published by Murray. Cf. no. 9.1 and no. 66.14.

· 5 ·

1727

MICHAEL DAHL (c. 1659-1743)

NOT LONG AFTER he had completed his painting of Pope as the profound modern
Homer, Kneller died (19 October 1723). His place as King's Painter was given to Pope's
friend Charles Jervas. But it might well have been given to a better painter, Michael
Dahl. Dahl was a Swede who had appeared first in England during 1682–85, had then
traveled on the continent, had painted Queen Christina at Rome, and had been one of
her converts to the Church of Rome.[1] Returning to England in 1689, he had soon found
powerful patrons in George, Prince of Denmark, and the "Proud" Duke of Somerset at
Petworth.[2] In 1698 he apparently could have stepped into the place of his old master
Ehrenstrahl at the Court of Sweden.[3] He remained in London and flourished during
the reign of Queen Anne. He made a sufficient fortune and enjoyed a considerable
continental reputation. After the accession of George I and the break with the Swedish
Legation (1717) on charges of Jacobite activity, he lost his Court patronage, but he continued, until about ten years after the death of Kneller, to be perhaps the most busily
employed portrait-painter in London.[4] He was active until within a few years of his
death in 1743. Lord Egmont records in his *Diary* that Dahl neglected to ask for the
place vacated by the death of Kneller, and that "besides, he refused to draw the Duke
of Cumberland when 2 years old, desiring the Lord who went down to ask for it to tell
his Majesty that not having had the honour of painting him or his Royal Consort, he

---

1. Wilhelm Nisser, *Michael Dahl and the Contemporary Swedish School of Painting in England*
(Uppsala, 1927), pp. 10–11 and notes 157, 163; Waterhouse, *Painting in Britain*, pp. 103–04; Whinney and
Millar, pp. 199–200; Vertue *1*.33; 2.68; 3.27–28, 118.

2. Vertue *3*.68, 118; *4*.21, 149.

3. Nisser, p. 10 and n. 137 and p. 19 and n. 185,
drawing on letters at the Riksarkivet, Stockholm.

4. Nisser, pp. 24–25; Waterhouse, *Painting in Britain*, p. 104.

90

was unwilling to begin with a child."[5] From 1696 to 1725 Dahl kept up a fancy studio and exhibition room, not far from the Swedish Legation, in Leicester Fields, and after that was in Beak Street, an artist's quarter, near Golden Square.[6] One of his close friends for thirty years was George Vertue, in whose *Note Books* much of our information about Dahl is preserved. At the National Portrait Gallery is a group painting (no. 1384) by Gawen Hamilton showing Dahl in his later days (1730–35) at the center of a circle of friends who met as a club at the King's Arms in New Bond Street. The roster of these veteran artists as set down by Vertue includes, besides Dahl and Vertue himself and other painters, several friends and acquaintances of the poet Pope: the landscape gardener and architect William Kent, the gardener Charles Bridgeman, the sculptor Michael Rysbrack, the architect James Gibbs.[7]

In his earlier work especially, Dahl is noted as a brilliant and tender colorist in the Venetian tradition, a successful painter of "grace," if not of stateliness or nobility. He was scarcely Kneller's competitor in the portrayal of conscious rank and power. He was at his best with delicate youth (the slender scarfed Verney lads, earnest over the terrestrial globe or adventurous with dog and fowling piece[8]) and lovely women (the faintly swelling white bosoms of the countesses at Petworth, the pouty little mouths and languorous eyelids, the delicately equine curves of neck, and dark tresses swept back from ears and brows).[9] In this department, Dahl was perhaps in his own way closer to Lely and much more seductive than Kneller. The full-length Hampton Court Beauties of Kneller are just as slender and long as Dahl's countesses but in comparison, cold, sharp, and chalky. Dahl's parallel but less inspired effort in the masculine range is the gallery of admirals commissioned by Prince George and complementing Kneller's,[10] today at Greenwich Hospital—square, bulky breasts, noses, and jaws, billowy wigs, swords, ships, flags, and cannon smoke.

He employed a somewhat less ample set of inventions when attempting to express the membership of his sitter in the commonwealth of learning and letters. Favorable instances of his work in this genre are the philosopher John Locke (1696), a fiercely aquiline countenance, with a characteristic dark wig and a knotted-up neckcloth,[11] and

5. Nisser, p. 26: Historical Manuscripts Commission, *Manuscripts of the Earl of Egmont, Diary of Viscount Percival Afterwards First Earl of Egmont, 3* (London, 1923), 275.

6. Nisser, p. 16 and n. 176 (citing Poor Rate Books, London City Hall) and nn. 177, 178—if I understand this part of a very obscure story.

7. Vertue 3.71 (diagram and key); *BMEP* 5.54, 93; Hilda F. Finberg, "Gawen Hamilton, An Unknown Scottish Portrait Painter," *The Sixth Volume of the Walpole Society 1917–1918* (Oxford, 1918), 51–58. NPG 1384 is illustrated facing p. 51 and also in A. S. Turberville, *Johnson's England* (Oxford, 1952), 2, facing p. 48, and in M. I. Webb, *Michael Rysbrack Sculptor* (London, 1954), facing p. 58. A similar picture at the Ashmolean Museum is illustrated in the *Oxford Illustrated Catalogue of a Loan Collection of Portraits* (Oxford, 1906), no. 83, facing p. 48. See also the Walker Art Gallery, *Painting and Sculpture in England*

land 1700–1750 (Liverpool, 1958), no. 22, p. 14. See pp. 97, 100–101.

8. Nisser, Plates VII and VIII.

9. Vertue 3.43 (1730): "at Petworth are several whole-length pictures of ladies, beauties, painted several years ago for the Duke of Somerset, that show the great skill of Mr. Dahl in art, beauty, of grace, genteel artful draperies finely painted and well disposed. These pictures and the admirals at Hampton Court will always be public demonstrations of his superior skill." Cf. 2.81; 4.21. See Waterhouse, *Painting in Britain*, pp. 103–04; Walpole, *Anecdotes* 2.265; Nisser, Plates XIII–XVIII.

10. Nisser, p. 25; Vertue 2.67 ("Tour to Hampton Court . . . the Gallery of Admirals. 15 half len. 8. by Dahl 7. G. Kneller"); Waterhouse, *Painting in Britain*, p. 104 and Pl. 86B.

11. NPG 114 and NPG Photograph 1932, collection of Mrs. W. A. Molyneux, Trewyn. See Piper, *Catalogue*

the Queen's Physician John Freind, wearing a pudgy smile, complacently addressed to his writing table, and confronting a bust of Hippocrates.[12] Using the same handsome oblong pewter inkwell as for Freind and the same stiff green and gold brocaded folds of stuff in the upper right background as for a portrait of Sir Watkin Williams Wynn (M.P. for Denbighshire),[13] Dahl also painted the statesman, poet and essayist Joseph Addison (1719)—solid in a yellow coat, but leaning uneasily back against a long, black, scroll-topped chair, a flat, cream-colored face framed in a soft gray wig knotted on his shoulder.[14] Dahl painted at least two portraits of his friend Matthew Prior: one a rather plain half-length, in lavender-gray cap and coat, now at the National Portrait Gallery[15]; another and more interesting, at Knole House, in coat and cap of port-wine color, with extremely black eyebrows and a generally brown and southern cast, standing with his left hand touching a table, and with his right hand confidently pointing to the works of Spenser. In the same dining room hangs Dahl's signed portrait of the poet John Gay—heavier, in a Rembrandtesque russet robe, wearing clearly the expression of the commoner.[16]

It may well have seemed unlikely—if not to Dahl himself, at least to Pope or to a friend—that the image of Pope which Kneller had but recently created—the professional Grecian, the wreathed and immortal Roman, the pensive Homer—was now to be improved upon or augmented in the studio of Dahl. The confrontation of painter and sitter may well have occurred without special inspiration or gratification for either. There is a scrap of contemporary evidence which one may be tempted to borrow. Dahl's most important patron during his later years was Pope's friend, the great collector, Edward Harley, Second Earl of Oxford, lord of Wimpole and of Welbeck Abbey.[17] At the sale of some of his pictures (1742) the year after his death, no fewer than eighteen portraits by Dahl went for very low prices—much to the distress of the aged painter himself.[18] A letter of 1730 to Oxford from one of his learned friends, the Reverend Dr.

---

of the Seventeenth-Century Portraits, p. 209. See Vertue 2.15–17 for another portrait of Locke by Dahl.

12. National Portrait Gallery no. 1322, on loan from the Royal College of Physicians, 1902–61: NPG Photograph; Piper, *Catalogue of the Seventeenth-Century Portraits*, p. 131.

13. NPG Photograph 1944: collection of David Minlore, 22d Kensington Court, London W.8; engraved by Vertue in 1742.

14. NPG no. 714. See Piper, *Catalogue of the Seventeenth-Century Portraits*, p. 2.

15. NPG no. 3682; see Piper, *Catalogue of the Seventeenth-Century Portraits*, p. 287 and Pl. 15d.

16. Nisser, p. 123 and nos. 64 and 120 in his "Catalogue of Pictures seen." Dahl is said to have painted himself several times (Vertue 2.68; 3.12, 28). One of his self-portraits has been engraved for editions of Walpole's *Anecdotes*. (See Nisser, pp. 10, 123, and no. 52 of Pictures seen, at Moreton, Dorchester.) A second portrait, which has come to light only in recent years, shows an Italianate countenance and an athletic figure three-quarter length. Leaning slightly back on

his right elbow against some object of furniture, in an attitude of ease and mastery, the swarthy young painter gestures from beneath heavy wraps toward a female Grecian head of white marble, beside which lie his big palette and brushes (NPG no. 3822, signed and dated 1691; illustrated in *British Historical Portraits*, Pl. 105; cf. p. 183. And see Piper, *Catalogue of the Seventeenth-Century Portraits*, pp. 100–01). These portraits show a kind of narcissistic energy which of course was not always available.

17. Vertue 3.79 (1736). Richard W. Goulding and C. K. Adams, *Catalogue of the Pictures Belonging to His Grace The Duke of Portland, K.G. at Welbeck Abbey* (Cambridge, 1936), pp. 166, 176, 437, describe two portraits of Harley by Dahl, one dated 1728 (engraved by Vertue in 1745), the other before 1719 (engraved by Vertue in 1746).

18. Nisser, p. 26–27. "Mr. Dahl had the mortification to be told that in the sale of the Earl of Oxford's . . . a picture of his was sold for 39 shillings, for which the Earl had paid 30 guineas, which greatly discomposed him, as well may be thought" (Historical

George Harbin, goes some way to suggest how portraits by Dahl were commissioned by Oxford and perhaps by other collectors:

> And I do most earnestly beseech you to consider what will be said of your Lordship when it is known you have made Mr. Dahl spend his time so ill as to draw my picture, but of pure obedience to your Lordship I was contented to sit for it; but so much out of my humour that I think Mr. Dahl has been so just to me as to discover it in my countenance.[19]

Pope's portrait by Dahl was, however, apparently not among the portraits collected by Lord Oxford.

The main contemporary evidence about the Dahl type of Pope portrait is the mezzotint engraving by J. Simon 1728 (no. 10.4), which has "M. Dahl Pinx. 1727." In a letter to the elder Jacob Tonson (7 June 1732) Pope wrote: "My portrait, by Dahl, I have sent a week ago to your nephew. You oblige me in the copy of . . . Garth."[20] Tonson had been the commissioner, and perhaps was still the owner, of the celebrated Kit-Cat suite of forty-two Whig portraits by Kneller (including a very fine one of Garth).[21] But about 1721 he had retired to his estate at Ledbury in Herefordshire, leaving his business and his house where the Kit-Cat Club had met, Barn Elms, to his nephew, Jacob II, who built an extra room for the portraits. After being lodged in three other houses during the eighteenth century, those portraits were taken in 1804 by William Baker, a grandson of Jacob II's, to Bayfordbury, in Hertfordshire. In 1854 we find Peter Cunningham's notation: "At Bayfordbury is the portrait by Dahl (engraved by Simon), which Pope presented to the nephew of old Jacob Tonson." The parenthesis *may* mean (it seems not quite clear that it does mean) that the portrait presented by Pope was only a Simon mezzotint. The Kit-Cat portraits remained at Bayfordbury until 1945. In that year they went to the National Portrait Gallery, but they brought with them no clue concerning any portrait of Pope.[22]

At Christie's on 4 July 1859, lot 24 was a "head" of Alexander Pope by Dahl. The owner was not named.[23]

Manuscripts Commission, *Manuscripts of the Earl of Egmont, Diary of Viscount Percival Afterwards First Earl of Egmont, 3* (1923), 275.

19. Nisser, p. 26, quoting Archives of the Duke of Portland, Welbeck Abbey.

20. *Correspondence 3.291.*

21. Waterhouse, *Painting in Britain*, pp. 99–100,

Plates 85A–B (Tonson and Garth). They may be seen at the National Portrait Gallery, nos. 3220 and 3208.

22. National Portrait Gallery, *The Portraits of Members of the Kit-Cat Club* (1945), pp. 4–5; Piper, *Catalogue of the Seventeenth-Century Portraits*, Appendix.

23. Wilhelm Nisser, *Michael Dahl* (Uppsala, 1927), no. 121 in "Catalogue of Pictures not seen," p. 71.

10.1. OIL PAINTING, BY OR AFTER MICHAEL DAHL. THE EARL OF PEMBROKE, WILTON HOUSE, SALISBURY.

A Description of the Antiquities and Curiosities in Wilton House . . . A New Edition, Salisbury, 1786, was followed by *Aedes Pembrochianae, A New Account and Description of the Statues, Bustos, Relievos, Paintings . . . in Wilton House . . . The 11th*

Edition, Wilton House and Salisbury, 1788 [by George Richardson]. Comparison between these two catalogues shows that a great accession of pictures had occurred at Wilton House in the interval 1786–88[1]—during the earldom of Henry, Tenth Earl of Pembroke (1734–94). (Noted as a cavalry leader, the Tenth Earl succeeded his father the "architect earl" in 1751.) One of these pictures was "A Portrait of Mr. Pope by Dall," in the Coffee Room (p. 115, 1788). The portrait is mentioned by Cunningham in 1854: "Jervas—one at Lord Pembroke's, at Wilton (startled look, pen in hand)." It is catalogued by Neville R. Wilkinson, *Wilton House Pictures* (1907), *1*.160, no. 149, as by Jervas, acquired before 1827.

1. British Museum 7706.h.22 and 290.b.14. Pope does not appear in Richard Cowdry, *A Description of . . . Wilton* (London, 1751), or in James Kennedy, *A New Description of the Pictures . . . at Wilton* (Salisbury, 1758).

10.2. PAINTING, BY OR AFTER MICHAEL DAHL. READING UNIVERSITY, FACULTY OF LETTERS.

This painting was presented to the University in 1937 by Sir William Mount, Bart., of Waring Place, Aldermaston, Berkshire, then Hon. Treasurer of the University. On the back of the frame at the bottom is an old inscription in large ink letters: "N° 14" or "44." At the top of the frame and the stretcher are small paper labels bearing the number 5339.

This picture was exhibited at the National Portrait Gallery Exhibition in 1961.

10.3. OIL PAINTING, BY OR AFTER MICHAEL DAHL. NATIONAL PORTRAIT GALLERY NO. 4132.

This painting was in the possession of B. F. Stevens and Browne Ltd. (New Ruskin House, 28–30 Little Russell Street) in 1939[1] and was offered for sale by them c. 1942.[2] It was acquired by the late Peter Murray Hill and while still a part of his estate was illustrated in an article on Dahl by C. H. Collins Baker, *Country Life, 124* (20 November 1958), 1164. Offered for sale in 1959 by William Dawson's of Pall Mall and illustrated on p. 116 of their *Catalogue No. 102*, it was acquired in that year by the National Portrait Gallery (no. 4132).[3]

1. National Portrait Gallery archives.

2. A sheet of a catalogue bearing a reproduction of the portrait, Plate IX, and a reference to no. 582, in the possession of the late Professor George Sherburn, was annotated by him "B.F. Stevens and Browne" and "1943." The same sheet at the Courtauld Institute (file on Michael Dahl) is annotated "London, 1942."

3. National Portrait Gallery, *One Hundred and Third Annual Report of the Trustees, 1959–60* (London, 1960), no. 4132.

10.4. MEZZOTINT ENGRAVING, BY JOHN SIMON AFTER MICHAEL DAHL, 1728.

J. Ch. Smith *3*.1110, John Simon no. 125, and Russell 2.261 describe three states: 1. "M. Dahll Pinx. 1727. / / J. Simon fec. 1728 / Mr Alexander Pope. / Sold by J. Simon

above 10.1. Oil on canvas. 29¼ x 24¼ in. Colors similar to those of no. 10.2, but the face has more gray shadow, the wig is painted in tighter, more generalized masses. The Earl of Pembroke, Wilton House, Salisbury.

above, right

10.2. Oil on canvas. 29⅛ x 24¼ in. Background an even olive gray, robe a brilliant cobalt blue with black (fur) lapel and cuffs, shirt grayish white, wig painted in free circlets, ashy gray with brown shadows, face plastery pink, a pallid impasto, eyes grayish blue, table reddish brown, quill white, inkwell black. Reading University, Faculty of Letters.

below, left

10.3. Oil on canvas. 28¾ x 24 in. Colors similar to those of no. 10.2, but a more bluish tinge suffuses the white areas, the face is pinker, and the whole painting is smoother. As in no. 10.1, the masses of the wig are tighter. National Portrait Gallery no. 4132.

'ow, right

4. Mezzotint engraving. 13⅞ x 9⅞ in. (including letters). "M hll Pinx. 1727. // J. Simon fec. 1728 / Mr Alexander Pope. / d by J. Simon in New Street near Convent Garden". *BMEP* 1. Ch. Smith 3.1110, Simon no. 125, state 1. National Portrait llery, London.

in New Street near Convent Garden." 2. Same, with "AEtat 38" added after Pope's name. 3. With "AEtat 38" erased, Pope's name erased ⅛ at bottom, address erased (cf. *BMEP* 1). A further state is recorded in an American Art Association Catalogue, 27 April, 1920: *Mezzotint Portraits . . . Collected by the Late Edwin B. Holden,* lot 192: "Sold by H. Overton at ye White Horse without Newgate.—Sold by J. Simon in New Street near Covent Garden." State 2 is reproduced in Paston, *Mr. Pope, 1.344.* State 1 is reproduced above.

The three oils (nos. 10.1, 2, 3) have in common a thinner and more astringent countenance than that of the mezzotint, which seems in some respects crude enough to have been executed by an engraver who had before him no more than a sketch of one of these oils or of another. C. H. Collins Baker is presumably alluding to the mezzotint when (in 1912) he speaks of "Dahl's *Alexander Pope* . . . with his great staring eyes and wooden face."[1] Yet the mezzotint has the individually stroked ringlets of the wig which distinguish the Reading oil (no. 10.2). The round inkwell of the paintings is squared in the mezzotint, which perhaps indicates that the inkwell suspended from the donkey's ear in the satiric engraving *His Holiness and His Prime Minister,* 1729 (no. 7.10), is derived directly from an oil rather than from the more likely engraving.

A single derivative from the above mezzotint is to be found: a stipple, 4 x 3¼ in. picture, "N [sic] Dahll pinxt 1727 / / Engraved by Robt Cooper / ALEXANDER POPE / Ætat 29 / Published by John Bell Proprietor of the Weekly Messenger Southamp / ton Str^t Strand for the 40th Number of La Belle Assemblee Jan. / 1st 1809." This appears as frontispiece to *Supplement to La Belle Assemblée; or, Bell's Court and Fashionable Magazine, For the Fifth Volume. Containing The Beauties of Alexander Pope. . . .* London, 1808. This is Grolier 85.

1. *Lely and the Stuart Portrait Painters* (London, 1912), 2.102, 178–81.

· 6 ·

1730
MICHAEL RYSBRACK (1694-1770)

GAWEN HAMILTON'S PAINTING of the thirteen virtuosi who about 1730–35 were in the habit of meeting at the King's Arms in New Bond Street includes, as we have already noticed, several acquaintances of Pope, and among these are actually three who portrayed him in one medium or another. Toward the left of the picture, seated in a position of honor and holding out a drawing toward another gentleman (the dilettante artist Matthew Robinson, who seems to be a patron or leader of the group), is the elderly painter Michael Dahl. At the extreme left is George Vertue. At the extreme right stands the gardener, architect, and history painter William Kent. And next to him, with hand on the crown of a classically sculptured female head, stands the newly flourishing sculptor Michael Rysbrack. Another figure in the group, at the back, holding a partly rolled sheet of paper in his hand, is the architect James Gibbs.[1]

Michael Rysbrack was a Fleming who arrived in London about 1720, already an accomplished sculptor. He had been trained in the "classical" school which had arisen at his native Antwerp in the workshops of Artus Quellin and Michael van der Voort, the latter of whom was apparently his master.[2] Rysbrack's first employer of importance in London was Lord Oxford's architect James Gibbs.[3] An early and important partner

---

1. See p. 91.

2. M. I. Webb, *Michael Rysbrack Sculptor* (London, 1954), pp. 22, 26, 27. Mrs. Webb's richly and carefully documented book is a main guide for the following brief perspective on Rysbrack.

3. Realized today most readily as the creator of the

Radcliffe Camera at Oxford and of the Church of St. Martin-in-the-Fields—at both of these places a bust of him by Rysbrack may be seen—and of Queen Anne's first Church, St. Mary-le-Strand and, close by, the steeple of Wren's St. Clement Danes. See H. M. Colvin, *A Biographical Dictionary of English Architects*

with Rysbrack in the designing of monuments and ornamental sculpture was Lord Burlington's architect William Kent.

We have been present already at the deathbed of Sir Godfrey Kneller, holding in his hand, said Pope in later reminiscence, the design for his monument which he had drawn himself.[4] The model, however, had been made by Rysbrack, and the monument was actually executed by Rysbrack, with a bust of Kneller, two cherubs, and a medallion of Lady Kneller. Today it may be found "skied" in the nave of Westminster Abbey. In all, sixteen monuments by Rysbrack occupy Westminster Abbey and its precincts, the greatest total by any single sculptor.[5] The labors of his early years in London survive today most conspicuously perhaps in the two great monuments, designed by Kent, which stand before the screen in the nave, that of 1731 to Newton and that of 1733 to the Peninsular General Lord Stanhope—both marvelously elaborate, handsome illustrations of what is now called the "classical" style of the period—in marbles only white and gray, with the tall pyramidal backgrounds to which Rysbrack was especially partial, the full-length figures in Roman drapes and reposeful postures. Newton reclines among a galaxy of symbols relating to his scientific triumphs, as the *Gentleman's Magazine* for April 1731 explains in lavish detail.[6]

Sarah, Duchess of Marlborough, was one of Rysbrack's early patrons. At Blenheim in the chapel towers the stupendous monument, again designed by Kent, to the First Duke of Marlborough (£2200 worth of richly colored marbles and no fewer than six full-length sculptured figures[7]). In the Great Gallery appears the standing full length of Queen Anne in her robes, with sceptre and orb, finished in 1738.[8] One of Rysbrack's most impressive public commissions was the equestrian King William III (derived from the bronze Marcus Aurelius in the Piazza del Campidoglio at Rome), which, for only £1800, he completed in 1735 for the Bristol Council and set up in Queen's Square.[9] For his highest patron of all, Queen Caroline (for whom he worked again in conjunction with Kent), he modeled in the mid-1730s busts of English sovereigns from Alfred to Elizabeth,[10] and he did four of the five marble busts (Newton, Locke, Boyle, Clarke, and Wollaston) for Queen Caroline's Richmond Hermitage,[11] which are now ranged along the King's Gallery in Kensington Palace. Among the more spectacular of his

1660–1820 (London, 1954); Bryan Little, *The Life and Work of James Gibbs 1682–1754* (London, 1955). Vertue reports that Rysbrack complained that Gibbs underpaid him, but the two apparently remained on good terms (Vertue *1.76; 3.17*).

4. Joseph Spence, *Anecdotes,* ed. S. W. Singer (1820), p. 165; Vertue *3. 43.*

5. Webb, *Rysbrack,* p. 86.

6. Webb, *Rysbrack,* pp. 81–83, 92, and figs. 19 and 20: "tho the design or drawing of it on paper was poor enough, yet for that only Mr Kent is honourd with his name on it (Pictor et Architect inventor.) which if it had been deliverd to any other Sculptor besides Rysbrack, he might have been glad to have his name omitted" (Vertue *3.50;* cf. p. 65). Over a period of thirty years, Vertue expresses his admiration for Rysbrack.

7. Webb, *Rysbrack,* pp. 91–94 and fig. 26; Vertue *3.65,* 115–16.

8. Webb, *Rysbrack,* pp. 163–64 and fig. 82.

9. Webb, *Rysbrack,* pp. 140–45 and fig. 66; Vertue *3.61,* 66, 76. "It is a felicity, which wee have reason to be proud of, that the two greatest Men whom the Modern Times have known, or the English Armies ever were led by, King William the Third and the Duke of Marlborough, have lately had a Rysbrack to give them life & likeness in Brass and Marble" (Vertue *3.66*).

10. Webb, *Rysbrack,* p. 146.

11. Webb, *Rysbrack,* pp. 146–48, 153–54; Vertue *3.66.* Rysbrack's terra-cotta and marble portrait busts of Queen Caroline and George II (all four now at Windsor) are illustrated by Mrs. Webb, figs. 73–76; cf. p. 155.

decorative works, the full-length stone statues of Palladio and Inigo Jones, done about 1730 for the front of Chiswick House,[12] still stand today—fantastic, in swirls of blackened and eroded drapery; and the visitor to Henry Hoare's Park at Stourhead who steps into the Pantheon will confront the marble Hercules, more than six feet high (1756), and in the House the terra-cotta statuette (1744), which Rysbrack modeled from selected "bruisers" at Broughton's Amphitheater.[13]

Perhaps the most handsome category of Rysbrack's works for the modern eye will be the numerous deeply carved marble reliefs of religious and peaceful classic scenes, which after his early "Roman Marriage" in the Cupola Room at Kensington Palace (where Kent and Burlington were much involved),[14] he continued to do as fireplace panels (sacrifices to Diana or Apollo) for such patrons as Walpole at Houghton and the Duke of Bedford at Woburn,[15] or for the East India Office and the Inner Temple.[16] His large relief of Charity and her children (1745) given to the Foundling Hospital was, along with Hogarth's "Captain Coram," the beginning of the Hospital's permanent collection and exhibition.[17] Toward the end of his life the terra-cotta models for these fireplaces were snapped up by such patrons as Henry Hoare at Stourhead and Sir Edward Littleton at Teddesley Hall.[18]

During the earlier years of his practice, Rysbrack had few rivals of any importance. Lord Burlington's protégé Guelfi, who seems for some reason to have been much admired by Pope, and who did the monument to Secretary Craggs, in flowing draperies and leaning on an urn, in Westminster (1727), and apparently began the series of busts for the Hermitage, soon lost favor and returned to Italy in 1734.[19] The "dull and puddingy" classicist Scheemakers was somehow more durable, and after a retreat to the continent c. 1726–28, returned and ran a shop where, doing less of his own carving than Rysbrack, he had as working pupils two sculptors, Joseph Nollekens and Thomas Banks, who were to become famous in the succeeding "neoclassical" age. Scheemakers, says Vertue, would always do a job more cheaply than Rysbrack.[20] His model for an equestrian William III to be placed at Bristol, having come second in the competition with Rysbrack's, and having been taken up by the city of Hull, was done in "hard metal lead pewter" for Market Square, a year sooner than Rysbrack's, and for just under £900.[21] Scheemaker's most ambitious bid for supremacy came in 1741, when by the "contrivance" of his friends, as Vertue puts it, he got his most famous commission, the monument to Shakespeare in Westminster Abbey—designed by Kent—paid for by public subscription at Covent Garden and Drury Lane.[22]

The arrival of the French baroque sculptor Roubiliac on the London scene during the 1730s is the theme of a later part of this book.

After the death of Kneller and during the dull period of English painting which

12. Webb, *Rysbrack*, pp. 101–03 and figs. 38 and 39.
13. Webb, *Rysbrack*, pp. 121–22, 125, and figures 52 and 53; Vertue 3.121–22, 162.
14. Vertue 3.19 (1723).
15. Webb, *Rysbrack*, pp. 128–30 and figs. 55, 56, 60.
16. Webb, *Rysbrack*, p. 131 and fig. 64.
17. Webb, *Rysbrack*, pp. 132, 135, and fig. 63; Vertue 3.132 (1746).
18. Webb, *Rysbrack*, pp. 126, 135.
19. Webb, *Rysbrack*, pp. 43–44, 153, 171; Vertue 3.73–74.
20. Webb, *Rysbrack*, pp. 63–69, 145; Vertue 3.116.
21. Webb, *Rysbrack*, p. 145; Vertue 3.72.
22. Webb, *Rysbrack*, p. 67; Vertue 3.101.

ensues until the arrival of Reynolds in 1754, Rysbrack may well be, as his recent biographer claims, the most impressive portrait artist working in England. In addition to his historical and decorative creations and the very successful derivative busts which were often produced along with his monumental sculpture, Rysbrack made many excellent terra cottas and marbles *ad vivum*—masterpieces not only of classical decorum but of sober lifelikeness. The delicate marble of Lord Harley's eight-year-old daughter, Pope's "Chum" "Lady Meg,"[23] Prior's "noble, lovely, little Peggy," at Welbeck, was done before the end of 1723.[24] Another impressive example of his art is the broad-headed Roman Sir Robert Walpole in terra cotta at the National Portrait Gallery (matching the marble bust built in over the fireplace at Houghton)[25]; another is the terra-cotta Sir Hans Sloane, at the British Museum, a towering composition of textures: cascading old-fashioned curls, lace cravat, and weathered visage[26]; or another, the marble Dr. Robert Freind, the Westminster Headmaster, at Christ Church, Oxford, with bulldog underlip, a Piltdown profile.[27] The world of English literature is represented by a scrupulously compiled marble bust of Shakespeare,[28] by the medallions of Nicholas Rowe and Gay,[29] and probably that of Ben Jonson, and the bust of Milton on the monuments in Westminster, and by the two separate marble busts of Milton—the old man and the young—which came to rest in the library at Stourhead.[30] Rysbrack also carved Lord Harley's monument to Prior in Westminster, but the bust was an importation, by the Versailles classicist Coysevox.[31]

By the summer of 1725 Rysbrack was established in the house and workshop which he occupied until his death. This was on Vere Street, in Lord Oxford's new suburban development around Cavendish Square (landscaped by Bridgeman), and near Lord Oxford's Chapel built by Gibbs (now St. Peter's). Gibbs and Bridgeman also lived in the neighborhood, and a few other artists, among them John Vanderbank (whose oil portrait of Rysbrack at the National Portrait Gallery gives our best idea of what the slender, wiry, dark little artist looked like).[32] Like Pope himself, and no doubt in the same inconspicuous way which the times necessitated, Gibbs the Scot and Rysbrack the Fleming were Roman Catholics. Still it was probably not so much religious sympathy as their common orientation toward Lord Oxford which brought it about that early in Rysbrack's career at London he should make a portrait bust of the reigning poet.

23. *Correspondence* 2.159, 364; 3.57, 187, 245, 266, 371 (1723–33).
24. Webb, *Rysbrack*, p. 53 and fig. 35.
25. Webb, *Rysbrack*, p. 128 and figs. 56, 149.
26. Webb, *Rysbrack*, p. 161 and figs. 77, 78.
27. Webb, *Rysbrack*, p. 180 and fig. 90.

28. Webb, *Rysbrack*, pp. 117–19.
29. Webb, *Rysbrack*, pp. 85, 87, and figs. 32, 49, and 31.
30. Webb, *Rysbrack*, pp. 112, 115, and figs. 50, 51.
31. Webb, *Rysbrack*, pp. 36, 49–50.
32. Webb, *Rysbrack*, frontispiece, NPG 1802.

11.1 and 2. CLAY OR TERRA-COTTA MODEL (UNTRACED). MARBLE BUST, BY MICHAEL RYSBRACK, 1725–30. THE ATHENAEUM CLUB.

The earliest evidence relating to a bust of Pope by Rysbrack is a letter to Pope from Gibbs written apparently in the late summer of 1725:

Sir,—Mr Rysbracks house is in the further end of Bond Street Just cross Tyburn Rode in Lord Oxfords ground upon the right hand, going to his Chaple—but I will wait on you att Williames coffie house near St Jameses about five in thursday. . . .[1]

A series of letters written by Rysbrack to one of his later patrons, Sir Edward Littleton, has in recent years come to light and has served not only to document a number of specific works by Rysbrack but to give us the most direct information we have about *one* of the techniques used for terra-cotta modeling in that day. The process of modeling, then drying for a number of months, then burning, then caulking (in the cracks) with plaster, then lightly painting, which Rysbrack explains to his patron in the course of an apologia for the length of time taken in delivering commissions,[2] ought to prepare us to recognize that a bust begun by Rysbrack at a given date need not have been completed, even as a terra cotta, for perhaps a year and a half or two years. As a marble sculpture it need not have been completed until after a considerably longer wait.[3]

But in the spring of 1729 some form of the bust was so well known (perhaps through visits of journalists and others to Rysbrack's shop)[4] as to elicit abusive attention in the newspapers.

To Mr. REISBRANK, on his Carving A POPE'S Busto

REISBRANK, no longer let thy Art be shown
In forming Monsters from the *Parian* Stone;
Chuse for this Work a Stump of crooked Thorn,
Or Logg of Poyson-Tree, from *India* born,
There carve a *Pert,* but yet a *Rueful Face,*
Half Man, half Monkey, own'd by neither Race. . . .

· · · · · · · · · · · · · · · ·

This his mishapen Form—But say, what Art
Can shape the monstrous Image of his Heart.[5]
—*The Weekly Journal or the British Gazetteer,*
No. 201, Saturday, 29 March 1729[6]

An EPIGRAM

· · · · · · · · · · · · · · ·

P[op]e too. . . .
Must needs, forsooth, bespeak his Bust;
The Sculptor to the figure just!
When Sawney saw the hideous Sight
He cry'd, Thou Dog! Thou'st done't in spite;
Let O[ldmi]x[on] or Th[eobal]d buy't.
—*Brice's Weekly Journal* No. 211, Exon, Friday,
25 April 1729[6]

11.2a. Marble bust. 20⅛ in. high (without pedestal), 17 in. across shoulders. 9 in. chin to crown. 7 in. across at hair over ears. Inscribed on the back: "ALEX: POPE Poeta / M——R——S / 1730." The Athenaeum Club, Pall Mall, London.

11.2b. Detail of Athenaeum bust. Royal Academy *British Portraits 1956–1957*. By permission of the Courtauld Institute.

In "The Second Edition, with some Additional Notes," of the *Dunciad Variorum,* published in November 1729, Pope attaches to 2.134 a garrulous Scriblerian annotation about physical appearances, working in a complaint that certain "Gentlemen of the Dunciad" have gone so far as to "libel an eminent sculptor for making our author's *Busto* in marble, at the request of Mr. *Gibbs* the Architect." As a retort to these "Rhimes" Pope produces two verse epigrams, one "by the Earl of B" and the other "by another Person of Quality."[7] Pope scholars seem to be agreed that at least the first is Pope's own composition,[8] a conclusion which is supported by the fact that at some time, apparently just after the newspaper assault of 29 March 1729, Pope wrote a version of this epigram on a sheet of paper and sent it as a note to Lord Oxford in Dover Street:

> 'Tis granted Sir: the Busto's a damn'd head
>   Pope is a little Elf
> All he can say for't, is, He neither made
>   The Busto, nor himself.[9]

In 1732 George Vertue reports: "[Rysbrack] had Modelled from the life many Noblemen Ladies & Learned men & others, a list of them folows. I had from himself—and I have seen the Models when done." A list of thirty-nine items follows, including "Mr Alex Pope a Marble."[10] In the same year a couplet by one of the *Dunciad* gentlemen, Leonard Welsted, contains another testimony:

> While Time, nor Fate, this faithful Sketch erase,
> Which shows thy Mind, as Reisbank's Bust thy Face.[11]

And one further satirical shot may proceed from some sort of truth which is significant for the subsequently mysterious history of this bust. In 1734 *An Epistle To the Egregious Mr. Pope, In Which The Beauties of his Mind and Body are amply display'd. By Mr. Gerard,*[12] attaches to a couplet (p. 13) the following note:

> *Pope* ordered several Pictures and Busts of Himself, in which he would have been represented as a comely Person; But Mr. *Rysbrack* scorning to prostitute his Art, made a Bust so like him, that *Pope* returned it without paying for it.

This may sound at first like no more than a translation of the logic of satire (Pope is deformed; therefore a bust of him either will be or ought to be a monstrosity) into the pretense of a fact. But it is unlikely that Pope refused to pay for the bust, for there is no evidence that he either then or ever agreed to pay for a portrait. At the same time it looks very much as if this bust actually failed to become an approved likeness. It was neither multiplied in plaster or porcelain nor celebrated by engravings.[13]

11.1. The terra-cotta or clay model, 1725–30

It seems not necessary to suppose that the clay model was made into a terra cotta. In the primary document quoted below the word "clay" may well be used with literal accuracy. On the other hand, it seems possible that it can mean "terra cotta." In either case, what became of this model? The absence of any word whatever concerning it is a context which seems to me to invite our taking quite literally the following testimony.

In December 1731 or January 1732 Lawton Gilliver published in octavo *A Collection of Pieces In Verse and Prose, Which have been publish'd on Occasion of the Dunciad. Dedicated to the Right Honourable the Earl of Middlesex, By Mr. Savage.* The Dedication in Savage's name to Lord Middlesex has been traditionally attributed to Pope himself. Whether he was Pope or Savage or someone else, the knowledgeable writer sets out to "relate . . . the war of the Dunces . . . which began in the year 1727, and ended in 1730." "The Dunces (for by this name they were called) held weekly clubs, to consult of hostilities against the author: one wrote a letter to a great minister, assuring him Mr. Pope was the greatest enemy the government had; and another bought his image in clay to execute him in effigy, with which sad sort of satisfaction the gentlemen were a little comforted."[14]

11.2. The marble bust, 1730

The most likely immediate fate of the marble was that it stood in a back room of Gibbs' house until his death in 1754. Gibbs left his properties to his friend the Scottish painter Cosmo Alexander—"my house I live in, with all its furniture as it stands, with pictures, bustoes, &c."[15] Alexander, a Jacobite who had been out in the '45 and wandered later as far as America, returned to Scotland to die in 1772. The first mention of Rysbrack's bust of Pope which I have found occurs in the will of Edward Lowth Badeley, barrister at law, of 3 Paper-buildings, Inner Temple, who died 29 March 1868: "My marble bust of Pope which was given to me by the Right Hono[ble] Sir William Garrow I give to the Athenaeum Club in Waterloo Place Pall Mall to be placed in their library or dining room."[16] The bust, signed on the back and dated 1730, is still at the Athenaeum Club. In 1934 it was exhibited at the Royal Academy *Exhibition of British Art c. 1000–1860*, and A. C. Cooper's photograph in the *Commemorative Catalogue* is perhaps the first reproduction of it ever published.[17] In 1956–57 it was again exhibited at the Royal Academy,[18] and in 1959 at the Kenwood Exhibition of Portrait Busts.[19]

The bust is scarcely a delicate rendering of Pope. Yet it is a noble portrait, heroic in size and handsome, in a sense a convincing, if not a typical, interpretation. Perhaps Rysbrack the Roman antiquarian and classicist here anticipates by almost a hundred years a more romantic ideal, something almost neo-Hellenic.

The bust was exhibited at the National Portrait Gallery Exhibition in 1961.

1. *Correspondence* 2.298. Gibbs writes from "Gerard street" to Pope "at the Rght Honble the Lord Bathursts House in St James sqr." The evidence for the date of the letter in the summer of 1725 is its position in the Homer Mss. Rysbrack began paying rates for his premises in Vere Street in August of 1725. In 1719 Pope had consulted Gibbs about plans for altering a house, probably the villa at Twickenham (*Cor-*

respondence 2.4).

2. The letters were first published by Mrs. Esdaile in *The Art of Rysbrack in Terra-Cotta* (London: Spink & Son, 1932). See p. 346. They are reprinted as Appendix One, pp. 192–209, of Mrs. Webb's *Michael Rysbrack Sculptor* (London, 1954). See esp. pp. 195–200.

3. Even if the second stage, the burning of the dried

clay into terra cotta, were omitted, the whole process might extend over a number of years.

4. Rysbrack was delayed in delivering his bust of Shakespeare to Sir Edward Littleton "by the Desire of a Great many people to keep back Shakespeare's Bust so long" (letter of 7 April 1761, in Webb, *Rysbrack*, pp. 204–05; Esdaile, *Art of Rysbrack*, pp. 24–26). Mrs. Esdaile illustrates the public interest in studios of sculpture by citing the *Annual Register, 1* (1758), 437, which tells how a visitor to Roubiliac's studio left a paper of verses in honor of the Shakespeare statue then in progress for Garrick.

5. These verses, with the name "Reisbrank" changed to "Artist," were reproduced on p. v of *Pope Alexander's Supremacy and Infallibility Examin'd* (1729) and are said to be the inscription engraved on one side of a pedestal on which sits the original of the frontispiece, Pope as a monkey with the thoughtful head taken from Kneller's painting of 1722 (see no. 7.10).

6. British Museum, Burney Collection.

7.   *Rysbrake, to make a Pope of Stone,*
     Must labor hard and sore;
     But it would cost him labour none,
     To make a Stone of Moor.

8. *Correspondence* 3.100; *Twickenham* 5.116; 6.305.

9. *Correspondence* 3.100. Postmarked 2 April; no year is indicated. It has sometimes been supposed (e.g. Elwin and Courthope 3.272 and Mrs. Webb, *Rysbrack*, pp. 76–77) that Lord Oxford had a bust of Pope, perhaps this bust, in his new library at Wimpole. But the passages in Vertue's *Note Books* and the letters of Pope to Oxford on which this idea rests all refer rather to an oil portrait (see no. 5.1).

10. Vertue 3.56. This passage (which includes a reference to a sculpture of Lord Nottingham, "from the life," "to a great degree of likeness") is doubtless the source of the statement by Horace Walpole (*Anecdotes* 3.35) that "Rysbrach made also a great many busts, and most of them very like, as of Mr. Pope. . . ."

11. *Of Dulness and Scandal, Occasion'd by the Character of Lord Timon. In Mr. Pope's Epistle To The Earl of Burlington . . . By Mr. Welsted*, a folio published 3 January 1732 (see Robert Rogers, *The Major Satires of Alexander Pope* [Urbana, 1935], p. 141). A "second edition" appeared in the same year. The poem was reprinted in *The Works in Verse and Prose of Leonard Welsted*, ed. John Nichols (London, 1787), pp. 196–99.

12. A folio "Printed for the Author; And sold by M. Harris, at the Bee-Hive, opposite St. Clement's-Church, in the Strand," published 12–14 February 1734 (see Rogers, *Major Satires*, p. 145).

13. Mrs. Webb, *Rysbrack*, p. 78, believes that a replica of the Rysbrack Pope appears in a plaster bust at the Victoria and Albert Museum [16⅞ in. high, "Portrait of a Gentleman," A.84.1921], similar to one in her own possession. The latter is painted bronze and signed "J.P. Paphern. 16 Marylebone St, Golden Square." The bust at the Victoria and Albert, however, is surely not Pope. Both it and a marble bust, 22 in. high, seen at Gerard Kerin's Ltd., 9 Mount Street W.1, in July 1961, resemble National Portrait Gallery photographs of a bust of John Locke at the Central Library, Paddington, 1958.

Cunningham 1854, followed by Dallaway-Wornum, ed. Walpole's *Anecdotes* 3.35, says a bust of Pope by Rysbrack was sold at Mrs. Garrick's sale in 1823, for £58.10, but this is clearly a mistake. See no. 60.1, the Garrick Roubiliac bust.

14. Quoted by Samuel Johnson, *Life of Pope*, in *Lives of the Poets*, ed. G. B. Hill (Oxford, 1905), 3.147–49. Griffith (no. 268) reports: "The dedication is signed (p. vii): R. Savage. It is commonly supposed to have been written by Pope." Robert Rogers, *The Major Satires of Alexander Pope* (Urbana, 1955), p. 141, accepts the attribution to Savage.

15. Sketch of his life and abstract of his will, reprinted from the *Scot's Magazine, 22* (September 1760), 475–76, in the *European Magazine, 16* (September 1789), 168–69.

16. Probate copy at Somerset House. Sir William Garrow (1760–1840) was a baron of the exchequer. Badeley was his executor. His will (Somerset House) does not mention the bust.

17. Royal Academy of Arts, *Exhibition of British Art c. 1000–1860, Full Catalogue* (London, Burlington House, Piccadilly, 1934), p. 67, no. 149; *A Commemorative Catalogue of the Exhibition of British Art, Royal Academy of Arts, London, January–March, 1934* (Oxford University Press, 1935), p. 266, no. 1190, and Pl. CCXVI.

18. *British Portraits, Winter Exhibition, 1956–57* (London: *Royal Academy of Arts*, n.d.), p. 181, no. 584.

19. The Iveagh Bequest, Kenwood, *Eighteenth Century Portrait Busts June to September 1959* (London County Council, 1959), p. 26, Pl. [2].

· 7 ·

1725-1735
WILLIAM KENT (1684?-1748)
DOROTHY BOYLE, COUNTESS OF BURLINGTON
(1699-1758)

WILLIAM KENT WAS a Yorkshireman who ran away from an apprenticeship as coach-and-house-painter, got to London, and thence to Italy. There, for the space of about nine years, from 1710 to 1719, he collected and copied works of art for several generous and hopeful English patrons. He tried his hand at original history painting, ceiling pieces, ornaments and architecture, and was supposed both by his patrons and by himself to be preparing for a return to England as a *Raphael Secundus,* to reintroduce "the Italian gusto." His leading patron, Burrell Massingberd, of Ormsby in Lincolnshire, had hopes that Kent might come back and settle down with him as a resident artist. But on the return journey, between Paris and London, Kent seems to have been kidnapped by another patron, whose acquaintance he had made midway of the Italian sojourn, the whirlwind young impresario of the new Palladian conspiracy in English architecture, the Third Earl of Burlington:[1]

> After a dismal journey from Paris . . . got safe here with my Ld. Burlington
> and am lodg'd in his house, and he will have me begin to paint for him the

1. Margaret Jourdain, *The Work of William Kent* (London: Country Life Limited, 1948), pp. 28–31, 36. An important primary source is George Vertue, who in addition to various anecdotal passages summarizes Kent's career in one extended narrative (Vertue 3.139–141). Vertue is on the whole as severely critical of Kent as he is enthusiastically appreciative of Rysbrack.

fierst thing that I do, wch is the fine roome in his new building. I have already made the design, which he seems to be much pleased with.

—10 December 1719

being quite a stranger to the extravagant Tast of ye English vertuosi in painting sculpture & Arch. . . . I don't now were I am when I am once out of the gates of Ld. Burlington's house, were I think you may see a true Palladian front. I have made a sketch in collers for the Great Roome in the front, and all the rest of the ornaments yt are to be al Italiano.

—19 January 1719/20

I am still at work here ye days being so short and cold to an Italian constitution yt I keep my little room, only twice a week yt I go to ye Operas where I am highly entertain'd, and then think myself out of this Gothick countery. Engagements I have for more work makes all these power-spirited English daubers raile, and make partys against me, but I hope to overcome ym all.

Lord Burlington is going to be marryed to Lady Dorothy Savill, so I hope ye *vertu* will grow stronger in our house & Architecture will florish more.

—30 January 1720/[21?][2]

Kent was a plastic personality, "soft" and "civil," "fluid and attaching."[3] He was drawn irresistibly toward "greatness." A certain strain of coarse overconfidence, even arrogance, which his portraits by Dandridge[4] intimate, seems not to have erupted in any surface harshness or angularity. This versatile and highly practical, though hardly exquisite or profound, reconstructed Englishman, convivial and bibulous—latterly a plump and "whisk"-playing, rather comic "Signior"—settled in for the rest of his life at Burlington House as a companion to Lord and Lady Burlington and chief "executant" of Palladianism. He was doubtless pushed forward more vigorously than he deserved, patronized and encouraged, as Vertue reports, "above any other Artist living."[5] And at the outset of his career he no doubt got some commissions to which other artists had a better claim, notably the Cupola Room at Kensington Palace (1721–25), which he took away from the incomparably superior decorative painter—Sergeant Painter to the Crown—Sir James Thornhill and thus earned the formidable hostility of Hogarth, who in 1729 became Thornhill's son-in-law.[6] But, as he had "hoped" in his letter of 1721 to his country patron Massingberd, Kent was able in one way or another to "overcome ym all." He held important posts in the Office of Works (Master Carpenter 1725–35, Master Mason 1735–, Deputy to the Surveyor-General 1735–42, Commissioner to the Board of Works from 1735[?] until his death).[7] He succeeded in becoming for about

2. The three letters, addressed to Burrell Massingberd, are quoted on pp. 36–37 of Jourdain's *Kent*. Lord Burlington married, 21 March 1720/21, Lady Dorothy Savile, daughter of the Marquis of Halifax.

3. Jourdain, *Kent*, p. 30.

4. Jourdain, *Kent*, p. 44 and frontispiece: NPG no. 1557, reproduced below no. Ex 4. The other portrait by Bartholomew Dandridge, Kent with a folio in his hand and an architectural motif in the background, is today untraced, but a photograph may be seen in the National Portrait Gallery archives.

5. Vertue *3.73*; cf. 79.

6. Vertue *1.100–01*; *3.55–56*, 68.

7. Jourdain, Kent, p. 38; cf. Vertue *3.81*, 140. *The Chronological Diary for the Year 1735* (London, 1735; published with *The Historical Register*, vol. 20, 1735), p. 25, has "*William Kent*, Esq; Master Carpenter of his Majesty's Board of Works, made Master Mason."

twenty years a dominant influence on English taste in building, decorating, and gardening. The Renaissance range of his ambitions, the versatility, the size at least, and the robustness of his achievements have brought about his revival by twentieth-century scholars as a figure neither too small nor too silly to fill out the space in the history of English taste that lies between the age of Wren and that of Adam and Reynolds.

Kent was weakest as a painter, though it was apparently as a painter that he entertained his first ambitions. Two small blue-and-whitish history paintings (1729), of Henry V and his French princess, to be seen today in the Presence Chamber at Kensington Palace, are perhaps not totally eclipsed by the larger histories of Benjamin West in the same room. The ceiling oval of Jupiter and Semele in the King's Drawing Room at Kensington, the story of Ulysses on the ceiling of the King's Gallery, and the rows of quasi-illusionistic contemporary portrait figures crowding over the painted balustrades of the King's Grand Staircase (1725–27), with Kent himself and his actress looking down from a painted ceiling aperture, today still present a conspicuously accessible and not entirely disagreeable evidence of Kent as a picture painter.[8] As an architect Kent realized himself in part through books of pictures, *The Designs of Inigo Jones* (1727) and the later book (1744) published by Vardy, *Some Designs of Mr. Inigo Jones and Mr. William Kent.*[9] He found a kind of realization as well in certain schemes for a monumentally reconstructed center of government, Westminster and Whitehall, which have come fully to light only in our own day with the publication of his drawings for the Houses of Parliament and a national memorial temple.[10] A number of the larger buildings actually erected from his designs (the Royal Stables in the Mews at Charing Cross in Trafalgar Square, the façades of Kew Palace erected for Frederick, Prince of Wales, Devonshire House in London, parts of the Savile Row development behind Burlington House, and the Library in St. James's Park) have long since been demolished.[11] Yet much is still standing, and impressively: the front of the Treasury Building overlooking the Horse Guards Parade, and answering it across the Parade the Horse Guards building itself (put up posthumously from his designs by John Vardy c. 1753), and in London also the exquisite town house, No. 44 Berkeley Square, built for the spinster Lady Isabella Finch. In the country, Kent's greatest monument was and remains the rectangular four-winged Palladian villa of Holkham in Norfolk (begun in 1734 for the Walpole courtier Thomas Coke, Lord Lovel, a patron who as a youth had known Kent in Italy). But he also designed Worcester Lodge, the great gatehouse at the northern end of the long avenue to the main front of Badminton, Gloucestershire, and Wakefield Lodge in Northamptonshire; he was responsible for alterations and additions at Rousham and Stowe, and he is frequently remembered by literary students for those "uninhabitable" structures, "points in a landscape," the Temples of Ancient Virtue, of the British Worthies, and of Venus, in the great gardens at Stowe.[12] As an architect Kent was, like

8. Ceiling and wall paintings which he did at Kensington, at Rousham, at Stowe, at Houghton, at Chiswick, and at Ditchley are illustrated in Jourdain, *Kent*, figs. 63, 85, 86, 88–92, 94, 97, 99–101.

9. Jourdain, *Kent*, pp. 40, 46 n.

10. Jourdain, *Kent*, pp. 46–47 and figs. 16, 21–27, 47.

11. Jourdain, *Kent*. pp. 49, 51–60, 39 n.3.

12. Jourdain, *Kent*, p. 49; and no. 19. And see Arthur Oswald, "Euston Hall, Suffolk III—The Seat of the Duke of Grafton," *Country Life, 121* (January 24, 1957), 148–51. "The Temple [a domed octagon], built

his patron and the other Palladians, "classical" only in an antiquarian and associative, "subjective" way. His manner nowadays is likely to seem both "unadventurous" and sentimental in contrast to the more toughly mathematical baroque, of rebuilt London and St. Paul's, which the Augustan ethical philosophy, Shaftesbury's softer harmony, and the proposals of Burlington had discountenanced.[13] As an interior designer and decorator, Kent was lavish and grand in a manner which subsequent generations have found it easy to patronize as a too flamboyant amateurism.[14] His elaborately columned and coffered, swagged and scrolled, paneled, stuccoed and gilded interiors are still to be seen in most of their glory at Holkham, Raynham, and Walpole's Houghton (all three within a six-mile radius in Norfolk), at Rousham, at Ditchley, at Burlington's Chiswick Palladian Villa, at Kensington Palace, and in the dramatic "scenery" of the staircase hall at No. 44 Berkeley Square. The gilded lead gods and goddesses which stand in the marble niches and on the consoles of the domed blue and gold Cupola (or "Cube") Room at Kensington, Kent's earliest London work in decoration, are likely to make upon even the casual visitor a lasting impression of his "robustness" and *bravura*.[15] His furniture designs were emphatically of a sort with his decorations. Finally, his great claim to originality, his most pronounced touch of genius, appeared in his landscape gardening, largely and inevitably altered in the passage of centuries, but still to be seen as an intact minor creation, integrated more or less with the surrounding countryside, at Rousham,[16] still discernible in vast overgrown blurred contours at Stowe, and still susceptible of sampling in miniature at Chiswick.[17] Kent arrived on the scene at the right moment and with just the right painter's eye to go beyond the beginnings by Bridgeman and Vanbrugh and to create for England perhaps her greatest and most indigenous contribution to eighteenth-century art, the "picturesque," or more correctly the "humanized," landscape, something which seemed to the age impressively open, irregular, sinuous, and "natural" (as it *was*, in contrast to the Versailles kind of formalism), but which was still very conveniently ordered and formal in contrast to any real wilderness—and in contrast to the more loosely naturalistic parks which would succeed in the age of the full picturesque.

In 1716 the Pope family had settled temporarily "under the wing of Lord Burlington,"[18] in a house close to his Chiswick grounds and Jacobean mansion. An affectionate and confident friendship between Pope and the Burlington family may be traced in a surviving correspondence which runs to within a few months of Pope's death.[19] Pope may be looked upon by an art historian as a "public relations officer" for the Academy at Burlington House.[20] Some degree of friendly association between the two protégés,

---

in 1746, is one of the least known and most successful of Kent's landscape buildings."

13. Christopher Hussey, Introduction to Jourdain, *Kent,* pp. 16–18, 20.

14. Pope's other patron, Lord Oxford, was ahead of his time in holding views about Kent the opposite of Burlington's (Hussey, Introduction to Jourdain, *Kent,* p. 18; Jourdain, *Kent,* pp. 63, 65).

15. Vertue 3.19 (1723): "Niches of Marble & pedestals with statues. gilt with burnished gold. which

makes a terrible glaring show. & truly gothic."

16. Hussey, Introduction to Jourdain, *Kent,* p. 23; Jourdain, *Kent,* p. 80.

17. "The famous gardens of the Georgian period, such as Claremont, Stowe, and Chiswick, are palimpsests upon which a succession of designers have written" (Jourdain, *Kent,* p. 78).

18. *Correspondence 1.*339–40.

19. *Correspondence 1.*371; *4.*490.

20. Jourdain, *Kent,* p. 20.

the resident artist and the resident poet, must have "come as naturally," as inevitably, "as the leaves to a tree," but its first stages are not recorded. Kent's capacities as a designer of houses and gardens, rather than his claims as a painter, were probably his closest avenues of sympathy with Pope. Kent and Burlington were both invoked in the design of Pope's portico for the front of the Twickenham villa in 1732–33.[21] And Kent had a hand in Pope's garden.[22] Another connection with literary men came through his designs for engravings in books. He did illustrations and ornaments for Gay's *Poems* (1720), for his *Fables* (1727), and for the first complete edition of Thomson's *Seasons* (1730).[23] In 1725 he contributed fifty designs for copper plates to Pope's Odyssey,[24] and in 1734 six head and tail pieces for Gilliver's edition of *An Essay on Man*.[25]

The three portrayals of Pope by William Kent which are known today all appear to date from the period 1725–35.[26] But it happens that the main surviving record of personal relations between the two comes later. Perhaps, however, it is not much later than 1735 that we should date a comic petition to Lord Burlington drawn in Pope's hand and signed by nine other residents of Chiswick, including Lady Burlington and her two daughters. The avowed purpose is to save an old and well-loved shade tree from the ruthless hand of Kent with his plans for the view from a new terrace: "Your Honours humble Petitioners . . . have many years . . . seen the said William Kent the Agent & Attorney of the said Sathan, solace himself with Syllabubs, Damsels, and other Benefits of Nature, under the said Tree."[27] During the latter half of the decade, as both Pope and Kent, equally high livers, begin to experience symptoms of premature decay, there are further hints of a certain over-ripeness in the personal relation. At the same time, the second of Pope's portraitists in the Burlington circle, Lady Burlington herself, becomes more clearly a central figure in the comic picture.

The public history of art hardly knows Lady Burlington—except perhaps in Vertue's report of a conversation picture of her and her two daughters "engaged together in the practice of the polite arts. . . . all disposed in the virtuosi way,"[28] and in his further

21. *Correspondence* 3.332, 328–29, 356: "My Lord,—The Zeal of my Portico has eaten me up."

22. "Mr. Pope . . . is going upon new Works in his garden that I design'd there" (Kent to Lord Burlington, 12 September 1738: *Correspondence* 4.124, n.1). See below no. 14.

23. He did illustrations for Lord Burlington's *Palladio*, 1730 (Jourdain, *Kent*, pp. 47 n.4, 73). See *Correspondence* 2.415–16, his plates for Gay's *Fables*. His plates for the 1751 edition of Spenser's *Faerie Queene* (Jourdain, pp. 73 and 99, Figs. 12, 13) were severely treated by Horace Walpole (*Anecdotes* 3.59–60).

24. *Correspondence* 2.287–88, n.1; Griffith no. 151. See *Correspondence* 2.532–33, the possibility that he designed something for the *Dunciad* of 1729, perhaps the headpiece of the first page; and 2.80–81, Pope to Jacob Tonson Jr., an interestingly technical reference to a plate for Addison's *Works* which did not materialize. "I have also ingagd Mr Kent to draw the Outline of Mr Addison upon the Copper plate itself. You must therefore get a Plate prepared to etch upon,

that I may send it to him for that purpose."

25. See no. 17.

26. See nos. 14, 17, 18.

27. *Correspondence* 4.323–24. Jourdain, *Kent*, p. 86 quotes part of this with a note: "(Dated by the 6th Duke of Devonshire 1741.)" Jokes at the expense of Kent seem to have been a favorite amusement in the Burlington Circle. Vertue records that the Earl himself had been guilty. "When the present Earl of Burlington was at Rome and took into his favor Mr. Kent painter, French the painter, who was there at the same time and looked upon to be the better painter of the two by much, having gained the first prize in the Academy . . . was very uneasy at this distinction in favor of Kent and took an occasion to write an expostulatory letter to the nobleman setting forth the difference of merit on his side. . . . But this had no other effect but only as sometimes Lord Burlington would read it to Kent, by way of mortification—and mirth" (Vertue 4.163).

28. Vertue 3.96; painting by Van Loo. See p. 314.

report of her being taught drawing by Kent and of a "great room" at Burlington House adorned all around with great numbers of heads copied by her in "crayon painting"—including one of Kent himself. "These works may well be esteemed an *honor* to the Art and a glory to this Nation when the Virtu is in so high esteem, and worthy of the regard of such a noble Lady."[29] A mass of caricature and fantasy sketches which passed with her daughter's marriage into the Devonshire collection and is now at Chatsworth shows her perhaps in this department the superior of her teacher.[30]

During a long autumn and winter period of 1738 the Burlingtons were absent at their Yorkshire estate of Lanesboro.[31] Both Pope and Kent yearned much for the company of their absent patrons; they encountered each other occasionally, but in a sort of unsatisfactory vacuum, and mainly as mutual targets from which they bounced off observations in letters to the north. Lady Burlington, who some time before had played amanuensis for Pope, transcribing some of his satires for the press, now took the trouble to copy out and send Pope two squibs against his *Dialogues of 1738,* from *The Daily Gazetteer,* along with two epigrams of her own. Her purpose is perhaps as difficult to estimate as the precise shade of his own laboriously jocular resentment:

> I know her Hand writing, tho she has disguised it a little; & so I believe you will, when you see them. Kent is clear in that opinion; but thinks there is an Allegory in one of the Epigrams & doubts if it is not a reflection upon him at the bottom? He is very Umbrageous in his Drink & says Lord H. writ the Gazetteer....[32]

About this time too a rich benefice which lay in the gift of Lady Burlington seemed about to become vacant, and Pope's fancy soared with the irresistibly funny idea of proposing no other than a certain very worthy friend of his—fit indeed to be a bishop:

> I think your Ladyship begins to find the Excellent Person at whom I point, (or rather to *Smoke* him, for he is very hot, & very fat)
>
> > Of Size that may a Pulpit fill,
> > Tho more inclining to Sit still.
>
> viz. Mr. William Kent. . . . He is totally ignorant of this Address, nor do I know any Motive he could have to accept of the Living, save to get into a Soft Pulpit, where is a Soft Cushion, to lay his Soft Head, & rest his tender Tail.[33]

Some of the lustre may seem to be taken off this spoof by the more phlegmatic version of Kent himself, which, as it happens, also survives in letters to Lord Burlington.

29. Vertue 3.115, 140; 5.73.

30. See nos. 15, 16, 65.

31. Or Londesburgh (*Correspondence* 3.323).

32. *Correspondence* 4.124–25; endorsed by Lady Burlington, "rec'd & answer'd Sept. 8 1738." A prose attack on Pope had appeared in *The Daily Gazetteer* for 24 August and a verse attack on 26 August. The two epigrams are at Chatsworth (Ms. 143. 76).

33. Pope to Lady Burlington, 29 October [1738] (*Correspondence* 4.139–40).

I forgot to tell you in my way to Esher on Sunday I call'd upon Mr Pope, he's going upon new works in his garden that I design'd there—he told me of a letter he had wrote to her of some witt that he had me a party of.[34]

In my way to **Windsor** a fortnight agoe, I call'd on Pope he had write me word twice he had great besnese with me, but when I came I found it was for some drawings. . . . & that he wanted to know if my Lord Bruce is friend that had the great liveing was dead or dying, and if my Lady Burlington had it not in her guift to all this I was Ignorant.[35]

Toward the end of November Kent gives his patron an account of a rainy-morning visit he has made with Pope to the home of the old painter Jonathan Richardson—this we shall see somewhat later.[36] Another part of the same letter draws a dismal enough picture of Pope.

> . . . my service to mr Bethell and tell him his friend Pope is the greatest Glutton I know, he now talk of the many good things he can make, he told me of a soupe that must be seven hours a making he dine'd with mr Murry & Lady betty & was very drunk last sunday night.[37]

And the aging retainer, left behind for the winter in London, concludes on a forlorn personal note.

> I hope you'll keep CristX at chiswick after so many years I have not mis'd that I shall be so fancefull as to think it will be the last I shall ever be there.[38]

We have seen how Pope had gradually lost touch with another and an even earlier and closer friend than Kent, the painter Charles Jervas, who in 1723 succeeded Kneller as Principal Painter to the King. Jervas died on 3 November 1739, and late in December it was announced that William Kent was to succeed as "His Majesty's Face Painter." Pope was at Bath.

> If his Majesty's Principal Painter (for so I read again in my Paper, the Gazeteer) would follow my example here for as many months, (for so many at least it will take) to cleanse his Pencil & purify his Pallat, from all that greasy mixture & Fatt Oyl they have contracted, he would paint like a Raphael, & look

34. Kent to Burlington, 12 September 1738: one of four letters from Kent to Burlington in the Althorp library, published in *Country Life, 63* (1924) and by H. Avray Tipping, *Architectural Review, 63* (May and June, 1928), 180–83, 209–11, and quoted in *Correspondence 4.*124–25, n.1. Nothing is left of the garden laid out by Kent at Esher Lodge for the Duke of Newcastle's brother, Henry Pelham, who bought it in 1729 (Jourdain, *Kent,* p. 78).

35. Kent to Burlington, 10 November 1738 (*Correspondence 4.*141 n.1). See preceding note.

36. See pp. 144–45.

37. *Correspondence 4.*150.

38. Kent to Burlington, 28 November 1738 (*Correspondence 4.*149–50). Pope to Burlington, 19 December 1738, and Kent to Burlington, 27 January 1738/39 (*Correspondence 4.*153–54, 162–63), continue the themes of the autumn.

like an Angelo, whereas if he proceeds in his Carnality and Carnivoracity, he must expect not to imitate Raphael in any thing but his untimely End.[39]

Thus tit for tat, Pope and Kent's carom shots at each other via Lord Burlington display a kindly interest in each other's health. Pope was of course the less durable of the pair. The closing chapter of his relations with Kent concerns a portrait for a Yorkshire friend, Hugh Bethel, which never got painted.

Your Friend Kent I understand has sent you Zeman's Picture without any alteration, for he says he cannot, or will not, mend it, but I must sit to him for another for you. Which you may be sure I shall readily do, whenever he will.[40]

That was in the autumn of 1740. During the winter and early spring of 1744, we find Pope and Bethel still bent on an exchange of images, from their sick beds.

. . . I ought not to finish this letter without acknowledging the Recceit (just now) of your Picture, which I do in the kindest manner. . . . If Kent will still put off my picture, will you have a Copy of Vanloo's?[41]

I told you in my last how very welcome was your kind present of your Picture. . . . The last thing I did before I was confind, was to sit the first time to Mr Kent, for you: It wants but one sitting more.[42]

In his will, drawn 13 October 1743, Kent had bequeathed "to Mr. Alexander Pope Raphael Head Busto and the Wooden Term and the Alabaster Vase."[43]

39. Pope to Burlington, 19 January 1739/40 (*Correspondence 4.*220). *The Daily Gazetteer* (British Museum, N.R. Burney 343.b.), Wednesday, 26 December 1739, reports: "William Kent, Esq. is appointed principal Painter to his Majesty, in the Room of Charles Jervase, Esq; deceased." Vertue (*3.*98 and n.4) makes an attempt at satirical verses "On the report that Mr. Kent was appointed the King's Face Painter. 1739."

40. Pope to Bethel, 28 November [1740] (*Correspondence 4.*229). A portrait of Pope by Enoch Seeman (d. 1744) or by Isaac Seeman (d. 1751) is otherwise unknown, unless, as seems possible, it is the copy of

a Kneller portrait mentioned by Bethel in his letter of 25 March 1744 (below note 42).

41. Pope to Bethel, 20 February 1743/4 (*Correspondence 4.*498–500).

42. Pope to Bethel, 19 March 1743/4 (*Correspondence 4.*508–09). On 25 March, Bethel wrote to Pope: "I have got a copy here of That I like best of those I have seen of you—Sir God. Kneller's. Vanloe's I never saw, but I much question if I should like it better" (*Correspondence 4.*511–12).

43. Jourdain, *Kent,* p. 90.

12. LINE ENGRAVING, ANONYMOUS. FRONTISPIECE TO *Gulliveriana,* ATTRIBUTED TO JONATHAN SMEDLEY, 1728.

This picture appears as frontispiece to an octavo volume published 12 August 1728,[1] and entitled: *Gulliveriana: Or, A Fourth Volume Of Miscellanies. Being a sequel of the Three Volumes, published by Pope and Swift. To which is added, Alexanderiana; or, A Comparison between the Ecclesiastical and Poetical Pope. And Many Things, in Verse and Prose, relating to the latter. With an ample Preface; and a Critique on the*

Third Volume of Miscellanies lately publish'd by those two facetious Writers. . . . London: Printed for J. Roberts, at the Oxford Arms in Warwick Lane. MDCCXXVIII.[2] The volume held up by Swift and Pope in the frontispiece is the "Last," i.e. Third, volume of their *Miscellanies,* published on 8 March 1728.[3] The word "Stella" at the top of the picture alludes no doubt to seven of Swift's "Stella" poems which are included in this volume of the *Miscellanies.*[4] The four Latin tags which appear in labels within the picture are from Virgil and Horace as follows: *socia arma capesse* (*Aeneid* 3.234—"sociis tunc arma capessant edico"—the invasion of the Harpies); *tantae molis erat* (*Aeneid* 1.33 —"Romanam condere gentem"); *me quoque vatem* (*Eclogue* 9.34—"me quoque dicunt vatem pastores"); *hoc genus omne* (*Satire* 1.ii.2—"mimiae, balatrones, hoc genus omne. . . ."). In his *Dunciad Variorum* of April 1729 Pope attributed the volume to Jonathan Smedley.[5] Pages xi–xii of the Preface are an attack on Pope's physical deformity, alleging that it makes him peevish, quarrelsome, waspish, ill-natured. As a matter of fact, the inventor of the picture (*Veritas Invenit*) seems to have kept a fairly close eye on Pope's actual physique. This picture seems far the best of the free satirical renderings of Pope. (For others, see Appendix 4.) The height of the figure and the degree of deformity seem quite consistent with full-length standing images of him drawn by Kent (no. 14) and by William Hoare (no. 64.1) and with the caricature of him seated, by Lady Burlington (no. 65). The somewhat too aquiline profile bears a degree of resemblance to the face of Pope according to Kent (nos. 17 and 18).

1. Robert W. Rogers, *The Major Satires of Alexander Pope* (Urbana, 1955), citing *Monthly Chronicle.*

2. Cf. Herman Teerink, *A Bibliography of the Writings in Prose and Verse of Jonathan Swift* (The Hague, 1937), p. 23, no. 32; Arthur E. Case, *A Bibliography of English Poetical Miscellanies, 1521–1750* (Oxford, 1935), no. 351.

3. Griffith 196.

4. Pp. 148, 150, 154, 160–63, 278–96, 300–08, 309–13. See Harold Williams, ed. *Poems of Swift* (Oxford, 1937), *1.*xxi.

5. *Twickenham* 5.208; Griffith 211.

13.1. LINE ENGRAVING, "TASTE," ANONYMOUS BROAD SHEET, 1731–32.

In his *Note Book* under March 1721 / 2 George Vertue reports how "a mighty mortification fell" on the King's Sergeant Painter and History Painter Sir James Thornhill when the painting of the new apartments at Kensington was taken away from him by a low bid from Lord Burlington's upstart William Kent.[1] Kent, as we have seen, flourished mightily, and in 1724 he became a target for the newly arriving satirical engraver William Hogarth in a work entitled *Masquerades and Operas.* In the background of this general assault on the "Taste of the Town," appears the gateway of Burlington's Palladian house in Piccadilly labelled "Accademy of Arts," and atop the gate stands a statue of William Kent. Raphael and Michelangelo appear on either side in postures of reverence.[2] In the following year, October 1725, Hogarth struck again, with a burlesque of Kent's debated *Altarpiece* at St. Clement Danes.[3] In 1729 Hogarth married the daughter of Sir James Thornhill—as Vertue reports, without the father's consent, but by 1732 the couple were living with Sir James in Covent Garden.[4] These preliminaries may relevantly be borne in mind as we move to consider the traditional idea about the authorship of the engraving "Taste," 1731–32, the subject of this entry.

Pope's Fourth Moral Epistle, *Of the Use of Riches,* originally entitled *Of Taste, An Epistle To The Right Honourable Richard Earl of Burlington. Occasion'd by his Publishing Palladio's Designs,* published in December 1731,[5] pays Burlington the high compliment of making him the restorer of Inigo Jones and Palladio, the Vitruvius of the present age:

> Till Kings call forth th' Idea's of your mind,
> Proud to accomplish what such hands design'd.
> > —11. 195–96.

At the same time the Epistle contains a now celebrated satiric passage (11. 99–168) on the extravagant Villa of Timon, in the Chapel of which, for instance,

> On painted Ceilings you devoutly stare,
> Where sprawl the Saints of Verrio and Laguerre.
> > —11. 145–46.

This satire was immediately,[6] and to Pope's great indignation, taken as an ungrateful attack upon his acquaintance the Duke of Chandos, who had an opulent palace called Cannons, near Edgware, in Middlesex, rebuilt by Gibbs about 1719[7] and decorated in part by Thornhill and Laguerre.[8] Pope's retorts to the slander and his vindication by modern scholarship[9] are not relevant to the present narrative. His supposed guilt was a public topic.

And so it happened that somebody, no doubt within a few weeks, got out a sixpenny sheet engraving, "Taste,"[10] which, picking up the motif of Kent aloft upon Burlington Gate (from Hogarth's *Masquerades and Operas* of 1724), made it the vehicle of a broad satire upon Pope's *Epistle.* The meaning of the satire is revealed in a key beneath the picture which reads as follows:

A. P—ᵖᵉ a Plasterer white washing & Bespattering / B. any Body that comes in his way / C. not a Dukes Coach as appears by yᵉ Crescent at one Corner [but with Ducal coronets at two corners—and part of the Chandos coat-of-arms on the coach door] / D. Taste / E. a standing Proof [i.e. Kent ("K–N–T") atop the gate admired by recumbent figures of "RAPHAEL URB. and "MIᴸ· ANGELO"] / F. A Labourer. [wearing a peer's ribbon, Lord Burlington].

John Nichols, in his second edition of *Biographical Anecdotes of William Hogarth* (London, 1782), pp. 24, 153, attributes the print to Hogarth, and this attribution has become traditional, in part because of Hogarth's supposed grudge against Kent as the supplanter of Thornhill. Here, turning back to the *Note Books* of George Vertue, we find late in 1731 or early in 1732: "a small print was formerly publishd where Mr Kent was sett up upon the pediment of Lᵈ Burlingtons Gate. with Inigo Jones & Paladio.— <a Caricature by Hogarth> lately upon Mʳ Popes. publishing book on *Taste* dedicated to ye Erl of Burlington another Caricature print came out where Mr Pope is white washing."[11] A little later, Hogarth himself having suffered two defeats similar to Thornhill's (being prevented, "by Mr Kents interest," from doing a group picture of the Royal family and from drawing the nuptials of the Prince and Princess of Orange), Vertue adds the comment: "these are sad Mortifications to an Ingenious Man But its the effect of carricatures wch he has heretofore toucht Mr Kent. & diverted the Town. which now he is like to pay for, when he least thought on it. add to that there is some other causes relateing to Sr James Thornhill. whose daughter is marryd to Mr Hogarth. and is blended with interest & spirit of opposition."[12]

Three main observations may be made: (1) that Vertue does not make it clear that he believes the second Burlington Gate ("Taste," 1731–32) to be the work of Hogarth ("Carricatures wch he has heretofore toucht Mr Kent" may mean *Masquerades and Operas,* 1724, and Kent's *Altarpiece,* 1725), and even if he does believe or suspect it to be by Hogarth, he may be wrong; (2) that a motif very closely copied from an earlier Hogarth engraving is an argument, not for, but against an attribution to Hogarth; (3) that the internal evidence, the very crude style of this unsigned engraving, is against giving it to Hogarth.[13]

The engraving is reproduced as frontispiece in F. W. Bateson's edition of the *Moral Essays, Twickenham* 3.ii.

1. Vertue *1*.100–01.

2. *British Museum Political & Personal Satires* no. 1742 (2.603–05); Austin Dobson, *William Hogarth* (London, 1907), p. 229, illustrated facing p. 16.

3. *British Museum Satires* no. 1764 (2.620–23); Dobson, *Hogarth* (1907), p. 230, illustrated p. 19.

4. Vertue *3*.38, 58.

5. Griffith nos. 264 and 265 (vol. *1*, pp. 198 and 201); *Twickenham 3.ii.* xxvii, 128. The title, as I quote it, is a conflation of the half-title and title of the folio first edition described in *Twickenham,* p. 129.

6. *Correspondence* 2.254–63.

7. Bryan Little, *The Life and Work of James Gibbs* (London, 1955), pp. 50, 90, 99.

8. Vertue *4*.196; *5*.94.

9. *Twickenham* 3.ii.164–68.

10. *British Museum Satires* no. 1873 (2.749–51); Dobson, *Hogarth* (1907), p. 234, illustrated facing p. 24.

11. Vertue 2.55–56.

12. Vertue 2.68 (1733). In the interest of the raw evidence, I have refrained from normalizing these passages.

13. I have been guided in this argument by generous advice from Professor Ronald Paulson, whose catalogue of *Hogarth's Graphic Works* has recently been published by the Yale University Press.

13.2. LINE ENGRAVING, FRONTISPIECE TO *A Miscellany on Taste,* 1732.

Within a few weeks, in January 1732, a reduced copy of the engraving "Taste" appeared as frontispiece to an octavo volume in half sheets entitled *"A Miscellany on Taste. By Mr. Pope, &c. Viz. I. Of Taste in Architecture. An Epistle to the Earl of Burlington. With Notes Variorum, and a Compleat Key. . . .* [five other titles] London: Printed; and Sold by G. Lawton, in Fleet-street; T. Osborn, below Bridge, and J. Hughes in High-Holborn. 1732."[1] This engraving[2] follows for the most part the details of the original, as expounded in the key above. The most important difference between the versions is that whereas in the original, only the back of Pope's head, in a large wig, is seen, in the derivative frontispiece, Pope's face is turned profile, and he wears a cap. The profile, however, is not a likeness of Pope. This illustration and the preceding are

12. Line engraving. 6⁷⁄₁₆ x 3¹¹⁄₁₆ in. frame. "Stella! . . . / Veritas Invenit, // Justitia Sculpsit". Frontispiece to *Gulliveriana*, 1728. For the other inscriptions, see the entry for no. 12. Yale University Library.

13.1. Line engraving. 9⅛ x 6⅝ in. plate mark. "TASTE. . . . Price 6ᵈ". *BMP&PS* 2.749–51, no. 1873. For the other inscriptions, see the entry for no. 13.1. Professor F. W. Hilles, Yale University.

right

13.2. Line engraving. 7⁷⁄₁₆ x 4½ in. plate mark. "TASTE". Frontispiece to *A Miscellany On Taste. By Mr. Pope, &c.*, London, 1732. *BMP&PS* 2.751–52, no. 1874. See the entries for nos. 13.1 and 13.2. Yale University Library.

introduced here for the sake of the satire linking Pope, Kent, and Burlington, and as fair examples of a kind of satiric engraving which, though in some sense intended to represent Pope, has no claim to be either a likeness of him or to be derived from any specific portrait. See Appendix 4 for some further examples of this category.

1. Griffith no. 266 (giving the date 15 January from the *Grub-Street Journal*); Rogers, *The Major Satires*, p. 141 (giving the date 20 January from the same source); Twickenham 3.ii.128.

2. *BMP&PS* no. 1874 (2.751–52). See also nos. 1875 and 1876 (copies of 1874) and nos. 1877, 1878, 1879 (copies of the original engraving no. 1873)—all except 1875 appearing in editions of Hogarth pictures, 1798–1822.

14. DRAWING, PEN AND INK, WITH SEPIA WASH, BY WILLIAM KENT. DEPARTMENT OF PRINTS AND DRAWINGS, BRITISH MUSEUM.

Pope leased his Twickenham villa and garden by the river toward the end of 1718. By 19 November, 1719, he had taken two more acres, across the highway.[1] "My present Employment is Gardening." The "grotto" or tunnel under his house connecting the riverside lawn with the main garden, was dug at least as early as the summer of 1722.[2] He was actively engaged in improvements to his garden throughout the years 1719–26, 1733–35. The best description occurs in his letter to Edward Blount 2 June 1725:

> I have put the last Hand to my works of this kind, in happily finishing the sub-terraneous Way and Grotto; I there found a Spring of the clearest Water, which falls in a perpetual Rill, that echoes thro' the Cavern day and night. From the River *Thames,* you see thro' my Arch up a walk of the Wilderness to a kind of open Temple, wholly compos'd of Shells in the Rustic Manner; and from that distance under the Temple you look down thro' a sloping Arcade of Trees, and see the Sails on the River passing suddenly and vanishing, as thro' a perspective Glass. When you shut the Doors of this Grotto, it becomes on the instant, from a luminous Room, a *Camera obscura;* on the Walls of which all the objects of the River, Hills, Woods, and Boats, are forming a moving Picture in their visible Radiations: And when you have a mind to light it up, it affords you a very different Scene: it is finished with Shells interspersed with Pieces of Looking-glass in angular forms; and in the Cieling is a Star of the same Material, at which when a Lamp (of an orbicular Figure of thin Alabaster) is hung in the Middle, a thousand pointed Rays glitter and are reflected over the Place. There are connected to this Grotto by a narrower Passage two Porches, with Niches and Seats; one toward the River, of Smooth Stones, full of light and open; the other toward the Arch of Trees, rough with Shells, Flints, and Iron Ore. The Bottom is paved with simple Pebble, as the adjoining Walk up the Wilderness to the Temple, is to be Cockle-shells, in the natural Taste, agreeing not ill with the little dripping Murmur, and the Aquatic Idea of the whole Place.[3]

In December 1735 the shell temple had "fallen down."[4] In June 1736 he was engaged in "Rebuilding of the Temple."[5] A good expression of Pope's lofty philosophy of gardening occurs in his letter to Swift of 25 March 1736:

> I have more fruit-trees and kitchen-garden than you have any thought of. Nay I have good Melons and Pine-apples of my own growth. I am as much a better Gardiner, as I'm a worse Poet, than when you saw me: But gardening is near a-kin to Philosophy, for Tully says *Agricultura proxima sapientiae*.[6]

Early in the year 1740, Pope after returning from an extended visit to Ralph Allen at Prior Park, began a feverish program of enhancing his grotto—sending for numerous loads ("baskets," "tons") of stones and fancy minerals from Allen and Dr. William Oliver at Bath and from William Borlase and Thomas Edwards of Penzance.[7] On 3 September 1740, he included in a letter to Bolingbroke the verses "On His Grotto at Twickenham."[8] As late as 18 July 1741, having recently announced that the grotto was completed, he was nevertheless planning two new rooms.[9] Shortly afterwards he was "still . . . Grottofying,"[10] and shortly afterwards again he arranged three waterfalls in the grotto.[11]

A sketch of Pope's grotto drawn by himself for Dr. Oliver, 29 December 1740, now in the Houghton Library, Harvard University, is reproduced by Carruthers, *Life of Pope* (1857), p. 175. *A Plan of Mr. Pope's Garden* . . . (with a diagram and a detailed description of the grotto) was published by Pope's gardener John Searle in 1745.[12]

On the back of the present drawing is an inscription, written in ink: "Mem: June [undecipherable mark]. 1790 An Original Drawing by Alexander Pope Esqr Purchas'd at Mrs. Shorts Sale—whose Mother Had been His House keeper." Apparently the housekeeper was Mrs. Searle, and she had lived for a long time. In the *Saint James Chronicle*, 11–13 December 1783, appears the following notice: "A Correspondent writes from Eccleshall, to say he rode day before to Newport and found alive Mrs. Serle, for many years housekeeper to Pope, whose husband is immortalized in verse: 'Tie up the knocker. . . .' She was 90 yrs. old."[13] The drawing was acquired by the British Museum in November 1872. The attribution to Pope himself was followed by Binyon in the *Catalogue* of 1902. But the style of Kent's garden designs is unmistakable.[14] The drawing is reproduced in Paston, *Mr. Pope*, vol. 2, facing page 622, and in Iolo A. Williams, *Early English Watercolors* . . . (London, 1952), Plate XII.

A painter, palette in hand (no doubt Kent himself, though not so rotund as we might expect), talks to a shorter companion, with slightly bowed back, who looks at the shell temple through a glass. The portraiture of Pope is slight and softened, but seems nevertheless intended and not quite a falsification. The large dog of the Bounce type will not serve to date the drawing (see no. 9). Pope's sketch of 1740 and Searle's Plan and description of 1745 give us a very elaborate ramification of chambers and porches. These need not be taken as inconsistent with the view through the central tunnel presented in this drawing. Aside from the obvious elements of fantasy (the fountain with Nereids and Tritons, the rainbow in the spray, and the dolphin on the tripod), the emphasis of

14. Drawing, pen and ink, with sepia wash. 11⅜ x 15⅝ in. Binyon, *Drawings by British Artists . . . in the British Museum*, 3.174. By permission of the Trustees of the British Museum.

this drawing accords remarkably with the description in Pope's letter to Edward Blount of 1725. The temple stands apparently at the near end of a corridor of trees, the stone archway, or tunnel entrance, perspectived (not quite successfully) at a distance in the center, showing a boat in the Thames beyond: "under the Temple you look down thro' a sloping Arcade of Trees, and see the Sails on the River passing suddenly and vanishing, as thro' a Perspective Glass."

The drawing was exhibited at the National Portrait Gallery Exhibition of 1961.

1. *Correspondence* 2.18.

2. *Correspondence* 2.125, 142. Cf. Frederick Bracher, "Pope's Grotto: the Maze of Fancy," *The Huntington Library Quarterly, 12* (February 1949), 141–62. Bracher p. 153 and Robert Halsband, *Lady Mary Wortley Montagu* (Oxford, 1956), p. 109, quote Lady Mary writing in the spring of 1722 to the Countess of Mar: "Mr. Pope . . . continues to embellish his house at Twickenham. He has made a subterranean grotto, which he has furnished with looking glass, and they tell me it has a very good effect" (*Letters and Works,* ed. W. Moy Thomas [1861], *1.*461). *Restoration and Eighteenth-Century Literature, Essays in Honor of Alan Dugald McKillop,* ed. Carroll Camden (Chicago, 1963), contains essays on Pope's grotto by Maynard Mack and Benjamin Boyce.

3. *Correspondence* 2.296–97.

4. *Correspondence* 3.512.

5. *Correspondence* 4.22.

6. *Correspondence* 4.6.

7. *Correspondence* 4.245 and thereabouts *passim.*

8. *Correspondence* 4.260–63.

9. *Correspondence* 4.340, 343, 351–52.

10. *Correspondence* 4.353–54.

11. *Correspondence* 4.267. Cf. 278, 281–82.

12. Bracher, pp. 148–51, quotes a further contemporary source, a rhapsodic correspondent to *The Newcastle General Magazine,* January 1748, p. 26.

13. Whitley Papers, Department of Prints and Drawings, British Museum. Lugt, *Répertoire des Vents,* does not report a sale for Mrs. Short.

14. See two of Kent's sketches of Chiswick garden reproduced in James Lees-Milne, *Earls of Creation, Five Great Patrons of Eighteenth-Century Art* (London, 1962), facing p. 128.

15 AND 16. DRAWINGS OF POPE IN HIS GROTTO. BY WILLIAM KENT? SEE ALSO NO. EX. 6 (SELF-PORTRAIT) AND NO. 65 (POPE AT CARDS), BY THE COUNTESS OF BURLINGTON. DEVONSHIRE COLLECTION, CHATSWORTH, BAKEWELL, DERBYSHIRE.

At Chatsworth, in the collections inherited by the Dukes of Devonshire through Lord Burlington's daughter Lady Charlotte Boyle, are two large albums of drawings, thought to have been put together by the bibliophile Sixth Duke of Devonshire, who succeeded to the dukedom in 1811. One of these albums, 22⅝ x 17½ inches, consisting of heavy wove-paper blank leaves in marbled board covers with a leather spine, is marked *Lord and Lady Burlington Drawings* ("Drawings XXIV" on the spine, and "Drawings 26" inside the front cover). More than eighty drawings, in pencil, pen and ink, and wash (with a few in crayons) are mounted in the album. These include a good many grotesque medleys of *Dunciad*-like subjects—monkeys, dogs, owls, other birds, bats, and toads, mingled with human figures, and sometimes in multiple perspectives on a single sheet.[1] There are several portraits of a buxom lady with a squarish freckled face, wearing a small flat, ruffled cap on the top of her head (and resembling very closely the portrait of Lady Burlington by Aikman at Chiswick House).[2] In one of these, she sits at an easel, drawing a picture of two youthful female heads.[3] In another, the figure of the lady, bust length, rises from behind a hill and is fantastically juxtaposed to a monkey and an owl in a tree—and apparently she is reaching toward the monkey.[4] In another, the lady's head and shoulders appear as from beside a table, on which a cat is killing a bird and several chicks are walking; an insect is flying above.[5] Another curious fancy, in pen and ink and wash, shows a lady in a garden wringing her hands, as an assemblage of fowls are pulling strings and hanging a dog over a branch of a tree. An owl in the top branch holds a book. Another dog crawls on the ground. In the background is a Palladian colonnade.[6]

The second volume, composed of similar paper and boards (watermark "1802" on p. 15), 24 x 18¾ inches, and marked *Chiswick & Chatsworth Miscellaneous Drawings* ("Drawings XXV" on spine, and "Drawings 26A" inside the front cover), contains most conspicuously a number of architectural and landscape drawings clearly by Kent. But other kinds of pictures appear also. Two elaborate allegorical drawings, for instance— one fairy-tale grotesque and one London satire—are much more complicated and ugly than the pictures of the other volume.[7] Another picture is a large and careful drawing of an owl holding in its bill a kind of hornbook.[8] Another portrait of Lady Burlington shows her petting a large owl which sits on the branch of a tree with a mouse hanging from its talons. Two small owls appear above, one sitting on a twig, one hovering.[9] See no. Ex. 6.

It seems possible, even likely, that in addition to the architectural and landscape drawings in the second volume, some of the drawings in each volume are by William Kent. Thus in *Lord and Lady Burlington Drawings*, p. 22, no. 59, ink and red crayon, is a dog snapping at a bull, while a man in a cap and jacket, with a sheath knife at his waist, throws up his hands. This, in subject matter at least, might be related to Kent's work for Gay's *Fables*.[10] But at the same time, associations with Kent's pupil Lady Burlington herself are numerous in both volumes.[11] Thus in *Lord and Lady Burlington Drawings*, on p. 24, no. 69 is a pencil sketch of an elderly woman in a nightcap, with coverlet up to her chin, lying apparently dead. Just above it, no. 70 is a scrap of paper with four lines in ink in Pope's hand: "Alas! what room for flattry, or for Pride! / She's dead!—but thus She lookd the hour she dy'd. / Peace, blubbring Bishop! peace thou flattring [lying] Dean! / This single crayon, Madam, Saints the Queen."[12] The reiterated appearance of Lady Burlington herself, especially in contexts of grotesque humor, suggests rather the self-portrait than the work of her retainer Kent. The style of the drawings in these volumes which I am inclined to attribute to Lady Burlington seems more crude yet more lively, certainly more grotesque and derisive, than the soft and professionally graceful washes of Kent. The hanging of the pet dog by the birds, and the other animal, bird, and lady pictures seem the work of a feminine, if somewhat macabre and cruel imagination. If the emphasis which I have placed on Lady Burlington's share in these volumes does only a little to frame one of the first two drawings I am about to mention, it has seemed to me nevertheless desirable, in order to explain fully the claim of a third drawing (no. 65) to be the work of this lady.

No. 39, on page 18 of volume XXIV–26, and no. 51, on page 20, are pen-and-ink and wash drawings of Pope in his grotto. The free style of these wash drawings does suggest Kent the professional designer rather than the lady his pupil. The winged creatures intrusive in the upper corner of the larger drawing (39), however, are very

15. Pen and ink and wash on paper. 8⅝ x 7⅜ in. Devonshire Collection, Chatsworth. Reproduced by Permission of the Trustees of the Chatsworth Settlement.

16. Pen and ink and wash on paper. 3½ x 5 in. picture, on 4¾ x 6½ in. paper. Devonshire Collection, Chatsworth. Reproduced by Permission of the Trustees of the Chatsworth Settlement.

close in pattern to similar figures in the grotesque backgrounds of some of the Lady Burlington self-portraits. The lepidopteron flying in the center of the group, for instance, is very close to the insect flying above a table in a drawing described above. And the small bird-like flying creature is similar, in reverse, to one of the two small owls in another drawing described above (and reproduced, no. Ex. 6). These figures do not have quite the appearance of doodles introduced at the edge of the picture by a hand other than the original.

No. 51 (reproduced above, no. 16) and a photograph of no. 39 (no. 15 above) were exhibited at the National Portrait Gallery Exhibition of 1961, and no. 51 was reproduced in the *TLS* for 7 April 1961, page 224. No. 39 is reproduced in James Lees-Milne, *Earls of Creation* (London, 1962), facing page 145.

In the second Chatsworth volume, XXV–26A, drawing no. 69, on page 34, is a pen-and-ink caricature of Alexander Pope, seated and playing cards—surely by Lady Burlington. This, because of the apparent age of the subject, I place at a later point in this book.[13]

1. For example, nos. 14, 16, 19, on p. 6; no. 28, on p. 12; no. 42, on p. 18; no. 66, on p. 24.

2. National Portrait Gallery photograph (1944); *Walpole Society* 16.23.

3. P. 8, no. 20. Nearby, she appears seated with one of the young ladies (her daughters, no doubt) on each hand.

4. P. 20, no. 49.

5. P. 26, no. 79.

6. P. 27.

7. P. 25, no. 44, and p. 32, no. 62.

8. P. 33, no. 64.

9. P. 33, no. 65.

10. See p. 111.

11. And in a number of separate papers in the Devonshire Collection. No. 143.76, for example, consists of two epigrams against Walpole in Lady Burlington's hand.

12. See *Twickenham* 6.390: "On a Picture of Queen *Caroline*, drawn by Lady *Burlington*." Cf. Joseph Warton, *Works of Pope* (London, 1797), 4.335-36: "The two following unpublished lines of our Author, have been communicated to me by a learned friend, on a picture of this Queen [Caroline], drawn by Lady Burlington: 'Peace! flattering Bishop, lying Dean! *This* Portrait only saints the Queen!'"

13. See no. 65. I am grateful to His Grace the Duke of Devonshire for the opportunity of seeing and using these materials. Professor John Butt, who examined the volumes in 1945 and who first brought them to my attention, left a number of helpful annotations. Professor George Sherburn, who also examined the volumes a number of years ago, took photographs which he lent me at the start of my studies. Mr. Thomas S. Wragg, Keeper of the Devonshire Collections at Chatsworth, has repeatedly been most helpful.

17. LINE ENGRAVING, BY P. FOURDRINIER, AFTER WILLIAM KENT, 1725. TAILPIECE TO POPE'S *An Essay on Man*, LONDON, 1734, P. [VII]. *See* page 127, note 3.

An Essay on Man, Being the First Book of Ethic Epistles. To Henry St. John, L. Boling-broke . . . London: Printed by John Wright, for Lawton Gilliver, MDCCXXXIV, quarto, is Griffith nos. 336, 337, 338, advertised in the *Grub-Street Journal* on 2 May. Griffith nos. 339 and 340 are folio printings, known to Griffith only through Gilliver's advertisement, but presumably they too have the tailpiece portrait at p. [vii],[1] P. Fourdrinier was employed to do six special head- and tail-pieces after Kent for this edition. The oval vignette of Pope appears again on p. 19 of *The First Satire of the Second Book of Horace*, 1734 (Griffith 341, Texas). Retouched and with its edges trimmed, the same plate appears yet again as title-page vignette to *The Works Of Mr. Alexander Pope.—Volume II.—. . . London: Printed by J. Wright, for Lawton Gilliver at Homer's Head in Fleetstreet, M DCC XXXV*, small folio, large folio, and quarto, published in April 1735 (Griffith nos. 370, 371, 372).[2] Retouched again and further trimmed, with loss of all but a part of the first two letters of P. Fourdrinier's signature, the same plate appears as title-page vignette of *The Works of Alexander Pope, Esq; Vol. II* . . . London: Printed for L. Gilliver, 1735, small octavo, published 31 July or earlier (Griffith no. 388).

The characteristically Kentian figures of the two putti, one holding a lyre, one having dropped the palette and brushes, meet above Pope's head in an embrace symbolic of a spontaneous affection between the arts. The motto inscribed about the medallion is "UNI AEQUUS VIRTUTI ATQUE EJUS AMICIS," from Horace, *Satire* 2.i.70. This line was inserted by Pope in the 1739 edition of his *Works* (Griffith 505) as a concluding motto to the Advertisement of his Horatian Imitations repeated from the 1735 editions of the *Works.* Cf. no. 59.

Peter Fourdrinier had been a pupil of Picart at Amsterdam. He came to England in 1720 and was known especially for architectural engraving. He did the plates of Lord Burlington's folio *Fabbriche antiche disegnati da Andrea Palladio, 1730.*[3]

1. Later (vol. 2, pp. 281, 592) Griffith had apparently seen a copy of no. 340, but he does not say where and does not confirm the presence of the tailpiece.

2. The large folio is known to Griffith from no. 63 in the Grolier Exhibition catalogue of 1911. Griffith reports numerous elaborate tailpieces by Fourdrinier after Kent in the quarto, a smaller number in the small folio (p. 286). This title page, "Vol. II" (with the vignette and date "M DCC XXXV") reappears in quarto sets of Pope's works made up as late as 1738, and serves in such sets also with "Volume II" changed by pen-and-ink to "Volume III" (Griffith 514, and

17. Line engraving. Oval: 3⅛ x 2½ in. Plate mark: 3⁹⁄₁₆ x 3¼ in. "VNI ÆQVVS VIRTVTI ATQ. EIVS AMICIS / W. Kent. / inv. / P Fourdrinier SC". Tailpiece to *An Essay on Man*, London, 1734, quarto, p. [vii]: Griffith 336. University of Texas Rare Book Collections.

515, and Vinton A. Dearing, "The Prince of Wales's Set of Pope's Works," *Harvard Library Bulletin, 4* [Autumn 1950], 323).

3. I learn very late that the same engraving, with-

out the motto, appears as early as June 1726, a tail-piece to Book XXIV of Pope's quarto *Odyssey*. See p. 111.

18 a,b,c. OIL PAINTING, BY WILLIAM KENT. CHISWICK HOUSE.

It was apparently between 1725 and 1729 that Lord Burlington, having pulled down a part of old Chiswick House, put up his translation of Palladio's Villa Rotonda into a somewhat differently shaped English pleasure house, octagonal and chimneyed, a casino for his receptions and a gallery for his pictures and statuary.[1] But as late as 1738 some of the work on the interior was still being tidied up. ("Polly *con grand labori di spalli* has done ye stucco Pavement and has *datto una semplici vernice* to some of ye pictures I desird he would let the rest alone.")[2]

A portrait of Pope by Kent at Chiswick House is mentioned in Robert Dodsley's *London and Its Environs Described* (1761), 2.116, and again in *The English Connoisseur, 1*, London, 1766. The latter account (pp. 33–38) places in the Blue Velvet Room [southeast corner] two pictures: "Lord Sandwich in a round, Sir *Peter Lely*," and "Inigo Jones in a round, Dobson;" and in the Bed Chamber [northeast corner] three pictures: "Earl of Cumberland in a round," "Mr. Pope in a round, *Kent*," and "Lady Burlington in a round, Aikman." (No doubt it was the proximity of Pope to Lady Burlington by William Aikman which had led Walpole in his *Visits to Country Seats* in 1760 to attribute the Pope to Aikman.[3]) Daniel Lysons' *Environs of London*, 1795, was published (or written) at a time when the Fifth Duke of Devonshire had just employed James Wyatt to add two wings (1788) to the south and north sides of the villa, so that the Burlington pictures were temporarily removed; Lysons appeals to Dodsley's *London and Its Environs* for a list of pictures, including Pope by Kent.[4] *The Beauties of England and Wales*, 1816, records the painting, still in company with Lady Burlington, and two others unnamed, all in circular frames, over the doors and chimney, in "a small apartment contiguous to the east saloon."[5] This is difficult to interpret. In September 1806 Charles James Fox had died at Chiswick House—in the Bed Chamber [northeast corner], giving his name to it for one or two generations. In May 1865 George Scharf visited Chiswick House and noted Pope "Over the door in Fox room . . . Dark eyes and eye brows, dark brown [and] red [background], dark brown white [shirt] life size, weakly painted, amateur-like by Kent. Shadows of face grey."[6] The portrait is poorly reproduced, without attribution, by Elizabeth Balch in "Glimpses of Old English Homes," *The English Illustrated Magazine*, no. 62 (November 1888), p. 103, and again in her *Glimpses of Old English Houses* (London, 1890), p. 137, and in John R. Green, *A Short History of the English People, Illustrated Edition* (New York, 1895), 4.1596.

In recent decades the villa has been taken over by the Ministry of Works, the wings added by Wyatt have been demolished (1952), and original features of the whole have been extensively restored. The *sopraporta* portrait of Pope now appears, adjacent to that of Inigo Jones, in the Blue Velvet (southeast corner) Room.[7] Apparently in the

18 a. Oil on canvas. 18 in. diameter. Cap light red, coat darker red, with brownish fur collar. Lips red; shadows on cheekbone pinkish; eyes gray. Background brown; shirt white. Chiswick House: The Ministry of Works. Photograph in the Witt Library, Courtauld Institute of Art.

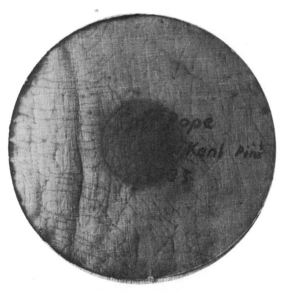

18 b. Back of oil painting of Pope at Chiswick House. "Mr Pope / W Kent Pinxt / 1735". Witt Library, Courtauld Institute of Art.

18 c. Pope and Inigo Jones in the Blue Velvet Room, Chiswick House. Ministry of Works. Crown Copyright Reserved.

course of the restorations, the picture was removed from its place and was photographed, front and back, prints of both photographs finding their way to the Courtauld Institute.[8] On the back of the picture is painted in bold dark letters: "Mr Pope / W Kent Pinx^t / 1735." This portrait has the same red coat and fur collar which appear in several Richardson portraits of Pope. The length of the face and aquiline nose are fairly close to Kent's other effort at a portrayal of Pope's face, the engraved vignette of 1726 (no. 17).

1. John Charlton, *A History and Description of Chiswick House and Gardens* (London: Her Majesty's Stationery Office, 1958), p. 9; R. Wittkower, "Lord Burlington and William Kent," *Archaeological Journal*, *102* (1945), 155, 163n.28. "In 1727 plans, elevations and a section through the cupola room were included in Kent's *Designs of Inigo Jones*."

2. Kent to Burlington, 10 November 1738, quoted in Jourdain, *Kent*, p. 87, and H. Avray Tipping, *Architectural Review*, *63* (May 1938), 182. I have arbitrated as well as I could between two divergent transcriptions of Kent's Italian.

3. Horace Walpole, *Journals of Visits to Country Seats, The Sixteenth Volume of the Walpole Society 1927–1928* (Oxford, 1928), p. 23. A person signing himself W. Aikman, most likely the painter, wrote from Suffolk Street, London, apparently in 1725, to thank Pope for a gift, no doubt the first three volumes of

his *Odyssey* (*Correspondence* 2.294).

4. Daniel Lysons, *The Environs of London*, 2 (London, 1795), 195. The appeal to Dodsley is repeated in the second edition of Lysons' *Environs*, 2.i, *Middlesex* (1811), 125.

5. J. Norris Brewer, *The Beauties of England and Wales*, *10.iv, Middlesex* (1816), 319.

6. National Portrait Gallery, Scharf *Sketch Book* 72.25, 22 May, 1865. Names of colors are indicated in part by initials, which I have expanded. Brackets indicate areas in Scharf's pencil sketch.

7. See John Charlton, *A History and Description of Chiswick House and Gardens* (London, Her Majesty's Stationery Office, 1958), pp. 22, 25. "Lady Burlington (by Aikman)" is still in the Bed Chamber or northeast corner room (the Fox Room).

8. From Ministry of Works negatives made 17 August 1951.

19 a,b,c. STONE GARDEN BUST, POSSIBLY BY MICHAEL RYSBRACK. STOWE SCHOOL, BUCKINGHAMSHIRE.

The vastly rolling and blurred landscape, with its surviving lakes, bridges, arches, and temples, which the schoolboys of Stowe today inherit, went through several stages in a development from formality, through "irregularity," to landscape, during the lifetime of Pope's friend Richard Temple, Viscount Cobham. Charles Bridgeman was the gardener who with his sunken fence or ha-ha opened the gardens to the countryside; at the same time he softened their internal symmetry. Cobham's first architect of garden buildings was his fellow Kit-Cat Whig Sir John Vanbrugh, who died in 1726 and was succeeded by James Gibbs. Among other buildings on the western fringe of the gardens which Gibbs designed was a small domed temple enclosed by a semicircle of busts.[1] It is this temple which is described by Cobham's nephew Gilbert West in his anonymous poem *Stowe, The Gardens Of the Right Honourable Richard Lord Viscount Cobham. Address'd to Mr. Pope*, published at London by Pope's publisher Lawton Gilliver in 1732:[2]

> Where yon high Firs display their darksome Green,
> And mournful Yews compose a solemn Scene,
> Around thy Building, *Gibbs,* a sacred Band
> Of Princes, Patriots, Bards, and Sages stand:
> Men, who by merit purchas'd lasting Praise,

Worthy each *British* Poet's noblest Lays:
Or bold in Arms for Liberty they stood,
And greatly perish'd for their Country's Good:
Or nobly warm'd with more than mortal Fire,
Equal'd to *Rome* and *Greece* the *British* Lyre:
Or Human Life by useful Arts refin'd,
Acknowledg'd Benefactors of Mankind.[3]

George Vertue, who copies these lines in his *Note Book* in 1734, breaks off the quotation to recite in brief the names celebrated through the next four pages of West's poem: "Q. Elis. Ld. Verulam. Shakespear. K. Wm. 3. Lock Newton Milton." And Vertue adds: "these busts made by Mr. Rysbrake."[4] Apparently about 1730, yet another architect and gardener, William Kent, had been recruited by Lord Cobham to supplement the labors of both Bridgeman and Gibbs. During the next ten or fifteen years Kent not only transformed the whole of the gardens more thoroughly into a softened landscape, but he went to work with a special will in two undeveloped areas to the east, the Grecian Valley and the Elysian Fields. Lord Cobham, we are told, resolved to make the Elysian Fields a visible counterpart to a moral essay or satire by Pope. The Boy Patriots, Cobham's circle of opposition Whigs, with whom Pope began to be acquainted during the summer of 1735 at Stowe, and whose bustos were soon enshrined at Stowe in the Temple of Friendship,[5] enjoyed a sophisticated game of landscape gardening. They had good fun fitting a social and moral meaning to a new kind of landscape whose very freedom from arbitrary rules reflected their own Shaftesburyan ideals.[6] A new circular colonnaded temple by Kent, designed from the Roman Temple of Vesta at Tivoli, was erected in the Elysian Fields and dedicated to Ancient Virtue. Nearby was Modern Virtue—a ruin. Just across the water, in conspicuous confrontation, rose a third temple, a shallow curved frame or screen with niches for a series of busts—the Temple of British Worthies.[7] On the right or south wing were enshrined (where they may still be seen) eight stone busts, from end to center: Sir John Barnard, Hampden, Drake, Raleigh, William III, Elizabeth, Edward Prince of Wales, Alfred. An oval niche in a central pyramid once contained a head of Mercury. Beneath this remain today the words: *Campos Ducit ad Elysios*. And in a square of black marble these lines from the Sixth Book of Virgil's *Aeneid*:

Hic manus ob patriam pugnando vulnera passi,
Quique pii vates, & Phoebo digna locuti,
Inventas aut qui vitam excoluere per artes,
Quique sui memores alios fecere merendo.

On the left or north wing may still be seen, from center to end: Bacon, Newton, Locke, Shakespeare, Milton, Inigo Jones, Sir Thomas Gresham, and Alexander Pope. (Pope, like Barnard at the opposite end, is around a corner and will not be seen in a frontal view of the Temple.[8]) These sixteen busts include the eight subjects recorded by West. It would seem that these identical busts and their inscriptions were transferred from

19 a. White limestone. 23 in. high; 20 in. below shoulders; 9¼ in. chin to crown; 6¼ in. at ears. Temple of Worthies, Stowe School, Buckinghamshire.

below, left

19 b. Corner of Temple of Worthies, showing Gresham and Pope.

below, right

19 c. Detail of bust of Pope, Temple of Worthies.

Gibbs' original Temple.[9] Early guidebooks record that Pope and Barnard, the two centemporaries at either end, are alone in being without any inscription.[10] The lengthy inscriptions for these two were added in the 1760s.[11]

We have seen that Vertue attributed to Rysbrack seven of the busts at Gibbs' temple mentioned by West—and the omission of the eighth, Hampden, may have been only an accident. Mrs. Webb, in her book on Rysbrack, observes that the Newton is not only documented [by Vertue] but is similar to the signed terra cotta of Newton by Rysbrack at Trinity College, Cambridge. The Milton, too, is similar to a known Rysbrack—apparently the documented marble of Milton as an older man at Stourhead.[12] Hampden, too, she thinks probably by Rysbrack. Of the eight busts added to Kent's Temple of Worthies she notes that Inigo Jones resembles the marble bust by Rysbrack that comes by descent from the Third Earl of Burlington, at Chatsworth.[13] Six others (Alfred, Barnard, Drake, the Black Prince, Gresham, Raleigh) she believes to be probably by Rysbrack.[14] All the busts of more antique subjects may indeed be said to resemble in style the sort of pastiche historical bust which Rysbrack was successful in creating after the model of George Vertue's antiquarian and patriotic series of engravings for the second edition (1732) of Tindal's English translation of Rapin de Thoyras's *History of England*.[15] Other figures—contemporary or but recently deceased—Locke and Newton are executed in a more severe classical or quasi-classical style—with shorter hair and toga-like garment over an open shirt.

It is true that Pope, who is the only one of the sixteen busts excluded by Mrs. Webb from her Rysbrack catalogue,[16] is somewhat more simply treated than either Locke or Newton.[17] And he does not look at all like the unsuccessful or "damned" head of Pope signed by Rysbrack in 1730. That fact, however, might be urged either for or against the probability of his having made the Stowe bust. As the Temple may have been completed (whenever it was completed) before some or any of the new busts were ready, perhaps all that can be said is that Pope was there when the earliest Stowe guide, the *Description* of 1744 was prepared.[18]

Photographs of the Pope bust taken in 1951 show that it had at some time before that lost the tip of the nose, with the result that the aspect of the whole face was spoiled. In May 1961 I took the liberty of restoring the nose temporarily in white clay and of putting a background of black paper inside the niche. The photographs above (nos. 19 a and b) are I believe the first of this bust ever published. The Temple of Worthies has been described at some length by F. Saxl and R. Wittkower, *British Art and the Mediterranean* (Oxford, 1948), p. 68.

1. See Laurence Whistler, "Stowe in the Making, Some Original Drawings," *Country Life, 122* (11 July, 1957), 68–71. Whistler draws upon "a set of Lysons' *Buckinghamshire* magnificently grangerized in eight elephant folios," formerly in the library at Stowe and at the time of the writing in the possession of the Hon. R. W. Morgan-Grenville. See also Laurence Whistler, *Stowe A Guide to the Gardens 1956* (London: Country Life, 1956), pp. 5–6; and Christopher Hussey, "Stowe, Buckinghamshire—I—II—III," *Country Life, 102* (12, 19, 26 September 1947), 526–29, 578–81, 626–29.

Charles Bridgeman died in 1738. In 1739 his widow Sarah Bridgeman published *A General Plan of the Woods, Park and Gardens of Stowe*—a volume 21¼ x 26¼ in. in size and consisting of a large folding Plan

(35 x 23 in.), 3 large folding plates and 12 smaller plates (Newberry Library, Chicago). Vertue (3.69; 6.194) under the years 1733 and 1736 describes the making of the plates by Jean Rigaud during a stay of twelve or eighteen months in England. All sixteen of the plates are lettered "Publish'd by S. Bridgeman May 12, 1739. // Rigaud & Baron del. & Sculp." Plate 7 in the second series, "View from Gibbs's Building," shows at the lower right three busts on pedestals placed at intervals about a domed temple. This corner of plate 7 is reproduced by Whistler, *Country Life*, *122* (11 July 1957), 70, Fig. 8.

2. Sometimes wrongly ascribed to George Bickham the younger, engraver of *Sixteen Perspective Views . . . at Stow . . . Correctly Drawn on the Spot 1752 . . . By Mons Chatelain*, London, n.d.

3. *Stowe, The Gardens . . . Address'd to Mr. Pope. Devenere locos laetos, & amoena Vireta. Fortunatorum nemorum, sedesque beatas. Virg.* (London: Printed by J. Wright, for Lawton Gilliver at Homer's Head against St. Dunstan's Church in Fleetstreet, 1732), p. 8. The poem, still anonymous, was joined even more closely with Pope's name in the same year: *Stowe, The Gardens . . . To which is added, Taste. A Poem. By Mr. Pope. London: Printed. And, Dublin, Reprinted by George Faulkner in Essex-Street, opposite to the Bridge, 1732* (Griffith no. 279).

4. Vertue 3.70–71. West names an eighth figure, Hampden. In July 1732 Vertue had visited Stowe and apparently about the same time entered in his *Note Book* (5.103): "a Poem. calld Stowe. by Mr. West a nephew of Ld Cobhams." A list of buildings "in the Gardens" includes both a "Temple of the Worthies" and "1 pavillion Gibbs."

5. "the following ten Bustoes of my Lord and his illustrious Friends, viz. the Prince of *Wales*—Earls of *Westmoreland, Chesterfield,* and *Marchmont*—Lords *Cobham, Gower,* and *Bathurst*—*Richard Greenville, William Pitt,* and *George Lyttleton*, Esqrs." (*A Description of the Gardens of Lord Viscount Cobham, At Stow in Buckinghamshire*, Northampton, 1744, p. 26).

6. The expansive gardener of the mid-century, Lancelot (Capability) Brown, entered service at Stowe in 1740 and remained until 1751. Either he or his disciple Woodward are thought responsible for the greater opening up of the vista, the unrolling of belts of woodland, which accompanied the final enhancement of the great house by Lord Cobham's nephew and successor Earl Temple, with the help of Robert Adam and the King of Sardinia's architect Giovanni Battista Borra (Whistler, *Stowe*, p. 7, and "Signor Borra at Stowe," *Country Life*, 111 [19 August 1957], 390–93; and Hussey, *Country Life*, *102* [26 September 1947], 626–629). During the 1750s the landscaping became social and political on a grander scale, heroic more than Arcadian, as Lord Cobham's other nephew William Pitt provided the victories of the Seven Years' War.

7. A "Temple of the Worthies" was seen by Vertue at Stowe in 1732 (5.103, note above). Whistler, *Country Life*, *122*, 69 and Fig. 6, referring to a recent discovery of drawings in a cupboard at Stowe, reproduces a design for the Temple of British Worthies which he attributes plausibly to Kent and which he dates about 1735. In Sarah Bridgeman's *Plan* of 1739 Kent's name appears only in the legend "Kent's Bastion and Building" [The Temple of Venus]; the shape of the Temple of Worthies may be distinctly made out in the "Elysian Fields," but it is designated "The Monument." Early guidebooks (e.g., *A Description*, Northampton, 1744, p. 17, and *Stowe*, London, 1762, p. 25) do not name the architect of the Temple, but later ones give Kent (e.g., *Stowe*, London, 1769, p. 24).

8. See Jourdain, *Kent*, p. 169, Figs. 128 and 129. Pope is just out of sight to the left of Gresham. On the back of the Temple is an inscription "To the Memory of Signor Fido, an Italian of good Extraction"—a greyhound.

9. Whistler points out that a couplet on Milton in West's poem is a rhymed version of the inscription which stands today above the poet's head (*Country Life*, *122*.70). It may be added that the lines from Virgil which appear on the central tablet of black marble are expanded in the passage by West quoted above, and that West quotes the Latin in a footnote—"an inscription on the Building."

10. *A Description of the Gardens of Lord Viscount Cobham, at Stow in Buckinghamshire* (Northampton, Printed by W. Dicey; and sold by B. Seeley . . . M.D.CC.XLIV), pp. 17–22; *The New Oxford Guide . . . to which is added, A Tour to Blenheim, Ditchley, and Stow, By a Gentleman of Oxford* (Oxford, 1759), p. 112. Vertue 3.133 quotes without comment a list of the busts (minus Milton) from a "Description of Ld Cobham's Gardens at Stow, 1745. . . . a small book printed & sold at Buckingham."

11. Absent in *Stowe: A Description . . .* (London, 1762), pp. 26, 28; present in *Stowe: A Description . . .* (London, 1769), pp. 24, 27.

12. I believe, too, that the Locke is somewhat like the Locke, documented as by Rysbrack, 1733, at Kensington Palace. Mrs. Webb points out (p. 154) that the face of the Kensington Locke differs considerably from the statue of Locke which Rysbrack was to make some twenty years later for Christ Church, Oxford (pp. 46, 166, 169–70).

13. I believe it resembles also the statue, documented 1733, by Rysbrack, at Chiswick House.

14. See especially p. 136 and the entries of the names in the alphabetical catalogue.

15. Webb, *Rysbrack*, p. 90.

16. Pp. 136, 233. Peter Scheemakers, who has a very tenuous connection with the annals of Stowe (p. 136), may perhaps be conjectured to have helped Rysbrack with the busts for the Temple of Worthies. In *Stowe A Description* (Calkins and Budd, Pall Mall, 1838), p. 19, we read, for the first time I believe, that the

busts in the Temple of British Worthies are "by Rysbrack and Scheemakers." This is repeated in Henry Rumsey Forster, *The Stowe Catalogue* (London, 1848), p. xxvii. See Appendix 2.12 for some allusions to a bust of Pope by Scheemakers.

17. The eyes of all sixteen busts in the Temple, except Locke, are uncarved. Like most of the other busts in the group, Pope is hollowed behind, with a central prop. The stone of all the busts is a white limestone, the Temple itself of a yellower limestone.

18. "*A Description of the Gardens of Lord Cobham, at Stow, in Buckinghamshire* (Northampton, Printed by W. Dicey, and sold by B. Seeley . . . M.D.CC.-XLIV)," pp. 17–22.

Alexander Pope. Attributed to Jonathan Richardson, c. 1738. National Portrait Gallery no. 1179.
See no. 54.

· 8 ·

1733-1742
JONATHAN RICHARDSON
(1665-1745)

I

IF OUR PREVIOUS ARGUMENT (see no. 8.1) is correct, the earliest date for a portrayal of Pope by Richardson is provided by Richardson's inscription on the back of a pencil-on-vellum drawing—a youthful face done in 1735 from a painting by Richardson himself, done about 1718. The thirty-three drawings of Pope by Richardson which remain to be presented give us no date earlier than 1733. Beyond question, some, even many, drawings of Pope by Richardson either have perished or at the moment are lying hidden. Nevertheless, the gap between the years 1718 and 1733 seems broadly representative of Pope's actual relations with Richardson as an artist. It fits well enough with Pope's cultivation of Kneller and his sitting to Dahl and Rysbrack during this period, and it fits the fact that Richardson's most intense devotion to portrait-*drawing* does not seem to have begun until about 1728, though it continued unabated until not long before his death.[1]

By about the year 1722, however, Pope at Twickenham and Richardson and his literary son Jonathan the younger, at their house in Ormond Street, Queen's Square, Bloomsbury, were on well-established terms of friendship. From a period of more than

1. See pp. 148, 154 for an account of the main collections of Richardson drawings known today. The dates inscribed on these drawings are distributed rather evenly from about 1728 to 1741. See especially the British Museum and Courtauld Institute catalogues cited on p. 148, notes 1 and 5.

twenty years running to the early spring of 1744, not long before Pope's death, some fifty-four notes and short letters written by Pope to Richardson survive in whole or in part. On the other side, a single letter, written by Richardson the younger, containing a note on Milton, survives, not because it was saved by Pope, but because it was returned by him for the author's convenience.[2] Pope's letters to Richardson are our main source of information about Richardson's later career, nearly all that rescues his personality and domestic life from oblivion.

The editor of Pope's *Correspondence* dates the beginnings with some uncertainty. But we are on firm ground if we quote a note which is clearly Pope's thanks for a copy of the Richardsons' *Account of Some of the Statues, Bas-reliefs, Drawings and Pictures in Italy, &c.*, published in 1722. Richardson Senior's Preface gave lavish credit both to his son's competence and to his filial piety.[3] Pope's note, dated 4 November, rejoices in the same harmony: "it is worthy Mr. Richardson and his son,—worthy two such lovers of one another, and two such lovers of the fine arts."[4] Another episode in the friendship which may be dated about the same year was Richardson's introduction of his neighbor in Queen's Square the celebrated surgeon William Cheselden, who thereafter reappears with great frequency in Pope's notes to Richardson and was to be one of Pope's main reliances near the end of his life. Pope's immediate concern was literary: "that you will tell your friend Mr. Cheselden I shall be obliged to him if he will put upon paper those conjectures of some passages of Shakespeare which he mentioned to Dr Arbuthnot."[5]

A few years later, in January of 1724/5 (or possibly 1725/6), Richardson lost his wife. "I had written you a letter by my waterman," wrote Pope, "before I received that melancholy one from your son, to which there can be no answer in words, but I assure you my heart is sorrowful for you."[6] A temporary move from Queen's Square to a house in Lincoln's Inn Fields in the spring of 1725 was perhaps an effort by Richardson to escape memories. Pope wrote on 10 June complaining that his friend had forgotten to give his new address—he directed the letter to Richardson "at the Golden ball in Holborne Row, Lincoln's Inn Fields."[7] In the Richard Bull album of English Portrait

---

2. *Correspondence* 3.331. Three of Pope's letters to Richardson are known only in summary and brief quotation in Thomas Thorpe's autograph catalogue of 1833 (*Correspondence* 3.457; *4*.81, 489). It seems likely that Pope attached small literary value to Richardson's notes and did not save them. Why none has survived by accident through Pope's paper-saving habits seems more puzzling. Pope's letters to Richardson contain frequent allusions to and echoes of the other side of the correspondence. See, for example, *Correspondence* 2.61, 106, 297; *3*.350, 353; *4*.78, 484.

3. "what he Principally intended in making, and noting down his Observations was to gratify Me. . . . He has from his Infancy accustom'd me to such an intire Resignation of Himself to Me; and that in so Obliging a manner, that I can never tell what his Real Sentiments Are, but by what I think they Should be" (*An Account*, pp. A2ᵛ–A4, Preface).

4. *Correspondence* 2.140–41.

5. 6 February [1721/22?] (*Correspondence* 2.100). Another note tells us that Pope invites Cheselden to join a party at Richardson's—one of those roundtables, guesses Professor Sherburn, with the help of which Pope was accomplishing his collation of Shakespeare (*Correspondence* 2.106). Pope's six-volume Shakespeare, begun in 1721, was published in March 1725. See Richardson's portrait of Cheselden reproduced by C. J. S. Thompson, "Historical Portraits at the Royal College of Surgeons of England," *The Connoisseur, 81* (June 1928), 82.

6. 20 January (*Correspondence* 2.284). John Nichols, *Literary Anecdotes of the Eighteenth Century, 4* (1812), 615 n., tells us that Mrs. Richardson "died in 1725 on her birthday, aged 51, after having been married 33 years."

7. *Correspondence* 2.297–98. Pope's letters to Rich-

Drawings at the Pierpont Morgan Library is a delicate pencil-on-vellum drawing by Richardson of two intimately joined profiles—a lady of youngish middle age, wearing a wimple drawn back to show her forehead and hair, and, looking out from close behind her, himself. "My Father," and "Mrs Knapp," the younger Richardson has written on the back. And another hand, Richard Bull's, I think, has added: "I believe his 2^d Wife."[8] Richardson made several other careful drawings of the attractive Mrs. Catherine Knapp.[9] He seems to have had no second wife,[10] but nothing that we know of his romantic, even sentimental, though orderly and cautious character, forbids our picturing the solace of a close friendship during his later years.

For about five years after 1725, the record of Pope's relation with the Richardsons is lost. Then on a 13th of January, probably in 1730/31, we have what is apparently the beginning of a renewed interest on the part of Pope in Richardson's talent as a portrait artist, and especially in his portrait *drawing*.[11] The facetiously flattering missive was published by Pope himself in a volume of his *Works* in 1739.

> I have at last got my Mother so well, as to allow myself to be absent from her for three days. As sunday is one of them, I do not know whether I may propose it to you to imploy in the manner you mention'd to me once. Sir Godfrey call'd imploying the pencil, the prayer of a painter, and affirm'd it to be his proper way of serving God, by the talent he gave him. I am sure, in this instance, it is serving your friend; and you know we are allowed to do that, (nay even to help a neighbour's oxe or ass) on the sabbath: which tho' it may seem a general percept, yet in one sense particularly applies to you, who have help'd many a human oxe, and many a human ass, to the likeness of man, not to say of God.[12]

The frequency with which Richardson sketched Pope during the decade of the 1730s and the loving punctilio with which this activity of friendly and mutual immortalizing was carried on may be suggested by the inscribed dates (coupled with the name of Pope),

ardson early and late have this address: "at his home in Queen's Square, Bloomsbury." A letter of 2 March [1732/3] (*Correspondence* 2.352) gives us "Ormond Street." An anecdote by Sir John Hawkins, *Life of Johnson* (1787), p. 347, which ought to date in 1743, speaks of Pope's coming to Richardson's house in Lincoln's Inn Fields, where Richardson was painting. I cannot explain this—unless by a confusion between Queen's Square and Great Queen Street, Lincoln's Inn Fields, where in fact several noted painters, including Kneller, had their homes. *Correspondence* 2.61–62 and 298 contain suggestions that the Richardsons went often to Hampstead and Bushy. Richardson the younger, in his *Richardsoniana*, 1776, Preface, p. iv, speaks of his father's having made a "yearly progress on horseback, for about a fortnight . . . taking elegant sketches . . . of the most beautiful prospects."

8. *English Portrait Drawings, Bull Collection*, p. 5.

9. See Courtauld Institute, *Hand-List of the Drawings in the Witt Collection* (London University, 1956), No. 583, pencil-on-vellum drawing, "Mrs. Cath: Knapp by R Aug. 25. 1731"; Laurence Binyon, *Catalogue of Drawings by British Artists . . . in the British Museum*, *3* (1902), 224–28: Richardson 25 (a) and (b). The second of these two profile drawings of Mrs. Catherine Knapp is dated 31 October 1733.

10. Pope, writing to Cheselden about 1741, happens to say of Richardson, that "he has no Wife" (*Correspondence* 4.372). There is no mention of such a person in Richardson's will (See below p. 147).

11. See below pp. 152–53.

12. *Correspondence* 3.160. Cf. 3.402, 8 January [1733/44]: Pope will "dedicate" himself to Richardson from 10 A.M. to 1 P.M.

running from June 1733 to July 1741, for the most part, if not always, in Richardson's hand, on seventeen of the drawings reproduced in this book.[13]

On 10 June 1733, Pope's aged mother died, and Pope sent Richardson a special call which is one of the most readily remembered notes that passed between them:

> there is yet upon her countenance such an expression of Tranquillity. . . . It wou'd afford the finest Image of a Saint expir'd, that ever Painting drew; and it wou'd be the greatest obligation which even That obliging Art could ever bestow on a friend, if you could come and sketch it for me. I am sure, if there be no very prevalent obstacle, you will leave any common business to do this: and I hope to see you this evening as late as you will, or to morrow morning as early, before this Winter-flower is faded. I will defer her interment till to morrow night. I know you love me, or I cou'd not have written this—I could not (at this time) have written at all.—Adieu! May you dye as happily![14]

II

During the years 1731–32 a principal topic of correspondence between Pope and Richardson was the commentary on Milton which the two Richardsons were preparing. Pope is willing to look over Richardson's "notes" on Milton and sends him an edition of Milton, first the wrong one, then the right one. He reads "notes" and returns them; he reasons about emending an epithet in Milton.[15] In January 1734/5[16] this work by the two connoisseurs and litterateurs appeared in octavo: *Explanatory Notes and Remarks on Milton's Paradise Lost. By J. Richardson, Father and Son. With the Life of the Author, and a Discourse on the Poem. By J.R. Sen.* It was "printed for" Richardson's friends the Knaptons—James (the father), John and Paul (the sons, brothers of Richardson's pupil George Knapton the painter), at the Crown in Ludgate Street, near the West End of St. Paul's.[17] The book drew unfriendly notice on account of Richardson's absurdly phrased acknowledgement of help from his son in the "Learned Languages."[18] It was actually remarkable for certain features of its life of Milton[19] and espe-

13. See below nos. 19(2), 19(13), 19(14), 20, 22–24, 26–32, 34, 37, 37(1). The fragmentary character of the surviving evidence is suggested in the fact that no one of these seventeen dates coincides with any one of the five dates (known or conjectured) when Pope in his letters promises to sit for Richardson: *Correspondence* 3.160 (13 January 1731; 3.402 (10 January 1734; 4.79 (30 June 1737); 4.91 (after 4 January 1738); 4.399 (? 3 June 1742).

14. *Correspondence* 3.374. If Richardson responded to this call and succeeded with the drawing, it is unknown today. He had also drawn Pope's father on his deathbed (1717); this drawing is known today in a copy. See p. 81, and no. 30.

15. *Correspondence* 3.231, 240, 269, 326–27 (2 November 1732), 330, 331.

16. Vertue 3.74. The title page bears the date 1734.

17. J. Knapton alone (the father) at the same address had been the publisher of *An Account of Some of the Statues* . . . (1722).

18. *Explanatory Notes,* p. cxli: "When therefore I, in my Own Person talk of Things which in my Separate Capability I am known to be a Stranger to, let Me be Understood as the Complicated *Richardson.* . . . In what depends on the knowledge of the Learned Languages my Son is my Telescope." This passage was the occasion for an indecent crude engraving which has been blamed, it would seem unjustly, on Hogarth. See *BMP&PS 3,* Part I, p. 4, no. 2018, "After a design by Hogarth?"

19. Republished in Helen Darbishire, ed. *The Early Lives of Milton,* London, 1932.

cially for an accent on Milton's appearance.[20] The frontispiece is an etching of Milton by Richardson himself from an excellent pastel, attributed to Faithorne, which was then in Richardson's possession.[21] In his *Burlington Magazine* article on the Richardsons' "Cult of Milton," J. F. Kerslake reproduces a large Richardson painting which he appropriately entitles: "Portrait of the Artist and his Son in the presence of John Milton." "In the foreground the light streams down on the forehead of their hero [a strange bust-length velvet-clad apparition of the Faithorne Milton], crowned once again with the laurel wreath. . . . Modestly in the background stand the two men for whom Milton lives again. The younger Richardson holds a book—presumably an allusion to his classical learning and literary ability—and gazes in admiration at his father. On the ledge in front of him is a pile of manuscripts. The writing on it cannot be read, but, if it could, surely the title would begin *Explanatory Notes. . . .*"[22]

The joke was perhaps partly deserved when a few years later Pope and Lord Chesterfield (according to a letter from George Vertue to Lord Oxford) collaborated to hoax the old "Connoisseur" with ten new lines by Milton, "Found in a Glass Window in the Village of Chalfont in Bucks": "As erst he Scourged Jessides sin of yore / For the fair Hittite, when on Seraph's Wings / He sent him War, or Plague or famine Sore." Pope throws in at the end of a hasty note: "The above was given me by a Gentleman, as I travelld.—I copyd it for you. You will tell me more of it perhaps than I can." With the authority of Richardson behind them, the lines got so far apparently as to be set up in type for an edition of Milton's prose by Thomas Birch, before the jokers intervened. "I could wish your Honour had been in view of Richardson when this discovery was made a day or two ago only. In short, they are obliged to reprint the sheet in the book in a hurry."[23] The incident does not throw the pleasantest light on Pope's attitude toward his elderly and less witty friend. It may disappoint us that he should have ventured so far, and so cruelly. Perhaps this kind of practical humor was almost the only form of the laughable in which he could participate with the serious old painter. "The father," says Walpole, "was a formal man, with a slow, but loud and sonorous voice, and, in truth, with some affectation in his manner."[24] We have a quoted snatch from a note in which Pope is joking with Richardson about their different kinds of religious orthodoxy.[25] But on the whole Pope seems not to have looked on Richard-

20. *Explanatory Notes*, pp. i–iv, xxxii, xxxvi. Richardson had taken "the trouble to make minute inquiries of Milton's descendants and acquaintance."

21. This pastel has recently come to rest in the Princeton Library and has been reproduced handsomely in color. See John Rupert Martin, *The Portrait of John Milton at Princeton and its place in Milton Iconography* (Princeton University Library, 1961), Illustration no. 25. And see esp. pp. 12, 16–17, 20, 27–28. Richardson's etching embellishes the Faithorne image with a laurel crown and adds beneath the picture an appropriate quotation from Milton's *Mansus*.

22. J. F. Kerslake, "The Richardsons and the Cult of Milton," *Burlington Magazine*, 99 (January 1957), 24. The painting was at Capesthorne, the property

of Lt.-Col. and Mrs. W. H. Bromley-Davenport. The illustrations for this article, especially a double drawing of Richardson and his son, serve admirably to clarify a matter until then confused, the difference in appearance between the two men. Richardson the younger may be known by his cleft chin, glaring hare-like eyes, and dome-like forehead. Richardson the elder is always the sober full-mouthed good man of National Portrait Gallery no. 706.

23. Pope to Richardson, 18 July [1737] (*Correspondence* 4.80) and note 1, quoting Vertue's letter to Oxford from Historical Manuscripts Commission. Portland, 6.66 (24 February, 1737/38).

24. Walpole, *Anecdotes* 2.275.

25. [July 1737] (*Correspondence* 4.81).

son as the kind of correspondent with whom it was worthwhile to employ the literary and facetious style in which he indulged so frequently with so many of his friends—even, at an earlier date, with the painter Charles Jervas.

Not long after Pope had given the Richardsons advice about their work on Milton, he seems to have been taking them into his own confidence about a major literary matter, the secret that he was the author of a certain unpublished poem, the *Essay on Man*, which was soon to be appearing in parts anonymously. Thus in February 1733: "the thing I apprehend is . . . a copy of part of . . . [a] work, which I have cause to fear may be got out underhand; but of how much, or what part, I know not. In that case pray conceal your having any knowledge of its belonging, either wholly or partly, to me; it would prejudice me both in reputation and profit."[26] A second note, written a little later, seems even more like part of a plot and suggests that Pope's sharing of this secret was one of his characteristic indirections:

the Essay on Man, which I hear so much of. Pray, what is your opinion of it? I hear some cry it extremely up; others think it obscure in part; and some (of whom I am sure you are not one) have said it is mine. I think I could shew you some faults in it, and believe you can shew me more, though, upon the whole, it is allowed to have merit, and I think so myself.[27]

This, as Professor Sherburn observes, looks like an exhibit which Richardson was expected to pass around among friends. Richardson wrote a poem on the *Essay* and sent it to Pope, Pope replying that "all in good time" he would find a use for this. In Volume 2 of his *Works*, 1739, he published, among other commendatory verses, lines "To the Conceal'd Author of the Essay on Man," by "J.R."

> Yes Friend! thou art conceal'd; Conceal'd? but how?
> Ever the Brightest, more Refulgent now,
> By thy own Lustre hid! each nervous Line,
> Each melting Verse, each Syllable, is thine.[28]

III

An equally devoted admirer of Pope's genius was the younger Richardson. He was the earliest textual critic or serious collator of Pope. In a letter of about 1737 Pope alludes to sending him a copy of all his *Works* with wide margins,[29] and in another of about 1741 he is sending him manuscripts.[30] In his anecdotal *Richardsoniana*, published posthumously in 1776, Richardson the younger would boast:

26. [18 February 1732/3] (*Correspondence* 3.350).
27. [February 1732/3] (*Correspondence* 3.351). The First Epistle of the *Essay on Man* appeared anonymously on 20 February 1732/3.
28. 2 November 1732 (*Correspondence* 3.326–27 and p. 327 n.1); Griffith no. 505; Pope's *Works* 2 (1739), 3–4, lines 1–4 of a considerably longer poem.
29. 17 June [1737] (*Correspondence* 4.78). Cf. 2.496 n.2.
30. [1 December 1741?] (*Correspondence* 4.374).

I was witness to the whole conduct of it [the *Essay on Man*] in writing, and actually have his original MSS. for it, from the first scratches of the four books, to the several finished copies, (of his own neat and elegant writing these last) all which, with the MS. of his *Essay on Criticism,* and several of his other works, he gave me himself, for the pains I took in collating the whole with its printed editions, at his request, on my having proposed to him the "making of an edition of his works in the manner of Boileau's."[31]

Richardson the younger is known to readers of Boswell's *Johnson* as the litterateur to whom Pope turned for information in vain when in May *1738* his own *1738, Dialogue I* happened to be published on nearly the same day as an anonymous imitation of Juvenal entitled *London*.[32] Pope's later note to Richardson the elder identifying the author was preserved by Richardson the younger and given to Sir Joshua Reynolds, who gave it to Bishop Percy, who gave the text to Boswell.[33] It is Richardson the younger, again, who tells a vivid little story, transmitted by Samuel Johnson, of Pope's sensitivity to satire:

I have heard Mr. Richardson relate that he attended his father the painter on a visit, when one of Cibber's pamphlets came into the hands of Pope, who said, "These things are my diversion." They sat by him while he perused it, and saw his features writhen with anguish; and young Richardson said to his father, when they returned, that he hoped to be preserved from such diversion as had that day been the lot of Pope.[34]

IV

The elder Richardson's etched frontispiece of Milton in his *Explanatory Notes* of 1735 was something of an experiment for him. "I have imitated it as well as I could in a Way of Working which I Never Practiced but on a Few Plates, and Those in my Youth, except an Attempt on One or Two near 20 Years ago."[35] The Milton plate was perhaps the beginning of a modest cultivation of the etcher's art, which reached a cli-

31. *Richardsoniana* (London, 1776), p. 264. From Richardson the younger the collection passed to Dr. Charles Chauncey (1706–77) and was owned by his heirs when the manuscripts were consulted for the edition of Elwin and Courthope (Griffith *1*.149; 2.282; Elwin and Courthope *1*.viii, 323, 324; *3*.x; 4.271 ff.). Having found their way latterly into research libraries, they have been published in sumptuous facsimile editions. See Robert M. Schmitz, *Pope's "Windsor Forest" 1712 A Study of the Washington University Holograph* (Saint Louis, 1952), pp. 10–14; Earl R. Wasserman, *Pope's "Epistle to Bathurst" A Critical Reading with An Edition of the Manuscripts* (Baltimore: The Johns Hopkins Press, 1960), p. 60; Maynard Mack, *Alexander Pope "An Essay on Man"* *Reproductions of the Manuscripts* (Oxford: The Roxburghe Club, 1962), pp. xxiv–xxv, xlviii–xlix.

32. Boswell, *Life of Johnson,* ed. G. B. Hill and L. F. Powell, *1* (Oxford, 1934), 128–29, May 1738; cf. 2.85. Johnson's poem appeared on 13 May (*Poems,* ed. Smith and McAdam, 1941, p. 1); Pope's on 16 May (Griffith no. 484: 2.380).

33. Boswell, *Life of Johnson,* *1*.143; *Correspondence* 4.194.

34. Johnson, *Pope,* in *Lives of the Poets,* ed. G. B. Hill (Oxford, 1905), 3.188; n.2 quotes a similar anecdote from Hawkin's *Life of Johnson* (1787), p. 347. *Richardsoniana* (1776), p. 311 touches the same theme.

35. *Explanatory Notes,* p. iii.

max about four years later. It was restricted to variations on the image of Milton and to portraits of himself, his son, and a few friends.[36] A profile etching of Bolingbroke, which appears as frontispiece of the posthumous *Letter to Sir William Windham,* 1753, has the inscription "H.S.L.B. / Nil Admirari / 1738."[37] An etching of Richardson's friend and neighbor in Great Queen Street, the virtuoso Dr. Richard Mead, is dated 1739.[38] The interest in the portraiture of Milton apparently reached out in a curious way to connect with the portraiture of Pope—as we shall illustrate later with a single plate containing three heads (no. 38). Ten other etched plates of Pope can be grouped around three superior images (nos. 41, 43.1, 48) done in 1736, 1737, and 1738. "Amicitiae Causa," Richardson inscribed on the first two, and on the third, "ΟΥΤΟΣ ΕΚΕΙΝΟΣ" ("The Very Man"), from a chapter of Aristotle's *Poetics* (4) which theorizes about the kinship between poetry and painting. The surviving correspondence of Pope with Richardson touches on the engravings only in a rapid flurry of three notes (quoted below no. 43.1) in the winter of 1737, as the title page for Pope's *Letters,* with its medallion, was in the course of manufacture.

No one of the seven types of oil paintings of Pope done by Richardson during this period (nos. 49–51, 52.1, 53.1, 54, 55.2) is distinctly alluded to in the correspondence. We can gather, however, that the late summer and autumn of 1738 was a period of great activity, both in etching and in oil painting. This was near the beginning of the long stretch during 1738 and 1739 when Bolingbroke was living with Pope, and Pope's admiration for him swelled so vastly. Pope and Bolingbroke were apparently in the process of exchanging portrait gifts. The correspondence with Richardson speaks of Bolingbroke's soon coming to see Richardson (?17 August 1738),[39] of Pope's coming to Richardson to get a "Picture" and meanwhile sending the "Case" (20 September),[40] of an "enamel picture" which is done, of "two originals" which Pope wishes Richardson to "take back" into his keeping for a while—"I desire you will cause mine of him, to be framed in the manner you best approve" (19 November),[41] and of a "Blue Picture" which Richardson is asked to keep "till my Lord comes" (December).[42] A kind of chaotic vignette of all this portrait frenzy is preserved in Kent's illiterate letter to Lord

36. See pp. 178–80.

37. This is no doubt the engraving of Bolingbroke alluded to by Pope in a letter to Richardson written perhaps early in the autumn of 1738 (*Correspondence* 4.123).

38. A wigged profile, inscribed "J. Richardson f 1739" (*BMEP 3*). An oil painting of Dr. Richard Mead by Richardson was acquired by the National Portrait Gallery in 1960, no. 4157. The identification and attribution are secured by a Richardson drawing in the Ashmolean Museum and another in the British Museum—red chalk, inscribed "Dr. Meade 5 Oct. 1738" (B.M. 1902–8–22–37). See National Portrait Gallery, *One Hundred and Fourth Annual Report of the Trustees 1960–61* (London, 1961), p. 11. And see below no. 52.1.

39. *Correspondence* 4.118–19.

40. *Correspondence* 4.128–28. The year is inferential, but seems certain enough.

41. *Correspondence* 4.147–48. The year again is not given.

42. *Correspondence* 4.151. It is tempting to think that one of these pictures is the small oil of Bolingbroke, "wearing a deep brownish old velvet turban cap . . . and a dark greyish lavender drapery about his shoulders . . . probably left unfinished by the artist," no. 1453 at the National Portrait Gallery, attributed to Richardson. It was acquired in 1908, with no past identification. See Piper, *Catalogue of the Seventeenth-Century Portraits,* p. 30. Once before, on 2 November 1732, Pope had thanked Richardson for a drawing of Bolingbroke (*Correspondence* 3.326). (See below no. 35, a copy of a drawing of Bolingbroke once at Strawberry Hill.) And again on 10 June, apparently in 1742, Richardson was painting Bolingbroke for Pope (*Correspondence* 4.400). Pope's will (*Works,* ed. Carruthers, *1* [1853], 326) mentions more than one portrait of Bolingbroke by Richardson.

Burlington written on 28 November. Another part of this letter has been quoted already in our account of Kent.[43] The following longer passage gives us, besides a picture of a dismal morning in London and Pope's desperate need for company, one of our few direct glimpses of Pope in conversation with the Richardsons.

> I had not seen Pope but once this two months before last sunday morning & he came to town the night before   the next morning he came before I was up   it had raind all night & rain'd when he came   I would not get up & sent him away to disturb some body else—he came back and sayd could meet with nobody, I got drest & went with him to Richardsons & had great diversion   he shew'd three picturs of Lord Baulingbrok   one for himself for Pope, another Pope in a mourning gown with a strange view of the garden to shew the obelisk as in memory to his mothers Death, the alligory seem'd odde to me, but after I found, its to be in the next letters as I suppose some of the witt that was write to Londesbrough will be in print—the son of Richardson & Pope agree'd that popes head was Titziannesco, the old long Glow worm sayd whe have done our best. . . . I forgot to tell you that Richerson give me all the prints he has grav'd, he has given me so many miltons, & three different popes, the last he has done is write behind his head in greek letters the English—thats the man, or this is the man, I cannot just tell—[44]

IV

In some of Pope's letters to Richardson, the high regard and affection expressed for the old painter may seem all too clearly connected with the poet's steady concern for the delineation and public projection of his own image. (He did look on Richardson as a famous painter. Thus to his new ally Warburton, about 1742: "If you are at leisure to breakfast at the Celebrated Mr Richardson's in Queens Square Bloomsbury, I am to be there before ten.")[45] No doubt Richardson's esteem for Pope was also partly nourished by the facepainter's satisfaction that the sisterhood of the arts and the friendship of artists was being illustrated for him in a partnership with the very highest. On the other hand, there is sufficient evidence of a genuine friendship and regard on both sides. An early family acquaintanceship, in mid-career a professional consultation of Richardson by Pope, and thereafter a series of mutually gratifying exchanges, seem to have ripened during later years into a homely and unaffected kind of intimate esteem.

> Pray let me enjoy yours and your Sons agreeable Conversation, in the place where I can have it most uninterrupted, (viz) Twickenham. This Saturday

---

In 1736 Richardson painted at full length in garter robes Pope's new friend Frederick Prince of Wales; the signed and dated canvas has come down at Warwick Castle (J. Ch. Smith 2.93, Andrew Miller no. 17, 1738; Goulding and Adams, *Portland Catalogue*, p. 475).

43. See p. 113.

44. *Correspondence* 4.150. Pope in mourning gown with a view of the garden and obelisk is unhappily not further known. For "the wit that was write to Londesbrough," see p. 112.

45. *Correspondence* 4.380.

Evening, & Sunday all day & night. I will be there attending you. It is but turning your Horses heads towards me.

—2.61: [undated]

I have been confined three days in town, still hoping daily to be able to get out to see you. In vain, I am still a prisoner.

—3.345: [1732–3]

Be assured we think alike, & alike warmly. . . . If you can pass Sunday Sennight here. . . . let it be so; if not, tell me any other Day, or take 2 days.

—4.78: 17 June [1737?]

If your Self & your Son can mount this day, & enjoy my Groves all to Ourselves all this day & as much of the night as the fine moon now allows, I am wholly yours for this day & till noon to morrow.

—4.79: [29 June 1737]

the Twitnam Coach . . . comes hither by 6 in the afternoon; by which time my Ladies will be gone, & leave us the peaceable Enjoyments of Philosophers in the Garden. All Sunday I may keep you.

—4.408: [30 July 1742]

On 12 December 1740 (two years before his latest, and only signed and dated, oil painting of Pope),[46] Richardson published in *The London Daily Post and General Advertiser* a notice of retirement:

Mr. Richardson having given over his Business, and his Continuance in Town being uncertain, is very desirous to discharge himself of the few Pictures, which are yet remaining in his Hands, especially those for which Money has been received in Part. He gives the publick Notice, in hopes that all concern'd will be pleas'd to further his honest Intention within the Space of three Months.

His Collection of Pictures, Plaister-Figures, &c. will be sold by Auction in a short Time, of which the Publick shall have further Notice.[47]

Illness, delaying or preventing visits in either direction, had been all along one of the most frequent topics of Pope's notes to Richardson. During the year 1743 and the spring of 1744 Richardson and Pope were declining toward the grave together.

Everything was welcom to me in your kind Letter, except the Occasion of it, the Confinement you are under. . . . I shall in the Course of the Winter prob-

46. See no. 55.2.
47. *The London Daily Post, and General Advertiser*, no. 1915, Friday, 12 December 1740, "Printed for H. Woodfall, jun. at the Rose and Crown, in Little-Britain; where Advertisements of moderate Length are taken in at Two Shillings each."

ably be an Evening Visitant to you if you sit at home, tho I hope it will not be by Compulsion or Lameness. We may take a Cup of Sack together, & chatter like two Parrots. . . . I am glad you Sleep better.

—*4.484*: 21 November [1743]

I am in a very ticklish State, dreading any Cold, from the Asthmatic Complaint; which follows me close, or I had been sooner there.

—*4.487*: [1743/4?]

I fear your own complaint of the same kind may press as heavy upon you.

—*4.489*: 3 January 1743/4

You had seen me had I been well. . . . I have not been abroad this Month, nor out of my Chamber, nor able to see any but Nurses.

—*4.513*: 26 March 1744

Richardson's will is dated only a few days after this note, 7 April 1744. He leaves most of his wealth to his beloved fellow connoisseur Jonathan Junior, but makes bequests also to four daughters, including one who had rebelled against him by running away with one of his pupils: "to Mr. Thomas Hudson and to my Daughter Mary his wife."[48] Richardson was more than twenty years older than Pope. He died a year later than Pope, almost to the day. George Vertue gives us an account of his character, last days, and death, with which we may well close our story.

Tuesday, May 28, 1745, died Mr. Jonathan Richardson Senior, a portrait painter of famous reputation in his art and of the first class in his time. He was a man of quick and lively spirits, diligent, studious, and of loud elocution, loved exercise and walking much in his latter days. Growing feeble some years before his death he had a paralytic fit, that weakened his right hand, for which he went to the Bath. He used in a coach to go from Queen's Square (at his house) to St. James's Park to walk for an hour or two with his son or his daughter. So daily almost—and return back to his dinner. This he did to his last, the day he died. As soon as he returned home, sat down in his chair and made his exit, anno Aetatis 80, his legs having swelled some time before, etc. This was the last of the eminent old painters that had been contemporaries in reputation—Kneller, Dahl, Jervas, and Richardson—for portrait-painting in England for many years.[49]

48. G. W. Snelgrove, *The Work and Theories of Jonathan Richardson (1665–1745)*, Thesis for the Ph.D. Degree at the University of London, June 1936, reports the date of Richardson's will (Somerset House, Seymour 178) and adds that it was proved 5 June 1745, by his son, the sole executor. His other three daughters were named Elizabeth, Harriot, and Frances. Vertue 3.66 (1733) tells how "Mr. Hudson Painter of Portraits learnt of Mr. Richardson . . . whose daughter he married without the father's consent."

49. Vertue 2.125. Richardson and his wife are said by Snelgrove to have been buried beside each other in the south part of St. George-the-Martyr's Parish Burial Ground—behind the site of the Foundling Hospital, now laid out as St. George's gardens. The stones could not be traced in 1936.

Drawings of Pope by Jonathan Richardson

G. W. Snelgrove, in his University of London doctoral thesis of 1936 on Jonathan Richardson, catalogues 205 drawings by Richardson, distributed as follows: (in ten public places) The Department of Prints and Drawings at the British Museum (by far the largest collection),[1] the Victoria and Albert Museum,[2] the Pierpont Morgan Library,[3] the Bodleian Library, the Ashmolean Museum, the National Portrait Gallery, the Fogg Art Museum, Windsor Castle,[4] the Fitzwilliam Museum, the Whitworth Gallery; (in four major private collections) Sir Robert Witt's (now in part at the Courtauld Institute),[5] Dr. G. C. Williamson's at Mount Manor House, Guildford,[6] Francis Wellesley's (dispersed in 1920),[7] Roger Warner's (still intact);[8] and in a few other miscellaneous places.

But the drawings by Jonathan Richardson the elder which can be located today are only about a fifth of the number which he left at his death.

Four Richardson sales ought to be noticed, in order to distinguish the one which is here of main concern. The sale of Richardson the elder's paintings, 3 and 4 March 1746/7 (Lugt 656), included no drawings.[9] The earlier sale of his *Italian and Other Drawings*, 22 January 1746/7 (Lugt 653), included no drawings of his own, unless some stray ones were hidden here and there under the word "various." It was preponderantly and obviously a sale of foreign-master drawings and various prints. Some oils by the elder Richardson, all copies after other painters, do appear in the March sale. But the drawings were the heart of a family aesthetic cult. All that we know of the filial piety of the younger Richardson makes the early disposal of his father's drawings seem improbable.[10] After the death of Richardson the younger, a sale of his *Pictures* 18 February 1772 (Lugt 1999) included only a few drawings by Richardson the elder, mostly copies after foreign masters. The vast body of Richardson the elder's drawings were dispersed at a separate sale, of *Prints and Drawings*, 5 February 1772 and seven following days

1. Lawrence Binyon, *Catalogue of Drawings by British Artists . . . in the British Museum, 3* (1902), 224–28, in his joint treatment of Richardson the elder and Richardson the younger, catalogues thirty-eight drawings, nearly all correctly attributed to Richardson the elder. Shortly after the appearance of this Catalogue, the Department of Prints and Drawings, in 1902, acquired the collection of thirty-nine drawings by Richardson the elder which had been in the Strawberry Hill sale of June 1842 (see no. 23).

2. More than a dozen drawings, from various sources.

3. Twenty-six drawings by Richardson, with others, are found in an album which belonged to the Walpolian devotee Richard Bull, of Ongar in Essex, and later to Charles Fairfax Murray.

4. See no. 25.

5. See *Hand-List of the Drawings in the Witt Collection* (London University, 1956), pp. 39–40, nos. 583, 1465, 1552, 1590, 1655, 1660, 1662, 1663, 1986, 2189, 3902, 3932; and C. H. Collins Baker, "Some Drawings by Jonathan Richardson in the Witt Collection," *The Connoisseur, 73* (December 1925), 195–202.

6. Dr. Williamson died 4 July 1942. At Sotheby's 31 January 1945, a sale of Williamson drawings included (lot 77) two self-portraits by Richardson. At a second sale, on 28 February, further Richardson drawings were sold (lots 2, 3, 9, 19, 23).

7. At Sotheby's, 28 June–2 July 1920. Nos. 648–660 on 1 July were drawings by Richardson.

8. See no. 20.

9. Typescript, at the National Portrait Gallery, from a photostat, at the National Gallery, of the unique copy belonging to W. Roberts recorded in Lugt (no. 656).

10. Mr. Parsons, the "ingenious picture cleaner and painter," who in 1789 sold eight drawings by Richardson to Edmond Malone, was clearly mistaken when he told Malone: "that the great sale of Richardson's drawings was in 1746–7. At that sale the younger Richardson was a considerable purchaser, and he afterwards added greatly to his collection" (James Prior, *Life of Edmond Malone*, London, 1865, pp. 397–98, in "Maloniana").

(not recorded in Lugt). Seventeen lots from antique and Renaissance models, with a few English seventeenth-century subjects, Cromwell, Milton, Charles II, totaled 292 drawings. Five lots of landscape "sketches" and "views" totaled 191. Ten lots of self-portraits and portraits of Richardson the younger totaled 102. Forty-four lots of various portrait heads totaled 481. Thus a total of 76 lots contained a total of 1,066 drawings, all by the elder Richardson.[11]

The name of Alexander Pope appears attached to six lots of drawings:[12]

II.39.   Four heads by Richardson, of Mr. Pope, on blue paper, in chalk.

II.43.   Eight by Richardson on vellum, of Milton, Pope, and Sir Isaac Newton &c.

III.33.   Eight heads by Richardson on vellum, of Shakespeare, Pope and Milton &c.

IV.43.   Eight drawings of Pope, different from each other, on vellum, by Richardson Senior.

V.31.   Eight heads, three Milton, four Pope, and one Sir Isaac Newton, on vellum by Richardson Senior.

VIII.12. Three, Pope, his father and mother.[13]

Most likely it was lot III.33 which Parsons the cleaner and painter acquired and sold in 1789 to Edmond Malone, who showed them to Reynolds: "eight drawings. . . . two of Pope; two of Milton, one of them very highly finished . . . two of Shakespeare . . . one of the elder Richardson; and one of the late Dr. Birch."[14] Almost certainly it was the same collection of drawings which later belonged to Malone's friend and fellow Shakespeare editor James Boswell, Jr., and appeared, only somewhat dwindled, in the sale of Boswell's Library (*Bibliotheca Boswelliana*) at Sotheby's in May 1825: "two beautiful" pencil-on-vellum drawings of Milton, one of Richardson Senior himself, one of Dr. Birch, and one of Pope (all acquired by Thorpe), and one of Shakespeare (acquired by Colnaghi).[15]

At the Chantry, near Ipswich, in July 1834 a sale of the books and pictures of the deceased Charles S. Collinson (heir of the eighteenth-century naturalist Peter Collinson) included twelve drawings by Richardson, one of these a landscape "sketch," on the back of which was inscribed: "From my chamber at Mr. Pope's, 21st June, 1737."[16]

11. British Museum, Department of Prints and Drawings, A.19(8)S.C. Lot 53 of the first day is "Eleven after the antique by Richardson jun. coloured." Twenty-one lots of engravings by Richardson Senior are described on p. 180.

12. The numbers, "II.39," etc. represent days and lots. I have translated "ditto"s into the words for which they stand.

13. Other portraits of Pope must have been hidden among the remaining thirty-eight lots of miscellaneous portraits. Twenty-eight portraits in four lots (II.42, V.29, VI.25, VI.28) are said to be of ladies. Other names of sitters which appear in the entries are: Lucy, Folkes, Mead, Cheselden, Locke.

14. Prior, *Malone*, pp. 397–98. The two of Pope are "marked at the back with Richardson's R—but have no date." For all the others, Malone gives the dates, from 1732 to 1739, "written in pencil with which the drawings were made" (pp. 399–400).

15. Yale University Library. At Sotheby's, 28 June 1824, in a sale of prints from the collection of Sir Mark Masterman Sykes, Bart., lot 308 included Pope and Milton "(small heads,) drawings in black lead pencil, by Richardson, fine" (Yale University Library).

16. Lugt 13734, British Museum Library. Six in this collection were said to be of Jonathan Richardson the younger. Two were of Mrs. Catherine Knapp, one dated 1733. Cf. p. 139.

Lot VIII.12 in the Richardson sale of 1772 ("Three, Pope, his father and mother"), or something very much like it, was apparently acquired at an early date by Horace Walpole. In Walpole's *Description of Strawberry Hill* (1774), the Red Bed Chamber (pp. 39–40) contains four drawings described as follows:

> The father of Pope as he lay dead; drawn by his father-in-law Samuel Cooper:
> bought by Richardson, junior, at the sale of Mrs. Martha Blount, to whom
> Pope had bequeathed this and the three following,
> Mrs. Editha Cooper, Mother of Pope. by John Richardson, senior
> Mr. Pope himself; ditto.
> Henry St. John Viscount Bolingbroke; ditto.[17]

The Catalogue for the first of the two Strawberry Hill sales in the spring of 1842, lot XX.72 (p. 224), repeats the account of the four drawings as Walpole had published it in 1774. They were bought for £4.10.0 by a Mr. Thomas Young, who had recently built a new house near the site of Pope's villa.[18]

We are fortunate in having a nearly contemporary description of the four drawings as they appeared at the Strawberry Hill sale. In *The Gentleman's Magazine* for November 1849 an anonymous writer reviewing the Reverend Robert Aris Willmott's *Journal of Summer Time in the Country,* adds to a remark about Pope's mother the following:

17. The miniaturist Samuel Cooper (1609–72) was not the poet Pope's grandfather, but his uncle by marriage, the husband of Pope's aunt Christiana Turner. Pope's father died in 1717. Some years after the printing of Walpole's *Description of Strawberry Hill* (1774), the Reverend William Mason wrote to him pointing out the mistake about Cooper. Walpole replied that he had picked up the idea in the manuscripts of George Vertue—of which he had purchased about fifty volumes in 1758 (*Horace Walpole's Correspondence with William Mason,* 2, ed. W. S. Lewis, Grover Cronin, Jr., and Charles Bennett [New Haven, 1955], pp. 278 ff., letters of 4 and 7. December 1782, and annotation). Vertue, however, in a note written about 1727, says, on the authority of Lord Oxford: "Mrs. Pope mother to Mr. Alex: Pope was Sister to Mrs. Cooper wife of the famous limner" (Vertue 2.41). There is some evidence that Jonathan Richardson the younger, rather than Vertue, was the source of Walpole's mistake. In 1885 there came to rest in the British Museum a drawing of Pope's mother in pen and ink washed with India ink, 6½ x 5½ in. (Binyon, Richardson 23: B.M. 1885-5-9-1895). This is inscribed on the back: "Mr. Pope's mother from the life at Twitnam. She was Daughter to Sam. Cowper ye Limner. This is the Scetch for a finished one in Black lead my F. made for Mr. Pope. Both extremely like Mrs. Pope. 5 July 173 . . . " (Binyon, Richardson 23, and see the inscription in facsimile in Frits Lugt, *Les Marques de Collections* [Amsterdam, 1921], p. 563, no. 2997 a). In volume 7 of *The Works of Alexander Pope,*

ed. Elwin and Courthope (1872), a good engraving of apparently the same drawing (before it came to the British Museum) appears as frontispiece. It was then in the possession of Edward Cheney, Esq. (Professor Sherburn, *Correspondence* 3.374n.6, believed that this was the drawing which Pope, 10 June 1733, asked Richardson to make of Mrs. Pope after her death.)

Walpole told Mason that he had corrected his mistake in the new edition of his *Description of Strawberry Hill.* He had actually stated the relation correctly in the first two editions of his *Anecdotes of Painting* (based on Vertue's *Note Books*), and had made an emendation in the passage about the four drawings in a copy of the 1774 *Description* now at Farmington (Allen T. Hazen, *A Bibliography of the Strawberry Hill Press* [New Haven, 1942], p. 109, copy 3 of the 1774 *Description*). But the text of the 1784 *Description* remained unrevised (p. 30).

18. *Catalogue of the Classic Contents of Strawberry Hill Collected by Horace Walpole . . . Mr. George Robins is Honoured by Having Been Selected by the Earl of Waldegrave, to Sell by Public Competition, The Valuable Contents of Strawberry Hill. . . . Monday, the 25th Day of April, 1842, and Twenty-three Following Days,* p. 224, day XXII, lot 72. *Aedes Strawberrianae. Names of Purchasers and the Prices . . . At Strawberry Hill . . . Printed for J. H. Burn,* p. 53, *12.72,* "Young, Esq. Pope's Villa 4 10 0." R. S. Cobbett, *Memorials of Twickenham . . .* (London, 1872), p. 289: "a new house was built by Mr. Thomas Young . . . neither like Pope's nor any other."

There was sold at Strawberry Hill a most interesting pencil drawing, by Richardson, of Pope's mother in her extreme age, Pope's father lying on his death bed, Pope himself, and Lord Bolingbroke, in one frame. They were formerly in Pope's possession.[19]

The drawings themselves are not further known. But the image of Pope's mother may be identified in an etching by Carter dated 1774.[20] What seems to be a copy of the drawing of Pope's father survives today in a collection at the Pierpont Morgan Library.[21] A copy of the Bolingbroke may be seen in an extra-illustrated *Description of Strawberry Hill* at Farmington.[22]

Our narrative of the dispersal and disappearance of the Richardson drawings of Pope brings us at length to those that are today known to survive: four collections, that recently acquired by Cornell University, that of Mr. and Mrs. Roger Warner of Burford, Oxfordshire, that of Her Majesty the Queen at Windsor Castle, and that of Dr. Dallas Pratt, of New York City; and four single drawings—at the British Museum, at Yale University, at the University of Texas, and at Farmington, in the possession of Mr. Wilmarth Lewis. The provenance of some of these is quite short; others take us back again as far as Strawberry Hill or to the drawing room of the poet Samuel Rogers. In the catalogue which follows, the drawings appear in two series (sketches and finished drawings), each series arranged in the order of dates or probable dates of execution. The provenance of each of the four collections (Cornell, Warner, Windsor, Pratt) is discussed in the entry for the earliest drawing in that group.

The Richardsons' Marks

Frits Lugt, *Les Marques de Collections de Dessins & d'Estampes* (Amsterdam, 1921), pp. 406–07, in his main article on Jonathan Richardson the elder, identifies two marks, nos. 2183 and 2184, as marks used by Richardson for his collection of drawings. Apparently Lugt has in mind, for the most part if not altogether, Richardson's collection of old-master drawings. The first of these marks, no. 2183, a rather elaborate stamp of a palette,

19. *Gentleman's Magazine, 186* (November 1849), 466–67. It is to be noted that this adds to *Strawberry Hill* (1774), pp. 39–40, the information that the drawings were in pencil, and that they were in one frame.

20. One reason for William Mason's complaint to Walpole (above note 16) was that before Mason realized the mistake he had set a "servant" of his, Charles Carter, to make an etching of Mrs. Pope, with the following legend: "J. Richardson delin 1731 // C. Carter fecit Aqua fortii 1774. / Mrs Pope. / Daughter of Samuel Cooper, Painter; & Mother of Alexander Pope, from / an Original Drawing of J. Richardson Senr now in the Collection / of the Honble Horace Walpole, at Strawberry Hill." The image and the substance of the legend are copied in a smaller stipple engraving: "Engraved by W. Evans . . . Published by Cadell & Davies, Strand, and the other Proprietors, May 1.

1807."—to be found in *The Works of Alexander Pope,* ed. W. L. Bowles (London, 1806), *1*, facing p. xvii; and vol. *6* of the "Ruffhead" quarto *Works,* added in 1807.

21. A pencil-on-paper drawing of a man with lightly bearded chin and closed eyes, in night shirt and cap, lying against pillows, is to be found in the Pierpont Morgan Library, at p. 162 of vol. *4* of an extra-illustrated set of *The Poetical Works of Alexander Pope, Esq.,* Glasgow, Printed by Andrew Foulis, 1785. (The set was apparently put together for Henrietta Frances, Countess of Bessborough, about 1796.) The face is tinted with water color. Beneath is a handwritten inscription: "Pope's Father. From a Drawing at Strawberry Hill."

22. See no. 30.

with brushes and a quill pen behind it, and a monogram JR inscribed upon it, I have not seen on any drawing done by Jonathan Richardson himself. The second mark, however, no. 2184, a monogram "JR," which Lugt reports as appearing in black on the face of drawings in Richardson's collection, does appear, almost regularly, as a stamp in black ink, either on front or back, of drawings which may be safely ascribed to Richardson himself. This mark is a strong corroboration of other kinds of evidence that a drawing is by Richardson himself. (For the question whether he ever inscribed the mark, with pen or pencil, rather than stamped it, see no. 30.) A second mark, a single and smaller letter "R" stamped in black, appears often, either alone or along with "JR," on drawings by Richardson the elder. It is most often, if not always, on the face of the drawing, very often in the lower right corner. This mark was happily indentified very early as that of Jonathan Richardson the younger's collection. The eminent virtuoso John Barnard (died 1784, son of Pope's companion among the busts in the Temple of Worthies at Stowe, Sir John Barnard) amassed a distinguished collection of drawings which was sold 16 February 1787, and seven days thereafter, by Greenwood in Leicester Square. The 43-page catalogue, quarto, of this sale is noted in collectors' annals as including a prefatory list of collection marks, with comments. It is considered the most ancient catalogue of such information, the embryo in fact of Lugt's *Les Marques de Collections.* Barnard's Catalogue says: "A very small R done with a stamp, is the signature of Jonathan Richardson jun. son of the painter, who, after he had sold his father's cabinet, made a very large collection in a hurry. Sold after his death at Langford's February 1772."[1] We have observed above (p. 148) that Richardson the younger sold his father's collection of old-master drawings, but seems to have retained and nursed very carefully the actual works of his father.

Examples of the handwriting of both Richardson the elder and Richardson the younger, taken from their notes on drawings and mounts, appear also in Lugt's *Les Marques de Collections,* pp. 562–63, nos. 2993, 2994, 2995, 2996 (the elder, in pencil and in ink), nos. 2997, 2997a (the younger, in pencil and in ink). Examples of inscriptions by both the elder and the younger are reproduced in the pages following. The writing of each varies a great deal, as influenced by deliberacy or haste, or by other circumstances. As Lugt remarks, the younger Richardson sometimes imitates his father. The inscriptions on face and back of the thirty-three drawings of Pope and one of his mother which follow and on one of Pope which is placed earlier (no. 8) seem to me to be safely ascribable to Richardson the elder—with the notable exception of the remark by Richardson the younger on the back of no. 23, the inscription probably in the hand of Richardson the younger on the face of no. 37(1), and the inscriptions on the front of nos. 30 and Ex. 9, Pope and his mother in Bull's *Strawberry Hill* at Farmington.

In the biographical sketch of Richardson carried to Bologna about 1723 by the London bookseller Andrew Hay and digested by him for Father Orlandi's *L'Abecedario*

1. Lugt, *Les Marques de Collections,* p. 403, no. 2170 (Richardson the younger); pp. 255–56, John Barnard and his sale of 16 February 1787. Review articles of Lugt's *Les Marques* by A. M. Hind, *The Connoisseur,* *61* (December 1921), 210–14, and by C. F. Bell, *Print* *Collector's Quarterly, 9* (February 1922), 43–44, raise some questions about Richardson marks, but do not I believe cast any doubt on the tradition which I outline.

above, left

Ex. 7. Oil painting, self-portrait, by Jonathan Richardson the elder. 29 x 24 in. National Portrait Gallery no. 706.

left

Ex. 8. Drawing in black, white, and orange crayons on dark blue paper, self-portrait, by Jonathan Richardson the elder. 18 x 12⅜ in. British Museum, Department of Prints and Drawings, 1902–8–22–40. By permission of the Trustees of the British Museum. The ink inscription to the left ("His Son has written on the back / Tranquilla Senectus.") and that in the center ("J. Richardson Senr / by himself.") are in the hand of Horace Walpole. See p. 171. The date "6 Ap. 33" in black crayon, to the right, is in the hand of Richardson the elder. His monogram stamp "JR" appears just to the right of the collar.

above, right

Ex. 9. Etching, Jonathan Richardson the younger, by Jonathan Richardson the elder. 6¾₆ x 4⅛ plate mark. Frontispiece to Richardson the younger's posthumous *Richardsoniana,* 1776.

Pittorico,[2] the drawings in Richardson's collection are said to be "mounted with great care, on the thinnest paper, and bordered with gold."[3] If the word "gold" be translated into "ochre" or "bistre," the mounts which survive with the drawings in the Warner collection and with the laureated head of Pope in the British Museum will perhaps satisfy this description.

2. Vertue 3.13 (1723): "he says it was such a long epistle of his own perfections, his son's qualifications, and his daughters, and his collection, that he was ashamed to show it, but made a small account of himself which is what is printed in the *Abecedario*. And that of Richardson's writing he says he has lost."

3. [Pellegrino Antonio Orlandi], *L'Ab[e]cedario Pittorico . . . In Firenze . . . M.DCC.XXXI*, p. 389: "i quali con somma diligenza, e studio affissi sopra finissima carta, perfilati d'oro riempiono circa trenta libri."

The Cornell Drawings

The following fourteen entries for drawings by Richardson in the Cornell collection are given parenthetical numbers, 19(1)—19(14), because the drawings came to light only in September 1964, after the rest of the manuscript had been prepared for the printer. They are placed at this point in the book, however, because they constitute a series of drawings on white paper parallel to the three other series of Richardson portraits in the book; drawings in pencil on vellum, with one in crayons on blue paper (nos. 20–37), etchings (nos. 38–48), and oil paintings (nos. 49–56). A fifteenth drawing in the same collection, pencil on vellum, dated 1738, is placed later as no. 37(1).

19(1). PENCIL DRAWING ON WHITE PAPER, BY JONATHAN RICHARDSON, C. 1734? THE KAUFMANN COLLECTION OF SWIFT AND POPE, CORNELL UNIVERSITY LIBRARY. CF. NOS. 23, 28.

In October 1760 Sir Harbord Harbord, of Gunston Hall, Norfolk, married Mary Assheton, coheiress of Middleton Hall, in Lancashire, near Manchester. In August 1786 he was created Baron Suffield. He died in 1810 and was succeeded by his son (born at Middleton in 1766) William Assheton Harbord, Second Baron. He died in August 1821 and was suceeded by his younger brother Edward Harbord, Third Baron, Member of Parliament and philanthropist (*DNB*). He died in July 1835 and was succeeded by his son Edward Vernon Harbord, Fourth Baron, who died in 1853. The Barons Suffield lived at their Norfolk seat but visited Middleton on occasion, the Third Baron "frequently." The last resident of the Hall was a steward, Theophilus Smith, who died in 1843.[1] The furniture was removed from the Hall and it was pulled down in 1845.[2] The relevance of this history to the present subject will appear below.

Samuel Hibbert-Ware, physician, antiquary, and geologist, author of works concerning Scottish and Lancashire subjects, resident in later years at Hale Barns, Cheshire, was born in 1782 and died in 1848 (*DNB*). His son Titus Herbert Hibbert-Ware, born in 1810, was a barrister, who lived during his later years at Bowdon, Altringham, Cheshire. He died in 1890.[3] In July 1888 Titus Herbert Hibbert-Ware sent to the

Pope Commemoration Loan Museum at Twickenham a collection of "38 drawings of heads . . . by Richardson . . . in a "quarto volume . . . morocco bound." They included fifteen of Pope.[4] The drawings were returned to Hibbert-Ware and after that seem not to have come again to public notice.[5] In September 1964 they were in the hands of Charles Sessler and Company, of Philadelphia, having recently been obtained from an owner in England. They were purchased by Eugene M. Kaufmann, Jr., of Philadelphia, and presented to the Cornell University Library in 1965.

The straight-grained red morocco cover of the volume is decorated with a tooled gilt border, and the spine with a similar pattern. A black label on the upper part of the spine is lettered in gilt: "DRAWINGS / BY / RICHARDSON." Marbled end papers of tannish color at front and back are pasted flat against the first and last leaves. The book contains in all fifty-two quarto leaves, in twos, of a thick white laid paper. At the inner margin of some leaves is a Strasburg Lily watermark, larger than but similar to the element of the Lily in Churchill's no. 437, Strasburg Bend & Lily, dated 1722; at the inner margin of other pages is the mark "I V" [Jean Villedary], very nearly identical, if not exactly identical, in size and design with that element as it appears in Churchill no. 437.[6]

The preliminary contents are as follows:

1. Armorial bookplate inscribed in pen and ink "S. Hibbert Ware," pasted to inside of front cover.

2. A sheet of thin laid paper, 7¼ x 6¾ inches, with a large crown watermark, hinged by the left margin onto the inside edge of the front cover. This bears (in the hand of Samuel Hibbert-Ware; see no. 3 below) a pen-and-ink note about the Richardsons, father and son, derived apparently from Walpole's *Anecdotes of Painting*. On the back of this sheet is a shorter pencil inscription (apparently in the hand of T. H. Hibbert-Ware) referring to a note on Richardson in the *Cornhill Magazine* for May 1860. This (vol. 1, p. 565) is a note to an article on Hogarth [by George Augustus Henry Sala, 1828–96; cf. Sala's *William Hogarth* (London, 1866), p. 116].[7]

3. The first and second leaves of the book are blank. Written in ink on recto and verso of the third leaf is an extended note, signed "T. Hibbert-Ware, F. S. A. Scot. Bowdon, Altringham." This reads in part: "The M.S. affixed at the beginning of this volume [i.e. no. 2 above] . . . is in the handwriting of my late father Samuel Hibbert-Ware, F. S. A. Scot, &c. of Hale Barns, Cheshire, who died in 1848, and in the possession of whose family it [the book] had been for a long time. To the best of my remembrance I have heard my father say that it had been bought at the sale at Middleton near Manchester of Lord Suffield's library."

Leaves [4]–[41] of the book are numbered in pen-and-ink in the upper right corner of each recto (or on the corner of the larger drawings) "1"—"38". Each of these leaves has pasted down, more or less tightly, on the recto a drawing by Richardson, as follows:

1. Self-portrait of Richardson the elder, full face, laureated, pencil on vellum, 7⅝ x 5⅜ inches, with Richardson the younger's collection mark "R" at lower right. On the lower back in pencil in Richardson the elder's hand is a poem of eight lines, dated "12

Ap. 1732." Following the date is Richardson the elder's stamped paraphe, "JR". For the poem see below p. 157. The drawing is similar to British Museum G. g.1–510 (Binyon 6).

2–8. Drawings of John Milton, after "Cooper" and [Faithorne].

9–23. Drawings of Alexander Pope, rearranged in a partially conjectural chronological order in the catalogue of this book, nos. 19(1)–19(14) and 37(1).

24. Pencil-on-vellum drawing of Annibale Carracci.

25–29. Self-drawings of Richardson the elder.

30–33. Drawings of Richardson the younger as a boy.

34–38. Drawings of Richardson the younger as a man.

The next leaf, [42], is blank on both sides.

Leaf [43] has hinged to it two different printed Twickenham Loan Museum forms, dated July 1888. The second consists of two leaves. The first lacks a second leaf, which was the "Museum Loan Form,"[8] presumably filled out by Hibbert-Ware and sent to Twickenham with the drawings. Leaf [44] has hinged to it three pen-and-ink letters: Henry R. Tedder, Hon. Secretary of the Pope Commemoration Committee, to Hibbert-Ware, 18 July 1888, requesting the loan of the drawings;[9] Edwin Maynard, Librarian of the Free Public Library, Twickenham, to Hibbert-Ware, 21 July 1888, acknowledging receipt of the drawings; Edwin Maynard to Hibbert-Ware, 8 August 1888, announcing return of the drawings by parcel post.

Laid down flat on the recto of the same leaf, [44], is a notice of "The Pope Museum" cut from the *Athenaeum*, 11 August 1888, p. 194. Leaves [45]–[52] are blank.

Despite the possibly early date of the paper which composes the volume (1722; see above), the drawings would seem to have been brought together in it at a date later than the dispersal of the Richardson collection in 1772. The label, "Drawings By Richardson," on the spine suggests this, and even more the loss of corners suffered by many of the drawings, as if they had been not very carefully pulled from an earlier setting, and beyond that the close clipping which has followed for some of them. Sir Harbord Harbord, Bart., who had married the heiress of Middleton in 1760, and who in 1786 became First Baron Suffield, seems a possible, even a likely, first owner of this volume.

The fancy mounts for which the Richardson collection was noted have been described above; see also no. 23. Many of the drawings in the present collection, however, may never have been fully mounted by the Richardsons. They seem to be the actual *ad vivum* sketches, or stages close to these, from which Richardson elaborated his pencil-on-vellum and chalk-on-blue-paper drawings and his etchings. Among the twelve pen-and-ink drawings by Richardson in the Bull album at the Pierpont Morgan Library, two are inscribed in Richardson's hand "for the vellum." Even a more elaborate pen-and-wash drawing of Pope's mother (British Museum, Binyon 23; p. 150, n. 17) is said by Richardson the younger to be the "Scetch for a finished one in Black lead."

On the back of the pencil-on-vellum drawing of himself laureated which is placed first in this volume, Richardson had written in pencil the following verses:

Yes Pope, yes Milton I am Bayes'd you see.
But Why—go ask my Oracle, not Me:
Shee, not Severe is Beautyfull, & Wise,
Shee Thus Commanded me, & Thus it is.
May You enjoy your plenitude of Fame!
While Shee with Smiles embellishes my Name
I ask not Your Applause, nor Censure Fear,
I am Pope, Milton, Virgil, Homer Here.

12 April 1732 JR

Just above this poem, somebody, presumably not Richardson the elder and not the younger, has sketched in pencil a small caricature wigged head in profile, nose and chin up, eyelid down—the very portrait of self-satisfaction. *Sublimi feriam sidera vertice.*

1. Information from Arnold Goldman, University of Manchester.

2. Richard James, *Iter Lancastrense; a Poem . . . 1636*, ed. Thomas Corser (Manchester, Printed for the Chetham Society, 1845), p. 31, note; William Farrer and J. Brownbill, eds. *The Victoria History of the County of Lancashire, 5* (London, 1911), 167–68. The *Victoria History* cites E. Butterworth, *Middleton* [1840], p. 18, in support of the statement that Middleton was visited "frequently" by the Third Baron. Cf. Richard Mackenzie Bacon, *A Memoir of the Life of Edward, Third Baron Suffield* (Norwich, 1838, privately printed), pp. 249, 488.

3. *Law Times* (30 August 1890), p. 319. The elder Hibbert-Ware was on the Council of the Chetham Society in 1845, and the younger was a member of the Society in 1858.

4. *Catalogue*, p. 35, no. 178, and p. 56; hectograph duplicate of a letter from Edwin Maynard, for the Loan Museum, to Hibbert-Ware 21 July 1888, at the Borough of Twickenham Public Library; *Athenaeum*, 11 August 1888, p. 194; *Richmond and Twickenham Times*, 4 August 1888, p. 7. col. 2; *Graphic, 38.* 152 (11 August 1888).

5. Mr. T. M. Murray-Rust informed me in 1961

that the drawings had not come down on the Hibbert-Ware side of the family. Mary Clementina Stewart Hibbert-Ware (the novelist Mrs. Hibbert-Ware), widow and surviving heir of the barrister, died in 1911, leaving all her personal property to her niece Agnes Stewart, of Southport, Lancashire.

6. W. A. Churchill, *Watermarks in Paper . . . in the XVII and XVIII Centuries* (Amsterdam, 1935), pp. [85], [CCCXXVII].

7. Lying loose inside the volume is a sheet of blue wove note paper, $6\frac{15}{16}$ x $5\frac{3}{8}$ in., having on it, in an unidentified hand, pen-and-ink notes about Richardson the elder, derived, at least in large part, from Walpole or Vertue, and identified as "Extract copied from a manuscript diary or pocket book of George Augustus Sala, Feb. 22nd. 1860." The contents of these jottings are very close to the material in Sala's note on Richardson in the *Cornhill* for May 1860.

8. Complete examples of the several forms used in advertising the Loan Museum during the summer of 1888 are preserved at the Borough of Twickenham Public Library.

9. A Mr. C. W. Sutton had told the Committee of their whereabouts.

19(2). PEN-AND-PENCIL DRAWING ON WHITE PAPER, BY JONATHAN RICHARDSON, 1736. THE KAUFMANN COLLECTION OF SWIFT AND POPE, CORNELL UNIVERSITY LIBRARY. SEE NO. 19(1). CF. NO. 32.

19(3). PEN-AND-WASH DRAWING ON WHITE PAPER, BY JONATHAN RICHARDSON, APPARENTLY 1736. THE KAUFMANN COLLECTION OF SWIFT AND POPE, CORNELL UNIVERSITY LIBRARY. SEE NO. 19(1). CF. NO. 32.

Richardson's self-drawing in pencil on leaf 27 of the Hibbert-Ware volume is similarly covered on the back with crayon.

19(1). Lead pencil on white paper. 4½ x 3¼ in. On leaf 20 in the Hibbert-Ware album. The Kaufmann Collection of Swift and Pope, Cornell University Library.

19(2). Pen and ink and pencil on white paper. 6 x 4¾ in. Inscribed on back in pen and ink "Pope", on front lower left in pen and ink "Pope", and at lower right in pencil "4 Sep. 1736". Above the date is stamped Richardson the elder's monogram "JR." On leaf 22 in the Hibbert-Ware album. The Kaufmann Collection of Swift and Pope, Cornell University Library.

right

19(3). Pen and ink and wash, over light pencil lines, on white paper cut to octagonal shape. The background is washed. The back of the paper is covered with crayon in several colors. 5 x 4¾ in. On leaf 21 in the Hibbert-Ware album. The Kaufmann Collection of Swift and Pope, Cornell University Library.

below

19(4). Black crayon over etching on white paper trimmed at upper corners to hexagonal shape and made up at lower left and near lower right corner. 6½ x 5¼ in. Inscribed at lower right in pen and ink "Mr Pope." On leaf 23 in the Hibbert-Ware album. The Kaufmann Collection of Swift and Pope, Cornell University Library.

19(4). BLACK-CRAYON DRAWING OVER AN ETCHING ON WHITE PAPER, BY JONATHAN RICHARDSON. THE KAUFMANN COLLECTION OF SWIFT AND POPE, CORNELL UNIVERSITY LIBRARY. SEE NO. 19(1). CF. NO. 40.

Richardson has drawn this image in black crayon over a counterproof and hence reversed image of his etching reproduced in this book as no. 40. The purpose of a counterproof, taken from a damp impression on paper, was apparently to provide an etcher with a printed image looking in the same direction as that on the plate. Corrections drawn on the counterproof could be more easily transferred to the plate (A. M. Hind, *A Short History of Engraving and Etching* [London, 1908], p. 15; William M. Ivins, *How Prints Look* [Boston, 1953], pp. 14, 140–41, 164). But Richardson has here apparently gone beyond such a purpose, to make in effect a new image. It is difficult to say whether the counterproof which he has all but covered with crayon represents an earlier state of the plate represented in no. 40.

19(5). PEN-AND-PENCIL DRAWING ON WHITE PAPER, BY JONATHAN RICHARDSON, C. 1738. THE KAUFMANN COLLECTION OF SWIFT AND POPE, CORNELL UNIVERSITY LIBRARY. SEE NO. 19(1). CF. NOS. 44 AND 45 (1738).

19(6). PENCIL DRAWING ON PAPER, BY JONATHAN RICHARDSON. THE KAUFMANN COLLECTION OF SWIFT AND POPE, CORNELL UNIVERSITY LIBRARY. SEE NO. 19(1).

No close counterpart to this profile appears in either the series of Richardson pencil-on-vellum drawings nos. (20–37) or the series of Richardson etchings (nos. 38–48). The face, however, seems younger, or at least not older, than that of the three drawings in the Cornell collection which I place next, nos. 19(7)–19(9). These may be dated approximately 1738.

19(7). PEN-AND-PENCIL DRAWING ON WHITE PAPER, BY JONATHAN RICHARDSON. THE KAUFMANN COLLECTION OF SWIFT AND POPE, CORNELL UNIVERSITY LIBRARY. SEE NO. 19(1). CF. NO. 19(9).

19(8). PEN-AND-PENCIL DRAWING ON WHITE PAPER, BY JONATHAN RICHARDSON. THE KAUFMANN COLLECTION OF SWIFT AND POPE, CORNELL UNIVERSITY LIBRARY. SEE NO. 19(1). CF. NO. 19(9).

19(9). PENCIL DRAWING ON WHITE PAPER, BY JONATHAN RICHARDSON, C. 1738. THE KAUFMANN COLLECTION OF SWIFT AND POPE, CORNELL UNIVERSITY LIBRARY. SEE NO. 19(1). CF. NOS. 19(7–8) AND NOS. 46, 47, 48 (ETCHING DATED 1738).

above, left

19(5). Pen and ink over pencil on white paper made up at lower right and left corners. 4⅛ x 3¹⁵⁄₁₆ in. Inscribed at lower left in pen and ink "Pope". Richardson the elder's monogram "JR" stamped near the nape. On leaf 12 in the Hibbert-Ware album. The Kaufmann Collection of Swift and Pope, Cornell University Library.

above, right

19(6). Pencil on white paper cut to ten sides. Maximum dimensions 4½ x 3 in. Inscribed in pen and ink at lower left with Richardson the elder's monogram "JR." On leaf 14 in the Hibbert-Ware album. The Kaufmann Collection of Swift and Pope, Cornell University Library.

right

19(7). Pen and ink over pencil on white paper. 3¾ x 2⅞ in. On leaf 10 of the Hibbert-Ware album. The Kaufmann Collection of Swift and Pope, Cornell University Library.

19(8). Pen and ink over pencil area lines on white paper, with a single curved stroke of red crayon behind the collar. 4½ x 3 in. Inscribed on front at lower right in pen and ink "Pope". On leaf 11 in the Hibbert-Ware album. The Kaufmann Collection of Swift and Pope, Cornell University Library.

19(9). Pencil on white paper. 5 x 3¾ in. Inscribed on the back in pen and ink "Pope" and on the front at lower left in pencil, apparently in Richardson the younger's hand, "A. Pope." Richardson the elder's monogram "JR" stamped behind the collar. On leaf 9 in the Hibbert-Ware album. The Kaufmann Collection of Swift and Pope, Cornell University Library.

19(10). PENCIL DRAWING ON WHITE PAPER, BY JONATHAN RICHARDSON. THE KAUFMANN COLLECTION OF SWIFT AND POPE, CORNELL UNIVERSITY LIBRARY. SEE NO. 19(1). CF. NOS. 24 AND 25 (DRAWINGS, THE FIRST DATED 1734).

19(11). PENCIL DRAWING ON WHITE PAPER, BY JONATHAN RICHARDSON. THE KAUFMANN COLLECTION OF SWIFT AND POPE, CORNELL UNIVERSITY LIBRARY. SEE NO. 19(1). CF. NO. 19(12).

The three-quarter face, which is close to that of the next entry, has no close counterpart in either the series of pencil-on-vellum drawings by Richardson (nos. 20–37) or the series of Richardson etchings (nos. 38–48).

19(12). PENCIL DRAWING ON WHITE PAPER, BY JONATHAN RICHARDSON. THE KAUFMANN COLLECTION OF SWIFT AND POPE, CORNELL UNIVERSITY LIBRARY. SEE NO. 19(1). CF. NO. 19(11).

Pope appears in a headdress (chaperon and liripipe[1]) and buttoned garment which are reminiscent of three-quarter-face miniatures of Geoffrey Chaucer found in manuscripts of Thomas Hoccleve's *De Regimine Principum* and published in several engravings during Pope's lifetime. George Vertue's frontispiece for the 1721 edition of Chaucer by John Urry shows two buttons and was perhaps taken from a Hoccleve miniature pasted into a miscellaneous manuscript book which was destroyed in the Cottonian fire of 1731. Another engraving by Vertue (with three buttons) derives in part from a manuscript of Hoccleve then in Lord Oxford's collection; this was issued in Vertue's series of *Twelve Heads of the Poets,* 1730. Another engraving (with three buttons) was that by Houbraken, dated 1741, which appears as the first plate in Birch's *Heads of Illustrious Persons,* published in 1743 by friends of Richardson, the Knaptons.[2] This was taken from Hoccleve indirectly, through a painting in the possession of Pope's friend Sir Hans Sloane (now National Portrait Gallery no. 532). A picture of Chaucer in a black frame hung in the "Little Parlor" at Twickenham at Pope's death.[3] No. 37(1), "A. Pope, as Milton," and the corresponding etchings, nos. 38b. and 38bx., support the notion that in the present drawing Pope may be represented in some sort of Chaucerian (or Canterburian?) role.[4] The loss of a corner of the paper, however, leaves us with the puzzling inscription "Pope as a C [?]. . . ."

1. Herbert Norris, *Costume and Fashion,* 2 (London, 1927), 384–85; Nevil Truman, *Historic Costuming* (London, 1936), p. 26; Nancy Bradfield, *Historical Costumes of England* (New York, 1958), pp. 34, 43.

2. I have examined the engravings in Urry and Birch, but my account of the Chaucer portraits relies mainly on George L. Lam and Warren H. Smith, "George Vertue's Contributions to Chaucerian Iconography," *MLQ,* 5 (September 1944), esp. 306, 308, 317–18, 320. M. H. Spielmann, *The Portraits of Geoffrey Chaucer* (London, 1900), pp. 7 and 12, illustrates the Hoccleve Chaucer in Harleian MS. 4866 and Sir Hans Sloane's Chaucer painted on an oak panel, National Portrait Gallery no. 532.

3. Mapledurham inventory, *Notes and Queries,* 6th Series, 5 (13 May 1882), 364.

4. In 1888 Pope's grotto at Twickenham was reported to contain, along with a bust of himself a bust of a "pilgrim." See no. 57–61.13. This was no doubt the bust (of white stone?) which on a visit in 1960 I saw occupying a niche in one of the chambers at the river end of the tunnel. This figure wears in the hat a cockle shell (badge of pilgrims to St. James of Compostella), and a similar shell appears in the wall above the niche.

above, left

19(10). Pencil on white paper cut to octagonal shape. 3¹⁄₁₆ x 2⅝ in. On leaf 16 of the Hibbert-Ware album. The Kaufmann Collection of Swift and Pope, Cornell University Library.

above, right

19(11). Pencil on white paper cut to octagonal shape. 2⅞ x 2¼ in. On leaf 15 of the Hibbert-Ware album. The Kaufmann Collection of Swift and Pope, Cornell University Library.

right

19(12). Pencil on white paper. 5⅛ x 3¹⁵⁄₁₆ in. Inscribed on back in pen and ink "Pope" and on front in pencil at lower center and right "Pope as a C [?] . . . . " Richardson the elder's monogram "JR" stamped near the collar. On leaf 19 of the Hibbert-Ware album. The Kaufmann Collection of Swift and Pope, Cornell University Library.

19(13). BLACK CRAYON AND PENCIL DRAWING ON WHITE PAPER, BY JONATHAN
RICHARDSON, 1741. THE KAUFMANN COLLECTION OF SWIFT AND
POPE, CORNELL UNIVERSITY LIBRARY. SEE NO. 19(1).

As in no. 19(14), Pope appears in this drawing "asleep." An inscription partly legible
on the back seems to say that he was sketched while napping in an easy chair in his
parlor. The Mapledurham inventory of furnishings at Twickenham after Pope's death
includes "Six Beach Chaires [and] 4 Windsor Arm Chaires" in the Great Parlor and
"two Arm Chaires covered with green Bays" and "two Arm Chaires Beach" in the
Library.[1] "I nod in Company, I wake at Night," says Pope as early as 1733 in *Satire* II.i
(l.13). "I sleep in company, & wake at night: which is vexatious," he echoes himself in
a letter to Richardson 21 November [1743].[2] Johnson in his *Life of Pope* adds that
Pope "once slumbered at his own table while the Prince of Wales was talking of
poetry."[3] After the Twickenham Exhibition of 1888, this drawing was reproduced by
the *Graphic* in a wood engraving as a "Portrait of Pope Apparently Taken after
Death."[4]

1. *Notes and Queries*, 6th Series, 5 (13 May 1882), 3, 198. Note 3 quotes Lord Marchmont, the Duchess
364. of Marlborough, and Warburton to a similar effect.
2. *Correspondence* 4.484. 4. *Graphic, 38.*152 (11 August 1888).
3. *Lives of the Poets*, ed. G. B. Hill (Oxford, 1905),

19(14). PENCIL DRAWING ON WHITE PAPER, BY JONATHAN RICHARDSON, 1741,
AT TWICKENHAM. THE KAUFMANN COLLECTION OF SWIFT AND POPE,
CORNELL UNIVERSITY LIBRARY. SEE NO. 19(1). CF. NO. 19(13).

For this drawing Richardson used a piece of paper the other side of which had apparently already been used for some notes in pen and ink on seventeenth-century
painters, partly lost at the top and left side when, either before or after the use for
drawing, the paper was trimmed: "the Conception} / Lanfran[c]? / Claude. / . . . ap. /
. . . shd} / Col[rd] / V. Dyck" (reading by Professor Donald Eddy).

20. PENCIL-ON-VELLUM DRAWING, BY JONATHAN RICHARDSON, 1733. MR. AND MRS.
ROGER WARNER, BURFORD, OXFORDSHIRE. SEE ALSO NO. 8, AND NOS. 22, 24,
27–29, 31, 32.

Mr. and Mrs. Roger Warner, of Burford, Oxfordshire, are the owners of a collection of thirteen pencil-on-vellum drawings by Richardson, of which nine are heads of
Pope. Mr. Warner tells me that his father and grandfather (Metford Warner, a designer and manufacturer of wallpaper—Messrs Jeffrey & Co., London) were on a walking tour in Sussex about 1905 or 1906, and at an auction or jumble sale at Bignor Park,
Frittlewell, they bought for a few shillings an old red morocco binding with unusual
gilt tooling of birds and insect design. It was only on their getting the book home that
the collection of drawings was found inside.[1] The drawings are recorded in G. W.
Snelgrove's University of London thesis of 1936. The present drawing has been reproduced at p. 144, Plate 8, of Robert Halsband's *Life of Lady Mary Wortley Mon-*

19(13). Black crayon over pencil on white paper
made up at upper right and left and lower left
corners. 5⅜ x 3¾ in. Inscribed in pencil on back
at lower left "July 1741 / . . . . / . . . n of easy chair
Parlor", and on front at lower left in pencil "a
Sleep". Richardson the elder's monogram "JR"
stamped on the front at lower right. On leaf 18 of
the Hibbert-Ware album. The Kaufmann Collection
of Swift and Pope, Cornell University Library.

19(14). Pencil on white paper. 5½ x 3⁵⁄₁₆ in. Inscribed on the back in pen and ink with notes about
seventeenth-century painters (see entry) and on the
front across the lower part in pencil "at Twitnam
11 July 1741 / Pope a S . . . p". Richardson the
elder's monogram "JR" stamped above the inscription at right. On leaf 17 in the Hibbert-Ware album.
The Kaufmann Collection of Swift and Pope, Cornell University Library.

tagu, Oxford, 1956. All nine of these drawings were exhibited at the National Portrait Gallery Exhibition of 1961.

1. Letter of 2 July 1956. The collection includes also four drawings by Richardson of subjects other than Pope, and two drawings apparently by Robert White.

21. CRAYON (CHALK) DRAWING, BY JONATHAN RICHARDSON, C. 1733. BEINECKE RARE BOOK AND MANUSCRIPT LIBRARY, YALE UNIVERSITY.

In 1854 Peter Cunningham wrote: "Mr. Rogers, the poet, has the head (I suspect by Jervas) so often engraved for his Letters and Poems: it was a present to Mr. Rogers from the poet Crabbe." I have searched the Catalogue of the Rogers sale, 28 April 1856, and eighteen following days, without being able to identify such a drawing. It was at the Rogers sale, however, that John Murray III acquired the Roubiliac terra cotta of Pope (see no. 57). Murray's granddaughter Lady Proby tells me that an old family catalogue has the entry: "Pope in red and black chalk by Richardson." On 9 November, 1894, George Scharf drew a pen-and-ink sketch of a head of Pope turned three-quarters to the left, in open shirt collar, with natural hair (pretty clearly the drawing known today—the subject of this entry). He inscribed it: "(original at Chiswick House) A. Pope drawn by Richardson in black & red chalk upon blue-gray paper belonging to Hallam Murray."[1] About 1936 or 1937, Professor John Butt was shown by Mrs. Hallam Murray (mother of Lady Proby) a drawing of Pope by Richardson "in terracotta and white crayon on blue paper." Like Cunningham in 1854, he was under the impression this was the original for the title page of Pope's *Letters*.[2] In an album of Popeana, once in the Hallam Murray collection, which came to the Yale Rare Book Room in 1939, is the drawing in crayons on blue paper which appears below as no. 21. Despite the difference between this and the profile etching which Richardson did for Pope's title page (see no. 43.1), it seems very likely that only one drawing is represented in the allusions just quoted—perhaps one of the four heads of Pope in "chalks" on blue paper, II.39 in the Richardson sale of 1772—and the only such drawing known today. The Yale drawing is reproduced as the frontispiece of vol. *1* of Professor Sherburn's *Correspondence of Alexander Pope* (Oxford, 1956) and in the review (by C. H.) of the *Correspondence* in *Country Life*, *121* (24 January 1957), 155.

1. Separate sheet of note paper in Pope file of photographs at the National Portrait Gallery. Scharf somewhat slants the drawing to look like the supposed original at Chiswick House (no. 18).

2. Letter of c. 1951.

22. PENCIL-ON-VELLUM DRAWING, BY JONATHAN RICHARDSON, 1733. MR. AND MRS. ROGER WARNER. SEE NO. 20.

23 a and b. PENCIL-ON-VELLUM DRAWING, BY JONATHAN RICHARDSON, 1734. DEPARTMENT OF PRINTS AND DRAWINGS, BRITISH MUSEUM.

To return to 1842 and the collections of Horace Walpole: a second sale was held for ten days in June. This was a sale of prints and drawings "removed from Strawberry Hill"

20. Lead pencil on vellum. 5⅞ x 4⅜ in. On a paper mount, with watermark of lion in a circle and crown above, similar to Churchill 93. Framed in two ruled ink lines, the inner one thicker. Inscribed on front lower right: "2 [?] June 1733" with Richardson the younger's stamp "R" following; on the back lower right "Pope by the Life" with Richardson the elder's monogram stamp "JR" following. Mr. and Mrs. Roger Warner, Burford, Oxfordshire.

21. Red, black, and white crayons (chalks) on blue paper. 8¹¹⁄₁₆ x 6⅜ in. Richardson the elder's monogram stamp "JR" in lower right corner. Yale University Library.

22 Lead pencil on vellum. 5¾ x 4⅞ in. On a paper mount, with watermark "I V." Framed in two ruled ink lines, the inner one thicker. Richardson the younger's stamp "R" on front lower right; inscribed on the back: "Alex Pope Esqr" with Richardson the elder's monogram stamp "JR" following, and then "16 June 1733." Mr. and Mrs. Roger Warner, Burford, Oxfordshire.

Your Friend but gives the Bay you had before,
Friendship wou'd fain, but Friendship Can no more.
31 Jan 1733

23 a. Lead pencil on vellum. 6⅜ x 5⅛ in. On a paper mount; framed in an outer thick line of black ink, a ruled line of brown ink just inside that, a space, then three ruled lines of brown ink, a lesser space, and, inside two ruled ink lines, a band of ochre paint. Inscribed in Richardson the elder's hand beneath picture on front: "Your Friend but gives the Bay you had before, / Friendship wou'd fain, but Friendship Can no more. / 31 Jan 1733/[4]". Richardson the younger's stamp "R". For a further note on the couplet, see no. 23 b. By permission of the Trustees of the British Museum Department of Prints and Drawings, 1902–8–22–17.

The Verses were my Father's, M.ʳ Pope made the Little
alteration, perhaps they were better before.
J.R. jun.ʳ

23 b. In the couplet inscribed under no. 23 a. the word "but" in the second line has been lightly drawn through and the word "evn" written lightly above. On the back of the mount appears an inscription in pen and ink: "The Verses were my Fathers, Mʳ Pope made the Little / alteration, perhaps they were better before. / J.R. junʳ" Richardson has given Pope a wreath composed mainly of bay leaves, but with what are apparently four or five ivy leaves intermingled. The couplet is perhaps a commentary on the earlier phase of Pope portraiture (see no. 6, by Kneller) where Pope is crowned only with the ivy. By permission of the Trustees of the British Museum.

to the premises of Mr. Robins in Covent Garden. On the twenty-second day, lot 1266 was "A folio volume of miscellaneous drawings, by various masters, ancient and modern, collected and arranged by Lord Orford, as follows"—116 pages itemized. Pages 60–87 held thirty-nine drawings by Richardson the elder, including, on p. 67, "One a laureated bust of Alexander Pope, from the life, 1733."[1] The folio volume was bought by Graves of Pall Mall for £ 53.11s.[2]

In May 1902 this collection of drawings by Richardson was in the hands of E. Parsons & Sons, 45 Brompton Road, London S. W.[3] Shortly afterwards, the entire collection, thirty-nine drawings in all, was acquired from P. & D. Colnaghi by the Department of Prints and Drawings of the British Museum. The portrait of Pope laureated was described in the first issue of the *Burlington Magazine* (March 1903) and was illustrated in *The Magazine of Art* at about the same time.[4] The drawing was exhibited at the National Portrait Gallery Exhibition in 1961.

1. *A Catalogue of the Collection of Scarce Prints Removed from Strawberry Hill . . . for Sale in London . . . By Mr. George Robins, At His Great Rooms in Covent Garden*, 13–23 June 1842, 10th Day, p. 122, lot 1266. On page 87 of this lot, two sketches by Correggio and one by Titian are not ascribed to Richardson, but in the event have turned out to be copies initialed by him.

2. *Aedes Strawberrianae, Names of Purchasers And The Prices . . . to the Collection . . . withdrawn From Strawberry Hill . . .* London, Printed for J. H. Burn . . . [n.d.], p. 19.

3. Document at the National Portrait Gallery.

4. "New Acquisitions at the National Museums," *Burlington Magazine, 1* (March 1903), 134; W. Roberts, "Recent Acquisitions at Our Public Museums and Galleries, The Print Room, British Museum," *The Magazine of Art*, New Series, *1* (London 1903), 40–44.

24. PENCIL-ON-VELLUM DRAWING, BY JONATHAN RICHARDSON, 1734. MR. AND MRS. ROGER WARNER. SEE NO. 20.

25. PENCIL-ON-VELLUM DRAWING, BY JONATHAN RICHARDSON, C. 1734. HER MAJESTY THE QUEEN, WINDSOR CASTLE. SEE NOS. 33 AND 35.

Four drawings said to be from Strawberry Hill, three of Pope, one of Milton, appeared in a sale of pictures from the collection of the "well-known connoisseur deceased" Charles Sackville Bale, Esq., at Christie's, 24 May 1881, and were bought by the Royal Librarian.[1] (It is impossible to identify the drawings sold in 1881 with anything which had been in either the Walpole Sale for April 1842, at Strawberry Hill, or the later one of June 1842, in London.) In 1888 Queen Victoria lent three drawings of Pope by Richardson, said to be "formerly in" the "Strawberry Hill Collection," "afterwards in the possession of Mr. C. Sackville Bale," to the Pope Commemoration Loan Museum at Twickenham.[2] These would be the three drawings of Pope, with one of Milton, now at Windsor Castle, which have on the back of their common mount an old vellum label bearing an ink inscription in an unidentifiable hand: "H Walpole's Sale / Purchased by me at Strawberry Hill / sketches from life by Richardson / of Alexander Pope." The subject of this entry, no. 493 in A. P. Oppé's *English Drawings . . . at Windsor Castle* (1950), was reproduced in reverse in *The Graphic, 38* (11 August, 1888), 152: "lent by the Queen from the Royal Library at Windsor." The three draw-

above

24. Lead pencil on vellum. 4¾ x 4⅛ in. On a paper mount, with watermark "Pro Patria," Britannia and Lion in a stockade, similar to Churchill 133 and 147. Framed in two ruled ink lines, the inner one thicker. Richardson the younger's stamp "R" on front lower right; inscribed on back: "K Mr Pope May 1734" followed by Richardson the elder's monogram stamp "JR." Mr. and Mrs. Roger Warner, Burford, Oxfordshire.

above, right

25. Lead pencil on vellum. 2½ x 3 in. Inscribed "Pope's" in an overset label in upper left corner. A. P. Oppé, *English Drawings . . . at Windsor Castle* (London 1950), p. 83, no. 493. Windsor Castle, by gracious permission of Her Majesty The Queen.

right

26 a. Lead pencil on vellum. 4 x 5 in. Inscribed in pencil on the back: "Pope by the Life / 5 Feb. 1734/5." Richardson the elder's monogram stamp "JR" above the date. See no. 26 b. Dr. Dallas Pratt, New York City.

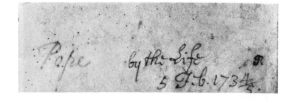

26 b. Inscription on back of 26 a. "Pope by the Life / 5 Feb. 1734/5." Richardson the elder's monogram stamp "JR" above the date.

ings are reproduced by Edmund Gosse, *English Literature, An Illustrated Record, 3* (London, 1903), 194. They were exhibited at the National Portrait Gallery Exhibition in 1961.

1. A. P. Oppé, *English Drawings Stuart and Georgian Periods. In the Collection of His Majesty The King At Windsor Castle* (London, The Phaidon Press, Ltd., 1950), p. 83, nos. 493–95. Bought by Holmes for £ 7.7s each.

2. *Catalogue* p. 34, no. 166: "Three portrait heads of Alexander Pope. Drawn in pencil by Jonathan Richardson, and signed at the back with his monogram. Drawn for Horace Walpole, and formerly in his Strawberry Hill Collection. Afterwards in the possession of Mr. C. Sackville Bale. Lent by Her Majesty the Queen."

26. PENCIL-ON-VELLUM DRAWING, BY JONATHAN RICHARDSON, 1735. DR. DALLAS PRATT, NEW YORK CITY. SEE NOS. 34 AND 37.

At some time during the 1930s, Dr. Dallas Pratt of New York acquired from an English dealer a set of three pencil-on-vellum drawings of Pope by Richardson.

27. PENCIL-ON-VELLUM DRAWING, BY JONATHAN RICHARDSON, 1735. MR. AND MRS. ROGER WARNER. SEE NO. 20.

A pencil-on-vellum self-portrait by Richardson, in the British Museum (Binyon, *Drawings by British Artists, 3*, Richardson no. 6: G.g 1–510) shows him full-face as a young man wearing a wreath of twenty-two visible bay leaves very similar to that in the present drawing of Pope. And see no. 19(1).

28. PENCIL-ON-VELLUM DRAWING, BY JONATHAN RICHARDSON, 1736. MR. AND MRS. ROGER WARNER. SEE NO. 20.

29. PENCIL-ON-VELLUM DRAWING, BY JONATHAN RICHARDSON, 1736. MR. AND MRS. ROGER WARNER. SEE NO. 20.

30 and Ex.10. PENCIL-ON-VELLUM DRAWINGS OF POPE (1736) AND HIS MOTHER (1703), BY JONATHAN RICHARDSON. W. S. LEWIS, FARMINGTON, CONNECTICUT.

The drawings of Pope and his mother and father, once in the Red Bed Chamber at Strawberry Hill, have (see p. 151) dropped out of sight. But it happens that good substitutes for the drawings of Pope and his mother have been preserved in connection with Strawberry Hill. The Walpolian collector Richard Bull of Ongar in Essex grangerized a copy of the 1784 *Description of Strawberry Hill,* now in the collection of W. S. Lewis at Farmington.[1] At the account of the four drawings in the Red Bed Chamber (p. 30) are inserted three pencil drawings: Pope, Pope's mother, and Bolingbroke. The Bolingbroke is finely drawn on wove white paper and is inscribed on the front "Lord Bolingbroke at Strawberry Hill—Page 30" (on the back, "Page 30 of the Catalogue"). But Pope and his mother are drawn on vellum. Each has an inscription, including a date,

27. Lead pencil on vellum. 5⅞ x 4¾ in. On a paper mount, with watermark "I V." Framed in two ruled ink lines, the inner one thicker. Richardson the younger's stamp "R" on front lower right; inscribed on back lower right: "Mʳ Pope / 18 June 1735" with Richardson the elder's monogram stamp "JR" above "1735." Mr. and Mrs. Roger Warner, Burford, Oxfordshire.

28. Lead pencil on vellum. 5 x 4 in. On a paper mount, with watermark of crown and letters "GR" below, like Churchill 139 or 254. Framed in two ruled ink lines, the inner one thicker. Richardson the younger's stamp "R" on front lower right; inscribed on back: "Mʳ Pope. / 24 Jan 1735/6" with Richardson the elder's monogram stamp "JR" above the date. Mr. and Mrs. Roger Warner, Burford, Oxfordshire.

29. Lead pencil on vellum. 6⅜ x 5¼ in. On a recent paper mount, framed and glazed. Richardson the younger's stamp "R" on front lower right; inscribed on back lower center "Pope" and on back lower right: "Feb. 8 1735/6" with Richardson the elder's monogram stamp "JR." Mr. and Mrs. Roger Warner, Burford, Oxfordshire.

30. Lead pencil on vellum. 5¼ x 3¾ in. With two ruled lines around the edge, in pencil and partly in ink, the outer line heavier. Inscribed lightly in ink on front lower left "A. Pope July 7. 1736" and in right lower corner in pen and ink with Richardson the elder's monogram "JR." At the right edge, nearly half way up, covered in part by the inner pencil line, is Richardson the younger's stamp "R." W. S. Lewis, Farmington, Connecticut.

on the front, written in a hand apparently used by Bull in imitation of Richardson inscriptions which he sometimes lost from backs of drawings in trimming them to the frames of double pencil line which he imposed on the fronts.[2] Both drawings have the elder Richardson's monogram "JR" written with a dry pen on the front, probably by Bull, and that of Pope has the younger Richardson's stamp "R". The image of Pope's mother is neither that of the C. Carter etching of 1774 (from the Strawberry Hill drawing—See p. 151) nor that of the British Museum pen-and-ink drawing. Whereas the drawing of Bolingbroke is a copy, Pope and his mother are authentic drawings by Richardson the elder—though not of course the drawings which were at Strawberry Hill until 1842 and have now disappeared. The drawing of Pope's mother in her middle age is inscribed on the back in Richardson's hand "1703" and "by Candle light" and thus is evidence for a friendship between the families going back fifteen years earlier than is indicated by the earliest date on a drawing of Pope (no. 8.1).[3]

1. Hazen, *Bibliography of the Strawberry Hill Press,* pp. 123–28, Copy 13 on p. 128, "extra-illustrated with prints, drawings by John Carter, and Detached Pieces. . . . Inlaid to folio (probably about 1790)."

2. Richard Bull's album of English drawings at the Pierpont Morgan Library includes twenty-six by Jonathan Richardson, and of these thirteen are pencil on vellum. Most of these thirteen have a pencil inscription on the back in the hand of Richardson the elder and also his stamped monogram "JR." A few have added inscriptions in the hand of Richardson the younger. The small stamped R of Richardson the younger (see p. 152) occurs here and there on the fronts. A few of the larger drawings are still on mounts with frames consisting of dark ink ruled lines and bands of ochre watercolor, very likely the original mounts of the Richardson Collection. (See the mount of Pope laureated 1733/4 in the British Museum, acquired in 1902, formerly at Strawberry Hill.) Others have a similar, but distinguishable kind of frame drawn around the drawings, on the actual paper of the album, presumably by Bull himself, who had a penchant for fancy frames and multiple rules. It was Bull apparently who drew a double pencil-line frame about the edges of each of these vellum drawings that had lost the original mount, and he trimmed the vellum close to this frame, thereby sometimes sacrificing all or part of Richardson the elder's inscription and stamp on the back at the bottom. Bull then wrote a similar inscription in pencil (reversing the order of elements in dates, however, putting month first, numbers second—and using the expression "Richardson Sen.") in a hand somewhat resembling Richardson's, across the bottom front of the vellum, and he imitated in pencil the monogram "JR", adding, however, a point ".", and once even writing "by JR." See, for example, on p. 5 of the album, no. 15, the double profile of Richardson the elder and Mrs. Knapp, where most of the features I have described may be observed. The top of Richardson's stamp "JR" appears unmistakably at the lower back edge of this drawing.

3. The Mapledurham inventory of Pope's goods after his death (*Notes & Queries,* 6th Series, 5.364, 13 May 1882) includes "a drawing of M*rs* Pope" in a black frame, "M*r* Pope Senior" (apparently a painting) in a black and gilt frame, and "M*rs* Pope" (also apparently a painting) in the same kind of frame.

31. PENCIL-ON-VELLUM DRAWING, BY JONATHAN RICHARDSON, 1736. MR. AND MRS. ROGER WARNER. SEE NO. 20.

32. PENCIL-ON-VELLUM DRAWING, BY JONATHAN RICHARDSON, 1736. MR. AND MRS. ROGER WARNER. SEE NO. 20.

33. PENCIL-ON-VELLUM DRAWING, BY JONATHAN RICHARDSON, 1736? HER MAJESTY THE QUEEN, WINDSOR CASTLE. SEE NO. 25.

34. PENCIL-ON-VELLUM DRAWING, BY JONATHAN RICHARDSON, 1737. DR. DALLAS PRATT. SEE NO. 26.

35. PENCIL-ON-VELLUM DRAWING, BY JONATHAN RICHARDSON, 1737. HER MAJESTY THE QUEEN, WINDSOR CASTLE. SEE NO. 25.

Ex. 10. Lead pencil on vellum. 5¾ x 5⅛ in. With two ruled lines in pencil around the edge, the outer one heavier. Inscribed in pencil on front: (1) to the lower left, "Pope's Mother" in a hand used apparently by Richard Bull in imitation of Richardson; (2) to the lower right, "Mʳˢ Pope" in an uncial printing hand often used by Richard Bull; (3) at the bottom left, "done by candle light 1703", possibly in Richardson the elder's hand. The date is written in ink over pencil figures, which too are apparently "1703." In the lower right corner by Richard Bull, Richardson the elder's monogram "JR" is written in a double line with a dry pen. Inscribed in pencil on the back: (1) in the center, "Pope's Mother ℈" in the same hand as the same phrase on the front. "℈" is apparently a Bull symbol meaning "query." (2) Across the bottom: "from a Dr: done by Candle light abᵗ the Year 1703." in a hand which looks like Jonathan Richardson the elder's. W. S. Lewis, Farmington, Connecticut.

31. Lead pencil on vellum. 5⅝ x 4⅛ in. On a paper mount, with watermark of crown and letters "GR" below, like Churchill 139 or 254. Framed in two ruled ink lines, the inner one thicker. Richardson the younger's stamp "R" on front lower right; inscribed on back bottom center "Pope" and on right "30 Aug: 1736" with Richardson the elder's monogram stamp "JR" above the date. Mr. and Mrs. Roger Warner, Burford, Oxfordshire.

above, left

32. Lead pencil on vellum. 6½ x 5⅜ in. On a paper mount, with watermark of lion in circle with crown above, similar to Churchill 93. Framed in two ruled ink lines, the inner one thicker. Richardson the younger's stamp "R" on front lower right; inscribed on back lower right: "Alex Pope Esqr 6 Sep 1736," followed by Richardson the elder's monogram stamp "JR." Mr. and Mrs. Roger Warner, Burford, Oxfordshire.

above, right

33. Lead pencil on vellum. 4 x 3 in. Inscribed on the back, under the mount, "15 Feb. 1736" (or "1738"). A. P. Oppé, *English Drawings . . . at Windsor Castle* (London 1950), p. 83, no. 495. Windsor Castle, by gracious permission of Her Majesty The Queen.

left

34 a. Lead pencil on vellum. 3½ x 5¼ in. Inscribed in pencil on the back: "Pope 22 Feb. 1736." with Richardson the elder's monogram stamp "JR" below the date. See no. 34 b. Dr. Dallas Pratt, New York City.

34 b. Inscription on the back of 34 a. "Pope 22 Feb. 1736." Richardson the elder's monogram stamp "JR" below the date.

36. PENCIL-ON-VELLUM DRAWING, BY JONATHAN RICHARDSON, C. 1737. UNIVERSITY
OF TEXAS LIBRARY.

The Popean collector Lieutenant Colonel F. Grant[1] had an extra-illustrated copy of
Carruthers' *Life of Alexander Pope*, London, 1857, in two volumes inlaid to folio,
which was acquired by the late Professor R. H. Griffith, and is now in the Rare Book
Collections at the Library of the University of Texas. On p. 391 of vol. 2 is a pencil
drawing on vellum, Pope, profile to left, laureated, inscribed apparently in Richardson's hand, with part of a couplet about bays and ivy from Pope's *Essay on Criticism*.
(See no. 6, and no. 54.1).

1. See, for example, Twickenham Loan Museum *Catalogue* (1888), pp. 10, 15–17, 55. Col. Grant lived at 109
Edith Road, West Kensington, W.

37. PENCIL-ON-VELLUM DRAWING, BY JONATHAN RICHARDSON, 1738. DR. DALLAS
PRATT. SEE NO. 26.

37(1). PENCIL-ON-VELLUM DRAWING, "A. POPE, AS MILTON," BY JONATHAN
RICHARDSON, 1738. THE KAUFMANN COLLECTION OF SWIFT AND
POPE, CORNELL UNIVERSITY LIBRARY. SEE NO. 19(1).
CF. NOS. 38 AND 38BX.

Richardson's undated etching of three heads on one plate (no. 38) suggests that he
played with approximating or assimilating the heads of Pope and Milton to each other.
The inscription on the front of this drawing, I believe in the hand of Richardson
the younger, is a sufficient corroboration of that idea. It seems to me, however, not
quite conclusive proof that the drawing was intended by Richardson the elder specifically for *Pope as* Milton, rather than, let us say, *Milton as* Pope, or a composite of Milton
and Pope. The Greek characters in which the name of Milton is drawn might be thought
to serve the purpose of distancing the name or putting it in quotation marks. But the
same form appears on the pedestal of Richardson's etched bust of Milton after Faithorne
used as frontispiece to Samuel Say's *Poems and Essays*, 1745,[1] and on a similar pencil-
on-vellum drawing in the Hibbert-Ware album (leaf 8). Richardson's etching dated
1738 and inscribed similarly "MIΛΤΩ" is a close counterpart of the present entry. Thinking this etching to be a portrait not of Pope but of Milton, I placed it originally not
in the Pope series but as no. 38bx. for the sake of throwing light on no. 38. There would
seem to be some advantage in its remaining there.

1. John Rupert Martin, *The Portrait of John Milton at Princeton* (Princeton, 1961), p. 17.

Engravings of Pope by Jonathan Richardson

G. W. Snelgrove's University of London Thesis of 1936 catalogues portrait engravings
by Richardson the elder of eight different subjects: himself, his son, Pope, Milton,

35. Lead pencil on vellum. 3⅜ x 2⅝ in. Inscribed "Pope's" on overset label at upper right corner, and on the back, under the mount, "1737." Richardson the younger's stamp "R" in the lower right corner. A. P. Oppé, *English Drawings . . . at Windsor Castle* (London 1950), p. 83, no. 494. Windsor Castle, by gracious permission of Her Majesty The Queen.

36. Lead pencil on vellum. 2⅞ x 3¾ in. Inscribed below oval with part of a couplet from Pope's *Essay on Criticism*, 3.705–06: "on whose honour'd brow / the Poet's Bays and Critick's Ivy grow. / Pope". Rare Book Collections, University of Texas Library, Austin, Texas.

37 a. Lead pencil on vellum. 3¼ x 4⅛ in. Richardson the younger's stamp "R" on front lower right. Inscribed on back: "Mr Pope / 13 Jan. 1737." Richardson the elder's monogram stamp "JR" above the date. Dr. Dallas Pratt, New York City.

37 b. Inscription on the back of 37 a. "Mr Pope / 13 Jan. 1737." Richardson the elder's monogram stamp "JR" above date.

Bolingbroke, John Lord Somers, Dr. Richard Mead, and one antique, Theophrastus.[1] The seven Englishmen are the same as those we find under "Richardson, J." in the index of artists in the British Museum *Catalogue of Engraved Portraits*.[2] We can extend the list of possibilities slightly by turning to Richardson the younger's sale catalogue of 5 February 1772, where we find (V.23) along with "Pope" and "Richardson Senior," in a batch of thirteen, the name "Sloane." Along with the 1,066 lots of drawings by Richardson the elder to which we have already alluded, Richardson the younger's sale of 5 February included 401 etchings in twenty-one lots. A conspicuous feature is the frequent repetition of the names of Richardson the elder and the younger, of Pope, and of Milton. Dr. Mead appears once, representing part of a lot of twenty-one etchings (III.28). Lots which include Pope, Milton, and the two Richardsons, repeatedly mention "proofs, variations, reverses." Thus V.21: "Seventeen etchings of Pope. Six different plates, various impressions, proofs, and reverses by J. Richardson . Sen."[3]

37(1). Pencil on vellum. 5¾ x 5⅛ in. Inscribed on back at lower left in **pencil** "25 Mar. 1738" (The "8" is in Richardson the elder's archaic style), and on front at lower left in pencil, apparently in Richardson the younger's hand, "A. Pope, as Milton." Richardson the younger's collection mark "R" on the front at the lower right corner. Drawn below the head: "ΜΙΛΤΩ". On leaf 13 of the Hibbert-Ware album. The Kaufmann Collection of Swift and Pope, Cornell University Library.

1. A bust, etched in 1739 (The Rijksmuseum, Amsterdam).

2. *BMEP 6* (by H. M. Hake, 1925), p. 670.

3. *An Essay on Prints,* published by William Gilpin in 1768 and several times thereafter and added anonymously to the 1792 edition of Richardson's *Works,* says (pp. 265–66): "*Richardson* etched several heads for Mr. Pope and others of his friends, they are slight, but spirited; Mr. Pope's profile is the best." Cf. Carl Paul Barbier, *William Gilpin* (Oxford, 1963), pp. 20 n. 4, 25.

The catalogue of *Engraved Portraits* in the British Museum lists five types of self-etching by Richardson (3.573) and six types of Milton.[4] Mead, Bolingbroke, and Richardson the younger[5] are listed only once each. John Lord Somers, a virtuoso and perhaps an early employer of the Richardsons,[6] appears once, and the etching stands apart from the others in being derived from a Richardson painting.[7] Richardson's phase of interest in etching, as we have seen, corresponds rather closely with that of his most intense phase of portrait-drawing. The etching begins apparently in the early 1730s and reaches a peak about 1738, the date on etchings of Bolingbroke, Milton, Pope, and Richardson the elder. Mead is dated 1739. The activity is obviously confined to a close circle of friends and heroes.

Certain details in the account of the etchings of Pope which follows (notably nos. 43.1 and 48.1) suggest to me, though I cannot demonstrate it, that "etching," an art not much cultivated in England at this time, was for Richardson indeed an art that did not go much if at all beyond drawing. That is, it was a kind of drawing with a needle, in which he enjoyed some facility and made many trials and experiments, using a prepared copper plate much as he used a sheet of paper or vellum. (The other etching stages, matters of such delicate concern to the masters in the history of the art, the biting with acid and the impressing with rollers, were very likely done by some other person— a shop down the street.[8]) The following passage in Richardson's essay of 1719 *On the Art of Criticism*, Section III, "Of Originals and Coppies" (pp. 194–96), seems closely relevant:

> Of Prints there are two kinds: [the first] Such as are done by the Masters themselves whose Invention the Work is . . . these may be Subdivided into three Kinds. 1. Those they have done after a Painting of their Own. 2. Those done after a Drawing also done by Themselves, or [3.] Lastly what is Design'd upon the Plate which has been Sometimes done especially in Etching. The 1st of these are Coppies after their Own Works; and so may the 2d, or they may not, according as the Drawing they have made previously to it happens to be: but Both are so but in Part; what is Thus done being a Different way of Working. But if it be Design'd on the Plate 'tis a kind of Drawing (as the Others are)

---

4. *BMEP* 3.242–43, 245: Milton 24–27, 29, 73. Nos. 29 and 73 are attributed, I believe mistakenly, to Richardson the younger.

5. Bolingbroke may be seen as the frontispiece to Bolingbroke's *Letter to Sir William Windham*, 1753; and Richardson the younger is the frontispiece to his *Richardsoniana*, published in 1776. (See above no. Ex. 9.) Mead is inscribed "J. Richardson f 1739." At Oxford in February 1745/6 William Gilpin saw "three Heads which Mr. Richardson etched for Dr. Mead" (Barbier, *William Gilpin*, p. 20).

6. See Lugt, *Les Marques de Collections*. p. 407; Richardson, *Theory of Painting* (London, 1715), p. 112, "Of Expression."

7. G. W. Snelgrove reports the painting in the collection of the Earl of Malmesbury, at Heron Court, and says that the etching (*BMEP* 4.142, John Somers, Baron, nos. 11 and 12) is done in Richardson's usual style. The same painting was engraved in mezzotint by J. Smith (J. Ch. Smith 3.1221, no. 234): "J. Richardson pinx. 1713."

8. See Pope asking for a prepared copper plate for Kent "to draw the Outline of Mr. Addison upon," *Correspondence* 2.81; and see no. 43.1. When William Gilpin, at Oxford in 1744 and 1745, made his first attempts at etching, he does seem to have applied the "Aqua-fortis" himself. He sent "an Impression" of his very first attempt, a head of Pope (cf. below no. 47), to his friend John Brown. Doubtless both the acid bath and the rollers were available at the establishment of "the only Engraver we have in Town, Mr. Cole," who had furnished Gilpin with a plate and taught him how to lay a ground (Barbier, *William Gilpin*, pp. 19–20).

tho' in a Manner Different from the rest, but 'tis purely, and properly Original.

It is not clear that Richardson published or sold his etchings, though he dated and otherwise inscribed some of them. A few of these were no doubt the accepted versions which were multiplied in greater numbers, distributed among the friends of Pope and Richardson, and used in various ways as memorials—for instance, by insertion as frontispieces in volumes of various made-up sets of Pope's collected *Works*.[9] Among his etchings of Pope, it is possible to distinguish three (nos. 41, 43.1, 48) which, on the grounds of their inscription, dating, attractiveness, and the frequency with which they are found today, may be said to have enjoyed a preferred status. These are most likely the three described by William Kent in his letter to Burlington of November 1738, after Pope had knocked him up on a rainy Sunday morning and dragged him around to Richardson's house:

> I forgot to tell you that Richerson give me all the prints he has grav'd, he has given me so many miltons, & three different popes, the last he has done is write behind his head in greek letters the English—thats the man, or this is the man, I cannot just tell—[10]

The smallest of the three best-known engravings—the medallion profile inscribed "Amicitiae Causa J. Richardson f."—was not dated, because it was intended for the dated title page of Pope's *Letters*, 1737. It was also used in volumes of later date. The variations on, or etchings similar to, each of these three main types, are apparently momentary experiments along the same lines, both approaches and afterthoughts. Richardson's drawings, etchings, and paintings of Pope are in general not related to one another in the way of copies or derivations, but seem rather multiple attempts along similar lines. I have treated the etchings, therefore, like the drawings—each as a separate type, with its own primary number in the series of Pope portraits.

9. See no's. 41 and 48.1.   10. *Correspondence 4.150; see p. 145.*

38 a,b,c. HEAD OF POPE, LAUREATED, PROFILE HEAD, APPARENTLY OF MILTON, AND INDETERMINATE PROFILE HEAD: THREE HEADS ON ONE ETCHED PLATE, BY JONATHAN RICHARDSON. DEPARTMENT OF PRINTS AND DRAWINGS, BRITISH MUSEUM.

The profile head (38b) in the lower left corner of this plate was developed by Richardson into a plate (38bx) inscribed "ΜΙΛΤΩ" and dated 1738.[1] At the same time the laureated head of Pope (38a) in the upper half of the plate is close to a drawing (no. 26) dated 1734/5. And this date fits well with the pitch of Miltonic interest which may be supposed to have accompanied the publication in January 1734/5 of the two Richardsons' *Explanatory Notes and Remarks on Milton's Paradise Lost,* to which the frontispiece was Richardson's larger etching of Milton, after Faithorne, laureated.[2]

The profile (38c) in the lower right compartment of the plate now under discus-

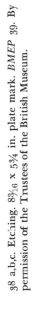

38 a,b,c. Etching. 8⁷⁄₁₆ x 5¾ in. plate mark. *BMEP* 39. By permission of the Trustees of the British Museum.

38 bx. Etching. 3⅞ x 3⁹⁄₁₆ oval. "ΜΙΛΤΩ / J. Richardson 1738." W. S. Lewis, Farmington, Connecticut.

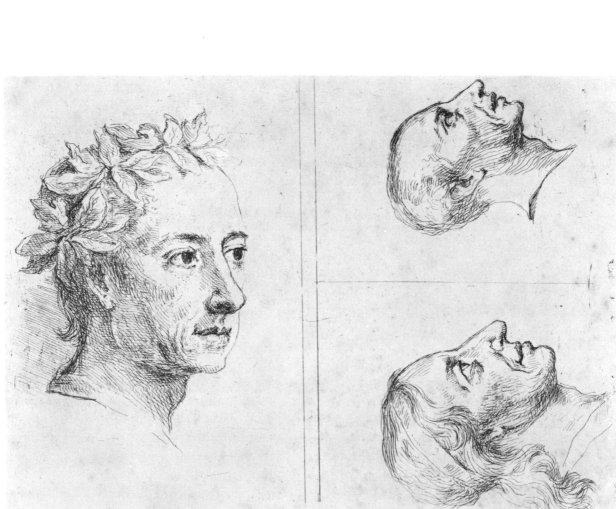

sion seems scarcely a satisfactory portrait of Pope. Nevertheless, the presence of Pope in the upper compartment of the plate and the juxtaposition of the profile in the lower right with that in the left tempt the speculation that Richardson, in line with the universalizing and characterizing ideas of his theoretical writing,[3] was here experimenting with an assimilation of the two great poetic features, or the construction of the ideal poetic profile. If this was so, his effort had a certain prophetic validity. For Thomas De Quincey would discover in Richardson's etching of Milton for the frontispiece to his book on Milton a "nearly perfect" likeness to the poet Wordsworth.[4]

No. 37(1), the recently discovered drawing "A. Pope, as Milton," should be noticed in connection with this entry.

I can locate three copies of this plate intact, one at the British Museum, *BMEP* 39, one in Thomas Dodd's extra-illustrated set of Roscoe's *Pope* (xx.144), now in the possession of Dr. Gordon Ray, and one in a reference collection of portrait engravings in the Yale University Library.[5]

1. Milton no. 73 in *BMEP* (3.245), attributed to J. Richardson Junior, for what reason is not clear. The example reproduced above (38 bx.) is in Lord Derby's extra-illustrated set of Spence's *Anecdotes* (*1*.xxxviii), in the collection of W. S. Lewis at Farmington.

2. *BMEP,* Milton 27. See p. 141.

3. See pp. 76–77.

4. *Recollections of the Lake and the Lake Poets* (1862), pp. 145, 148, quoted by Frances Blanshard, *Portraits of Wordsworth* (Ithaca, New York, 1959), pp. 56–57, and Plate 19b; cf. DeQuincey, "Wordsworth," *Tait's Edinburgh Magazine, 6* (January 1839), 9.

5. J. L. Graham Album [15], Pope no. 18.

39. ETCHING, BY JONATHAN RICHARDSON. WIDENER MEMORIAL LIBRARY, HARVARD UNIVERSITY.

Four examples of this etching are known to me: the one at Harvard in the Widener Memorial Library, which I reproduce below (Clarence S. Bement extra-illustrated copy of Johnson's *Life of Pope,* vol. 1, p. IX), one in the Department of Prints and Drawings at the British Museum (50–10–14–352), one in the Thomas Dodd extra-illustrated Roscoe's *Pope* owned by Dr. Gordon Ray (vol. 15. front.), and one in my own collection. The lighter etching and somewhat thinner and slighter features are close to two Richardson drawings in the Warner Collection, nos. 31 and 32. Perhaps this etching was a trial for no. 41.

40. ETCHING BY JONATHAN RICHARDSON. NATIONAL PORTRAIT GALLERY, LONDON.

There is an impression of this etching at the British Museum (Cracherode Q.1–119); another as frontispiece of vol. 19 of Dodd's extra-illustrated Roscoe, owned by Dr. Gordon Ray; another at the Pierpont Morgan Library (Bathurst Album of Popeana, p. 44); and another in my own possession. The National Portrait Gallery example, which I reproduce below, is inscribed at the lower left, with pen and ink, perhaps in the hand of Richardson the elder, "JR. fec" (underlined) and in the center "Mr Pope." The image is reversed from nos. 39 and 41 and nos. 31 and 32 (drawings). The squarish arrangement of the garment below is close to no. 32, dated 6 September 1736, and even closer to no. 19(2), dated 4 September 1736.

See no. 19(4), a black crayon drawing done over a reverse or counterproof of this etching.

41. ETCHING: "ALEX. POPE. AMICITIAE CAUSA. J. RICHARDSON F. 1736." BEVERLY
   CHEW BEQUEST, THE NEW YORK PUBLIC LIBRARY.

In the Lefferts Collection in the Harvard College Library is a four-volume set of Pope's works bound in red morocco for his friend Frederick, Prince of Wales. It consists of impressions on thick paper of Pope's one-volume *Works*, 1717, his *Works*, volume 2, 1735 (divided into two volumes), and his *Letters*, 1737, quarto. In the first and fourth volumes appear inserted copies of this etching as frontispiece, but lacking the date "1736." Professor Dearing, who describes this set, reports that a third example of this etching without the date is to be found at Harvard in a copy of the large-paper folio edition of the 1737 *Letters* (Griffith 456), formerly in the Gay Collection.[1] A fourth is to be found in the Widener Memorial Library Clarence S. Bement extra-illustrated

39. Etching. 8⅛ x 5⅝ in. plate mark. From the Harry Elkins Widener Collection, Harvard College Library.

40. Etching. 8¼ x 5¾ in. plate mark. Inscribed at lower left, in pen and ink: "*J R. fec*" and in the center: "Mr Pope." National Portrait Gallery, London.

Alex. Pope.

Amicitiæ causa.

J. Richardson f. 1736.

41. Etching. 7¼ x 5⅜ in. plate mark. "Alex. Pope. / Amicitiae causa. // J. Richardson f. 1736." *BMEP* 33. *Grolier* 32. Beverly Chew Bequest, Prints Division, The New York Public Library.

Johnson's *Life of Pope, 1,* p. 54. Another is at the National Portrait Gallery, another is *BMEP* 33 (Cracherode Q.i–118), and another is in my own collection. Another, without lettering, is frontispiece of vol. 13 of Dodd's extra-illustrated Roscoe, owned by Dr. Gordon Ray. The only example with the date which I have seen, reproduced below (no. 41, *Grolier* 32), is that in the Beverly Chew Bequest at the New York Public Library.

The drawing which seems closest in facial features (though reversed), is no. 34, dated 22 February 1736/7. But the wig and clothes resemble drawings no. 31 and no. 32. So far as I have discovered, this plate was not imitated by any other engraver.

1. Vinton Dearing, "The Prince of Wales's Set of Pope's Works," *Harvard Library Bulletin,* 4 (Autumn 1950), 320, 324.

42. ETCHING, BY JONATHAN RICHARDSON, SIMILAR TO NO. 43.1. PROFESSOR
     JACOB ISAACS, QUEEN MARY COLLEGE, UNIVERSITY OF LONDON.

Apparently a trial, in the reverse direction from that adopted, for the medallion used the year following on the title page of Pope's *Letters.* The method of stipple, which Richardson characteristically mingles with line etching, here gets a little out of hand. Under the medallion Richardson has written in pencil, in part along a guide line, "Amicitiae Causa Richardson 1736." Professor Isaacs kindly brought this engraving, unique so far as I know, to my attention and helped to arrange for the photograph.

43.1. ETCHING, MEDALLION: "AMICITIAE CAUSA. J. RICHARDSON F." ON TITLE PAGE
     OF POPE'S *Letters,* 1737.

Three surviving notes from Pope to Richardson bear on the use of this etching for the title page of the 1737 *Letters.* Apparently in February of 1736/7, Pope wrote from Lord Cornbury's to Richardson in Queen's Square, Bloomsbury: "The business of this, next to the Assurances of my true affection, is to desire you to send me inclosd to my Lord Cornbury's near Oxford Chappel the Exact size of the Plate for the title page of my book. Which is wanted so far as to stop the printing the Title."[1] On 3 March 1737, he wrote from Twickenham:

> Dr Sir,—I hope your Friend has done justice to your Work, in rolling off that excellent Etching in My Titlepage which will be the most Valuable thing in the book. As soon as they, together with the Headpiece & Initial Letter to the Preface are done, & the Sheets quite dry, I must desire your Care again to cause them to be very cleanly packed up & sent to the Printer's Mr Wright on St Peter's hill, who should give his Receit for them & return him also the Copper Headpiece & Letter to the Preface. You know the *least Dirt* thrown on the best Work, or best character, will spoil the whole Grace of it. And pray acquaint Mr Knapton, that I will satisfy him in the amplest manner he pleases, as well as be obliged for his Care.[2]

On 20 April Pope wrote again:

> I desire, you dear Sir, to give the Bearer ye little Plate of my Profile, wch is wanted for another Book.[3]

On 18 or 19 May was published Pope's authorized edition of the *Letters of Mr. Alexander Pope, And Several of his Friends,* in two nearly identical quarto variants (Griffith 454 and 455) and in large and small folio (Griffith 456 and 457). These issues were all "Printed by J. Wright for J. Knapton in Ludgate-street, L. Gilliver in Fleetstreet, J. Brindley in New Bond-street, and R. Dodsley in Pall-mall."[4] The same plate was used for another title page dated 1737 and prepared for persons who wished to bind into one quarto volume pieces of Pope's satires and epistles purchased separately. This title page reads: *The Works of Mr. Alexander Pope: Containing his Epistles and Satires: With some never before printed. London: Printed by J. Wright for J. Knapton in Ludgate street, L. Gilliver in Fleet-street, J. Brindley in New Bond-street, and R. Dodsley in Pall-Mall. MDCCXXXVII.*[5] The veteran bookseller James Knapton, who with his sons John and Paul had published Richardson's book on Milton in January 1734/5, died in November 1736, and was succeeded by his sons John and Paul at the Crown in Ludgate Street.[6] Another brother was George Knapton, the painter, who had been Richardson's pupil.[7] He became portrait painter to the Society of Dilettanti (1740–63),[8] and he is said to have done drawings for the engraved heads by Houbraken in Birch's *Lives,* published by John and Paul.[9] Yet a fourth brother was the artist Charles Knapton, who had been engaged with Arthur Pond in producing a series of engraved imitations of landscape drawings by old masters.[10] The "Mr. Knapton" of Pope's note, who is to be acquainted by Richardson that Pope will satisfy him in the amplest manner he pleases, is scarcely Pope's publisher John Knapton (though doubtless he, too, was one of Richardson's friends) but someone, a "friend," to whom Richardson has delegated the "rolling off" of the portrait etching along with one of the headpieces (by Fourdrinier after Kent) and an initial letter. Either George Knapton, Richardson's pupil and an engraver as well as painter, or Charles, who seems to have specialized in engraving, seems likely.

The same plate was used later on, with the medallion flattened out and Pope's head oppressed under a lowered ceiling for the sake of two extra lines of type, on the title page of *The Works of Mr. Alexander Pope in Prose, vol. II,* 1741 (Griffith 531).

---

1. *Correspondence* 4.54.

2. *Works,* ed. Elwin and Courthope, 9.505; *Correspondence* 4.58.

3. Yale University Library.

4. Griffith 2.357–61.

5. Griffith 474, quoting the catalogue of the Lefferts Collection at Harvard; and photostatic copy of the title page of a copy at Harvard. One copy of this volume in the Lefferts Collection, that forming volume 2 of the Prince of Wales's set of Pope's *Works,* has in addition an example of Richardson's etching of 1736, "Amicitiae Causa," as an inserted frontispiece (see no. 41), and a second copy (see no. 48.1) has an example of Richardson's etching of 1738, "ΟΥΤΟΣ ΕΚΕΙΝΟΣ."

6. Henry R. Plomer, *A Dictionary of the Printers and Booksellers . . . from 1668 to 1725* (Oxford, 1922), p. 181, and *A Dictionary of the Printers and Booksellers . . . from 1726 to 1775* (Oxford, 1932), p. 148, follows John Nichols, *Literary Anecdotes, 1* (1812), 236, in making John and Paul Knapton brothers of James Knapton. But this can scarcely be correct. Paul Knapton was married in 1741 and died in 1755; John Knapton died in 1770 aged 75. See Nichols, *Literary Anecdotes,* 3.607, and William Musgrave, *Obituary* (London, 1900), 3.383–84.

7. Vertue 3.62.

8. Lionel Cust, *History of the Society of Dilettanti,* ed. Sidney Colvin (London, 1898), pp. 64, 217–19.

9. Cust, *History of the Society of Dilettanti,* p. 217; Joseph Strutt, *A Biographical Dictionary . . . of All the Engravers* (London, 1786), 2.70.

10. See Henry M. Hake, "Pond's and Knapton's Imitations of Drawings," *The Print Collector's Quarterly, 9* (December 1922), 324–49; Vertue 6.194; no. 66.16.

43.2. COPY OF NO. 43.1. FRONTISPIECE TO A VOLUME OF POPE'S *Letters* PUBLISHED BY EDMUND CURLL IN JUNE 1737.

Apparently in November of 1736, Curll published a small octavo volume of letters of Pope and Swift to Bolingbroke, the title page of which can only be conjectured (Griffith 429). In June 1737, Curll's octavo volume of Pope's letters, *Mr. Pope's Literary Correspondence, Volume the Fifth* (Griffith 462) incorporated the few letters of November 1736 into a larger collection made possible by Pope's own publication on 19 May of his *Letters Of Mr. Alexander Pope, And Several of his Friends* (see above 43.1). In the Yale Rare Book Library (IK P810 737n) is a book containing about five-sevenths of the contents of Curll's *Mr. Pope's Literary Correspondence, Volume the Fifth*[1] and having three extraordinary features. (1) The title-page reads *New Letters of Mr Alexander Pope, And Several of his Friends.—Vellem Nescire Litteras! Cum desiderio Veteres, Revocamus Amores; atque olim missas, flemus Amicitias. London: Printed, Anno Reformationis, 1737.* The two Latin sentences (the first from Suetonius, *Nero 10,* the second a couplet misquoted from Catullus *96*) are lifted by Curll verbatim from the engraved ornaments, by P. Fourdrinier after Kent, which appear at the beginning and end of the "Preface" (and the second also after the table of "Contents," at top of the first page of the text) in Pope's authorized *Letters* of 18 or 19 May.[2] (2) In the same vein of mimicry, Curll supplies the frontispiece to this volume. Quite unlike the crude line-cuts after Kneller and Jervas (no. 5.15) with which Curll had so far been content in volumes of the *Correspondence,* this frontispiece is a very careful replica etching after the medallion which, "Amicitiae Causa," Richardson had supplied for the authorized *Letters* (see no. 43.1). (3) The full promptitude of this polite attention on the part of Curll, and its quality of riposte, comes out only when we notice the "Advertisement" put at the end of the volume. This concludes with the words: "E. Curll / Rose Street, June 8, 1737. / Die Nat A. Pope, / Ætat. 49."[3]

1. I.e. as far as p. "242" (misprint for 252), in Griffith's collation of no. 462.

2. The Emperor Nero, asked to sign a death warrant, had exclaimed, "How I wish I had never learned to write." (" 'Quam vellem,' inquit, 'nescire litteras' ") The two Latin quotations are Pope's sardonic and his sentimental summation of feelings about his letters.

3. Curll himself had earlier published this version of Pope's birthday and was perhaps the original propagator of it—though perhaps too it had been supplied to him by Pope himself either in some way connected with Giles Jacob's *Poetical Register* of 1720 or through the mysterious correspondents, "P.T." and

"E.P.," who involved Curll in the publication of Pope's *Letters* in May 1735. In his "Anecdotes of the Life and Family of Mr. Pope," published in July 1735 in *Volume the Second of Mr. Pope's Literary Correspondence,* Curll had written: "I shall begin my labor with the account Mr. Pope has given of himself. . . . Mr. Alexander Pope was born in Cheapside, London, on the 8th day of June, in the year 1688; so that one week produced both Pope and the Pretender. Memorable era!" (See Elwin and Courthope 6.419, 426–27, 439–40; Griffith 2.309, no. 386. The correct date of Pope's birth is 21 May 1688. See Elwin and Courthope 1.ix and Spence, *Anecdotes,* ed. S. W.

Singer, 1820, p. 259.) Perhaps the allusion to the Pretender (born 10 June 1688) actually explains why somebody had conjured 8 June as Pope's birthday. At any rate, Curll's date for Pope's birthday gained some currency. It appears in the first sentence of William Ayre's *Memoirs of the Life and Writings of Alexander Pope, Esq.*, 1745. And it appears incised, along with an incorrect date for Pope's death, under the shoulder of one of the four marble busts of Pope signed by Roubiliac (no. 61).

For further details relating to the subject of this entry and to Curll's use of other portraits of Pope, see my article " 'Amicitiae Causa': A Birthday Present from Curll to Pope," in *Restoration and Eighteenth-Century Literature, Essays in Honor of Alan Dugald*

McKillop, ed. Carroll Camden (University of Chicago Press for William Marsh Rice University, 1963) pp. 341–49.

In my possession are three other etched copies, in reverse, of Richardson's profile of 1737: (1) uninscribed, but the same etching is said in a pencil note by Thomas Dodd (extra-illustrated Roscoe's *Pope*, 3.18: Dr. Gordon Ray) to be the work of Thomas Worlidge (1700–66); (2) inscribed beneath: "Mʳ // Pope." // "Darly Exᵗ in Round Court." (Matthew Darly flourished 1778.); (3) a reduced image printed on tissue paper, inscribed in pencil on the front: "Alexander Pope Esqʳ // private plate," and on the back: "Mʳ J. Becket fecit, Lloyds."

43.3. LINE AND STIPPLE, MEDALLION: "ÆPOND F." SERIES OF SIMILAR PLATES ON TITLE PAGES OF WARBURTON'S EDITIONS OF THE *Essay on Man*, 1745–53.

Warburton's octavo editions of the *Essay on Man*, beginning with that of 1745, have on the title pages (opposite a frontispiece of Roman ruins designed by Pope) a series of small engravings, profile, facing left in a stipple medallion, with the signature of A. Pond inscribed to the lower left outside the medallion. The likeness to Pope is very poor, and the image may not be a direct copy from Richardson. Nevertheless, the attitude of head and neck, without garment, is more reminiscent of Richardson's 1737 medallion than of anything else.[1] Editions of the *Essay on Man* are to be noted as follows:

(1) Griffith 607: *An Essay on Man. By Alexander Pope Esq. Enlarged and Improved by the Author. With Notes by William Warburton, M.A. London, Printed for John and Paul Knapton in Ludgate street.* MDCCXLV.[2] Plate reproduced below, no. 43.3. Signed "ÂPond f."

(2) Griffith 620: *An Essay on Man . . . with Notes by Mr. Warburton . . . Printed by John and Paul Knapton . . . MDCCXLVI.* A copy with this title page at Yale has a new and slightly superior plate (1⅞ x 1⅞ in. plate mark; 1⅝ in. medallion), but inscribed in the same way.[3] The same plate appears in nos. (4) and (6) below.

(3) Griffith 631: *A [sic] Essay on Man . . . with the Commentary and Notes of Mr. Warburton . . . Printed for John and Paul Knapton . . . MDCCXLVIII.* Griffith reports a title-page "vignette" signed at the lower left "A. Pond f."

(4) [Not in Griffith] *An Essay on Man . . . With Notes by Mr. Warburton . . . Printed for John and Paul Knapton in Ludgate-street. MDCCXLVIII.* The plate (apparently *BMEP* Pope no. 60) is the same as in (2) above.

(5) Griffith 637: *An Essay on Man . . . with Notes by William Warburton, A.M. . . . Dublin: Printed by George Faulkner . . . M DCC XLIX.* 12mo. Griffith reports that the plate is signed "A. Pond f.—P. Simms scᵗ".

(6) [Griffith 656]: *An Essay on Man. . . . With the Notes of Mr Warburton . . . London . . . J. and P. Knapton . . . MDCCLI* (Yale). The plate is the same as in (2) and (4).

42. Etching. On an irregularly shaped plate, 4½–4¾ x 3⅝–4 in. Inscribed beneath in pencil: "Amicitiae Causa // Richardson 1736". Professor Jacob Isaacs, Queen Mary College, University of London.

43.1. Etching. 3¹⁵⁄₁₆ x 3¹³⁄₁₆ in. plate mark. 2¹⁵⁄₁₆ x 2⅜ in. image. "Amicitiae Causa. // J. Richardson f." On the title page of Pope's *Letters*, 1737. *BMEP* 31. *Grolier* 34. Reproduced from a copy of the small folio of Pope's *Letters* (Griffith 457), in the Yale University Library.

43.2. Etching. 3¼ x 3 in. plate mark. 2⅞ x 2¼ in. image. "Amicitiae Causa. // J. Richardson f:" Frontispiece to a volume of Pope's *Letters* published by E. Curll in June 1737.

43.3. Line engraving and stipple. 1¹⁵⁄₁₆ x 2 in. plate mark. 1¹¹⁄₁₆ in. medallion. "Æpond f." On title page of *An Essay on Man*, edited by William Warburton, London, 1745.

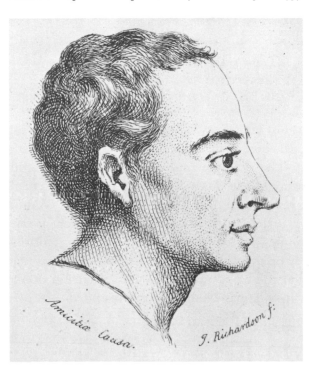

43.4. Red sulphur cast. Height (without frame) 1¹⁄₁₆ in. Tassie *Catalogue* 1791, no. 14375. Scottish National Portrait Gallery, Edinburgh.

Warburton's next edition, in 1753, introduced a new portrait medallion. See no. 48.3.

1. There is no curl at the nape, as in the ΟΥΤΟΣ ΕΚΕΙΝΟΣ of 1738, yet the heavily lined muscles at the mouth may owe something to that engraving.

2. Griffith reports that no. 608, nearly line for line the same book, but a different setting of type throughout, has a different plate from 607 (though the same image, I infer), and that names inscribed in both left and right lower corners have been heavily inked over.

3. An inferior medallion of this type but lacking the signature of A. Pond appears on the title page of a volume which I once saw in the collection of Professor George Sherburn: *Ethic Epistles. by Alexander Pope Esq; London, Printed for J. and P. Knapton in Ludgate-street. MDCCXLVII* (not recorded in Griffith). This volume contained the *Essay on Man* and *Moral Essays*. It had a frontispiece from Pope's design.

43.4. RED SULPHUR CAST BY JAMES TASSIE, FROM A GEM AFTER RICHARDSON'S ETCHING NO. 43.1. TASSIE *Catalogue* 1791, NO. 14375. SCOTTISH NATIONAL PORTRAIT GALLERY. SEE NO. 62.8.

44. ETCHING, SIMILAR TO NO. 43.1. "MR. POPE AMICITIAE CAUSA. J. RICHARDSON F." THE PIERPONT MORGAN LIBRARY.

The increased size of the image and the more elaborate inscription suggest that the success of the small medallion done for the 1737 *Letters* led Richardson to experiment in producing a similar image in a form suitable for multiplication on separate sheets. The relative scarcity of the engraving suggests that it was not actually multiplied to the extent that 41 and 48 were. The example reproduced below, from Henrietta Frances, Countess of Bessborough's extra-illustrated set of the Foulis *Poetical Works of Pope*, 1785 (*1.67*), at the Pierpont Morgan Library, is the only example which I have seen with the inscription. The plate occurs in an earlier state, without inscription, and with a large bump in the line of the nose near the tip, in the Thomas Dodd set of Roscoe's *Pope* now in the possession of Dr. Gordon Ray (*2.75*), and in my own collection.

45. ETCHING, SIMILAR TO NO. 43.1. "YES, HAPPY MAN! BE EVR'Y HONOUR THINE; / STILL MORE THAN WIT SHALL HONEST FRIENDSHIP SHINE. / J. RICHARDSON / 1738." W. S. LEWIS, FARMINGTON, CONNECTICUT.

Like no. 44, this seems an attempt to develop the successful medallion of 1737 into an engraving for a separate sheet. This engraving, with couplet and date, occurs with somewhat greater frequency than no. 44. The example reproduced below appears in Lord Derby's extra-illustrated set of Spence's *Anecdotes* (*4.308*) in the collection of W. S. Lewis at Farmington. Two other examples are in Lieutenant-Colonel F. Grant's extra-illustrated Carruthers' *Life of Pope* at the University of Texas; and there is one in my own collection. At the Loan Museum, Twickenham, 1888, no. 194, p. 37 of the Catalogue was apparently this etching. It occurs also in an earlier state, without the inscription and with the hair or shadow at the nape of the neck somewhat less developed; the only example I have seen is in Thomas Dodd's extra-illustrated Roscoe's

Pope (*1*, after 110, insert no. 64) now in the possession of Dr. Gordon Ray. See no. 19(5), a drawing which seems to be a sketch for this engraving.

In a characteristic couplet, Richardson the elder expresses his appreciation at enjoying the friendship of the great poet. See no. 23a, his couplet beneath the laureated drawing of Pope, 1733/4. Beneath an etching of himself dated 1738 (in his own hair), he inscribed:

> These Features must in Silent Darkness Rot.
> No Reason why my Heart shou'd be Forgot.
> J. Richardson. 1738.

And beneath another dated 1738 (in wig) he inscribed:

> Me, as you find my Soul, Neglect or Love,
> and show by Virtue Virtue you approve.
> JR. 1738.[1]

1. *BMEP* 3.573, Richardson nos. 1 and 5.

44. Etching. 5¾ x 4⅛ in. plate mark. 3¾ x 3 in. image. "Mʳ Pope / Amicitiae causa. // J. Richardson f." Pierpont Morgan Library, New York City.

45. Etching. 4⅝ x 3⅞ in. plate mark. 3⅝ x 3½ in. medallion. "Yes, Happy Man! be Evr'y Honour Thine; / Still more than Wit shall Honest Friendship Shine. / J. Richardson / 1738." W. S. Lewis, Farmington, Connecticut.

46. ETCHING, BY JONATHAN RICHARDSON, SIMILAR TO NO. 48.
DEPARTMENT OF PRINTS AND DRAWINGS, BRITISH MUSEUM.

The absence of inscription and the lightly sketched branch of bay leaves which intrudes in the lower left corner make this look like a trial plate for no. 48, which the image closely resembles. The example reproduced below is in the Department of Prints and Drawings at the British Museum (50–10–14–361). I have seen one other impression, a slightly different state, in volume 1 of an extra-illustrated large-paper set of Singer's edition of Spence's *Anecdotes,* having the bookplate of Henry William Poor. In 1963 this set was in the hands of W. H. Lowdermilk & Co., booksellers in Washington, D.C., and was acquired by the University of Illinois Library.

47. ETCHING, BY JONATHAN RICHARDSON, SIMILAR TO NO. 48.

Apparently another trial, a reverse profile, and a smaller image, on a smaller plate, but very similar to 48. The only example I have seen is in my own possession and was sent to me by a friend, who got it from G. David, Bookseller, in Cambridge, England. Beneath the fur collar appear in pencil the letters "A P," the "A" drawn with two fancy flourishes and linked to the "P." To the left, drawn with a fine ink line over pencil, is the monogram "WG"—perhaps a testimony that this etching was once in the possession

46. Etching. 6 x 4½ in. paper, trimmed inside plate mark. 4¹⁵⁄₁₆ x 3¹¹⁄₁₆ in. image, including shadow and bay leaves. Probably *BMEP* 37. By permission of the Trustees of the British Museum.

47. Etching. 4¼ x 3¼ in. plate mark. Inscribed at the lower left in ink over pencil: "WG" and lower center in pencil: "AP".

of William Gilpin? At Queen's College, Oxford, in November 1744, the future tourist of the picturesque attempted the art of etching and as a first trial copied a head of Pope, dashing "the Strokes out any how." About a year later he had made another attempt at Pope and planned to do it again, taking "a little more Pains."[1] In the period of his maturity he would mark his own landscape drawings with a blind stamp "W G."[2]

1. Carl Paul Barbier, *William Gilpin, His Drawings, Teaching, and Theory of the Picturesque* (Oxford, 1963), pp. 16, 19, 20: letters of Gilpin to John Brown, 12 November 1744; Brown to Gilpin, 5 January 1745/6; Gilpin to his father, 8 February 1745/6. Cf. p. 180 n.3.

2. Barbier, *William Gilpin*, later chapters, *passim*.

But Barbier observes (p. 29, n. 1) that Gilpin "never signed or initialled a drawing on the face." See Lugt, *Les Marques de Collections, Supplément* (1956), p. 377, for a facsimile of a fancy monogram "WG" in an oval line frame, used by Gilpin "sur ses propres dessins."

ΟΥΤΟΣ ΕΚΕΙΝΟΣ

Mr Pope

J. Richardson fecit. 1738.

48.1. Etching. 5¾ x 4½ in. plate mark. 4⅜ x 3⅜ in. image. "ΟΥΤΟΣ ΕΚΕΙΝΟΣ / Mr Pope / J. Richardson. fecit. 1738." *BMEP* 36. *Grolier* 33.

48.1. ETCHING: "ΟΥΤΟΣ ΕΚΕΙΝΟΣ / Mʳ POPE / J. RICHARDSON FECIT 1738."

The plate of this etching survives in the possession of Sir John Murray, who in 1951 sent me an excellent impression from it and in 1961 kindly allowed me to examine it. The plate seems to be composed of copper but washed over on the face and on the margins of the back with a silvery metal. Traces of brown varnish appear on the back. It is wrapped in a piece of thin bluish wove paper bearing on the front of the package an impression of the image. A small white paper label pasted on at the lower left bears the number "1" stamped in black ink and after it in faint pen and ink "40." Written above the image in light ink is: "Very Curious. The Original / Copper's. Etched. by / . . . G: D: Canonbury . . ." On the top fold of the paper at the back of the package a pasted label of white laid paper bears in heavy black ink the inscription: "The copper plate of / Pope, etched by / the late Mʳ G. Daniel / from—his collection." (George Daniel, 1789–1864, miscellaneous writer and book collector, lived at 18 Canonbury Square, London.) An impression of this plate in my possession, on a piece of heavy laid paper of the type called "French" paper and employed much in England for engravings during the middle years of the eighteenth century,[1] has pasted on the back a small paper label bearing in pencil the words "Leicester Square" and below this label in pencil, " . . . Daniel . . . 37 Cranbourn St." The numerous impressions of this plate to be found today are likely enough to be on a paper which dates after the death of Pope.

The image was apparently well known to Pope's friends from the start (see Kent's letter of November 1738 quoted above), and impressions were apparently multiplied and used in the same way as the two examples of no. 41 inserted as frontispieces in volumes of the Prince of Wales' set of Pope's *Works* at Harvard. Among the books of the Henry A. Colgate bequest in the Yale Rare Book Library is a set of Pope's quarto *Iliad*, 1715–20 (Griffith 40, 47, 76, 94, 113, 117), on heavy paper, extra-illustrated with mounted plates, and bound in contemporary red gilt-tooled morocco. Volume 1, 1715, has inserted before the title page and facing George Vertue's frontispiece of the Farnese Homer (no. 3.2x) an impression of the present etching, which I reproduce above. The same bequest includes also a similarly illustrated and bound set of Pope's quarto *Odyssey*, 1725 (Griffith 151, 155, 159, 166, 170), the first volume having inserted before the title page and facing Vertue's engraving of Dr. Mead's Arundel Homer, another example of the same etching. In the Lefferts collection at Harvard, one copy of the made-up volume *The Works of Mr. Alexander Pope: Containing his Epistles and Satires*, 1737 (Griffith 474) has an example of this plate as frontispiece.[2]

The motto "ΟΥΤΟΣ ΕΚΕΙΝΟΣ" is from Aristotle's *Poetics*, chapter 4, where Aristotle discusses the pleasure of recognition in art. The phrase meant to Pope and his friends, and perhaps (despite recent editorial qualms) still means: "The very man," or "The man himself."

---

1. I am indebted for this information to Professor Allen T. Hazen.

2. See Griffith 474 and M. C. Lefferts, *Alexander Pope Notes towards a Bibliography* (1910), pp. 38, 46.

48.2. LINE ENGRAVING, AFTER RICHARDSON NO. 48.1, BY "PARR." FRONTISPIECE TO WILLIAM AYRE'S *Memoirs of . . . Pope*, 1745.

A kerchief-like drape is substituted for the fur collar, and the image is reversed, but the curl at the nape of the neck, the generally longer hair and the muscular lines around the mouth show the source of this popularization to be no. 48.1 rather than no. 45.1. The engraving appears as frontispiece to each of the two octavo volumes of William Ayre's *Memoirs of the Life and Writings of Alexander Pope, Esq; . . . London: Printed by his Majesty's Authority, For the Author, and Sold by the Booksellers of London and Westminster. M DCC XLV.*

An engraver named Parr had copied two of the Kneller types of Pope portrait in 1735 (see under nos. 6.13, 7.8). "Parr" might be either N. Parr or Remi (Remigius) Parr, both apparently active in London portrait-engraving at this time (*Bryan's Dictionary*, 1903–05; *BMEP 6*, Index of Engravers).

48.3. LINE AND STIPPLE, MEDALLION: "A WALKER SCULP." ON TITLE PAGE OF WARBURTON'S EDITIONS OF THE *Essay on Man*, 1753 AND LATER.

See no. 43.3 for medallions by A. Pond in Warburton's editions of the *Essay on Man*, 1745–51.

Warburton's next edition (*An Essay on Man. By Alexander Pope Esq. Enlarged and Improved by the Author. Together with his MS. Additions and Variations, as in the Last Edition of his Works. With the Notes of Mr. Warburton. London, Printed for J. and P. Knapton in Ludgate-street. M DCC LIII*) has a vastly improved title-page portrait. The profile to right in a stipple medallion is without garment, but the pattern of hair and facial muscles places it unmistakably in the family of Richardson's profile of 1738. The plate is inscribed to the lower left outside the medallion: "A. Walker sculp." The same medallion appears on the title page of at least two later Warburton editions of the *Essay: An Essay on Man . . . with his MS Additions and Variations. . . . with the Notes of Dr. Warburton . . . Printed for J. and R. Tonson, and A. Millar . . . M DCC LX;* and *An Essay on Man . . . with the Notes of William, Lord Bishop of Gloucester . . . Printed for W. Strahan; and T. Cadell . . . M DCC LXXI.*[1]

"A. Walker" is no doubt Anthony Walker (1726–65) and the same artist whose name appears on plate III of the first volume of Warburton's edition of Pope's *Works* in 1751 (Griffith 643): "Anty. Walker Del: et Sculpt."

---

1. An inferior small reversed head of Pope (in a medallion 2⅛ in.) appears on the title pages of John Hawkesworth's two folio *Adventurer* volumes, printed for J. Payne, at Pope's Head in Paternoster Row; vol. *1* (1753), "B. Ross // 1753," and vol. 2 (1754), plate badly retouched, "B.R.f. // 1754."

48.4. DRAWING, AFTER RICHARDSON, BY WILLIAM MASON. HARTLEBURY CASTLE, WORCESTERSHIRE.

On 30 May 1747 Richard Hurd at Emmanuel College, Cambridge wrote to William Mason (at his father's vicarage in Hull):

You are very kind in not forgetting Pope's Head, which I want very much to preside over the little band of worthies, which I am collecting for the ornament of my Study. If you would but, at some leisure time, contrive to give me a Sketch of your own from Hayman's picture, it would complete the Obligation.

And soon after he wrote again:

I am much oblig'd by your favor of Pope's head, which I received safe, & shall value, as it deserves, extremely.[1]

We shall come to Hayman's picture in due course.[2] With regard to "Pope's head," Leonard Whibley, the editor of the Hurd-Mason *Correspondence,* wrote in 1932: "The reference is to a sketch . . . which Hurd must have transferred from his study at Emmanuel to his study at Thurcaston, and thence later to Eccleshall and to Hartlebury, where his successors have had charge of it to this day. It hangs in his library in a group."[3] The late Reverend James Nankivell, Librarian at Hartlebury, describes the same picture in his posthumously published work *The Collection of Portraits in Oils of Bishop Richard Hurd at Hartlebury Castle,* Worcester, 1953.[4] In July 1961 I visited Hartlebury and found the drawing, not quite in such a group as Whibley describes, but still on the wall of the "classic" library which Hurd in 1782 added to the Gothic castle.[5]

The word MVSAEVS which Mason has put on the drawing (balanced against Richardson's ΟΥΤΟΣ ΕΚΕΙΝΟΣ) is from the title of his *Monody to the Memory of Mr Pope,* published by Dodsley on 17 April 1747. Mason had sent an early copy to Hurd.[6] The frontispiece of this work elicited Hurd's request for a sketch from "Hayman's picture." See Appendix 4.8.

1. *The Correspondence of Richard Hurd & William Mason And Letters of Richard Hurd to Thomas Gray,* ed. Leonard Whibley (Cambridge, 1932), pp. 5–6, Letters II and III. Cf. John W. Draper, *William Mason* (New York, 1924), pp. 18, 20, 25–27.

2. See Appendix 4.8.

3. *Correspondence of Hurd & Mason,* p. 6, n. 2.

4. Ebenezer Baylis & Son, Ltd., Worcester, 1953, p. 37.

5. Dr. A. P. Grimbly of Worcester very kindly took the photograph here shown.

6. *Correspondence of Hurd & Mason,* p. 1, Letter I.

48.5. DRAWING, AFTER RICHARDSON, BY TIMOTHY SHELDRAKE. IOLO A. WILLIAMS, 1960.

A lead-pencil drawing of this image, signed in ink "Timothy Sheldrake" (fl. 1740–1756), appeared in the Francis Wellesley sale at Sotheby's beginning 28 June 1920 (lot 711), and was bought by "Roberts" (Catalogue in Yale Library). It was in the possession of the late Iolo A. Williams, who in 1960 kindly showed it to me.

48.6. DRAWING, AFTER RICHARDSON, BY A. LINNELL. PROFESSOR MAYNARD MACK.

Professor Maynard Mack, of Yale University, is the owner of a drawing of this type,

above, left

48.2. Line engraving. 6¼₆ x 3¹¹⁄₁₆ in. plate mark. "Pope / Parr sculp". Frontispiece to William Ayre, *Memoirs of the Life and Writings of Alexander Pope, Esq;*, London, 1745. Probably *BMEP* 38.

left

48.3. Line engraving and stipple. 1⅝ in. medallion. 2¹⁄₁₆ x 2⅜ in. plate mark. "A. Walker sculp." On title page of *An Essay on Man,* edited by William Warburton, London, 1753.

above, right

48.4. Lead pencil on paper. 8 x 6¼ in. paper. Inscribed in ink: "ΟΥΤΟΣ ΕΚΕΙΝΟΣ // MVSAEVS / Mr Pope / E Descriptione J. Richardson. // W. Mason Delineavit". Hartlebury Castle, Worcestershire.

below, left

48.7. Red sulphur cast. Height (without frame) ¹⁵⁄₁₆ in. Tassie *Catalogue* 1791, no. 14367. Scottish National Portrait Gallery, Edinburgh.

below, center

48.8. Wedgwood intaglio. 1³⁄₁₆ x ¾ in. Impression from intaglio mold no. 393. Wedgwood Museum, Barlaston.

below, right

48.9. Wedgwood intaglio. ⅝ x ½ in. Impression from intaglio mold no. 660. Wedgwood Museum, Barlaston.

facing to right, in pen-and-ink, on a sheet of laid paper (the image 4⅝ x 3⁹⁄₁₆ in., the paper 8⅛ x 6⅜ in.), signed in ink "A. Linnell fecit 1750."[1]

1. Richardson's "ΟΥΤΟΣ ΕΚΕΙΝΟΣ" etching of 1738 was apparently a favorite subject for amateur copyists. In the same category as the three drawings just described, should perhaps be placed the following: (1) a soft-ground etching inscribed "Mr Pope / T. Preston Fecit," in my possession (cf. Griffith no. 622); (2) a reversed engraving in bistre ink, apparently in dry-point, uninscribed, in my possession; (3) a very neatly executed reverse etching, the same size as Rich-ardson's, inscribed "Mr. Pope. / R. Blyth fecit" (Robert Blyth, engraver, lived 1750–84), in my possession; and (4) in the Bathurst Album of Popeana at the Morgan Library (see no. 6.10), p. 36, a very close copy of Richardson, inscribed in the same style "ΟΥΤΟΣ ΕΚΕΙΝΟΣ / Mr Pope." Cf. above no. 47, the efforts of William Gilpin to copy an etching of Pope, at Oxford in 1744.

48.7. RED SULPHUR CAST BY JAMES TASSIE, FROM A GEM RESEMBLING RICHARDSON'S ETCHING NO. 48.1. TASSIE *Catalogue* 1791, NO. 14367. SCOTTISH NATIONAL PORTRAIT GALLERY.

See no. 62.8. Nos. 14372, 14373, and 14377 in the Tassie *Catalogue* of 1791, also repre-sented at the Scottish National Portrait Gallery, show a vaguer resemblance to both no. 43.1 and no. 48.1, Richardson's etchings of 1737 and 1738. No. 14377 owes something perhaps also to the Roubiliac type of bust. See no. 57–61.17, a gem by Lorenz Natter.

48.8–9. WEDGWOOD INTAGLIO MOLDS (AND A CORRESPONDING CAMEO), AFTER RICHARDSON NO. 48.1. WEDGWOOD MUSEUM, BARLASTON.

The first edition of the *Wedgwood Catalogue* (1773) lists one Cameo of Pope, no. 735, under the heading "Illustrious Moderns," a "chalcedony."[1] The second edition of the *Wedgwood Catalogue* (1774) repeats the cameo (735) and adds one intaglio of Pope (no. 12 among "Modern Subjects").[2] The fifth edition (fourth in English, 1779) repeats cameo 735 and intaglio 12 and adds three other intaglios of Pope, nos. 50, 100, 269, and one cameo, no. 1699.[3] In the sixth edition of 1787, only one intaglio reappears (no. 100, which, no. 62.8, I identify as the Dassier type), and only one cameo, no. 735.[4]

Today the Barlaston Museum has in addition to the mold of intaglio 100, two other intaglio molds of Pope (nos. 393 and 660), and, identical with the second of these, a cameo mold (no. 354).

Intaglio 393 (1³⁄₁₆ x ¾ in.) is a clear derivative from Richardson's etching of 1738 (no. 48.1), facing to right, with fur collar. An impression of it is reproduced above, no. 48.8.

Intaglio 660, with its corresponding cameo 354 (each ⅝ x ½ in.), is a derivative from the same source, but in the reversed direction, the vertical line of hair at the temple, and the drape at the neck strongly reminiscent of no. 48.2, Parr's line engraving for Ayre's *Memoirs of Pope*, 1745. An impression of it is reproduced as no. 48.9.

1. Eliza Meteyard, *The Wedgwood Handbook* (London 1875), p. 98.

2. Meteyard, *Handbook*, pp. 98, 123.

3. Reprinted in Wolf Mankowitz, *Wedgwood* (London, 1953), pp. 218, 222–24, 227.

4. *Wedgwood's Catalogue of Cameos, Intaglios, Medals, Bas-Reliefs, Busts, and Small Statues, Reprinted from the edition of 1787*, ed. Eliza Meteyard, 1873.

OIL PAINTINGS OF POPE BY JONATHAN RICHARDSON

49. OIL PAINTING, BY JONATHAN RICHARDSON. THE BARON EGREMONT, PETWORTH HOUSE, SUSSEX.

A folio ledger notebook at the National Portrait Gallery, entitled *Royal and Private Picture Galleries, Sales, Etc.,* volume 1, compiled by George Scharf and dated 1870, has in it, pp. 207 ff., an entry for Petworth House: "Extracts taken from Mr. Knox's Catalogue. Lent me by Mrs. Smith the Housekeeper 2nd and 3rd August 1866: . . . North Gallery, p. 2, no. 53, Alexr. Pope, Richardson. . . . Library, p. 6, no. 270, Alexr. Pope. (Comp. ante 53)." The first of these pictures is no. 52.1. For the second, it is worth noticing that Scharf records no attribution. Another early *Catalogue of Pictures at Petworth House,* compiled by Thomas Sockett, was printed in 1856. In a copy of this at Petworth House one finds, for the picture in question (no. 270), the word "Jervas" entered in pencil in the hand of a secretary named Whitcomb who flourished at Petworth toward the end of the nineteenth century.[1] This apparently is the source of the heading "Jervas (attributed to)" for no. 270, at p. 64 of C. H. Collins Baker's *Catalogue of the Petworth Collection of Pictures in the possession of Lord Leconfield* (London, The Medici Society, Ltd., 1920). The face seems too elderly for the time when Jervas was painting Pope. The brown coat and the fur collar suit the period in the 1730s of Richardson's most frequent portrayals. The image is sufficiently like several of Richardson's drawings: nos. 28, 29, 37. The portrait is reproduced by Edmund Gosse, *English Literature An Illustrated Record* (London, 1903), 3.198. It was exhibited at the National Portrait Gallery Exhibition in 1961.

1. Information kindly given by Miss D. Beatrice Harris, Petworth House.

50. OIL PAINTING, BY JONATHAN RICHARDSON. MRS. H. W. POORE, SOUTHDOWN HOUSE, PATCHAM, SUSSEX.

The Harcourt Papers, of. c. 1880, following the "Catalogue which was drawn out by . . . [the Second Earl] Harcourt," report as no. 102, in the Library: " 'Pope, by Richardson.' " "This picture," the entry adds, "was engraved by Vertue, for a large folio edition of Pope's works."[1] The resemblance between Jervas' portrait of 1714 (no. 2.1) and the present picture is not very close, but is close enough to explain the mistake. On 6 January 1866, George Scharf visited Nuneham and noted in the Library: "Pope by Richardson. A powerful and well painted head with strong shadows well massed and gray half tones but mellow. Oval, wig, cravat."[2] The picture next appears at a sale of pictures from Lord Harcourt's collection held at Christie's 11 June 1948, lot 170. It was acquired by the late H. W. Poore, of Southdown House, Patcham, Sussex, and is now in the possession of Mrs. Poore. It was exhibited at the National Portrait Gallery Exhibition in 1961.[3]

1. *The Harcourt Papers. Edited by Edward William Harcourt, of Stanton Harcourt, at Nuneham Courtenay, In The County of Oxford, Esquire, 3* (printed for Private Circulation by James Parker and Co., Oxford), p. 252. See no. 5.1.

2. Scharf *Sketch Book* 75.48 (National Portrait Gallery).

3. See no. 5.1, the account of Lord Harcourt's por-

50. Oil on canvas. Oval, 29 x 24 in. Background dark, black to green; coat dark, black to blue; wig painted in gray-brown masses; face pallid; eyes blue-gray. Mrs. H. W. Poore, Southdown House, Patcham, Sussex.

49. Oil on canvas. 18½ x 14¾ in. (cut down from a larger canvas). Background dark, wig brownish gray, complexion sallow, eyes brownish to hazel, fur collar and cloth garment brownish. On frame: "270. Attributed to Jervas". The Baron Egremont, Petworth House, Sussex.

trait of Pope by Kneller, 1722. It would be plausible to argue that the better-known Kneller was the portrait of Pope lent by Harcourt in 1792 to Lord Onslow for copying. Lord Onslow in return lent his portrait of Milton to Lord Harcourt for copying by Benjamin Van der Gucht. Lord Onslow's copy of Pope was presumably lot 105 "Pope," in his sale at Christie's 23 June 1827, bought by "Moore" (or "Moon") for £ 4-12 0. It has disappeared. His original Milton was lot 104 and was bought by the same buyer. A picture thought to be the Milton has recently come to light and has been acquired by the National Portrait Gallery. A curious circumstance is that, whereas this picture of Milton is smaller and rectangular, the copy made for Lord Harcourt is a larger oval and framed identically with the Harcourt-Poore Richardson portrait of Pope, presumably to hang with it and make a pair. Query: Was the portrait of Pope lent by Harcourt to Onslow not actually the Kneller but the oval Richardson? See Piper, *Catalogue of the Seventeenth-Century Portraits*, pp. 394–97, citing a priced copy at Christie's of the 1827 Catalogue, for the Milton, to which Mr. Piper has kindly added for this note the data for the Pope.

51. OIL PAINTING, BY JONATHAN RICHARDSON. MUSEUM OF FINE ARTS, BOSTON, MASSACHUSETTS.

The picture seems to enter the record for the first time in John Britton's *Beauties of England and Wales*, 9 (1807), 400, in the account of Donington Park, Leicestershire, a seat of the Earl of Moira: "Portraits . . . Alexander Pope." Presumably it was this picture which was sold as lot 84 at Christie's 25 February 1869, from the collection of the Marquis of Hastings at Donington Park. In his copy of the Catalogue (at the National Portrait Gallery) George Scharf noted: "10 guineas bid, 84 gns. observe shorn hair under flaxen wig." The picture was bought by "Graves." In his *Yesterdays with Authors*, first published in 1872, the Boston litterateur James T. Fields describes at some length his purchase of the picture from Mr. Graves at no. 6 Pall Mall. "When I dropped in upon him that summer [!] morning he had just returned from the sale of the Marquis of Hastings' effects. . . . One of the best preserved pictures inherited by the late Marquis was a portrait of Pope, painted from life by Richardson for the Earl of Burlington."[1] The best reproduction of the picture in the period of its possession by Fields and later his widow is the frontispiece of the Cambridge *Complete Works of Pope*, ed. H. W. Boynton (Boston, 1903). In F. O. Matthiessen's *Sarah Orne Jewett* (Boston, 1929), facing p. 112, a photograph of Miss Jewett and Mrs. Fields in the drawing room at 148 Charles Street shows the portrait of Pope over the fireplace. In 1924 the picture came from the estate of Mrs. Fields to the Boston Museum of Fine Arts.[2] In the winter of 1945 it was exhibited at the Rhode Island School of Design in Providence, R.I.[3] It is included in a portfolio of reproductions entitled *Life in 18th-Century England*, edited by Robert J. Allen and published by the Boston Museum of Fine Arts. It is plate 34 in Frances Sharf Fink, *Heads Across the Sea, An Album of Eighteenth-Century English Literary Portraits in America* (Charlottesville, 1959). Since about 1952 it has hung on loan in the Houghton Library, Harvard University.

1. James T. Fields, *Yesterdays with Authors* (17th Edition, Boston, 1880), pp. 4–6. A small reproduction of the picture, head and shoulders, appears in the *New Illustrated Edition* of the same work (Boston, Houghton, Mifflin and Company, 1882), facing p. 4, and in James T. Fields and Edwin P. Whipple, *The Family Library of British Poetry from Chaucer to the Present Time* (Boston, 1878), facing p. 312. This picture was no doubt the "head" or "portrait" of Pope which Fields once showed to the painter Elihu Vedder (*The Digressions of V.*, London, 1911, p. 263).

2. Cf. *Museum of Fine Arts Bulletin*, 22 (February 1924), 19.

3. *The Catalogue of Old and New England, an Exhibition of American Painting . . . in the Museum of Art of the Rhode Island School of Design, Provi-*

51. Oil on canvas. 30 x 25 in. Background dark brown; coat dark blue; table light brown; cover of book tan; page edges pink; wig gray-white; flesh tints pallid pinkish. On a label at the back of the stretcher: "Henry Graves & Co. / 2111/6, Pall Mall, London". Courtesy, Museum of Fine Arts, Boston.

dence, R.I. from January 19th through February 18th, 1945, p. 47, no. 94; reproduced in a review of the Exhibition in The Art Quarterly, published by the Detroit Institute of Arts, 8 (Winter 1945), facing p. 9, figure 6.

52.1. OIL PAINTING, BY JONATHAN RICHARDSON. THE BARON EGREMONT,
PETWORTH HOUSE, SUSSEX.

Dr. Richard Mead, a neighbor and friend of the painter Richardson,[1] was one of the most eminent virtuosi of his day. "His large and spacious house in *Great Ormond Street,* was converted into a Temple of Nature, and a Repository of Time."[2] "He was the friend of *Pope,* of *Halley,* of *Newton,* and placed their portraits in his house near the Busts of their great Masters, the antient Greeks and Romans."[3] After his death in 1754, his collections, of books, pictures, gems, bronzes, marbles, and coins, were auctioned in five great sales.

Mead apparently owned at least two nearly identical portraits of Pope by Richardson. Doubtless the first of these to be painted is the one alluded to by Pope in his letter to Richardson in Queen's Square of 4 January 1737: "I keep my promise in acquainting You a day before, that I will come to you to morrow by eleven, to sit till one if you please for ye D^{r}'s Picture."[4]

A picture of Pope was lot 34 on the second day of the sale of Mead's Pictures by Langford in Covent Garden, 20, 21, and 22 March 1754: "Mr. Richardson . . . Mr. Pope. 3 qrs." It was bought for £15.4.6.[5] In a second edition of the *Catalogue of Pictures,* dated in 1755, with added notes, we find, p. vi: "Mr. Alexander Pope, a Profile by Mr. *Richardson,* who also etched this picture." This allusion is presumably to the profile etching, OYTOΣ EKEINOΣ, dated 1738, but I think that neither oil nor etching should be considered as the model of the other.

To turn now to the profile portrait of Pope at Petworth House: On the bottom of the frame at the back and crumbling off in three pieces, in November 1960, was a very old laid-paper label inscribed: "From Dr Mead   Alexr / Popes Picture by Richardson / bought by Mr. Chetwynd / who left it Dr. Cooke." A larger vellum label (18½ x 3½ in.) at the top of the frame is inscribed: "This Portrait of Pope was taken from Life by Richardson for Dr. Mead the Physician and given by him to Mr. Chetwyn of Kings College who left it by will to Dr. Cooke then Provost of Kings, my Father. A. Way. July 1825."[6] Elizabeth Anne Cooke, daughter of Dr. William Cooke (rector of Denham in Buckinghamshire, who was in succession Headmaster of Eton, Provost of King's College, Cambridge, and Vice-Chancellor of the University) was married in 1767 to Benjamin Way, squire of Denham Place, who became M.P. for Bridport, High Sheriff of Buckinghamshire, a sub-governor of the South Sea Company, and F.R.S. In recent years it has come to light that the agreeable Mrs. Way was a correspondent of Samuel Johnson's during 1782 and 1783.[7] The ownership of the portrait of Pope by Benjamin Way and later his widow may be traced in the lettering of the engravings to be noticed below (no. 52.2).

A note in pen and ink in a British Museum copy of the Catalogue of the Mead sale of Prints and Drawings, no. 69, 13th day, 28 January 1755, says that Walter Chetwynd,

52.1. Oil on canvas. 29½ x 24½ in. Background light umber brown; collar darker brown; hair dark brown, grayish at temple; cloth of coat dark red to plum; flesh tint sallow with heavy pink strokes in cheek; ear, nostril, lips deep red; eye hazel to brown. The Baron Egremont, Petworth House, Sussex.

Fellow of King's College, Cambridge, was a purchaser at that sale.[8] Mrs. Way's vellum label, written when she was about 79 years old, repeating the substance of the older paper label, should not be allowed to contradict the more plausible testimony of the older label that Chetwynd (not a friend of Mead's so far as I have found out) acquired the portrait of Pope by purchase, no doubt at the Picture Sale of March 1754.

The picture is noted by Cunningham in 1854, who alludes to it as "Sir William Wyndham's." Very likely it was brought to Petworth by Sir George O'Brien Wyndham, 3rd Lord Egremont (d. 1837), the patron of Nollekens, Constable, and Turner, the last of whom had a studio at Petworth.

It was exhibited at the National Portrait Gallery Exhibition in 1961.

The red cloak which appears conspicuously in Pope portraits of this Richardson type and in one other type (see nos. 55.1 and 55.2) is the subject of an anecdote in Thomas Davies' *Memoirs of David Garrick:* The play, Mallet's "opposition" tragedy of *Mustapha*, was acted [13 February 1739] with great applause; and at its close Pope went behind the scenes, where he had not been for some years. "He expressed himself to be well pleased with his entertainment; and particularly addressed himself to Quin, who was greatly flattered with the distinction paid him by so great a man; and when Pope's servant brought his master's scarlet cloak, Quin insisted upon the honour of putting it on him" (New Edition, London, 1780, 2.35–36).

1. See pp. 144, 180.

2. *Authentic Memoirs of the Life of Richard Mead, M.D.* (London, 1755), p. 51. The *Memoirs* (Preface) are translated from the notice in the *Journal Britannique* and may be ascribed to Dr. M. Maty.

3. *Memoirs*, pp. 62–63. Cf. Pope's *Epistle to Burlington*, 1. 10.

4. *Correspondence* 4.91.

5. *A Catalogue of the Genuine and Capital Collection of Pictures . . . of that Late Great and Learned Physician, Doctor Richard Mead, Deceased . . . March 1754*, p. 6 (British Museum 7805.e.5 [4]). The sale and the price are noted by Cunningham in 1854.

6. Cf. C. H. Collins Baker, *Catalogue of the Petworth Collection of Pictures* (London, 1920), p. 109, no. 53.

7. James L. Clifford, "A New Johnson Correspondent," *TLS*, 30 May 1952, p. 368.

8. Whitley Papers, Department of Prints and Drawings, British Museum. Whitley reports that this note appears in a copy of the Mead Prints and Drawings Catalogue bound up with a copy of the 1755 Catalogue of Mead's Pictures. I have not seen it. The drawing purchased by Walter Chetwynd is said to have been a Holbein of Anne of Cleves, later in the Royal Collection.

52.2. LINE ENGRAVING, BY T. HOLLOWAY, AFTER JONATHAN RICHARDSON. FOR WARTON's *Pope*, 1797.

A small line engraving from an unidentified portrait of this type appears at an earlier date (*Grolier* 42: "Richardson. Thornthwaite sculp. Printed for John Bell near Exeter Exchange Strand London Mar. 1st 1777"). But Thomas Holloway's engraving for the first volume of Joseph Warton's edition of the *Works of Pope*, 1797, is securely connected by its lettering with the portrait in the possession of Benjamin Way. Both the oil painting (no. 52.1) and the engraving have a larger mass of fur collar behind the neck than other oils of the type. Two original documents relating to the picture in Warton's edition survive. One is Holloway's acknowledgement of being paid: "Received Nov.r 29th 1796 of Messrs. Cadell & Davies twenty Guineas for engraving a Head of Mr Pope. £.21. .o. .o   Thos. Holloway."[1] The other is a note from Joseph Warton to Thomas Cadell, 11 December 1795, saying that Benjamin Way's portrait of Pope formerly belonged to Dr. Mead.[2]

Holloway's plate was used again by Cadell and Davies as an illustration (facing p. xv) in the first volume of W. L. Bowles' edition of the *Works of Pope,* 1806. Several similar engravings, possibly copies from Holloway's work, are to be found. For example: 4⅛ x 3⅜ inches, "Alexander Pope Esq. / Engraved by R. Cooper, from the original Picture, painted by J. Richardson / in the possession of Benj[n] Way, Esq[e] / Published by Richard Priestly, High Holborn, London" (British Museum 1868–8–22– 1411); and 3¼ x 2⁹⁄₁₆ oval, "Neagle sc. / . . . Sep. 1. 1802 by Longman and Rees, Paternoster Row" (*Grolier* 40). The history of the engraving of this portrait apparently ends with W. H. Worthington's plate for the second volume of William Roscoe's edition of the *Works* of Pope in 1824. The portrait is now "in the possession of Mrs. Way." Her note to Cadell, Bookseller, Strand requesting the return of the painting has survived: "Mrs Ways Compliments to Mr Cadell & wishes to see her Picture of Mr Pope in its Place, as she concludes it must be done with by the engraver by this time. 9 Chandos Street April 23, 1824."[3]

1. Thomas Dodd's extra-illustrated set of Roscoe's *Pope,* 20, insert no. 20 (Dr. Gordon Ray).

2. *The R. B. Adam Library Relating to Dr. Samuel Johnson and His Era* (London and New York, 1929), 3.254.

3. On black-edged note paper, in Thomas Dodd's extra-illustrated Roscoe's *Pope,* 20, insert no. 9 (Dr. Gordon Ray). The plate, as it appears in Roscoe's volume 2, has: "Published, March 1, 1824, by T. Cadell, Strand, London." An impression in the J. L. Graham Collection of reference engravings ([xv.Pope 5]) in the Yale University Library, has instead: "Published by Longman, Brown, Green & Longmans, Paternoster Row."

A large etching in greenish-gray ink, framed within a fancy scroll design, which appears as frontispiece to *An Essay on Criticism by Alexander Pope* (San Francisco, printed for William Andrews Clark, Jr., by John Henry Nash, 1928), is a reversed image of this type, which shows, I believe, some signs of having been taken from Worthington's version.

52.3. OIL PAINTING, BY JONATHAN RICHARDSON. SIR ROBERT ARTHUR WILMOT, BART., PITCAIRLIE, NEWBURGH, FIFE.

A second profile painting of Pope, by Richardson, which belonged to Dr. Mead is that now in the possession of Sir Robert Arthur Wilmot, Bart., of Pitcairlie, Newburgh, Fife. Edward Wilmot (1693–1786), husband of the eldest daughter of Dr. Richard Mead, was Physician in Ordinary to George II and was created Baronet in 1759. His descendant, Sir Henry S. Wilmot, 4th Baronet, of Chaddesden, in Derbyshire, lent a portrait of Pope, once belonging to Dr. Mead, to the Manchester Art Treasures Exhibition in 1857,[1] and in 1867, to the South Kensington Museum Second Special Exhibition.[2] Sir Robert A. Wilmot tells me that a manuscript catalogue of the family collection, compiled at Chaddesden in 1881, has a note against this picture and a number of others: "From Dr. Mead's collection." About seven years ago the portrait of Pope was damaged in a fire. The photograph which I present below, with the kind approval of Sir Robert, is a detail from a negative, now somewhat deteriorated in the lower part, made at South Kensington in 1867 (Victoria and Albert no. 6400).

1. *Catalogue* p. 131, no. 371: "Pope the Poet, By Richardson. In Profile. This picture belonged to Dr. Mead." At Manchester, 9 October 1857, George Scharf entered in his notebook: "Obviously by Richardson" (NPG Scharf *Sketch Book* 49.17).

2. *Catalogue* p. 44, no. 149: "Bust, profile to r.; furred dark dress. Formerly in Dr. Mead's Coll. . . . 30 x 25 in." At this exhibition George Scharf filled out a form for notes on the colors of this picture: "brown fur collar to maddery brown coat. no spandrils, dark yellow brown background" (NPG archives).

52.4. OIL PAINTING, SIMILAR TO NOS. 52.1–3. THE BARON WALPOLE, WOLTERTON PARK, ERPINGHAM, NORWICH.

Cunningham in 1854 says: "Richardson. Lord Walpole's (a profile) is at Wolterton." A label on the back of the picture reads: "sold at the Wolterton Sale, June 1856, to Mrs. Sterling of Keir—Purchased by me for the same price, I think £16. Given to Horatio Walpole of Wolterton according to a tradition in the family, Orford."[1] The present Lord Walpole kindly informs me that the picture was brought back to Wolterton by the late Lord Orford, who died in 1931. On the front of the frame is a plate which reads: "Given with his Works / by Alexander Pope, this picture by Richardson / to Lord Walpole of Wolterton." Pope's acquaintance with Sir Robert Walpole's brother "Mr. Horace Walpole," later First Baron Walpole of Wolterton, may be noted in the *Correspondence* (2.323 and 3.6) during 1725 and 1729.

1. The painting is no. 136 in G. W. Snelgrove's Catalogue in his Thesis of 1936 at the University of London. I take the reading of the label from Snelgrove.

52.5. OIL PAINTING, SIMILAR TO NOS. 52.1–3. NATIONAL PORTRAIT GALLERY NO. 561.

A manuscript copy at the National Portrait Gallery from the Minutes of the British Museum Trustees reads: "June 6 1794 Mr. [Francis] Annesley having proposed to give to the museum an original portrait of Mr. Pope in exchange for a picture of Sir Robt. Cotton, which is a duplicate. Resolved that his proposal be accepted." The transfer of this picture from the British Museum to the National Portrait Gallery is recorded in *Twenty-Second Annual Report of the Trustees of the National Portrait Gallery* (1879), p. 7, no. 216. In George Scharf's *Historical and Descriptive Catalogue of Pictures in the National Portrait Gallery* (London, 1888), the picture is no. 561, on p. 361: "wearing his natural hair and a dark yellow-brown dress, with brown fur over the shoulder, leaving the neck bare. The eyes are very dark and lustrous. Eyebrows dark, broad and strongly marked. The cheek is sunk and the face entirely shaven. The lips broad and full, of a deep red. The hair a dark brown. Background a plain deep brown. The old canvas is plain at the back." The picture was for many years during the present century on loan to the Scottish National Portrait Gallery, Edinburgh. It returned to London a few years ago.

52.6. OIL PAINTING, SIMILAR TO NOS. 52.1–3. SEEN AT TWICKENHAM, 1901.

In June 1901 Edwin Maynard, Librarian of the Free Public Library, Town Hall, Twickenham, and Secretary to the Twickenham Library Committee (and in 1888

ALEXANDER POPE ESQ.

Engraved by I. Holloway, from a Picture painted by I. Richardson

in the profession of Benjⁿ Way Esqʳ

Published January 1ˢᵗ 1797 by Cadell and Davies Strand London.

left

52.2. Line engraving. 5 x 4⅛ in. "ALEXANDER POPE ESQ. / Engraved by T. Holloway, from a Picture painted by J. Richardson, / in the possession of Benjⁿ Way Esqʳ / Published January 1ˢᵗ 1797 by Cadell and Davies Strand London." *Grolier* 38. Frontispiece to vol. 1 of *Works of Alexander Pope*, ed. Joseph Warton, London, 1797.

above, right

52.3. Oil on canvas. 30 x 25 in. Colors similar to those of no. 53.1. Detail from a photograph made at the South Kensington Exhibition, 1867. Victoria and Albert Museum Photograph. Sir Robert A. Wilmot, Bart., Pitcairlie, Newburgh, Fife.†

52.4. Oil on canvas. 29½ x 24½ in. Colors similar to those of no. 53.1. Label at bottom of frame: "Given with his Works / by Alexander Pope, this picture by Richardson / to Lord Walpole of Wolterton." The Baron Walpole, Wolterton Park, Erpingham, Norwich.†

52.5. Oil on canvas. 16½ x 14 in. Colors similar to those of no. 52.1. National Portrait Gallery no. 561.

member of the Twickenham Loan Museum Sub-Committee) had on loan, "or for sale," an "oil painting—2 feet by 1 ft. 8 in.—a Portrait, in profile, of Pope." This was "similar" to the picture once owned by Benjamin Way and engraved for the editions of Warton, Bowles, and Roscoe. It was "as nearly as possible the same" as NPG 561, a photograph of which was sent to Maynard by Lionel Cust, Director of the Gallery. In October Cust had seen the portrait and reported that he "considered it to be a genuine old portrait & probably one of Richardson's numerous repetitions."[1] The dimensions of this oil would seem to preclude its identification with any one of the others listed in this group.

1. Letters from Maynard to Cust, 13 and 22 June 1901, and Gallery Memorandum dated October 1901 (National Portrait Gallery archives).

52.7. OIL PAINTING, SIMILAR TO NOS. 52.1–3. KELJIK GALLERIES, SAINT PAUL, MINNESOTA, 1965.

The picture reproduced below (no. 52.7) is taken from a photograph in the *Illustrated Catalogue of Old and Modern Paintings by the Great Masters Forming the Important Collection of Mr. John Anderson, Jr. To be sold . . . April 16, 1916 . . . The American Art Association . . . New York City.* This was lot no. 35: "Jonathan Richardson . . . Portrait of Alexander Pope," 30 x 25 inches. The entry mistakenly asserts that this picture belonged to Benjamin Way, Esq., and that it was engraved by T. Holloway for Warton's *Pope* in 1797 (see nos. 52.1 and 52.2). It says further that the picture is "From the Collection of Evert Jansen Wendell, Esq., New York." Evert Jansen Wendell, collector and philanthropist, was brother of Barrett Wendell, Professor of English at Harvard University. His large *Artistic and Literary Collections* were sold in six parts by his executors for the benefit of Harvard University at the American Art Galleries, New York, 15–25 October 1919. He had died 28 August 1917.

In February 1965 Mr. Var Keljik, of Keljik Galleries, Saint Paul, Minnesota, sent me a photograph which convinces me that the painting sold in 1916 is in his hands.

52.8. OIL PAINTING, SIMILAR TO NOS. 52.1–3. MR. AND MRS. JAMES M. OSBORN, NEW HAVEN, CONNECTICUT.

At a sale of *First Editions, Autograph Letters and Manuscripts, Association Books & Other Items,* 24 and 25 April 1935, at the American Art Association Anderson Galleries, New York, lot 254 (p. 128) was "A Portrait in Oils of Alexander Pope by Jonathan Richardson. . . . in profile, bust length facing left, with abundant brown curly hair, clad in a dark maroon coat with fur collar exposing a white shirt at the throat, against a very dark brown background," 30 x 25 inches. The entry continues, mistakenly, that the portrait was engraved by T. Holloway for Warton's *Pope* of 1797 and was in the collection of Benjamin Way (see nos. 52.1 and 52.2). It says also that the portrait had been in the collections of Evert Jansen Wendell, Esq., and John Anderson, Jr.

Dr. Dallas Pratt of New York told me in 1952 that he had acquired the portrait which is the subject of the present entry at a book sale at the Anderson Galleries, in the thirties, before 1937. It seems likely that the portrait described for the sale of 1935 was the one acquired by Dr. Pratt. But Dr. Pratt's picture is clearly a different picture from the one sold at the John Anderson, Jr., sale of 1916 (no. 52.7), although the cataloguer of 1935 seems to have copied from the American Art Association Catalogue of 1916.

Dr. Pratt put his portrait up for sale at Parke-Bernet Galleries, 1 May 1951, lot 574 (p. 138 of the Catalogue, where the history of the portrait is again traced mistakenly from Benjamin Way and T. Holloway through Wendell and John Anderson, Jr.). It was acquired by Mr. James M. Osborn, of New Haven, Conn.

52.9. OIL PAINTING, BY EDWARD WRIGHT, AFTER RICHARDSON. GUILD HALL, BATH.

An oil painting of Pope, profile to left, which hangs in the Guild Hall at Bath has in the upper right quarter on the back a large paper label inscribed in pen and ink:

Edward Wright the painter of this / picture was an intimate friend of / Mr. Richardson and obtained leave from / him to copy the portrait of Mr. Pope / which Mr. R. was then painting and / had nearly finished. When the outline / was sketched out by E. Wright he happ / ened to meet Mr. Pope at dinner and on / mentioning to him how he was employed / Mr. Pope said "Why should you take a / copy when the original is at your service / I will come and sit to you." He did so and / this picture was finished from Mr. / Pope himself.

52.7. Oil on canvas. 30 x 25 in. From a photograph in the Catalogue of John Anderson, Jr.'s sale, American Art Association, 16 April 1916.

52.8. Oil on canvas. 30 x 25 in. Colors similar to those of no. 52.1. Mr. and Mrs. James M. Osborn, New Haven, Conn.

This account I had from the late William Wright / Esq. my honoured uncle who had the / picture from the painter himself. / At Mr. Wright's death it came to his / widow who gave it to my brother / at whose decease it came to me. / Bath / March 21, 1803. [signed] William Falconer.[1]

Dr. William Falconer came to Bath in 1770 and died at his home in the Circus in 1824. One of his grandsons, Dr. Randle Wilbraham Falconer, was Mayor of Bath in 1858, and lent a portrait of Pope to an exhibition at the Archaeological Institute Museum, where it was noted by George Scharf.[2] It was doubtless the same person ("R.W.F. Bath") who communicated a transcript of the note quoted above to *Notes and Queries,* First Series, 7 (1853), 294. The picture was bequeathed to the Victoria Art Gallery at Bath in 1940.

1. From a typescript Catalogue of Pictures in the Victoria Art Gallery. I have seen the picture and the label.

In the album of drawings assembled by Richard Bull now in the Pierpont Morgan Library, New York City, is an ink drawing by Richardson the elder, inscribed in Richardson's hand, "Mr. Wright Senior of Cheshire," and another inscribed, "Mr. Wright, Junior" (p. 40, nos. 65, 66). G. W. Snelgrove reports another drawing of Wright (Senior or Junior?) in the Ashmolean Museum, dated 10 December 1736, and another in the possession of J. H. J. Mellaart, Rotterdam (no. 660, "Edward Wright," in the Wellesley

Sale, Sotheby's 28 June ff., 1920). Snelgrove speculates that Richardson's friend may have been Edward Wright, author of *Some Observations Made in Travelling through France, Italy, &c. in . . . 1720, 1721, and 1722,* 2 volumes, London, 1730. And indeed on the back of no. 65 in the Morgan Bull album appears the pencil inscription: "(auth of the Travels) Mr Wright / of Cheshire."

2. National Portrait Gallery, Scharf *Sketch Book* 52.21, 30, 22 July 1858. "Portrait of Pope, profile to left . . . resembles profile by J. Richardson. Coll. Mayor of Bath."

52.9. Oil on canvas. 28½ x 24 in. Colors similar to those of no. 52.1. For text of label on back, see the entry for no. 52.9. Guild Hall, Bath. By Courtesy of the Victoria Art Gallery, Bath.

53.1. OIL PAINTING, ATTRIBUTED TO JONATHAN RICHARDSON. VICTORIA AND ALBERT
MUSEUM.

The portrait seems to be first recorded in the South Kensington Museum's *Dyce Collection, A Catalogue of the Paintings, Miniatures, Drawings, Engravings, Rings, and Miscellaneous Objects Bequeathed by the Reverend Alexander Dyce* (London, 1874), p. 3, no. 13. The entry reads: "Jonathan Richardson the Elder, Portrait Head, life-size, of Alexander Pope . . . Canvas, 25¼ in. by 20½ in." Dyce's will was dated 9 March, 1869. The same picture is listed in the Museum's *Catalogue of the National Gallery of British Art at South Kensington* (1893), p. 124.

This painting represents a less well-known type than nos. 52.1–9, but seems similar enough in conception and technique to be safely ascribed to Richardson. Along with the change in the character of the profile, the change in the garment, especially the shape of the small portion of white shirt, suggest a transitional stage between no. 52.1 (the Petworth profile) and Richardson's momentary triumph in no. 54 (National Por-

53.1. Oil on canvas. 25¼ x 20½ in. Brown background recessed behind painted brown spandrels; cloak nearly the same shade of brown; hair nearly the same, with black lines; flesh tints sallowish; lips light pink; shirt white. Victoria and Albert Museum Crown Copyright.

trait Gallery 1179). The following passage is from Richardson's *Theory of Painting,* 1715, pp. 184–186, "Of Grace and Greatness":

'Tis of Importance to a Painter to consider well the Manner of Cloathing his his People. . . . the truest Taste in this Matter the Ancient *Greeks* and *Romans* seem to have had; at least the great Ideas we have of those brave People prejudices us in Favor of whatever is theirs, so that It shall appear to Us to be Graceful and Noble: Upon either of which Accounts, whether of a Real, or Imagin'd Excellence, that *manner* of Cloathing is to be chosen by a Painter when the Nature of his Subject will admit of it. . . . *Portrait-Painters* seeing the Disadvantage they were under in following the Dress Commonly Worn, have Invented one peculiar to Pictures in their Own Way, which is a Composition partly That, and partly something purely Arbitrary.

53.2. OIL PAINTING, SIMILAR TO NO. 53.1. INDIANA UNIVERSITY.

This picture came to the Indiana University Library about 1958 from the Eli Lilly Collection. The back is covered with a cardboard shield, with openings to show the following: "C 274" (in ink on the frame at the top); "The Schneider-Gabriel Galleries Inc. 71 East 57th Street New York" (a small printed label near the top); "Alexander Pope by Jonathan Richardson bought from Miss Mary Lockwood Hanover N.Y. John

53.2. Oil on canvas. 29¼ x 24¼ in. Painted for an oval frame; background brown; hair darker brown; robe brown; flesh tints yellowish, with bright red on lips and ear, and in front of the eye socket. University Library, Indiana University, Bloomington, Indiana.

53.3. Oil on canvas. 29 x 24 in. Colors similar to those of nos. 53.1 and 2. Inscribed in paint at lower left: "Alexander Pope Ob—1744." Charles Jones, Esq., New York City.†

Frederick Everett Providence R.I. 1902" (handwritten ink label near center); a small line engraving of the type of no. 52.1 (near the bottom); "Francis Harvey" (engraved or printed on a small label at the bottom).

53.3. OIL PAINTING, SIMILAR TO NO. 53.1. CHARLES JONES, NEW YORK CITY.

Mr. Charles Jones tells me he acquired this picture at an auction 13 November 1959, at Savoy on East 59th Street, New York City, lot 711.

53.4. OIL PAINTING, SIMILAR TO NO. 53.1. SIR EDWARD CLIVE MILNES-COATES.

This picture has been at the City of York Art Gallery, on loan from Sir Edward Clive Milnes-Coates since 1952. A photograph of it is to be seen in the National Portrait Gallery archives.

53.5. OIL PAINTING, SIMILAR TO NO. 53.1. CARNEGIE BOOKSHOP, NEW YORK, 1956.

William Duff (1696?–1763), First Earl Fife, built Duff House, County Fife, in 1740–1745. It was perhaps during the Earldom of James, Second Earl Fife (1729–1809), that someone compiled the list of pictures at Duff House which is included in Sir William Musgrave's MS. *Notes on Portraits in Scottish Country Houses*, at the British Museum. Here we find (p. 32),—along with "Garrick studying . . . Hamlet . . . Reynolds"—"Alexander Pope, profile, three quarters, Kneller," with the added note: "Lord Marchmont had one at the same time.)"[1] In a *Catalogue of the Portraits and Pictures in the Different Houses Belonging to James, Earl of* [sic] *Fife, 1807*, the picture of Pope is no. 10 at Duff House, hanging in the vestibule with portraits of other literary figures, including Prior, Swift, and Garrick.[2] The collateral descendant and heir of the Earls Fife, Alexander William George, First Duke of Fife (1849–1912), married, at Buckingham Palace 27 July 1889, H.R.H. Princess Louise Victoria Alexandra Dagmar (d. 1931), eldest daughter of Prince Edward, later King Edward VII. At Christie's on 26 June 1925, lot 83, sold "by order of H.R.H. The Princesss Royal," was "J. Richardson, Portrait of Alexander Pope, in red coat edged with fur, 29 in. by 24½." This was bought for six guineas by H. L. Puckle, Esq., 1 Angel Court, Finsbury, E.C.[3] In 1954 the painting was found in an antique shop in England by Charles Stonehill of New Haven. It came to America, and in 1956 was at the Carnegie Bookshop in New York. The photograph which I reproduced below was taken while the painting was at Stonehill's in New Haven in 1954. Although this painting has the fur collar of the 52.1–9 type, in other features, both of face and garment, it seems closer to nos. 53.1–3.

1. British Museum Add. MS. 6392, quoted in the Whitley Papers, Department of Prints and Drawings, British Museum. Cf. no. 53.6.

2. Information from the Scottish National Portrait Gallery, Edinburgh.

3. A letter of 8 May 1935, from Christie's to Puckle, enclosing an inquiry from Gordon W. Snelgrove (This letter was still with the picture when it reached New Haven in 1954).

53.6. OIL PAINTING, PROBABLY SIMILAR TO NO. 53.5. THE THIRD EARL OF
MARCHMONT AND GEORGE ROSE, C. 1805.

See no. 53.5, the allusion to Lord Marchmont in the Duff House inventory. The friendship between Pope and Hugh, Third Earl of Marchmont, seems to date from about the
time of the latter's succession to the title in the winter of 1739/40 (*Correspondence*
4.217), when he is more likely to have gotten a Richardson replica than a Kneller. On
12 May 1778, James Boswell records in his *Journal:* "Then Ld Marchmont's. Large
Library. Intermediate Pannels w^t prints, Heads, glazed, but fixed in ye Wall. I said, 'No
good one of y^r friend Pope' " (Boswell Mss., Yale University). In a later source (E. W.
Brayley and J. Britton, *The Beauties of England and Wales, 6* [1805], 181) we read that
the Right Honorable George Rose, who had a large house called Cuffnells, near Lynd-
hurst, in Hampshire, had in it a fine library which had come into his possession from
the late Earl of Marchmont (d. 1792), to whom Mr. Rose was sole executor. The house
contained "a few . . . original portraits of intimate friends of the late Earl: Lord
Bolingbroke, Sir William Wyndham, the late Earl of Chatham, and Pope, by Richardson."

54. OIL PAINTING, ATTRIBUTED TO JONATHAN RICHARDSON. NATIONAL PORTRAIT
GALLERY NO. 1179.

In 1898 this picture was in the collection of Mr. Alfred A. de Pass at Cliffe House, Fal-
mouth, Cornwall. After conversations with Lord Ronald Sutherland Gower, a Trustee

53.5. Oil on canvas. 29½ x 24½ in. Colors similar to those of no. 53.1.
Last traced at the Carnegie Bookshop, New York City, 1956.

217

54. Oil on canvas. 23¼ x 17¼ in. Background dull brownish (raw umber or Vandyke brown—with no red); cloak gray-blue, with shadows brown like the background—the effect is silvery; laurel wreath deep blue-green, about twenty leaves, with berry clusters in three places; short gray hair at temple above ear; flesh tints of face cream and gray, in rough twisted strokes; dull orange red in ear and behind jaw under ear; red shadows in nostril and behind nostril and under cheekbone; lips grayish, reddish only at center; eyebrows gray smudgy; neck gray and shadowy, and heavy shadows under chin; ear painted in large coarse strokes; eyes grayish to blue. National Portrait Gallery no. 1179.

of the National Portrait Gallery, Mr. De Pass wrote the following note to Lionel Cust, the Director: "15 Nov. 1898—Lord Ronald Gower thought a portrait I had of Pope by Kneller ought to be in the National Collection. I have sent it to you today, & if the Trustees think it is good enough I shall be pleased to present it to the Gallery." The donation is recorded in the *Forty-Second Annual Report of the Trustees of the National Portrait Gallery* (London, 1899), p. 4.

The quality of this painting is a surprising contrast to that of the oils of Pope by Richardson so far presented. In freedom and strength, it surpasses the best of Richardson's earlier achievements in oil. On the other hand, its similarity to two pencil drawings of Pope by Richardson, one of them dated "1737" (see above nos. 35 and 36), is good reason for the attribution. The management of the clothing, especially the exposed strip of white shirt, suggests a development through earlier profiles by Richardson, nos. 52.1 and 53.1. At the National Portrait Gallery, no. 1493, apparently a portrait of Bolingbroke, nearly the same size (22½ x 19 inches) and painted in a somewhat similar plastic style, with a "deep brownish red velvet turban cap" and "dark greyish lavender drapery" about the shoulders, and a white shirt open at the throat, is thought most likely to be by Richardson.[1] See p. 144, my account of Richardson's painting for Pope and Bolingbroke in 1738. I have heard it suggested that the portrait of Pope looks like something which the dissipated but brilliant young artist John Vanderbank (Rysbrack's neighbor in Vere Street—he died in 1739) might have painted toward the end of his life, as a kind of joke, to show a new style of painting. But Richardson had all along had successes in painting, and during the thirties he experiences many moments of release and power, especially in his larger chalk drawings on blue paper of himself and his son. One other well-authenticated late portrait of Pope (see no. 55.1) shows, if not the same noble success as National Portrait Gallery 1179, at least something of the same loose brush work. It seems to me plausible to suppose that the aging Richardson, who painted Pope so many times rather drably during the later 1730s, did achieve his one lucky spurt of freely directed artistic energy and, "Amicitiae Causa," succeeded in conferring upon Pope the deep blue-green crown of bay leaves.

The painting has been reproduced in Lionel Cust, *The National Portrait Gallery, I* (London, 1901), 215, and as frontispiece to volume 2 of George Paston's *Mr. Pope His Life and Times* (London, 1909); as frontispiece to Edith Sitwell's *Alexander Pope* (London: Faber & Faber Limited, Second Impression, March 1930), and (reversed) as frontispiece to the New York edition (Cosmopolitan Book Corporation, 1930);[2] and in the *TLS* for 3 June 1944, to illustrate a bicentenary middle-page article.

It was exhibited at The National Portrait Gallery Exhibition in 1961.

---

1. Piper, *Catalogue of the Seventeenth-Century Portraits*, p. 30.

2. In at least one copy of the first Faber and Faber impression which I have seen, the frontispiece is replaced by a special leaf before the half title. This is tinted green on the recto and bears a monochrome gray facsimile drawing (4½ x 4 in.) which shows a bust of Pope on a pedestal, against which Miss Sitwell in a flowery long dress, dainty high-heeled shoes, and a heavy string of round beads, is leaning with one elbow. She holds a garland of bay leaves draped in part about the pedestal. A few wisps of grass are growing between the base of the bust and the pedestal. The bust, which faces three-quarters to the left, owes something in the fold of the garment perhaps to the Roubiliac type (see no. 61.25, Angelica Kauffmann's Muses

Crowning a Bust of Pope), but the open shirt collar, the face itself, especially the nose, and the crown of bay leaves, derive clearly from NPG 1179. The picture is signed in the grass near the front of the pedestal "Rex Whistler." I have seen the same picture in a larger size (5⅞ x 5 in.) on front and back of a green-tinted dust jacket on a copy of the second Faber and Faber impression.

55.1. OIL PAINTING, BY JONATHAN RICHARDSON. COLIN BROUN LINDSAY, ESQ., YOUNGER, COLSTOUN, HADDINGTON.

In Jonathan Richardson the younger's sale of Pictures held after his death by Langford on 18 February 1772 (Lugt 1999; see p. 148), lots 45 and 46 were "Richardson Senior, His own portrait," and "Richardson Senior, Mr. Pope, from the life." Today at Colstoun House, Haddington, the home of Major Sir George Humphrey Maurice and Lady Broun Lindsay and their son Colin Broun Lindsay, are two pictures, the same small size: one of Richardson the elder (similar to NPG 706) and one of Alexander Pope. These look very much as if they are the pictures of the 1772 sale.

George, Ninth Earl of Dalhousie, married in 1805 Christian Broun, heiress of Colstoun. Their son James Andrew, Tenth Earl and Marquis of Dalhousie, died in 1860, when the marquessate and barony of Dalhousie of the United Kingdom became extinct, the Scottish title going to a cousin, the Eleventh Earl. The 10th Earl left, however, two daughters: one, Edith Christian, was grandmother of the present Lady Broun Lindsay; the other, Susan Georgiana, married in 1863 Robert Bourke, First Baron Connemara; she died in 1898 without issue.

In *The Spectator, 124* (10 January 1920), 45, after a flurry of correspondence concerning portraits of Pope, appeared the following communication: "Sir,—In this house there is a small head painted in oils of Alexander Pope. The head is turned towards the right shoulder; he is wearing a red coat trimmed with fur and a plain white shirt well up to the neck. On the back of the frame is this inscription: 'This picture Mr. Pope sat[e] to my father for at my request for me 1742.' . . . It was formerly in the possession of my grandfather, the Marquis of Dalhousie.—I am, Sir, etc. Susan G. Baird, Colstoun, Haddington." Susan G. Baird was the mother of Lady Broun Lindsay, who has sent me the information that the original label bearing the inscription dated 1742 was removed by a restorer, who, however, copied the words onto the frame. In 1961 Lady Broun Lindsay kindly allowed the painting to come to the National Portrait Gallery, where I had the opportunity of seeing it. Along with the restorer's purple pencil along the bottom of the stretcher, appears at the top an ink inscription on a paper label: "Head of Pope / Brought from Dalhousie. / In 1861. Susan G.B. Bourke / Colstoun 1884."

The picture seems to be rather more freely and tentatively painted than its close counterpart, no. 55.2.

55.2. OIL PAINTING, BY JONATHAN RICHARDSON, 1742. FITZWILLIAM MUSEUM, CAMBRIDGE.

This picture is catalogued in F. R. Earp, *A Descriptive Catalogue of the Pictures in the Fitzwilliam Museum Compiled Largely from Materials Supplied by Sidney Colvin*

right

55.1. Oil on canvas. 11⅝ x 10 in. Background dull brown; garment red-brown; hair and fur collar dark brown. See no. 55.2. Colin Broun Lindsay, Esq., Younger, Colstoun, Haddington.

below, right

55.2. Oil on canvas. 13 x 11¼ in. Background a warm reddish brown; cloak bright red; fur collar brown and gray in loose strokes; hair dark, touched with gray, painted in long twisting strokes over ear and behind neck; facial tints gray and pinkish, in twisting strokes; lips pink obscured by gray; bright pink in inner corner of left eye; eyes light brown to hazel. Inscribed in thin brown or black lines of paint, middle right: "[Richardson's monogram] JR. / 1742." By permission of the Syndics of the Fitzwilliam Museum, Cambridge.

below

56.1. Stipple engraving. 4⁵⁄₁₆ x 3¹¹⁄₁₆ in. "R Clamp Sculp / A Pope Esqʳ / From an Original Picture by Richardson. / in the Possession of Antony Storer Esqʳ / Pub, Feb, 20, 1793, by E & S Harding Pall Mall." *Shakespeare Illustrated*, 1793.

(Cambridge, 1902), p. 167, no. III.16. It came to the Fitzwilliam Museum in the important collection of 248 pictures bequeathed to the University by Daniel Mesman in 1834. Like other pictures in that collection, it was said to have been formerly in the collection of "Lord Mitford," a person whose name is not known in the peerage.[1] It was seen at the Second Special Exhibition of National Portraits at the South Kensington Museum in 1867 (p. 41, no. 136). It is reproduced facing p. 166 of the Fitzwilliam *Catalogue* cited above and in C. R. L. Fletcher and Emery Walker, *Historical Portraits 1700–1850* (Oxford, 1919), *3.40*.

It is the only known oil portrait of Pope by Richardson which bears a signature or date.

It was exhibited at the National Portrait Gallery Exhibition in 1961.

1. F. R. Earp, *A Descriptive Catalogue*, pp. vii and 167, and communication from J. W. Goodison, The Fitzwilliam Museum.

56.1. ENGRAVING, BY R. CLAMP, AFTER RICHARDSON. *Shakespeare Illustrated*, 1793.

Shakespeare Illustrated By an assemblage of Portraits & Views appropriated to the Whole Suite, of that Author's Historical Dramas; to which are added Portraits of Actors, Editors, &c., was published, according to the Act of Parliament, by S. & E. Harding, N. 102 Pall Mall, in 1793. The fifth plate after the title page is a stipple engraving of Pope with the lettering: "R Clamp Sculp / A Pope Esqr / From an Original Picture by Richardson. / in the Possession of Antony Storer Esqr / Pub, Feb, 20, 1793, by E & S Harding Pall Mall." This is *Grolier* 46. The same plate reappears, with the original inscription erased, a facsimile of Pope's handwriting and signature substituted, and the following inscription: "Richardson Pinxt. / Published as the Act directs from the Original Jan. 1, 1806." This is *Grolier* 47. Examples occur in Grant's extra-illustrated Carruthers at the University of Texas, and inserted as frontispiece in the first volume of a set of Joseph Warton's *Essay on Pope*, 1806 (Yale University Library).

Antony Morris Storer (1746–99), collector and engraver, left his library and prints to Eton College. The painting of Pope remains untraced. The engraving bears a sufficient resemblance to nos. 55.1 and 55.2 to tempt momentarily the theory that Storer's painting went either to Lord Dalhousie or to "Lord Mitford." But a number of differences seem to rule this out.

Another engraving (*Grolier* 43 and 44), similar to no. 56.1, appears as illustration to a Memoir of Pope in *The Literary and Biographical Magazine, and British Review* for November 1793 (2.321): "Harding Sculp^t / Alexander Pope Esqr / From an Original Painting by Mr Richardson." In this engraving a head nearly identical with that in no. 56.1 sits on a body swung around to a nearly left-profile, the garment having the familiar fur collar.

· 9 ·

1738-1741
LOUIS FRANÇOIS ROUBILIAC (1705?-62)

THE FRENCH ROCOCO ARTIST who is today usually thought of as the finest sculptor working in England during the middle of the eighteenth century, died after a full career—
three marriages and much business—a bankrupt in 1762. He had achieved a triumphant
vogue only rather late in life. Shakespeare at full length leaning on his fancy lectern,
done for Garrick's Temple at Hampton (1759) and now to be seen in the King's Gallery at the British Museum; Handel, beating time with his left foot, looking for inspiration to an angel in the clouds above his head, in the south transept of Westminster
Abbey (1759); Sir Isaac Newton (designed from the mask and bust by Rysbrack) at
full length holding the prism and rolling his eyes to heaven, in the ante-chapel at Trinity College, Cambridge (1755); Death launching his dart at Lady Elizabeth Nightingale,
her distracted husband attempting to ward it off (1761), in the north transept at Westminster; and in the nave General Hargrave rising from his tomb as Time breaks the dart
of Death and the Angel's trump topples a background of dark marble (carved with the
almost illusory precision of a mezzotint) (c. 1752)—these and other similar works all executed by Roubiliac in the latter part of his career, stand today as conspicuously accessible illustrations of his bravura realism, his spiritually picturesque, energetic and in-
ventive talent.[1]
  It was several years after the death of Alexander Pope that Roubiliac first reached

  1. Katherine A. Esdaile, *The Life and Works of Louis François Roubiliac* (London, 1928), is my principal guide in this sketch of Roubiliac's career. M. I. Webb, *Michael Rysbrack* (London, 1959), has suggested a few counter-emphases.

the eminence of a monumental sculpture in Westminster Abbey. The incident (1749) seemed to George Vertue striking enough and yet typical enough of a trend of the times to be framed in a brief history of English sculpture:

> Of all the arts now practised in England none has shone late years more apparently than that of sculpture or statuary works.

> Of that kind of artists three or four different masters have established a reputation here equal to any others in foreign cities or countries from whence these artists came and have indeed learnt and brought their skill with them by the English encouragement and rewards.

> now having completed the grand monument for the late Duke of Argyle, erected in Westminster Abbey,[2] therein Mr. L. F. Roubiliac sculptor has shown the greatness of his genius. . . . this monument now outshines for nobleness and skill all those before done, by the best sculptors, this fifty years past. such monuments have cost, some, five hundred pounds each, some, seven or eight hundred, some, a thousand, and some, hundreds more—by reason of which it may be concluded that so long as that vanity or humor remains in the mind of the noble and wealthy persons, there will be works to be done hereafter of the same kind.[3]

> In this month of May 1749 was finished and erected in Westminster Abbey church the Monument of the Duke of Argyle. . . . Whilst Mr. Rysbrack statuary had all the most considerable employments of that kind—and after him Mr. Scheemaker had also the run of business in making monuments with other works, after he had done the monument of Shakespeare, this Mr. Roubiliac scarce had any considerable capital work till this noble monumant of the Duke of Argyle, which being of a grand composition strikes the spectators with admiration, for its work and loftiness. The beauties and richness of the marbles etc. is beyond all others, but to speak of the sculptor's skill and artful performance, I observe the whole is masterly, in the design noble and grand.[4]

Roubiliac was from Lyons and had worked with the Lyonnais Nicholas Coustou, nephew and pupil of another Lyonnais, the sculptor of Versailles and the Tuileries, Antoine Coysevox.[5] It seems uncertain when Roubiliac arrived in England, but apparently a good deal later than his Flemish and classical rival Michael Rysbrack. The *Procès-Verbaux de l'Académie Royale* show that as late as 1730 (his old master Coustou being President) Roubiliac submitted a sculptural group of Daniel rescuing Susanna, for which he was awarded in June of that year the second *Grand Prix*.[6] The earliest

---

2. Roubiliac's model for the monument, signed and dated 1743, is in the Victoria and Albert Museum (Esdaile, *Roubiliac*, p. 62 and Plate XVI). Mrs. Webb, *Rysbrack*, p. 86, as we have seen (p. 98), gives six monuments in Westminster Abbey to Roubiliac, against sixteen for Rysbrack, ten for Scheemakers, nine for Sir Henry Cheere, and nine for Francis Bird.

3. Vertue 3.145–46.

4. Vertue 3.149.

5. Esdaile, *Roubiliac*, p. 11; Webb, *Rysbrack*, p. 36. Coysevox is represented in Westminster Abbey by the bust of Prior on the tomb which Rysbrack made to Lord Oxford's order.

6. Esdaile, *Roubiliac*, pp. 11–12.

sure date for Roubiliac in England seems to be that of his application for his first marriage license in April 1735. At about this time he was a member of the Huguenot congregation in St. Martin's Lane.[7] He was not yet independent but was apparently working in the employ of one of the brothers Cheere, who had shops in St. Margaret's, Westminster, and at Hyde Park Corner, the latter noted for its production of the stone and lead "gods of Athens and of Rome" which lurk in so many grottoes and stand against the sky along so many rooftops of the era.[8] Then in 1738 came his first notable success in London. A later pupil of Roubiliac's, the sculptor Nathaniel Smith, is responsible for the story that Jonathan Tyers, the developer of Vauxhall Gardens, took up a suggestion thrown out by Henry Cheere: "I conclude you will have music . . . therefore you cannot do better than to have a carving of an Apollo. What do you say to a figure of Handel?" The figure would be inexpensive if done by "an uncommonly clever fellow" whom Cheere had working for him.[9] Roubiliac was paid £300 for the famous statue of Handel set up in Vauxhall Gardens in May 1738. Seated upon a pedestal and leaning his elbow on a stack of his own works (*Operas, Oratorios, Alexander's Feast, Lessons*), Handel fingers a stone lyre bearing the image of Apollo and is attended by a cupid sitting at his feet and taking down the strains as they come. Nevertheless, the great composer lolls at his ease, in the working negligé of cap and long coat, knees crossed and one flat slipper off and lying beneath his stockinged foot, the other flapping, and the floor strewn with modern musical instruments. "Every button," Peter Cunningham would say, "seems to have sat for its likeness."[10] This elegant piece of naturalism, at once classical, rococo, and domestic, was an immediate sensation. It elicited essays in the magazines and newspapers, poems and congratulations to the proprietor of Vauxhall.[11] It brought Vertue for the first time to Roubiliac's studio.[12] Roubiliac's recent biographer sees "no exaggeration" in saying that this statue "marked an era not in English sculpture only, but in European."[13] It has suffered some vicissitudes in the course of two centuries,[14] but has never been lost sight of. In 1961 it could be seen throned at the top of the stairs in the lobby of Novello's music store in Wardour Street. In 1965 it was acquired by the Victoria and Albert Museum. The terra-cotta statuette from which the marble was modeled was noticed in 1751 by Vertue in Hudson's studio,[15] belonged later to Nathaniel Smith, to Nollekens and to Hamlet the silversmith and today may be seen, signed and dated 1738, in the Fitzwilliam Museum at Cambridge.[16]

Roubiliac's pictorial chisel, his lively realism and homely accuracy, were the more remarkable in a full-length statue. The same extraordinary quality appears, however, in his portrait busts done both earlier and later. Handel himself, a marble bust in nightcap and tasselled gown, was done in 1739; it may be seen today at Windsor Castle.

7. Mrs. Esdaile dug up the Marriage Allegation in Doctors' Commons (*Roubiliac*, p. 33). Mrs. Webb, *Rysbrack*, p. 69, stresses the uncertainty of earlier evidence for Roubiliac in England.

8. Webb, *Rysbrack*, pp. 74–75; Esdaile, *Roubiliac*, p. 36.

9. J. T. Smith, *Nollekens and His Times*, ed. Whitten (London, 1920), 2.166; Esdaile, *Roubiliac*, p. 36.

10. Esdaile, *Roubiliac*, p. 39.

11. Esdaile, *Roubiliac*, pp. 36–38; *London Magazine* (1738), pp. 250, 302.

12. Vertue 3.84 (1738).

13. Esdaile, *Roubiliac*, p. 39.

14. Esdaile, *Roubiliac*, p. 38.

15. Vertue 3.157.

16. Esdaile, *Roubiliac*, Plate VII and pp. 41–42.

A terra cotta miniature model for a different Handel bust is at the National Portrait Gallery.[17] Another prime example of his art in marble is the jaunty, beak-nosed, and broad-shouldered bust which came to light in London during 1851 and, on the ground largely of family resemblance in a descendant, was identified as a self-portrait and is today on exhibition at the Portrait Gallery.[18] The startling painted plaster bust of Colley Cibber, embroidered, smiling, puckered, also at the Gallery, seems surely the work of the same hand.[19] Roubiliac had an exquisite chisel; he had at the same time perhaps an even more exquisite touch as a modeler. The clay busts were perhaps all shaped originally as models for marbles, but modeling is not carving, and the terra cottas or baked clays of Roubiliac exert their own peculiar and striking claim.[20]

The very solidity of the thick clay mass employed by Rysbrack produced at its best its own special aesthetic effect. Consider, for instance, his Sir Hans Sloane in the King's Gallery at the British Museum, a towering composition in cascading curls and seamy visage,[21] or his neolithic Sir Robert Walpole at the National Portrait Gallery.[22] Roubiliac, on the other hand, in the usual Italian or French manner,[23] made a clay bust with a hollow head and with a shoulder span deeply concave at the back, supported by a central post or prop, which was often hollowed out as well. The main technical reason for this parsimony in material was no doubt that the thinner sheet of clay was less subject to shrinkage in baking and was thus saved from the cracks which developed in Rysbrack's busts and had to be filled with plaster and the whole given a coat of paint.[24] Roubiliac's models exhibit the fair surface and mellow earthy hues of the actual terra cotta. They have a springy, vital, soaring character, the impress of his deft hand and tool, but apparently also corresponding in some secret way to the lightness of their internal structure. A triumphant instance is the Hogarth at the National Portrait Gallery.[25]

The date 1738 on the earliest of the four signed and dated marble busts of Pope by Roubiliac which are known today shows that Pope sat for Roubiliac at the latest not long after the statue of Handel was placed in Vauxhall Gardens. There is no real evidence that the sittings did not occur somewhat earlier, perhaps even as early as 1737 (for the dates on the marbles in the cognate group are obviously the dates for the marbles themselves). On the other hand, nothing that is known of Roubiliac's procedures prevents our supposing that a clay bust, even while quite fresh, and before being itself made into a permanent object by baking, could serve as a model or point of departure for a marble. The absence of terra-cotta counterparts for many marble busts of that era

17. Esdaile, *Roubiliac,* p. 51 and Plate VII.

18. Esdaile, *Roubiliac,* pp. 191–92; *Athenaeum,* 15, 16 July 1851, p. 811. Sotheby's, 18 July 1851, no. 162 (Whitley Papers, Department of Prints and Drawings, British Museum).

19. Esdaile, *Roubiliac,* pp. 108–09, Plate XXXIII.

20. "When a meeting of Statuaries was held about the Alto Relievo at the Mansion House, the late celebrated Roubiliac, among others, attended. The other artists delivered drawings, & when Roubiliac was asked for his, he said, 'I have brought no plan— I do not draw—but if you will give me a lump of

clay & let me be shut up in a room I will do something for you.' It is remarkable of this great artist that though he was so famous a statuary he could never give an adequate sketch in drawing of his design" (*Middlesex Journal,* 18 September 1770 [Whitley Papers]; Esdaile, *Roubiliac,* p. 61).

21. Webb, *Rysbrack,* p. 152, Plate 77.

22. Webb, *Rysbrack,* p. 149, Plate 71.

23. See p. 228.

24. See p. 228.

25. Esdaile, *Roubiliac,* p. 50 and Plate IX.

which are known today would seem in fact to argue that not every clay model was turned into a permanent object by baking.

We may well imagine, then, though we cannot demonstrate, that a certain opportunism in having himself handsomely portrayed, latent perhaps since the death of Kneller, awoke in Pope in the spring of 1738—that perhaps entirely on his own initiative or perhaps at the prompting of some friend, he took an early occasion to seek out the new celebrity in Saint Martin's Lane.[26]

26. This address, which is questioned by Mrs. Esdaile, *Roubiliac*, p. 34, is quoted by her, on p. 36, from *The London Daily Post*, 18 April 1738.

Roubiliac Busts

Four marble busts of Pope by Roubiliac, signed and dated (1738, 1740, 1741, 1741) are known today. There is also a terra-cotta model, and a plaster molded from the terra cotta. All six of these busts were assembled on one table at the National Portrait Gallery Exhibition in April 1961 (see photograph p. 249). It is a judgment based on aesthetic, psychological, and economic probability, but to me it seems irresistible: that all four of the marbles were made by Roubiliac from the same original model, the terra cotta, which, from the date of the earliest marble, we must place no later than 1738. At the same time, no one of these four busts is a simple replica of the terra cotta, if indeed a bust in the medium of marble, made by carving, can ever be a replica of a bust in the medium of clay, made largely by modeling.[1] The size and attitude of the head remains the same in the six busts. But Roubiliac individuated each of the marble busts, not only in the mass of body and garment which he balanced with the head, but much more subtly in the chiseling of the features. In the earliest and smallest marble, of 1738, the features are somewhat rejuvenated and sweetened in comparison to those of the terra cotta. In the largest, and probably the latest to leave Roubiliac's shop (as it bears, in addition to 1741, the date of Pope's death, 1744), the approximation of the whole image to that of the terra cotta is closest of all, but a new appearance results, notably from a flattening and tightening of the facial planes and the polish put on the marble. It seems possible, though perhaps not likely, that Pope was called in for secondary sittings as each of these marbles, "ad vivum," was being worked in the shop.

The rough grooving of the marble at the back of the three busts inscribed apparently before Pope's death (nos. 58, 59, 60) makes the lettering rather informal, though in general the lower-case script and block capitals are comparable to the inscriptions on such larger specimens of Roubiliac's work as the full-length Isaac Newton (1755) in the ante-chapel at Trinity College, Cambridge; Garrick's Shakespeare (1755), in the British Museum; or the seated Handel (1738), now in Novello's Music Store on Wardour Street. The style of inscription on these busts seems at any rate characteristic enough to warrant the reproduction below of that on the earliest, the Temple Newsam bust, of 1738.

1. Even though the surface of the clay is worked over with a carving tool.

As we have noticed earlier,[2] a series of letters which the rival sculptor Michael Rysbrack wrote to his patron Sir Edward Littleton during the late 1750s, concerning a posthumous bust of Pope and some others, gives us a fortunately authoritative glimpse of how one kind of terra cotta was made at this date. The Flemish sculptor Rysbrack built his clay busts up solid and straight at the back, with solid heads. He let them dry for several months, and then he fired them. Being solid, they developed cracks. He filled the cracks with plaster and painted the whole bust over with a light coat of tan. On the other hand, and no doubt just for the purpose of avoiding the disadvantages of the solid clay mass, the rival French sculptor Roubiliac made his clay busts by a different method. He made the backs hollow or concave, with a prop at the center, and sometimes the prop too, as with the Pope bust, is hollowed out. The chest and garment of a Roubiliac bust are no more than a curved sheet of clay. He made the head and neck hollow too, empty, though fully sculptured all around.[3] He employed perhaps some kind of removable core. Room 63 at the Victoria and Albert Museum provides a convincing exhibit of the difference between the terra-cotta construction of Rysbrack and that of Roubiliac: Rysbrack's Inigo Jones, Shakespeare, and "Unknown Man" (signed and dated 1728) are all three solid and straight up the back, in contrast to Roubiliac's Francis Willoughby, Jonathan Tyers, and Oliver Cromwell, all three concave at the back, with hollow heads. Another terra-cotta bust in the same room, Giovanni Battista Guelfi's Anne, Duchess of Richmond, datable 1722, is hollowed or curved at the back, though it has a solid prop and a solid head. The hollow method of modeling, perhaps more favored in the south than in the north, can also be seen as one enters the Museum from Brompton Road, in the large early sixteenth-century terra cotta of Saint Philip Neri. Another fine example of Roubiliac's hollow modeling is his Hogarth at the National Portrait Gallery.

In an appendix (pp. 218–29) to her *Life and Works of . . . Roubiliac* (Oxford, 1928), Katherine A. Esdaile reproduced, from the unique copy, then in possession of Mr. A. J. Finberg (p. 176), the contents of *A Catalogue of the Genuine and Entire Collection of Models, Moulds, Casts and Busts in Terra Cota, Marble and Bronze, of Mr. L. F. Roubilliac, Statuary, Deceas'd; At his late Dwelling House in St. Martin's Lane*, sold by Langford in Covent Garden on 12 May 1762, and three following days. Roubiliac's sale (cf. Esdaile, p. 185) included a number of objects relating to Pope, as follows (numbered by day and lot):

4.75, marble bust; 4.76, marble head
3.76, terra-cotta bust
1.9; 2.3 and 14; 3.2, 5, and 10, plaster busts
1.42 and 48, molds in plaster for busts or basso relievos

2. See no. 11.

3. I am much indebted for instruction in this matter to Mr. T. W. I. Hodgkinson, of the Department of Sculpture, Victoria and Albert Museum.

Modern works on sculpture speak emphatically of the need for scooping or hollowing out the interior of sculpture in clay designed for firing, in order to allow for even expansion and contraction. See, for instance, Jack C. Rich, *The Materials and Methods of Sculpture* (New York, Oxford University Press, 1947), p. 31, "Hollow Forms;" and Joshua C. Taylor, *Learning to Look, A Handbook for the Visual Arts* (University of Chicago Press, 1957), p. 118.

1.67, medal or design for medal; 2.22 and 4.33, plaster medals

2.51, plaster mold for medal; 3.61, plaster mold for small medal

2.93, bronze basso relievo

It seems wholly probable that Roubiliac made only one terra-cotta bust of Pope (3.76), and that no. 57.1 in this book is that one. One of the six plaster busts (1.9 etc.), we shall see, was bought at the sale and presented to the British Museum (no. 57.2). The bronze basso relievo (2.93) seems accounted for in no. 57–61.1. I am unable to give any account of the "marble bust" (4.75) or the "marble head" (4.76), or of the plaster medals and molds for medals (1.67, 2.22, 4.33, 2.51, 3.61), though these medals are mentioned again below in the article on the basso relievo, no. 57–61.1.

Mrs. Esdaile's own list of eight Roubiliac sculptures of Pope, (a) to (h), pp. 47–48, is accounted for at various places in my catalogue which follows—except for (f), a marble version, "whose fate is unknown . . . left unfinished at Roubiliac's death," by which no doubt she refers to either 4.75 or 4.76, known only from Roubiliac's catalogue, as above.

57.1. TERRA-COTTA BUST, BY L. F. ROUBILIAC. MRS. COPNER, ELTON HALL, HUNTINGDONSHIRE.

One anecdote concerning the making of this bust comes down from the younger Flaxman, whose father had been Roubiliac's assistant. "His father found him one morning at work upon it in his studio, when Pope was sitting to him in his arm chair there."[1] Sir Joshua Reynolds told another to Malone. "Roubiliac the statuary, who made a bust of him from life, observed that his countenance was that of a person who had been much afflicted with headache, and that he should have known the fact from the contracted appearance of the skin above the eyebrows, though he had not been otherwise apprised of it."[2] Of the four signed and dated marbles which Roubiliac apparently executed after this single terra cotta, the earliest is dated 1738 (see no. 58). On 2 June 1741, George Vertue entered in his *Note Book:* "Mr. Roubiliac sculptor of marble, besides several works in marble, models in clay; had modelled from the life several busts or portraits extremely like:—Mr. Pope, more like than any other sculptor has done I think."[3] After Roubiliac's death, as we have seen, a sale of his "Genuine and Entire Collection" was held by Langford at his "late Dwelling House in St. Martin's Lane" on 12 May 1762 and three following days. Lot no. C 76 was a "terra-cotta bust" of Alexander Pope.[4] One of the accomplished virtuosi of this day was the surgeon John Belchier or Belcher (1706–85), who seems to have had some acquaintance with Pope and Handel,[5] who himself sat to Roubiliac,[6] and who bequeathed a bust of Newton to the Royal Society.[7] There is no record that he bought the terra cotta of Pope at Roubiliac's sale. But on 29 March 1805, Christie held a sale for a "Man of Fashion," two of the lots being Roubiliac's terra-cotta models for busts of Handel and Pope.[8] In the record of this sale surviving today at Christie, Manson & Woods, the name of the man of fashion appears to be "Belcher." The bust of Pope, lot 119, made 5 guineas, and the purchaser's name was "Rogers."[9]

57.1. Terra cotta. Height (without pedestal) 18¾ in. Chin to crown 8½ in. Width above ears 6½ in. Hollowed behind, with central prop, and head hollow. A label in the hand of A. H. Hallam Murray pasted on the bust's left side just above the pedestal records the purchase at the Rogers sale by John Murray III. Mrs. Copner, Elton Hall, Huntingdonshire.

230

57.1. View 2

For fifty years the terra-cotta bust of Pope remained in possession of the banker, collector, and poet Samuel Rogers, and during this period it seems to have become one of the most noted objects of virtu in London. In Rogers' later years, it was likely to be one of the chief conversation pieces during a breakfast with him in St. James's Place. Macaulay saw it on such an occasion in June 1831, and thought it was a cast taken after death.[10] In February 1834, the poet Tom Moore, apropos of a visit to Sir Robert Peel and a view of his marble bust (below no. 61), remarked in his *Journal:* "Rogers's is the original clay or model from which this bust was made, and is remarkable for the fine lines and markings with which it abounds, and which were afterwards softened down or omitted in the marble."[11] In *The Athenaeum* for 29 December 1855, we learn that "to the right of the door [of the dining room] on entering is a sideboard supporting ancient painted Greek vases, and Roubiliac's terra-cotta model of the head of Pope."[12]

"The Very Celebrated Collection of Works of Art . . . and the Extensive Library" of Samuel Rogers were sold at Christie's 28 April 1856, and eighteen following days. On the seventh day (5 May) "Roubiliac's original bust of Pope, in terra-cotta," was bought by Skeffington for Murray for 137 guineas.[13] The bust now entered on a second phase of fame, in which it has continued while in the possession of John Murray III (1808–92) and afterwards in that of his son Alexander Henry Hallam Murray (d. 1934) and of his heirs. It appears as the frontispiece of Courthope's *Life of Pope,* which is volume 5 of the Elwin-Courthope edition of Pope's *Works,* published by Murray in 1889. It is no. 316 (p. 53) of the Catalogue of the Twickenham Loan Museum in 1888: "The sculptor's original clay model converted into terra-cotta. From this all the marble busts have been modelled."[14]

It is discussed and illustrated in Katherine A. Esdaile's *Life and Works of Louis François Roubiliac* (Oxford, 1928), pp. 46–47 and Plate VIII. Today the bust is the property of the former Mrs. Michael R. H. Murray, now Mrs. Copner, of Jesmond, Liss, Hampshire. It is kept at the seat of Major Sir Richard Proby, Bart., Elton Hall, Huntingdonshire.[15]

It was exhibited at the National Portrait Gallery Exhibition of 1961.

1. *Catalogue of the Very Celebrated Collection of . . . Samuel Rogers, Esq., Deceased . . .* Christie and Manson, 28 April, 1856, 7th day, p. 83, lot 836. I have not found an earlier source. The statement is quoted in the *Times,* 6 May 1855, p. 7.

2. James Prior, *Life of Edmond Malone* (London, 1860), pp. 428–29, "Maloniana."

3. Vertue 3.105.

4. See above pp. 228–29.

5. Charles Burney, *An account of the Musical Performances in Westminster-Abbey, and the Pantheon . . . in Commemoration of Handel* (London, 1785): "When Pope found that his friends, Lord Burlington and Dr. Arbuthnot, thought so highly of Handel, he not only lashed his enemies in the *Dunciad,* but wished to have his *Eurydice* set to Music by him. Mr.

Belchier, a common friend, undertook to negotiate the business" (p. 33).

6. Esdaile, *Roubiliac,* pp. 42, 111, Plate XXXIV.

7. Esdaile, *Roubiliac,* pp. 20, 42. *The Gentleman's Magazine,* 55 (February 1785), 156 has: "Feb. 1. Mr. John Belcher, surgeon, F.R. & A.SS., aged 80, in Suncourt, Threadneedle-street. He was buried in the founder's vault in the chapel of Guy's Hospital."

8. Rupert Gunnis, *Dictionary of British Sculptors 1660–1851* (Harvard University Press, 1954). "Roubiliac."

9. Information from Messrs. Christie, Manson and Woods, Ltd. The sale catalogue is Lugt 6917.

10. George O. Trevelyan, *The Life and Letters of Lord Macaulay* (London, 1876), *1.*225, letter of 25 June 1831 to his sister Hannah.

11. *Memoirs, Journal, and Correspondence of Thomas Moore*, ed. Lord John Russell (London, 1853–56), 7.24–25. Cf. Edward M. Goulburn, *John William Burgon, Late Dean of Chichester. A Biography with Extracts from his Letters and Early Journals* (London, John Murray, 1892), *1*.27. About 1835 Burgon and his brother Tom breakfasted with Rogers in St. James's Place at 9.30. "We happened to be contemplating a most interesting bust of Pope by Roubiliac, when he ceased writing. He came near us, and talked to us about Pope, and that bust." See for this period also: Mrs. Jameson, *Companion to the Most Celebrated Galleries of Art in London* (London, 1844), p. 411; *Art Journal*, 1847, p. 85; Carruthers, *Pope's Works* (1853), *1*.ix.

12. In *The Illustrated London News* for 5 January 1856, appears an engraving of Samuel Rogers' breakfast room, showing the mantel with busts on it, but unhappily not the sideboard (Whitley Papers, Department of Prints and Drawings, British Museum).

13. Annotated copy of the Catalogue at the National Portrait Gallery. The same information appears in *The London Gazette*, 10 May 1856, with a poor engraving of the bust.

14. Reproduced as an illustration to Austin Dobson's "Little Roubiliac," *Magazine of Art*, *17* (London, 1894), 204. Its history is sketched up to this date in a communication from A. H. Hallam Murray in *Notes & Queries*, 9th Series, *11* (3 January, 1903), 12.

15. A good photograph of the bust, in the library, appears in Arthur Oswald's article on Elton Hall (III) in *Country Life*, *121* (7 March, 1957), 427. I am grateful to Major Sir Richard and Lady Proby for repeated assistance in the study and photographing of the bust.

57.2. PLASTER CAST, FROM L. F. ROUBILIAC'S TERRA COTTA. DEPARTMENT OF BRITISH AND MEDIEVAL ANTIQUITIES, BRITISH MUSEUM.

After the death of Roubiliac, Nicholas Read his assistant made an effort to keep the business going. He advertised: "To all Lovers of Sculpture. By the death of the late ingenious artist Mr. L.F. Roubiliac, his business at present is likely to drop: It is to be hoped they will for the future command Mr. Reed, a person who for sixteen years past has studied under him and executed great part of his most capital works; and, thus encouraged, means to succeed him."[1] Somewhat later apparently: "Among the valuable collection of the late Mr. Roubiliac, statuary, are found moulds of busts, modell'd by him, chiefly from the following persons themselves." "Alex. Pope" heads a list of fourteen subjects, which includes also Garrick, Newton, Milton, Shakespeare, Dr. Richard Mead. "Any persons who are related to the said gentlemen, or holding them in esteem, and are willing to have casts from those moulds, shall be furnished with them considerably cheaper than their usual price. The present opportunity is particularly recommended, as these moulds will shortly be disposed of by publick auction. Orders for such casts shall be punctually executed by applying at the late Mr. Roubiliac's."[2] The catalogue of Roubiliac's sale on 12 May and three following days includes six "plaster busts" of Alexander Pope: 1.9, 2.3 and 14; 3.2, 5, and 10.[3] One of these apparently was acquired, along with fifteen other plasters and terra cottas, by Dr. Matthew Maty, at that time a librarian of the British Museum. An old minute book at the British Museum, *Department of Antiquities & Coins, Donations*, has for 28 May 1762, an entry recording Dr. Maty's gift of the whole collection: "The following busts of great Men and Authors, being casts and models of the late Mr Roubiliac; purchased by Dr Maty at his sale and presented by him to the Museum:" five terra cottas from the antique, six terra cottas of English heads (three of these "original models in terracotta from which the marble Busts in Trinity College, Cambridge were executed"), and five "casts in plaster" of English heads—Milton, Pope, Dr. Mead, Mr. Folkes, and Lord Chesterfield.[4]

The bust is noticed by Katherine A. Esdaile, *The Life and Works of Louis François Roubiliac* (Oxford, 1928), pp. 103, 185.

It was cleaned in 1951. The photograph reproduced here represents it, I believe, before the cleaning.

It was brought to the National Portrait Gallery Exhibition of 1961 for comparison with the terra cotta and marbles. It stands on a lower pedestal than the Elton Hall terra cotta. Except for a general softening and blurring of the tool strokes, it is a mechanically exact replica of that terra cotta.

1. A newspaper cutting, undated, quoted in Horace Walpole, *Anecdotes of Painting in England*, ed. F. W. Hilles and P. B. Daghlian (New Haven, 1937), p. 151.

2. *Anecdotes*, ed. Hilles and Daghlian, pp. 151–52, a cutting dated March 1762.

3. Esdaile, *Roubiliac*, pp. 185, 218–30. Cf. above p. 228.

4. Department of British and Medieval Antiquities, British Museum. The full list is given by Mrs. Esdaile, *Roubiliac*, p. 103.

57.2. Pink plaster. Height (without pedestal) 18¾ in. Width across shoulders 16½ in. Incised on the back, just above the pedestal: "16". By permission of the Trustees of the British Museum. Department of British and Medieval Antiquities.

58 a and b.   MARBLE BUST, BY L. F. ROUBILIAC, 1738. TEMPLE NEWSAM HOUSE,
     LEEDS.

Pope's friend William Murray, Solicitor General, and later Lord Chief Justice and Earl of Mansfield, the rebuilder of Kenwood House, had a fine oil portrait of Pope done in 1742 by Van Loo. Along with this painting of Pope at Kenwood in the later eighteenth and the early nineteenth centuries, there was the head of Betterton said to have been painted by Pope after Kneller,[1] and there was a "bust" of Pope.[2] William Murray, a friend of Pope's latter days, had a late oil painting of Pope, and a very good one. Almost certainly his bust of Pope was late, of the Roubiliac type. There was really no other. Almost certainly it was a good one. The Kenwood collection was not broken up until 6–9 November 1922, when by order of the Earl of Mansfield a sale was held by C. B. King & Co. Ltd. (28 Church Row, Hampstead). The catalogue of the sale was notably vague. For example, a marble bust of Lord Mansfield by Nollekens, inscribed and dated 1779 (returned to Kenwood in 1955), was described (lot 1028) as "24 in. marble bust of a Gentleman."[3] The Van Loo oil of Pope and Pope's own oil of Betterton went to Scoon Palace, Perth, with the Earl of Mansfield. But today there is no rumor of a bust of Pope at Scoon.

Mr. A. R. A. Hobson thinks that his father, the late G. D. Hobson, M.V.O. (of Sotheby's), acquired the bust which is the subject of this entry about 1922.

The bust first comes clearly to light in 1932 in the possession of G. D. Hobson. It is illustrated in a wall niche on a staircase at his home No. 1 Bedford Square, W.C. 1, in an article in *Country Life*, *71* (February 1932), 152. It was sold at Sotheby's on 17 November 1933 (lot 63, p. 15 of the Catalogue, illustrated), and a few years after that was in the possession of R. H. Muir, Esq., of Pope's House, Binfield, Bracknell.[4] It was sold by Mrs. R. H. Muir at Sotheby's on 21 November, 1941, and was bought by H. Calmann.[5] In June 1942 the Leeds Art Gallery, with the help of Mr. F. F. Madan, of Oxford, acquired the bust from Calmann for Temple Newsam House.[6] Mrs. Esdaile celebrated this "lovely signed head" in a bicentenary tribute to Pope in the *TLS* for 3 June 1944 (p. 273). It is reproduced, with quotations from Richardson and Reynolds, in an eloquent account of the eighteenth-century bust made according to the ideal and universal Roman tradition, by F. Saxl and R. Wittkower, *British Art and the Mediterranean* (Oxford, 1948), p. 68. It has subsequently been seen in Liverpool at the Walker Art Gallery's *Exhibition of Painting and Sculpture in England 1700–1750*, 1958 (p. 24, no. 43 of the Catalogue),[7] and again at Kenwood House in the exhibition of *Eighteenth Century Portrait Busts* held during the summer of 1959 (no. 21, p. 22, and second plate).

It was exhibited at the National Portrait Gallery Exhibition in 1961.

The inscription along the base at the front, *Qui nil molitur inepte*, is from the *Ars Poetica* of Horace, l.140, a passage eulogizing Homer.

---

1. See p. 12, n. 34.

2. *Ambulator*, 8th edition, 1796, p. 154; J. Norris Brewer, *The Beauties of England and Wales, 10*, Part IV (1816), 177.

3. Information from Miss Elizabeth Johnson, Assistant Curator at Kenwood.

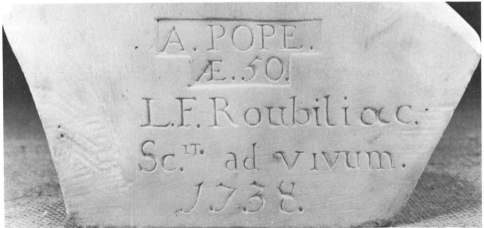

58 a. Marble. Height 14¼ in. Chin to crown 8½ in. Width above ears 6½ in. Across base at front: "Qui nil molitur inepte." On back: "A. POPE. / Æ. 50 / L. F. Roubiliac. / Sc^IT. ad vivum. / 1738." Temple Newsam House, Leeds.

58 b. Inscription on back of 58 a.

4. Memorandum dated 18 July 1939, in National Portrait Gallery archives.

5. *Art Prices Current 20.668.*

6. *The Times*, Friday, 24 July 1942; Leeds Art Gallery and Temple Newsam House, *Exhibition of the Acquisitions of 1942*, No. 13.

7. Cf. Geoffrey Beard, *Leeds Art Calendar, 12* (Summer 1958), No. 40, pp. 5–6 and Figure 2.

58 X. "MASK," PERHAPS FROM NO. 58.a. KATHERINE A. ESDAILE, C. 1928.

At the National Portrait Gallery are two photographs (profile to right and full face) of an object which belonged to the late Mrs. Arundell Esdaile and was thought to be a life mask of Pope. It has rather the appearance of having been taken from a bust, possibly that now at Temple Newsam. Copies of the photographs are to be found also in the files of the Warburg Institute, and negatives from the Warburg Photographic Portrait Exhibition of 1943. Mrs. Esdaile, *Roubiliac* (1928), p. 48, refers to "A bronzed life-mask . . . in my possession."

59.1. MARBLE BUST, BY L. F. ROUBILIAC, 1740. THE EARL FITZWILLIAM, MILTON, PETERBOROUGH.

A notable collection of classical sculpture was formed during the later eighteenth century at Wentworth Castle, the Yorkshire seat of the Earls Fitzwilliam. The present Earl kindly informs me that so far as he knows the bust of Pope has always been at Milton. It seems first to come to public notice in the exhibition *English Taste in the Eighteenth Century* held at Burlington House during the winter of 1955 and 1956 (no. 139 in the Catalogue). It was illustrated, with other portraits and objects of art at the exhibition, in *The Times*, Saturday, 3 December 1955, p. 12. The inscription around the front edge, *Uni Aequus Virtuti Atque Ejus Amicis*, from Horace's *Satire* 2.i.70, is the motto which Pope had added in 1739 to the Advertisement to his *Satires and Epistles of Horace Imitated,* and which had appeared around the portrait engraved by Fourdrinier after Kent used in several of his books, 1734–35 (no. 17).

The bust is illustrated in Peter Quennell and Alan Hodge, *The Past We Share, An Illustrated History of the British and American Peoples* (London, 1960), pp. xi, 160. It was exhibited at the National Portrait Gallery Exhibition in 1961.

59.2. MINIATURE MARBLE BUST, SIMILAR TO NO. 59.1. VICTORIA ART GALLERY, BATH.

This bust seems first to come to public notice in a letter from John Lane (The Bodley Head, Vigo Street, W.) to the editor of *The Spectator*, 3 January 1920, p. 12: "it may interest your readers to know that some eighteen months ago I picked up in Bath a bust of Pope in marble by Prince Hoare." The bust was at about that time on loan from Mr. Lane to the Victoria Art Gallery, Bath. After his death it was presented to the gallery by Mrs. John Lane. (Her letter to Reginald Wright, Director of the Gallery, is dated 30 August 1925.) The hollow wooden pedestal into which the bust is fitted has painted on it "Prince Hoare, Sculpt. Obit 1769." On 3 August 1961, I was fortunate enough

59.1. White marble, on a pedestal of black marble. Height (without pedestal) 14¼ in. Chin to crown 8½ in. Width above ears 6½ in. Inscribed around front: "UNI ÆQUUS VIRTUTI ATQUE EJUS AMICIS". On back: "A. POPE. Æⁱˢ 52. / L. F. Roubiliac. / SCⁱᵀ· AD VIVUM. / 1740." The Earl Fitzwilliam, Milton, Peterborough.

to have an interview with Mr. Wright at the Victoria Art Gallery. He told me that he himself had had the lettering added to the pedestal, on the authority of Mr. Lane.

In *The Gentleman's Magazine, 11* (February 1741), 102, appears an epigram with the title: "On Mr. Nash's present of his own Picture at full Length, fixt between the Busto's of Mr. Pope, and Sir Is. Newton, in the Long Room at Bath."

> Immortal Newton, never spoke
>> More truth, than here you'll find;
> Nor Pope himself, e'er penn'd a joke
>> More cruel on mankind.

> This picture plac'd the busts between,
>> Gives satyr all his strength,
> *Wisdom* and *Wit* are little seen,
>> But *Folly* at full length.[1]

In the Broadley Collection of papers and pictures relating to Pope and Allen in the Victoria Art Gallery and Municipal Library, Bath (vol. 1, p. 264) is a wash drawing, 8¾ x 7⅝ inches, showing an assembly room with a full-length painting of a male figure hung between two busts. Under this drawing is pasted a cutting from a dealer's catalogue, making a statement derived from ink inscriptions written on the back of the drawing itself, in what is apparently a late eighteenth-century hand. One of these is a version of the epigram from *The Royal Magazine or Quarterly Bee,* vol. 2 [1750–51], p. 424, with the title "On seeing the Picture of Beau Nash . . . in the Pump Room," to which the transcriber has added: "(I fancy this shd. have been in Wiltshire's long Room as in this Drawing at Bath)." At the bottom of the sheet a second inscription reads: "This drawing is by Mr James Vertue of Bath." (George Vertue's brother James was a pupil of Richardson and Vanderbank; he showed promise but suffered from a nervous paralysis of the hands and lived at Bath and taught drawing to "persons of distinction."[2]) The meaning of the epigram is of course that the busts of genius are small ("little") in contrast to the full-length painting of folly. In the drawing the busts seem larger than miniatures, but if they were smaller, they would hardly be visible.

Wiltshire's [Long] Rooms in the Walks and Harrison's Rooms in the Walks (both known as Lower Assembly Rooms) disappeared in 1794 and 1820 respectively. But it was not until just after World War I that a number of objects of historic association which seem to have survived at the Upper Assembly Rooms were dispersed at a sale.[3]

At about the same period it would appear that John Lane "picked up" at Bath the small marble bust of Pope which is the subject of this entry. It seems likely, though scarcely certain, that this was a bust which had come down in the Assembly Room collection.

It seems unlikely, however, that the bust alluded to in *The Gentleman's Magazine* for February 1741 could have been the work of the Bath sculptor Prince Hoare. For Vertue, writing under the date of January 1749/50, says that the "young statuary" Prince Hoare has just returned to Bath from studies in Italy, after an absence of seven or eight years. With the encouragement of his brother William Hoare the painter, the citizens of Bath are proposing to raise money for a marble statue of Richard Nash. Prince Hoare, Vertue adds, was "educated [i.e. was apprenticed] under Mr Scheemaker" —presumably before his going to Italy.[4]

The bust is not a generalized instance of the Roubiliac type, but seems rather a specific replica, though miniature, of no. 59.1, the bust dated 1740, now in the possession of the Earl Fitzwilliam at Milton, Peterborough.

1. Subsequent versions of this epigram appeared in Goldsmith's *Life of Nash* (1762), in Jane Brereton's *Poems* (1744), and in Chesterfield's *Works*, 1777, and elsewhere. See A. Barbeau, *Life & Letters at Bath in the XVIIIth Century* (London, 1904), pp. 43–44; Lewis Melville, *Bath Under Beau Nash* (London, 1907), p. 219; *Notes and Queries*, 5th Series, *10* (30 November 1878), 429.

2. Vertue 3.157.

3. Information from Victoria Art Gallery. And see A. Barbeau, *Life & Letters at Bath in the XVIIIth Century* (London, 1904), p. 59.

4. Vertue 3.152. On 26 August 1749, Horace Mann at Florence had written to Horace Walpole that "Hoare the Sculptor," whom he had in his house, was to return to England by land from Marseilles (*Horace Walpole's Correspondence with Sir Horace Mann, 4*, ed. W. S. Lewis, W. H. Smith, and G. L. Lam [New Haven, 1960], 86).

On Scheemakers' career in London and his apprentices, see M. I. Webb, *Rysbrack* (London, 1954), pp. 64–68.

Several dates in the 1740s and one as early as 1730 for sculpture by Prince Hoare, in Rupert Gunnis, *Dictionary of British Sculpture 1660–1851* (Harvard University Press, 1954), pp. 203–04, should be scrutinized very closely. The bust of Chesterfield dated "1741," with a reference to Chesterfield's *Works, 4.* 241, is presumably the bust referred to by Chesterfield in his letter to Bishop Chenevix, 22 May 1752 (*Miscellaneous Works*, ed. M. Maty [London, 1779], 4.241). The signed monument to Bishop Maddox in Worcester Cathedral is said to be dated 1743. But in 1743 Maddox was translated to the see of Worcester; he died in 1759. Both dates appear on the monument.

Prince Hoare was married to an heiress in 1751 and died at Bath in 1769. See Appendix 1, for his authorship of Warburton's monument to Pope in 1761.

59.2. White marble. Height (without pedestal) 10 in. Width at shoulders 6 in. On a hollow wooden pedestal, 3½ in. high, lettered in gilt: "Alexander Pope / 1688–1744 / Prince Hoare, Sculpt. / Obit 1769". By Courtesy of the Victoria Art Gallery, Bath.

59.4. Marble. Height (without pedestal) 13 in. Eyes uncarved. "POPE" inscribed on black marble pedestal. Mr. and Mrs. Roger Warner, Burford, Oxfordshire.

59.3. PLASTER BUST, REPLICA (?) OF NO. 59.1. MRS. RICHARD WIGSTON, MUNDESLEY, 1903.

In 1903 Mrs. Richard Wigston at The Creaseys, Mundesley, Norfolk, seems to have had another replica of the Milton bust. This was a plaster bust which was inscribed on the back: "A. Pope AE^{is} 52 / L.F. Roubiliac Sc. / Ad Vivum 1740." And around the edge: "Uni AEquus VI[r]tuti atque ejus amicis."[1]

1. Memorandum at the National Portrait Gallery, London.

59.4. MARBLE REPLICA OF NO. 59.1. MR. AND MRS. ROGER WARNER, BURFORD, OXFORDSHIRE.

In 1963 Mr. and Mrs. Roger Warner, of Burford, Oxfordshire, had recently acquired a marble bust, cut in a style suggestive of a date about 1800, and modeled after no. 59.1.

60.1. MARBLE BUST, BY L. F. ROUBILIAC, 1741. SHIPLEY ART GALLERY, GATESHEAD.

The appearance today of a plaster replica of this bust in a house which was the home of Garrick's friend William Windham (1717–61) (see no. 60.2) suggests that Garrick owned the bust at a fairly early date. But that Garrick commissioned the bust in the year of its execution, 1741, when Garrick himself was a young man realizing his first Shakespearean success as Richard III, is an assumption that hardly seems required.

The bust is first mentioned in the catalogue of the sale of Garrick's small but valuable collection of pictures, "Brought from the Mansion of Mrs. Garrick, Deceased, on the Adelphi Terrace, and from his Villa at Hampton," sold at auction by Mr. Christie at his Great Room in Pall Mall, 23 June 1823. It was lot no. 72, "Roubiliac, 1741. A Bust of Pope, in marble." It was bought by the art expert [William] Seguier[1] for 56 guineas, apparently for "Mr. Lambton," later the 1st Earl of Durham.[2]

In her *Life and Works of Louis François Roubiliac* (1928), pp. 47–48, Mrs. Esdaile says that she is indebted to the Earl of Durham for the information that the bust then in his possession (and described as below) had been bought at the Garrick Sale by William Seguier "for Lord Durham."

In 1932 the Earl of Durham ordered a sale of objects in his collection at Lambton Castle. Shortly before the sale, Messrs. Anderson and Garland of Newcastle upon Tyne purchased the bust of Pope for Mr. G. L. Collins of South Dene Towers, Low Fell, Gateshead. At the death of Mr. Collins, Messrs. Anderson and Garland held a sale of his property, 13 September 1937, at which the bust (lot 140) was purchased by Mr. Samuel Smith, who presented it in the same year to the Shipley Art Gallery, Gateshead, Newcastle upon Tyne.[3]

The bust was exhibited at the British Portraits Exhibition at Burlington House in the winter of 1956–57 (no. 663 in the Catalogue, p. 202). It appears as frontispiece to volume 6 of the *Twickenham* Pope, *The Minor Poems*, ed. Norman Ault and John Butt, 1954.

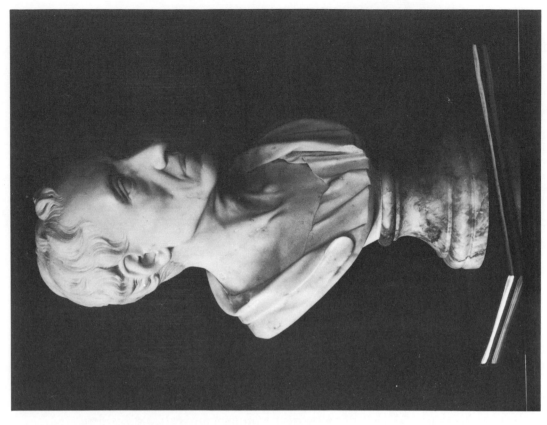

60.1. White marble, on a round pedestal of rose marble. Height (without pedestal) 16¼ in. Chin to crown 8¾ in. Width above ears 6½ in. Inscribed on back: (on left side) "L. F. ROUBILIAC / SC. AD VIVUM / MDCCXLI."—(on right side) "A. POPE / ÆTⁱˢ LIII." Shipley Art Gallery, Gateshead.

It was exhibited at the National Portrait Gallery Exhibition in 1961.

1. Spelled "Seguird" by the annotator of the Victoria and Albert copy of the Catalogue (Lugt 10483), which I follow. This person also wrote "John Soand" for the name of John Soane, the purchaser of lot 63, the four Hogarth Election paintings. The bust had apparently been brought from Garrick's Villa (*Morning Chronicle*, 8 May 1823—Whitley Papers, Department of Prints and Drawings, the British Museum).

2. In *The Gentleman's Magazine* for July 1823, pp. 62–64, the purchase of the bust for 56 guineas is assigned to "Mr. Lambton," who is also noted, in the Victoria and Albert copy of the Catalogue, as the purchaser of lot 53, a Zoffany conversation piece of the Garrick family at the Hampton villa.

Cunningham in 1854 and Dallaway-Wornum, ed. Walpole's *Anecdotes* 3.35, make the mistake of saying that the bust which sold for 56 guineas was by Rysbrack. The sale is correctly reported in Algernon Graves, *Art Sales*, 3 (London, 1921), 106.

3. This paragraph is derived from the admirable account of the bust (with illustration) published in the County Borough of Gateshead's *Shipley Art Gallery and Saltwell Park Museum Annual Report 1st April, 1951 to 31st March, 1952*, p. 9.

60.2. PLASTER BUST, REPLICA OF NO. 60.1. ROBERT WYNDHAM KETTON-CREMER, FELBRIGG HALL, NORWICH.

William Windham the Statesman (1750–1810), friend of Dr. Johnson and of Burke, is a better-known figure than his father William Windham the Elder (1717–61), officer of hussars for Queen Maria Theresa in Hungary and M.P. for Aldeburgh, 1754. The latter, however, was a close friend of David Garrick from about 1743 (after his return from the Grand Tour)[1] until his death. Windham was the owner of Felbrigg Hall, near Norwich, Norfolk, today the home of Robert Wyndham Ketton-Cremer. The bust is hollow plaster. The mold for it, however, seems to have been taken not from the original bust but from a freely modeled replica, 2½ inches higher than the original.

60.2. Plaster, painted black over tan. Height (without pedestal) 17 in. Eyes uncarved. Robert Wyndham Ketton-Cremer, Felbrigg Hall, Norwich.

60.3. Engraving. 3¾₁₆ x 3⅝₁₆ in. plate mark. Robert Dodsley, *A Collection of Poems by Several Hands*, volume 3, Second Edition, 1748.

In October of 1964 Mr. Kulgin D. Duval (Books & Manuscripts, Brunton Street, Falkland, Fife) had recently acquired from Propert Williams Ltd., Victoria Street, Edinburgh (who had acquired it from a dealer in England), a plaster bust of Pope, 16½ in. high, on a round pedestal 4 in. high, the whole painted black. The bust is "lettered" on the back at the left "L. F. ROUBILIAC / SC. AD VIVUM / MDCCXLI" and at the right "A POPE / Æ T. LIII." A photograph which Mr. Duval has kindly sent me, though taken at a different angle from that of no. 60.2, goes far to convince me that the two busts are from the same mold.

1. Arthur Murphy, *Life of Garrick* (1801), *1*.66, cited by R. W. Ketton-Cremer, *The Early Life and Diaries of William Windham* (London: Faber and Faber, 1930), p. 38.

60.3. LINE ENGRAVING, FROM NO. 60.1. DODSLEY'S *Collection of Poems, 3*, 1748.

"Whose the bust was," says Mrs. Esdaile (*TLS*, 3 June, 1944, p. 273), "which was engraved at the end of the third volume of Dodsley amid a border of bays, pipes, trumpet and lyre is unknown." Mrs. Esdaile had in 1928 not been able to see the Garrick bust. The engraving, which appears first in the Second Edition (1748) of volume 3 of Robert Dodsley's *A Collection of Poems by Several Hands*,[1] cannot be called a close rendering of the Garrick bust; the expression is sweetened and etherealized. But the segment of body and garment included, the arrangement of the garment, and the fact that the eyes are uncarved argue very strongly for the identification. The engraving appears at p. 345 as an ornament for Dodsley's poem *The Cave of Pope. A Prophecy* (pp. 344–45).

In a Third Edition of *A Collection of Poems*, volume 3 (1775) p. 347, the same image appears, re-engraved with the signature "J. Basire. S." James Basire (1730–1802) was engraver to the Society of Antiquaries, c. 1763–1802. William Blake was his apprentice, 1771–78.

1. London: Printed by J. Hughs, for R. Dodsley, at Tully's-Head in Pall Mall, 1748.

61.1. MARBLE BUST, BY L. F. ROUBILIAC, 1741. THE EARL OF ROSEBERY, DALMENY HOUSE, SOUTH QUEENSFERRY, WEST LOTHIAN.

It was in the year 1791 that Malone is reported to have said, after repeating Reynolds' remarks on Roubiliac and Pope (quoted above p. 229): "This bust of Roubilliac is now . . . in possession of Mr. Bindley, Commissioner of Stamps."[1] James Bindley (1737–1818), Commissioner of Taxes at Somerset House (lover of the arts to whom Nichols' *Literary Anecdotes*, 1812, are dedicated), built up a *Very Extensive, Choice, and Valuable Collection of Medals in Gold, Silver, and Bronze . . . Likewise a Small Select Collection of Marbles, Bronzes, Abbey Seals, and other Curiosities*, which were auctioned by Mr. Sotheby in Wellington Street on 3 March 1819, and seven following days. On the third day, lot 243 (pp. 18–19 of the Catalogue) was "The Bust of Alexander Pope, in Marble, a most masterly Performance by Roubiliac."[2] I have not seen an annotation of the purchaser. But a notice in the *Morning Chronicle* of 26 June 1823 (p. 3), recording the Garrick sale, alludes to the bust of Pope "which was purchased by Mr. Watson Taylor at a sale of the late Mr. Bindley." In his *Art in England, 1821–1837*, William T. Whitley says that Watson Taylor got his bust of Pope by Roubiliac at the Bindley sale, and that Bindley had "acquired it many years before, for £40, from the collection of Joseph Brown of Shepton Mallet."[3] The collection of "Joseph Browne" of Shepton Mallet was sold in London during March 1791. No bust of Pope or of any other subject appears in the Catalogue.[4] But, as we have noted above, it is in the same year that Malone says that a bust of Pope by Roubiliac "is now" in possession of Mr. Bindley.

Watson Taylor's possession of the bust during a decade following 1819 is fairly conspicuous. In 1820 he lent it to the exhibition held by the British Institution for Promoting the Fine Arts, of which he was a Governor and Director.[5] In the same year S. W. Singer mentions the bust in his Dedication of Spence's *Anecdotes* to Taylor. In 1824[6] it is the subject of an excellent engraving by J. Thomson which serves as frontispiece to the first volume of William Roscoe's edition of the *Works of Pope*.[7]

Taylor, as we know (see no. 3.2), went bankrupt some years later, and the bust, along with Jervas' painting of Pope and the lady, was in the vast sale beginning 9 July 1832, at Erlestoke Mansion in Wiltshire. On the 15th day, it was lot 163 (p. 167 of the Catalogue): "A Bust in statuary marble, of Alexander Pope, modelled from the life in 1741, and sculptured by Roubiliac." Sir Robert Peel was the purchaser, for 70 guineas.[8] In a well-known exchange of letters he speaks somewhat reservedly of his triumph (preferring portrait art to the osier pools of Hobbema), and John Wilson Croker replies exuberantly, "I give you joy! Pope—Dryden—Johnson for £300! . . . I should have given £300 for the Pope alone. It is to my taste, the finest bit of marble which I ever saw."[9]

A visitor to Peel's town house who saw the bust during the early years of his possession was the poet Thomas Moore, whom we have quoted above concerning the terra cotta (no. 57.1). Moore's entry in his *Journal* for 7 February 1834 seems to report an interesting belief about the bust on the part of Peel. "Called upon Sir Robert Peel, and found him at home.[10] . . . [He] took me into another room, to show me what he said *I* ought to see, the original bust of Pope, by Roubillac, which was done for Lord Bolingbroke."[11] I have been unable to find any earlier expression of this idea. Soon after Pope's death, Bolingbroke, as is well known, made a discovery concerning a secretly printed edition of *The Patriot King* which reversed a lifetime of cordial feeling.[12] The bust has on its sides under the shoulders two inscriptions, one giving the year 1741 for its making, and the other, incorrect dates for Pope's birth and death.[13]

Mrs. Jameson in 1844[14] and Cunningham in 1854 report the bust at Drayton Manor. It appeared in Robinson and Fisher's sale of *Peel Heirlooms* held 10 and 11 May 1900 (lot 142) and was bought for 510 guineas by T. Agnew & Sons for the Earl of Rosebery.[15] It is discussed by Mrs. Esdaile, *The Life and Works of . . . Roubiliac* (Oxford, 1928), pp. 47–48, 50.

After Watson Taylor's loan of it to the British Institution in 1820, it was apparently not seen again at a public exhibition until it came to the National Portrait Gallery Exhibition of 1961.

61.1. Polished white marble. Height (without pedestal) 19¼ in. Width across shoulders 17 in. Chin to crown 8¾ in. Width above ears 6½ in. Inscribed on white marble pedestal: "POPE". Inscribed on right side: "Anno Dom. / MDCCXLI. / L. F. Roubiliac / Sc^{1t} ad vivum". Inscribed on left side: "ALEX · POPE nat^{g} LONDINI, / die 8º junii anno MDCLXXXVIII. / Obiit in vico Twickenham prope / Urbem, die 8º maii MDCCXLIV." The Earl of Rosebery, Dalmeny House, South Queensferry, West Lothian.

246

1. James Prior, *Life of Malone* (1860), pp. 428–29, "Maloniana." We read at p. 326 that Bindley was a friend of Malone's He added notes to Boswell's *Life of Johnson* (ed. Hill–Powell, *1*.15, Advertisement to the Third Edition, signed by Malone, 8 April 1799).

2. Lugt 9526, in the British Museum Library, S.C. 828. (14).

3. Whitley, *Art in England, 1821–1837* (Cambridge University Press, 1930), p. 44. Whitley does not name his source for this statement. I have searched the Whitley Papers for it in vain.

4. *The Intire and Valuable Museum of that well-known Collector, the Late Joseph Browne, Esq. of Shepton-Mallet, Somersetshire* was auctioned by Mr. Gerard in Soho on 16 March 1791, and three following days (Part I, coins and medals) and on 23 March and following days (Part II, books). This is Lugt 4689, in the British Museum, Department of Coins and Medals.

5. It is no. 45 on p. 19 of the *Catalogue:* "Alexander Pope (a Bust). Roubiliac;" the same on p. 16 of the *Descriptive Catalogue* for the same year.

6. On 13 and 14 June 1823, Watson Taylor had held an important sale. W. T. Whitley says (in the same mysterious passage of his *Art in England, 1821–1837*, p. 44, which I have quoted above) that the bust of Pope "figured" in this sale, and on a later page that the bust, along with certain paintings by Reynolds, was "bought in." If so, it was "bought in" without getting as far as the catalogue of the sale (British Museum Library 7870.i.47; cf. *The Gentleman's Magazine*, June 1823, pp. 546–48).

7. See no. 61.2.

8. A copy of the catalogue consulted in the British Museum Library (B.M. 788.f.28) is not annotated. I take the price from *The Gentleman's Magazine*, August 1832, p. 163.

9. Peel's letter of 10 August 1732, and Croker's reply of 15 August appear in *The Croker Papers*, ed. Louis J. Jennings (1884), 2.189. Croker's holograph, or

a first part of it, in which he speaks of the busts, is now at the Fitzwilliam Museum, Cambridge, in a volume (MS2-1949) containing autograph material relating to artists and Sir Robert Peel.

10. Mrs. Esdaile, *Roubiliac*, p. 48, interprets Moore's anecdote (correctly, I believe) as referring to Peel's town house. *The Athenaeum*, 19 May 1900, pp. 631–32, takes it as referring to Drayton Manor. In a letter of 25 October 1832, David Wilkie the painter, having just returned from a week at Drayton Manor, reports to Andrew Wilson that Peel has just bought a head of Johnson by Reynolds and a bust of Pope by Roubiliac at Watson Taylor's sale, but his description of building plans at Drayton Manor does not seem to imply that the portraits are there (Allan Cunningham, *The Life of Sir David Wilkie* [London, 1843], 3.61).

11. *Memoirs, Journal, and Correspondence of Thomas Moore*, ed. Lord John Russell (London, 1853–56), 7.24–25.

12. Samuel Johnson, *Life of Pope*, in *Lives of the Poets*, ed. G. B. Hill (Oxford, 1905), 3.193–94, 407.

13. The inscriber follows Curll in making the *day* of Pope's birth 8 June (see no. 43.2), and gives the day of his death as 8 May.

14. *Companion to the Most Celebrated Private Galleries of Art in London* (1844), p. 380. See also Henry Rumsey Forster, *The Stowe Catalogue* (London, 1848), p. 48; Carruthers, *Poetical Works of Pope*, 1853, *1*.324; 2. Front.; *Life of Pope*, Second Edition (1857), p. 417. Norman Gash, *Mr. Secretary Peel* (London, 1961), p. 273, refers to the bust and, p. 275n.2, to Sir Walter Armstrong, *The Peel Collection*, 1904, a work which I have not seen.

15. The earliest statement I know that Lord Rosebery was the purchaser appears in A. H. Hallam Murray's communication to *Notes & Queries*, 9th Series, *11* (3 January 1903), 12. The identity of the bust owned by Lord Rosebery today with that owned by Watson Taylor, 1820–32, is confirmed by J. Thomson's engraving for Roscoe's *Works of Pope*, 1824.

61.2. STIPPLE ENGRAVING, BY J. THOMSON. FRONTISPIECE TO *Works of Pope,* ED. WILLIAM ROSCOE, VOLUME 1, 1824.

Published 1 July 1824, by T. Cadell, Strand, London, this is the first readily identifiable engraving of a specified Roubiliac bust, or the first to present full credentials in its lettering. It may be said to close a period of almost total obscurity concerning the whereabouts and appearance of the authentic busts.[1]

1. See no. 60.3 and nos. 57–61.24, 25, 26, four of the more presentable early engravings.

Grolier 84 (*BMFP* 40) is a small line-and-stipple engraving, oval in a rectangle 4⅛ x 2½ in., inscribed: "Alex: Pope Esq. AEta. LIII. to front Vol. 7." I have not discovered the series of volumes for which this was executed. The derivation from the Roubiliac type is very crude.

An even stranger derivation from "Roubiliac," invested with coat, ruffed shirt collar, and wig, appears in a series of small oval engravings, the earliest perhaps dated 1795. I have a duodecimo sheet bearing an oval engraving of this type, with the words: "Cooke's Edition of Select Poets. Engraved by W. Ridley, from a Bust of Roubilliac's, in the possession of the Proprietor. POPE. Printed for C. Cooke, 17, Paternoster Row. July 18, 1795." I have also a German version, a stipple engraving, of octagonal shape, a 3¼ x 2½ in. picture, and plate mark 7¼ x 4½ in.: "Roubiliacs det. F. Rosmäsler jun. sc. Leipzig. Alexander Pope. in Zwickau b.d. Geb. Schumann." See

also *Grolier* 100, "W. Haines Sculpt," and *Grolier* 101, "M.I. Danforth sc." The latter is found facing the title page of *An Essay on Man*, Hartford, Conn., 1824 (Grolier) and 1832 (Yale).

GROUP PICTURE: NOS. 57.1, 57.2, 58, 59.1, 60.1, 61.1. AT NATIONAL PORTRAIT GALLERY EXHIBITION, APRIL 1961. *See* page 249, bottom.

The Roubiliac Type. The multiplication of signed marbles, doubtless for Pope's more eminent friends, is itself good evidence that Pope approved of the image fashioned by Roubiliac. The early popularity of the image is attested by replicas in several media. Of the four signed and dated marbles, no. 61.1, that owned today by Lord Rosebery, is the closest in size and general appearance to the terra cotta, the extent of body and garment and the arrangement of garment being the same. The most frequently encountered kind of replica follows this pattern, which we may call the "Roubiliac type," but without any implication as to which of Roubiliac's busts—the marble, the terra cotta, or a plaster—is the source. It will be convenient if all the examples which follow are given the combined primary numbers 57–61. I group them roughly according to media, though this may in part obscure the probable chronology.

57–61.1. BRONZE HIGH RELIEF, BY L. F. ROUBILIAC. MR. AND MRS. F. J. B. WATSON, LONDON.

The Catalogue of Roubiliac's sale held in May 1762 includes a number of "medals," "small medals," medals "in plaister," and "moulds in plaister" for medals. On day 1,

61.2. Stipple engraving. 3⅝ x 2⅞ in. frame. "ALEXANDER POPE, / Engraved by J. Thomson, from a drawing by R. Lane, after a bust by Roubiliac, / 1741, in the possession of Watson Taylor, Esqʳ, M.P. / Published July 1, 1824 by T Cadell, Strand, London." *BMEP* 41. Frontispiece to *Works of Pope,* ed. William Roscoe, Volume 1, London, 1824.

lot 67 under "Designs for Monuments, Basso Relievo's, &c.," is "Three medals of *Pope, Mr. Garrick* and Dr. Middleton." On day 2, lot 51, under "Moulds in Plaister," is "*Three* medals of Sir *Isaac Newton, Mr. Middleton* and Mr. *Pope.*" On day 3, lot 61, under "Moulds in Plaister," is "A small medal of Mr. *Garrick,* and 1 of Mr. *Pope.*"[1] Mr. J. V. G. Mallet, whose article in the *Burlington Magazine*[2] is my chief guide in this account, argues very plausibly that Roubiliac's "plaister medals" are in fact small medallions, closely parallel to a series of bronze basso-relievos which also appear in the catalogue. On day 2 of the sale, 13 May 1762, under the heading "BRONZES, etc." occurs lot 93, "Three ditto [i.e. basso relievos] of Mr. *Handell,* Sir *Isaac Newton,* and Mr. *Pope.*" In one of the earliest Christie sales, held either in 1766 or 1767, appeared "Sir Isaac Newton, Pope and Handel in bronze finely repaired [i.e. finished] by the late ingenious Mr. Roubiliac."[3]

In recent years there have come to light several medallions by Roubiliac, both in terra cotta and in bronze. These do a good deal to explain the rather numerous catalogue entries of 1762 and to leave with us the impression that Roubiliac, hard pressed by financial difficulties toward the end of his life, turned extensively to this kind of high quality reproductive work. Mr. Mallet illustrates three bronze medallions (of Pope, Handel, and a clergyman, probably Conyers Middleton) collected some years ago by Mr. F. J. B. Watson, and a fourth in gilt-bronze of Garrick, at the Garrick Club, London. The last has on its reverse the flourished inscription: "*DAVID GARRICK. Arm*[r] */ L.F. Roubiliac Sc*[t] *ad Vivum. /* 1758." All four of these medallions, I take it, are hollow cast, by the *cire perdue* process. The Garrick is screwed to its backplate, Pope and Middleton are welded, and Handel is cast in one piece with the backplate. These four bronze medallions are not a single set, but they do form a distinct group, with a close similarity in size—the height of the oval being about 10 inches. The terra

61.1   57.2   58   57.1   60.1   59.1

cottas described and illustrated in the same article are somewhat larger. The relief of
Pope was exhibited at the National Portrait Gallery Exhibition in 1961.

1. Cf. p. 228. Plaster "medals" of Pope appear on day 2, lot 22; day 4, lot 33.

2. "Some Portrait Medallions by Roubiliac," *Burlington Magazine, 104* (April 1962), 153–58.

3. Henry Currie Marillier, *Christie's* (London, 1926), p. 10, quoted by Mallet, *Burlington Magazine, 104*.154.

57–61.2. MINIATURE MARBLE BUST, ROUBILIAC TYPE. MISS GLADYS SINGERS-BIGGER, THE GRANGE, KENNINGHALL, NORWICH.

Miss Gladys Singers-Bigger acquired this bust in 1917 at Bath in the shop of an antique
dealer named Kirk in Walcot Street. Early in 1925 she was in correspondence with
Mrs. Esdaile about it, and her diary records that on 18 January 1927, on the occasion of
Mr. and Mrs. Esdaile's opening an Exhibition of Bath Treasures at the Guild Hall,
Mrs. Esdaile came to her home in Marlborough Buildings to examine the bust. This
would seem to be the miniature bust alluded to by Mrs. Esdaile in her *Roubiliac*.[1] (The
other miniature bust, no. 59.2, at the Victoria Art Gallery, Bath, is never mentioned by
Mrs. Esdaile. It was doubtless considered as simply a work of Prince Hoare.) A distinctive feature is the long hair piled at the nape of the neck. The overall height, 14¾
inches, is slightly greater than that of the Temple Newsam signed bust (14½ inches),
but it should be borne in mind that the size of the present bust is accounted for by the
vertical slope of the shoulders and the elongation of the lower garment. The head is
only 6¼ x 5 inches.

1. *Roubiliac,* 1928, p. 48.

57–61.3. MARBLE BUST, ROUBILIAC TYPE. VICTORIA AND ALBERT MUSEUM.

The bust was the property of Lady Neave, at Dagenham Hall, Dagenham, Essex,
whence it passed into the hands of a dealer in statuary, Bert Crowther, Syon Lodge,
Isleworth. From him it was acquired in 1947 by Dr. W. L. Hildburgh, F.S.A., who
presented it to the Victoria and Albert Museum.[1]

It was exhibited at the loan exhibition "Eighteenth Century Art in England and
France" in 1950 at the Montreal Museum of Fine Arts, and is illustrated in an article
on the exhibition, "Les Anglais Rococo: the Georgian French," by Algy S. Noad, in
Art News, 49 (May 1950), 30–35.

1. Victoria and Albert archives.

57–61.4. MARBLE BUST, ROUBILIAC TYPE. THE CECIL HIGGINS MUSEUM, BEDFORD.

This bust appeared at a sale, by Browns of Chester Ltd., of the contents of Greenbank,
Chester, the home of the late E. Peter Jones, 25–27 April 1961. It was lot 252 on the
first day (p. 14 of the Catalogue): "A marble Bust of Pope probably by Roubiliac, on

57–61.1. Bronze. Oval 9¹³⁄₁₆ x 8 in. Bust 6⅝ x 5⅜ in., and 2³⁄₁₆ in. deep. Bust hollow cast, soldered to oval chased (or stippled) background, set in a red velvet frame. Mr. and Mrs. F. J. B. Watson, London.

57–61.2. White marble. Height 14¾ in. Breadth of shoulders 13 in. Crown to chin 6¼ in. Breadth above ears 5 in. Miss Gladys Singers-Bigger, The Grange, Kenninghall, Norwich.

57–61.3. White marble. Height (without pedestal) 19 in. Uninscribed. Victoria and Albert Museum. Crown Copyright.

a brown marble plinth." It was purchased by Montague Marcussen Ltd., 98 Crawford Street, London W.1, and from them by the Cecil Higgins Museum, Bedford, in July 1961.

The head is turned more to the right than in any of the four "ad vivum" Roubiliac marbles. The eyes are uncarved (as with the Garrick marble), but in other respects the face is closer to the Temple Newsam or the Rosebery. There is no drapery. The overall length of 16¾ inches results from the considerable elongation of the chest. The slightly tapered cylindrical prop at the back and the inscriptions in small capital and lower-case Roman letters (capitals ⁵⁄₁₆ inch high) are not reminiscent of the signed Roubiliac marbles.

57–61.5. MARBLE BUST, ROUBILIAC TYPE. HER MAJESTY THE QUEEN, WINDSOR CASTLE.

This enlarged marble version of the Roubiliac type is recorded in Windsor archives as present in the "Grand Corridor" in 1874. It was removed in 1905 to the Library, where it remains. The "Grand Corridor" was built during the 1820s by George IV. Today it contains a numerous collection of large marble busts, many signed by Nollekens, Chantrey, and other sculptors active in the early nineteenth century. The stout cylindrical prop fortifying a back of shallow depth is characteristic of this collection, as it is generally, I believe, of busts executed in the later eighteenth and the early nineteenth centuries.

57–61.6. MARBLE BUST (OR BUSTS), AFTER ROUBILIAC, BY JOSEPH NOLLEKENS.

Joseph Nollekens the sculptor (1737–1823) met Sterne at Rome in 1766 and did a bust of him which contributed much to the sculptor's fame.[1] At Nollekens' sale by Christie, 3, 4, and 5 July 1823, the original terra cotta of Sterne was bought (third day, lot 22) by Agar Ellis for £46.4, and a copy of it, apparently in marble, was bought (second day, lot 79*) by Russell Palmer for £60.18s. "A Bust of Pope, copied from the original by Roubiliac" (second day, lot 79) was bought for £14.14s by the "Rev. Mr. Este"[2] (probably the Rev. Charles Este, formerly of the Chapel Royal, Whitehall, author of *My Own Life*, 1787; d. 1829).[3] The sale of this bust of Pope is noted by Mrs. Esdaile, *Roubiliac*, p. 47. A marble copy of the Sterne was c. 1900 in the possession of J. T. Wharton, Esq., at Skelton Castle.[4] And National Portrait Gallery no. 1891 is a marble bust of Sterne by Nollekens, given by G. B. Croft-Lyons in 1920.

R. J. Minney, in his *Private Papers of Hore-Belisha* (London: Wm. Collins Sons & Co. Ltd., 1960), p. 81, reports a Nollekens marble bust of Pope and one of Sterne at Leslie Hore-Belisha's house in Stafford place near Buckingham Gate, in 1937. These busts were left to Miss Hilde Sloane and in 1961 were in her hands in London. At Sotheby's, 18 June 1965, Pope was lot 81, 21½ in., "Nollekens ft.," sold to R. A. Lee.

1. John Thomas Smith, *Nollekens and His Times*, ed. Wilfred Whitten (London, 1920), *1*.8; Henri Fluchère, *Laurence Sterne* (Paris, 1961), p. 162 n. 4.

2. A copy of the catalogue in the British Museum

above, left

57–61.4. White marble. Height 16¾ in. Chin to crown 8½ in. Breadth above ears 6½ in. Eyes uncarved. Inscribed at edge of shoulders on back: (to left) "A. Pope." and (to right) "L. F. Roubiliac". By courtesy of the Trustees of the Cecil Higgins Museum, Bedford.

above, right

57–61.8. Terra cotta. Height 22 in. Inscribed beneath on terra-cotta pedestal: "Pope". National Portrait Gallery 2483.

left

57–61.5. White marble. Height (without pedestal) 21⅜ in. Width of shoulders 19 in. Chin to crown 9 in. Breadth above ears 6¾ in. Inscribed on front of pedestal "ALEX- ANDER POPE." and on back of bust with crown and number ".77". Windsor Castle, Copyright Reserved.

Library (555.(3816)) has an annotation attributing the purchase for £14.14 to "Bridge." But an annotated copy in the Victoria and Albert Museum Library and *The Gentleman's Magazine*, 1823, p. 167, give the purchase to "Este," "Rev. Mr. Este."

3. *The Gentleman's Magazine*, *99* (Supplement 1829), 643.

4. Smith, *Nollekens*, *1*.8 n. 2.

57–61.7. MARBLE BUST, ROUBILIAC TYPE. SIR KENNETH MCKENZIE CLARK.†

Sir Kenneth McKenzie Clark has a marble bust of Pope at Saltwood Castle, Hythe, Kent. In a letter to me of June 1961 he kindly describes it as "a standard example of the Roubiliac type, . . . it appears to be a more or less contemporary version."

57–61.8. TERRA-COTTA BUST, ROUBILIAC TYPE. NATIONAL PORTRAIT GALLERY NO. 2483.

This large terra cotta was purchased by the National Portrait Gallery in 1930 from Gaston Demeter, of the Musée Royaux des Beaux Arts, Brussels, who said that it had been in a garden at Antwerp and had been brought many years previously from England. It is a reworking of Roubiliac's conception, apparently by another hand. It is reproduced as frontispiece by W. L. Macdonald, *Pope and His Critics, A Study in Eighteenth Century Personalities*, London, 1951. It was exhibited at the National Portrait Gallery Exhibition of 1961.

57–61.9. PLASTER BUST, ROUBILIAC TYPE. STOURHEAD, WILTSHIRE.

The Palladian house at Stourhead was built, 1721–24, by Henry Hoare the London banker, and improved by his son Henry (who laid out the gardens) after 1741, and by the second Henry's grandson Sir Richard Colt Hoare, Second Baronet, the county historian. The library, added by Sir Richard Colt Hoare, was decorated after 1800. Here, along with Rysbrack's two white marble busts of Milton, young and old, are four busts in plaster painted black: Milton, Dryden, Bolingbroke, and Pope.[1]

Like no. 59.2, the plaster replica of the Garrick marble, the bust at Stourhead is a cast replica, more closely related to the Rosebery marble (and hence to the terra cotta) than to the other three signed marbles, but yet so free in its relation as to be indeed an example of what should be called the "Roubiliac type." The marked inclination of the head especially sets this bust apart.

Mrs. Esdaile notices this bust[2] and believes (for a reason which is not apparent) that three of the four Stourhead busts may be the same sort as three of the four busts (Shakespeare, Milton, Dryden, Pope) of which Lord Chesterfield promised two to Madame de Bocage in June 1750 and sent all four in May 1751.[3] Madame de Bocage's four busts were seen in her Paris drawing room in 1775 by Mrs. Thrale.[4]

1. James Lees-Milne, *Stourhead Wiltshire, A Property of the National Trust*, 5th ed., 1958 (London, Country Life Limited for the National Trust), pp.

5–6, 20–21, 23. The bust of Pope may be seen in the view of the library in *Stourhead Wiltshire* (*National Trust Properties in Pictures*) (London, Country Life

Limited, 1952), Second Impression, 1959. See M. I. Webb, *Rysbrack* (London, 1954), p. 115, for the history of Rysbrack's Miltons.

2. *Roubiliac,* pp. 48, 106–07.

3. Chesterfield, *Works* (1779), *3.*338, 372; cf. Mrs.

Esdaile, *Roubiliac,* pp. 106–07.

4. *The French Journals of Mrs. Thrale and Doctor Johnson,* ed. Moses Tyson and Henry Guppy (New York, 1932), p. 102.

57–61.10. PLASTER BUST, ROUBILIAC TYPE. RUPERT GUNNIS, ESQ., HUNGERSHALL LODGE, TUNBRIDGE WELLS.

Like no. 57–61.9, this library bust is a cast made from a very free modeling of the Roubiliac type.[1]

1. In his *Dictionary of British Sculptors 1660–1851* (Cambridge: Harvard University Press, 1954), p. 147, Mr. Gunnis notes that John Flaxman the elder (1726–95) was employed by Roubiliac (cf. no. 57.1), Scheemakers, and later Wedgwood (cf. no. 57–61.20). He draws on the Archives of the West family of Alscot Park, Stratford-on-Avon, to reveal that Flaxman made busts of Milton and Pope and figures of "Flora" and "Zingara" for James West in 1767.

57–61.11. PLASTER BUST, ROUBILIAC TYPE. JOHN JOLLIFFE TUFNELL, LANGLEYS, GREAT WALTHAM, ESSEX.†

Mr. John Jolliffe Tufnell, of Langleys, Great Waltham, near Pleshey, Essex, believes that this bust was acquired and brought to Langleys by his ancestor Samuel Tufnell (d. 1758), one of the Trustees of the Founding of the State of Georgia. M. I. Webb, "Henry Cheere, Sculptor and Businessman and John Cheere—II," *Burlington Magazine, 100* (August 1958), 277–78, argues that Henry Cheere probably made Tufnell's monument at Pleshey and also that of his uncle Sir William Jolliffe (d. 1749) in the same Parish Church, erected by Tufnell and his cousin John Jolliffe of Petersfield. Tufnell and Jolliffe were also the erectors in 1757 of an equestrian statue in lead of William III at Petersfield, commissioned in the will of Sir William Jolliffe, designed probably by Henry Cheere, and probably cast in his brother John Cheere's yard at Hyde Park Corner. Cf. no. 57–61.22.

57–61.12. PLASTER BUST, ROUBILIAC TYPE. ASTON HALL, BIRMINGHAM, AND TRINITY COLLEGE, CAMBRIDGE.

Five large plaster busts painted black (Shakespeare, Milton, Newton, Locke, and Pope) were brought in 1959 from Shardeloes in Buckinghamshire to the City Museum and Art Gallery collection, Birmingham, and were placed at Aston Hall. In the Library at Trinity College, Cambridge, an identical bust of Pope, painted white over dark, is part of a similar set of 26 busts of classical and English subjects (including Shakespeare, Milton, Newton, and Locke) which stand atop the bookcases.[1] This type of plaster bust of Pope is characterized by an elongated body and garment, embroidered patterns along the hem of both inner and outer garments, and a youthful head turned in the opposite direction from that of the Roubiliac signed busts. The bust of Pope at Cambridge is on

above, left
57–61.9. Plaster, painted black. Height (without pedestal) 16½ in. Breadth at shoulders 16½ in. Stourhead, Wiltshire, The National Trust.

left
57–61.10. Plaster, painted brown. Height 17 in. Rupert Gunnis, Esq., Hungershall Lodge, Tunbridge Wells. Photograph by Alan Lamboll.

above, right
57–61.11. Plaster, painted white. Height 15 in. Breadth 11 in. John Jolliffe Tufnell, Esq., Langleys, Great Waltham, Essex.†

below, left
57–61.12. Plaster, painted black over bronze. Height (without pedestal) 23 in. Breadth below shoulders 18½ in. Chin to crown 9¾ in. Breadth above ears 7¼ in. Aston Hall, Birmingham.

below, right
57–61.13. Plaster, painted bronze. Height (without pedestal) 17¼ in. Inscribed on back (across shoulders): "D. Landi 36 Charles St. ⟨Late⟩ 11 Leather Lane" and beneath, on a cylindrical prop, "POPE". National Book League, 7 Albemarle Street, London.

the third bookcase from the north end, west side, not far from Rysbrack's terra cotta and marble, and Roubiliac's marble, of Newton.

1. The 26 plasters of this set are to be distinguished from Anacreon and Ben Jonson (both wooden) and from plasters of Coleridge and Porson and a second of Shakespeare (from the Stratford tomb effigy). I believe that (like Pope) Shakespeare, Milton, Newton, and Locke are identical with the Aston Hall images.

A bust of Pope which I have not further identified is said to appear in a set of black plaster literary busts in the library at Littlecote, formerly the home of the Popham family, in Wiltshire.

57–61.13. PLASTER BUST, DERIVED FROM THE ROUBILIAC TYPE. NATIONAL BOOK LEAGUE, 7 ALBEMARLE STREET, LONDON.

In a letter of 10 June 1944 to the TLS, p. 283, Mrs. Esdaile writes: "When *The Ambulator* was published, there was in a grotto in Pope's grounds 'a most beautiful bust of Pope.' " The eighth edition of *The Ambulator* (1796) has the following sentence in a description of the grotto: "In two adjoining apertures in the rock are placed a Ceres and a Bacchus, an excellent bust of Pope, and some other figures."[1] *The Richmond and Twickenham Times Supplement*, 4 August 1888, reports that the two corners of the grotto nearest the river lawn are "adorned" with busts: "that on the left being a representation of a pilgrim, while that on the right is devoted to a bust of Pope himself."[2] In 1907, when the quasi-Elizabethan half-timbered house which had been built approximately on the site of Pope's villa by Thomas Young, c. 1840, was up for sale, *The Daily Graphic* carried an article with several illustrations, one of which showed a bust on a round pedestal against a background of rocks with the caption "Bust of Alexander Pope in the Grotto."[3]

The relatively remote derivative in plaster from the Roubiliac type reproduced above was presented to the National Book League in 1959 or 1960 by Messrs. Bumpus of London. The name of the maker inscribed on the back, "D. Landi," does not appear in Rupert Gunnis's *Dictionary of British Sculptors 1660–1851*.

The photograph in *The Daily Graphic* is obscure. Nevertheless, certain prominent features (e.g., the left turn of the head, the shape of the nose, the arrangement of the garments) suggest that the bust in Pope's grotto was of the same sort as the plaster now at the National Book League.

1. P. 267. A second bust is mentioned. "Over an arched way, leading to the new gardens, is a bust of Pope in white marble, under which are these lines by Earl Nugent: 'The humble roof, the garden's scanty line, / Ill suit the genius of the bard divine: / But fancy now displays a fairer scope, / And Stanhope's plans unfold the soul of Pope.' " A stone bearing this inscription is, I believe, still to be seen at the back of the gardens, belonging now to Saint Catherine's School.

2. Cols. 4–5.

3. Cutting from *The Daily Graphic*, Saturday, 2 November 1907, in a scrapbook of Popeana compiled by George Potter (Yale University, Beinecke Rare Book and Manuscript Library).

57–61.14. ENGRAVED GEM, BY LORENZ NATTER, C. 1740.

Late in 1740 George Vertue enters in his *Note Book:* "Mr. Nattieres Sculptor of Stones Gemms. has done the head of Dr Mead. very like from a drawing in Crayons. Mr Alex

Pope—from a bust—."[1] Lorenz Natter (1705–63), a Swabian gem-engraver and medalist, was in England for a few years, c. 1740–43, and again at a later period after 1754. The gem of Pope, in all likelihood of the Roubiliac type, seems to be unknown today. But see nos. 48.8 and 62.9.

1. Vertue 3.100–01.

57–61.15. PLASTER STATUETTE, BY "CHEERE." CASTLE MUSEUM, YORK.

At the Castle Museum, York, are ten statuettes in plaster, and nine busts, acquired in 1950 from Kirkleatham Hall, near Redcar, North Yorkshire. The statuettes are Homer, Inigo Jones, Van Dyck, Rubens (the latter three after Rysbrack), Locke, Newton, Spenser, Shakespeare, Milton, and Pope. All except Shakespeare have the signature and date "Cheere Ft.1749." Shakespeare has "P. Scheemakers F. 1740." The statuettes and busts were presented to Sir William Turner's Hospital, Kirkleatham, in 1749–50.[1] Pope (19 inches high) and Spenser are similar to lead statuettes in the Victoria and Albert Museum. See no. 57–61.16. Sir Henry Cheere (1703–81), the businesslike statuary and monumental sculptor, had a shop in St. Margaret's, Westminster, where he was the partner or neighbor of Scheemakers and the employer for a while, as we have noticed (p. 225), of L. F. Roubiliac. His brother John Cheere had a casting yard at Hyde Park Corner, noted for the production of ornamental lead statuary.[2] See no. 57–61.11.

The standing figure with elbow on a fancy lectern is a pattern deriving from such classical statues as the Farnese Hercules and the Capitoline Leaning Faun, and established in England by Guelfi's Secretary Craggs (above Pope's epitaph) in Westminster Abbey (1727) and Scheemakers' Shakespeare in Westminster Abbey (1741). It appears again notably in Roubiliac's Shakespeare for Garrick's Hampton Temple (1758), now in the British Museum.[3] The Shakespeare monument of 1741 was put up at the direction of a Palladian committee which included the Earl of Burlington, Dr. Richard Mead, and Alexander Pope (Vertue 3.101; *Gentleman's Magazine, 11* [1741], 105). See David Piper, *O Sweet Mr. Shakespeare, I'll Have His Picture, The Changing Image of Shakespeare's Person, 1600–1800* (London: National Portrait Gallery, 1964), pp. 20–25.

1. Communications from D. T. Piper, the National Portrait Gallery, and R. Patterson, Curator, the Castle Museum, York.

2. See M. I. Webb, *Rysbrack* (London, 1954), pp. 68, 70, 75; and "Henry Cheere, Sculptor and Business Man and John Cheere,—I and II," *Burlington Magazine, 100* (July and August 1958), 232–40, 274–79 (especially p. 235, resuming the author's earlier article in the same *Magazine* for April 1957).

3. Webb, *Rysbrack*, pp. 171–72.

57–61.16. LEAD STATUETTE, WITH HEAD OF THE ROUBILIAC TYPE. VICTORIA AND ALBERT MUSEUM.

This lead figure (Victoria and Albert A.4–1955) was given by Dr. W. L. Hildburgh in 1955. He had acquired it with a similar figure of "Milton" (actually Spenser) at Sotheby's 29 May 1953, in a sale of various properties: "A pair of lead figures of Shake-

57–61.15. Plaster. Height 19 in. Inscribed at base of lectern "POPE" and half way up "Cheere Fᵗ 1749". Castle Museum, York.†

57–61.15x. Plaster. Height 19⁷⁄₁₀ in. Inscribed at base of lectern: "P. Scheemakers F. 1740". (After Peter Scheemakers' statue of Shakespeare placed in Westminster Abbey in 1741.) Castle Museum, York.

57–61.16. Lead. Height 18⅜ in.
Victoria and Albert Museum. Crown Copyright.

speare and Milton standing beside pedestals." The figures are similar to the plaster statuettes by Cheere described in no. 57–61.15. Both are reproduced (Plate ten, facing p. 24) in David Piper's *O Sweet Mr. Shakespeare* cited in that entry.

57–61.17. MINIATURE WHITE PORCELAIN BUST, ROUBILIAC TYPE. CHARLES WOOLLETT & SON, LONDON, 1961.

The bust was photographed in April 1961 by the courtesy of Charles Wollett & Son, 59 & 61 Wigmore Street, London, W.1. It is apparently not listed in the literature on Bow Porcelain, but is of the style produced by the Bow factory c. 1750. See R. L. S. Bruce-Mitford and Hugh Tait, *Bow Porcelain 1744–1776,* British Museum, 1959; Frank Hurlbutt, *Bow Porcelain,* London, 1926.

57–61.18. MINIATURE TORTOISE-SHELL-WARE BUST, ROUBILIAC TYPE. BRIGHTON ART GALLERY AND MUSEUM.

In 1899 the Bethnal Green Branch of the Victoria and Albert Museum published a *Catalogue of a Collection of Pottery and Porcelain Illustrating Popular British History, Lent by Henry Willett, Esq. of Brighton.* On p. 72 appears: "952. Bust. Tortoiseshell

57–61.17. White glazed porcelain. Height (including pedestal) 9 in. Charles Woollett & Son, London, April 1961.

57–61.18. Tortoise-shell ware. Height 8¼ in. Brighton Art Gallery and Museum.†

ware. Alexander Pope. . . . H. 8¼ in. *Staffordshire (Burslem)*. c. 1750." The Willett collection was bequeathed at the beginning of the present century to Brighton Art Gallery and Museum, where the bust of Pope is now to be found.

57–61.19. MINIATURE GLAZED EARTHENWARE BUST, ROUBILIAC TYPE. VICTORIA
AND ALBERT MUSEUM.

This bust is no. 79.—1874 in the Victoria and Albert Museum Ceramics collection.[1] It is of the type known generally as Staffordshire, attributable to the second half of the eighteenth century. The mold number "90" is impressed at the back of the pedestal. Frank Falkner, *The Wood Family of Burslem* (London, 1912), Appendix, in a list of Burslem mold numbers gives Pope as "90."[2] A bust apparently from the same mold, though differently colored, is illustrated by D. M. & P. Manheim, of 7 Manchester Street, London, W.1, in *The Connoisseur Souvenir of the Coronation Year Antique Dealers' Fair and Exhibition, Held at Grosvenor House June . . . 1953*, ed. L. G. G. Ramsey, 1953, p. 62 (Courtauld Institute Library). Here Pope is said to wear a brown cloak, with turquoise lining, and to have been modeled by Ralph Wood c. 1780.

1. A second enameled earthenware bust (6¾ in. high) at the Victoria and Albert Museum (*Catalogue of English Porcelain, Earthenware . . . Collected by Charles Schreiber, Esq. M.P., and Lady Charlotte Elizabeth Schreiber and presented to the Museum in 1884, I* [1928], 74, no. 360, bought at Utrecht in 1869), is said to be Pope but is surely not. This is glazed ware of the Derby type. Neither John Haslem, *The Old Derby Factory*, London, 1876, nor William Bemrose, *Bow, Chelsea, and Derby Porcelain* (London, 1898), pp. 69–88, "A List of Moulds and Models, which belonged to the Estate of the late Mr. Duesbury in 1795," record

any image of Pope. In February 1965 Mr. R. J. Charleston kindly informed me that the bust in question is now recognized as being after the bust of Matthew Prior by Antoine Coysevox in Westminster Abbey.

2. Mr. J. V. G. Mallet, to whom I owe the above information and the color notes in the legend for this bust, tells me that impressed mold numbers of the type in question are found mostly on enameled figures dating from the time of Ralph Wood the younger (1748–1795). Ralph Wood the elder lived 1715–1772.

57–61.20. BLACK BASALT WEDGWOOD BUST, ROUBILIAC TYPE. WILLIAM ANDREWS
CLARK MEMORIAL LIBRARY, UNIVERSITY OF CALIFORNIA, LOS ANGELES.

The Wedgwood basalt bust of Pope had a slight shadow cast on it when in *Apollo*, 27 (May 1938), 248–53, an article by John Thomas, M.A., "Edward Gibbon and His Circle Portrayed by Wedgwood Medallions and Busts," included, in an illustration of six out of twelve busts that adorned Gibbon's library at Lausanne in 1788, one identified as "Pope," but actually Laurence Sterne.[1] The same bust, grouped with the same Shakespeare and Milton, reappears as "Pope" in "Portrait Busts in Black Basaltes," by G. Bernard Hughes, in *County Life, 132* (16 August 1962), 360.

The celebrated Wedgwood basaltes busts appear in strength first in the second edition of the Wedgwood Catalogue in 1774.[2] That of Pope first appears in the fourth edition, of 1777, where it is in a group described as "About 15 inches high." The same bust reappears in the fifth and sixth editions, of 1779 and 1787.[3] From Josiah Wedgwood's letters during the summer of 1774 to his partner in the Etrurian factory, Thomas

Bentley, we know that a large number of busts were derived or improved from plaster casts provided by James Hoskins and Benjamin Grant, who appear to have kept a shop somewhere near Westminster Bridge. A chief modeler and improver of busts at Etruria was William Hackwood.[4] Hoskins and Grant are said to have supplied a bust of Pope.[5] Today the Wedgwood Museum, at Barlaston, Stoke-on-Trent, has a photograph of a bust of Pope, apparently of black basalt, but the bust itself is no longer present. A notation "12″" on the photograph perhaps refers to the height of the bust. Both the bust and the pedestal appear nevertheless to be identical with the black basalt bust (9⅞ in. with pedestal) now at the William Andrews Clark Library.[6]

1. After the Nollekens bust of 1766 (NPG no. 1891). Cf. no. 57–61.6.

2. Eliza Meteyard, *The Wedgwood Handbook, A Manual for Collectors* (London 1879), pp. 202–09.

3. Meteyard, *Handbook,* p. 208, and *Wedgwood's Catalogue of Cameos, Intaglios, Bas-Reliefs, Busts, and Small Statues, Reprinted from the Edition of 1787,* 1873. See also Wolf Mankowitz, *Wedgwood* (London 1953), p. 254, in "A Transcript of the 1779 Wedgwood & Bentley Catalogue."

4. Meteyard, *Handbook,* p. 203. See also Mankowitz, p. 215.

5. Rupert Gunnis, *Dictionary of British Sculptors, 1660–1856* (Cambridge, Harvard University Press, 1954), p. 211.

6. A black basalt bust of Pope, then in the possession of Mr. C. Cox, was shown in the Liverpool Art Club's Exhibition of Wedgwood held in 1879 (*Catalogue* no. 1134).

57–61.21. WEDGWOOD CAMEO MEDALLION, ROUBILIAC TYPE. *Bulletin of the Russell-Cotes Museum,* 1930.

The five English editions of the *Wedgwood Catalogue* (1773, 1774, 1777, 1779, 1787) all listed a portrait medallion of Pope, apparently under some such head as "Portrait Medallions, modern," or "Heads of Illustrious Moderns."[1] This is possibly the medallion listed as "22" of the "English Poets," under the general head "Class X Heads of Illustrious Moderns from Chaucer to the Present Time," in Wolf Mankowitz's 1950 transcript of the 1779 (5th edition) *Wedgwood & Bentley Catalogue.*[2] The size for cameos in this group is here given as 2 x 1¾ inches (without frames). This seems too small, however, for either of the two cameo medallions of Pope known today in the working molds at the Barlaston Wedgwood Museum. For one of these, no. 271–A–8, see no. 62.5, the Dassier type. The other, no. 271–8, a profile to left, of the Roubiliac type, is said to produce a plaque which after firing measures 4³⁄₁₆ x 3³⁄₁₆ inches. A photograph in my possession, of an impression from this mold, shows, however, that the image is the same as that illustrated in the *Bulletin of the Russell-Cotes Art Gallery & Museum,* 9 (June 1930), 20 (said to measure 4½ x 2¾ inches). I reproduce this illustration below, no. 57–61.21. The light shades probably represent the frequently used white on blue jasper.[3] In February 1965 Mrs. Robert D. Chellis, of Wellesley Hills, Massachusetts, kindly sent for my inspection a jasper medallion of this type, white on black, made at the Etruria Wedgwood factory during the 1920s for the collection of Helen Sard Hughes. This measures 3¹⁰⁄₁₆ x 2¹⁰⁄₁₆ inches (plaque, unframed), and the image is 3 inches high.

1. Eliza Meteyard, *The Wedgwood Handbook,* (London, 1875), pp. 187, 198; *Wedgwood's Catalogue of Cameos . . . Reprinted from the Edition of 1787,* 1879, "Heads of Illustrious Moderns."

2. Wolf Mankowitz, *Wedgwood* (London, 1953), p. 250.

3. Mankowitz, p. 250; Meteyard, *Handbook,* p. 186. Meteyard (pp. 188, 190) says that Wedgwood's first

57–61.19. Enameled earthenware. Height 9¼ in. Hair gray, flesh color natural, tunic lilac with brown hem, cloak canary yellow with blue dots in green circles and blue lining; line decoration and inscription on pedestal, brown. Victoria and Albert Museum. Crown Copyright.

57–61.20. Black basalt, Wedgwood. Height 9⅞ in. without pedestal; screwed to a round pedestal of black basalt, 1⅞ in. high. "Pope" in Roman capitals slightly less than ⅛ in. high impressed at back of collar; "Wedgwood" in Roman capitals about 1⁄16 in. high impressed at inside back of base of bust. William Andrews Clark Memorial Library, University of California, Los Angeles.†

57–61.21. Wedgwood cameo medallion. 4½ x 2¾ in. Beneath image: "Pope." *Bulletin of the Russell-Cotes Art Gallery & Museum, 9* (Bournemouth, June 1930), no. 2, p. 20, no. 11.

57–61.23. Bronze. Height about 9 in. Professor Douglas Grant, University of Leeds.

modeler of portrait medallions of any note was Joachim Smith, residing in Bemers Street, Oxford Street, but their relation lasted only a year or two, for in January 1775 Wedgwood discovered that Smith was sending models to the Derby works. About the same moment he secured the services of the younger Flaxman. In 1777 Flaxman executed a new set of English Poets. See no. 62.5.

57–61.22. CEILING RELIEF, ROUBILIAC TYPE. TRUMPETERS' HOUSE, RICHMOND.†

In an article contributed to *Country Life*, *95* (21 April 1944), 686–88, Christopher Hussey describes Trumpeters' House, built on the site of Richmond Palace about 1708, by persons close to Queen Anne, and owned from 1730 to 1771 by Mr. Lewis Way. Hussey believes it was Way who, about 1740, added to a paneled room overlooking the lawn a fine rococo ceiling with two plaster relief busts which he identifies as Pope and Milton. The illustration, Fig. 5, shows a profile to left, apparently quite similar to 57–61.21, the Wedgwood cameo of 1773 or later. The resemblance is so close as to suggest a date later than 1773 for the Trumpeters' House relief.

57–61.23. MINIATURE BRONZE BUST, ROUBILIAC TYPE. PROFESSOR DOUGLAS GRANT, THE UNIVERSITY OF LEEDS.

This small bronze derivative of the Roubiliac type was found by Professor Grant some years ago in a shop at Oxford.

57–61.24. LINE ENGRAVING, AFTER ROUBILIAC, BY H. GRAVELOT.

This line engraving is an adaptation of Roubiliac's image, fitted into a medallic frame similar to that of the same artist's engraving from the Dassier medal (no. 62.3). Hubert François Gravelot (properly Bourguignon) (1699–1773) was a designer and book illustrator who came to England about 1732 and stayed until 1746.[1] He designed the symbolic ornaments for the heads in Thomas Birch's *Heads of Illustrious Persons*,[2] published by the Knaptons, in two folio volumes, 1743 and 1751. An impression of the present plate in my possession has a heavier hatched shading under the lower right quarter of the medal and in general a heavier shading of hair, face, neck, and garment, than the British Museum impression which I reproduce below. My impression bears the initial "G" in pencil at the lower left corner.

1. Vertue 3.89, 131; and *Le Nécrologe des Hommes Célèbres De France, Par Une Société de Gens de Lettres* (Paris, 1774), "Éloge de Monsieur Gravelot," pp. 134–35, 137. The "Éloge" is by his brother, [J. B.] d'Anville (pp. 132, 145), Premier Géographe du Roi.
2. The title-page allegorical vignette has "Des. and Eng. by H. Gravelot who invented the Ornaments for the Heads."

57–61.25. STIPPLE ENGRAVING, FROM A DRAWING AFTER ROUBILIAC BY ANGELICA KAUFFMANN, 1783: "THE MUSES CROWNING THE BUST OF POPE."

Grolier 83, but missing from the Chew collection at the New York Public Library in 1951. An impression in black ink in the Countess of Bessborough's extra-illustrated

The MUSES crowning the BUST of POPE.

Immortal Bard! for whom each Muse has wove
The fairest garlands of th' Aonian Grove.—

L.ᵈ Lyttelton

57–61.25. Stipple. 4 x 5 in. oval. "Ang. **Kauffman** invᵗ // **P. W. Tomkins** sculp. Pupil of F. Bartolozzi. / The MUSES crowning the BUST of POPE. / Immortal Bard! for whom each Muse has wove / The fairest garlands of th' Aonian Grove.— / Lᵈ Lyttelton / Published as the Act directs 1 March 1783, by S. Watts, Nº 3 Featherstone Buildings Holborn." *Grolier* 83. The Pierpont Morgan Library, New York City.

ALEXANDER·POPE.

above

57–61.24. Line engraving. 2⁵⁄₁₆ x 2⁵⁄₁₆ in. rectangle. 2¼ x 2¼ in. medal. "ALEXAN- // DER POPE. / H. Gravelot del. et sculps." *BMEP* 4. By permission of the Trustees of the British Museum.

right

57–61.26. Stipple engraving. 10⅜ x 8 in. oval. "Drawn by J. Brown. // Engraved by Mᵣˢ Bovi, Pupil to F. Bartolozzi R.A. / ALEXANDER POPE. / From the fine Original Bust by Rysbrack, in the Possession / of Wᵐ Seward Esqᵣ / London Publish'd by Mᵣˢ Brown, at Mᵣ Middleton's Nº 162, Strand, Febᵧ 1788." *BMEP* 42–43. *Grolier* 79 and 80.

Works of Pope (1785), *1*.67, at the Morgan Library, is reproduced above. An impression in bistre ink is in the album of Bathurst Popeana at the same library, and another (showing an earlier state of the lettering) is in my own collection. The type of stipple or roulette technique employed here in imitation of drawing is sometimes called "chalk-line" engraving. The couplet inscribed below the picture is the opening of *An Epistle to Mr. Pope, from Rome*, 1730, which may be found in the *Works* of George Lord Lyttelton (London, 1776), *3*.97. This pleasant allegorical engraving invites comparison with Sir Joshua Reynolds' painting of the daughters of Sir William Montgomery as "The Graces adorning a term of Hymen," exhibited at the Royal Academy in 1774.[1] And see no. 54.2, Miss Sitwell draping the pedestal of a crowned bust of Pope.

C. B. Tinker, ed. *Dr. Johnson and Fanny Burney* (New York, 1911), facing p. 150, reproduces a satirical print, "Old Wisdom. Blinking at the Stars. Pub. March 10th 1782 by W. Raint [?]." Johnson as an owl in a library perches on a volume of *Lives of the Poets* beneath busts of Milton, Pope, and other poets. Pope is a token image of approximately the Roubiliac type. This picture reappears in E. L. McAdam, Jr. and George Milne, *Johnson's Dictionary A Modern Selection* (New York, 1963), facing p. 4, "By James Gillray . . . Prints Division, New York Public Library."

---

1. E. K. Waterhouse, *Reynolds* (London, 1941), p. 152. Angelica Kauffmann (1741–1807) was a Tyrolese who settled in London in 1766 and practiced decorative historical painting. In 1781 she married the Italian painter Antonio Zucchi and went to Rome, where later she was a member of the Goethe circle. See Waterhouse, *Painting in Britain*, p. 195.

57–61.26. STIPPLE ENGRAVING, AFTER ROUBILIAC, BY "M^{no} BOVI," 1788.

The attribution to Rysbrack can scarcely be substantiated; the bust seems clearly of the Roubiliac type. If the drawing by J. Brown and the engraving by Marino Bovi (1758–1805)[1] render faithfully the shape of the pedestal, it is difficult to identify this with any Roubiliac bust now known. But it may possibly represent one of the five plaster casts, in addition to the one acquired by Dr. Maty, sold at the Roubiliac sale of 1762. William Seward (1747–99), man of letters, F.R.S. and F.S.A., and friend of Dr. Samuel Johnson, published much in the anecdotal and biographical way, but a search of his books (*Anecdotes of Some Distinguished Persons*, 1795–97, and *Biographiana*, 1799) has failed to discover any allusion to this bust. The engraving of 1788 is reproduced in illustration of Austin Dobson's "Alexander Pope," *Scribner's Magazine*, *3* (May 1788), 534.

---

1. Born at Naples, worked in London. Thieme-Becker gives the first name as "Marino" and says he was bankrupt in May 1805. Lugt 6958 gives the name as "Mariano" and places the sale on 28–30 May 1805, after his death.

· 10 ·

1741
JACQUES ANTOINE DASSIER
(1715-59)

THREE GENERATIONS of the family of Dassier were chief engravers to the Mint of Geneva. Domaine Dassier died in 1719 and was succeeded by his son, Jean Dassier, who died in 1763 and was succeeded in 1777 by his son, Antoine Dassier. Other members of the family were also medalists—a brother of Jean, whose name seems uncertain,[1] and another son of Jean, named Jacques Antoine. This family of artists, eminently successful in their own country, seem nevertheless to have been strongly attracted towards London —where two restrictions, one on the employment of foreign artists in government posts[2] and the other on the setting up of coining presses, worked to discourage the medallic art, but may have seemed to artists at a distance to have created an inviting opportunity. "My proposal in this case," writes George Vertue on 28 June 1731, "is to apply to His Majesty or parliament to have one coining press set up in the Stamp Office, Lincoln's Inn . . . which shall be under the inspection of the commissioners of the Stamp Office, to have three keys to lock it up. . . . when any engraver has any medal to stamp off, he should show the commissioners the die and an impression in wax and be allowed to stamp off as many as he pleased in presence of those persons entrusted with the keys."[3]

The family of the Dassiers had begun their attack on the English mint about the

1. According to the Index of the Walpole Society edition of the Vertue *Note Books,* this brother's name was Jacques. But Leonard Forrer, *Biographical Dictionary of Medallists,* vol. *1* (1904) and Supplement, vol. 7 (1923), lists only one brother, named Paul, 1681–1768.

2. Vertue *3.47, 53.*

3. Vertue *3.53.*

year 1728 or earlier. The member of doubtful name had come "twice" and had "offered his service to the government," but failing to overcome the obstacles had returned to Geneva.[4] At about the same time, or precisely in 1728, Jean Dassier, though he held the post of chief Engraver at Geneva, came also to London, but at first had no great success. ("Though from Geneva and no Papist, yet could not obtain favor").[5] Jean Dassier, however, was more resourceful than his brother. About the year 1720 he had begun an excellent series of seventy-two medallic portraits of the French rulers and a series of the Protestant Reformers.[6] And now we find in Vertue's notebook the following announcement:

> Beginning from William Conqueror to the present time—a set of medals, engraved by J. Dassier of Geneva and dedicated to King George 2nd., 1731. Eighteen of them delivered to subscribers at four guineas—the other fifteen, when done, to be two guineas more, struck in copper. In silver, fifteen pounds, each medal weighing about five shillings.

Vertue thought that six of these historic portraits, "not done from a genuine picture," were "bad." To give Dassier due credit, however, he told Vertue he would "grave these over again from true originals."[7] As a result of this kind of campaigning, it was not long before the rule was broken. "Sir Andrew Fountaine and Mr. Conduitt offered to place Mr. Dassier in the Mint at London, allowing him £50 yearly to work under Mr. Croker," until Mr. Croker died. Mr. Dassier, however, "did not care for" Mr. Croker. This kind of "uncertainty . . . made him resolve to return to Geneva."[8]

In April 1733, nevertheless, Vertue was still in touch with Dassier; he records giving him "assistance" ("designs," "prints," and advice—whether by post to Switzerland or directly at London, is not clear) in a project for "engraving medals of English great men." A few—Cromwell, Newton—were done already. More than a dozen others—Chaucer, Shakespeare, Milton, Spenser, Bacon, Locke—had "proofs done."[9]

Then toward the end of 1740, the third Dassier arrives in London. "Lately come over into England from Geneva the young Mr. Dassier medallist or graver of medals, son of John Dassier living at Geneva. He has made some essays that way, but the difficulty of getting them struck off prevents the publication of them."[10]

> 1740 / 1, February. James Anthony Dassier has published proposals for cutting several medals or dies—the portraitures of famous men living in England. Martin Folkes Esq. is done very like him—but was struck at **Geneva** from the die done here, because here is not engines allowed for that purpose, or because it is cheaper. The subscription is four guineas for thirteen medals.

4. Vertue 3.51–52, 100.
5. Vertue 3.47.
6. Forrer, *Biographical Dictionary of Medallists, 1* (1904), 515–16.
7. Vertue 3.51. Page 52 gives a transcript and pat-
tern of the reverse of the medals.
8. Vertue 3.52.
9. Vertue 5.106.
10. Vertue 3.100.

This is a young man, son of John Dassier of Geneva. . . . Names of the illustrious persons to be done:

See the printed Proposals:

Duke of Argyle	Earl of Chesterfield	Richard Mead, M.D.
Robert Barker, M.D.	Abraham De Moivre	Alexander Pope
Sir John Barnard	Martin Folkes	William Pulteney
Lord Carteret	Edmund Halley	Sir Hans Sloane
		Sir Robert Walpole[11]

And at about this time something happened which made it possible for the ambition of the father to be realized by the son.

> 1741. Mr. John Croker principal Engraver to the Mint for coins and medals died (1740, aged 70). Towards his latter end of life he . . . was much assisted in his business of the Mint by Mr. Tanner.[12]

> April 1741. Mr. John Christopher Tanner, Esq., his warrant passed from the King to be the first Graver of the Mint in London for coins and medals.

> At the same time was admitted as second Graver in the Mint Mr. James Dassier of Geneva, who has lately made three medals: Mr. Folkes, Mr. Pope, and Mr. De Moivre. He is gone over again to Geneva for a little or take his farewell in order to settle here.[13]

By August 1745 the young medalist had finished a medal of Sir Andrew Fountaine and seven or eight more of an English series (price each 7s.6), and Vertue records again that he is "gone to Geneva . . . to his father for a small time—to return here again."[14] He kept his post in the English Mint until the end of November 1757, at about which time apparently he left to go to the Mint at St. Petersburg. He died at Copenhagen in 1759 on his way back to Switzerland, "or as some say, to England."[15]

Dassier apparently acquired some reputation for the rapidity and liveliness of his *ad vivum* sketching. An anecdote, perhaps not apocryphal, which comes to light in the later nineteenth century, tells how in 1752 he went over from London to Paris for the express purpose of drawing a profile of the philosopher Montesquieu. Obtaining a breakfast interview with Montesquieu through the offices of a friend, Dassier sprang his request. Montesquieu, after a flattering preamble ("Monsieur Dassier, je n'ai jamais voulu laisser faire mon portrait à personne. . . . Mais . . . je sais qu'on ne resiste pas au burin de Dassier."), threw the challenge back at Dassier by insisting that the job be done on the spot. Nothing daunted, Dassier whipped out his materials ("tira ses crayons de sa poche") and in about half an hour produced the drawing for the medal dated 1753

11. Vertue 3.101.

12. Vertue 3.101.

13. Vertue 3.102. Forrer, *Biographical Dictionary of Medallists*, 7 (1923), 206, cites an article in *Schweizer Künstler-Lexicon*, Supplement, p. 117, which draws on Public Record Office materials to argue that Dassier succeeded John Tanner, not as "second," but as "third" Engraver.

14. Vertue 3.127.

15. Forrer, *Biographical Dictionary of Medallists*, 1 (1904), 511, corrected by 7 (1923), 206.

which may be seen illustrated in the *Tresor de numismatique et de glyptique*[16] or as frontispiece of Robert Shackelton, *Montesquieu,* Oxford, 1961.

George Vertue seems to perceive something of such a method and style in three English medals which Dassier made. A few pages after the notice of April 1741 which we have already quoted, he returns to the subject:

> I observe three medals in copper. I have lately seen one of Mr. Folkes, Esq., Mr. Alexander Pope, and Mr. De Moivre—done by Dassier of Geneva in London. They are done from the life and are free and boldly cut, but not so elaborately, nor so high finished as others. There appears a little of the *fa-presto.*[17]

16. See Fernand Mazerolle, "Dassier et Montesquieu," *Revue Suisse de Numismatique, 5* (Geneva, 1895), 96–98. Mazerolle quotes *Revue Universelle des Arts, 18* (1863–64), 283–84, edited by P. Lacroix—a letter supposed to have been written in 1778 to the son of Montesquieu by the friend who had introduced Dassier to the philosopher, "M. Risteau, directeur de la Compagnie des Indes."

17. Vertue 3.104.

62.1, a and b. COPPER MEDAL, BY JACQUES ANTOINE DASSIER, 1741.

This medal is illustrated in Count Pier Antonio Gaetani, *Museum Mazzuchellianum seu Numismata Virorum doctrina praestantium, 2* (Venice, 1763), Pl. clxxxv.3; and in Thomas Snelling, *Thirty Three Plates of English Medals* (London, 1776), Pl. 31.3.[1] An example appeared (along with a marble bust of Pope, no. 61.1) in the sale of James Bindley beginning 3 March 1819 (Lugt 9526), pp. 3–4 of the Catalogue, Lot 40, medals by the Dassiers.

It is catalogued in Edward Hawkins, *Medallic Illustrations of the History of Great Britain,* ed. Augustus W. Franks and Herbert A. Grueber (London, 1885), 2.565, no. 198. Both face and reverse are illustrated in *Medallic Illustrations of the History of Great Britain and Ireland, Plates CLI–CLX* (London, British Museum, 1911), Plate CLX, no. 9. Hawkins, ed. Franks and Grueber, calls it "not uncommon." In addition to the example in the British Museum Collection, I have seen one in the possession of Professor George Sherburn, the reverse of which is illustrated below, 62.1b. One presented to me by a friend in London (illustrated below, no. 62.1a), was exhibited at the National Portrait Gallery Exhibition in 1961.

1. I take the reference to Gaetani from Hawkins (1885), 2.565 (see above). The competent reportorial line engravings of the face and reverse of this medal in Snelling were done by "C. Hall," presumably Charles Hall (1720–83). See Plate 31 and title page.

62.2 a and b. COPPER MEDAL, APPARENTLY BY JACQUES ANTOINE DASSIER, 1743.

This medal appears in Thomas Snelling's *Thirty Three Plates of English Medals* (London, 1776), Pl. 31.4. Hawkins, *Medallic Illustrations,* ed. Franks and Grueber (1885), 2.582, no. 221, calls it "Rare," and asserts, apparently on grounds of the medal's appear-

62.1a. Copper. Diameter 2.15 in. "ALEXA- // NDER POPE. // I. A. DASSIER F."

62.1b. Reverse of no. 62.1a. "POETA / ANGLUS • / M.DCC.XLI." The late George Sherburn.

62.2a. Copper. Diameter 1.1 in. Edge milled. "ALEXA- // NDER POPE." By permission of the Trustees of the British Museum. Department of Coins and Medals.

62.2b. Reverse of no. 62.2a. "POETA / ANGLUS • / M.DCC.XLIII." By permission of the Trustees of the British Museum.

62.3. Line engraving. Rectangle 2¼ x 2¼ in. "ALEXAN- // DER POPE. / H. Gravelot sculps."

62.4. Line engraving. 4⅜ x 3 in. "ALEXANDER POPE / "Dessiné et Grave sur la Medaille de Dassier // Par G. Ph. Benoist." *BMEP* 3. By permission of the Trustees of the British Museum. Department of Prints and Drawings.

ance, that it was "copied" from no. 62.1 "by James Anthony Dassier himself." Both face and reverse are illustrated in *Medallic Illustrations of the History of Great Britain, Plates CLXI–CLXX* (London, British Museum, 1911), Plate CLXIII, no. 1, where the medal is said to occur in copper and also in silver.

62.3. LINE ENGRAVING, BY HUBERT FRANÇOIS GRAVELOT, AFTER DASSIER.

A similar line engraving by Gravelot, slightly larger, has been described in no. 57–61.24. In that one, Gravelot joins a right profile very freely derived from the Roubiliac bust with a medallic frame and arrangement of letters clearly reminiscent of Dassier's medal. In the present engraving the actual image of Dassier is reversed, to left, in a similar frame and letter arrangement. The example reproduced above is in my own collection and is the only one I have heard of.

62.4. LINE ENGRAVING, BY G. PH. BENOIST, AFTER DASSIER.

An example of this engraving at the Pierpont Morgan Library (Bathurst Album of Popeana, p. 52) has below the image the additional lettering: "Poëte et Philosophe il réunit tous les suffrages, / Et vécut honoré ches un peuple de sages." / Æaris chés Lattré rue St Jacques."[1] Guillaume Philippe Benoist, French line-engraver, was born near Coutances, Normandy, in 1725, is said to have been educated in England, to have lived at Paris about 1760, and to have died at London in 1770 or at Paris in 1800. He specialized in small portrait engravings copied from medals (G. K. Nagler, *Neues allgemeines Künstler-Lexicon, 1*, München, 1825; E. Bénézeit, *Dictionaire . . . des Peintres, Dessinateurs et Graveurs, 1*, Librairie Gründ, 1948).

1. At the New York Public Library, in the Prints Division, is an engraving after Dassier (42a in their Grolier list) on an octavo sheet with five other heads in compartments, with the lettering: "Stahlstich von Carl Mayer's Kunst-Anstalt in Nürnberg. Verlag von C. A. Hartleven in Pesth." The firm of Carl Mayer was founded by him in Nürnberg in 1828. He died in 1868.

62.5. WEDGWOOD CAMEO MOLD, AFTER DASSIER. WEDGWOOD MUSEUM, BARLASTON.

We have noticed above (no. 57–61.21), that the five English editions of the *Wedgwood Catalogue* (1773, 1774, 1777, 1779, 1787) all listed a "Portrait Medallion" of Pope under the heading of "Modern" or "Illustrious Moderns." The size, however, was apparently 2 x 1¾ inches, which seems too small for either of the two cameo medallions of Pope known today in the working molds at the Barlaston Wedgwood Museum. One of these, a profile of the Roubiliac type, we have already seen (no. 57–61.21). The other, of the Dassier type, is known to me only in a photograph of an impression made at Barlaston from a "Plaster of Paris Working Mould" (no. 271–A–8). This is reproduced as no. 62.5. In a letter to his partner Bentley written in 1777 Josiah Wedgwood reports that John Flaxman the younger (1755–1826) has executed a new set of medallions of English poets.[1] The superiority of the Dassier derivative to the Roubiliac suggests that the Dassier is the replacement rather than the original.

The Dictionary of English Furniture (by Ralph Edwards and Percy Macquoid, revised by Edwards, London, 1954), *1*.293 and 296 (Fig. 223) describes and illustrates a neoclassic armchair, c. 1780, at Brocklesby Park, Lincolnshire, seat of the Earl of Yarborough. The top rail of this chair is "mounted with a blue Wedgwood medallion." The chair is one of a set, two of which were exhibited at the Royal Academy of Arts Winter Exhibition 1955–56, *English Taste in the Eighteenth Century*, no. 380 (Catalogue, p. 102). I am told that this set of chairs consists of eight, four having Wedgwood medallions of ancient authors, and four having Shakespeare, Milton, Dryden, and Pope. The size shown in the *Dictionary of Furniture* seems to accord literally with the term "medallion" used in the description. The dating as late as 1780 would suggest the Wedgwood medallion derived from Dassier rather than that derived from Roubiliac (no. 57–61.21).

1. Eliza Meteyard, *The Wedgwood Handbook, A Manual for Collectors* (London, 1875), p. 190.

62.6. GRISAILLE CEILING MEDALLION, C. 1781, BY BIAGIO REBECCA, AFTER DASSIER. VIVIENNE, LADY CAWLEY, BERRINGTON HALL, HEREFORDSHIRE.

Berrington Hall in Herefordshire was built about 1778–81 by the banker, Lord Mayor of London, and M.P. for London and Herefordshire Thomas Harley, a younger son of the Third Earl of Oxford and Mortimer. The architect was Henry Holland, Jr., and the grounds were landscaped by his father-in-law Capability Brown. The ceiling of the library is adorned with eight grisaille medallion portraits of English poets and savants,

left

62.5. [Wedgwood cameo medallion] 2⅞ x 2⁵⁄₁₆ in. plaque. Image 1½ in. high. Impression, from plaster working mold, no. 271 A–8. Wedgwood Museum, Barlaston.†

center

62.6. Grisaille ceiling medallion. Diameter about 18 in. Vivienne, Lady Cawley, Berrington Hall, Herefordshire.†

right

62.7. White paste on black 1⁵⁄₁₆ x 1³⁄₁₆ in. In a coiled paper frame gilt on front. Inscribed in relief letters vertically before the face: "BURCH R A". In pencil on paper backing: "Pope." In ink on side of paper frame: "125."

attributed to the decorative artist Biagio Rebecca (1735–1808).[1] Rebecca had come to England in 1761. He excelled in arabesques and in deceptive painting.[2] The Berrington medallions are painted with emphatic shadows, to look as much like stucco relief as possible.[1]

1. Christopher Hussey, "Berrington Hall, Herefordshire—II," *Country Life, 116* (9 December, 1954), 2102-05. See Plate 4 and p. 2105: "The painter, according to the sale catalogue of 1887, is 'reputed to be Rebecca the Dutch artist [sic] who spent many years on the work.' " And see James Lees-Milne, *Berrington Hall, Herefordshire, A Property of the National Trust* (London, Country Life Limited, for the National Trust, 1958), esp. pp. 1–6, 10, 16, and plate facing p. 9.

2. *Examiner,* 1808, p. 141 (Whitley Papers, Department of Prints and Drawings, British Museum), and W. T. Whitley, *Art in England, 1800–1820* (Cambridge, 1928), pp. 139–40.

62.7. CAST CAMEO MEDALLION, AFTER DASSIER, BY "BURCH, R.A.," C. 1777.

A friend found this in a London shop in 1951 and presented it to me. Edward Burch, miniature-painter and art-student was R.A. in 1771, exhibited at the Academy from 1771 to 1808, and was librarian of the Academy in 1780. At the Academy Exhibition of 1777, no. 24 was a head of Pope, a sulphur cast from a gem, by "E. Birch" [sic].

62.8. REPRODUCTIONS OF GEMS, BY JAMES TASSIE, MOSTLY AFTER DASSIER. SCOTTISH NATIONAL PORTRAIT GALLERY.

James Tassie (1735–99), a Glasgow Scot, settled in London in 1766 and achieved celebrity for his original portrait medallions in a vitreous paste or white enamel composition which he had earlier invented with a Dublin physician Henry Quin. Tassie made also many reproductions of gems, in "pastes . . . of the colour and lustre of the originals." His *Catalogue of Impressions . . . of Antique and Modern Gems* (1775) lists eight portraits of Pope, with names of three owners of the originals and the name of one artist, as follows:

2823. Mr. Pope, (Dr. Plumtree). *Cornelian.*
2824. —— ——
2825. —— ——
2826. —— —— (by Wray).
2827. —— —— (Bishop of Gloucester). *Cornelian.*
2828. —— —— *Onyx.*
2829. —— —— (Dr. Chauncey). *Berryl.*
2830. —— —— *Chalcedony.*[1]

A second catalogue of Tassie's gems, compiled by Rudolf Eric Raspe (Baron Munchausen), published in 1791, includes no fewer than twenty portraits of Pope, as follows:

Heads and busts of Alex. Pope.
14358 —— —— Octagon.
14359 —— ——

14360 CORNELIAN. Rev. *R. Burnside. Engraved by Wm. Pownall.*

14361 ———

14362 ———

14363 ———

14364 CORNELIAN. —— *Engraved by Wray.*

14365 —— —— WRAY. F.

14366 ———

14367 CHALCEDONY. ——

14368 CORNELIAN. Dr. *Warburton,* Bishop of Gloucester.

14369 ———

14370 CORNELIAN. Dr. *Plumtree.*

14371 CORNELIAN. Dr. *Chauncey.*

14372 ONYX. —— *(With a bezle.)*

14373 ———

14374 ———

14375 JASPER. ——

14376 ———

14377 —— ——[2]

Robert Bateman Wray (1715–79) was a gem-engraver and draftsman at Salisbury. A number of his intaglios appear in Tassie's catalogues, both classical and modern subjects. A portrait of Pope comes twelfth in a list of his works which he is said to have considered his best. He signed himself either WRAY FEC or ΟΥΡΑΙΟΣ ΕΠΟΙΕΙ (Leonard Forrer, *Biographical Dictionary of Medallists, 6* [London, 1907], 555). Laurence Binyon, *Catalogue of Drawings by British Artists . . . in the British Museum, 4* (London, 1907), 366–68, describes an album containing 54 outline drawings for gems by Wray, mostly classical subjects.

William Pownall was an engraver who seems known today only in the considerable series of his gems which appear in Tassie's catalogue (Forrer, *Biographical Dictionary of Medallists, 4* [1909], 677).

On the death of James Tassie in 1799, his business in Leicester Square was carried on by a nephew, William Tassie, and he on his death in 1860 left a large collection which is today housed at the Scottish National Portrait Gallery, in Edinburgh. James Tassie's reproductions of gems (nearly 16,000 in number) are represented by a complete set of casts in red sulphur, a complete corresponding set of white glass cameos, and a complete corresponding set of intaglios in transparent glass, each the color of the original stone.[3] The twenty gems identified as portraits of Pope in the 1791 *Catalogue,* nos. 14358–14377, may be described as follows:
Eleven of them, nos. 14358–14366, 14368, and 14370, are derived from Dassier's medal. Photographs of the red sulphur casts of these gems are reproduced here as no. 62.8. No. 14366 in this group, the only one without the fur collar, is identical with a mold preserved today at the Barlaston Wedgwood Museum, no. 816,[4] and with a basalt seal owned by Mr. Alfred Fairbank.

No. 14368, described in the 1791 *Catalogue* as a cornelian, the property of Dr. Warburton, Bishop of Gloucester (presumably the same as no. 2827 in the 1775 *Catalogue*—though Warburton died in 1779), perhaps is the same, or perhaps is not the same, as a cornelian which Warburton at some earlier time had given to Dr. John Brown, who died in 1766, the year when Tassie came to London.[5]

No. 14367 is derived from Richardson's etching ΟΥΤΟΣ ΕΚΕΙΝΟΣ of 1738 and is entered and illustrated as no. 42.8.

No. 14375 seems to be derived from Richardson's medallion for the title page of Pope's *Letters*, 1737. It is entered and illustrated as no. 43.4.

Nos. 14372, 14373, and 14377 possibly owe most to one or the other of Richardson's etchings of 1737 and 1738 just alluded to. No. 14377 possibly owes something also to Roubiliac. Cf. nos. 42.7, 43.4, and 57–61.17, a gem by Lorenz Natter.

Nos. 14369, 14371, 14374, 14376, are apparently not Pope. With no. 14374 compare Wedgwood medallion mold 271.B–8, Appendix 3, no. 26.

---

1. James Tassie, *A Catalogue of Impressions in Sulphur of Antique and Modern Gems from Which Pastes Are Made and Sold* (London: Printed for J. Murray, 1775), pp. vi, 96 (Library of Congress).

2. Rudolf Eric Raspe, *A Descriptive Catalogue of a General Collection of Ancient and Modern Engraved Gems, Cameos as Well as Intaglios* (London: James Tassie, 1791), pp. 747–48 (Library of Congress). Entries in French parallel those in English.

3. Leonard Forrer, *Biographical Dictionary of Medallists*, 6 (London, 1916), 22–34; John M. Gray, *James and William Tassie*, Edinburgh, 1894; Scottish National Portrait Gallery, leaflet *James and William Tassie, An Account of the Collection of Portrait Medallions and Gem-stone Reproductions at the Scottish National Portrait Gallery*; supplementary information in a letter from B. C. Skinner, Assistant Keeper, Scottish National Portrait Gallery.

4. The second edition of the *Wedgwood Catalogue* (1774) lists one intaglio of Pope, no. 12 among "Modern Subjects" (Eliza Meteyard, *The Wedgwood Handbook* [London, 1875], p. 123). The fifth edition (fourth in English, 1779) lists four intaglios of Pope, nos. 12, 50, 100, 269 (reprinted in Wolf Mankowitz, *Wedgwood* [London, 1953], pp. 223, 224, 227). Intaglio 100 reappears in the sixth edition of 1787 (*Wedgwood's Catalogue of Cameos, Intaglios, Medals, Bas-Reliefs, Busts, and Small Statues, Reprinted from the Edition of 1787*, ed. Eliza Meteyard, 1873). This would seem very likely to be the intaglio known today at the Barlaston Museum as "Intaglio Mould Catalogue no. 816," but bearing on its oval frame the lettering "Pope. / 100."

5. Dr. John Brown (1715–66), best known as the author of the *Estimate of the Manners and Principles of the Times*, 1757, had become the friend of Warburton through his *Essay on Satire, Occasioned by the Death of Mr. Pope*, published in 1745. In 1766 Brown committed suicide. On 9 October Warburton wrote to Hurd: "Poor Browne is dead. . . . the ring mentioned in his Executor's letter I suppose, is one I gave him, with Mr. Pope's head" (*Letters from a Late Eminent Prelate to One of his Friends* [London, *circa* 1808], p. 283). In the *Gentleman's Magazine*, *61* (February 1791), 104 and plate facing, Fig. 9, a correspondent describes and illustrates with a crude cut: "a portrait from an impression of a seal, under which, in the hand-writing of Bp. Warburton, it is said, "I have given this impression of Mr. Pope's head, lest the medal cannot be got. It is equal in workmanship and likeness.' Round the edge is a Greek inscription, too much worn to be read, but ending with. . . . ΛΗΣ." See Appendix 1, 67.3, for a suggestion of the context of Warburton's writing. The correspondent of 1791 was apparently not in possession of the seal itself.

In Volume 2 of his *Poetical Works of Alexander Pope* (London, 1853), Advertisement, p. iv, Robert Carruthers reports that he has received from Sir Edward F. Bromhead, Bart., of Thurlby Hall, Lincolnshire, "an impression of a portrait seal, on a ring presented by Pope to Warburton. . . . a good likeness of the poet, apparently reduced from Richardson's profile. The ring is inscribed, 'Don. A. Pope, G. Warburton— G. Warburton, John Brown.' . . . Dr. Brown left the ring to Dr. William Stephens, who left it by will, to his wife, now Mrs. Butt, Trentham, Staffordshire. . . . Mrs. Butt says: 'The ring has been much worn, but the lettering is quite legible. The red cornelian is also slightly scratched, but the portrait is perfect and uninjured.' " A small line cut is "subjoined." (The same account and the cut appear in Carruthers' *Life of Alexander Pope* [2nd Edition, 1857], p. 461.)

The two crude line cuts (*Gentleman's Magazine* 1791 and Carruthers 1853) are different enough from each other and from the Tassie gem no. 14368 to raise a question whether Warburton did not own more than one seal portrait of Pope.

14358   14359   14360   14361

14362   14363   14364   14365

14366   14368   14370

62.8. Red sulphur casts. Height of no. 14360 (without frame) 1 in. Tassie *Catalogue* 1791, nos. 14358–14366, 14368, 14370. No. 14365 is inscribed vertically along the right lower edge: "WRAY. F." Scottish National Portrait Gallery, Edinburgh.

62.9. Impression in sealing wax from a glass intaglio. Diameter 1⅛ in. "ALEXA // NDER POPE". Professor Geoffrey Tillotson, Birkbeck College, University of London.

62.10a. Copper. Diameter 1.65 in. "ALEXANDER // POPE // VIVIER F". By permission of the Trustees of the British Museum. Department of Coins and Medals.

62.10b. Reverse of no. 62.10a. "NATUS / LONDINI / AN. M.DC.LXXXVIII. / OBIIT / AN. M.DCC.XLIV." Exergue: "SERIES NUMISMATICA / UNIVERSALIS VIRORUM ILLUSTRIUM / M.DCCC.XXIV. / DURAND EDIDIT".

277

62.9. GLASS INTAGLIO, AFTER DASSIER. PROFESSOR GEOFFREY TILLOTSON.

Professor Geoffrey Tillotson, Birkbeck College, The University of London, is the owner of a transparent colorless glass intaglio about 1⅛ inches in diameter and about ¼ inch thick with a frosted rim. Professor Tillotson kindly sent me the excellent impression in sealing wax which I reproduce.

62.10 a and b. COPPER MEDAL, AFTER DASSIER, BY M. VIVIER, 1824.

Hawkins, *Medallic Illustrations,* ed. Franks and Grueber (1885), *1.*4 and 2.584, no. 225, describes this as "one of an extensive series of medallic portraits, executed in Paris, and representing illustrious men of all countries." Colonel M. H. Grant, *Catalogue of British Medals Since 1760,* Part I (reprinted from *The British Numismatic Journal,* 22, 1936–37), p. 30, says that this medal was made by "M. Vivier" and that "The Durand Series was issued twice, first in Paris, later in Munich, when *Monachii* was engraved on the rims." Matthias Nicolas Marie Vivier was born at Paris in 1788, was active at the Paris Salon from 1819 to 1833, and died about 1859. He did a number of medals for Durand's *Galerie métallique* (L. Forrer, *Biographical Dictionary of Medallists,* 6 [London, 1916], 291). Amedée Durand, Parisian *éditeur* of medals, died c. 1848 (Hawkins, 2.724).

Professor Paul Fussell, Jr., of Rutgers University, is the owner of a plaster medal apparently molded from Vivier's, with blank reverse. A set of several hundred similar plaster medals, depicting British and Continental worthies of the seventeenth and eighteenth centuries, came from a Connecticut family collection to the Lyman Allyn Museum at New London.

Alexander Pope. By William Hoare, type of 1739–1740. Collection of Mr. and Mrs. James M. Osborn. See no. 63.4.

·11·

1739-1740, c. 1742
WILLIAM HOARE OF BATH
(1707?-92)

THE MAIN EVIDENCE concerning the early career of William Hoare is the article in Chalmers' *Biographical Dictionary*, 1814.[1] The source of this article is said to be information communicated by Hoare's son, Prince Hoare (1755–1834), Foreign Secretary of the Royal Academy. According to this account, William Hoare was born at Eye, near Ipswich, came to London, presumably at a rather early age, studied under the history painter Giuseppe Grisoni, and then went to Italy. At Rome he lived with the sculptors Scheemakers and Delvaux (whom he had known in London); he studied in the school of Francesco Fernandi, called Imperiali, and was a fellow student with Pompeo Batoni. He stayed for nine years. At the end of the year 1738, George Vertue records in his *Note Book:* "Mr. Hoarde Crayon painter, returned from abroad."[2]

He must have gained a reputation very rapidly at Bath, for in 1742, on the opening of the Bath Mineral Water Hospital, he was appointed to the Committee of Assistants (or Governors).[3] In this year, the year of the opening of the Hospital, he is said to have

1. Alexander Chalmers, *The General Biographical Dictionary, A New Edition, 18,* London, 1814.

2. Vertue 3.85. At the British Museum is a large red crayon (or "chalk") head of Newton framed by an ouroboros (1894-12-19-1: Binyon 2.313-15, Hoare no. 12). A corresponding large reversed etching in black ink (P. 8-217–not in BMEP) is inscribed "Hoare ft aquâ forti 1734." These may well have been done in Italy.

3. Committee Book and Book of House Visitors, 25 June 1742, Royal Mineral Water Hospital archives, Bath. Mr. H. Bond, Senior Non-Medical Officer of the Hospital, tells me that the Committee Book shows that Hoare was appointed to the Committee of Governors 1 May 1742. The British Museum preserves a letter concerning a copy of a picture of "Thurlow," written by Hoare at Bath to the London litterateur Thomas Birch, 23 February 1740 (Add. MS. 4310, Birch Letters, *11,* no. 390).

painted the lively and realistic oil picture, still hanging on the main stairs at the Hospital, of Doctor William Oliver and Mr. Jeremiah Peirce, surgeon, examining patients—with an elevation and ground plan lettered "BATH HOSPITAL" in the background.[4] "1742" again is the date inscribed on one of his crayon paintings of Lord Chesterfield,[5] who in 1744 was the third President of the Hospital.[6] In the same year (1742) he did the crayon painting of himself which many years later at the request of the Governors he presented to the Hospital.[7] And in the same year or the next he is said to have married a London merchant's daughter, Elizabeth Barker. His eldest daughter Mary was baptized at Walcot Church, Bath, 4 September 1744.[8]

In Vertue's *Note Book,* under the year 1742, appears the following entry:

Crayon painting has met with so much encouragement of late years here that several painters, those that had been in Italy to study, as Knapton, Pond, Hoare, etc., for the practice of painting in oil, found at their return that they could not make any extraordinary matter of it, turned to painting in crayons, and several made great advantage of it. It looking pleasant and covered with a glass (large gold frames), was much commended for the novelty—and the painters finding it much easier in the execution than oil colors, readily came to it.[9]

The Chalmers *Dictionary* account says that in his early days at Bath Hoare found the demand for crayons so great that he sent to Rosalba the celebrated Venetian crayon "paintress" and got two of her fancy pictures as models—"Apollo with his Lyre" and "A Nymph Crowned with Vernal Flowers." Later entries by Vertue are more respectful of the new art and its leading professor. Thus by 1749:

amongst many ingenious artists that are in England in several degrees or sorts of painters, Mr. Hoare of Bath has had great employments at Bath by most or many people of distinction for many years. He chiefly excelled in portrait-

4. The label on the frame, giving the date 1742, seems early. The hospital opened for the reception of patients 18 May 1742. Dr. William Oliver was Physician of the Hospital, 1740–61, and Jeremiah Peirce was Surgeon, 1740–61 (*History of the General Hospital Now Known as The Royal Mineral Water Hospital,* Bath [c. 1888], pp. 27, 156). Hoare's painting was shown in London at the *Exhibition of The Society of Artists of Great Britain* in 1762, no. 38, as "A picture intended to be given to the Bath Hospital." Horace Walpole adds the identification, "Middling; Drs. Oliver and Pierce examining patients" (Algernon Graves, *The Society of Artists of Great Britain 1760–1791* [London, 1907], p. 119; and NPG copy of *Catalogues of the Exhibitions Held by the Society of Artists 1760–1791* [with Walpole annotations], 1762, p. 3).

5. In the Stanhope collection at Chevening (NPG Photograph 4366, 1947). A similar crayon painting, 28 x 14 in., may be seen at the Victoria and Albert Museum (P. 11–1943), and an oil painting, 36 x 26¼ in., at the National Portrait Gallery (158).

6. The second President of the Hospital was Ralph Allen, in 1742; the fourth was The Lord Viscount Palmerston, 1750 (*History of the General Hospital,* p. 153). On Palmerston, see also no. 64.1.

7. *History of the General Hospital,* p. 44, for the presentation in 1780. The date of painting is recorded on the label attached to the gilt carved-wood-and-gesso frame of this softly modeled and attractive picture, which still hangs in the Board Room of the Hospital.

8. Reginald W. M. Wright, "William Hoare, R. A., of Bath," *Apollo, 31* (February, 1940), 39–43.

9. Vertue 3.109.

crayon-paintings, for which he was reckoned amongst the best of the professors, as also in oil-painting from the life. . . . he lived in a handsome genteel manner, being of a fruitful genius, with great variety in his decoration or dresses. . . . this summer he set out for France, Flanders, and Holland. . . . he makes that [Bath] his continual residence—he has had better success than any other painter there before him.[10]

A measure of the early and rapid success of William Hoare appears in the fact that in 1751 he had succeeded in placing five of his crayon portraits, or copies, in the Earl of Pembroke's collection at Wilton. These were reported in a Wilton guide book of that year, and the "honour" thus done to "Mr. Hoare of Bath" was duly noted by Vertue.[11]

Hoare's early and middle years were crowded with labors for the greater statesmen of the day and their families—especially the political clique of the Pitts, Grenvilles, and Pelhams. He is most readily consulted today in his portraits of this caliber—larger oils and a certain number of pastel paintings, the oils especially done in the style of metallic rotundity (firm, expressionless faces, hard wigs, sloping shoulders, heavy coats and vests occasionally popping open, embroidered lapels, feathers, seals, ribbons, and stars), the conservative convention which he developed from Riley and Richardson and shared with Richardson's son-in-law Thomas Hudson so closely as to make their conceptions of the affluent or eminent middle-aged male scarcely distinguishable. At the National Portrait Gallery, for instance, may be seen the massive squadron of William Pitt, First Earl of Chatham (no. 1050, from Hoare's studio), Charles Fitzroy, Second Duke of Grafton (no. 723), John Carteret, Second Earl Granville (no. 1778, wondrously blue, stuffed and uncomfortable), Thomas Pelham-Holles, First Duke of Newcastle (no. 757), Henry Pelham (no. 221), and Richard Temple Grenville, Second Earl Temple (no. 258).

The more delicate and interesting style of which Hoare was capable as a crayon artist (both in drawings and "paintings") is less well known today. At the British Museum, are a considerable number of large crayon drawings ascribed to Hoare, nearly all very coldly if finely worked on squared gray paper, apparently studio models for paintings or perhaps engraver's copies. But another, a three-quarter-length drawing in black and red crayon of the aged artist Christian Friedrich Zincke at work on a miniature, stands apart from the rest in the freedom and interest of its technique, and this has under it an extended pencil inscription with the date 1752, apparently in the hand of Hoare.[12] At the Courtauld Institute of Art, in the Witt Collection, three black and red crayon drawings, all profiles, show the same qualities of line and a certain tender humor: a full-length of a little girl in an embroidered dress, seated, inscribed in ink "Anne Hoare"; a bust-length of an elderly lady in a wide-brimmed hat; and a bust-

10. Vertue 3.149. See no. 59.2 and Vertue 3.152 for the return from Italy in January 1750 of Hoare's "young" brother, the sculptor Prince Hoare.

11. Richard Cowdry, *A Description of the Pictures . . . At Wilton* (London, 1751), pp. 40, 72. Vertue alludes to all five pictures apparently as "coppys in Crayons." Though the name of Cowdry, a Wilton guide, is attached to the work, Vertue believes it is

inspired by the Norfolk virtuoso Sir Andrew Fountaine, subject of one of the crayons (Vertue 3.156–157). Vertue's last reference to Hoare (3.161) records his [temporary] removal to London in the spring of 1752.

12. Binyon, *Catalogue of Drawings*, 2.313–315, Hoare no. 13 (1860–7–28–167).

length of a gentleman with a squarish head, inscribed in contemporary pencil: "Dr. Charlton. W. Hoare d^t 1755."[13]

There can hardly be any doubt that one of Hoare's patrons and friends at Bath was the philanthropist Ralph Allen, of Prior Park, and that Hoare was a familiar figure in his household. One contemporary, the Reverend Richard Graves (1715–1804), a protégé of Allen's, recalled meeting at Prior Park three persons especially—Dr. Warburton, Mr. Fielding, and "Mr. William Hoare, the Painter. . . . not only one of the most virtuous, friendly and inoffensive men, but one of the best classical scholars, both in Greek and Latin, with whom I was ever acquainted."[14] Graves was a teacher of the younger Prince Hoare. The Chalmers *Dictionary* article also speaks of Hoare's "soon" getting to know Allen, of his "always being a welcome visitor" at Prior Park, and of his meeting there Warburton and Pope.

We may be left in some doubt as to the earliest date when Hoare portrayed either Allen or his nephew-in-law Warburton.[15] If he met Pope at Prior Park, he must have met him no later than the summer of 1743.[16] It is certain enough that he drew at least one sketch of Pope at Prior Park—surreptitiously (see no. 64.1). This was not widely known until 1797. But when Hoare died at Bath in 1792, he seems to have enjoyed the reputation of having been honored by Pope as a sitter.

> Whose pencil Pitt and Pelham have approv'd,
> Nay, Pope has dignify'd and Allen lov'd.[17]

About eleven years after his death, his son Prince Hoare, Corresponding Secretary of the Royal Academy, in a conversation with the Academician Joseph Farington, "mentioned that when Pope sat to His Father for a Portrait, He showed an anxiety to conceal the deformity of his person, & had a cloak thrown over his shoulders, & while Mr. Hoare

13. Courtauld Institute of Art, *Hand-List of Drawings in the Witt Collection* (London University, 1956), nos. 733, 1975, 3574.

14. Richard Graves, *Trifling Anecdotes of the Late Ralph Allen*, quoted by F. Kilvert, *Ralph Allen and Prior Park* (Bath, 1857), pp. 4, 17.

15. It was in September of 1758, for example, that he went to Allen's summer residence at Weymouth to "draw a picture of Mr. Allen, for the Exeter Hospital" (*Letters from a Late Eminent Prelate to One of His Friends* [London, c. 1808], p. 196, Warburton to Hurd, from Weymouth, 3 September 1758). Another portrait of Allen by Hoare is the small medallion profile to the left engraved by R. H. Cromek and dated at Bath, 1764. An earlier possibility is the crayon three-quarter-length standing, in the British Museum (Binyon, Hoare 5). Only in 1765 (after Allen's death) do we hear of his drawing Warburton—apparently at Prior Park—the picture being intended for Hurd. Yet it is apparent that he had drawn Warburton before, perhaps a good many times. "Your picture is finished. Hoare says it is much the best he has ever drawn of me" (*Letters from a Late Eminent Prelate*, p. 270, Warburton to Hurd, from Prior Park,

6 October 1765). Two portraits of Warburton by Hoare, both dated 1765 and both given by Warburton to Hurd, are today at Hartlebury Castle: an oil and a crayon (James Nankivell, *The Collection of Portraits in Oils of Bishop Richard Hurd at Hartlebury Castle*, Worcester, 1953, pp. 22–24). The crayon is apparently the source of the profile engraving by J. Neagle ("from the original sketch made by Mr. Hoare of Bath in 1765") which appears as one frontispiece of the *Letters from a Late Eminent Prelate*. An engraving after Hoare by Jn. Hall which is the frontispiece of *The Works of . . . Warburton*, *1*, with *Life* by Hurd, London, 1811, is from an "Original Picture in Gloucester Palace."

16. *Correspondence* 4.436.

17. Reginald W. M. Wright, "William Hoare, R. A., of Bath," *Apollo, 31* (February 1940), 43, quotes this couplet after a description of the monument to Hoare by Chantrey in Bath Abbey which Hoare's son Prince Hoare erected in 1828. The couplet does not appear on the monument. It has, however, the authentic ring of the period. It may well be from a newspaper or periodical notice of Hoare at the time of his death.

was painting that part of the picture He came behind Him & said 'He need not be very particular about the Shoulders.' "[18]

18. Joseph Farington, R. A., *The Farington Diary*, ed. James Greig, 2 (London, 1923), 190: 12 February 1804.

63.1 and 2. ENGRAVINGS FROM AN UNTRACED OIL PAINTING, BY WILLIAM HOARE OF BATH, ONCE IN THE BUCKINGHAM COLLECTION AT STOWE.

In November and December of 1739 Pope, in search of mineral waters and health, was off on a trip to Bristol and then Bath and Prior Park. He wrote back long journal-like letters to Martha Blount. On 27 December, lodged securely with Ralph Allen at Prior Park, outside Bath, he wrote her a gossipy letter in which among a great many other things he said: "tell Mr. Nugent that I will sit for my Picture for him, as I once did for his Lady,[1] and that I believe that it will be a very excellent picture, because I am very much alterd for the better."[2]

Pope stayed on at Prior Park (going little into the city of Bath)[3] until mid-February, when he returned to Twickenham and, with his new-found health, immediately fell into a prolonged fury of "grottofying." Some weeks later, on 2 April of this year, his friend Mr. Robert Nugent was himself at Bath. Perhaps he had just seen or picked up a new property at the studio of William Hoare when he sat down to write a letter to Mrs. Whiteway (Swift's cousin, nurse, and amanuensis) in Dublin. Taking up with her a delicate matter of some letters of Alexander Pope's which Pope wished Dean Swift would return, Mr. Nugent threw in parenthetically:

> I shall say nothing of the picture [of Swift], because I am sure you remember it. I must beg that you will let Mr. Bindon know I would have the picture no more than a head upon a three-quarter cloth, to match the one I now have of Mr. Pope.[4]

Mr. Nugent was at that date married, for a second time, and as a third husband, to Pope's friend Mrs. Anne Craggs-Newsham-Knight. After her death in 1756 Nugent inherited the estate of Gosfield in Essex. In less than two months he married a third time, and he had by this marriage a daughter, Mary Elizabeth, who became in 1775 the wife of George Grenville, who in 1784 became Marquis of Buckingham and master of the great house at Stowe, where we have seen in Pope's own day his friend William Kent engaged in reshaping the garden for Lord Cobham and putting up the Temple of Worthies with its niche for the stone bust of Pope. Robert Nugent became in 1776 Earl Nugent. He lived in his later years at Gosfield, the family home of the Knights.[5] About the time of his death in 1788, a number of paintings (including miniatures of the Craggs, Newsham, Knight, and Nugent families and their friends) seem to have passed into the Stowe collection.[6] The pictures with which we are immediately concerned are traceable for the first time in J. Seeley's *Stowe. A Description of the House and Gardens,* published at Buckingham in 1797 Thus:

pp. 50–51 The Billiard Room
Dr. Swift, by Samuel Bindon, sent to Lord Nugent, with a copy of verses, by
   Dr. Dunkin.
Mr. Pope, given by him to Mr. Craggs; by Hudson.

Craggs had died in 1721, rather early for him to be associated with the image of Pope in middle age which we are to discover. But Pope's early devotion to Craggs (publicized in the Westminster Abbey epitaph) was of course better known than his later and more casual relation with Craggs' posthumous brother-in-law Nugent. In the next Stowe guide which I have seen, J. Seeley's large and fancy *Stowe. A Description of the House and Gardens* (Buckingham, 1817), the portraits of Pope and Swift have been moved to "The Hall" (p. 34), but the entries read the same except for the addition of the term "(original)" to Pope. The large collection of miniatures, which in 1788 and 1797 were in her Ladyship's Dressing Room, have been moved to the Manuscript Room (pp. 51–53), and here we find for the first time the names of certain ancestors and family friends, including "Opposite the Chimney. . . . Alexander Pope, given by him to Anne Knight, afterwards wife of Robert Nugent." (See no. 5.12.)[7]

Meanwhile, however, another source of information, and misinformation, must be reckoned with. The oil painting of Pope had been engraved, along with the miniature, from drawings by Gardner, for the edition of Pope's *Works* by Bowles in 1806. And here the lettering gives the oil painting to "Richardson." (See no. 63.1.) Subsequent engravings within a few years cast two votes for Hudson and one more for Richardson (no. 61.2).

The Second Duke of Buckingham (grandson of Mary Nugent), after succeeding to the title in 1839 and immediately sweeping out nearly 1,000 pictures and selling them at Christie's for only about £600,[8] was forced to sell nearly the whole of the collections in a second, grand Stowe sale of forty days beginning 15 August 1848. These collections are described in a Christie *Catalogue of the Contents* and more amply in Henry Rumsey Forster's subsequent *Stowe Catalogue Priced and Annotated*, London, 1848. The family miniatures were withheld for a later sale in London.[9] Something, however, of the old guidebook entry for the Pope miniature seems to come over into the entry for the oil painting in the Christie *Catalogue* and thence into Forster's enlargement. The name of Mrs. Knight now replaces that of her indeed less plausible brother. The entry for the painting is a curious conglomerate:

Private Dining-Room
No. 296. Pope; this was given by him to Mrs. Knight—(Richardson).
                           —Forster, p. 176

The compiler has apparently capitulated to the engravers in the matter of the attribution.[10]

Thomas Hudson, a Devonshire man, pupil and son-in-law of Jonathan Richardson, worked in the neighborhood of Exeter for several years in the later 1730s, but by the autumn of 1740 he had a house in London and there became the teacher of Joshua Reynolds.[11] About the same time he made visits to Bath.[12] Pope's friend and principal painter, the aging and failing Jonathan Richardson, announced his retirement at the end of the year 1740 (p. 146), yet we know that he painted Pope as late as 1742. There is no reason why either Hudson or Richardson could not have painted a portrait of Pope which got into the Stowe collection. Nevertheless, the contradictory attributions of the period 1797–1848 (unhappily repeated often since then) cannot be taken seriously. It would seem nearly certain that the painting of Pope which was sold at Stowe in 1848 was one which Pope had given to Robert Nugent (not to Craggs, and not to Mrs. Knight), and that this painting was done at Bath during the winter of 1739–40.

That the painting at Stowe, which we know through engravings of the period 1806–35, was the original of a type which was the property, not of Richardson or of Hudson, but of the Bath painter William Hoare, is a conclusion which I hope will emerge clearly from the immediately following entries.

The painting of Pope was bought at the Stowe sale for 70 guineas by Farrer, for Sir Robert Peel.[13] It does not reappear until the sale of *Peel Heirlooms—Pictures from the Statesmen's Gallery at Drayton Manor,* held 6 and 7 December 1917, by Robinson,

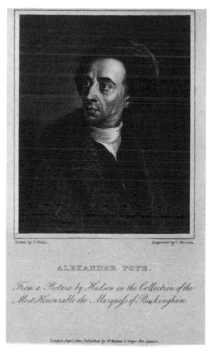

63.1. Stipple engraving. Picture 4 x 3¼ in. "Engraved by C. Picart, from a drawing by Gardner. / ALEXANDER POPE, / From a Picture by Richardson, / in the Marquis of Buckingham's Collection at Stowe. / Published by Cadell & Davies, Strand, and the other Proprietors, May 1. 1807." *Grolier* 48. *BMEP* 26. Frontispiece to vol. 1 of W. L. Bowles's edition of Pope's *Works,* 1806.

63.2. Line engraving. Picture 3¾ x 3 in. "Drawn by T. Uwins. // Engraved by C. Warren. / ALEXANDER POPE. / From a Picture by Hudson in the Collection of the / Most Honourable the Marquess of Buckingham. / London, Sept.ᵣ 1, 1821; Published by W. Walker, 8 Grays Inn Square." *Grolier* 49. *BMEP* 28. *Effigies Poeticae or The Portraits of the British Worthies* (1824), 2.53.

Fisher, and Harding: p. 9, lot 90, "A Portrait of Pope. Richardson. 30 in. by 25." It was sold to Swift for 210 guineas.[14]

The portrait has not been further traced.[15] Two engravings are reproduced above. The first, Picart's engraving after Gardner's drawing, dated 1807, and used in Bowles' edition of the *Works of Pope,* 1806, bears, despite an odd tilt of the head, a stronger facial resemblance to nos. 63.3 and 63.4, the two best authenticated repetitions from the hand of Hoare himself. This interpretation is followed in a later engraving of smaller size: "Alexander Pope. / Engraved by Alais from a Picture in the Possession / of the Marquis of Buckingham. / London, Published Sep^t 1st 1821, by Thos McLean, 26, Haymarket;" and in another, embellished with a background of column, drape, and landscape features, with the lettering: "Alexander Pope. / From a Picture by Richardson, / in the Duke of Buckingham's Collection at Stowe. / London: William Darton, 58, Holborn Hill, 2 mo. 26. 1824."

The second of the two engravings now reproduced, by C. Warren, after T. Uwins' drawing, for the collection entitled *Effigies Poeticae* (1824),[16] has the head more upright but at the same time a somewhat knottier or craggier face. This interpretation is followed and heightened in what seems a better, even though perhaps derivative, engraving, that by J. Posselwhite for the *Gallery of Portraits* published by Charles Knight, Under the Superintendence of the Society for the Diffusion of Useful Knowledge, in 1835.[17] This image and the attribution to Hudson which accompanies it are the clues to the Stowe portrait perhaps best known today.[18]

Edward W. Brayley and John Britton, *The Beauties of England and Wales, 1* (1801), 313, find Pope, by Hudson, in the State Drawing Room at Stowe and observe: "This great Poet is represented with a care worn and sallow countenance."

For thirty years, at least, or from the engraving by Picart in 1806 to that by Posselwhite in 1835, this picture, always meticulously located in the Buckingham collection at Stowe, must have been the best-known portrait of Pope.

William Hoare lived and practiced portrait-painting at Bath for about 50 years after the winter of 1739–40 when Pope, staying at Prior Park near Bath, seems to have had his portrait painted. The series of paintings which now follow suggest that Hoare had a property in this image of Pope and that from time to time he turned out examples of it, in oil or in pastel, with variations of color, at the demand of various patrons.

1. This perhaps refers to the miniature discussed in no. 5.12 and p. 284, though presumably Pope did not sit directly for that miniature. The date when Allen got into his new house Prior Park is uncertain. See no. 64.1, n. 10.

2. *Correspondence 4.*212.

3. *Correspondence 4.*205, 211: to Bethel 27 November 1739, and to Martha Blount 27 December 1739.

4. *Correspondence 4.*233. Phrases such as "half length" and "three quarters," as used in the artists' language of this time, often refer, not to the figure, but to the canvas. See a bill of Richardson's quoted by R. W. Goulding and C. K. Adams, *Catalogue of the Pictures Belonging to His Grace the Duke of Portland* (Cambridge, 1936), p. 475.

5. Henry Rumsey Forster, *Stowe* (1848), p. 151: "The collection had been formed out of the accumulation of several families; from Gosfield, the Seat of Earl Nugent. . . ." And see Claud Nugent, *Memoirs of Robert Earl Nugent,* London, 1898.

6. See B. Seeley, *Stowe. A Description of the House and Garden,* Buckingham, 1788, p. 43, "Her Ladyship's Dressing Room." A variety of crayons and drawings by Lady Buckingham herself and her copy of Mrs. Siddons as the Tragic Muse are recorded.

7. The same three pictures appear in J. Seeley's

Stowe. A Description (Buckingham, 1827), pp. 45, 49, 199; in R. Chandler's *Stowe. A Description* (Buckingham, 1832), pp. 41, 45, 64; and in Calkin and Budd's *Stowe. A Description* (London, 1838), pp. 41–42, 90. "Mr. Craggs" in the miniature entry progresses to "Secretary Craggs" (1827) and "the Right Honourable James Craggs" (1838). And in 1838 the name of the painter of Swift's portrait, always incorrect in the "Samuel," is lost entirely.

8. "For some weeks after this sale, it is said the shops in Wardour Street and the neighborhood were lined with old pictures—many of them sufficiently large to cover the side of a room" (Forster, *Stowe*, 1848, p. 151).

9. See no. 5.12.

10. "The names of the painters are given as in the original catalogue: in cases where no name appears, the artist is unknown" (Forster, p. 151). Cf. *Catalogue of the Contents of Stowe House . . . which will be Sold by Auction, by Messrs. Christie and Manson, On the Premises, . . . August 15th, 1848*, p. 182 (23rd Day's Sale): "Richardson. 296 Pope: This was given by him to Mrs. Knight."

The portrait of Swift was no. 301 on p. 177 (Forster), West Staircase. For its subsequent fate, so far as known, see Frederick Falkiner's account of Swift's portraits in Swift's *Prose Works,* ed. Temple Scott, *12* (1908), 24. The name of the painter was not Samuel but Francis Bindon.

Falkiner accepts both the Swift and the Pope portraits at Stowe in 1848 as the ones alluded to by Nugent in his letter of April 1740 to Mrs. Whiteway.

11. Evelyn M. Davies, *The Life and Works of Thomas Hudson (1701–1779)* (unpublished M.A. Thesis at the University of London Library, 1938), p. 27, quotes documents for Exeter. William Cotton, *Sir Joshua Reynolds and his Work* (London, 1856), pp. 43–49, quotes letters of 1740 concerning Reynolds' apprenticeship to Hudson.

12. When Reynolds reached London on 13 October 1740 and went to Hudson's house, Richardson's daughter (Hudson's wife) told him that Mr. Hudson was not at home. He was "at the Bath" (Cotton, *Reynolds,* 1856, p. 47). The lettering of a mezzotint by Faber after a portrait by Hudson of the Bath arbiter Beau Nash says the portrait was painted in 1740 (J. Ch. Smith *1.399*, Faber 253). Faber's mezzotint (1754) after Hudson's portrait of Ralph Allen (J. Ch. Smith

1.302, Faber 6) shows Allen holding a piece of paper on which appears a date which looks like 1744. A good example of the portrait inscribed "T. Hudson pinx" is at Hartlebury Castle. Hudson had much employment by 1742 and 1744 (Vertue *3.111*, 121).

The Stowe guides, 1788–1838, list a number of pictures which suggest connections between both Hudson and Reynolds and the amateur painter Mary Nugent, Lady Buckingham. Such connections tend to explain but not to validate the attribution in 1797 of the portrait of Pope to Hudson.

13. Forster, *Stowe* (1848), p. 176, lot 296. Peel's autograph note recording his purchase of the portrait from Farrer and setting down some facts about Mrs. Knight and Earl Nugent and his daughter is today at the Fitzwilliam Museum (MS2–1949–No. 77).

14. A copy of the catalogue at the National Portrait Gallery has the dates 29 and 30 November 1917 on the cover corrected in ink to 6 and 7 December, and the price "220.10" entered for lot 90. I take the name of the buyer from a manuscript continuation of Redford's *Art Sales* seen in 1952 at Parke-Bernet Galleries by a friend.

This portrait of Pope is nowhere, so far as I have noticed in the documents, specifically referred to as an "oil painting." But Nugent's reference in 1740 to a "three-quarter cloth," the size 30 x 25 inches (supplied for the first time in 1917), and the absence of the term "pastel" from the record, are good grounds for supposing an oil.

15. Mr. F. H. Swift told me in 1961 that he could remember nothing of the portrait, and that his records had been destroyed during World War II by enemy action.

16. *Effigies Poeticae or the Portraits of the British Worthies,* 2, 53, Pl. 96, published by James Carpenter and Son, Old Bond Street.

17. Vol. 5, p. 164. And see *Cabinet Portrait Gallery of British Worthies* (London, 1847), *12.16*; George C. Craik and Charles MacFarlane, *Pictorial History of England* (New York, 1851), *4.707*; Joseph Gostwick, *English Poets* (New York, 1875), p. 88; Charles W. Moulton, *Library of Literary Criticism of English and American Authors* (New York, 1902), *3.145*.

18. See *Pope and his Poetry,* ed. E. W. Edmunds, (*Poetry and Life* Series, ed. W. H. Hudson), George Harrap and Co., 1913; and H. V. D. Dyson, ed. *Pope* (Oxford, 1933), frontispiece.

69.9 a and b. CRAYON PAINTING (PASTEL), BY WILLIAM HOARE. NATIONAL PORTRAIT GALLERY NO. 299.

National Portrait Gallery No. 299 is a pastel "painting" 23¼ x 17¼ inches on rough gray paper folded back over a stretcher on all four sides. Written down the back on the right-hand fold of the paper, in a bold, squarish pencilled hand (the capitals being about ¾ inch high) is this inscription: "This Picture belongs to Mr Andrews / of Hill-

63.3a. Crayons on paper. 23¼ x 17¼ in. Background reddish brown; outer garment bright blue (like BCC 196 Larkspur); cap and waistcoat dark blue (like BCC 90 Midnight); eyebrows brown-gray; eyes dark indigo-blue. Inscribed in pencil on back: "This Picture belongs to Mr Andrews / of Hillhouse. // Wm Hoare / Bath. / 1784". National Portrait Gallery no. 299.

63.3b. Part of inscription on back of 63.3.

house. / / Wm Hoare / Bath. / 1784."[1] (The hand bears a sufficient resemblance to that of a long inscription, clearly by Hoare, below a crayon drawing of Hoare's friend, C. F. Zincke, the miniaturist, at the British Museum.) John Andrews, Esq., of Hillhouse, in Gloucestershire, died in September 1786 near Exeter.[2] I believe the most plausible interpretation of the inscription is that it is a memorandum of identification made by Hoare in his studio after Mr. Andrews, traveling through Bath, had ordered the picture, had perhaps even paid for it, but had failed to return and claim it. (See no. 63.9.)

At any rate, the picture later belonged to William Hoare's son Prince Hoare, the Foreign Secretary of the Royal Academy, and either at his death in 1834 or before it, he conveyed it to a good friend, the Rev. Charles Townsend, of Preston, near Brighton, who in turn, dying in 1870, bequeathed it to the National Portrait Gallery.[3]

The portrait is described by George Scharf in the National Portrait Gallery *Catalogue* of 1888, p. 360. It is reproduced in *The Academy, 52* (3 July 1897), 13, to illustrate Francis Thompson's essay on Pope, "Academy Portrait XXXIV"; in Lionel Cust, *The National Portrait Gallery, 1* (London, 1901), 215; in *Zeitschrift für bildende Kunst,* New Series *15* (1904), 90; in Edmund Gosse, *English Literature* (1906), 3.196; and in George Paston, *Mr. Pope* (London, 1909), 2.500; in W. L. Macdonald, *Pope and His Critics* (London, 1951), p. 123; and on a postcard by the National Portrait Gallery.

It was exhibited at the National Portrait Gallery Exhibition in 1961.

1. A note at the National Portrait Gallery in the hand of George Scharf shows that when he found the inscription, on removing the outer paper 28 July 1882, he first read "1784," then corrected this to "1734," the date which appears in the Gallery *Catalogue* of 1888, p. 360. The date seems to me to be clearly 1784. Hoare was presumably in Italy in 1734.

2. *Gentleman's Magazine,* 56.ii (October 1786), 908. On the assumption that the date on the back is actually "1734," an earlier "Andrews, Esq. of Hill House, Gloucestershire" might be invoked. He died in June 1758 (*Gentleman's Magazine, 28* [July 1758], 340).

3. *Thirteenth Report of the Trustees of the National Portrait Gallery,* 1870, p. 1, no. 81. The documents are obscure, but not substantially so. Prince Hoare's will (Probate 1834, Somerset House), executed in 1831, has several codicils in favor of Rev. Charles Townsend, one dated 4 November 1832, leaving him "works of art in the flower room in my home at Brighton," but the only portrait of Pope mentioned in

the will is a painting left to Sharon Turnor, Esq. of Red Lion Square. In Townsend's will (Probate 5 March 1870): "I give to Wm. Twopenny Esq. of the Middle Temple & Upper Grosvenor St. the portrait of Pope by Hoare." At the National Portrait Gallery an extract transcribed by George Scharf from a postscript to a letter from Wm. Twopenny (the barrister who made the will) to A. W. Franks, Esq., 10 February 1870, explains that his friend Charles Townsend "has left . . . a Crayon Portrait of Pope by old Hoare of Bath, life size head & shoulders to the National Portrait Gallery. Prince Hoare left it to Townsend, who at first by his will left it to me—I wrote for him a cod[1] & witnessed it, revoking that gift, substituting the Portr. Gallery." In the same file at the gallery is a letter from Henry Townsend (nephew of the Rev. Charles), 22 February 1870: "This Portrait was given by Prince Hoar (the son of the Artist) to his dear & most intimate friend my uncle."

63.4. OIL PAINTING, BY WILLIAM HOARE. MR. AND MRS. JAMES M. OSBORN, NEW HAVEN, CONNECTICUT.

Pope bequeathed most of his library to Ralph Allen and by reversion to William Warburton. At Warburton's death a part of the books were purchased by Richard Hurd,[1] who died in 1808, leaving his library, including the books once owned by Pope, and a collection of pictures, to the See of Worcester. Among the papers of Hurd still at Hartlebury Castle are two lists of pictures, one rough, one fair copy headed "Pictures at Worces-

63.4. Oil on canvas. 30 x 25 in. In a painted oval. Background dark brown; cap dark blue; loose coat, dark green, with six green buttons under right lapel; waistcoat brown; shirt gray where vest is open. Inscribed upper left in yellow paint: "Pope." Lower left: "W. Hoare pinx." Mr. and Mrs. James M. Osborn, New Haven, Connecticut.

ter Palace, 1813," both in the hand of Hurd's nephew, executor, and editor Richard Hurd.[2] One portrait in this list is "Mr. Pope—painted by Mr Hoare of Bath from an original in Crayons by himself."[3] At some time, most likely during the lifetime of Hurd, a group of portraits of literary and ecclesiastical figures today hanging in the Hurd Episcopal Library at Hartlebury Castle were given inscriptions in yellow paint naming the subjects and the painters. At some time during the mid-nineteenth century a number of pictures escaped from Hartlebury Castle. These included a Joseph Addison by Dahl and the Pope by Hoare.[4] A comparison of the lettering on National Portrait Gallery no. 714, "Addison / M. Dahl pin 1719," and on several portraits still hanging in the Hurd Library, e.g. "Ralph Allen / T. Hudson pinx.,"[5] "T. Balguy Archdeacon of Winchester 1739 / W. Hoare pinx.," establishes the style beyond reasonable question. (The portraits of Addison and Pope once at Hartlebury have been replaced by copies in oil made by Mrs. Joyce Aris from National Portrait Gallery no. 714, Addison, and no. 299, the Hoare pastel of Pope.[6])

The portrait now being discussed was Lot 299 [sic] of a sale held 12–15 August 1947 by Samuel T. Freeman & Co. of Boston, at Belton Court, Barrington, R.I., the home of the deceased Frederick Stanhope Peck. It is said in the sale catalogue (p. 44) to have been exhibited at the Rhode Island School of Design in 1940. It was bought by the Brodney Gallery, Boston, and from the Brodney Gallery, in 1957, by James M. Osborn, of New Haven, the present owner. It is illustrated in color in *Season's Greetings from the Osborns,* January 1964.

The two painted inscriptions leave little if any doubt that this example of Hoare's Pope was once a part of the Hartlebury Collection.

1. James Prior, *Malone* (1860), pp. 344–45; Ernest Harold Pearce, *Hartlebury Castle* (London, 1926), pp. 286, 290–92; Francis Kilvert, *Remains* (1860), p. 134.

2. Volume 9 of bound MSS., "Correspondence About Portraits," pp. "35"(or "13")–"36" and "37"(or "14")–"38."

3. Vol. 9, both the rough list and the fair copy, pp. 36 and 37.

4. James Nankivell, *The Collection of Portraits in Oils of Bishop Richard Hurd at Hartlebury Castle* (Worcester, 1953), pp. xii, 30, 37.

5. A painting of Warburton is embellished more elaborately at the upper left with coat of arms, mitre and keys, "Warburton" at upper right, and at lower left "Wm. Hoare p[t] / 1765."

6. Nankivell, *The Collection of Portraits,* pp. 30, 37.

63.5. OIL PAINTING, BY OR AFTER WILLIAM HOARE. DAWSONS OF PALL MALL, 1963.†

Mr. Wolfe Cherrick, of 67 Leinster Road, Rathmines, Dublin, owned this painting in 1961 and kindly sent the photograph reproduced below. He had bought it about twenty years earlier in Dublin at the auction of a "Mr. Murphy" deceased. In the winter of 1962–63 the picture was for sale by Messrs. Dawsons of Pall Mall, and is described and illustrated in their *Catalogue 120, pot-pourri, A Small Collection of Books.*

63.6. OIL PAINTING, BY OR AFTER WILLIAM HOARE. JAMES GALVIN, WEXFORD, IRELAND.†

Mr. James Galvin, Park Cottage, Wexford, Ireland, in a letter to the Director of the National Portrait Gallery, 16 August 1961, writes that he is the owner of a portrait of

Pope, "virtually identical" in "face and dress" with the National Portrait Gallery pastel by Hoare (no. 299, above no. 63.3a). The portrait was purchased about 70 years ago at a sale of the effects of the deceased Hon. Martin Ffrench, Ballinamore Bridge, Co. Galway.

The following nine entries, 63.7–63.15, represent allusions to portraits which I have not been able to trace. All these portraits seem to be of the Hoare type. They are listed chronologically in the order of the dates of the allusions. It is possible that some of these refer to the same portrait at different moments in its career, or to 63.4, 63.5, or 63.6. The numeration .7–.15 must therefore be looked on as tentative.

63.7.

A manuscript list of portraits at Wimpole in 1798 (during the ownership of the Third Earl of Hardwicke) includes "No. 48. Alex^r Pope poet" (B.M. Musgrave collection, Add. MS. 6391, Fol. 19, NPG photostat). Presumably the same picture is mentioned by John Britton and E. W. Brayley, *The Beauties of England and Wales*, 2 (1801), 122. On 15 December 1879 George Scharf saw a portrait of Pope at Wimpole (National Portrait Gallery, *Trustees' Sketch Books* 26.76) and noted: "Pope in green turban, to waist same

63.5. Oil on canvas. 29 x 24 in. Background brown; cap and cloak green; waistcoat brown; neckcloth white; eyes dark blue. Dawsons of Pall Mall, 1963.†

as N.P.G. Crayon" [i.e. no. 299, above no. 63.3a]. In his copy of the Wimpole Sale Catalogue (Christie's, 30 June 1888, p. 6) Scharf notes: "Alexander Pope in cap, face & eyes to L. Like our crayon."

63.8.

On 12 February 1804, Prince Hoare, son of William, in the conversation with Joseph Farington quoted on p. 282, showed Farington "3 original portraits executed by His Father,—Mr. Hoare of Bath, viz.: a painting in Oil of Pope,—a portrait in Crayons of *Handel*,—& a drawing in Chalk of Lord *Chatham*. He sd. He proposed to have engravings made from them."[1] In his will executed 9 December 1831 and proved in 1834 (see no. 63.3a), Prince Hoare bequeathed to Sharon Turnor of Red Lion Square [*DNB* Sharon Turner, 1768–1847, historian and attorney] "paintings" of Handel and Pope "executed by my father."

1. Joseph Farington, R.A., *The Farington Diary*, ed. James Greig, 2 (London, 1923), 190.

63.9.

At Colnaghi's 28 March 1863, George Scharf (National Portrait Gallery, *Trustees' Sketch Books* 7.82) drew a sketch of a painting of this type in a painted oval, to which he added rather elaborate notations: "[spandrels] dk. brown; [background] opaque yellow brown with much of yellow ochre in it and some parts dark with either grey or bt siena; [cap and coat] grass green; [waistcoat] brown black; [undergarment where waistcoat is open] grey; [neckcloth] w. Canvas, 2 ft 5—by 2 ft ¼ inch (sight measure). Has been new-lined. Eyeballs pale blue grey, Eyebrows sepia[.] Coarsely painted in crude colours red brown white & grey which have stood well. The woolly and lumpy manipulation would seem to show the work of an old man. It is very like the style of Ld Lyttelton now in the Gallery. Cross piece of original wooden strainer preserved on which was written in ink. This Picture of Mr. Pope was commanded and paid for by Captain Martin and to be delivered to him or his order without frame   William Hoare."

63.10.

Again, at Christie's, 17 March 1864, on p. 14 of the Catalogue Lot 152 was: "William Hoare (of Bath), Portrait of Alexander Pope, in a green dress and cap." And Scharf (in the copy at the National Portrait Gallery) sketched it in an oval, inside a "br" painted rectangle, and noted: "life size canvas"; [background] "y. br."; [coat or cloak] "dk. g"; [waistcoat] "br."; [neckcloth] "wh."

63.11.

In the *Remains* of Francis Kilvert, the Somerset historian, published 1866, is an essay entitled "On the Connection of Pope with the West of England in General, and Bath in Particular." On p. 128, Kilvert imagines Pope in the gallery of Prior Park "in his usual morning dishabille consisting of a dark grey waistcoat, a green dressing-gown, and a blue cap (as he is represented in the crayon painting of him by Hoare)." The crayon portrait to which he refers was no doubt the model for Kilvert's painting for the lithograph reproduced as no. 63.21.

63.12.

At the South Kensington Museum in 1869 (Third Exhibition of National Portraits) No. 790 (p. 159) was a loan by Major Morton Jeffery: Alexander Pope, by William Hoare, "Bust, looking to r.; blue cap and drapery. Pastel, paper, 24 x 18."

63.13.

At the Twickenham Loan Museum in 1888, no. 152 was Pope painted by W. Hoare, lent by Messrs. P. and D. Colnaghi. This picture is described in the *Richmond and Twickenham Times,* 4 August 1888, as showing Pope in a "loose green jacket, green skull cap, with a thin, womanish face." A small yellowing photograph, laid down on a stiff cardboard mount, is to be seen at the Borough of Twickenham Public Library in a file of various documents relating to the Loan Museum of 1888. It seems to me very likely that this photograph represents no. 152 in the Twickenham 1888 Catalogue.

63.14.

In the catalogue of the Grolier Club *Exhibition of English Literary Portraits,* 4–19 November 1898, on p. 28 appears a "Portrait of Alexander Pope . . . Pastel, by William Hoare of Bath."

63.15.

At Christie's 11 April 1913, in a sale of properties of J. R. Hallond and others, lot 95 was "W. Hoare, R. A. Portrait of the young son of Bishop Warburton in white dress, holding some skittles; and Portrait of Pope, the Poet, in blue coat and cap. Pastels." Sold for £22.1 to Lawrence (Yale copy). The same two portraits reappear at Christie's 15 March 1929, among various properties (sold along with property of the late Thomas B. Gabriel, Esq.). Dimensions, apparently for both, are given as 23½ x 17½ inches. Bought by Spiller for £12.12 (*Art Prices Current,* New Series, *8a,* 162, no. 7909).

63.16. OIL PAINTING, BY GEORGE LUMLEY, 1750, AFTER WILLIAM HOARE.
BUTLER LIBRARY, COLUMBIA UNIVERSITY, NEW YORK.

At the Anderson Galleries (sale no. 1845, paintings from the estate of Benno Loewy and other sources, 29 April 1924), lot no. 168, the seller not named, was: "George Lumley.

English, 18th Century. Portrait of Alexander Pope. Bust, shoulders to the front, head turned to the left, wearing black cap and white neckcloth; complementary background. Canvas. Height, 22 inches; width, 18 inches." A photograph of this painting, made presumably at this sale, and now at the Frick Art Reference Library, is that reproduced below, no. 63.16. The painting was acquired in New York about 1940 by Robert M. Halsband, who in 1958 presented it to Columbia University, where it hangs in the Butler Library. The picture was cleaned and restored in 1964. It is discussed and illustrated by Robert Halsband, "Alexander Pope at Columbia," *Columbia Library Columns, 14* (November 1964), 13–15.

George Lumley was a solicitor and amateur painter and mezzotint engraver who lived at York. He died there 12 October 1768, aged 60.

63.17.

Lot 10 of a sale at Christie's 23 February 1934, "Different Properties," was: "William Lumley Portrait of Pope the Poet, in black gown and hat. *Signed.* 22 in. by 18 in." This was bought for 7 guineas by "Veser" (*Art Prices Current*, New Series, *13*, no. 2770).

63.18. OIL PAINTING, AFTER WILLIAM HOARE. LADY NICHOLS, LAWFORD HALL, MANNINGTREE, ESSEX.

At Lawford Hall, Manningtree, Essex, the home of Sir Philip Bouverie Nichols (d. 1962) and Lady Nichols, is an oil painting which belongs in the present group. On the back of the frame are inscriptions or labels to the effect that the picture came from the Earl of Arran's sale, at Christie's, 2 March 1865, lot 27, as by Richardson; and that it was exhibited at the Moot Hall, Colchester, in 1951, no. 26, again as by Richardson. (Philip Yorke Gore, Fourth Earl of Arran, was born in 1801, succeeded his uncle to the title in 1837, and died at London in 1884.)

63.19. OIL PAINTING, AFTER WILLIAM HOARE. ST. EDMUND HALL, OXFORD.

This small portrait was found by Mr. Harold Lilley in an antique shop at Maidenhead and was presented by him to St. Edmund Hall, Oxford, in 1941. It now hangs in the Principal's drawing room.

63.20. OIL PAINTING, AFTER HOARE. A. N. L. MUNBY, KING'S COLLEGE, CAMBRIDGE.

Mr. A. N. L. Munby, Librarian of King's College Library, Cambridge, is the owner of an oil painting which he acquired at a book sale at Sotheby's about 1935–36. This is 29¾ x 25 inches, an old canvas on an old stretcher in an old carved and gilt wood frame, the name "Bull" appearing in black ink upside down on the bottom of the frame at back. Within dimly painted spandrels, Pope wears a green cap, brown coat, black waistcoat, and a gray garment where the waistcoat is popped open. The flesh

63.16. Oil on canvas. 22 x 18 in. Cap black; coat dark. After cleaning and restoration of the picture in 1964, an inscription in orange paint in the lower left corner reads: "Geor: Lumley. Pinx. / .13 April 1750." Butler Library, Columbia University.

63.18. Oil on canvas. 18 x 15 in. Colors similar to those of 63.19. "Dark steely grey eyes." Lady Nichols, Lawford Hall, Manningtree, Essex.†

63.19. Oil on canvas. About 18 x 15 in. Background dark brown; coat and cap black; waistcoat dark brown; flesh tints bright. Label on frame: "AVLAE SANCTI EDMVNDI d.d. HAROLDVS LILLEY MCMXLI." St. Edmund Hall, Oxford.

tints are chalky. This portrait is unique among those of the present group in that it has, instead of a neckcloth, an open shirt collar. The jaw is more pronounced and square than in the Hoare paintings. It seems like a copy by another hand.

63.21. OIL PAINTING, AFTER HOARE. WILLIAM HEINEMANN LTD., LONDON.

This picture hangs in the office of Mr. Alan Hill at William Heinemann Ltd., Queen Street, London. It is painted on a joined wooden panel, 27 x 20⅞ inches. The features suggest the influence of the Warren or the Posselwhite engraving of the Stowe portrait.

63.22. LITHOGRAPH, BY R. J. LANE, AFTER F. KILVERT, 1840: "POPE, ALLEN & WARBURTON (AT PRIOR PARK)."

R. J. Lane had completed this lithograph on 23 November 1840 and on 25 January 1841 received payment for it from the Reverend F. Kilvert.[1] It appears as frontispiece to a selection of Warburton's miscellaneous writings edited by Kilvert as volume 14 of Warburton's *Works,* 1841.[2] From a passage in his essay *On the Connection of Pope*

Painted by F. Kilvert   On Stone by R J. Lane

POPE, ALLEN & WARBURTON.
(At Prior Park)
M & N Hanhart, lith Printers

63.22. Lithograph. Picture (without lettering) 3⁷⁄₁₆ x 4¹⁵⁄₁₆ in. "Painted by F. Kilvert • // On Stone by R. J. Lane. / POPE, ALLEN & WARBURTON. / (At Prior Park.) / M & N Hanhart, Lith. Printers." Frontispiece to *A Selection from Unpublished Papers of . . . William Warburton,* 1841. *Grolier 88.*

with the West of England (quoted on p. 294) we may infer that Kilvert was familiar with a specific "crayon painting" of Pope by Hoare (dark gray waistcoat, green dressing-gown, blue cap). The figure of Allen in the lithograph may be drawn from the painting by Hudson, which today hangs over the mantel in the Hurd Library at Hartlebury[3]—though in the lithograph Allen seems to have dropped to the floor the letter which he holds in the painting. The head and shoulders of the standing Warburton in the lithograph might well enough be derived from the Warburton by Hoare which today hangs to the right of the mantel in the Hurd Library.[4]

Kilvert seems to have had in mind his own painting (today untraced) when he wrote the poem dated in his *Remains* 1853 and entitled *On a Picture of "Pope, Allen, and Warburton, at Prior Park."*

> Ye who embodied seek the informing mind,
>
> WIT, WORTH and WISDOM here behold enshrined;
>
> Each in the form it loved on earth to own
>
> As POPE, as ALLEN and as WARBURTON.
>
> Thus in sage council did the trio meet,
>
> Where Widcombe's classic shades and letter'd seat
>
> To haunts Pierian woo'd the studious pilgrim's feet.[5]

The chamber at Prior Park represented in the lithograph seems to adjoin a lofty portico opening over the valley toward Bath. Kilvert, in the passage which we have quoted from *On the Connection of Pope with the West of England,* imagined Pope "surrounded" by a "distinguished circle" of "divines and politicians . . . assembled" in the "gallery which formed the library at Prior Park."

The gallery seems actually to have been a kind of narrow second-story passage. See nos. 64.1 and 64.2.

1. Lane's MS. Account Books, 2.43 and 5.19 (National Portrait Gallery).

2. *A Selection from Unpublished Papers of the Right Reverend William Warburton, D.D.* (London, John Bowyer Nichols and Son, Parliament Street, 1841) appears also with a title page identifying it as vol. *14* of *The Works.*

3. See James Nankivell, *The Collection of Portraits . . . at Hartlebury Castle* (Worcester, 1953), pp. 16–18.

4. See Nankivell, pp. 22–24.

5. *Remains in Verse and Prose of the Rev. Francis Kilvert, M.A.* (Bath and London, 1866), p. 33, poem xxxvi. On p. 32, poem xxv, *On the Pictures of Bishop Hurd and Dr. Parr, in the Library of Hartlebury Castle,* 1858, celebrates this reconciliation in effigy of the two theological antagonists. (Cf. Kilvert, *Memoirs of the Life and Writings of the Right Rev. Richard Hurd* [London 1860], p. 174.) Nankivell, *Portraits at Hartlebury Castle,* pp. 36, 37, seems to confuse the occasions of the two poems.

64.1 a and b. RED CRAYON DRAWING, BY WILLIAM HOARE. NATIONAL PORTRAIT GALLERY NO. 873.

In the first volume of his edition of the *Works* of Alexander Pope, published in 1797, Joseph Warton included an engraving of Pope in profile to right standing full length (no. 64.2). On the opposite page, "[ix]," appeared a legend: "This is the only Portrait that was ever drawn of Mr. POPE at full Length. It was done without his knowledge, as he was deeply engaged in conversation with Mr. ALLEN in the Gallery at Prior Park, by

Mr. Hoare, who sat at the other end of the Gallery.—Pope would never have forgiven the Painter had he known it—He was too sensible of the Deformity of his Person to allow the whole of it to be represented.—This Drawing is therefore exceedingly valuable, as it is an Unique of this celebrated Poet."

The drawing had presumably not been well known before, and although various satiric full-length engravings of Pope had appeared during his lifetime, this was the first time any such authentic revelation had been put in either a biography of Pope or in an edition of his works. Warton was the object of some public censure for his daring,[1] and he was also publicly defended: "We, for our parts, most heartily thank the editor for inserting the whole length sketch of his author: we agree with him, that as an unique, it is valuable and curious."[2] In his *Biographical Memoirs of the Late Rev⁴ Joseph Warton*, 1806, Warton's friend the Reverend John Wooll was prompted to the following disclosure: "The late Lord Palmerston possessed the picture, and knowing that his friend Dr. Warton was employed in an edition of this poet's works, sent it to him both as a curiosity and an interesting addition to the publication."[3]

On 24 April 1891, Christie's held a sale of a *Collection of Engravings and Drawings, Formed by the Second Viscount Palmerston (1770–1801)*.[4] Lot 176 (p. 129 of the *Catalogue*) was "A Curious Full-Length Portrait of Pope, by Hoare—*vide* note on the back." This drawing was purchased by Colnaghi, and in June was purchased from Colnaghi by the Trustees of the National Portrait Gallery.[5]

Among the Palmerston papers which have come down until recently at Broadlands, near Romsey, Hampshire, is a notebook inventory of pictures, drawings, and furniture in her own apartment at Broadlands, drawn up 4 February 1797, by Mary Mee, second wife of the Second Lord Palmerston. This records several acquisitions, apparently by gift to members of her family, made at Bath in 1796 or thereabouts—e.g. "a Drawing," "Seventeen Profiles." Another document, Lord Palmerston's Diary, records extended visits to Bath by Lady Palmerston in 1791 and 1792.[6] William Hoare, as we have seen, died at Bath in December 1792. On 18 February 1794, at No. 10 Milsom Street, Bath, Mr. Plura sold by auction *The Genuine, Valuable Collection of Paintings and Drawings, by Ancient and Modern Masters. . . . and many much-esteemed, genuine Performances in Crayons and Oil, of the late William Hoare, Esq. Deceased.*[7]

National Portrait Gallery no. 873 is a drawing in red crayon (or "chalk") on white laid paper, 8⅛ x 6¼ inches, backed by a similar-looking sheet of paper pasted to it around the edges. The front edges are concealed by a pasted-on paper frame washed ochre and brown and inscribed. Between a double inner and a first outer rule appears in ink: "A:Pope Esqʳ" and between the first outer and a second outer rule, on the left "ad Vivum" and on the right "Wm Hoare." Written in pencil on the paper of the drawing and partly covered by the paper frame at top is "Mr Pope".

The chain spaces of both sheets of paper measure about 23½ millimeters. The first sheet, or that with the drawing on it, has part of a watermark consisting of a bell, with the word "JURE," hanging from a segment of a circular frame which seems to be a buckled belt and contains parts of a design, perhaps the Hanoverian coat of arms. This is similar to watermark no. 164 dated 1741 by W. A. Churchill, *Watermarks in Paper*

(Amsterdam, 1935), pp. 73 and cxxxiv. The other sheet of paper, the backing sheet, has a countermark consisting of a single-line circle containing at each side a branch with leaves ("support") and in the center the initials "IV" surmounted by a crown. This is a type of countermark common during the mid-eighteenth century.[8]

Written on the backing sheet in ink is a note which, except for differences in punctuation and capitalization and correction of the word "was" to "sat" in the phrase "Mr. Hoare who sat," is the same as the note printed on the page opposite the drawing in Warton's edition of 1797. The handwriting of this note is apparently not that of William Hoare. It is not that of Joseph Warton, and not that of Lady Palmerston. At the National Portrait Gallery is an autograph letter of Prince Hoare, dated 8 May 1829. Despite some differences in detail and the general deterioration of the hand, the basic slant and character of this handwriting seems very similar to that on the backing paper of National Portrait Gallery 873. It cannot be clearly proved but it seems a plausible guess that this note was written, either toward the end of William Hoare's life or shortly after his death in 1792, by his son Prince Hoare (1755–1834), artist and author, foreign secretary of the Royal Academy in 1799.[9]

In a letter and invitation sent from Prior Park to William Warburton on 12 November 1741, and now celebrated as the beginning of Warburton's rise to fame, Pope describes among the attractions of Prior Park "a Gallery ninety foot long to walk in."[10] Kilvert believed that "this gallery . . . formed the library."[11] But he quotes a letter written in 1763 by the Master of Ceremonies at Bath, Samuel Derrick, which perhaps gives a more essential description: "I am no great admirer of a gallery up one pair of stairs, which runs almost the whole length of the house, and is, in my opinion, too narrow: its terminations are, an apartment, in which Mr. Allen sits to dispatch business; and a good gallery or pew, looking into one of the neatest chapels I ever saw, where the family constantly attend divine service."[12] In a communication to *The Monthly Magazine, or British Register, 41* (London, May 1816), 290–91, a writer signing himself "W" says that about 1780 at St. Blazy, Cornwall, he knew a Mrs. Elliott, Ralph Allen's sister, who had lived at Prior Park during the years when Pope was a visitor. "Lord, Sir, when I was at brother's at Prior Park, Mister Pope, the great poet, used to come there. He was a leet hump-backed man, with a long nose, and a large wig."[13]

National Portrait Gallery no. 873 has been reproduced by Lionel Cust, *The National Portrait Gallery, 1* (London, 1901), 215; by Reginald Wright in his article on William Hoare in *Apollo, 31* (February 1940), 40; and by W. L. Macdonald, *Pope and His Critics* (London, 1951), p. 302. It is mentioned with something of its history in *TLS*, 7 October 1920, p. 656.

It was exhibited at the National Portrait Gallery Exhibition in 1961.

1. [Thomas James Mathias], *The Pursuits of Literature, A Satirical Poem*, 6th ed. (London, 1798), pp. 328–29: "Like *Warton* driveling on the page of Pope; / While o'er the ground that WARBURTON once trod, / The Winton Pedant shakes his little rod, / . . . Nor e'en the Bard's deformity can 'scape, / 'His pictur'd person and his libel'd shape.' " The "Fourth Dialogue," in which the passage occurred, was first published in July 1797 (p. 2).

2. *The British Critic, 10* (November 1797), 509.

3. John Wooll, *Biographical Memoirs of the Late Rev.ᵈ Joseph Warton, D.D.* (London, T. Cadell and W. Davies, 1806), p. 84.

4. Henry Temple, Second Viscount Palmerston, born

in 1739, died in 1802. He became M.P. for Winchester in 1796. See p. 280, n. 6.

5. *Thirty-Fourth Annual Report of the Trustees of the National Portrait Gallery* (1891), p. 16, no. 458.

6. I am grateful to Mr. C. K. Adams and to Mrs. Blois, Librarian of the late Lady Mountbatten. Mrs. Blois examined Lord Palmerston's diary and very kindly brought the notebook inventory to the National Portrait Gallery. The Palmerston papers are in the course of being transferred on loan to the Public Records Office.

7. An unidentified newspaper cutting at the Victoria and Albert Museum Library, *Press Cuttings From English Newspapers on Matters of Artistic Interest, 1686–1835,* 3.694 (P.P.14.G).

8. See, for instance, Churchill, *Watermarks,* nos. 165, 406, 408 (p. CCCI), and no. 52 (p. XXXIII), "I. Villedary."

9. This A.L.S. by Prince Hoare consists of four quarto pages (one folded sheet), furnishing recollections of Christopher Anstey to a correspondent and concluding with an account of the monument in Bath Abbey to William Hoare, which Prince Hoare had commissioned Chantrey to execute. The year date is entered in another hand. A second A.L.S. by Prince Hoare at the National Portrait Gallery is without year date (in William Brockedon's Album of Drawings and Autographs). The hand is similar. A third autograph of Prince Hoare which I have seen, a short note written apparently about the year 1813 (collection of Professor F. W. Hilles, New Haven), shows some inconclusive differences in the hand from that of 1829.

10. *Correspondence* 4.371. As late as 14 May 1741, Pope, writing to Allen, inquired: "Are you got into your New House?" (4.344). On the other hand, on 15 May 1740, he had written: "It is my firm resolution to inhabit the Room at the end of your Gallery one Fortnight at least in September, & as much longer as I can, to see your Gardens finish'd" (4.238).

11. *Remains in Verse and Prose* (1866), p. 128, "On the Connection of Pope with the West of England."

12. Samuel Derrick, *Letters* (Dublin, 1767), 2.58: Bath, 10 May 1763; cf. Kilvert, *Remains,* p. 24, "Ralph Allen and Prior Park."

13. "He used to lie a-bed till twelve or one o'clock; and zumtimes, out of fun, I have goed up to his bedroom, and put a candle and lanthorne to the door; zo—when he comed out o's room, and seed lanthorne, he laughed leek a piskey. Mister Pope and I have made many rhimes together—but he hath never mentioned my name in his books. . . . though he hath those of many other vokes that hath made rhimes for un."

64.2. STIPPLE ENGRAVING, BY P. CONDÉ, AFTER WILLIAM HOARE. WARTON'S EDITION OF POPE'S *Works,* 1797, VOLUME 1.

For the source of the image, see no. 64.1. The engraving seems close enough in dimensions to the drawing to have been done with the aid of a tracing. This engraving, in sepia ink,[1] appears facing p. ix of volume 1 of Joseph Warton's edition of the *Works* of Pope, 1797. The same plate reappears in black ink, facing p. xi of volume 1 of Bowles' edition of Pope's *Works,* 1806. Page xi has the note "This is the only Portrait" etc., with the omission of one sentence, "Pope would never . . . allow the whole of it to be represented." The name "Warton" is added, as if a signature. A re-engraving printed in sepia ink appears as a recto following the full text of the note on p. vi in volume 1 of Pope's *Works,* edited by Joseph Warton and others, "A New Edition," London, 1822, "Printed by J. F. Dove, St. John's Square: For Richard Priestley, High Holborn." This plate is lettered only: "Published by Richard Priestley, High Holborn, London." Grolier 96 and 98, under the heading "American Portraits," are described as small stipple engravings of this type, 3⅝ x 2⅝ inches, the first inscribed "C. Tiebout Sct." and "Published by B. J. and R. Johnson, 1804." Examples of what I believe are these two engravings, in double-line frames, 3½ x 2⅝ inches, stipple, and 3⅝ x 2⅝ inches stipple and line, both without lettering, may be seen in a collection of engravings of Pope in the Museum Arbuteanum (W. S. Lewis), Farmington, Conn. A woodcut apparently derived from Warton's engraving appears in Carruthers' *Life of Pope* (1857), p. 407.

A: Pope Esq.

ad Vivum   W. Hoare

This is the only Portrait that was ever drawn
of Mr Pope at full length. It was done
without his knowledge, as he was deeply engaged
in conversation with Mr Allen in the Gallery at
prior Park; by Mr Hoare, who sat at the other
end of the Gallery. — Pope would never have
forgiven the Painter had he known it. He was
too sensible of the deformity of his Person to allow
the whole of it to be represented. This Drawing
is therefore exceedingly valuable as it is an
Unique of this celebrated Poet.

To front Page IX [A 5] of Vol.1.

Published June 1 1797. by Cadell & Davies Strand.

left

64.1a. Red crayon on white laid paper, in paper frame pasted around edges. (With frame) 8 x 6 in. (Within frame) 6⅝ x 4½ in. Image including ground shadow 6¹/₁₆ x 3⁹/₁₆ in. For a description of the paper frame, backing paper with inscription, and watermarks, see entry no. 64.1. National Portrait Gallery no. 873.

64.1b. Inscription on backing sheet of 64.1a.

above

64.2. Stipple engraving, sepia ink. Line frame 6¹¹/₁₆ x 4⁶/₁₆ in. Image including ground shadow 5¹⁵/₁₆ x 3⁷/₁₆ in. "To front Page IX [A5] of Vol. I. // P. Condé sculp^t / Published June 1. 1797, by Cadell & Davies, Strand." On page [ix]: "This is the only Portrait that was ever drawn of Mr. POPE at full Length.—It was done without his knowledge, as he was deeply engaged in conversation with Mr. ALLEN in the Gallery at Prior Park, by Mr. HOARE, who sat at the other end of the Gallery.—POPE would never have forgiven the Painter had he known it—He was too sensible of the Deformity of his Person to allow the whole of it to be represented.—This Drawing is therefore exceedingly valuable, as it is an Unique of this celebrated Poet." *BMEP 5 Grolier 87 Works of Alexander Pope*, ed. Joseph Warton (London, 1797), Vol. 1, facing p. [ix].

Jean Condé (d. 1794) and Pierre Condé (still living in 1840) were French artists, brothers, active in London.

1. I describe copies which I have seen. An impression on large paper in my possession is in black ink. The colors may well vary in different copies of the same edition.

64.3–64.14. *Full-Length Drawings, Copies After Hoare.*

The full-length image of Pope established by Condé's stipple engraving in Warton's edition of Pope, 1797, became apparently a favorite subject for copying by amateur draughtsmen. In the following list of drawings I place first and illustrate (64.3) the only example which seems to me at all likely to have been copied from the primary drawing itself, rather than from an engraving in the editions of 1797, 1806, or 1822. Variations in both the vertical and horizontal dimensions of the other examples in this list are likely to be due to the amorphous character of the ground shadow. It seems possible that some or most of these drawings are based on tracings from an engraving. The use of red crayon may be due to imitation not of the original but of an engraving printed in sepia ink. None of these drawings has any serious claim to priority over Lord Palmerston's, National Portrait Gallery no. 873. A widespread if vague familiarity with this image of Pope during the mid-nineteenth century may be illustrated in the following passage from the Reverend Robert Aris Willmott's *Summer Time in the Country,* first published in 1849: "I always find it pleasanter to let authors . . . tell their own history. . . . We catch the form and face in a looking-glass, of which the person is unconscious. He has no opportunity of making up his countenance, but is sketched, like Pope while in conversation with a friend in the gallery of Prior Park, and transferred to the canvas before he knows that an eye is on him—hump and all."[1]

1. Robert Aris Willmott, *Summer Time in the Country* (London and New York, 1858), p. 42. Cf. *Gentleman's Magazine, 186* (1849), 349.

64.3. CRAYON DRAWING, AFTER WILLIAM HOARE. PROFESSOR MAYNARD MACK, YALE UNIVERSITY.

In August 1960, Mr. L. W. Wildgoose of 11 St. Flora's Road, Littlehampton, Sussex, presented to Professor Maynard Mack a drawing of Pope in profile to right, standing full-length, which he said had been given to him years before "by a lady who had a distant family connection with Prior Park." This is a drawing in red crayon (the image approximately 6¾ x 5 inches, including the ground shadow, which projects in front of the finger), on a piece of cream-white wove paper, 10⁄16 x 7¹³⁄16 inches. Three lines written in the same red crayon, in a hand that seems of the late eighteenth or early nineteenth century, appear just below the image: "Portrait of Mr Pope when deeply engaged in conversation with / Mr Allen in the Gallery at Prior Park. Drawn by Mr Hoare / who sat at the other end of the Gallery—." This drawing, which, if only because of the kind of paper it is on, cannot be the original, shows a much wider deviation from the type (nos. 64.1 and 2) than any of those I am to list below. It seems possible that this is a copy made by an amateur from the original Hoare drawing, perhaps while that was still in possession of William Hoare or Prince Hoare at Bath.

I arrange the following five drawings in a chronological order according to the dates of their first coming to public notice, even though obscurely. The dates of their execution would make a more satisfactory order, but here for the most part information is lacking.

64.4.†

At the Samuel Rogers sale, Christie's, April–May 1856, lot 391, p. 150, on the fourteenth day, Tuesday 13 May, was Garth's *Dispensary*, in a morocco case, 1703. This volume is now in the Victoria and Albert Library (*The Dispensary*, 5th edition, 8vo., 1703). The Rogers sale catalogue gives a description which is verified and amplified in the South Kensington Museum's *Forster Collection. A Catalogue of the Printed Books Be-*

64.3. Red crayon on cream-white wove paper. Sheet 10⅟₁₆ x 7¹³⁄₁₆ in. Inscribed below in red crayon: "Portrait of Mr Pope when deeply engaged in conversation / with Mr Allen in the Gallery at Prior Park. Drawn by Mr Hoare / who sat at the other end of the Gallery—". Professor Maynard Mack, Yale University.

queathed by John Forster (1888), p. 185, no. 3325. The volume contains MS. notes by Pope, a comment in the hand of William Mason on a flyleaf at the end, and pasted to the inside of the end cover a pen-and-ink drawing of the Hoare type. The provenance of the volume appears in Latin notes on a front fly leaf: "E Libris Alexandri Pope. Donum autoris. Alexander Pope Gulielmo Warburton moriens legavit 1744. Gulielmus Warburton Gulielmo Mason dedit 1752. Gulielmus Alderson (cujus patri (ὁμώνυμῳ) Gul⁵ Mason legaverat,) Alleynio Barⁱ de Sᵗ Helens dono dedit. 1815. D.D. Samueli Rogers A B Sᵗ Helens. 15 Nov. brevè moriturus." The Reverend Christopher Alderson was for many years Mason's curate at Aston, succeeded him as rector there, and was one of his legatees (John W. Draper, *Mason*, 1924, pp. 120–21). A sheet of paper accompanying the volume records that it was purchased at the Rogers sale for £12.15.0 by George Daniel, Canonbury. (For George Daniel, 1789–1864, print collector, of 18 Canonbury Square, London, see no. 48.1.) John Forster, who bequeathed the book to the Museum, died in 1876. A photostat shows the drawing of Pope to be identical with the unidentified drawing reproduced by Edmund Gosse, in *English Literature, An Illustrated Record* (London, 1903), 3.204. Both the photostat and the reproduction show the following manuscript inscriptions in the background: (at the top) "ALEXᴿ. / / POPE. / aetat: 52. / A.D. 1740."; and (at the bottom right) "by Hoare of / Bath". Beneath the drawing appears on the same sheet of paper (in type, with spelling corrected and the punctuation slightly changed, under the reproduction): "The only full-length Portrait of Pope. / Drawn, without his knowledge, while conversing with Mʳ Allen at Prior Park".[1]

Gosse's reproduction has apparently been the source of the image of Pope in yellow, purple, and maroon which appears on the cover of the 11th printing, August 1961, by Holt, Rinehart, and Winston, New York, of *Alexander Pope, Selected Poetry & Prose*, first published by Rinehart & Company in 1951.

---

1. In *Notes and Queries*, 8th Series, *4* (16 December 1893), 482, Col. Harold Malet describes this volume in the South Kensington Museum and speculates: "Hoare managed on the cover of a book to take a hasty outline of him in ink." Pope's copy of *The Dispensary* (said to be a gift from Garth, and apparently among the books bequeathed to Allen and Warburton) seems an unlikely drawing pad (or board) for Hoare's surreptitious and offensive sketch. The sketch is pasted down on the back cover, so that the character of the paper is not readily ascertainable. The drawing seems on the whole to be a much cruder effort than either NPG 873 or Condé's engraving of 1797. The date, which appears on no other drawing of this group, must be approximately correct. It suggests the hand of a person who at least had a fairly clear idea of Pope's life during his last years.

64.5.

At the Twickenham Loan Museum of 1888, no. 325 (p. 54 in the *Catalogue*) was a "Casket known as 'The Feather Box,' containing a Portrait of Pope, described as the only Portrait that was ever drawn of Mr. Pope at full length." The box itself was "made from the wood of a Willow planted by Pope, and it was given as it is by Mrs. Pope (whose husband was connected with the poet) to the grandmother of the present owner." It was lent by Captain Thomas Hincks, of Breckenborough, Thirsk, Yorkshire. A small wood engraving of the box, with the lid up showing the profile full-length drawing in the lid and a large label on the back inside of the box, appears in *The Illustrated London News, 93* (11 August 1888), p. 170; and the drawing itself is reproduced by a wood engraving in *The Richmond and Twickenham Times Pope Commemoration Supplement*, 4 August 1888, p. 4.

64.6.

The drawing here considered is said to have been once in the collection of G. H. Bohn.[1] It is described in the Grolier Club catalogue of *An Exhibition* [of the Beverly Chew Pope Collection] (1911), p. 45, no. 102, as an "Original crayon sketch of Pope, full-length in profile, by Mr. Hoare; with autograph note by Joseph Wharton [sic] on back." The same description appears in the Anderson Galleries' catalogue of *The Library of the Late Beverly Chew*, 8 and 9 December 1924, lot 322, and to it is appended a mistaken identification with Dr. Raymond Crawfurd's drawing (see below no. 64.7 in this list), and an allusion to National Portrait Gallery 873 as a "replica."[2] The drawing next appears in the Anderson Galleries' sale of *The Library of Jerome Kern*, 22 January 1929, where it is lot 964, reproduced on p. 317 of the catalogue; it is also reproduced in connection with this sale in the *International Studio: Associated with The Connoisseur, 91* (December 1928), 52, 96. At this sale it was purchased by Barnet J. Beyer,[3] and in 1951 it was part of the Beyer Estate, at the Seven Gables Bookshop in New York City. It is a drawing in red crayon, the image $5^{15}\!/_{16}$ x $3^{7}\!/_{16}$ inches (including ground shadow), on a piece of white wove paper, $7\frac{1}{4}$ x $4\frac{3}{8}$ inches. On the back is written in ink in perhaps an early nineteenth-century hand a note which follows with a few slight variations the printed note of 1797. Given to the Library of Congress, 1957.

1. A manuscript note in the Barnet J. Beyer copy of the Jerome Kern catalogue (1929) communicated to me by Mr. Michael Papantonio of the Seven Gables Bookshop.
2. A copy of this catalogue in the Yale Library has a

note that lot 322 was purchased for "270" by "Dr. R."
3. Note in the Beyer copy of the Kern catalogue, communicated by Michael Papantonio. A copy of the catalogue in the Yale Library has a note that the price was $525.00.

64.7.

In *The Library* (*Transactions of the Bibliographical Society*), 4th Series, *1* (September 1920), 97–101, "A Portrait of Alexander Pope," the late Sir Raymond H. Payne Crawfurd, F.R.C.P. (d. 1938), reproduced a profile full-length drawing, very similar, in general appearance, to both National Portrait Gallery no. 873 and the 1797 engraving—though by no means a facsimile of either. "There has recently come into my possession," he wrote, "along with other relics of Alexander Pope, a portrait of the poet in red chalk, which is here reproduced. On the lower margin of the drawing is the following inscription: 'This is the only portrait that was ever drawn of Mr. Pope at full length and was done without his knowledge, as he was deeply engaged in conversation with Mr. Allen, in the Gallery of Prior Park, by Mr. Hoare, who sat at the other end of the Gallery.' This portrait has been in the possession of my family certainly for more than a hundred years, and . . . some of them were on friendly terms with Pope." After an allusion to the engraving in Warton's *Pope* of 1797, Dr. Crawfurd adds, "William Hoare . . . also was a friend of my family." The article is reviewed in the *TLS*, 7 October 1920, p. 656.

Mr. Stephen Crawfurd very kindly made a search of his father's collection of autographs and other papers and inquired of several colleges with which his father had been associated, but has been unable to discover the whereabouts of the drawing today. He tells me that his grandfather Charles Walter Payne Crawfurd's collections had been formed at the family home Ardmillan, near East Grinstead, Sussex, which passed out of the family possession in 1918.

64.8.

In the *Letters of Thomas J. Wise to John Henry Wrenn,* ed. Fannie E. Ratchford (New York, 1944), p. 429, a letter written by Wise on 26 November 1905 tells Wrenn: "This is the lot about which I have written you hastily already. Calder brought it to me on Friday, and I did not need to look at it for more than two minutes before I made up my mind to secure it at any reasonable cost. I bought the collection of 6 books, one letter, and one portrait for £42.0.0, plus 10% Calder's commission. Please therefore give me 'with pleasure,' credit for £46.4.0." Four days earlier, on 22 November (in a letter still unpublished but in the Wrenn Collection at the University of Texas), Wise had written to Wrenn: "I have had today what *looks like* being news of something very attractive for you. The report came through Calder, who told me today that there is coming up to him from Leith a small collection of Pope books, all entirely uncut:—and with them, 'a small unpublished Portrait of Pope drawn from Life'! This sounds promising."[1]

In the Wrenn Collection at the University of Texas, bound in a Rivière binding (WK P810 6730ha) is a profile full-length of Pope which is no doubt the "Portrait" mentioned in the letters. This is actually a tracing in ink, with pencil shading, on very thin wove paper, the overall dimensions of the image being $6\frac{1}{8}$ x $3\frac{7}{8}$ inches. On a conjugate leaf facing the picture, is written in ink the note: "This is the only Portrait that was ever drawn of Mr. Pope at full length," etc.

1. For William Calder, "bookseller, unidentified," said later by Wise to have gone into the army in World War I and not to have returned, see *Letters*, pp. 18, 75, 296, 300.

The following five drawings have, I believe, never heretofore come to public notice.

64.9.

At the Victoria and Albert Museum is a folio album of drawings, bequeathed by the Rev. Chauncy Hare Townshend, 1798–1868 (Townshend: Drawings 93.E.15). This volume contains, among a variety of drawings by several hands dated during the 1820s and 1830s, a neat pencil sketch (no. 20, p. 9) of the type with which we are concerned. The paper is apparently wove paper, 8¾ x 7¼ inches. The figure is 5¹⁵⁄₁₆ x 4³⁄₁₆ inches (including ground shadow). An ink inscription beneath the figure is the same as that found alike with NPG 873 and the engraving of 1797, except that instead of "at Prior Park" it has "of Prior Park."

64.10.

In a folio folder (B.6.a) at the Victoria and Albert Museum (apparently also a part of the Townshend bequest) is a similar but rougher pencil drawing on a sheet of wove paper 8¾ x 7¼ in., watermarked "1812." The figure is 5¹⁵⁄₁₆ x 4³⁄₈ in. (including ground shadow). In pen and ink beneath the figure, apparently in the same hand as that of no. 64.9, is the same inscription, except that it reads "at Prior Park." Above, on a longer piece of paper, on which the drawing is mounted, is written in ink in apparently a different hand: "Copied by George Baillie, at Burbridge, Octr 1816."

64.11.

At the Morgan Library, New York City, volume 2 of *A Collection of Political Caricatures, Broadsides, Portraits, Etc., 1642–1830, From the Library of Sir Robert Peel, Bart., Drayton Manor, Tamworth, Twelve Volumes* (B32m), contains on p. 19, item 66, a full-length drawing of Pope in pen and ink over pencil on thick white paper, pasted down—but apparently wove. The image, 5⅞ x 3⅜ inches, follows the pattern of NPG 873 and the 1797 engraving rather closely, even to the doubling of the finger.

64.12.

In October 1941, Mr. W. Allan Tanner, Wateredge Hotel, Ambleside, Westmorland, sent to the National Portrait Gallery a description and a partly traced pencil copy of a watercolor drawing which he had seen in a small hotel nearby. Beneath the picture in faded ink was an inscription which he transcribed. Mr. C. K. Adams of the Portrait Gallery noted that the inscription was apparently the same as the note printed by Warton in 1797, and that the drawing was apparently the same size as the engraving in Warton's edition and as the drawing at the Gallery.

64.13.†

In August 1954 Mr. R. J. Baker Wilbraham, F.L.A.S. of Rode Hall, Scholar Green, Stoke-on-Trent, in a note to the National Portrait Gallery, said that a full-length drawing of Pope in possession of his family was a watercolor, the height of the figure about 6 inches. "Underneath is written the following:—This is the only Portrait that was ever drawn of Mr. Pope at full length," etc. The note as transcribed is identical with that in Warton 1797 and on the back of NPG 873, except for punctuation and capitalization and except for the last phrase, which instead of "celebrated poet," reads "illustrious

65. Pen and ink on paper. 7 x 6¼ in. Devonshire Collection, Chatsworth. Reproduced by permission of the Trustees of the Chatsworth Settlement.

Poet." It seems possible that the watercolor drawing now at Scholar Green is the same as that seen in 1941 at Ambleside.[1]

1. On 13 October 1901, a Mrs. Bradstreet, living at 2 Grove Road, Windsor, wrote to the Director of the National Portrait Gallery to say that she owned a red-chalk portrait sketch of Pope by Hoare, about six inches in height. It seems impossible to be sure that this drawing was not 64.3, 64.5, 64.6, or 64.7, described above.

65. PEN-AND-INK DRAWING, BY LADY BURLINGTON. CHATSWORTH.

For the artistic activity of Dorothy Savile, Countess of Burlington, and the two albums containing drawings by her, now at Chatsworth in the Devonshire Collection, see no. 15. The drawing reproduced above is no. 69 on page 34 of the second of the two albums, *Drawings XXV* [or 26 A], *Chiswick & Chatsworth Miscellaneous Drawings*. This is a pen-and-ink drawing, over pencil guide lines, on a piece of paper 7 x 6¼ inches, from which a strip about 3⅛ x 1 inches has been cut out at the top left. It was first brought to my attention by Professor John Butt, who saw it and identified it as a portrait of Pope in 1945. It seems clearly an example of the coarser and more malicious draughtsmanship which distinguishes Lady Burlington from Kent. I have put it here in the sequence of Pope images because both the age indicated in the profile face and the likelihood that it was done surreptitiously make it an appropriate companion to the Hoare full-length. The rosette or flower which appears on the background just above Pope's head has not been explained. Perhaps it illustrates Lady Burlington's habit of medley drawing, or mingled perspective, and perhaps it was related to some other image drawn in the area cut away at the left. In 1719 Sir Godfrey Kneller, inviting Pope to a party at Whitton, says, "I belive ther will be Card playrs enoug, and we may do how we please. If you Come about 4: a Clock, you may see me paint."[1] On 2 April 1731, Swift writes Pope urging him to repair his health by recreation. "Learn to play at Cards, or Tables, or Bowls; . . . contrive new tramgams in your Garden."[2] In 1738 Kent's love of cards perhaps helps to interfere with his seeing Pope. "Whe have begun a weekly meeting at Whist. . . . I had not seen Pope but once this two months."[3] By 1739 Pope is perhaps playing cards occasionally but not liking it. At Stowe on 4 July 1739, he writes to Martha Blount of a routine of contented leisure: "no Politicks [and] no Cards, nor much Reading. This agrees exactly with [m]e, for the Want of Cards sends us early to bed."[4] Perhaps Pope was sometimes dragooned into filling out a game of whist among his friends of the Burlington circle.

1. *Correspondence* 2.9.
2. *Correspondence* 3.191. Professor Sherburn's note on this passage observes "there is at Chatsworth a small drawing that has been thought possibly of Pope with cards in his hand as if playing."
3. *Correspondence* 4.150.
4. *Correspondence* 4.186.

· 12 ·

1742
JEAN BAPTISTE VAN LOO[1]
(1684-1745)

BORN TO THE PROFESSION in the fourth generation of a numerous and migratory family of Flemish painters,[2] Jean Baptiste Van Loo had a restless and perhaps unlucky career in the Italian and French courts. About the year 1713 at Turin, his services were the object of a jealous competition between Victor Amedeo II, Duke of Savoy,[3] and that potentate's son-in-law, the Prince of Carignan. The latter got him away from Turin with a pension to study at Rome, where in 1717 he achieved such notability that his name first comes into the record of George Vertue in London.[4] About 1719 he followed Carignan to Paris, was patronized there briefly by the Regent (until that Prince's death), painted the Royal family with great success, and became a member of the Royal Academy (1731) and a Professor (1735). He was an assiduous teacher, both of his own

1. Vertue's entries during the years 1737–46, besides giving some first-hand glimpses of Van Loo in London, include anecdotes, apparently told by Van Loo himself, of his years on the Continent. I have not found it possible to reconcile these entirely with the chief biographical source, Antoine Joseph Dezallier D'Argenville, *Abrégé de la vie des plus fameux Peintres*, Nouvelle Edition, Tome *4* (Paris, 1762), pp. 385–96. This account first appeared in 1752 in Tome *3* of the first edition and professes to derive from information furnished by friends and relatives at Aix. Another early account is Michel François Dandré-Bardon,

Vie de Jean Baptiste Vanloo (Paris, 1779). I am familiar with this only as it is digested in the *Abecedario de P. J. Mariette*, ed. Ph. de Chennevières and A. de Montaiglon, *5* (Paris, 1858–59), 381–82. Mariette noted on a transcript of Bardon's *Vie* that it had been read before the Academy 5 May 1753.

2. See the *Stammtafel* and articles in Thieme-Becker, *Allgemeines Lexikon der bildenden Künstler*, vol. *23*, 1929.

3. King of Sicily (1713) and of Sardinia (1720).

4. Vertue *1.45*: "Excellent painters now at Rome: Mr. Van Loo, Painter to the King of Sicily."

sons, one of whom, Louis-Michel, went to Spain as First Painter to the King in 1736,[5] and of his younger brother Charles André, who was to become head of the French Academy. At Paris, however, he lost a considerable amount of money in the Mississippi bubble."[6] His fortunes continuing for a number of years in some disrepair, he left France and arrived in London with one of his sons during December 1737[7]—a painter with a considerable reputation in portraiture but perhaps even better known for such earlier achievements as his two ceilings, one of the four seasons and one of Minerva and Pygmalion, painted for the Duke of Savoy in the castle at Rivoli.[8] He was still talking about a piece of bad luck he had suffered at Rome when a picture prepared for an Academy competition was spoiled by a blot of ink, so that he had to whip up another overnight, and won only second prize.[9] He liked to tell, too, how when he painted the deposed King of Poland Stanislaus and his Queen at Weissenburg, he was invited by his royal subject to smoke a pipe. ("So they did. King and painter smoke together.")[10] At London he had not, as Vertue remarks,[11] the advantage of an "importunate invitation from any nobleman or grandee of Court." His "prospect of staying or flourishing" seemed "very doubtful." He began by doing portraits of two noted theatrical characters, Colley Cibber and Owen Mac Swinney ("whose long silver-grey hairs were extremely picturesque and contributed to give the new painter reputation").[12] About the same time he painted a close friend of Pope and Kent, General James Dormer of Rousham.[13] His rise to eminence in London was, in fact, very rapid. Vertue's *Note Book* erupts in a series of little explosions of surprise and applause. "Soon after, being less than three or four months, had a most surprising number of people of the first quality sat to him. Did immediately only the faces." "Monsieur Van Loo, his increase of business by this time (April and May) fully employs him, having daily (as he says) five sittings . . . every day."[14]

> Monsieur Van Loo has had great approbation of his works from people of all
> condition, quality, and lately the Prince of Wales sat to him for his picture,
> the Princess, etc., the Princess Amelia. The great employment in six months

5. D'Argenville, p. 393. This incident as reported by D'Argenville sounds somewhat mysterious and perhaps is the same as an obscure imbroglio alluded to by Vertue 3.82, in which J. B. Van Loo lost a commission from the King of Spain to his brother and pupil Charles.

6. D'Argenville, pp. 386–94, and Vertue 3.82–83.

7. Vertue 3.82. D'Argenville, p. 394, says his wife and two sons came with him, and that one son, Claude, died in London, aged seventeen years.

8. D'Argenville, p. 389.

9. Vertue 3.82; D'Argenville, p. 388.

10. Vertue 3.83; D'Argenville, p. 392.

11. Vertue 3.82. Van Loo first had lodgings in Henrietta Street, Covent Garden; then, from 1740 to October 1742 he was at Nos. 55 and 56 Great Queen Street, the house to which Hudson moved in 1743 (Evelyn M. Davies, *The Life and Works of Thomas Hudson*, unpublished M.A. Thesis, University of London, 1938, pp. 35–37, citing Holborn Parish *Poor-Rate Books*, Holborn Municipal Offices). Cf. Vertue 3.130, 132.

12. Walpole, *Anecdotes* 2.330.

13. Vertue 3.82.

14. Vertue 3.82–83. "Crowds of coaches flocked to Mr. Vanloo's door, for several weeks after his arrival, just as they crowd the playhouse. He soon reckoned the pictures he had in hand, by hundreds, and was obliged to take five sittings a day: the man who kept the list of these sittings, was very handsomely rewarded for putting your name down before it came your turn, which was oftentimes six weeks after you had first presented yourself to have your picture drawn" (J. A. Rouquet, *The Present State of the Arts in England* [London, 1755], p. 38).

from his first coming exceeds any other painter that is come to England in the memory of any one living.

The English painters have had great uneasiness. it has much blemished their reputation and business.[15]

Perhaps the peak of Van Loo's felicity is represented in the following vignette:

Sir Robert Walpole, having had one picture drawn of himself by Van Loo, lately, since the death of Mr. Jervas [2 November 1739], whilst sitting mention was made of the death of the King's Principal Painter, and Sir Robert Walpole made Van Loo this compliment: that he so well liked and approved of his painting that if it had not been for an Act of Parliament that prevents foreigners of any nation to have or enjoy places of salary in the government, he would have presented him with the place of King's Painter.[16]

Vertue notices especially Van Loo's sometimes offensive realism: "his great success in likeness, naturally without flattery—or raising the character, but in that it's remarkable that Sir Robert Walpole and the Duke of Grafton were done too grossly—and Heidegger rather homelier than he was, but the generality were always pleased with his likeness of portrait."[17] The modern historian of Van Loo's work in England sees him as having been content to conform pretty closely to the prevailing realism of the school of Richardson, adding, however, a "tinge of modishness," a seasoning of "high French affectation," a certain chic of frills or embroidery, a curl to the edges of the draperies of the tablecloth, a slightly greater animation in the disposal of hands and arms.[18] These qualities of his painting are well enough illustrated in his General Dormer, seated with sword-hilt at his elbow on a table and a folio held on his knee (signed and dated 1738, the painting is still at Rousham),[19] or in the three-quarter-length standing portrait of Walpole, complacently smiling in wig, chins, brocaded arm, and ribboned stomach, with the Great Seal Case beneath his right hand (National Portrait Gallery 70).[20] One painting, which seems not to be known today but which may be evoked in the prose of Vertue, brings Van Loo well inside the circle of Pope toward the end of the year 1739:

Mr. Van Loo, having drawn a family piece in large of Lord Burlington, his lady, and two daughters—this noble Lord is sitting at a table, leaning on it, a port-crayon in his hand, some draughts, papers, books lying by them,—the lady is sitting richly dressed in brocades, flowered silks, a pallet of oil colours in her left hand. She is giving it to a blackamoor behind her, as if she had done with it. The eldest daughter has a music book which she opens on her mother's lap.

15. Vertue 3.84 (1738).
16. Vertue 3.97. "This Mr. Van Loo said."
17. Vertue 3.84.
18. Waterhouse, *Painting in Britain*, p. 149.
19. NPG Photograph 149404 (1947).

20. The same subject, by Van Loo, seated three-quarter-length with the Seal between left hand and knee (in the King's Gallery, Kensington Palace) exhibits the grossness of countenance to which Vertue alludes.

Thus they are all disposed in the virtuosi way. The whole picture is well drawn, the faces like, the attitudes graceful and natural, the coloring strong, and a free pencil. This masterpiece will remain as a testimony here of his skill and knowledge in art.[21]

Van Loo, however, was not destined to enjoy any long duration of good luck. By the winter of 1741 he was not feeling well. He often talked "of retiring into Provence his country" as soon as he could get "his work . . . finished here."

Monsieur Van Loo, painter, his illness increasing, ebbing, and flowing—being a complication of dropsy, gout, and rheumatism—though relieved by Dr. Ward's pills—still his greatest hopes was the air of his own country Provence in France at Aix, where he was born. All physicians and others advised him to retire there. Perhaps if not too much fatigued in the journey, he had a chance to recover or lengthen his days. However, here he left London, on October 16, 1742, this last year having not begun any new works, only employed his time to finish those begun.[22]

He had been getting along with the help of two assistants, Eccardt and Root (or Ross), who remained in London, finished some of his pictures, and then set up for themselves.[23] At Aix-en-Provence in September 1745 Van Loo died.[24] The two closely related oils of Alexander Pope to be discussed below (nos. 66.1 and 2) must have been finished rather late during the French painter's London sojourn. Yet they are both excellent examples of his art, and the larger and more elaborate perhaps shows him close to the height of his powers.

21. Vertue 3.96. Van Loo's portrait of Pope's friend Richard Temple Viscount Cobham was at Stowe and later (1947) at Chevening (NPG Photograph 4380, 1947).

22. Vertue 3.110.

23. Vertue 3.110, 125, 127, 130, 132. John Giles Eccardt was the portrayer of Thomas Gray and Horace Walpole, both at the National Portrait Gallery. Root or Ross was the drapery painter of the team. Vertue notes that the week after Van Loo's departure a newspaper puff of Mr. Stephen Slaughter, a rival for royal favor as portraitist, had a "sting in the tail." "Mr. Slaughter . . . finishes the whole with his own hands—not common" (3.111).

24. Sometime during the year 1745 Vertue entered in his notebook: "Q. when did Van Loo die? <at Aix en provence>." Then after October 1746 he wrote: "From France it is said that Monsieur Van Loo died about April last—1746" (Vertue 3.127, 132). But Dezallier D'Argenville says quite firmly that he died at Aix on 19 September 1745.

66.1. OIL PAINTING, BY J. B. VAN LOO. THE EARL OF MANSFIELD, SCONE PALACE, PERTH.

The mezzotint by John Faber (no. 66.15; J. Ch. Smith, *1*.413, Faber no. 294) says that Faber humbly presents the work to the Honorable William Murray, Solicitor General, and furthermore that it is derived from the "Archetype" painted by Van Loo in 1742 and in the possession of William Murray. Hugh Bethel's letter to Pope, 25 March 1744, confirms the fact that a portrait of Pope had been painted by Van Loo.[1]

66.1. Oil on canvas. 35½ x 28½ in. Background raw Siena and black; wig smoky gray; chair half-tone black; coat burnt umber and gray, representing velour material; book yellow ochre and raw Siena; table top Indian red; flesh tints umber, Venetian red and white. Seal of the First Earl of Mansfield, Lord Chief Justice of England, on back of canvas. The Earl of Mansfield, Scone Palace, Perth.†

William Murray became Lord Chief Justice in 1756 and First Earl of Mansfield in 1776. In 1754 he acquired Kenwood House in Hampstead, and ten years later he employed Robert Adam to remodel it.

A "portrait" of Pope (in addition to a bust of Pope and Pope's own oil painting of Betterton after Kneller) is reported at Kenwood by Daniel Lysons, *The Environs of London* (1795), 3.349; and in *The Ambulator*, 8th ed. (1796), p. 154.[2] Presumably it was the same portrait which was lent by the Earl of Mansfield in 1846 to the Exhibition at the British Institution (no. 119, attributed to Jervas). Cunningham in 1854 again attributes it to Jervas but at the same time assures us of the identification ("right arm resting on his folio Homer, right hand against his forehead, fingers beneath his wig, slate-coloured dress").[3] An engraving of the picture by George T. Doo appears as frontispiece to vol. 4 of Elwin and Courthope's *Works of Pope* in 1871: "From the original Picture by Jervas in the possession of the Earl Mansfield at Caen Wood." See no. 66.14. The portrait became so firmly attached to Jervas that along with the version in the Lansdowne Collection (no. 66.2) it is mentioned in the *DNB* article on Jervas by Lionel Henry Cust in 1892.

At the dispersal of the Kenwood Collection in 1922, the portrait of Pope (along with Pope's head of Betterton) seems to have gone to Scone Palace, Seat of the Earls of Mansfield, near Perth, where at any rate these pictures are today.[4]

The details of the picture—e.g. the pencil on the table and the more central position of the left hand—became well known through Faber's mezzotint (no. 66.15). This picture, rather than the larger and more elaborate Lansdowne version (no. 66.2), is the model for a large family of derivatives in oil, crayon, and line engraving.

1. *Correspondence* 4.512.

2. J. N. Brewer, *Beauties of England and Wales, 10*, Part IV (1816), p. 177: "In an apartment termed the School Room is an original portrait of Pope, presented by him to the Earl of Mansfield when Mr. Murray." On 22 June 1792, Fanny Burney visited Kenwood and saw a portrait of Pope, presumably this one, which she thought was by Pope himself and much in the style of Jervas. No doubt she remembered what she was told about the Betterton (*Diary & Letters of Madame D'Arblay*, ed. Charlotte Barrett and Austin

Dobson, 5 [London, 1905], 98–99).

3. The portrait is said to be mentioned also in Thomas James Barratt, *The Annals of Hampstead* (London, 1912), *1.*275.

4. Professor E. K. Waterhouse saw the picture at Scone in 1951. He assures me it is an authentic Van Loo.

Mr. R. F. Adam, of the Scone Estates Office, kindly sent me a detailed set of color notes on this picture, made by a professional friend.

66.2. OIL PAINTING, BY J. B. VAN LOO. W. S. LEWIS, FARMINGTON, CONNECTICUT.

John Fitzpatrick Baron Gowran (1719–58) was created Earl of Upper Ossory in 1751. He had married in 1744 Evelyn, daughter of Pope's friend John Leveson-Gower, 1st Earl Gower, and niece of Lady Mary Wortley Montagu. His son John Fitzpatrick (1745–1818), Second Earl of Upper Ossory, married in 1769 Anne, divorced wife of the Third Duke of Grafton, the "charming Duchess" of the correspondence with Horace Walpole. She died in 1804. The Second Earl on his death in 1818 left no legitimate male heir. Two daughters, Lady Anne Fitzpatrick (illegitimate) and Lady Gertrude Fitzpatrick, lived on at their father's estate of Farming Woods, Brigstock, and died both in 1841.

66.2. Oil on canvas. 44 x 35½ in. Background obscure; statue in right background greenish black monochrome; back of chair dark green with yellow nail heads; cloth over table dark emerald green; chair arms red brown; book yellow with pinkish leaf ends; paper in hand grayish; coat and breeches yellow brown; wig yellowish gray; neckcloth and cuffs white, with yellow links; flesh tints sallow; eyes blue gray. Column and drape in left background; a lofty colonnade in center. Inscribed in upper right with yellow paint: "Alexʳ Pope." On spine of book: "ΟΜΗΡΟΣ". Wilmarth S. Lewis, Farmington, Connecticut.

On 21 May 1842, Christie held a sale of the Earl of Upper Ossory's pictures from Ampt-hill Park. The portrait which is the subject of this entry comes to light as lot 52 on this day. It was bought, as a portrait of Pope by Charles Jervas, for 143 guineas by the Marquis of Lansdowne,[1] a nephew of the Second Earl of Upper Ossory. Mrs. Jameson, *Companion to the Most Celebrated Private Galleries of Art in London* (1844), p. 288, remarks that Lord Lansdowne's pictures frequently change their location, moving back and forth between Lansdowne House in London and the country seat of the Marquis, Bowood. On page 325, no. 134, Pope by "Jervas," is described as "Three quarters. Seated, leaning on his hand, in a contemplative attitude, the head raised." The same portrait, by "Jervas," "very animated," is reported at Lansdowne House by Waagen, *Treasures of Art in Great Britain* (1854), 2.152, and in 1854 by Cunningham, at Bowood. In 1892 Lionel Cust in the *DNB,* placing the portrait at Lansdowne House, attributes it to Charles Jervas.[2]

The picture was lot 50, correctly attributed to Van Loo, at the Lansdowne Sale, Christie's, 7 March 1930. The name of the buyer was "ffennell."[3] It reappeared at Christie's, 5 October 1956, as no. 34, p. 7, still attributed to Van Loo, in a sale of pictures and drawings, *The Property of Mrs. Raymond ffennell deceased, removed from Wytham Abbey near Oxford.*[4] It was bought by Frost and Reed of Bristol.[5] It was bought the following year, through Zeitlin & Ver Brugge, of Los Angeles, by Wilmarth S. Lewis, of Farmington, Connecticut. Professor E. K. Waterhouse saw the picture in New Haven in 1957 and pronounced it to be an original Van Loo, agreeing entirely in style with some dozen pictures which he has seen in England, documented works by Van Loo. It was shown in the exhibition of works of art collected by Yale Alumni, at the Yale University Art Gallery in June 1960, and was illustrated in Alfred Frankfurter's article on the exhibition, *Art News, 59* (Summer 1960), 48.

1. Lugt 16608 (annotated catalogue, E. K. Waterhouse, Barber Institute, Birmingham). The Upper Ossory pictures were part of a mixed sale, 20–21 May. The picture in question is described as "Portrait of Pope seated in his library, his head resting on his hand."

2. See also *Catalogue of the Collection of Pictures Belonging to the Marquis of Lansdowne, K.G. At Lansdowne House, London and Bowood, Wilts.,* 1897,

p. 48, no. 34: "Jervas, Charles."

3. Notation on photograph at the Warburg Institute, London; *Art Prices Current,* New Series, *10a,* no. 5468.

4. Cf. *The Times,* 25 May 1956, p. 13, and 11 June, p. 14.

5. Notation on photograph at the Courtauld Institute, London.

66.3. OIL PAINTING, AFTER J. B. VAN LOO. MR. AND MRS. A. M. D. PERRINS, BURE HOUSE, AYLSHAM, NORWICH.

The collection of pictures once at Cobham Hall, near Rochester, was mainly formed by John Bligh, Fourth Earl of Darnley, a patron of the fine arts and friend of Reynolds, Gainsborough, and Hoppner. The earliest allusion to the portrait of Pope at Cobham is apparently in John Preston Neale, *Views of the Seats of Noblemen and Gentlemen* (London, 1819), 2, page [6] following plates [42, 43, 44]: "A good half-length portrait of Pope, from which the print prefixed to some editions of his works, appears to have been taken." On 10 August 1868, George Scharf visited Cobham and recorded: "Pope resting head on r hand & elbow on book on a round table. A paper held in his left hand. White ruffles—long y. grey silky hair, . . . shadows brownish full pale crimson lips. Eyeballs indigo dark blue. Eyebrows broad & very dark sepia. Dark y. grey velvet coat. . . . Dark sepia background. No. 186."[1]

This portrait (attributed to Jonathan Richardson) was lot 68 (p. 24) of Christie's sale of *Important Pictures By Old Masters, The Property of the Rt. Hon. The Earl of Darnley, Removed from Cobham Hall, Kent,* 1 May 1925. This and a smaller companion portrait (lot 35, p. 14) "Charles Jervas. Portrait of Dean Swift," 29½ x 24½ inches, were purchased by Permain for 110 and 70 guineas respectively.[2]

These two portraits were in the winter of 1934 apparently the property of (Sir) Ernest Royden and were either intended by him for the *Loan Exhibition Depicting Marlborough and the Reign of Queen Anne* held that winter at Chesterfield House and were at the last minute withdrawn, or they were actually in the Exhibition but arrived too late to be properly catalogued.[3] Both Pope and Swift reappeared, as lot 517 (Pope attributed to Richardson) and lot 578, in a sale held by Messrs. Talbot Wilson & Co. (West Kirby, Cheshire) at the home of the late Sir Ernest Royden, Hill Bark, at Frankby, Cheshire, 19 December 1960, and both were acquired by a daughter of Sir Ernest, Mrs. A. M. D. Perrins, of Bure House, Aylsham, Norwich.[4]

The portrait of Pope was exhibited at the National Portrait Gallery Exhibition in 1961.

1. National Portrait Gallery, Scharf *Sketch Book 81.44*; cf. *63.113* and *86.26* (1871), "Pond?"

2. Sale Catalogue at National Portrait Gallery; cf. *Art Prices Current 4.237* (no. 5006).

3. See *A Loan Exhibition Depicting Marlborough and the Reign of Queen Anne*, Chesterfield House (By kind permission of the Earl of Harewood) *29th January–March 1934*, p. 109 (Index to Contributors), "Royden, E. B., Esq." But no exhibit numbers are entered for this name. Two labels on the back of the Swift indicate that it was no. 202 at the Exhibition, but in the Catalogue, no. 202 (p. 31) is a "Blue Dash Charger." Each Picture has a label of "James Bourlet & Sons, 17–18 Nassau Street, Mortimer Street W.1." handlers of pictures.

4. A photograph of this picture at the Frick Art Reference Library, originating at the sale of 1925, shows that it was once in a smaller frame, which cut off about an inch all around. The present frame has on the back an old paper label with these words in ink: "Palma Vecchio / The Holy Family / Sir Berkeley Sheffield Bart."

66.4. OIL PAINTING, AFTER J. B. VAN LOO. THE BARON SACKVILLE, KNOLE HOUSE, SEVENOAKS, KENT.

This portrait seems to be first mentioned ("168 Alexʳ Pope") in a manuscript list of paintings at Knole House dated 1775, among the Manuscripts of Sir William Musgrave at the British Museum.[1] It is no. 388, attributed to Van Loo, in S. J. Mackie, *Knole House, Its State Rooms, Pictures, and Antiques* (Sevenoaks and London, [1858]), pp. 99–102, "The Dining Room"—where it was seen and sketched by George Scharf, 7 May 1859.[2] It is still in the private dining room at Knole, along with portraits of Prior and Gay by Dahl and other literary portraits of the eighteenth century.

1. Photoextract from British Museum Add. MS. 5726E.6, *6.12* at the National Portrait Gallery.

2. National Portrait Gallery, Scharf *Sketch Book 55.46*.

66.3. Oil on canvas. 36¼ x 28½ in. Background brownish; chair olive green, with reddish nail heads; table mahogany red; leaf ends of book salmon, label blurred red; coat and breeches brown; cheeks reddish. Mr. and Mrs. A. M. D. Perrins, Bure House, Aylsham, Norwich.

below, left

66.4. Oil on canvas. c. 36 x 27¾ in. Colors similar to those of no. 66.3. Inscribed (at top): "ALEXᴿ POPE. OBᵀ 1744." On spine of book: "ΟΜΗΡΟΣ". The Baron Sackville, Knole House, Kent.

below, right

66.5. Oil on canvas. 36 x 28 in. Colors similar to those of no. 66.3. Earle W. Newton, St. Augustine, Florida.†

66.5. OIL PAINTING, AFTER J. B. VAN LOO. EARLE W. NEWTON, ST. AUGUSTINE RESTORATION COMMISSION, ST. AUGUSTINE, FLORIDA.

This picture first comes to light, attributed to Van Loo, as lot 140, without frame, in a Christie's sale, 16 December 1949. It was purchased by Mr. Murray Adams-Acton, 37 Palace Gate, Kensington, W.8. In April 1961 it was acquired at Eton by Mr. Earle W. Newton, then Director of the Museum of Art, Science and Industry, Bridgeport, Connecticut, where in September and October 1962, the picture was exhibited (no. 23, "Jonathan Richardson") in an exhibition assembled by Mr. Newton, *British Painting XVII–XVIII Centuries*. Mr. Newton is now Director of the St. Augustine Restoration Commission, St. Augustine, Florida. This picture is distinguished from all others in this group by the bookmark projecting from the leaves near the spine, a detail which it shares with the Faber mezzotint (no. 66.15).

66.6. OIL PAINTING, AFTER J. B. VAN LOO. WILLIAM ANDREWS CLARK MEMORIAL LIBRARY, UNIVERSITY OF CALIFORNIA, LOS ANGELES.

This picture was in 1951 in the hands of B. F. Stevens & Brown Ltd., 28–30 Little Russell Street, W.C.1. It was acquired by the William Andrews Clark Memorial Library, Los Angeles, California. In what seems a late-eighteenth-century hand, on a small label pasted to the top of the stretcher at the back, is "Mr Philips." At the middle of the stretcher is a clipping of printed paper, apparently from a dealer's catalogue: "This portrait was formerly in the Tennyson D'Eyncourt Collection." "⑨ D'Eyncourt" appears in chalk at the top back of the frame. Charles Tennyson D'Eyncourt, 1784–1861 statesman and antiquary, of Bayons Manor and Usselby House, Lincolnshire, was the founder of the family which seems most likely to have owned this picture. The picture is reproduced following page 10 of the William Andrews Clark Memorial Library's *Report of the Second Decade, 1945–55* (Los Angeles, 1956).

66.7. OIL PAINTING, AFTER J. B. VAN LOO. EMILY DRISCOLL, NEW YORK CITY, 1959.

In October 1959 Miss Emily Driscoll, 115 E. 40th Street, New York City, had this picture on consignment from a London dealer. An inkwell showing a brown geometric design on a bluish ground distinguishes the picture from all the others of this group. On the back of the stretcher a printed paper clipping, as from a dealer's catalogue, reads: "Mrs. H. N. Redmond. / Popefield / At. . . . "

66.8. OIL PAINTING, AFTER J. B. VAN LOO. UNIVERSITY OF PENNSYLVANIA LIBRARY, PHILADELPHIA.

At Christie's, 25 January 1929, in a sale of "The Property of the late Sir William Ingram, Bart.", appeared: "Jervas. Portrait of Alexander Pope, in lavender dress, seated by a table—28½ x 23." It was bought for £46/4 by "Newton" (*Art Prices Current*, New

Series, *8a*, p. 110, no. 4718). In *Parnassus*, *1* (April 1929), 16, under the heading "The Art Market," appears, courtesy of Arthur U. Newton, 655 Fifth Avenue, New York City, a photograph of a "Portrait of Alexander Pope, by Charles Jervas." This is similar to the portraits listed just above (nos. 66.3–66.7), except that it is cut off at both elbows and the waist. In 1963, or shortly before, an anonymous owner put this painting on loan in the University of Pennsylvania Library. An advertisement by Arthur Newton is attached to the back.[1]

1. John Preston Neale, *Views of the Seats of Gentlemen, in England, Wales, Scotland, and Ireland*, Second Series, *3* (London, 1826), with Plate [44], Shalford House, Surrey, the Seat of Henry Edmund Austen, Esq., gives a list of the "principal pictures," including "The well-known Portrait of Pope, by Jervis, which has been engraved. This was the last Portrait taken of the poet, and tradition says it was finished or corrected by himself." This no doubt was an oil painting of the Van Loo type—possibly no. 66.5, no. 66.6, no. 66.7, or no. 66.8.

66.9. OIL PAINTING, AFTER J. B. VAN LOO. ROBERT HALSBAND, COLUMBIA UNIVERSITY, NEW YORK.

This portrait first comes to light, illustrated and described, in *Catalogue Number Eighty-Six, Autograph Letters, MSS., and a Few Literary Portraits*, issued by P. H. Muir for Elkin Matthews, Ltd., at Takeley, Bishops Stortford, 1941. The portrait was bought in the same year by Mr. David A. Randall for the Scribner Book Store, 597 Fifth Avenue, New York City, where it was acquired by Robert Halsband in 1956.

66.6. Oil on canvas. 36 x 28 in. Colors presumably similar to those of no. 66.3. William Andrews Clark Memorial Library, University of California, Los Angeles.†

66.7. Oil on canvas. 36¼ x 27¾ in. (out of frame). Colors similar to those of no. 66.3. Background dark bluish. Emily Driscoll, New York City, 1959.

66.9(1) OIL PAINTING, AFTER J. B. VAN LOO. SOTHEBY'S, 24 JULY 1963.

At Sotheby's, 24 July 1963, in a sale of *Various Properties*, lot 21, attributed to "Troost," was an oil painting, "Portrait of a Gentleman, three-quarter length, seated at a desk on which are books and papers. In a sculptured oval, on metal, 11 in. by 9½ in." It was purchased by Jarvis for £15. This picture is like no. 66.9 in being painted on metal, and is approximately the same small size. The details of the composition (National Portrait Gallery Reference Photograph 11367), aside from the painted oval, very strongly resemble those of no. 66.9.

66.10. OIL PAINTING, AFTER J. B. VAN LOO. MR. AND MRS. R. W. ROBERTSON-GLASGOW, HINTON CHARTERHOUSE, SOMERSET.†

An oil portrait, 48½ x 39½ inches, of the Van Loo type, is in the collection of Mr. and Mrs. R. W. Robertson-Glasgow, Hinton Charterhouse, Somerset. A photograph of it taken by the Courtauld Institute of Art, c. 1960, shows a column in the left background, a drape coming down from the center behind the column and encircling it to fall in large folds on a massive marble-topped table with an elaborately carved leaf-and-scroll leg. The table holds a folio book, supporting Pope's right elbow. The back of the chair (straight with nail heads along the edge in all other examples of this type) here has a wood frame curving out in a heart-shaped lobe at the right, with a central ornament like a shell just behind Pope's head.

66.11. CRAYON "PAINTING" (PASTEL), AFTER J. B. VAN LOO. WILLIAM H. ROBINSON LTD., 16 PALL MALL, LONDON.

In a sale of various properties at Sotheby's, 3 March 1952, lot 161 (p. 19 of the Catalogue) was "The Property of T. W. Sandeman, Esq.," "a portrait in oils of Alexander Pope" 24 x 18½ inches, "Attributed to Arthur Pond." This picture, actually a pastel, or "crayon painting," was purchased by William H. Robinson Ltd., of 16 Pall Mall, and remains in their offices. It is a freely and cleanly executed crayon "painting," a very attractive picture. The back is covered with a paper shield, on which is pasted a label bearing the ink inscription: "This is the Property of Capt. Sandeman." Also attached to the paper shield is a decorative engraving of the Houbraken type, "A. Pond Pinxt. Goldar Sculpᵗ". For the role of Arthur Pond in the multiplication of portraits of the Van Loo type, see no. 66.16.[1]

1. At Knight, Frank, and Rutley's, 15 February 1929, in a sale of Various Properties, appeared: "Pond, A. Portrait of Alexander Pope. Pastel—24½ x 20." It was bought for £5/5 (*Art Prices Current*, New Series, *8a*, 131, no. 5899).

66.12. CRAYON "PAINTING" (PASTEL), AFTER J. B. VAN LOO. ALBERT VON FRANK, ELKINS PARK, PENNSYLVANIA.

At Christie's, 3 December 1910, lot 2 was: "W. Hoare, R.A., Portrait of Alexander Pope, in brown coat, *pastel*. 24½ x 18½ in." A copy of the catalogue at the National

above, left

66.8. Oil on canvas. 27⅞ x 24¾ in. (out of frame). Inscribed (upper left): "ALEXANDER POPE / B. 1688 D 1744". Colors similar to those of no. 66.3. The University of Pennsylvania Library, Philadelphia.†

above, right

66.9. Oil on copper. 11¾ x 9³⁄₁₆ in. Chair dark green; coat snuff brown; table and chair arms red brown; inkwell lead-gray. The back of the copper plate has on it small graph squares and numbers, but nearly effaced. Robert Halsband, Columbia University, New York.

right

66.11. Crayon painting (presumably on paper). 24 x 18½ in. Background steely gray; coat leathery brown but soft; table cover greenish; wig feathery ash-gray; letters and ornament on spine of book golden; eyes dark blue. On spine of book: "OMHPOΣ". William H. Robinson Ltd., 16 Pall Mall, London.

Portrait Gallery is annotated: "? Hoare. Seated resting his head against his r. hand & looking slightly upward, face ¾ R." In *The Connoisseur, A Magazine for Collectors, 80* (April 1928), p. LXXIII is a quarter-page advertisement by Blumenthal, Napoleon House, King Street, St. James, containing an illustration of a "Pastel Drawing of Alexander Pope by William Hoare," 24 x 18½ inches. The photograph actually shows a crayon "painting" of the Van Loo type. On 1 March 1935, a picture, offered by G. G. Blumenthal, appeared as lot 5 in a Christie's sale, catalogued as "Portrait of Alexander Pope, Esq., in brown coat—pastel—24 x 18¾ inches." It was "bought in" at 2½ guineas.

In 1952 Mr. Cecil S. Keeley, then of 159 Streetsbrook Road, Shirley, Birmingham, sent to the National Portrait Gallery a photograph of a crayon "painting" of the Van Loo type, 24 x 19 inches, with the name "George Romney" written on the back, and the Christie stencil "79.FZ.", a reference apparently to the 1935 sale. Comparison of this photograph with that in *The Connoisseur* for April 1928 reveals the same picture. Mr. Keeley could not be traced in October 1960.

In February 1965 this picture came to light once more, in the possession of Mr. Albert von Frank, of Elkins Park, Pennsylvania.

66.13. CRAYON "PAINTING" (PASTEL), AFTER J. B. VAN LOO. F. C. LETTS, ESQ., 1952.

In a Christie's sale, 7 January 1947, lot 40 was a similar pastel, 23½ x 17½ inches, "Alexander Pope by Russell." This was apparently a picture bought about this time by Mr. F. C. Letts, of London, who could not be traced in the winter of 1961. A photograph of this picture deposited at the National Portrait Gallery by Mr. Letts c. 1952 shows it to be very similar to no. 66.11 (Messrs. William H. Robinson Ltd.), and I should think possibly the work of the same hand. The word "ΟΜΗΡΟΣ" appears more faintly than in the other picture.

66.14. WATERCOLOR, AFTER J. B. VAN LOO. JOHN MURRAY, 1888.

No. 180, on page 35 of the Twickenham Loan Museum *Catalogue* of 1888 is a "Water Colour Copy of Lord Mansfield's portrait of Pope (by Jervas?), Lent by Mr. John Murray, 50 Albemarle St. W2." Perhaps this was an engraver's copy for the engraving by Geo. T. Doo, R. A., cut off inside both elbows and above the waist, which appears as frontispiece to volume 6 of Elwin and Courthope's *Works of Alexander Pope* in 1871: "From the original Picture by Jervas in the possession of the Earl Mansfield at Caen Wood." John Murray was publisher of the Elwin-Courthope Pope. Cf. no. 9.6.

66.15. MEZZOTINT ENGRAVING, BY J. FABER, AFTER J. B. VAN LOO, C. 1744.

J. Ch. Smith *1.413* (Faber no. 294) reproduces this engraving and, as corrected by Charles E. Russell, *English Mezzotint Portraits* (1926), 2.96, describes three states: 1. before any inscription ("Three examples known"—but not located); 2. with lettering as shown below; 3. with publication line: "Printed for John Bowles at the Black Horse in Cornhill & Carington Bowles in St. Paul's Church Yard London." At the British

Museum an example of this print (Q.1–122) has the original lettering removed and new lettering, which includes a passage slightly adapted from Dryden's praise of Ben Jonson in the *Essay of Dramatic Poesy:* "He Invaded Authors like a Monarch, And what Would Have Been Theft In Other Poets, was Only Victory In Him." See no. 66.1 for the relation of this mezzotint to the oil paintings. The mezzotint appears to be the only contemporary external evidence for the origin of this type of picture.

66.16. LINE ENGRAVING, BY J. HOUBRAKEN, AFTER A. POND, 1747. FOR THOMAS BIRCH'S *Heads of Illustrious Persons of Great Britain,* VOLUME 2.

The Heads of Illustrious Persons of Great Britain, Engraven by Mr. Houbraken and Mr. Vertue.[1] *With Their Lives and Characters by T. Birch, London,* printed for John and Paul Knapton, appeared in two folio volumes: volume 1, 1743, and volume 2, 1751.[2] The plate of Pope appears at the end of volume 2, facing p. 55 (his biographical sketch). This is a reversed image of the Van Loo type, cut off above the waist and with the arm which props the head (now the left arm) resting on a plain table or block.

H. Gravelot, as we are told by the lettering of the allegorical scene (Britannia amid symbols of civilization) on the title-page of each volume, invented the ornaments "for the Heads." Those for Pope consist of elaborate classical symbols of art and inspiration surmounting, and fortifying at lower right and left, the oval containing the portrait. Beneath the portrait, a sun bursting forth in splendor from behind sullen clouds, sheds its rays into a panel having a scene of the nine muses grouped around Apollo, who extends a crown of bays toward an aged Homeric-looking figure as he approaches, supported on either side by youthful escorts, who point forward and spurn back the reaching arms of satyr-like and deformed creatures lying tangled in shadow. For Gravelot, see no. 57–61.24.

We have seen the signature "A. Pond" before, attached to the very inferior profile medallion of Pope, derived apparently from Richardson for the title page of Warburton editions of the *Essay on Man* (no. 43.3). Arthur Pond (1705?–38), pupil of Vanderbank, was a painter and engraver and also a picture-framer, glazer, and dealer in art supplies for elite amateurs.[3] His shop was in Great Queen Street, Lincoln's Inn Fields. He achieved some success at portrait-painting, mostly in crayon "paintings"; he did landscape etchings, and portrait etchings in the rough or "scratched" manner of Rembrandt. He seems to have worked a good deal in collaboration with the Knapton brothers, both the publishers and the artists[4] (cf. no. 43.1). On the evidence doubtless of the medallion engraving just mentioned and of the lettering of the present engraving, the *DNB* article on Pond says that among the most notable of his original portraits were two of Alexander Pope. The obvious relation of Houbraken's engraving in 1747 to the Van Loo type of portrait would seem to forbid interpreting "A. Pond pinxit" as other than a reference to an intermediate portrait (either in crayons or oils). Pond seems to have been called in by the Knapton brothers precisely for the purpose of making a copy which could be used as a model for the engraver in Amsterdam. Vertue tells us that in the summer of 1737 "Mr Pond began his circuit in the Country to Noblemen and Gentle-

above, left

66.15. Mezzotint. 14 x 10 in. (with lettering). "ALEXANDER POPE, / Poeta
Anglus. / OB: Aº 1744 ÆTAT: 57 / Hanc Imaginem ex ipso Archetypo
a VANLO picto 1742 expressam / viro HONORABILI GULIELMO MUR-
RAY SOLICITATORI GENERALI apud quem Deponitur / Humillime D.D.D.
/ JOHANNES FABER / Price 2 Shill. Sold by J. Faber at the Golden Head
in Bloomsbury Square." *BMEP* 43. *Grolier* 124. *J. Ch. Smith 1.214*
(Faber no. 294). The example reproduced here is British Museum Por-
trait Q.1–121. By permission of the Trustees of the British Museum.

above, right

66.16. Line engraving. Plate mark 13⅞ x 8½ in. "ALEXANDER POPE
Esq. / A. Pond pinxit. // In the Possession of Mʳ Arthur Pond. // J.
Houbraken sculps. Amst. 1747. / Impensis J. & P. Knapton Londini."
BMEP 45. *Grolier* 51. For *The Heads of Illustrious Persons of Great
Britain . . . With Their Lives and Characters, By T. Birch*, vol. 2, 1751.
Professor John C. Pope, Yale University.

left

66.17. Line engraving. Picture 5½ x 3½ in. At top: "Plate XVI // Vol.
IV. facing p. 9." At bottom: "F. Hayman inv. et del. // C. Grignion
sculp. / Shut, shut the Door, good John! fatigu'd I said / Tye up the
Knocker, say I'm sick, I'm dead. / Ep: to Arbuthnot." *The Works of
Alexander Pope Esq.*, ed. William Warburton, 1751, 4.9.

mens houses in quest of business. or to coppy heads in Chiaroscure.—for Knaptons Illistrions [sic] to be gravd after."[5]

Pond's copy of Van Loo's Pope, of course, need not have introduced, probably did not introduce, either the reversal or the truncation and simplification of Houbraken's engraving. Pond may very well have been the painter of any one of several derivative portraits in oil and crayon listed above (nos. 66.3–66.13). But there is no evidence that any one of these is actually the work of Pond. Still less is there any warrant for saying that any one of these was painted by Pond "ad vivum."

The Van Loo type of Pope portrait would seem to have the distinction of being the model for a larger number of poor derivative engravings than any other during the second half of the eighteenth century. See *Grolier* nos. 51–74 and *BMEP* 46–59, which do not exhaust the list. So far as I am aware, this was the best-known image of Pope for the period, only the lugubriously amorphous cap and gown multiplied in France from the Kneller painting of 1722 being a near competitor. The name of Pond appears frequently with these engravings. When Pope's elbow rests on a book on a table, the source of the engraving is presumably the Faber mezzotint.[6] When the elbow rests on a simple table or block, the Houbraken engraving has apparently intervened in the sequence of sources.[7]

1. See, for example, no. 4, William Warham, "G. Vertue Sculp. 1737," and no. 25, Thomas Sackville, "G. Vertue Sculp;" and Vertue *1*.5, 18–19.

2. Republished: vol. *1*, J. and P. Knapton, 1747; vol 2, J. and P. Knapton, 1752; in one volume, John Knapton, 1756; in one volume, William Baynes, London 1813.

An impression of the plate of Pope showing the face heavily reworked is in the National Portrait Gallery reference collection.

3. Notes from Pond's Account Book, 1734–50 (British Museum Ad. MS. 23724), about art supplies, and Pond's letter, 10 May 1757, to John Moffatt (John Smibert's nephew) in Boston (Ad. MS. 23724–5), quoted in the Whitley Papers, Department of Prints and Drawings, British Museum. See also W. T. Whitley, *Artists and Their Friends in England 1700–1799* (London, 1928), *1*.29, 64–66.

4. Vertue *3*.125; *4*.194–95. A series of 69 engravings after old-master landscape drawings (in the collections of such connoisseurs as Richardson and Dr. Mead) was done by Pond and Charles Knapton between 1732 and 1736, and a series of 26 caricatures was done by Pond alone between 1736 and 1747. Sets of these two series preserved in the Cottonian Library at the Plymouth Corporation Art Gallery and Museum and in the British Museum Print Room are described by Henry M. Hake, "Pond's and Knapton's Imitations of Drawings," *The Print Collector's Quarterly*, *9* (December 1922), 324–49. Vertue *6*.194 says, "1734, 1735, 1736. . . . in all 70 plates." See no. 43.1.

5. Vertue *3*.79–80. "Principally from paintings by Vandyke."

6. See for instance *Grolier* 72, *BMEP* 44, in *The Universal Magazine of Knowledge and Pleasure*, *1* (October 1747), facing p. 217, the head and supporting hand reversed and cramped into an oval, but with the book showing and "Vanlo pinx. // C. Grignion Sculp." The accompanying biographical sketch is entitled "The Life of Alexander Pope, Esq; With his Head engraved by Mr. Grignion, from an original painting of Van Loo."

7. *Grolier* 67, to be found in *The London Magazine*, *20* (July 1751), 320, is a poor copy of the Houbraken engraving of 1747, which no doubt was circulated as a separate sheet before its inclusion in vol. 2 of Birch, 1751.

Professor Maynard Mack is the owner of an oil on canvas, 29¾ x 24⅜ in., acquired in London during 1960. Here Pope in the reversed pose of the Houbraken engraving is cut off inside a similar painted oval and rests his left elbow on a covered table or block. This is the only oil painting I know which seems derived from the Houbraken engraving.

66.17. ENGRAVING BY C. GRIGNION AFTER F. HAYMAN. *Works of Pope,* ED. WILLIAM WARBURTON, 1751, VOLUME 4.

The team of Francis Hayman and Charles Grignion the elder had not so long after Pope's death collaborated in a sheerly fanciful illustration for William Mason's obituary poem *Musaeus*, 1747. Here Chaucer, Spenser, and Milton stand by in a grotto scene, while a figure of A. Pope which has little claim to look like Pope, seated on a stone seat and attended by a goddess,[1] droops his head and dies. In a number of illustrations for Warburton's edition of Pope's *Works*, published in 1751, Hayman and Grignion produce a semi-allegorical, bardic Pope, dressed apparently in a shirt or waistcoat beneath a long gown.[2] In other illustrations the scene is modern and realistic, and here, especially in the illustration for the opening lines of Pope's *Epistle to Arbuthnot* (volume 4, facing p. 9), it seems clear enough that Hayman's figure of Pope is derived from the Van Loo type.

1. See Appendix 4.8.
2. See especially *The Works of Alexander Pope, Esq.* (London 1751), *4*, Plate XVIII, facing p. 299, *Epilogue to the Satires*, 2; and *6*, Plate XXIV, facing p. 1, *Essay on Criticism*.

66.18. MINIATURE, LEAD PENCIL ON VELLUM, BY SOLOMON POLACK. PARKE-BERNET GALLERIES, 10 MAY 1955.†

In an exhibition of miniatures at the Victoria and Albert Museum during 1914–18, no. 509 was a miniature of Pope lent by Francis Wellesley. This was an oval, 3 x 2⅜ inches, in a metal frame with a bow-knot ornament at top, lead pencil on vellum, by Solomon Polack, signed on the back.[1] Polack was a miniature painter born at the Hague in 1757. He settled in London and exhibited at the Academy almost every year from 1790 to 1835. He died at Chelsea in 1839.[2] A photograph of this miniature at the National Portrait Gallery (Photographs: Miniatures A–Z. 1725–1750) was presented by Wellesley in October 1918. A similar photograph is to be found in the Department of Prints and Drawings at the British Museum (Engraved Portraits of Pope 1918–8–28–16). The drawing was lot 636 at Sotheby's sale of the *Francis Wellesley Collection of Drawings and Miniatures*, 1–2 July 1920. It reappeared in a sale at Parke-Bernet Galleries, 10 December 1952, lot 575, consigned by Roger Barrett, with a note saying it was "Bought at the Wellesley sale." The same picture appeared once more at a Parke-Bernet sale, 10 May 1955, lot 358, "N.Y. Collector." It is derived from the Van Loo type.

1. I take this description, and the reference to the Victoria and Albert Museum Exhibition, from the sale Catalogues of 1920 and 1952. Labels on the back of the picture are reported to say "Exhibited at the Victoria and Albert Museum 1914–1918" and "509."
2. Michael Bryan, *Dictionary of Painters and Engravers*, ed. G. C. Williamson (London, 1904), *4*.139.

66.19. CONVERSATION PIECE, AQUATINT, 1786–94, BY SAMUEL IRELAND, AFTER HOGARTH AND HOUBRAKEN.

In the first volume of his *Graphic Illustrations of Hogarth From Pictures, Drawings, and Scarce Prints in His Own Possession* (London 1794), the "picturesque" engraver Samuel Ireland (d. 1800, father of William Henry Ireland the Shakespeare forger) published aquatints made by himself from four pen-and-brown-wash drawings which he believed Hogarth had done at Button's Coffee House ("at fit opportunities") "about the year 1720, when he was only three and twenty years of age."[1] The plates face pp. 25, 31, 34 and 38 of the volume. Three of them have the engraved title: "Characters who frequented Button's Coffee-house about the year 1720,"[2] and Ireland makes them the occasion for a running account of coffee houses and literary figures in the age of Queen Anne. Characters whom he identifies either in his text or by engraved names within the frame of the pictures[3] are Daniel Button, Martin Folkes, Addison, Dr. Arbuthnot, Count Viviani, Dr. Garth, Pope. In Plates 3 and 4 appears a figure identified by Ireland as follows (p. 38): "The character with a paper in his hand standing at the table [Plate 3], has much the countenance of Pope; but in that which occurs in the next print, plate IV, there is a peevishness and anxiety in the lineaments of the face, that we find in most of his finished portraits, and which are so strongly characteristic of the man, as to leave no doubt of the identity." This figure is seated in Plate 4, with the label "Pope" above his head, and at his right stands a fat-faced figure with cane in hands and a long wig, labeled above his head "Dr Garth." On p. 43 Ireland explains: "The portrait of Dr. Garth, in conversation with Pope, has some similitude to that introduced into Birch's Lives of Illustrious Persons."

The four wash drawings from which Ireland worked were acquired by the British Museum in April 1861, at the George Smith Sale.[4] A statement of provenance, handwritten in ink on a sheet of laid paper, which accompanies them repeats the statements and phrasing of Ireland, *Illustrations* (1794), pp. 24–25. Laurence Binyon, *Catalogue of Drawings by British Artists . . . in the British Museum*, 2 (1900), 321, says, "These drawings are undoubtedly by Hogarth," but he is doubtful of the identifications. A. P. Oppé, *The Drawings of William Hogarth* (New York 1948), p. 30, believes that Binyon has

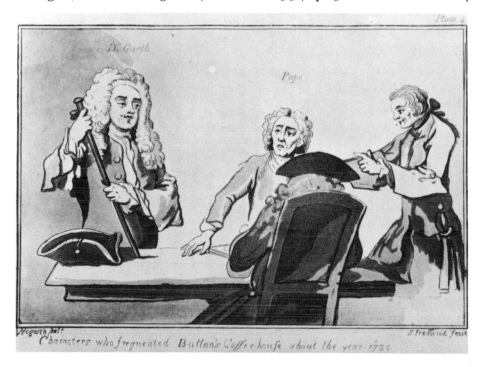

66.19. Aquatint. 5 x 7⅜ in. (outer frame line). "Plate 4 / Dr Garth // Pope / Hogarth Del^t // S. Ireland fecit / Characters who frequented Button's Coffee-house about the year 1720". Samuel Ireland, *Graphic Illustrations of Hogarth From Pictures, Drawings, and Scarce Prints*, vol. 1, 1794.

"sufficiently disposed of the identification." A certain coarseness in the drawings suggests that they may be early works of Hogarth.[5] The most learned collector of Hogarth in the later eighteenth century, George Steevens, annotated this set of the Ireland coffee-house aquatints: "These drawings, pretending to exhibit resemblances of Pope, Arbuthnot etc are all fictitious."[6] If we try to interpret either the drawings or the engravings in Ireland's terms, they are clearly pastiches. Garth died in 1719. The face of "Pope" in the drawing is elderly. 1712–14 would be plausible years at Button's for the scenes represented, rather than either the 1730 of the first state (see n.2) or the 1720 of the correction. In such respects, the engravings are interpretations, perhaps even developments, of the drawings. Ireland had later sources than Hogarth. The allusion to Birch's *Heads of Illustrious Persons* in his account of Garth does something to explain his not implausible identification of Garth in Plate 4.[7] The figure of "Pope," standing in Plate 3 and seated in Plate 4, if it is Pope, is the Van Loo image of Pope, and no other (despite Ireland's allusion to "most of his finished portraits"), and most likely the source of Ireland's inspiration is the Pond-Houbraken version of this image, which is the last plate in Birch's *Heads*,[8] separated from Garth by only one other plate.[9] The Pond-Houbraken plate in Birch's *Heads* would seem to be the source of a certain improvement in the resemblance to Pope which Ireland has conferred, along with a portion of "peevishness and anxiety," upon the seated figure in Plate 4. (Hogarth's drawing, in which the figure looks somewhat less like Pope, may be seen well reproduced in Oppé's *Drawings of Hogarth,* Plate 17.) With the names "Pope" and "Garth" engraved above the heads of these figures in the aquatint (Plate 4), there can be small doubt that Ireland intended them as portraits. He had the authority, if not of Hogarth, at least of Houbraken, for whatever degree of resemblance he attained in this forgery.

1. Pp. 24–25. "The authenticity of them may be relied on: they were purchased by me (with three of the original drawings of the Hudibras) of the executors of a Mr. Brent, an old gentleman who was for many years in the habits of intimacy with Hogarth." See A. P. Oppé, *The Drawings of William Hogarth* (New York, 1948), pp. 28, 30.

2. A line of lettering just beneath ("From the original drawing," etc.—see above) has in each case been imperfectly deleted, and the plate has been trimmed in closer to the bottom of the remaining line. These engravings appear in an earlier state, printed on two large sheets 17½ x 10⅜ in. (Plates 2 and 3 of Ireland's 1794 numbering on one sheet and Plates 4 and 1 on the other) in the British Museum Collection. With some minor variations each has the inscription: "Hogarth del^t // S. Ireland fecit / Characters who frequented Button's / Coffee house about the year 1730 / From the original drawing by Hogarth / in the Collection of Sam Ireland / Publish'd April 1st 1786, by W. Dickerson / no. 158 New Bond S^t" (Department of Prints and Drawings, British Museum, C.C.3—51–52–53–54).

3. Lacking in the earlier state.

4. See Oppé, *Drawings of Hogarth,* p. 30, for the intermediate provenance.

5. Oppé, *Drawings of Hogarth,* p. 30; A. C. Sewter, "Some Early Works of Hogarth," *Burlington Magazine, 80* (January 1942), 5–10.

6. W. S. Lewis, Farmington, Connecticut: Steevens Hogarth Albums, vol. 3, p. 232.

7. The portrait of Garth for Birch's *Heads* ("J. Houbraken sculps. Amst. 1748") represents the Kit-Cat oil painting of Garth, no doubt through J. Faber's mezzotint of 1733. A. P. Oppé (pp. 30–31) takes the head of "Garth" in the fourth Hogarth drawing (Plate 4, Ireland) and that of "Arbuthnot" (Plate 3, Ireland) as the head of a generic "fat man" or of the "same personage, slightly altered in feature," and he groups them further with the heads of fat men in two drawings in the Royal Collection. The difference not only in facial features but in wigs would seem more important than Oppé believes.

8. Facing p. 215 in the edition of 1813.

9. Samuel Clarke, D.D. So in the first and second editions of vol 2, 1751 and 1752. In a copy of the one-volume edition of 1756 at the Library of Congress, Garth is two places further back. In William Baynes' one-volume edition of 1813, he resumes his former position.

66.20. OIL AND TEMPERA PAINTING, BY WILLIAM BLAKE, AFTER VAN LOO, C. 1800. MANCHESTER CITY ART GALLERY.

Blake's friend the poet and patron of poets William Hayley lived at Turret House, Felpham by the Sea in Sussex, whither in 1800 Blake came to stay and work.[1] Among his earliest commissions was a set of eighteen life-sized heads of poets (wreathed with leaves and supported by appropriate ornaments and accessories) in oil and tempera for a frieze in the library.[2] The English poets are Chaucer, Spenser, Shakespeare, Milton, Dryden, Otway, Pope, and Cowper (with his favorite dog). Gilchrist records that within twenty years of Hayley's death the villa passed from the hands of the family, and the poets were dispersed. In 1860 five of them were in the hands of a bookseller, Mr. Toovey.[3] But in 1863 William Michael Rossetti, who added the Catalogue of Pictures to Gilchrist's *Life of Blake*, was able to report that eighteen pictures, "the entire series," had been reassembled by Mr. William Russell.[4] At some later date the eighteen found their way into the Manchester City Art Gallery,[5] where they remain to the present.

Of the eight English poets in the series, only three (Dryden, Otway, and Pope) could have been derived by Blake from engravings in Birch's *Heads* (Otway, after Mary Beal; Dryden, after Kneller; Pope, after "Pond"), and these three need not have been taken from that source. But Blake's Pope is in any event clearly taken from the Van Loo type—though much rejuvenated. If the rejuvenation of itself does not say something about Blake's attitude toward Pope, the two flanking vignettes from Pope's poems of 1717 clearly do so—Eloisa in her chapel on the right, of course, and on the left a female figure which W. M. Rossetti found "not easy to identify," but which, as

66.20. **Oil and tempera on canvas.** 15 x 30½ in. Leaves of tendrils wreathing head, deep (chrome) green; background to left lighter green, with dark green branches and spaces between tree trunks; figures to left and right, light brownish green; moon yellowish creamy; lamp flame in chapel orange; head of poet creamy white shades, with greenish tints; lines of eyes and eyebrows sharp black. Manchester City Art Gallery.

I believe, Kenneth Povey first noticed in 1926, represents the moonlit ghost of the "Unfortunate Lady." With the orange lamp flame which burns in the niche above her head as Eloisa prays, Blake has picked out one of the most persistent symbols of Pope's passionate poem:

> Ah hopeless, lasting flames! like those that burn
> To light the dead, and warm th' unfruitful urn.   ll. 261–62
>
> I waste the Matin lamp in sighs for thee.   l. 267
>
> In seas of flame my plunging soul is drown'd,
> While Altars blaze, and Angels tremble round.   ll. 275–76
>
> Here, as I watch'd the dying lamps around,
> From yonder shrine I heard a hollow sound.   ll. 307–08

In the sword which the other lady holds in her right hand and the broad dagger which she holds in her left, Blake apparently tries to render both Pope's actual word and his implied meaning, in an *Elegy* which shares symbols with *Eloisa* and like *Eloisa* vibrates in a range not very alien to that Blake who sang the contrary states of soul:

> What beck'ning ghost, along the moonlight shade
> Invites my step, and points to yonder glade?
> 'Tis she!—but why that bleeding bosom gor'd,
> Why dimly gleams the visionary sword?
> Oh ever beauteous, ever friendly! tell,
> Is it, in heav'n, a crime to love too well?   ll. 1–6
>
> Most souls, 'tis true, but peep out once an age,
> Dull sullen pris'ners in the body's cage:
> Dim lights of life, that burn a length of years,
> Useless, unseen, as lamps in sepulchres.   ll. 17–20

To the left, Pope's head is framed by branches which bear what are apparently bay leaves, though much elongated. To the right, the flame-like curling tongues of a strange plant bear some dark tricorne leaves which are no doubt what Rossetti alludes to in the word "ivy." Thus Blake, in a highly stylized way, continues the tradition of "the poet's bays and critic's ivy" (*Essay on Criticism,* l. 706) which we have seen variously illustrated in portraits of Pope by Kneller and Richardson.

The Blake oil and tempera of Pope was exhibited at the National Portrait Gallery Exhibition of 1961.

---

1. Mona Wilson, *The Life of William Blake* (London, 1948), pp. 133–34.

2. Wilson, *Life,* p. 138; Thomas Wright, ed. *The Heads of the Poets (Eighteen in number—of which seventeen have not hitherto been published) By William Blake* (The Blake Society . . . Cowper School, Olney, near Bedford, 1925), Introduction. Allan Cunningham, *The Lives of the Most Eminent British Painters and Sculptors,* 2 (New York, 1831), 136–37, reports that Blake, wandering by the seashore of evenings at Felpham, held converse with dead authors (Homer, Moses, Pindar, Virgil, Dante, Milton). "They are all majestic," Blake said, "gray but luminous, and superior to the common height of men." Gilchrist in his *Life of Blake,* chapter VIII (Everyman, p. 138), makes this into an explicit gloss on the library heads.

3. Alexander Gilchrist, *Life of William Blake* (London and Cambridge, 1863), *1.*166.

4. Gilchrist, *Life of Blake* (1863), 2.204; Gilchrist

(*1.*166) had thought there were originally ten pictures.

5. Wright, *The Heads of the Poets,* Introduction; Laurence Haward, *Illustrated Guide to the Art Collections in the Manchester Corporation Galleries* (Printed for the Manchester Art Galleries Committee, 1938) p. 12. P. 50 illustrates William Cowper and Thomas Otway. Wright in his Introduction says that the heads were originally twenty, that two now lost were Ariosto and Ercilla. K. Povey, "Blake's Heads of the Poets," *Notes and Queries, 151* (24 July, 1926), 57–58, renames several, including Wright's no. 6, "Sidney," which he suggests is actually Ercilla. Wilson, *Life,* p. 366, quotes the eighteen most recent identifications as communicated by the Curator of the Manchester Gallery.

APPENDIXES

APPENDIX 1:
THE WARBURTON TYPE

IN THIS APPENDIX I place a series of roughly similar posthumous portraits, nos. 67.1–67.5, all of which can be related to the promotional efforts of William Warburton, Pope's literary executor and editor. This group might also have included no. 48.9, the medallion by Anthony Walker on the title page of Warburton's 1753 edition of the *Essay on Man*—except that this is clearly and directly derived from a single source, Richardson's etching "ΟΥΤΟΣ ΕΚΕΙΝΟΣ" dated 1738. The portraits in the present group seem to be taken more or less freely—perhaps in a progressively derivative sequence—from Dassier and from Richardson's etching of 1738, "ΟΥΤΟΣ ΕΚΕΙΝΟΣ." Another possible source is the Roubiliac type of bust (see especially no. 67.3). I have grouped these images together under the number 67 in my primary sequence simply for ease in handling the exposition. The main purpose of the appendix may be considered as that of establishing the approximate source and identity of the two best-known and most troublesome of the group, the Twickenham Church medallion (no. 67.3) and the Rysbrack terra cotta (no. 67.5).

67.1. LINE ENGRAVING BY THOMAS MAJOR AFTER A DRAWING BY NICHOLAS BLAKEY. FRONTISPIECE TO VOLUME 1 OF WARBURTON'S *Works* OF POPE, 1751.

The lean and rather sour profile of Pope, looking to the left, at the top of the monument in this engraving is a different image from any in the series by Hayman and Grignion which illustrate some of the poems in Warburton's edition of 1751 (see no. 66.17). Here for the first time this sort of profile, derived in this instance, I think, mainly from Dassier, is used in close association with the image and name of Warburton. Edmond Malone is the source of the following relevant anecdote:

> Mr. Burke, who avowed he knew little of art, though he admired it and knew many of the professors, was acquainted with Blakey the artist, who made the drawing for the frontispiece to Warburton's edition of Pope's works. He told him it was to Warburton's particular desire that he made him the principal figure, and Pope only secondary; and that the light, contrary to the rules of art, goes upward from Warburton to Pope. A gentleman who was present when Mr. B. mentioned this circumstance, remarked that it was observable the poet and his commentator were looking different ways.[1]

Nicholas Blakey (fl. 1753), designer and engraver, was an Irishman who lived much at Paris. He was associated with Francis Hayman in designing a series of prints of subjects from English history. Thomas Major (1720–99) became engraver to the King and to the Stamp Office.

---

1. James Prior, *Life of Malone* (London, 1860), pp. 370–71, "Maloniana."

A smaller and inferior re-engraving of this frontispiece, unsigned, appears in the first volume of the octavo printing of Warburton's edition published in 1757.

A further departure from the Warburton 1751 frontispiece appears as the frontispiece (*Grolier 82,* "JW.M. inve: et fecit 1762.") to a volume of a reprint of Warburton's edition, "Berlin, Printed for FREDRICK NICOLAI Bookseller. MDCCLXII."

67.2. MEZZOTINT OF WARBURTON, WITH MEDALLION OF POPE IN THE BACKGROUND —BY THOMAS BURFORD, AFTER A PAINTING BY CHARLES PHILIPS.

Charles Philips' oil painting of Warburton, 49 x 38 inches, is National Portrait Gallery no. 23, purchased by the Gallery in 1857. *The Divine Legation of Moses* (the manuscript under Warburton's pen in both painting and engraving) was published in two volumes by Warburton in 1738 and 1741. Philips the painter died in 1747. Warburton became Bishop of Gloucester in 1759. The date of the painting would seem, therefore, to lie between 1738 and 1747, and Burford's engraving, which adds the medallion of Pope, must have been executed before 1759. The medallion, a heavy rendering, indebted perhaps mainly to Richardson's profile etching "ΟΥΤΟΣ ΕΚΕΙΝΟΣ" dated 1738 (no. 48.1), the relation being advertised by the motto "ΟΥΤΟΣ ΕΚΕΙΝΟΣ," is not necessarily an invention of the engraver. Nos. 67.3 and 67.5 below suggest that Warburton owned some such plaque or sculptor's model, no doubt in plaster or terra cotta.

67.3. MARBLE MEDALLION ON MONUMENT, BY PRINCE HOARE, ERECTED BY WARBURTON IN TWICKENHAM PARISH CHURCH, 1761.

The monument to Pope attached to the main wall of the north gallery in Twickenham Parish Church, St. Mary the Virgin, is a gray marble pyramid rising from a rectangular base of two entablatured sections. The whole structure is about 225 inches in height,

67.1. Line engraving. 5 x 3¼ in. frame. "Plate I. // Vol. I. facing the general Title. / Blakey del. // Major Sculp". Frontispiece to vol. 1 of Pope's Works, octavo, edited by William Warburton, 1751.

67.2. Mezzotint. 13¾ x 9⅝ in. "ΟΥΤΟΣ ΕΚΕΙΝΟΣ / The Divine Legation of Moses / Cha:ˢ Philips pinxᵗ // Thoˢ Burford fecit ex. / Mʳ Warburton." J. Ch. Smith *1*.131 (Burford no. 19). *BMEP 4*.398.

and the base is 60 inches at the bottom, the lower entablature 69 inches. The white marble medallion, sculptured with the profile head of Pope and simulated ring and cord above, is fixed to the pyramid about half way up. The lower section of the base has attached to it a white marble panel bearing Pope's verses, "For one who would not be buried in Westminster Abbey."[1] The upper section has, sunk behind an aperture in the gray marble, a white marble panel bearing this inscription:

ALEXANDRO POPE

M.H.

GULIELMUS EPISCOPUS GLOCESTRIENSIS

AMICITIÆ CAUSA FAC. CUR.

MDCCLXI.

The white marble tablet by Francis Bird erected by Pope himself for his father and mother and with provision for himself, duly completed ("et sibi qui obiit anno 1744, aetat. 57"), is attached to the east wall of the same gallery.[2]

Warburton's monument is represented in an engraving which appears in Ruffhead's *Life of Pope,* 1769, and in two derivatives from this (see below no. 67.4).

Accounts of Twickenham Church and its memorials appear in Daniel Lysons, *Environs of London* (1795), 2.580; Edward W. Brayley and John Britton, *The Beauties of England and Wales, 10,* iv (London, 1801), 425–26; J. Norris Brewer, *The Beauties of England and Wales, 10,* iv (London, 1816), 426.[3]

The profile sculpture of Pope is in reversed direction from the profile in Burford's mezzotint of Warburton and is generally not so close to Richardson's etching of 1738. The garment and the arrangement of the hair perhaps owe something to Roubiliac; the hard features are an injustice perhaps to Dassier.[4]

In his letter of 1920 to the editor of *The Spectator,* in which he announced his discovery of the miniature bust now in the Bath Museum and attributed this to Prince Hoare (no. 59.2), the late John Lane went on to say:

> Recently in Bath I discovered, thanks to the accomplished Mr. Reginald Wright, Curator of the Victoria Art Gallery, that Prince Hoare also made a bas-relief of Pope put up by Bishop Warburton in 1761 in Twickenham Church, where it still remains, but the sculptor's name was not attached to it, nor does it appear to have been known before.[5]

In her *English Church Monuments,* 1946, Katherine A. Esdaile, attributing the Twickenham monument to Prince Hoare, added a note: "The late Mr. John Lane told me he had documentary evidence of the fact."[6] Lane had died in 1925. At the British Museum, Additional Manuscript 50857 is a collection of papers concerning Prince Hoare, deposited by Lane, all apparently dating from 1918. In a draft of a letter to an unspecified editor, Lane quotes the following as from *Boddely's Bath Journal,* 28 December 1761: "We hear that a monument erected at Twickenham in memory of Mr. Pope is finished by Mr. Hoare." In another draft of the letter, he quotes the same sentence as from the *Bath Chronicle.* "Why," asks Mrs. Esdaile in her *TLS* memorial to Pope in 1944, "why did Bishop Warburton, who erected the monument to Pope at Twickenham, choose a relatively obscure provincial sculptor to carry it out . . . ?" To which she answers: "Prince Hoare, the younger brother of William, R.A., was patronized by Ralph Allen and belonged to the Prior Park group; he lived at Bath, and so was easily got at by a bishop resident at Gloucester." By a bishop, she might have added, who was married to Ralph Allen's niece and who, even after his consecration in 1759, was frequently resident at Prior Park. By the late 1750s Prince Hoare was well enough established at Bath and elsewhere in the west of England as a monumental sculptor.[7] The style of the heavy baroque pyramid with its medallion is characteristic enough of his known work, even if this style can hardly be called uniquely his. The pyramid monuments and medallions of Jerry Peirce (d. 1768) and of Paul Bertrand (d. 1755)—both likely enough by Prince Hoare—in Walcot Parish Church, Bath (where William Hoare the painter too has a tablet) may be consulted as parallels to the Twickenham Pope monument. (The much more elaborate monument signed "Prince Hoare Fec.," to Bishop Maddox, d. 1759, in Worcester Cathedral, exhibits in its white marble low relief of the Good Samaritan a very favorable instance of Hoare's work.) Another not distant relative of the Pope monument appears in the bust of Ralph Allen, signed "Hoare Sculpt 1759," which stands today on a wooden pedestal in the hall of the Mineral Water Hospital at Bath.[8] This bust, as one might plausibly anticipate, was commissioned by Warburton.

RADULPHO ALLEN. O.V. / AMICITIÆ GRATIA / H.M. PUB. POSUIT / GULS WARBURTON.[9]

1. *Twickenham 6.376*. This quatrain, scarcely intended by Pope as a self-epitaph, first appears in Pope's collected *Works*, vol. 2, Part 2, 1738.

2. See *Correspondence* 2.26 and frontispiece, a facsimile of Pope's drawing sent to Bird; cf. Rupert Gunnis, *Dictionary*, p. 54.

3. An accurate drawing of the monument, in ink washed with gray watercolor, may be seen at p. 72 of vol. 1 of a Grangerized Johnson's *Life of Pope* in the Widener Library at Harvard.

4. In the *Gentleman's Magazine*, 56, Part I (February 1791), facing p. 104, is a plate showing a collection of coins and seals. No. 9 is a medallion profile to right, the features looking scarcely like Pope, but the hair and especially a curl at the nape being reminiscent of Richardson's 1738 etching "ΟΥΤΟΣ ΕΚΕΙΝΟΣ." A letter to the editor signed "M.G." on p. 104 says: "Fig. 9 is a portrait from an impression of a seal, under which, in the handwriting of Bp. Warburton, it is said, 'I have given this impression of Mr. Pope's head, lest the medal cannot be got. It is equal in

workmanship and likeness.' Round the edge is a Greek inscription, too much worn to be read, but ending with . . . . ΛΗΣ." Cf. no. 62.8.

5. *The Spectator*, 3 January, 1920, p. 12.

6. *English Church Monuments* (London, 1946), p. 116. Similar statements of the attribution, but without the allusion to Lane, appear in the same author's *English Monumental Sculpture Since the Renaissance* (London, 1927), p. 140; *The Art of John Michael Rysbrack in Terracotta* (London: Spink & Son, Ltd., July 1932), p. 27; and Pope anniversary article in the *TLS*, 3 June 1944, p. 273.

7. The date of his beginning at Bath as a sculptor is discussed under no. 59.2. He did not begin later than 1750.

8. Now Royal National Hospital For Rheumatic Diseases.

9. Inscribed on a marble shield attached to the pedestal. Miss E. D. Abbott. Matron of the Hospital, and Mr. H. Bond, Senior Non-Medical Administrative Officer, gave me every assistance in my inquiry.

67.4. LINE ENGRAVING OF THE TWICKENHAM MONUMENT, BY SIMON FRANÇOIS RAVENET AFTER A DRAWING BY SAMUEL WALE, FOR RUFFHEAD'S *Life of Pope*, 1769.

In 1769 C. Bathurst, H. Woodfall, W. Strahan, and other London booksellers issued in quarto *The Works of Alexander Pope, Esq., Complete With His Last Corrections,*

67.3. Marble medallion. 30 in. wide.
Warburton's monument to Pope, 1761, Twickenham Parish Church.

67.4. Line engraving. 7⅛ x 4⁵⁄₁₆ in. plate mark.
6⁵⁄₁₆ x 3¹⁵⁄₁₆ in. frame. "S. Wale delin‡ // Ravenet
Sculpsit". For Owen Ruffhead's *Life of Pope*,
1769, quarto and octavo. *Grolier* 81.

67.5. Terra cotta. 23 x 18 in. Inscribed on back: "Mich¹ Rysbrack Fecit 17—". By permission of the Syndics of the Fitzwilliam Museum, Cambridge.

Additions, and Improvements: Together With the Commentary and Notes of His Editor [i.e. Warburton]. *A New Edition in Five Volumes. To Which is Annexed The Life of the Author, Compiled from Original Manuscripts, with a Critical Essay on His Writings and Genius. By Owen Ruffhead, Esq.* The phrase "in Five Volumes" on the title pages of the four volumes of *Works* is misleading. The "Annexed . . . Life of the Author" has a title page which bears no volume number and is not otherwise explicitly connected with the *Works:—The Life of Alexander Pope, Esq. Compiled from Original Manuscripts; with a Critical Essay on His Writings and Genius.*[1] *By Owen Ruff-Head, Esq.,* 1769.[2] The "original manuscripts" were notes "entrusted" to Ruffhead by Warburton, who for some years had been "teazed" by the booksellers to bring out his own life of Pope.[3] In the same year, the *Life* was issued also, by the same publishers, in octavo format.

In a copy of the quarto *Life* which I have examined (Yale University Library) the frontispiece is the "Kneller"-Ravenet line engraving of Pope, described in no. 8.2; facing page 1 is a profile of Warburton by W. Hoare, 1765; and facing p. 25 is the Wale-Ravenet engraving of the monument. In a set of the quarto *Works* and *Life* in the British Museum (no. 77.1.3), the "Kneller"-Ravenet engraving of Pope is the frontispiece of volume 1 of the *Works,* Juvenile Poems, etc.; the frontispiece of the *Life* is the Wale-Ravenet monument. The same engraving of the monument appears as frontispiece to copies of the octavo *Life.*

Samuel Wale (d. 1786) was a draughtsman and painter, who in 1751 had a shop in Long Acre called "Palladio's Head."[4] He became a member of the Royal Academy in 1768, later first professor of perspective to the Academy, and in 1768 the first pensioner of the Academy. For Ravenet, see no. 8.2.

Wale and Ravenet have altered the image of Pope considerably from that of the actual monument, the garment being now discarded and the features restored in the direction of the Dassier medal.

A near facsimile of this plate may be readily identified by the generally darker engraving, by the absence of the signatures of Wale and Ravenet, and by the presence, inside the frame at the top, of heavy funereal drapes parted over the point of the monument. This occurs on separate sheets; I have not seen it as a book illustration.

In the same year as the London edition (1769), there appeared at Dublin a two-volume 12mo edition of Ruffhead's *Life of Pope . . . To which are added Mr. Pope's Letters to a Lady. (Never before published).* In a copy at Yale, the frontispiece of volume 1 is an anonymous line engraving (5½ x 3 inches) of Pope's monument, reversed in direction from the engraving by Ravenet, but clearly derived from it.

1. This phrase announces the book as a competitor to the first volume of Joseph Warton's *Essay on the Writings and Genius of Pope,* which had appeared in 1756.

2. In 1807 Cadell and Davies brought out a quarto volume "VI" of the *Works,* embellished with a number of new plates of Pope and his friends—the same as those which appear in the Bowles edition of Pope's *Works,* 1806.

3. *The Life of Alexander Pope,* 1769, quarto, advertisement, *Letters from a Late Eminent Prelate* [Warburton] *to One of his Friends* [Richard Hurd] (London, circa 1808), p. 247, Prior Park, 27 December 1761.

4. *London Evening Post,* 25–28 May 1751 (Whitley Papers, Department of Prints and Drawings, British Museum).

67.5. TERRA-COTTA BUST, BY MICHAEL RYSBRACK, C. 1761. FITZWILLIAM MUSEUM, CAMBRIDGE.

In 1932 Messrs. Spink and Son, Ltd., 5–7 King Street, St. James, London, S.W.1, held an exhibition and sale of a collection of terra-cotta sculpture by Michael Rysbrack, brought to London from Teddesley Park, Staffordshire, by Lord Hatherton, a collateral descendant of Sir William Littleton, who during the middle years of the eighteenth century had commissioned a set of historical busts and various other works by Rysbrack. The discovery was celebrated by Mrs. Arundell Esdaile in *The Art of John Michael Rysbrack in Terracotta, Illustrated Catalogue,* July 1932, Spink & Son Ltd. A feature of unusual interest was Mrs. Esdaile's publication of a series of letters concerning the sculptures sent by Rysbrack from his shop in Vere Street to his patron at Teddesley during the period 1756–66. These letters have since been republished by Mrs. M. I. Webb in her *Michael Rysbrack, Sculptor* (London, Country Life Limited, 1954). I have appealed to these letters earlier to illustrate Rysbrack's method of working in terra cotta, apropos of his original bust of Pope finished c. 1730 (nos. 11.1, 2). The following passages tell us something of a later bust of Pope which he furnished for Sir Edward:

> As for the Bust of Mr. Pope you must Instruct me how to Dress it, because he is not in that antient Dress which the Others are, neither has he that Character in his Face, Tho' as Great a Man.
>
> —11 December 1759

> the Busts of Shakspear and Pope. are intirely ready whenever you Please to Order them to be sent to You.
>
> —15 January 1761

> On Monday next I shall send the Busts of Shakespeare and Pope. . . . The Bishop of Gloucester sent for the Model of Mr Pope and I returned it soon after I had modelled the Bust.
>
> —7 April 1761[1]

As I have suggested above (no. 67.2) Warburton seems to have had some sort of sculptural model of Pope (possibly a medallion such as that represented in the Burford mezzotint). This he seems to have lent to Rysbrack as a guide for his pastiche terra cotta of Pope and about this time to have recalled it, most likely for Prince Hoare's work on the Twickenham monument. Rysbrack's appeal to the Bishop of Gloucester had no doubt been suggested by Sir Edward Littleton himself, for this "amiable young man" had been a pupil of the Reverend Richard Hurd of Emmanuel College, Cambridge, and through him he had come to know Warburton. Sir Edward and Lady Littleton had visited Allen and Warburton at Prior Park in 1754.[2]

"The profile of that medallion" (on the Twickenham monument), says Mrs. Esdaile, "is identical with the profile of the bust before us" (the Rysbrack terra cotta for Littleton).[3] Not quite identical, but sufficiently close, one might say. The truth is that the terra-cotta bust completed by Rysbrack in 1761, and derived most likely only from a derivative low-relief model, is not a very good likeness of Pope.

It is inscribed on the back: "Mich¹ Rysbrack Fecit 17—," the last two figures of the date being uncertain.

A notation on a photograph in the Library of Sculpture at the Courtauld Institute indicates that at some time this bust was seen at the Maritime Museum, Greenwich. It was illustrated, Plate III, facing p. 13, in Mrs. Esdaile's *Art of John Michael Rysbrack*, 1932, the Catalogue of the Spink Exhibition. The bust was bought through Messrs. Spink in 1932 by the Fitzwilliam Museum, Cambridge, where it may be seen today, along with Rysbrack's Milton from the same set, in the Lower Marlay Gallery. It was exhibited at the National Portrait Gallery Exhibition of 1961.

1. Mrs. Esdaile, *The Art of Rysbrack*, pp. 24–26; Mrs. Webb, *Rysbrack*, pp. 204–05.

2. *Letters from a Late Eminent Prelate* [Warburton] *to One of his Friends* [Hurd] (London, *circa* 1808), pp. 116–17 (27 June, 2 July 1754), 120 (7 September 1754), 131 (1 January 1755), 133 (1755), 158 (30 December 1756), 186 (12 September 1757).

3. *The Art of Rysbrack* (1932), p. 27. Mrs. Esdaile, pp. 27 and 36–37, believes that the "model" which Rysbrack borrowed from Warburton was a bust which Rysbrack himself had executed c. 1735. "Therefore the present work [the Littleton terra cotta] is a copy of a lost bust modelled from the life for the Bishop of Gloucester, and reproduces the type selected by Pope's ardent friend and champion for reproduction on his monument at Twickenham." I have been able to discover no reason for thinking that the "model" which Rysbrack borrowed and returned in 1761 was something which he himself had made c. 1735 for Warburton from the life. Warburton and Pope became friends in 1740. The obscure origins of the profile of Pope which may be associated with Warburton are discussed in nos. 67.1–67.3.

APPENDIX 2:
UNEXPLAINED ALLUSIONS
TO POPE PORTRAITS

Pope and his Portrait* are fools to me. . . .
*Vide *Pope's* Portrait.
— *Tristram Shandy* VIII.ii

AT VARIOUS places in the catalogue I have quoted allusions to Pope portraits concerning which I have little or no other clue. All these allusions, however, are to portraits which can be more or less securely identified at least as to type of image. To some I have even assigned numbers, for the sake of precision in future reference. Each of these latter can not only be identified as to type but can be shown to be not individually identifiable with any other portrait of this type to which I give a number. See especially nos. 5.9–5.11 (Kneller 1716 type), 6.3 (Kneller 1721 type), 7.5 (Kneller 1722 type), 8.3 (Richardson 1718 type), 9.3–9.6 (Hagley Richardson type), 52.6–52.7 (Petworth Richardson profile type), 58.x, 59.3, and 57–61.14 (Roubiliac type), 62.8 n.5 (Tassie gems), 63.1–2 (Stowe portrait), 63.7–63.15, 63.17 (Stowe type), 66.12–66.14, 66.18 (Van Loo type).

In this appendix I place a collection of allusions which do not meet either of the requirements named above. This is a list, not of portraits, but of allusions to portraits. Some of these allusions may well belong to portraits which appear in my catalogue, or some which I place under different numbers here may well belong to the same portrait at different moments in its career.

I arrange the allusions in the order of their dates, without regard to names of painters attached, which in many instances may well be incorrect. The list makes no pretense to completeness.

1. Pope, writing to his friend Caryll, 25 June 1711, says: "I keep the pictures of Dryden, Milton, Shakespeare, &c., in my chamber, round about me, . . . I wish I had Mr. Caryll's there. . . . The extreme goodness with which you accept the offer I too imprudently made you of mine, can never be enough acknowledged (*Correspondence 1.*120).

2. George Vertue, writing in 1726, records that Mr. [James Francis] Maubert [active c. 1711–1746], chiefly noted for copying portraits of the English poets in small ovals, had painted Dryden, Congreve, Wycherley, and Pope from the life (Vertue *3.*28). About 1737, on a visit to the Honorable Mrs. Charles Stanhope's, Vertue reports "a picture of Mr. Alex. Pope, painted by Mr. Maubert about 1717." And again he says that Maubert has copied many poets' heads in small ovals (Vertue *4.*120). Cf. C. H. Collins Baker, *Lely and the Stuart Court Painters* (London, 1912), 2.71. John Gay's poem "Mr. Pope's Welcome from Greece," 1720, speaks of "grave Mawbert" among a crowd of friends greeting Pope. Cf. Carruthers, *Life of Pope* (1857) pp. 201, 209.

3. *The Family Memoirs of the Rev. William Stukely, M.D.* . . . ed. W. C. Lukis, *Surtees Society Publications*, 73 (1882), 121: "My pictures 1726. . . . Pope's profile, an original, by Kneller."

4. Kent to the Earl of Burlington, 28 November 1738: "He [Richardson] shew'd . . . another Pope in a mourning gown with a strange view of the garden to show the obelisk as in memory to his mothers Death. . . . the son of Richardson & Pope agree'd that popes head was Titziannesco, the old long Glow worm sayd whe have done our best" (*Correspondence 4.*150).

5. Pope to Ralph Allen, 15 May 1740: "[Johan] Vandiest has made an Excellent Picture of Mr. Hook, which I hope will fall to your Lott. I will sit to him too, when we meet at your house" (*Correspondence 4,* 239). See also *Correspondence 4.*13, 23, 195, 247, 253, *343,* 360. Cf. below no. 18.

6. Pope to Hugh Bethel, 28 November 1740: "Your Friend Kent I understand has sent you Zeman's [Enoch or Isaac Zeeman or Seeman's] picture without any alteration, for he says he cannot, or will not, mend it, but I must sit to him for another for you" (*Correspondence 4,* 299).

7. At Lord Oxford's sale of Monday 8 March and five following days, 1741/2, II. 36 (p. 7) was "Mr. Alexander Pope, half length, by Mr. Richardson," bought by Dunn for £12/12/0; and VI. 11 (p. 16) was "Mr. Pope, half length, by Mr. Richardson," bought by Governor Horne for £7/7/0 (Sale Catalogue at NPG).

8. Hugh Bethel to Pope, 25 March 1744: "I have got a copy here of that I like best of those I have seen of you—Sir God. Kneller's (*Correspondence 4.*511–12).

9. *Notes and Queries,* 6th Series, 5 (13 May, 1882), 363–65 prints a document at Mapledurham, "A Catalogue of the Goods at Twickenham," apparently a probate list made shortly after Pope's death. "In the Parlor / Mr. Pope's pictture in Gold Frame . . . / Mr. Pope when a boy in a Black and Gilt Frame. . . . / a drawing of Mr. Pope in Ditto [a Black Frame]."

10. In 1720 Charles Lord Bruce (son of the exiled Warden of Savernake Forest) married Lady Juliana Boyle, sister of the Third Earl of Burlington. Burlington soon drew plans, and between 1730 and 1740 Tottenham House on the Savernake Estates, Wiltshire, was rebuilt. The scheme is represented in drawings which are preserved at Chatsworth. An inventory of objects in Lord Bruce's study includes: "10 poetts heads on painted and gilt bracketts; one Ditto of Mr. Pope" (The Earl of Cardigan, *The Wardens of Savernake Forest*, 1949, pp. 245–46). Lord Ailesbury (The Earl of Cardigan) has kindly sent the added information that the date of the inventory is 14 November 1744, and that all the poets' heads have disappeared, he believes when the First Marquis of Ailesbury remodeled the house shortly after 1814.

11. *London Evening Post*, 13–15 September 1753: "To be sold. At Mr. Vander Gucht's at the Golden Head in Bloomsbury Square. Portrait pictures painted by various masters of the following eminent poets, viz– . . . Pope" (Whitley Papers, Department of Prints and Drawings, British Museum).

12. Dr. Richard Mead's sale of sculpture (*Museum Medianum*), 11 March 1755 (Lugt 871—second part of Lugt 859, 11–19 February) lists on p. 251 busts of Shakespeare, Milton and Pope, life-size, in white marble, by Peter Scheemakers (British Museum Library; cf. Rupert Gunnis, *Dictionary of British Sculptors*, 1954, p. 342). In Scheemakers' sale of 6–7 June 1771, on his retirement from business (Lugt 1938), lot 44 was "Three heads ditto [i.e. casts], an head of Fiammingo, Pope and another" (British Museum Library). Cf. no. 19.

13. Society of Artists of Great Britain, *Catalogue*, 1760, p. 11, no. 91: a head of Pope, intaglio, from a picture by Kneller, by [Christopher] Seaton. Cf. Algernon Graves, *The Society of Artists of Great Britain 1760–1791 . . . A Complete Dictionary . . .* (London 1907), p. 229.

14. At Lord Ferrers' sale, Christie's, 2 June 1779, three portraits by Jonathan Richardson—Bolingbroke, Swift, and Pope—sold to Fitzpatrick for £5.15.6 (George Redford, *Art Sales*, 1888, *1*.461; 2.107).

15. In Sir William Musgrave's collection at the British Museum (Add. MS. 6391), a manuscript inventory made at Lord Bessborough's house, Roehampton, in 1785, includes a portrait of Pope by Kneller. At Lord Bessborough's sale, Christie's, 7 February 1801, lot no. 5 was a profile of Pope by Kneller. See no. 3.2.

16. In *The Monthly Magazine, 16* (November 1803), 304 (wrongly numbered 403), a correspondent writes: "Travelling lately in the county of Berks, I had the good fortune to meet with and purchase a beautiful miniature of Alexander Pope, the poet; it is mounted in a brass carved and gilt frame: the back was soldered down, which, upon removing, had this inscription, '*Benj. Arlaud, pinxit*, 1707.' . . . this picture . . . had a wreath of oak-leaves curiously engraved on the back. . . . Nothing can exceed the lustre expressed in the eyes and the countenance. . . . It differs from all the pictures of

a more advanced age. . . . He is dressed in a light blue velvet coat, with gold buttons; his face perfectly round; the hair white, with a tinge of the red, and the eyes hazel."

17. The Fifth Duke of Rutland, successor of George Crabbe's patron, lost a number of valuable pictures at Belvoir Castle in a fire on 26 October 1816. I. Eller, *History of Belvoir Castle* (1841), p. 131, lists among pictures destroyed in the Music Room: "The Portraits of Pope, Wycherley and Gay," valued together at £15. Cf. below, no. 24.

18. Joseph Spence, *Anecdotes,* ed. S. W. Singer (1820), p. 369, alludes to a picture of Mr. Pope at Ralph Allen's. On 29 August 1859, George Scharf saw and sketched a picture (dubiously Pope) which was said to come from Prior Park and then belonged to an owner named Pinckney (NPG, *Trustees' Sketch Books 3.31*).

19. At Donhead Hall, Wiltshire, the home of Godfrey-John Kneller, Esq., c. 1821–25, was a collection of pictures which had been formed by his ancestor Sir Godfrey. "On the staircase hung a beautiful portrait of Pope by him" (W. T. Whitley, *Art in England, 1821–1837,* 1930, p. 15, quoting a letter from Archdeacon Fisher to William Constable). Whitley describes a sale by Phillips in 1821, but it is not clear that Pope was in that sale. Cf. William Roscoe, ed. *Works of Pope* (1824), 3.373–74; Sir Richard Colt Hoare, Bart., *History of Modern Wiltshire* (1829), 4.33. Hoare says that Godfrey-John Kneller sold the estate in 1825 to Charles Wyndham.

20. John Preston Neale, *Views of the Seats of Noblemen and Gentlemen, in England, Wales, Scotland and Ireland*, Second Series, *4* (London, 1828), after plate [29], "Hinton St. George, Somersetshire, the seat of The Right Honourable John Poulett, Earl Poulett. . . . principal pictures. . . . Alexander Pope—Sir G. Kneller / John Dryden—Ditto."

21. The preface to the *Post-Office Reading Directory,* 1842, is said to refer to "the famous picture . . . of Pope, Addison and Steele," hung at the Bear Inn in Bridge Street, Reading.

22. In a letter of 1843 to Crabb Robinson Quillinan says that in his youth he used to go to the house of Sir Thomas Plomer's widow at Malvern, in the owner's absence, "solely to gaze on an excellent original oil-portrait of Pope, that hung in her drawing-room. By whom was that portrait? How came it into the Plomers' possession, and where is it now? E.R." (*Notes and Queries, 179* [10 August 1940], 101).

23. *Gentleman's Magazine, 186* (October and November 1849), 467: "We . . . saw not long ago a small bronze or copper medallion of Pope—his head with a wreath of laurel 'round it, and with this inscription—ΜΟΙ ΑΥΤΟΣ ΗΔΩΚΗΝ." ΕΔΩΚΕΝ would be more plausible.

24. *The Life of George Crabbe, by his Son,* with Introduction by Edmund Blunden (London: The Cresset Press, 1947), p. 109: "[c. 1783] . . . At parting, the Duke [of Rutland] presented him with a portrait of Pope, by Sir Godfrey Kneller." Cf. above, this appendix, no. 17. Crabbe lived for a while at Belvoir Castle after his marriage in

1784, but presumably did not leave his portrait of Pope behind until the fire of 1816. At Samuel Rogers' sale, 5th Day, 3 May 1856, lot 573 (p. 11) was: "Jarvis Portrait of Pope, in a crimson dress and black cap. This capital portrait was presented by the Duke of Rutland to Crabbe, and by the sons of Crabbe to Mr. Rogers." It sold for 78 guineas to Radclyffe (Redford, *Art Sales*, 2.61). Cunningham 1854 alludes to this portrait in the possession of Rogers.

25. A correspondence in *The Builder, 9,* 16 January, 13 February 1864, discusses a portrait of Pope once "walled up" in the house of the Guise family in Gloucester, then temporarily in possession of a Mr. Thomas Baylis, Thames Bank, Fulham (*Notes and Queries,* 3rd Series, 5 [23 January and 13 February], 72, 137).

26. *Catalogue of the Pictures of Coombe Abbey, Warwickshire, The Seat of William Earl of Craven* (1866), p. 15, no. 216, Alexander Pope, no. 220, John Locke (NPG *George Scharf Private Houses*). At Christie's, 13 April 1923, lot 64, from the collection of the Right Honourable Cornelia Countess of Craven, Coombe Abbey, was A. Pope by Richardson, feigned oval, 29 x 24 inches, a pair with a portrait of John Locke. This portrait of Pope is no. 134 in G. W. Snelgrove's catalogue in his University of London doctoral thesis *Jonathan Richardson,* 1936. He remarks, on what evidence is not clear, that the portrait was similar to Dyce no. 13 in the Victoria and Albert (see no. 53.1).

27. At the sale of John Green, Christie's, 22 July 1871, lot 48 was a head of Pope, with an engraving (George Scharf noted cryptically, "by Richardson, not really the same"). Lot 62 was also a portrait of Pope (NPG copy of catalogue). A third lot, "Pope, From Malone's," is discussed in no. 8.2.

28. A correspondent, "J.C.J.," in *Notes and Queries,* 6th Series, 2 (30 October 1880), 348, reports owning six wax medallions, of Pope, Sidney, Shakespeare, Addison, Lansdowne, and Swift, each with a gilt border and the artist's signature in gold, ΜΩΤΛΕΙΟΣ ΕΠΟΙΕΙ. Motley worked in London during the reign of George II (*Country Life, 124* [20 November 1958], 1168).

29. *Pope Commemoration Loan Museum Catalogue* (Twickenham, 1888), no. 151: "Sketch in oils, probably by Jervas, Mr. T. W. Jackson, Worcester College, Oxford." In 1951, Mr. J. C. Masterman, Provost of Worcester College, informed me that T. W. Jackson had died in 1914, leaving a considerable collection of pictures, which were dispersed. Francis Kilvert (d. 1863) was a Fellow of Worcester College. Cf. no. 63.9.

30. *Pope Commemoration* (Twickenham, 1888), no. 179: "Large Portrait Sketch of Alexander Pope from Life, by G. Vertue. Lent by Sir Charles W. Dilke, Bart., Sloane Street, S.W." At the *Exhibition of the Royal House of Guelph* (The New Gallery, Regent Street, 1891), no. 1896 (p. 295) was "Alexander Pope, Pencil Drawing. By G. Vertue. Lent by the Rt. Hon. Sir Charles Wentworth Dilke, Bart." In 1951 Sir John Fisher Wentworth Dilke, Bart., informed me that this drawing was no longer known to members of his family.

31. *Pope Commemoration* (Twickenham, 1888), no. 261 (p. 46); "Frame of ten photographs of oil paintings and miniatures: 'Pope from the crayon portrait in the Bodleian.

. . .' Lent by South Kensington Museum." In 1951 this collection was not known at the Victoria and Albert Museum.

32. At Bath in 1889 occurred an auction of pictures the property of F. Shum. Lot 89 was "Pine. Fine Portrait of Pope." It sold for £19. Professor Benjamin Boyce sends me this information, taken from an annotated copy of the catalogue in the Bath Reference Library. The best-known painter of the name was Garrick's friend Robert Edge Pine (c. 1730–88), who in 1772 inherited property from his brother Simon at Bath and went to live there. A painter called by Vertue "young Pine" was apparently, c. 1742, doing crayon portraits at Bath. See Vertue 3.110; W. T. Whitley, *Artists and Their Friends* (London, 1928), *1*.146, 242; 2.293; Waterhouse, *Painting in Britain,* pp. 196–97.

33. Between 1866 and 1871 the Seventh Earl of Chesterfield removed from Chesterfield House the original library set of poets' heads (placed there by the Fourth Earl), and they were not returned until c. 1918, by the Sixth Earl of Harewood. See no. 5.7. In the interim, however, a different set of portraits seems to have occupied the Chesterfield House Library. A letter to Lionel Cust, 5 June 1896, from Philip Norman, gives a list of these pictures drawn up 20 June 1893: No. 17 is "Alexander Pope (J. Richardson)" (NPG archives, Chesterfield House).

34. *The Athenaeum,* no. 3899, 19 July 1902, announces that in a sale to take place at Sotheby's on Monday 21 July there will appear "A well-authenticated portrait of Alex. Pope by Jonathan Richardson, on Canvas, 24 x 19 in."

35. Prince Frederick Duleep Singh, *Portraits in Norfolk Houses,* ed. Rev. Edmund Farrer, *1* (Norwich n.d., 1928), pp. 332, 335, at Tutwood Hall, the property of Colonel Clement William Joseph Unthank, 21 September 1907, no. 13: "Alexander Pope. H. L. Body turned quite towards the sinister, face but slightly so, dark eyes full, clean shaven, gold-brocaded turban on the head, turned back with blue. *Dress:* Olive brown coat, sleeve slashed at the wrist, brown robe with shiny lining over the right shoulder, open collar, tight wristband; the left hand bent to the neck holding the robes." In 1961 Miss M. B. Unthank informed me that the portrait could be traced at Tutwood Hall as recently as 1943, but she believed that shortly after that date it was sold at Sotheby's.

36. At Christie's, 14 July 1916, lot 124, from the collection of the deceased Alexander Huth, 67, West Hill, Putney, was "Alexander Pope. In a sculptural oval and the Ettrick Shepherd." A rough pen sketch in the NPG copy of the catalogue shows a face looking three-quarters to right with wig, and body also three-quarters right. An obscure pencil note seems to read "after Richardson."

37. At Christie's, 20 May 1921, in a sale of the property of Sir Richard Brooke, Bart., removed from Norton Priory, Holton, Cheshire, lot 111 was "J. Richardson, Portrait of Alexander Pope, the Poet, in dark dress, seated, holding a quill pen. 49½ in. by 39½ in." It was bought by Spiller for £14.3.6 (Yale University Library).

38. At Christie's, 4–5 May 1922, in a sale of "Pictures and Drawings of the late Baroness Burdett-Coutts" was sold a portrait of "A. Pope in brown dress, white shirt and green cap, 29 x 24," by C. Jervis. It was bought by Samuel for £120.15.0 (*Art Prices Current,* N.S., *1* [1921–1922], 250 [40]).

39. At Christie's, 1 February 1923, from the collection of Sir J. G. Thorold, Bart., Syston Park, Grantham, lot 44 was a portrait of Pope (NPG archives).

40. At the Archibald G. B. Russell sale, Sotheby's, 15 May 1923, lot 19 was a painting of Pope by Richardson, half-length, seated, his head resting on his hand, canvas, 29 x 24 inches, formerly in the collection of Reginald Corbet, Adderley (no. 142 in the catalogue in G. W. Snelgrove's University of London thesis *Jonathan Richardson,* 1936).

41. At Sotheby's, 15 July 1952, lot 280 (p. 34) was "The Property of a Gentleman. . . . Portrait of Alexander Pope, half-length, his head half turned to the left, in oils, canvas, unframed (28 in. by 24 in.)." The purchaser was Mr. J. A. Pearson.

APPENDIX 3:
PORTRAITS MISTAKENLY CALLED POPE, AND SOME OTHERS

1. HOGARTH's line engraving of 1721, "An Emblematical Print on the South Sea Scheme," shows amid a wild medley of satiric detail, a dwarfish man in a wig and long coat picking the pocket of a taller fat man who wears at his girdle a hornbook. The third edition of *Biographical Anecdotes of William Hogarth*, by J. Nichols, G. Steevens and others, 1785 (p. 177), apparently originates the interpretation that the small figure is Pope (who gained something in the South Sea speculation) picking the pocket of Gay (who lost heavily by it). The "ABC" hornbook is said to represent Gay's *Fables*. These ideas thereafter echo through the several collections of Nichols and Steevens, John Ireland, and Samuel Ireland. Hogarth was supposed to be the author of the "Burlington Gate" print satirizing Pope. It seemed logical that he should attack him further, as Pope was the friend of Kent and Lord Burlington, who together had stolen jobs and prestige from Hogarth's father-in-law, Thornhill. The wonder was that Pope had never retaliated against Hogarth. Perhaps he was afraid (John Ireland, *Hogarth Illustrated* [1791], Third Edition [1806], 2.179–80; Samuel Ireland, *Graphic Illustrations, 1* [1794], 107). See Austin Dobson, *William Hogarth* (London, 1907), p. 228; A. P. Oppé, *The Drawings of William Hogarth* (London, 1948), p. 27 (no. 3) and Plate 2.

The attribution of "Burlington Gate" to Hogarth has been discussed in no. 13.1. See Appendix 4, no. 4, for the nominal image of Pope in an engraving of 1732, "Rich's Glory," which has been wrongly attributed to Hogarth. And see the same appendix, no. 6, for Hogarth's actual token image of Pope, a compliment to him, as he is shown thrashing Curll, in "The Distressed Poet," 1736. The painting of c. 1730 from which this engraving was derived represents a satiric engraving of Pope as monkey (see no. 7.10) on the attic wall of the indigent author, with Pope's lines from the *Dunciad*, "Studious he Sate," inscribed beneath. This I believe exhausts the loci where Hogarth may be said to be glancing at Pope. They seem to have treated each other with mutual respect and almost complete silence.

For Samuel Ireland's improvement of a Hogarth drawing to make it look like Pope, see no. 66.19.

2. Robert Carruthers, *Life of Alexander Pope*, 2nd ed. (1857), is apparently the first to describe "An original specimen of the poet's artistic powers—a pictorial satire . . . preserved in Ketley parsonage, Wellington, Salop . . . representing the Prodigal Son with other allegorical designs and inscriptions. . . . It has long been in the family of the present owner, the Rev. Thompson Stoneham" (p. 90; cf. p. 462). A note in the archives of the National Portrait Gallery, dated May 1930, says the picture was then in possession of the granddaughter of the Rev. Thompson Stoneham, Miss Maud E. Edalji, Ingleside, Colebrookdale, near Ironbridge, Salop. At Sotheby's, 2 July 1935, lot 328 (p. 39) was: "The Property of the grandchildren of the late Revd. Thompson Stoneham. Pope (Alexander) Self Portrait as a rake out at elbow reflecting among the ruins of Rome and holding in his hand a sepia drawing of the Prodigal Son, *in a contemporary black and gilt frame* (4 ft by 3 ft.)." The painting was acquired by Messrs. Robinson in Pall Mall and from them by the late A. E. Newton. It is said to remain today in the possession of Miss Caroline Newton of Berwyn, Pennsylvania. In this picture a spindly rake, who does not look like Pope, sits amid a background of classical decay, a free counterpart of the engraved capriccio scene which ("A. Pope inv.") appears as frontispiece of Warburton's editions of the *Essay on Man*, 1745, and later (cf. no. 43.3). Two drawings for this frontispiece are known today, one in red chalk said to be by Pope, but not available to study, and the other a sepia wash drawing in the collection of W. S. Lewis, inscribed beneath in ink: "Author Ipse Invt:. & I. M. Delineavit" (Benjamin Boyce, "Baroque into Satire: Pope's Frontispiece for the Essay on Man," *Criticism, a Quarterly for Literature and the Arts*, 4 [Winter, 1962], 14–15). The oil painting seems on the whole better executed than one would expect of Pope. See p. 12. Both oil painting and sepia drawing are reproduced in *Twickenham* 3.i, ed. Maynard Mack, 1950. The oil is reproduced also by A. Edward Newton, *Pope, Poetry and Portrait*, Privately Printed, "Oak Knoll," Daylesford, Berwyn P. O., Pennsylvania, 1936. Pages 15–19 tell of the purchase of the picture from Messrs. Robinson.

3. In the Burlington Fine Arts Club, *Exhibition of Portrait Miniatures* (London, 1889), no. XXIII. 9 (p. 65) is "Alexander Pope, lent by Edwin H. Lawrence, Esq." This seems most likely to have been the miniature acquired by James Ward Usher (before 1904) and in a catalogue issued by him, *An Art Collector's Treasures*, described as "Alexander Pope, from the Lawrence Collection," by Jacques Bisson, "signed and dated, 1722." Mr. F. T. Baker, Director, City of Lincoln Libraries, Museum and Art Gallery, in sending me a photograph and writing to me about this small oval oil painting, remarks that the inscription "must be on the back of the miniature itself as it is not

on the frame." George C. Williamson, *The History of Portrait Miniatures*, 2 (London, 1904) p. 140, says "Mr. Ward Usher's Collection at Lincoln . . . has Alexander Pope by Bisson." And Basil Long, *British Miniaturists* (London 1929), says that Bisson "worked in Paris, where he died in 1737," adding significantly, "The only reason I have for thinking that he worked in England is that the museum at Lincoln contains a miniature portrait of Pope by him."

4. At Sotheby's, 18 June 1892, among relics of Lord Byron in the collection of Robert Francis Cooke, Esq., late partner in the firm of John Murray, lot 1014 (p. 57) was "Alexander Pope, by Boit, enamel miniature, in original shagreen case." This seems most likely the miniature, surely not Pope, illustrated in *Munsey's Magazine*, *17* (June 1897), 330 in an article on Byron relics in the collection of Salvador de Mendonca, Brazilian minister to the United States. In 1955 Mrs. Nathan H. Fink of Brookline, Massachusetts, learned from a daughter of the late Brazilian Ambassador that her father's collection had been dispersed by auction in New York about 1914.

5. A photograph in the National Portrait Gallery archives sent in 1901 from the Council of the Shakespeare Memorial, Stratford-on-Avon, and annotated in the back "Pope by Hogarth (?)," might represent a painting poorly copied from Richardson's etching in profile, OYTOΣ EKEINOΣ, of 1738.

6. A head of a man with aquiline nose, in a wig, drawn in "chalks" on gray paper, at the British Museum, Department of Prints and Drawings in 1951 (1910-2-18-43), was inscribed in pencil at lower left "Kneller," and at right center "Pope." In the recent *Catalogue of British Drawings*, by Edward Croft-Murray and Paul Hulton, *1* (British Museum, 1960), this seems not to be included with Kneller's drawings, or elsewhere.

7. A small fancy book (Yale WA 16066), *The Ante Room of a Georgian Library Adorned with portraits as limned from the Life by Jonathan Richardson*, by Horace Townsend (New York, 1917), copyright 1917 by Karl Freund, and reprinted in part from *The Spur*, November 1916, describes a collection formed by the New York amateur interior decorator and antiquary Karl Freund. Six group oil paintings, "Portraits of Bygone Worthies" (illustrated), had been acquired by Freund from the collection of "a noted French connoisseur." They are said to have been painted by Richardson early in the eighteenth century and to be inscribed on the back in "quaintly picturesque Flemish script" with the names of the subjects. The third picture is a group of authors said to be Addison, Steele, Pope, Prior, Rowe, Samuel Clarke, and Roger North.

8. In Mrs. R. L. Poole, *Catalogue of Portraits . . . in the . . . Bodleian Library* (Oxford, 1926), no. 244 (p. 98) is a watercolor miniature on ivory, of an Unknown Man, English School about 1775. It was "labelled Alexander Pope." This picture could no longer be found in 1961.

9. In Bernard Rackham, *Catalogue of English Porcelain . . . Collected by Charles Schreiber . . . and Lady Charlotte Elizabeth Schreiber and presented to the* [Victoria and Albert] *Museum* in 1884, *1* (London 1928), no. 360 (p. 74) is a colored ceramic bust, 6¾

inches high, bought in Utrecht in 1869, said to be Pope adapted from the Kneller paint-ing of 1716. Cf. no. 57–61.19.

10. C. M. Newman, Esq., of 76 Brondesbury Park, London N.W. 2, about 1950 bought at an auction in Ryde, Isle of Wight, an oil painting called "Alexander Pope." In the photograph which he kindly sent me, a sitter with narrow brows and aquiline nose wears clerical bands.

11. An oval ivory relief, 5⅛ x 3⅞ in., thought to be English, mid-eighteenth-cen-tury, acquired by the Victoria and Albert Museum in 1931 (A44–1931), shows a bust pro-file to right. The hair and the classical garment are somewhat reminiscent of the Rou-biliac type of Pope bust. At the Walters Art Gallery, Baltimore, Maryland, is an oval ivory relief (71.428) very similar to that at the Victoria and Albert. It is 5⁵⁄₁₆ x 4¹⁄₁₆ inches and has on the back in black paint "Pope / Aut^r Ang^l" and in brown ink (an older in-scription) "A^r / Pope / Auteur Anglais". (A medallion called Pope once in the Dyce collection at the Victoria and Albert [Catalogue, p. 307, n. 3328] has disappeared.)

12. A photograph in the National Portrait Gallery archives represents a half-length painting of a man in a light cap with long hair, "called Alexander Pope, J. Richardson, Jr. (?)." In 1932 this was in the possession of W. de Belleroche, Manor House, Rusting-ton, Surrey.

13. At Sotheby's, 22 February 1944, was sold a drawing of a man with a baldish round head, in crayons on gray paper, said to be Pope by Richardson (NPG photo 129190). The same drawing is now at the Victoria and Albert Museum, Department of Engraving, Illustration and Design, inscribed in pencil on the back "Alex Pope" and on the mount "Alex Pope by J. Richardson" (*Accessions 1948*, vol. 2, *Henry Herbert Harrod Bequest* [London, 1957], p. 19).

14. In the National Portrait Gallery archives, a photograph of a painting in Lord Dyne-vor's Collection at Dynevor Castle, sent in 1932, shows a man thought perhaps to be "Pope," standing before a draped table, with quill and inkpot.

15. At the David Martin Currie sale, Christie's, 18 February 1921, lot 64 (p. 11), from the collection of Earl Cowley, Draycott House, Chippenham, was a conversation piece, showing a man in a loose gown and cap, seated at a table, receiving a letter from a boy. Through Scott and Fowles, New York (c. 1925), this picture passed into the Emily Crane Chadbourne Collection, at the Art Institute of Chicago (Frick Art Reference Library archives). A label pasted on the back of the canvas read: "Alexander Pope in his Villa / at Twickenham / Painted By / Jos. Highmore 1728" (photograph found at the Univer-sity of Texas Library). The painting is reproduced in the Detroit Institute of Arts, *Catalogue, Exhibition of English Conversation Pieces of the 18th Century*, 27 January– 29 February 1948, pp. 15, 20, no. 12, lent by the Art Institute of Chicago. The picture is said to be more recently re-described as "Gentleman Receiving a Letter—British School."

16. At Christie's, 29 October 1948, lot 18 was a painting from the collection of C. Shenstone, formerly in the collection of Captain Manning, called "Alexander Pope," with "R. Taylor pinx 1737" inscribed on a modern stretcher. A photograph at the National Portrait Gallery (no. 5376) shows a gentleman in cap and loose gown.

17. At Raynham Hall, Norfolk, a painted ceiling medallion by William Kent, c. 1730, is said in Margaret Jourdain, *Works of William Kent* (London, 1948), pp. 66, 148, Fig. 95, to represent Fame seated before a bust of Pope inscribing his name. A larger photograph seen at the National Portrait Gallery shows that the subject is not Pope. The presence of a column decorated with rostra suggests a naval hero.

18. A . P. Oppé, *English Drawings, Stuart and Georgian Periods In the Collection of His Majesty the King at Windsor Castle* (London, 1950) no. 423 (p. 73 and Fig. 34) describes and illustrates a caricature drawing in pencil and body color of a standing male figure, signed "P. Lens Pinx 1737" and inscribed on the back "Moggedorio the Good Clerk." When George Scharf saw this in 1863, he wrote beside his sketch of it, "Supposed to represent Pope" (NPG, Scharf *Trustees' Sketch Books, Windsor* 2.43, 26 May 1863).

19. At Sotheby's, 12 July 1950, lot 80 was a portrait by Mercier, catalogued as Pope, but reported to be not Pope, perhaps a member of the Carnival Club (National Portrait Gallery archives).

20. At Sotheby's 1 August 1951, lot 89 (p. 11) was: "Jervas. Portrait of Alexander Pope, half-length, in a yellow coat and furred cap, with purple mantle, 35 *in.* by 28 *in.*" This was the property of F. G. H. Storey, Esq., M.A., Wheat Hill, Sandon, Buntingford, Herts., who kindly informed me that he had acquired the picture at a sale of the contents of Frampton Court, Dorset, the family seat of the descendants of Richard Brinsley Sheridan. The painting was bought by M. Blum, 54 Goldhurst Terrace, London N.W. 6, and from him by S. Birnbaum, 32 Moreland Court, Finchley Road, N.W. 2. The photograph sent by Mr. Birnbaum shows a round-faced and dark-browed subject wearing a fancy coat and laced shirt and a fur cap.

21. Mr. Ronald A. Lee, Antiquarian, of Ormeley Lodge, Ham Common, Surrey, in 1956 sent me a photograph of a portrait, painted on a mahogany panel, of a Wordsworthian-looking subject, with piercing dark eyes, in black cap and coat and white cravat. A faded label on the back bears the name "Pope." Mr. Lee had acquired the painting in the city of Nottingham.

22. At W. and F. C. Bonham and Sons, Ltd., Knightsbridge, 6 September 1962, lot 23, from an anonymous vendor, was a "Portrait of Alexander Pope as a young man, oil on canvas, in a carved frame, 10 in. x 9 in.," attributed to Arthur Pond (indistinctly signed). A small-scale half-length of a young man in a turban, holding a book, with pillar and shelves behind, it is described for me by a friend as a genuine early-eighteenth-century painting of a man of letters or scholar.

23. At Christie's, 5 April 1963, lot 56 (p. 12), from the collection of Lord Leigh of Stoneleigh Abbey, Warwickshire, was: "Jervas. Portrait of Alexander Pope, three-quarter length, in red cloak and turban and white lace shirt—48½ *in. by* 37 *in.*" The portrait is said to bear a nineteenth-century label on the frame identifying it as Pope. This elegant large picture shows a richly costumed young man, with aquiline nose, soft chin, and pouty mouth. It was acquired by Mr. William Rees-Mogg, of *The Sunday Times.*

24. In 1962 J. S. Maas and Co., Ltd., 15a Clifford Street, New Bond Street, W.1, were in possession of a profile drawing, crayons (and perhaps lead pencil) on buff paper, with the name "POPE." in capital letters in a panel on the bottom. This drawing (16⅞ x 9⅜ inches) reappeared in the spring of 1963 as no. 319 in Catalogue 62 of Alister Matthews, 12 Eaton Road, Branksome Park, Poole, Dorset. In December 1963 the same drawing had come via Zeitlin & Ver Brugge of Los Angeles into the hands of Joseph Rubinstein, 2039 E. Juanita, Tucson, Arizona.

25. At Ditchley Park, Oxfordshire, built in 1722 by James Gibbs, a Palladian entrance hall was designed and decorated by William Kent. Above a niche in the west wall, is a blunt-nosed profile head in plaster relief, crowned with bay and surrounded with oak leaves. What appears to be a moustache adorns the upper lip. This apparently is sometimes thought of as Pope. The niche may be seen reproduced, with the head dimly visible, in *Country Life, 16* (22 October 1904), 601; and again in *66* (16 June 1934), 622. My description of the plaque is based on an excellent photograph sent to me by Mr. J. L. Ashton, Bursar, The Ditchley Foundation.

26. Among the Wedgwood molds, dating in design between about 1773 and 1787, preserved at the Barlaston Museum, are five, representing the Richardson 1738, the Roubiliac, and the Dassier types of Pope image. These are illustrated above, nos. 48.8, 48.9, 57–61.21, 62.5, and 62.8, and in addition the Wedgwood Roubiliac bust, no. 57–61.20. A sixth cameo mold, profile, no. 271.B–8, is also said to be Pope, but appears to me to be misnamed. Cf. no. 62.8 and no. 57–61.18, a wrong illustration for the Wedgwood Roubiliac bust.

27. In February 1963 Holleyman & Treacher, Ltd., Duke Street, Brighton, were in possession of an oil portrait of Pope, on canvas 20 x 18 inches, in a gilt wood and gesso frame, with a gilt wood label "A. POPE. 1744." This had been purchased at a local auction and came from the estate of an elderly lady, Mrs. Isaacs, who had died in Hove early in the previous year. The style of the frame and the condition of the paint suggest a date not much later than 1800. Pope in short natural hair faces right, nearly full profile, his body turned nearly full front, bust length; he wears a brownish garment, open across the chest, with a white undershirt showing on both sides. This rather drab painting, somewhat uncertain in the anatomy of chin and ear, is clearly Pope, but corresponds to none of the eighty-one types which are identified in this book. Derivation from one or more Richardson types seems likely, with perhaps a trace of the Roubiliac. The portrait was acquired by the present writer.

28. At Christie's 3 July 1964, lot 90 (seller not named) was a portrait described as follows: "Jervas—portrait of an unknown poet, half length in brown dress seated writing at his desk, inscribed Alexander Pope at the age of XVI—in frame—29½ x 24½ inches. Collections Tom Davies; Mr. Davies of Cadell and Davies." The portrait was acquired by Mr. William Rees-Mogg, of *The Sunday Times,* who kindly tells me that a label on the back, apparently a cutting from an auction catalogue of the nineteenth century, reads as follows: "C. Jervas—Flour. 1720 Pope (Alexander) the poet; a three-quarter. He is here represented very young, about the sixteenth year of his age; and in the act of writing, probably his Pastorals, which appeared about this time. This curious and interesting portrait of our great poet, is the earliest one known of him, at least it was always esteemed so and highly prized on this account by its late possessor Mr. Davies (of the firm of Cadell and Davies) and originally belonged to his father, the well-known Tom Davies, the author of the life of Garrick, &c." Mr. Rees-Mogg reports that the inscription, at the upper left, seems very recent, but that the painting is signed at the lower right corner: "C. Jervas Pinxit."

Thomas Davies died in 1785. His son William, partner with the bookseller Thomas Cadell the younger, died in 1820. Pictures that had belonged to a late William Davies, Esq., of the Strand, were sold with others at Christie's on 9 June 1821 (Lugt 10056) and included, no. 134, by "Kneller," a portrait "of Pope, when young." The firm of Cadell and Davies were chief conveyors of the portraiture of Pope in that era, publishing engravings of four Pope portraits (See nos. 5.13, 52.2, 63.1, 64.2), used as illustrations to Warton's Pope, 1797, Bowles' Pope, 1806, and the booksellers' volume VI, 1807, supplementary to the "Ruffhead" Pope of 1769. This latter volume contained also engravings of Pope's mother and a large collection of his friends and contemporaries.

The slender oval face of the young man in the picture is turned full to the viewer and wears a softly pensive expression. He wears a tight dark cap and a cassock-like garment open at the collar. In his right hand he holds a white quill pen. Pope's friendship with Jervas is not recorded before 1713, though Jervas on his return from Italy appears in full swing as a painter of society shepherdesses and "country girls" during the spring of 1709. See pp. 8–9.

APPENDIX 4:
NOMINAL PORTRAITS OF POPE

THESE ARE ALL ENGRAVINGS, satirical and conversation pieces, where the intention of the artist to represent Pope is clear from the lettering or from adjuncts in the picture, but where the image, except perhaps for crude features of stature and deformity, is merely a counter. Nos. 13.1–2, above, Pope whitewashing Burlington Gate, are of this sort. In contrast, no. 12, I believe, shows observation of Pope's actual appearance. For bibliographical guidance in this appendix I am indebted to an unpublished Yale doctoral dissertation, Joseph V. Guerinot's *Pamphlet Attacks on Alexander Pope, 1711–1744: A Descriptive Bibliography*, 1962.

I end with the death of Pope and thus leave out of account a few mysteriously unlike portrait engravings of the later eighteenth century, and the nineteenth-century fictions, which may be sampled plentifully in Carruthers' *Life of Pope*, 1853, and perhaps reach their finest in W. P. Frith's scene of Pope rejected by Lady Mary (Royal Academy Exhibition, 1858, engraved by F. Joubert; *The Art Journal*, 29 [1867], 172, engraved by C. W. Sharpe, the painting being then in the collection of John Hicks, Esq., Bolton). A print of Sharpe's engraving after Frith may be seen at the Frick Art Reference Library.

1. An octavo satirical volume entitled *A Complete Collection of all the Verses, Essays, Letters and Advertisements, Which Have been occasioned by the Publication of Three Volumes of Miscellanies, by Pope and Company*. . . . London; Printed for A. Moore, near St. Paul's, M. DCC. XXVIII, has as frontispiece an engraving which shows standing on a pedestal composed of Pope's books a dwarfish figure on crutches with satyr's feet and legs and a horn-like snake cropping out of his turban at the forehead. Owls

above and a monkey below complete the adjuncts. The motto on a scroll above his head, "Hic Est Quem Quaeris. Mart.," suggests that the figure is in some sense intended as Pope. For the volume see *Twickenham* 5. 209–10.

2. An octavo allegorical poem, *The Progress of Wit: A Caveat For the Use of an Eminent Writer. By a Fellow of All-Souls* . . . . London: Printed for J. Wilford, at the Crown in Stationers-Court. M DCC.XXX, has as frontispiece an engraving ("G. Vander Gucht inv^t: et sculp:") which illustrates the poem. The goddess Fancy from beside a chariot in the clouds admonishes "Tuneful Alexis," "Pope," a laureled figure in toga and tights, who turns in horror from a scene of dangers on the stream of Life and Fame. The poem is attributed to Aaron Hill.

3. A folio pamphlet *Ingratitude: To Mr. Pope Occasion'd by a Manuscript handed about, under the Title of Mr. Taste's Tour from the Land of Politeness, to that of Dulness and Scandal.* . . . London: Printed and Sold by J. Dormer, next Ludgate, 1733, had a crudely engraved frontispiece showing Pope in the center held under the arm of one nobleman, while a second stands at the left laughing, and a third at the right is urinating on Pope. The frontispiece is missing from the Yale copy of this pamphlet. The British Museum detached example (*BMP&PS* [2. 808–09], no. 1935) is a fragment, but the missing part may be inferred from the text of the pamphlet, p. 3, which implies also that one of the noblemen taking revenge on Pope is the Duke of Chandos. The folio poem *Mr. Taste's Tour* . . . London: Printed for S. Sloe . . . 1733, appeared on 31 May, two days after *Ingratitude*. The introduction pretends to be by Pope. See Robert Rogers, *Pope's Satires,* p. 144; *TLS,* 10 January and 14 February 1935.

4. *BMP&PS* no. 1899 (2.766–767), a line engraving 12 x 6½ inches, "Rich's Glory on his Triumphant Entry into Covent Garden. . . . WHIESCULP [W. Hogarth invenit et sculpsit]" celebrates both John Gay's success with *The Beggar's Opera* and John Rich's removal in December 1732 from Lincoln's Inn Fields and his opening of the Covent Garden Theatre. A small hunched figure appears to one side, marked by the letter "P" over his head, and in what seems a gratuitous and meaningless detail of the satire, he is "treating with contumely" sheets of the "*Beg*[gar's]. *Oper*[a]." *BMP&PS* nos. 1900 and 1901 are copies of no. 1899. This print has been traditionally, though with reservations, included in Hogarth's canon. See, for instance, Samuel Ireland, *Graphic Illustrations of Hogarth, 1* (London, 1794), 108; John Nichols, *et al., Biographical Anecdotes of William Hogarth* (London 1785), p. 164; Austin Dobson, *William Hogarth* (London, 1907), p. 236. I am indebted to Professor Ronald Paulson for the judgment that (if perhaps Hogarth was responsible for the "invention" of this design) the engraving is much unlike his style in the year 1732.

5. A folio poem, *A Tryall of Skill Between a Court Lord, and a Twickenham 'Squire. Inscrib'd to Mr. Pope.* . . . London: Printed and sold by J. Dormer, at the Printing-Office, the Green Door, in Black and White Court in the Old Bailey. . . . M. DCC. XXXIV, apparently an attack on Pope's antagonist Lord Hervey, has a crudely engraved frontispiece showing a short humpbacked man, wigged and coated (seconded by a wild

man with a club) crossing swords with a man in shirt sleeves and open collar, without hair or wig (seconded by a coated figure with fox's head). Pens, ink-pot, and paper litter the ground. Ink spots (?) appear on the face and around the head of the taller duellist, and from his mouth comes a label bearing the words: "With foul Disgrace—He daubs my face."

6. Hogarth's painting *The Distressed Poet,* showing a satiric engraving of Pope as monkey with tiara (no. 7.10) on the garret wall, was the model for a large line engraving "Invented Printed Engraved and Publish'd by Wm Hogarth March the 3rd 1736." On the wall here a small man in hat, wig, and long coat has his foot on the shoulder of another man and is using what is apparently a printers' stick to thrash him. The upraised stick has attached to it a sheet bearing the words "Pope's Letters." The prone figure holds another stick with a sheet bearing the words "To Curl." From Pope's mouth come the words "Veni Vidi Vici 1735." (In a later state of the print, "December the 15, 1740," the picture on the wall becomes *A View of the Gold Mines of Peru*). See Austin Dobson, *William Hogarth* (London, 1907), pp. 63–64, 201, 241–42; Frederick D. Leach, "Hogarth's Distressed Poet: The Riddle of the Garret," *The Ohio University Review,* 2 (1960), 15–16.

7. Provoked especially by Pope's *New Dunciad* of March 1742, the aged Whig dramatist and Poet Laureate Colley Cibber published in July 1742, *A Letter From Mr. Cibber To Mr. Pope, Inquiring into the Motives that might induce him in his Satyrical Works, to be so frequently fond of Mr. Cibber's Name. . . .* London, Printed: And Sold by W. Lewis in Russel-Street, Covent-Garden. MDCCXLII. On p. 44 of this octavo volume is a passage alleging that Cibber once rescued Pope from the pleasures of a whorehouse. This passage was the occasion for four illustrative engravings, exhibiting various degrees of indecency. They are described in the British Museum catalogue of *Political and Personal Satires* (*BMP&PS* 3.i.452–455) in the following order: no. 2571, [line] engraving 9⅛ x 7¼ in., "The Poetical Tom-Titt perch'd upon the Mount of Love. *Being the Representation of a Merry Description in Mr. Cibber's Letter to Mr. Pope.* Published according to Act of Parliam^t, July 31. 1742. Price 6d."; no. 2572, [line] engraving, 10¼ x 6⅝ in., "An Essay on Woman, *by the* Author *of the* Essay *on* Man: Being *Homer* Preserv'd, Or the Twickenham Squire Caught By the Heels. July 31 1742"; no. 2573, [line] engraving and etching [?], 13¼ x 10⅝ in., "*And has not* Sawney *too his* Lord *and* Whore? *Vide Cibber's Letter. Publish'd according to Act of Parliament by P. Uriel in Temple Lane* over against Chancery Lane. August 9th 1742"[1]; no 2574, [line] engraving, 4½ x 2¾ in., "*And has not* Sawney *too his* Lord *and* Whore?", reversed and adapted to the vertical dimension from no. 2573, as frontispiece to an octavo third edition of Cibber's *Letter,* Glasgow: Printed for W. Macpharson [1742?]. Cf. Norman Ault, *New Light on Pope* (1949), pp. 302–03.

8. In volume 4 of Warburton's octavo edition of Pope's *Works,* 1751, an illustration by

1. The B.M. account says that this engraving is by Gravelot. So too South Kensington Museum, *Dyce Collection, A Catalogue of the Paintings* (London, 1874), p. 251, no. 2594. A photograph in my possession of Dyce 2594 (Victoria and Albert Museum) fails to show any lettering other than what I quote above.

Hayman and Grignion for the opening of the *Epistle to Arbuthnot,* "Shut, shut the door, good John, I said," presents an image of Pope, hand to forehead, which is derived from a specific source, Van Loo's painting of 1742 (see nos. 66.1–2 and 66.17). Other illustrations by Hayman and Grignion in the same edition give us Pope, the speaker of his poems, in a much more generalized, almost allegorical, bardic image. An earlier effort made by the same team—Francis Hayman the painter of Vauxhall (1708–76) and Charles Grignion the elder (1717–1810)—was a title-page vignette for William Mason's quarto poem *Musaeus: A Monody to the Memory of Mr. Pope, In Imitation of Milton's "Lycidas."* London: Printed for R. Dodsley at Tully's Head in Pall-Mall; and sold by Mr. Cooper in Pater-noster-Row, 1747.[2] In entry no. 48.4, we have quoted Hurd's acknowledgement, sent to Mason on 30 May 1747, for a "Head of Pope, which Mason was either working on or had already sent, the pencil drawing after Richardson which today still hangs in the library at Hartlebury Castle. In the same letter Hurd adds: "If you would but, at some leisure time, contrive to give me a sketch of your own from Hayman's picture, it would complete the obligation."[3] But

F. Hayman inv. et del.   C. Grignion Sculp.

Appendix 4.8. Line engraving. 2¹⁴⁄₁₆ x 4³⁄₁₆ in. frame. "F. Hayman inv. et del. // C. Grignion Sculp." Title-page vignette for William Mason, *Musaeus: A Monody to the Memory of Mr. Pope,* 1747.

2. See Philip Gaskell, *The First Editions of William Mason* (Cambridge, 1951), pp. 1–2. In a "Third Edition," Dodsley, 1748, the engraving, slightly reworked at the right side, appears as headpiece to the text [p. 5].

A re-engraving of this picture, unsigned, appears in Dodsley's *Collection of Poems,* 3 (1775), 303.

3. *The Correspondence of Richard Hurd & William Mason* . . . ed. Leonard Whibley (Cambridge

Mason, in response to this, did better than send a sketch of his own. The neatly executed wash drawing (3⅜ x 4⅝ inches, in reverse direction to the engraving), which still hangs, along with Mason's more amateurish head of Pope ("ΟΥΤΟΣ ΕΚΕΙΝΟΣ / / MVSAEVS"), in the library at Hartlebury, is inscribed beneath in ink, "Hayman delin. 1747."[4]

Chaucer, Spenser, and Milton (in both poem and picture) convene at Pope's grotto to witness his death. Each speaks some verses in a parody of his own style. A goddess of "Virtue" (in the picture apparently translated into a goddess of poetic fame) steps from a cloud to praise and comfort Pope.

> But what might that avail? Blind Fate before
> Had op'd her shears, to slit his vital thread;
> And who may hope gainsay her stern behest?
> Then thrice he wav'd the hand, thrice bow'd the head,
> And sigh'd his soul to rest.

University Press, 1932), p. 5. In an earlier letter (p. 1) Hurd had thanked Mason for a present of *Musaeus:* "ev'ry one here reads & admires it, nothing ever pleas'd so generally. It has caught all sorts of Readers from Heads of Colleges down to little Coffee-House Critics."

4. The drawing is very similar in style to a set of five small wash drawings by Hayman, for engravings by Grignion, to illustrate the Baskerville-Tonson *Works of Congreve*, 1761 (at the Victoria and Albert Museum, E656–660–1949 and E662–665–1949).

INDEX

This is an index of proper names: persons, places, institutions, a few periodical titles, a few book titles, and the like. Identifications are generally more complete than in the text. Italicized page numbers indicate illustrations; when the same page also contains a text reference, the page number is not repeated. A key to the sequence of chapters is printed at the bottom of each double page; slant lines indicate chapter divisions.

Key to chapter sequence: xiii–xxxiii Introduction / 3–6 Anon. c. 1695 / 7–26 Jervas c. 1714–15 / 27–72 Kneller 1716, 1721, 1722 / 73–89 Richardson c. 1718 / 90–96 Dahl 1727 / 97–106 Rysbrack 1730 / 107–36 Kent and Countess of Burlington

368

1725–35 / 137–222 Richardson 1733–42 / 223–66 Roubiliac 1738–41 / 267–78 Dassler 1741 / 279–311 Hoare 1739–40, c. 1742 / 312–35 Van Loo 1742 / 339–47 Warburton Type / 348–54 Unexplained Allusions / 355–66 Mistaken and Nominal Portraits

Key to chapter sequence: xiii–xxxiii Introduction / 3–6 Anon. c. 1695 / 7–26 Jervas c. 1714–15 / 27–72 Kneller 1716, 1721, 1722 / 73–89 Richardson c. 1718 / 90–96 Dahl 1727 / 97–106 Rysbrack 1730 / 107–36 Kent and Countess of Burlington

1725–35 / 137–222 Richardson 1733–42 / 223–66 Roubiliac 1738–41 / 267–78 Dassier 1741 / 279–311 Hoare 1739–40, c. 1742 / 312–35 Van Loo 1742 / 339–47 Warburton Type / 348–54 Unexplained Allusions / 355–66 Mistaken and Nominal Portraits

373

Key to chapter sequence: xiii–xxxiii Introduction / 3–6 Anon. c. 1695 / 7–26 Jervas c. 1714–15 / 27–72 Kneller 1716, 1721, 1722 / 73–89 Richardson c. 1718 / 90–96 Dahl 1727 / 97–106 Rysbrack 1730 / 107–36 Kent and Countess of Burlington

374

Key to chapter sequence: xiii–xxxiii Introduction / 3–6 Anon. c. 1695 / 7–26 Jervas c. 1714–15 / 27–72 Kneller 1716, 1721, 1722 / 73–89 Richardson c. 1718 / 90–96 Dahl 1727 / 97–106 Rysbrack 1730 / 107–36 Kent and Countess of Burlington

1725–35 / 137–222 Richardson 1733–42 / 223–66 Roubiliac 1738–41 / 267–78 Dassier 1741 / 279–311 Hoare 1739–40, c. 1742 / 312–35 Van Loo 1742 / 339–47 Warburton Type / 348–54 Unexplained Allusions / 355–66 Mistaken and Nominal Portraits

Key to chapter sequence: xiii–xxxiii Introduction / 3–6 Anon. c. 1695 / 7–26 Jervas c. 1714–15 / 27–72 Kneller 1716, 1721, 1722 / 73–89 Richardson c. 1718 / 90–96 Dahl 1727 / 97–106 Rysbrack 1730 / 107–36 Kent and Countess of Burlington

1725–35 / 137–222 Richardson 1733–42 / 223–66 Roubiliac 1738–41 / 267–78 Dassier 1741 / 279–311 Hoare 1739–40, c. 1742 / 312–35 Van Loo 1742 / 339–47 Warburton Type / 348–54 Unexplained Allusions / 355–66 Mistaken and Nominal Portraits

381

Key to chapter sequence: xiii–xxxiii Introduction / 3–6 Anon. c. 1695 / 7–26 Jervas c. 1714–15 / 27–72 Kneller 1716, 1721,
1722 / 73–89 Richardson c. 1718 / 90–96 Dahl 1727 / 97–106 Rysbrack 1730 / 107–36 Kent and Countess of Burlington

1725–35 / 137–222 Richardson 1733–42 / 223–66 Roubiliac 1738–41 / 267–78 Dassier 1741 / 279–311 Hoare 1739–40, c. 1742 / 312–35 Van Loo 1742 / 339–47 Warburton Type / 348–54 Unexplained Allusions / 355–66 Mistaken and Nominal Portraits

383

Key to chapter sequence: xiii–xxxiii Introduction / 3–6 Anon. c. 1695 / 7–26 Jervas c. 1714–15 / 27–72 Kneller 1716, 1721, 1722 / 73–89 Richardson c. 1718 / 90–96 Dahl 1727 / 97–106 Rysbrack 1730 / 107–36 Kent and Countess of Burlington

1725–35 / 137–222 Richardson 1733–42 / 223–66 Roubiliac 1738–41 / 267–78 Dassier 1741 / 279–311 Hoare 1739–40, c. 1742
/ 312–35 Van Loo 1742 / 339–47 Warburton Type / 348–54 Unexplained Allusions / 355–66 Mistaken and Nominal Portraits

Key to chapter sequence: xiii–xxxiii Introduction / 3–6 Anon. c. 1695 / 7–26 Jervas c. 1714–15 / 27–72 Kneller 1716, 1721,
1722 / 73–89 Richardson c. 1718 / 90–96 Dahl 1727 / 97–106 Rysbrack 1730 / 107–36 Kent and Countess of Burlington

Key to chapter sequence: xiii–xxxiii Introduction / 3–6 Anon. c. 1695 / 7–26 Jervas c. 1714–15 / 27–72 Kneller 1716, 1721, 1722 / 73–89 Richardson c. 1718 / 90–96 Dahl 1727 / 97–106 Rysbrack 1730 / 107–36 Kent and Countess of Burlington

Key to chapter sequence: xiii–xxxiii Introduction / 3–6 Anon. c. 1695 / 7–26 Jervas c. 1714–15 / 27–72 Kneller 1716, 1721, 1722 / 73–89 Richardson c. 1718 / 90–96 Dahl 1727 / 97–106 Rysbrack 1730 / 107–36 Kent and Countess of Burlington

1725–35 / 137–222 Richardson 1733–42 / 223–66 Roubiliac 1738–41 / 267–78 Dassier 1741 / 279–311 Hoare 1739–40, c. 1742 / 312–35 Van Loo 1742 / 339–47 Warburton Type / 348–54 Unexplained Allusions / 355–66 Mistaken and Nominal Portraits